TAKING SIDES

Clashing Views on

Global Issues

SEVENTH EDITION, EXPANDED

TAKING SIDES

Clashing Views on
Global Issues

SEVENTH EDITION, EXPANDED

Selected, Edited, and with Introductions by

James E. Harf
Maryville University

and

Mark Owen Lombardi
Maryville University

Mc Graw Hill

Connect
Learn
Succeed™

TAKING SIDES: CLASHING VIEWS ON GLOBAL ISSUES, SEVENTH EDITION, EXPANDED

Published by McGraw-Hill, a business unit of The McGraw-Hill Companies, Inc., 1221 Avenue of the Americas, New York, NY 10020. Copyright © 2013 by The McGraw-Hill Companies, Inc. All rights reserved. Previous editions © 2010, 2009, and 2007. Printed in the United States of America. No part of this publication may be reproduced or distributed in any form or by any means, or stored in a database or retrieval system, without the prior written consent of The McGraw-Hill Companies, Inc., including, but not limited to, in any network or other electronic storage or transmission, or broadcast for distance learning.

Some ancillaries, including electronic and print components, may not be available to customers outside the United States.

Taking Sides® is a registered trademark of the McGraw-Hill Companies, Inc.
Taking Sides is published by the **Contemporary Learning Series** group within the McGraw-Hill Higher Education division.

This book is printed on acid-free paper.

1 2 3 4 5 6 7 8 9 0 DOC/DOC 1 0 9 8 7 6 5 4 3 2

MHID: 0-07-8050448
ISBN: 978-0-07-8050442
ISSN: 1536-3317

Managing Editor: *Larry Loeppke*
Senior Developmental Editor: *Debra A. Henricks*
Content Licensing Specialist: *Rita Hingtgen*
Marketing Director: *Adam Kloza*
Marketing Manager: *Nathan Edwards*
Project Manager: *Erin Melloy*
Cover Graphics: *Studio Montage, St. Louis, MO*
Buyer: *Jennifer Pickel*
Media Project Manager: *Sridevi Palani*

Compositor: MPS Limited
Cover Image: © Digital Vision/Getty Images RF

www.mhhe.com

Editors/Academic Advisory Board

Members of the Academic Advisory Board are instrumental in the final selection of articles for each edition of TAKING SIDES. Their review of articles for content, level, and appropriateness provides critical direction to the editors and staff. We think that you will find their careful consideration well reflected in this volume.

TAKING SIDES: Clashing Views on GLOBAL ISSUES
Seventh Edition, Expanded

EDITORS

James E. Harf
Maryville University

and

Mark Owen Lombardi
Maryville University

ACADEMIC ADVISORY BOARD MEMBERS

Editors/Academic Advisory Board continued

Preface

This volume reflects the changing nature of the contemporary world in which we live. Not only are we now witnessing a dramatic leap in the *scope* of global change, but we are also experiencing a *rate* of change in the world unparalleled in recorded history. Change in the international system is not a new phenomenon. Since the creation in the early 1500s of a Euro-centric world system of sovereign nation-states that dominated political, economic, and social events throughout the known world, global change has been with us. But earlier manifestations of change were characterized by infrequent bursts of system-changing episodes followed by long periods of "normalcy," where the processes and structures of the international system demonstrated regularity or consistency.

First, the Catholic church sought to recapture its European dominance and glory during the Middle Ages in a last gasp effort to withstand challenges against its rule from a newly developed secularized and urbanized mercantile class, only to be pushed aside in a devastating continental struggle known as the Thirty Years' War and relegated to irrelevant status by the resultant Treaty of Westphalia in 1648. A century and a half later, the global system was again challenged, this time by a French general turned emperor, Napoleon Bonaparte, who sought to export the newly created utopian vision of the French Revolution beyond the boundaries of France to the rest of the world. Napoleon was eventually repelled by a coalition of major powers intent on preserving the world as these countries knew it.

Soon nineteenth-century Europe was being transformed by the intrusion of the Industrial Revolution on the daily lives of average citizens and national leaders alike. Technological advances enhanced the capacity of countries to dramatically increase their military capability, achieving the ability to project such power far beyond their national borders in a short time. Other threats to the existing world order also emerged. Nationalism began to capture the hearts of various country leaders who sought to impart such loyalties to their subjects, while new ideologies competed with one another as well as with nationalism to create a thirst for alternative world models to the existing nation-state system. The result was another failed attempt by a European power, this time Germany, to expand its influence via a major war, later to be called World War I, throughout the continent. The postwar map of Europe reflected major consequences of the abortive German effort.

Almost immediately, the international system was threatened by a newly emergent virulent ideology of the left intent on taking over the world. Communism had gained a foothold in Russia, and soon its leaders were eager to transport it across the continent to the far corners of the globe, threatening to destroy the existing economic order and, by definition, its political counterpart. Shortly thereafter, a competing virulent ideology from the right, fascism, emerged. Under its manipulation by a new German leader, Adolph Hitler, the international system was once again greatly threatened. Six long years of war and unthinkable levels of devastation and destruction followed, until the fascist threat was turned back. The communist threat persisted, however, until late in the millennium, when it also virtually disappeared, felled by its own weaknesses and excesses.

In the interim, new challenges to global order appeared in the form of a set of issues like no other during the 500-year history of the nation-state system. The nature of these global issues and the pace at which they both landed on the global agenda and then expanded were to quickly affect the international system. The first new global issue to emerge grew out of World War II and Nazi atrocities. The concern for human rights throughout the globe and the recognition that the international community had responsibility for ensuring them to all global citizens irrespective of where they lived was settled when the United Nations Charter was adopted. A little over a decade later, other issues in this new agenda took root, when astute observers began to identify disquieting trends: quickening population growth in the poorer sectors of the globe, growing disruptions in the world's ability to feed its population, increasing shortfalls in required resources, and expanding evidence of negative environmental impacts, such as a variety of pollution evils. Some of these issues—like decreasing levels of adequate supplies of food, energy, and water—emerged as a result of both increased population growth and increased per capita levels of consumption. Dramatic population increases, in turn, resulted in changes in global population dynamics—increasing aged population or massive new urbanization patterns. The emergence of this set of new issues was soon followed by another phenomenon, globalization, which emphasized increasing speedy flows of information through innovative technology and a resultant diffusion of regional cultures throughout the globe and the emergence of a global macroculture. Globalization not only affected the nature of the international system in these general ways but also influenced both the manner in which these global issues impacted the system and how the latter addressed them.

The major consequence of the confluence of these events is the extent to which and the shortened time frame in which the change affects them. No longer is the change measured in centuries or even decades. It is now measured in years or even months. No longer are likely solutions to such problems simple, known, confined to a relatively small part of the globe, and capable of being achieved by the efforts of one or a few national governments. Instead, these global issues are characterized by increased rapidity of change, increased complexity, increased geographical impact, increased resistance to solution, and increased fluidity.

One only has to compare the world as it existed when these issues first appeared to the world of today to grasp the difference. When students first began to study these issues in the early 1960s, their written analysis was accomplished either by putting pen to pad or by engaging an unwieldy typewriter. Their experience with a computer was limited to watching a moon landing through the eyes of NASA Mission Control. The use of phones was relegated to a location where a cord could be plugged into a wall socket. Their written correspondence with someone beyond their immediate location had a stamp on it. Their reading of news, both serious and frivolous, occurred via a newspaper. Visual news invaded their space in 30-minute daily segments from three major TV networks.

Being entertained required some effort, usually away from the confines of their homes or dorm rooms. Today, of course, the personal computer and its companions, the Internet, the Kindle, and the iPad, have transformed the way students learn, the way they communicate with one another, and the way they entertain themselves. Facebook and Twitter have joined our vocabulary.

The age of globalization has accelerated, affecting and transforming trends that began over three decades ago. No longer are nation-states the only actors on the global stage. Moreover, their position of dominance is increasingly challenged by an array of other actors—international governmental organizations, private international groups, multinational corporations, and important individuals—who might be better equipped to address newly emerging issues (or who might also serve as the source of yet other problems).

An even more recent phenomenon is the unleashing of ethnic pride, which manifests itself in both positive and negative ways. The history of post–cold war conflict is a history of intrastate, ethnically driven violence that has torn apart those countries that have been unable to deal effectively with the changes brought on by the end of the cold war. The most insidious manifestation of this emphasis on ethnicity is the emergence of terrorist groups who use religion and other aspects of ethnicity to justify bringing death and destruction on their perceived enemies. As national governments attempt to cope with this latest phenomenon, they too are changing the nature of war and violence. The global agenda's current transformation, brought about by globalization, demands that our attention turn toward the latter's consequences.

The recent economic collapse, or what some now call "the Great Recession," is evidence of this rapid globalization. Economic shifts were greatly accelerated throughout the global community by technology, interdependence, and connectivity such that governments, analysts, and the public at large were unable to comprehend the destabilizing events as they happened. Further, relations between states such as Russia, China, and the United States rapidly altered as a result. And the Middle East remains unsettled as Israel copes with an ever threatening potentially nuclear-armed Iran.

The format of *Taking Sides: Clashing Views on Global Issues*, Seventh Edition follows the successful formula of other books in the Taking Sides series. The book begins with an introduction to the emergence of global issues, the new age of globalization, the effect of 9/11, the recent global economic crisis, a reemerging Russia, and the rise of revolutionary movements throughout North Africa and the Middle East—and the international community's response to these events—that characterize the first decade of the twentieth century. It then addresses 22 current global issues grouped into four units. Population takes center stage in Unit 1 because it not only represents a global issue by itself, but it also affects the parameters of many other global issues. Population aging, urbanization, and global policy making are considered. Unit 2 addresses a range of problems associated with global resources and their environmental impact, such as energy, food, and climate change. Units 3 and 4 feature issues borne out of the emerging agenda of the twenty-first century. The former unit examines widely disparate expanding forces and movements across national boundaries, such as illicit drugs, global pandemics, and human trafficking, as well as the contemporary global economic crisis and social media. Unit 4 focuses on new security issues in the post–cold war and post–September 11 eras, such as whether the world is headed for a nuclear 9/11, a nuclear Iran is a global security threat, China will become the next superpower, Al-Qaeda and its jihad against the United States have been defeated, or the Middle East is undergoing a democratic revolution. The two new issues are placed following Issue 20.

Each issue has two readings, one pro and one con. The readings are preceded by an issue *introduction* that sets the stage for the debate by laying out both sides of the issue as well as alternative viewpoints or approaches, and briefly describes the two readings. Each issue concludes with an exploration of critical thinking and reflection questions, seeking common ground, and a list of additional resources for further reading. At the back of the book is a listing of all the *contributors to this volume*, with a brief biographical sketch of each of the prominent figures whose views are debated here.

Changes to this expanded edition This seventh expanded edition adds two new issues. The first is "Is the International Community Making Effective Progress in Securing Global Human Rights?" (Issue 21). The second new issue is "Should Israel Preempt Against Iran's Nuclear Program?" (Issue 22).

A word to the instructor An instructor's manual with test questions (multiple choice and essay) is available through the publisher for the instructor using Taking Sides in the classroom. A general guidebook, *Using Taking Sides in the Classroom,* which discusses methods and techniques for integrating the pro–con approach into any classroom setting, is also available. An online version of *Using Taking Sides in the Classroom* and a correspondence service for Taking Sides adopters can be found at http://www.mhhe.com/cls. *Taking Sides: Clashing Views on Global Issues* is only one title in the Taking Sides series. If you are interested in seeing the table of contents for any of the other titles, please visit the Taking Sides Web site at http://www.mhhe.com/cls.

James E. Harf
Maryville University

Mark Owen Lombardi
Maryville University

To my daughter, Marie: May your world conquer those global issues left unresolved by my generation. (J.E.H.)

For Betty and Marty, who instilled a love of education and a need to explore the world. (M.O.L.)

Contents In Brief

Contents

Terry M. Redding, a communications consultant to The Population Institute, suggests that population *growth* is being unfortunately neglected in international development discussions, as the latter's focus has been on other aspects of population such as reproductive health and women's empowerment. Steven W. Mosher, president of the Population Research Institute, an organization devoted to debunking the idea that the world is overpopulated, argues in an interview with Michael J. Miller of *The Catholic World Report* that self-interest was the motivation for past efforts on the part of international funding agencies, including the World Bank, to curb population by pressuring developing countries to adopt fertility reduction programs.

Neil Howe and Richard Jackson of the Center for Strategic and International Studies argue that global population aging is likely to have a profound and negative effect on global economic growth, living standards and conditions, and "the shape of the world order," particularly affecting China, Russia, Pakistan, Iran, and countries of the West. Mark L. Haas, Duquesne University professor, suggests that global aging will likely have a positive effect on the United States as its chief competitors will have a far more difficult time coping with their aging populations.

Stephen Lendman, a research associate of the Centre for Research on Globalization in Montreal, argues that the global food crisis is related to rising prices in an economically troubled time rather than to a lack of food production. Lester Brown, founder and president of Earth Policy Institute, argues that unlike in the past when weather was the culprit, the spike in food prices is now caused by trends on both sides of the food supply/demand equation that are causing higher food prices.

Issue 7.   Is the Threat of Global Warming Real?   126

Bill McKibben, author of numerous books on ecological issues, addresses seven myths about climate change, arguing that the global community must act now if it is to save the earth from a climate catastrophe. Richard Lindzen, Alfred P. Sloan professor of meteorology at MIT, cautions us not to act too hastily in addressing assumed climate change as the evidence does not support such a conclusion or the need for hysteria.

Issue 8.   Can the Global Community Successfully Confront the Global Water Shortage?   143

Peter Rogers, professor of environmental engineering at Harvard University, suggests that existing technologies exist for averting a global water crisis, but the global community must act soon. Mark Clayton, staff writer for *The Christian Science Monitor*, suggests that changes in population, pollution, and climate are creating water shortages around the globe, leading private companies to take advantage of the increased demand for clean water while governments are slow to act.

UNIT 3   EXPANDING GLOBAL FORCES AND MOVEMENTS   161

Issue 9.   Can the Global Community "Win" the Drug War?   162

This 2010 report by the United Nations Office on Drugs and Crime suggests that "drug control has matured" and efforts are paying off as the world's supply of the two main problem drugs, opiates and cocaine, has been declining over the past 2 years since the previous UN report. According to

The International Strategy for Disaster Reduction Secretariat, a unit within the United Nations, suggests that countries are making "significant progress" in strengthening their capacities to address past deficiencies and gaps in their disaster preparedness and response. At the center of progress is the plan, *Hyogo Framework for Action 2005–2015,* which is aimed at reducing human and nonhuman disaster losses. David Rothkopf, president of Garten Rothkopf (an international consulting agency) and a member of former president Bill Clinton's international trade team, argues that the efforts of international organizations to prevent natural disasters from escalating into megadisasters "have fallen short of what is required."

Issue 13. Is the Global Economic Crisis a Failure of Capitalism?   270

Katsuhito Iwai, professor of economics at the University of Tokyo, argues that the current economic collapse is a sign of the inherent instability of global capitalism. He argues that capitalism's failure in this crisis is inherent because capitalism is based on speculation and therefore belief or faith in the strength of the system and its various parts. Dani Rodrik, professor of international political economy at Harvard University's John F. Kennedy School of Government, contends that the current economic downturn is not a sign of capitalism's failure but rather its need for reinvention and adaptation. Rodrik argues that this is precisely why capitalism will survive and thrive because it is so changeable based on new trends and conditions.

Issue 14. Is Social Media Becoming the Most Powerful Force in Global Politics?   280

Clay Shirky argues that social media has and will empower individuals and groups in profound ways giving political movements power, reach, and access. He contends that it will change the power dynamic between these groups and the state (often the object if not adversary of political action) and make insurrection and revolution more likely to occur and potentially to succeed. Evgeny Morozov contends that the social media revolution cuts both ways. He argues that rather than social media being a tool for overcoming oppression and empowering groups, it has and will be a mechanism for regimes to exercise greater control and dominance. He argues that rather than a panacea, it is a multiedged sword whose full impact, wielded by whom, is yet to be determined.

UNIT 4   THE NEW GLOBAL SECURITY DILEMMA   295

Brian Michael Jenkins, senior advisor to the President of the Rand Corporation, in testimony before the U.S. Senate Committee on Homeland Security and Governmental Affairs, posited that a team of terrorists could be inserted into the United States and carry out a Mumbai-style attack as terrorism has "increasingly become an effective strategic weapon." Graham Allison, Harvard professor and director of the Belfer Center for Science and International Affairs, affirms that we are not likely to experience a nuclear 9/11 because "nuclear terrorism is preventable by a feasible, affordable agenda of actions that . . . would shrink the risk of nuclear terrorism to nearly zero."

Hussein Solomon argues that when religious extremism, which is a security threat in and of itself, is merged with state power, the threat to global security is potentially catastrophic and must be met with clear and uncompromising policies. He contends that this is present across all religions, and he uses both a born-again George Bush and a fundamentalist Mahmoud Ahmadinejad as his examples. Shibley Telhami, on the other hand, does not argue that religious extremism is the threat, but rather that global security threats are from political groups with political agendas and not extremism as such.

Dore Gold contends that a nuclear Iran is a global security threat because of the nature of the fundamentalist regime, its antipathy for both Israel and the United States, and its clear support for international terrorism. He argues that evidence clearly indicates that it is developing a bomb and its past behavior means it will be likely to use it. Scott Horton contends that through media misrepresentation, governmental propaganda, and outright falsehoods, the myth has been created that a nuclear Iran is a global security threat. Horton argues that Iran has acted within its rights and treaty obligations and as such presents no more a threat than any other country that may or may not develop nuclear weapons.

Shujie Yao analyzes the current state of the Chinese economy and policy and postulates several possible scenarios for development. Ultimately, he surmises that China will develop as the next superpower by the mid-twenty-first century. Minxin Pei argues that the political and economic situation in China is not as stable and robust as we believe. He contends that there are structural economic concerns and growing political unrest that will mitigate China's ascension to superpower status and for the foreseeable future.

Fareed Zakaria argues through the acts of moderate Muslims across the Islamic world, "We have turned the corner on the war between extremism and the West and . . . now we are in a new phase of clean up and rebuilding of relationships." His argument rests on the actions of Muslim regimes in Saudi Arabia, Pakistan, and Indonesia who are fighting back against jihadism, engaging in military and political policies that are marginalizing extremists and consequently winning the war. Scott Stewart contends that despite Western victories against Al-Qaeda based in the Afghan–Pakistan border region, regional groups and cells have taken up the slack and the threat of extremism and jihad is still strong and ominous. He focuses on the work of these groups in Somalia, Yemen, and North Africa to illustrate this continued fight.

Fareed Zakaria argues that there are strong strands within the Egyptian polity and around other parts of the Middle East to indicate that the Arab Spring is truly a democratic revolution. Although he cautions that democracy results are dependent on a host of complex factors, he sees several reasons for optimism, including a strong and secular military and an independent judiciary system. Adam Shatz argues that it is far too early to determine whether the Arab Spring, as some are calling it, will lead to democracy of the type and form the west would favor. He contends that the revolt against autocratic rule may indeed lead to the exchange of one form of authoritarianism with another and that worries in parts of the United States and Israel about authoritarian, anti-Western regimes replacing governments in Egypt, Tunisia, and other places are quite justified.

UNIT 5   BONUS ISSUES   381

The Council on Foreign Relations, an independent nonpartisan and essentially American think tank, in *Issue Brief* summarizes the development of an elaborate global system of governmental and nongovernmental organizations developed primarily over the past few decades to promote human rights throughout the world, while recognizing that the task is still far from complete. Amnesty International's annual report on the state of human rights around the world suggests major failures in all regions ("Failed leadership has gone global in the last year . . ."), with specific restrictions on free speech in at least 91 countries and cases of torture and other ill-treatment in over 101 countries.

Issue 22. Should Israel Preempt Against Iran's Nuclear Program? 414

Elliott Abrams argues that a nuclear-armed Iran represents a unique and existential threat to the survival of the state of Israel and therefore is unacceptable. He contends that some states when faced with such a threat should act to prevent destruction since the approach and policy of the Iranian regime is clear and unequivocal in its hostility to Israel's very existence. Colin H. Kahl argues that Israel's attack on the Osirak reactor in Iraq had the reverse impact it wished. Saddam Hussein became even more determined to acquire nuclear weapons. Given the greater strength and resiliency of the Iranian regime, its geographic position, and its resources, an Israeli preemption on Iran would merely galvanize hard liners to regroup and continue the work toward nuclear weapons. And this is something that Israel or the United States cannot ultimately stop.

Correlation Guide

The Taking Sides series presents current issues in a debate-style format designed to stimulate student interest and develop critical-thinking skills. Each issue is thoughtfully framed with an issue summary, an issue introduction, learning outcomes, and critical thinking and reflection questions. The pro and con essays—selected for their liveliness and substance—represent the arguments of leading scholars and commentators in their fields.

Taking Sides: Clashing Views on Global Issues, 7/e, Expanded is an easy-to-use reader that presents issues on important topics such as *global population, global resources and the environment, expanding global forces and movements*, and *the new global security dilemma*. For more information on *Taking Sides* and other *McGraw-Hill Contemporary Learning Series* titles, visit http://www.mhhe.com/cls.

This convenient guide matches the issues in *Taking Sides: Clashing Views on Global Issues, 7/e, Expanded* with the corresponding chapters in one of our best-selling McGraw-Hill Political Science textbooks by Rourke/Boyer.

Taking Sides: Clashing Views on Global issues, 7/e, Expanded	*International Politics on the World Stage, Brief, 9/e by Rourke/Boyer*
Issue 1: Should the International Community Continue to Focus on Programs to Help Developing Countries Curb Population Growth?	**Chapter 1:** Thinking About International Relations in a Changing World **Chapter 12:** The Global Environment: What Does It Mean to Make the Global-Local Link?
Issue 2: Is Global Aging a Major Problem?	**Chapter 2:** Power Politics **Chapter 12:** The Global Environment: What Does It Mean to Make the Global-Local Link?
Issue 3: Does Global Urbanization Lead Primarily to Undesirable Consequences?	**Chapter 10:** Global Development: Why Is Prosperity and Development so Hard to Achieve?
Issue 4: Should Environmentalists Continue to Be Alarmists?	**Chapter 12:** The Global Environment: What Does It Mean to Make the Global-Local Link?
Issue 5: Should the World Continue to Rely on Oil as the Major Source of Energy?	**Chapter 7:** Pursuing Security: Threats More Than Enemies? **Chapter 9:** International Political Economy: How Is the World Organized Economically? **Chapter 12:** The Global Environment: What Does It Mean to Make the Global-Local Link?
Issue 6: Will the World Be Able to Feed Itself in the Foreseeable Future?	**Chapter 9:** International Political Economy: How Is the World Organized Economically? **Chapter 10:** Global Development: Why Is Prosperity and Development so Hard to Achieve? **Chapter 12:** The Global Environment: What Does It Mean to Make the Global-Local Link?
Issue 7: Is the Threat of Global Warming Real?	**Chapter 1:** Thinking About International Relations in a Changing World **Chapter 12:** The Global Environment: What Does It Mean to Make the Global-Local Link?
Issue 8: Can the Global Community Successfully Confront the Global Water Shortage?	**Chapter 12:** The Global Environment: What Does It Mean to Make the Global-Local Link?

(Continued)

Taking Sides: Clashing Views on Global issues, 7/e, Expanded	*International Politics on the World Stage, Brief, 9/e by Rourke/Boyer*
Issue 9: Can the Global Community "Win" the Drug War?	
Issue 10: Is the International Community Adequately Prepared to Address Global Health Pandemics?	**Chapter 11:** Human Rights: Does International Human Rights Law Make a Difference?
Issue 11: Do Adequate Strategies Exist to Combat Human Trafficking?	**Chapter 11:** Human Rights: Does International Human Rights Law Make a Difference?
Issue 12: Is the International Community Making Progress in Addressing Natural Disasters?	**Chapter 11:** Human Rights: Does International Human Rights Law Make a Difference? **Chapter 12:** The Global Environment: What Does It Mean to Make the Global-Local Link?
Issue 13: Is the Global Economic Crisis a Failure of Capitalism?	**Chapter 4:** Globalization: Politics from Above and Below **Chapter 9:** International Political Economy: How Is the World Organized Economically? **Chapter 10:** Global Development: Why Is Prosperity and Development so Hard to Achieve?
Issue 14: Is Social Media Becoming the Most Powerful Force in Global Politics?	
Issue 15: Are We Headed for a Nuclear 9/11?	**Chapter 7:** Pursuing Security: Threats More Than Enemies?
Issue 16: Is Religious and Cultural Extremism a Global Security Threat?	**Chapter 4:** Globalization: Politics from Above and Below **Chapter 6:** International Law: What Are the Laws of War and Do They Really Matter? **Chapter 7:** Pursuing Security: Threats More Than Enemies? **Chapter 8:** Conventional and Unconventional War
Issue 17: Is a Nuclear Iran a Global Security Threat?	**Chapter 1:** Thinking About International Relations in a Changing World **Chapter 2:** Power Politics **Chapter 7:** Pursuing Security: Threats More Than Enemies?
Issue 18: Will China Be the Next Superpower?	**Chapter 1:** Thinking About International Relations in a Changing World **Chapter 2:** Power Politics **Chapter 10:** Global Development: Why Is Prosperity and Development so Hard to Achieve?
Issue 19: Have Al-Qaeda and Its Jihad Against the United States Been Defeated?	**Chapter 7:** Pursuing Security: Threats More Than Enemies?
Issue 20: Is the Middle East Undergoing a Democratic Revolution?	**Chapter 1:** Thinking About International Relations in a Changing World **Chapter 2:** Power Politics **Chapter 3:** Humans, States and Systems
Issue 21: Is the International Community Making Effective Progress in Securing Global Human Rights?	**Chapter 11:** Human Rights: Does International Human Rights Law Make a Difference?
Issue 22: Should Israel Preempt Against Iran's Nuclear Program?	**Chapter 1:** Thinking About International Relations in a Changing World **Chapter 2:** Power Politics **Chapter 7:** Pursuing Security: Threats More Than Enemies?

Topics Guide

This topic guide suggests how the selections in this book relate to the subjects covered in your course. You may want to use the topics listed on these pages to search the Web more easily. On the following pages, a number of Web sites have been gathered specifically for this book. They are arranged to reflect the units of this *Taking Sides* reader. You can link to these sites by going to http://www.mhhe.com/cls.

All issues and the articles that relate to each topic are listed below in the bold-faced term.

Aging

2. Is Global Aging a Major Problem?

Al-Qaeda

15. Are We Headed for a Nuclear 9/11?
16. Is Religious and Cultural Extremism a Global Security threat?
19. Have Al-Qaeda and Its Jihad Against the United States Been Defeated?

Capitalism

13. Is the Global Economic Crisis a Failure of Capitalism?

China

18. Will China Be the Next Superpower?

Democracy

14. Is Social Media Becoming the Most Powerful Force in Global Politics?
20. Is the Middle East Undergoing a Democratic Revolution?
21. Is the International Community Making Effective Progress in Securing Global Human Rights?

Drugs

9. Can the Global Community "Win" the Drug War?

Energy

4. Should Environmentalists Continue to Be Alarmists?

5. Should the World Continue to Rely on Oil as the Major Source of Energy?

Food

5. Should the World Continue to Rely on Oil as the Major Source of Energy?
6. Will the World Be Able to Feed Itself in the Foreseeable Future?
8. Can the Global Community Successfully Confront the Global Water Shortage?

Global Environment

4. Should Environmentalists Continue to Be Alarmists?
5. Should the World Continue to Rely on Oil as the Major Source of Energy?
6. Will the World Be Able to Feed Itself in the Foreseeable Future?
7. Is the Threat of Global Warming Real?
8. Can the Global Community Successfully Confront the Global Water Shortage?
12. Is the International Community Making Progress in Addressing Natural Disasters?
15. Are We Headed for a Nuclear 9/11?
17. Is a Nuclear Iran a Global Security Threat?

Global Resources

1. Should the International Community Continue to Focus on Programs to Help Developing Countries Curb Population Growth?
2. Is Global Aging a Major Problem?
3. Does Global Urbanization Lead Primarily to Undesirable Consequences?
4. Should Environmentalists Continue to Be Alarmists?

(Continued)

Introduction

Global Issues in the Twenty-First Century

James E. Harf

Mark Owen Lombardi

Threats of the New Millennium

As the new millennium dawned a decade ago, the world witnessed two very different events whose impacts have been far reaching, profound, and in many ways have shaped the discourse of global issues. The first was the new era of terrorism, ushered in by the tragedy of 9/11. It burst upon the international scene with the force of a mega-catastrophe, occupying virtually every waking moment of national and global leaders throughout the world and seizing the attention of the rest of the planet's citizens who contemplated both the immediate implications and the long-term effects of a U.S. response. The focused interest of national policymakers was soon transformed into a war on terrorism, while average citizens sought to cope with changes brought on by both the tragic events of September 2001 and the global community's response to them. Both governmental leaders and citizens continue to address the consequences of this first intrusion of the new millennium on a world now far different in many ways since the pre-9/11 era. Unfortunately, as the millennium's first decade ended, other challenges to global welfare and security also emerged. At the global level, a severe financial crisis forced world leaders to question the major tenets of contemporary capitalism. At the national level, a reemerging Russian presence, flexing its new economic muscles based on energy and backed by a growing military might, brought back fears of a new cold war. And throughout North Africa and the Middle East, citizens took to the streets to protest decades of autocratic rule by despotic rulers and to seek more democratic government. The second event at the beginning of the millennium was less dramatic and certainly did not receive the same fanfare, but still has had both short- and long-term ramifications for the global community in the twenty-first century. This was the creation of a set of ambitious millennium development goals by the United Nations. In September 2000, 189 national governments committed to eight major goals in an initiative known as the UN Millennium Development Goals (MDG): eradicate extreme poverty and hunger; achieve universal primary education; promote gender equality and empower women; reduce child mortality; improve maternal health; combat HIV/AIDS, malaria, and other diseases; ensure environmental sustainability; and develop a global partnership for development. This initiative was important not only because the UN was setting an actionable 15-year agenda against a relatively new set of global issues but also because it signified a major change in how the international community would henceforth address such problems confronting human-kind. The new initiative represented recognition of

(1) shared responsibility between rich and poor nations for solving such problems; (2) a link between goals; (3) the paramount role to be played by national governments in the process; and (4) the need for measurable outcome indicators of success. The UN Millennium Development Goals initiative went virtually unnoticed by much of the public, although governmental decision makers involved with the United Nations understood its significance. As we approach the 15-year timeline for implementation of these millennium goals, the success rate has been mixed at best.

These two major events, although vastly different, symbolize the world in which we now find ourselves, a world far more complex and more violent than either the earlier one characterized by the cold war struggle between the United States and the Soviet Union, or the post–cold war era of the 1990s, where global and national leaders struggled to identify and then find their proper place in the post–cold war world order. Consider the first event, the 9/11 tragedy. It reminds us all that the use and abuse of power in pursuit of political goals in earlier centuries is still a viable option for those throughout the world who believe themselves disadvantaged because of various political, economic, or social conditions and structures. The only difference is the perpetrators' choice of military hardware and strategy. Formally declared wars fought by regular national military forces publicly committed (at least on paper) to the tenets of just war theory have now been replaced by a plethora of "quasi-military tactics" whose defining characteristics conjure up terrorism, perpetrated by individuals without attachments to a regular military and/or without allegiance to a national government and country, and who do not hesitate to put ordinary citizens in harm's way. At the same time, a few rogue states, Iran and North Korea for example, have opted for more bellicose approaches to international behavior, whether seeking nuclear weapons or choosing to use natural resources as a weapon.

On the other hand, the second event of the new century, the UN Millennium Goals initiative, symbolizes the other side of the global coin, the recognition that the international community is also beset with a number of problems unrelated to military actions or national security, at least in a direct sense. The past four decades have witnessed the emergence and thrust to prominence a number of new problems relating to social, economic, and environmental characteristics of the citizens who inhabit this planet. These problems impact the basic quality of life of global inhabitants in ways very different from the scourges of military violence. But their impact is just as profound. Consider that in the first months of this millennium's second decade, for example, two major natural disasters struck the planet, the devastating earthquake in Haiti, which followed on the heels of a similar disaster in Chile, and the equally destructive earthquake and tsunami in Japan with its resultant nuclear dangers. These events illustrate that in today's world, natural disaster phenomena are just as threatening. And they also unite us as global citizens in the same way that terrorism separates us. At the heart of this global change affecting the global system and its inhabitants for good or for ill is a phenomenon called globalization.

The Age of Globalization

The cold war era, marked by the domination of two superpowers in the decades following the end of World War II, has given way to a new era called globalization. This new epoch is characterized by a dramatic shrinking of the globe in terms of travel and communication, increased participation in global policymaking by an expanding array of national and nonstate actors, and an exploding arrey of problems with ever-growing consequences. While the tearing down of the Berlin Wall two decades ago dramatically symbolized the end of the cold war era, the creation of the Internet, with its ability to connect around the world, and the fallen World Trade Center, with its dramatic illustration of vulnerability, symbolize the new paradigm of integration and violence.

Globalization is a fluid and complex phenomenon that manifests itself in thousands of wondrous as well as disturbing ways. In the past couple of decades, national borders have shrunk or disappeared, with a resultant increase in the movement of ideas, products, resources, finances, and people throughout the globe. This reality has brought with it great advances and challenges. For example, the ease with which people and objects move throughout the globe has greatly magnified fears like the spread of disease. The term "epidemic" has been replaced by the phrase "global pandemic," as virulent scourges unleashed in one part of the globe now have greater potential to find their way to the far corners of the planet. The world has also come to fear an expanded potential for terrorism, as new technologies combined with increasing cultural friction and socioeconomic disparities have conspired to make the world far less safe than it had been. The pistol that killed the Austrian Archduke in Sarajevo in 1914, ushering in World War I, has been replaced by the jumbo jet used as a missile to bring down the World Trade Center, snuffing out the lives of thousands of innocent victims. We now live in an era of global reach for both good and ill, where a small group or a single individual can touch the hearts of people around the world with acts of kindness or can shatter their dreams with acts of terror.

This increase in the movement of information and ideas has ushered in global concerns over cultural imperialism and religious/ethnic wars. The ability both to retrieve and to disseminate information in the contemporary era will have an impact in this century as great as, if not greater than, the telephone, radio, and television in the last century. The potential for global good or ill is mind-boggling. Finally, traditional notions of great-power security embodied in the cold war rivalry have given way to concerns about terrorism, genocide, nuclear proliferation, cultural conflict, rogue states, and the diminishing role of international law.

Globalization heightens our awareness of a vast array of global issues that will challenge individuals as well as governmental and nongovernmental actors. Everyone has become a global actor and so each has policy impact. This text seeks to identify those issues that are central to the discourse on the impact of globalization. The issues in this volume provide a broad overview of the mosaic of global issues that will affect students' daily lives.

What Is a Global Issue?

We begin by addressing the basic characteristics of a *global issue*.[1] By definition, the word *issue* suggests disagreement along several related dimensions:

1. whether a problem exists and how it comes about;
2. the characteristics of the problem;

---

[1] The characteristics are extracted from James E. Harf and B. Thomas Trout, *The Politics of Global Resources*, Duke University Press, 1986. pp. 12–28.

3. the preferred future alternatives or solutions; and/or
4. how these preferred futures are to be obtained.

These problems are real, vexing, and controversial, because policymakers bring to their analyses different historical experiences, values, goals, and objectives. These differences impede and may even prevent successful problem solving. In short, the key ingredient of an issue is disagreement.

The word *global* in the phrase *global issue* is what makes the set of problems confronting the human race today far different from those that challenged earlier generations. Historically, problems were confined to a village, city, or region. The capacity of the human race to fulfill its daily needs was limited to a much smaller space: the immediate environment. In 1900, 90 percent of all humanity was born, lived, and died within a 50-mile radius. Today, a third of the world's population travel to one or more countries. In the United States, 75 percent of people move at least 100 miles away from their homes and most travel to places their grandparents could only dream about.

What does this mobility mean? It suggests that a vast array of issues are now no longer only local or national but are global in scope, including but not limited to food resources, trade, energy, health care, the environment, disease, natural disasters, conflict, cultural rivalry, populism, rogue states, democratic revolutions, and nuclear Armageddon.

The character of these issues is thus different from those of earlier eras. First, they transcend national boundaries and impact virtually every corner of the globe. In effect, these issues help make national borders increasingly meaningless. Environmental pollution or poisonous gases do not recognize or respect national borders. Birds carrying the avian flu and nuclear radiation leaking from disabled power plants have no knowledge of political boundaries.

Second, these new issues cannot be resolved by the autonomous action of a single actor, be it a national government, international organization, or multinational corporation. A country cannot guarantee its own energy or food security without participating in a global energy or food system.

Third, these issues are characterized by a wide array of value systems. To a family in the developing world, giving birth to a fifth or sixth child may contribute to the family's immediate economic well-being. But to a research scholar at the United Nations Population Fund, the consequence of such an action multiplied across the entire developing world leads to expanding poverty and resource depletion.

Fourth, these issues will not go away. They require specific policy action by a consortium of local, national, and international leaders. Simply ignoring the issue cannot eliminate the threat of chemical or biological terrorism, for example. If global warming does exist, it will not disappear unless specific policies are developed and implemented.

These issues are also characterized by their persistence over time. The human race has developed the capacity to manipulate its external environment and, in so doing, has created a host of opportunities and challenges. The accelerating pace of technological change suggests that global issues will proliferate and will continue to challenge human beings throughout the next millennium.

In the final analysis, however, a global issue is defined as such only through mutual agreement by a host of actors within the international community. Some may disagree about the nature, severity, or presence of a given issue. These concerns then become areas of focus after a significant number of actors (states, international organizations, the United Nations, and others) begin to focus systematic and organized attention on the issue itself.

Defining the Global Issues Agenda

The election of President Barak Obama has opened up opportunities for the United States to adopt differing policies to the new global agenda. After four years, there are signs of differing approaches to issues such as terrorism, civil conflict, nuclear proliferation, and resource use. The long-term impacts of these changes are yet to be determined. And the next national election could bring yet a different set of values as guiding principles in foreign policy decision making.

The Nexus of Global Issues and Globalization

Since 1989, the world has been caught in the maelstrom of globalization. Throughout the 1990s and into the twenty-first century, scholars and policymakers have struggled to define this new era. As the early years of the new century ushered in a different and heightened level of violence, a sense of urgency emerged. At first, some analyzed the new era in terms of the victory of Western or American ideals, the dominance of global capitalism, and the spread of democracy versus the use of religious fanaticism by the have-nots of the world as a ploy to rearrange power within the international system. But recent events call into question assumptions about Western victory or the dominance of capitalism. Others have defined this new era simply in terms of the multiplicity of actors now performing on the world stage, noting how states and their sovereignty have declined in importance and impact vis-à-vis others such as multinational corporations and nongovernmental groups like Greenpeace and Amnesty International. Still others have focused on the vital element of technology and its impact on communications; information storage and retrieval; global exchange; and attitudes, culture, and values.

Whether globalization reflects one, two, or all of these characteristics is not as important as the fundamental realization that globalization is the dominant element of a new era in international politics. The globalization revolution now shapes and dictates the agenda. To argue otherwise is frankly akin to insisting on using a rotary phone in an iPhone world. This new period is characterized by several basic traits that greatly impact the definition, analysis, and solution of global issues. They include the following:

- an emphasis on information technology;
- the increasing speed of information and idea flows;
- the ability of global citizens to access information at rapidly growing rates and thus empower themselves for good or for ill;
- a need for greater sophistication and expertise to manage such flows;
- the control and dissemination of technology; and
- the cultural diffusion and interaction that come with information expansion and dissemination.

Each of these areas has helped shape a new emerging global issues agenda. Current issues remain important and, indeed, these factors help us to understand them on a much deeper level. Yet globalization created a new array of problems that is reshaping the global issues landscape and the dialogue, tools, strategies, and approaches that the next U.S. president and indeed all global actors will take.

For example, the spread of information technology has made ideas, attitudes, and information more available to people throughout the world. Americans in Columbus, Ohio, had the ability to log onto the Internet and speak with their counterparts in Kosovo to discover when NATO bombing had begun and to gauge the accuracy of later news reports on the bombing. Norwegian students can share values and customs directly with their counterparts in South Africa, thereby experiencing cultural attitudes firsthand without the filtering mechanisms of governments or even parents and teachers. Scientific information that is available through computer technology can now be used to build sophisticated biological and chemical weapons of immense destructive capability, or equally to promote the dissemination of drugs and medicines outside of "normal" national channels. Ethnic conflicts and genocide between groups of people are now global news, forcing millions to come to grips with issues of intervention, prevention, and punishment. And terrorists in different parts of the globe can communicate readily with one another, transferring plans and even money across national and continental boundaries with ease. And antagonists against autocratic regimes can also communicate with their counterparts within their own society as well as those in neighboring countries, as witnessed by communication flows throughout North Africa and the Middle East among groups and individuals seeking democracy in the early months of 2011.

Globalization is an international system and it is also rapidly changing. Because of the fluid nature of this system and the fact that it is both relatively new and largely fueled by the amazing speed of technology, continuing issues are constantly being transformed and new issues are emerging regularly. The nexus of globalization and global issues has now become, in many ways, the defining dynamic of understanding global issues. Whether dealing with new forms of terrorism and new concepts of security, expanding international law, solving ethnic conflicts, dealing with mass migration, coping with individual freedom and access to information, or addressing cultural clash and cultural imperialism, the transition from a cold war world to a globalized world helps us understand in part what these issues are and why they are important. But most importantly, this fundamental realization shapes how governments and people can and must respond.

Identifying the New Global Issues Agenda

The organization of this text reflects the centrality of globalization. Units 1 and 2 focus on the continuing global agenda of the post-cold war era. The emphasis is on global population and environmental issues and the nexus between these two phenomena. Has the threat of uncontrolled world population growth subsided or will the built-in momentum of the past four decades override any recent strides in slowing birth rates in the developing world? Should the international community recommit to addressing this problem of population growth because of its built-in momentum, or are growth-related problems disappearing and in no need of policy intervention by global actors? Is global aging about to unleash a host of problems for governments of the developed world? Is rapid urbanization creating a whole new set of problems unique to such urban settings? Do environmentalists overstate their case or is the charge of "crying wolf" by environmental conservatives a misplaced attack? Is the world running out of natural resources or is the concern of many about resource availability, be it food, oil, water, air, and/or pristine land, simply misguided? Should the world continue to rely on oil or should the search for viable alternatives take on a new urgency? Will the world be able to feed itself or provide enough water in the foreseeable future? Is global warming for real?

Unit 3 addresses the consequences of the decline of national boundaries and the resultant increased international flow of information, ideas, money, and material things in this globalization age. Can the global community win the war on drugs? Is the international community prepared for the next global health pandemic? Has this community also designed an adequate strategy to address human trafficking and natural disasters that quickly cross national boundaries? Does the global financial crisis represent a failure of modern capitalism? Are social media becoming the most powerful force in global politics?

Unit 4 addresses the new global security dilemma. Are we in a new cold war as a consequence of a resurgent Russian foreign policy? Are cultural and ethnic violence and wars the defining dimensions of conflict in this century? Is this the China century? Is a nuclear Iran a global security threat? Have Al-Qaeda and its jihad against the United States been defeated? Is the Middle East undergoing a democratic revolution?

The two new issues in this expanded edition represent important emerging concerns for the international community. Global human rights, a fixture on the international agenda since the end of World War II, is entering a new phase in its evolution as citizens throughout the globe are increasingly adopting an attitude of "we are not going to take it any more" and have begun to actively rebel against abuses perpetrated by national governmental leaders and others. Meanwhile, regarding a potentially nuclear-armed Iran, the world watches as Iran makes increasingly bellicose statements toward Israel and the latter contemplates how it might address this expanding dangerous situation.

The revolutionary changes of the last few decades present us with serious challenges unlike any others in human history. However, as in all periods of historic change, we possess significant opportunities to overcome problems. The task ahead is to define these issues, explore their context, and develop solutions that are comprehensive in scope and effect. The role of all researchers in this field, or any other, is to analyze objectively such problems and search for workable solutions. As students of global issues, your task is to educate yourselves about these issues and become part of the solution.

Internet References . . .

Population Reference Bureau

The Population Reference Bureau provides current information on international population trends and their implications from an objective viewpoint. The PopPov Research Network section of this Web site offers maps with regional and country-specific population information as well as information divided by selected topics.

www.prb.org

United Nations Population Fund (UNFPA)

The United Nations Population Fund (UNFPA) was established in 1969 and was originally called the United Nations Fund for Population Activities. This organization works with developing countries to educate people about reproductive and sexual health as well as about family planning. The UNFPA also supports population and development strategies that will benefit developing countries and advocates for the resources needed to accomplish these tasks.

www.unfpa.org

Population Connection

Population Connection (formerly Zero Population Growth) is a national, nonprofit organization working to slow population growth and to achieve a sustainable balance between Earth's people and its resources. The organization seeks to protect the environment and to ensure a high quality of life for present and future generations. More recently, it has focused on women's population issues.

www.populationconnection.org

The CSIS Global Aging Initiative

The Center for Strategic and International Studies (CSIS) is a public policy research institution that approaches the issue of the aging population in developed countries in a bipartisan manner. The CSIS is involved in a two-year project to explore the global implications of aging in developed nations and to seek strategies on dealing with this issue. This site includes a list of publications that were presented at previous events.

www.csis.org/gai/

The Population Council

The Population Council is an international, nonprofit organization that conducts research on population matters from biological, social science, and public health perspectives. It was established in 1952 by John D. Rockefeller, III.

www.popcouncil.org

The Population Institute

The Population Institute is an international, educational, nonprofit organization that seeks to voluntarily reduce excessive population growth. Established in 1989 and headquartered in Washington, D.C., it has members in 172 countries.

www.populationinstitute.org

Global Population

*I*t is not a coincidence that many contemporary global issues in this book emerged at about the same time as world population growth exploded. No matter what the issue, the presence of a large and fast-growing population alongside it has exacerbated the issue and transformed its basic characteristics. In the new millennium, declining growth rates, which first appeared in the developed world but are now also evident in many parts of the developing world, pose a different set of problems. The emergence of a graying population throughout the globe, but particularly in the developed world, has the potential for significant impact. And the rapid growth within urban areas of the developing world continues to pose a different set of problems.

The ability of the global community to respond to any given issue is diminished by certain population conditions, be it an extremely young consuming population in a poor country in need of producers, an expanding urban population whose local public officials are unable to provide an appropriate infrastructure, a large working-age group in a nation without sufficient jobs, or an ever-growing senior population for whom additional services are needed.

Thus we begin this text with a series of issues directly related to various aspects of world population. It serves as both a separate global agenda and a context within which other issues are examined.

- Should the International Community Continue to Focus on Programs to Help Developing Countries Curb Population Growth?

- Is Global Aging a Major Problem?

- Does Global Urbanization Lead Primarily to Undesirable Consequences?

1

ISSUE 1

Should the International Community Continue to Focus on Programs to Help Developing Countries Curb Population Growth?

YES: Terry M. Redding, from "The Population Challenge: Key to Global Survival," *The 21st Century Papers* (The Population Institute, 2007)

NO: Michael J. Miller, from "The Under-Population Problem: An Interview with Steven W. Mosher on the Demographic Consequences of Birth Control Policies," *The Catholic World Report* (August–September 2008)

Learning Outcomes

After reading this issue, you should be able to:

- Gain an understanding of why certain groups and individuals still believe that population growth rates left unchecked by public policy will lead to undesirable consequences.
- Have an appreciation for why certain groups and individuals believe that population control is no longer necessary in today's world.
- Discuss how national and international governmental population issue officials have redefined today's basic population issue from an emphasis on population growth to a focus on women's reproductive health.
- Discuss the linkage between population growth and the environment defined broadly.
- Discuss the linkage between population growth and global security.

ISSUE SUMMARY

YES: Terry M. Redding, a communications consultant to The Population Institute, suggests that population *growth* is being unfortunately neglected in international development discussions, as the latter's focus has been on other aspects of population such as reproductive health and women's empowerment.

NO: Steven W. Mosher, president of the Population Research Institute, an organization devoted to debunking the idea that the world is overpopulated, argues in an interview with Michael J. Miller of *The Catholic World Report* that self-interest was the motivation for past efforts on the part of international funding agencies, including the World Bank, to curb population by pressuring developing countries to adopt fertility reduction programs.

T he history of the international community's efforts to lower birth rates throughout the developing world goes back to the late 1960s, when the annual growth rate hovered around 2.35 percent. At that time, selected individuals in international governmental organizations, including the United Nations, were persuaded by a number of wealthy national governments as well as by international nongovernmental population agencies that a problem of potentially massive proportions had recently emerged. Quite simply, demographers had observed a pattern of population growth in the poorer regions of the world quite unlike that which had occurred in the richer countries during the previous 150–200 years.

Population growth in the developed countries of the globe had followed a rather persistent pattern during the last two centuries. Before the industrial revolution, these countries typically experienced both high birth rates and high death rates. As industrialization took hold and advances in the quality of life for citizens of these countries occurred, death rates fell, resulting in a period of time when the size of the population rose. Later, birth rates also began to decline, in large part because the newly industrialized societies were better suited to families with fewer children. After awhile, both birth and death rates leveled off at a much lower level than that during preindustrial times.

This earlier demographic transition throughout the developed world differed, however, from the newer growth pattern in the poorer regions of the globe observed by demographers in the late 1960s. First, the transition in the developed world occurred over a long period of time, allowing the population to deal more readily with such growth. On the other hand, post-1960s' growth in the developing world had taken off at a much faster pace, far outstripping the capacity of these societies to cope with the changes accompanying such growth. Second, the earlier growth in the developed world began with a much smaller population base and a much larger resource base than that in the developing world, again allowing the richer societies to cope more easily with such growth. The developing world of the 1960s, however, found percentages of increase based on a much higher base. Coping under the latter scenario proved to be much more difficult. Finally, industrialization accompanied population change in the developed world, again allowing for those societies to address resultant problems more easily. Today's developing world has no such luxury.

New jobs are not available, expanded educational facilities are nonexistent, unsatisfactory health services remain unchanged, and modern infrastructures have not been created.

The international community formally placed the population issue—defined primarily as excessive birth rates in the developing world—on the global agenda in 1974 with the first major global conference on population held in Bucharest, Romania. There was much debate over the motives of both sides. Both rich and poor countries eventually pledged to work together. Finally, each side bought into the assumption that "the best contraceptive was economic development," but until development was achieved, national family planning programs would help lower growth rates. A decade later at the 1984 Mexico City global population conference, the international community and national governments had joined forces to combat high growth rates. By 1994 when nations of the world reconvened in Cairo to assess progress, considerable success had been achieved in getting developing countries to accept such programs. At Cairo, however, a major change occurred. Calls for population planning were replaced by cries for reproductive health and women's empowerment. For over a decade and a half, the focus and funds to accompany it have moved away from family planning to these other issues.

There are at least two basic dimensions to this issue. First, should the international community have involved itself in the first place in reducing fertility throughout the developing world? That is, was it a violation of either national sovereignty (a country should be free from extreme outside influence) or human rights (an individual has the right to make fertility decisions unencumbered by outside pressure, particularly those from another culture)? And what should its motives have been? To put it another way, was advocacy of population control really a form of ethnic or national genocide? And second, has the international community erred in moving away from emphasizing family planning and focusing, instead, on other population-related aspects, such as reproductive health and women's empowerment?

The first question was answered succinctly by Robert S. McNamara in "The Population Explosion," *The Futurist* (November/December 1992). His belief that the international community has an obligation to get involved is based on his assessment of the resultant damage to both the developing world where such high levels of growth are found and the rest of the world that must compete with the poorer countries for increasingly scarce resources. McNamara suggested that consequences include environmentally unsustainable development, food shortages, worsening of poverty, and negative impacts on the welfare of women and children. These consequences appear to make an overwhelming case for fertility reduction. And the cost of policy intervention is small, in his judgment, compared with both gross national products and overseas general development assistance.

Those who oppose such intervention point to several different reasons. The first, originally articulated at the 1974 Bucharest conference, argues that economic development is the best contraceptive. The demographic transition worked in the developed world and there was no reason to assume that it will not work in the developing world. This was the dominant view of the developing countries at Bucharest, who feared international policy intervention and at the same time wanted and needed external capital to develop. They soon came to realize that characteristics particular to the developing world in the latter part of the twentieth century meant that foreign aid alone would not be enough. It had to be accompanied by fertility reduction programs, wherever the origin. Second, some of those who oppose intervention do not see the extreme negative environmental consequences of expanding populations. For them, the pronatalists (those favoring fertility reduction programs) engage in inflammatory discourse, exaggerated arguments, and scare tactics devoid of much scientific evidence. And finally, cultural constraints can counteract any attempt to impose fertility reduction values from the outside. Children are valued in most societies. They, particularly male heirs, serve as the social security system for most families. They become producers at an early age, contributing to the family income.

The bottom line is that each has a valid point. Environmental stress is a fact of life, and increased consumption does play a role. If the latter originates because of more people, then fertility reduction is a viable solution. Left to its own devices, the developing world is unable to provide both the rationale for such action and the resources to accomplish it. The barriers are too great. Although the international community must guard against behavior that is or appears to be either genocidal in nature or violating human rights, it must nonetheless move forward.

An alternative approach is found by examining the 1994 Cairo population conference, where the debate over whether external intervention in family planning was a good idea was pushed aside. Calls for dropping demographic and family planning benchmarks were replaced by the broader set of issues that centered on women's empowerment. The previously central issue of population, high growth rates in the developing world, was barely mentioned at Cairo and was almost completely ignored after the conference. Funding priorities changed as well. Within a decade, only about 10 percent of 1994 levels of expenditures were targeted for family planning. Now, however, voices are beginning to be heard once again calling for a return to the central question of yesteryear.

In the YES selection, Terry M. Redding argues that ignoring "serious consideration of high fertility and family planning has been a mistake" and suggests a return to the earlier emphases. In the NO selection, Steven W. Mosher, president of the Population Reference Institute, an organization devoted to debunking the idea that the world is overpopulated, argues in an interview with Michael J. Miller that even if there was a reason for past global efforts to curb population by international funding agencies, these reasons no longer exist.

YES

Terry M. Redding

The Population Challenge: Key To Global Survival

Neglecting the Human Connection

Stabilizing the growth of the world's human population is a goal that must be achieved if we are to preserve our options for the future and improve the odds for the world's sustainability. Challenges such as climate change and global warming, fragile and failed states, migration and refugee crises, food and water insecurity, poverty, disease, debt, and illiteracy are caused or exacerbated by unchecked rapid population growth.

Discussions on addressing these challenges, however, often neglect serious consideration of high fertility and family planning. Former U.S. President Bill Clinton singled out population growth as the key issue that candidates in the 2008 presidential election were avoiding. This is puzzling and troubling, as population growth is the single world issue that binds all the others together; it is the root of many problems affecting the tree of humanity.

Indeed, trees provide an apt analogy to the current global reality: In countries with quality reproductive health services and policies serving as the roots, the branches—including economics, health, and education—are stable. As this paper will demonstrate, in countries with poor reproductive health services and policies for their roots, many branches are not healthy and cannot thrive; the tree may even fail. Just as the health and even the survival of a tree rely on strong roots, the health and viability of a country and indeed the planet can be traced to population.

Still, unlike many other global problems and crises, the technology to meet the population challenge is readily available and extremely cost effective, if we have the will to supply it to those in need.

By the year 2050, world population is projected to grow from its current 6.7 billion to 9.3 billion; less optimistic calculations, based on fertility not declining from 2006 rates, place the figure at nearly 12 billion. Practically all growth is estimated to occur in the developing countries, especially in the poorest of those countries, which already produce virtually all of the world's human numbers.

While many nations have reduced rapid population growth, more than 3 billion people currently under 25 years old will soon enter their prime reproductive years. Providing this largest youth generation in history with appropriate sexual and reproductive health services and education is essential to ease poverty, increase educational opportunities, preserve the environment, improve health, and provide political security. Meeting this challenge will be especially important in developing countries considered "fragile states," wherein booming populations would further stress already limited resources.

For population growth to slow and birthrates decline, Christopher Flavin, President of the Worldwatch Institute, has said, "It is essential that women and men around the world have increased access to sound information, a range of contraceptive options, and related health services. Access to voluntary family planning allows women and couples to time their births and choose the size of their families."

But at this critical moment, international support for family planning services faces ongoing annual reductions as the political climate has chilled and funds from many sectors are diverted to HIV/AIDS programs. In many countries, contraceptive use has risen only slowly or has stalled.

Ironically, in many developing countries, sexual and reproductive health education and services, especially meeting family planning needs, presents a cost-effective component in mitigating any of the above-mentioned issues.

The Challenge of Unmet Need

At the core of addressing population growth is managing unmet need. There is well documented unmet need for family planning, especially among the 2 billion people living on less than $2 a day.

Slower population growth offers a demographic dividend, allowing a country to invest more in education and health, thus serving the broader agendas of social and economic development.

It is also recognized that women are at the center of reproductive health efforts and addressing unmet need. As demographer Ruth Dixon-Mueller explains:

> Population control policies and programs would probably be unnecessary if women could exercise their basic economic, political and social rights and genuine reproductive choice. In addition, programs need to address the widespread unmet need in many countries for reproductive health services that would enable women to regulate the timing of their childbearing and, in particular, help women to avoid unwanted and mistimed pregnancies and unsafe abortion.

The definition of unmet need has undergone refinements over 25 years of discussion, but the basic objective is to estimate the proportion of women not using contraception who either want to cease further childbearing or want to postpone the next birth at least two years. The greatest need is in sub-Saharan Africa, where an average of 26 percent of married women are in the unmet need category. Other reports estimate the need among never-married women at 9 percent.

One calculation shows 113.6 million women (both married and unmarried) have an unmet need for contraception in the developing world. The World

Health Organization (WHO) estimates that over 120 million couples worldwide do not use contraceptives, despite wishing to limit or space their children.

While unmet need has lessened globally in recent decades, there are many more women now, in absolute numbers, than in years past, and many more younger women. Today there are almost 3 billion people under the age of 25, the largest generation of young people in history, 87 percent of whom live in the developing world. Meeting their sexual and reproductive health needs is central to their well being, as well as to population stabilization, poverty reduction, and sustainable development. The decisions of this "critical cohort" in the timing, sizing and spacing of their families will be a key factor in whether world population growth will be stabilized.

Where the need is met, family planning services work. In the 28 most populous countries receiving U.S. family planning assistance, the average number of children per family has dropped from 6.1 in the 1960s to 4.2 in 2003. In Colombia, Indonesia, and Mexico, the family average is three children, and in Taiwan and Thailand, early recipients of U.S. assistance, the average is two children.

The West African country of Ghana made family planning a public health priority in the early 1980s, and since then modern contraceptive use among married women has risen from 5.2 percent in 1988 to 18.7 percent in 2003. Ghana's rate of 64 infant deaths per 1,000 live births stands out from the regional average of 100 deaths, and the rate of HIV infection (2.2 percent) is half the West African average.

Further, one estimate shows that family planning services are preventing three-quarters of the induced abortions that would otherwise occur in the developing world. In addition, if every woman in the developing world with unmet need for a modern method used one, 52 million unintended pregnancies could be avoided annually.

Of the 46 million pregnancies that are terminated every year, only 60 percent are carried out under safe conditions. Almost all unsafe abortions take place in the developing world, with South America having the highest ratio. Although age patterns differ regionally, two-thirds of unsafe abortions occur among women aged 15 to 30.

The Cost-Effective Alternative

Prevention would seem a better policy. The cost to provide the services and supplies is estimated at $3.9 billion annually, but the savings would be much greater.

One example cited is a typical low-fertility Latin American country where every dollar spent on family planning saves $12 in health and education costs. Unfortunately, inflation-adjusted family planning spending has fallen since the mid-1990s. In the United States, President Bush's requests for overseas family planning program funding have been reduced from $425 million during the tenure of Secretary of State Colin Powell to $357 million under Secretary Condoleezza Rice.

The $34 million appropriated by Congress annually to the United Nations Population Fund (UNFPA) but blocked by the Bush administration, by one estimate, could have prevented 2 million unintentional pregnancies, nearly 800,000 abortions, 4,700 maternal deaths, and 77,000 infant and child deaths.

The planet now carries more people of child-bearing age than ever before, and yet a desired and cost-effective component in addressing the world's booming population is largely ignored in most policy discussions. The funds invested now in population programs will prevent conflicts, benefit the planet, and yield higher returns than any other investments in humanity's future. A convergence of potential calamities looms; offering couples the freedom to determine their own fertility is perhaps the only practical, the only realistic, option.

Population and the Millennium Development Goals

One notable example of how population growth is being overlooked in international development discussions comes through the Millennium Development Goals (MDGs) of the United Nations (UN). Eight MDGs (with 18 individual targets), based on the Millennium Declaration adopted in September 2000 by all 189 member states of the UN General Assembly, outline critical areas to be addressed by 2015, but did not originally cite population growth. One population researcher efficiently sums up the oversight: "Although reproductive health was not specifically included as an independent goal or a measurable target in the MDGs, for years experts have provided evidence that investing in reproductive health services is integral to meeting them all."

A 2007 report from the All Party Parliamentary Group (APPG) on Population, Development and Reproductive Health in the United Kingdom explores the impact of population on the first seven goals, and concludes "The evidence is overwhelming: the MDGs are difficult or impossible to achieve with the current levels of population growth in the least developed countries and regions."

The last half of the twentieth century provides the foundation for this conclusion:

> On the whole, those countries and regions where information and contraceptives were made available saw a moderate to rapid decline in the birth rate. In addition, there was an improvement in the economy, the health of women and their families, and the autonomy, education and status of women. The countries where many pregnancies remained unwanted and the birth rate did not fall are now seeing an explosive growth of urban slums, a failure of the state to keep pace with educational demands and, in some cases, the continuing oppression of women.

On a positive note, the APPG report states that the UN has approved a new target of universal access to reproductive health care by 2015, to be placed under Goal 5, Improve Maternal Health.

Still, "It is clear that the MDGs are difficult or impossible to achieve without a renewed focus on, and investment in, family planning." The recommendations in the report include targeting 10 percent of international development aid to population and reproductive health, putting the availability of contraceptive supplies as a top priority, and eliminating barriers to family planning.

Rising from Poverty

One country claims to have already met the first MDG target. The People's Republic of China reported to the APPG that through a combination of lowered birth rates and economic reform, 150 million people have been lifted out of abject poverty, thus meeting the MDG for poverty reduction a decade earlier than the target date. Nonetheless, controversy surrounding China's "One Child" policy will make others uncertain of the means to achieve the end. In fact, China is one case cited by population experts as having created an unwarranted stigma among critics and commentators on the topic of reproductive health.

Economists acknowledge that the link between slower population growth and economic development is complex and does not always result in an escape from poverty. Still, a "demographic dividend" occurs when family sizes drop rapidly, leaving relatively more people of working age with fewer dependents, and the ability to invest more resources in those dependents in terms of health and education. In developing countries where the birth rate has fallen, between 25 and 40 percent of economic growth is attributable to the demographic change.

Population Growth Outpacing Education

The second MDG, achieving universal primary education, seems especially daunting in the face of rising population pressures. In Tanzania, literacy rates fell from 90 percent in 1986 to 68 percent in 1995, attributed to increased school fees as the government was unable to keep pace with public service costs for its growing population. The country's population during the period grew from just under 22 million to nearly 30 million.

Almost 30 percent of the world population is under age 15, and the United Nations Children's Fund (UNICEF) estimates there are 115 million children of primary school age who are not in school. In high growth countries, the number of school-aged children doubles every 20 years. Assuming a class size of 40, an extra 2 million school teachers per year are required just to meet existing needs.

According to one World Bank report, the annual cost of meeting the MDG education goal ranges from $10 to $30 billion. In another report, World Bank researchers estimate the annual costs in low-income countries would be $9.7 billion annually, of which $3.7 billion would be needed from international assistance, many times higher than actual aid flows. Africa, for example, would need 75 percent of their total from external support.

While hope comes from countries that have registered an improvement of 20 percent or more within a decade in the primary school completion rate (e.g., Brazil, Nicaragua, Cambodia, South Africa, The Gambia), progress is fragile, and other countries, even some with strong financial resources, have lost ground (e.g., Albania, Zambia, Qatar, Bahrain, United Arab Emirates, Kenya, and Venezuela).

Success in achieving universal primary education nonetheless raises an interesting series of questions. Should countries meet the goal, will they have follow-on capacity to meet the needs of the large numbers of students who would like to continue their education to various levels? Do they have the capacity to satisfy the employment options for newly educated students? Would a brain drain result as students go abroad seeking higher education? No doubt many students would not be satisfied to return to a simple or subsistence lifestyle, but it is doubtful that most countries would have the capacity to build yet more schools and train enough staff to accommodate the greater ambitions of their students.

A slowing of the exponential rate of increase in the population of young people would allow countries to more realistically over time create the infrastructures to accommodate their numbers and ambitions. Thus the attainment of access to education for all children presents a powerful argument for the immediate and urgent need to extend access to family planning.

Although there may be potential local obstacles, the curricula for these children should include health education, and reproductive health education should be considered as students enter reproductive age.

Gender Educational Parity Missing Mark

The second and third millennium goals are closely intertwined. The first part of the target for MDG 3 has already passed without being met: "Eliminate gender disparity in primary and secondary education preferably by 2005." While 125 countries, both developing and industrialized, were on course to eventually achieve gender parity, overall enrollment remains low.

Some 94 countries missed the 2005 target for gender parity, and 86 may not achieve this by 2015, according to the United Nations Educational, Scientific and Cultural Organization (UNESCO). By contrast, Iran (where family size has declined to replacement level fertility) has already achieved a 90 percent gender balance, and more women than men enter Iran's universities.

High Fertility and Child, Maternal Mortality

Reducing child mortality and improving maternal health, MDGs 4 and 5, respectively, are essential aspects in addressing population stability. High fertility is strongly associated with child mortality and greatly increases a woman's lifetime risk of dying from pregnancy-related causes. Women will never be empowered until they achieve full control over their reproductive health.

The data indicate that much progress is required. Since 1990, there has been less than a one percent annual decline in deaths of women from pregnancy and childbirth complications. In 2005, 536,000 women—one each minute—died of maternal causes. The world's poorest countries account for

99 percent of these, the vast majority of which are preventable with at least minimal prenatal care and the assistance of skilled birth attendants. According to estimates, access to voluntary family planning could reduce maternal deaths by 20 to 35 percent.

Population and Fragile/Failed States

The issues affected by population range well beyond those promoted by the MDGs. In recent years the term "fragile states" has been used by the World Bank and other prominent international organizations, not without some controversy, to describe countries at risk from a mix of internal and outside factors.

The World Bank publishes a list of low-income countries under stress (LICUS), or fragile states, from among the 82 International Development Agency (IDA) borrowing countries. In fiscal year 2007 there were 34 countries on the list, up from 25 in 2005. The designation refers to countries scoring 3.2 and below on the Country Policy and Institutional Assessment (CPIA), which is the primary tool to assess the quality of country policies and the main input to IDA's Performance-Based Allocation system. In general terms, they are states that lack either the capacity or the will to deliver on core state functions, and where international partners find it difficult to engage.

Although country contexts vary considerably, the fragile states are home to almost 500 million persons, with child mortality rates twice as high as other low income countries, life expectancy 12 years lower, maternal mortality rates some 20 percent higher, and gross domestic product (GDP) rates typically half that of the others. Additional challenges these fragile states must confront are extreme poverty, low levels of human and social development, weak institutional capacity, and slow growth. Three out of four are affected by ongoing armed conflicts.

In a policy and principle strategy document for dealing with fragile states, Europe's Organization for Economic Cooperation and Development expressed its intent to focus on state building as the central objective, including "ensuring security and justice, mobilizing revenue, establish an enabling environment for basic service delivery, strong economic performance, and employment generation." The document notes that efforts must recognize the interdependence of political, security, economic and social spheres, and that gender equity, social inclusion, and human rights must be consistently promoted.

However, a special focus on population stabilization is needed as well. A state's natural resources are usually known and finite: arable land, port access, available water and forest lands, as well as infrastructure: roads, bridges and major buildings, which take medium to long-term planning to develop. However, population growth may often be much more difficult to quantify. What is known is that if a state is having trouble delivering services to its existing citizens, rapid population growth will surely hamper development planning and strategies. And common among nearly all the fragile states is high population growth. . . .

Population and the Environment

Any modern consumer of mass media is familiar with climate change and interrelated topics such as global warming, greenhouse gases, environmental degradation, and pollution. Of the challenges discussed so far, expanding population is perhaps most closely intertwined with climate change, and yet population is routinely ignored in most discussions. As such, population growth should become a second front in the battle against climate change, as one of the easiest and least costly, yet most neglected, options available.

It is recognized that the industrialized world, especially the United States, is among the major contributors to global warming through the burning of fossil fuels. No real progress can be made until industrialized countries address their high consumption and resulting effects on the planet. Least developed countries produce only a fraction of the emissions of the industrialized world. Total emissions from the developing world are expected to exceed those from the industrialized world by 2015.

Nonetheless, programs addressing the various issues of climate change that neglect the incorporation of population growth strategies are seriously flawed. In March 2007 the Associated Press reported that the head of the U.S. National Oceanic and Atmospheric Administration (NOAA) said the biggest challenge facing the world is population growth and people's desire to live in coastal areas where they can be endangered by storms.

Although wealthier, industrialized countries with large populations account for much of the consumption and greenhouse gases, environmental degradation in many less-industrialized countries is increasing as their rising populations struggle to survive, and this will have serious, long-term consequences. Such activities as clearing forests for grazing, crops, and living space, chopping wood for fuel, over-fishing and abuse of local marine ecosystems, diversion and overuse of fresh water systems, illegal strip mining and forestry, and unchecked burning for agriculture will only increase as populations grow. The environments in resource-poor countries will be especially at risk.

Addressing population growth is not an issue of limiting numbers of specific groups of human beings. But it is clear that many regions will remain at risk until their populations are stabilized and the capacity to adequately support more people is created. One economic report notes the evidence shows that ignoring climate change will eventually damage economic growth, but that tackling it does not cap the aspirations for growth for rich or poor countries.

The Intergovernmental Panel on Climate Change reports that many human systems are sensitive to climate change, including water resources, agriculture and forestry, fisheries, human settlements, energy, industry, insurance and other financial systems, and human health. The IPCC projects adverse impacts such as a general reduction in potential crop yields in most tropical and subtropical regions; decreased water availability for populations in many water-scarce regions; an increase in the number of people exposed to vector-borne and water-borne diseases; an increase in heat stress mortality; and increased energy demand for space cooling.

Nonetheless, population seems to be missing from many environmental discussions. Of the few voices making the connection between population and global warming, perhaps the most well known is Chris Rapley, head of the Science Museum in London. Quoted in a July 2007 *Telegraph* newspaper article, Rapley said, "My position on population is that I am disturbed that no one will talk about it." Among other things, Rapley told the newspaper that saving a gigaton of carbon emissions through education for women and birth control programs would cost 1,000 times less than any of the other technical options available, such as nuclear power, renewables, or increased car efficiency.

A year earlier, Rapley opined on a British Broadcasting Corporation website that population was a "Cinderella" subject, rarely visible in public or even private, and noting that it is in fact ". . . A bombshell of a topic, with profound and emotive issues of ethics, morality, equity and practicability."

Along with the issues discussed in international global warming meetings, Rapley noted that attention is merited by a much broader range of human impacts contributing to global warming, such as land cover, the water cycle, the health of ecosystems, and biodiversity, as well as the release of other chemicals into the environment, the massive transport and mixing of biological material worldwide, and the unsustainable consumption of resources. All of these effects interconnect and add up to the collective footprint of humankind on the planet's life support systems:

> Although reducing human emissions to the atmosphere is undoubtedly of critical importance, as are any and all measures to reduce the human environmental "footprint," the truth is that the contribution of each individual cannot be reduced to zero. Only the lack of the individual can bring it down to nothing. So if we believe that the size of the human "footprint" is a serious problem (and there is much evidence for this) then a rational view would be that along with a raft of measures to reduce the footprint per person, the issue of population management must be addressed.

In describing how environmental writers are part of the problem for not mentioning population growth in their discussions, environmental writer and activist John Feeney notes that it is well known among scientists that the size and growth of the global population is a root cause of environmental degradation, including climate change. He comments on one author who avoids the subject because it is "political poison," stemming from negative reactions to news of coercive family planning policies in some countries, free market capitalism that stresses growth, and political wrangling by concerned groups.

In an online article about peak oil and carrying capacity, Canadian writer Paul Chefurka calls population the "elephant in the room:"

> At the root of all the converging crises of the World Problematique is the issue of human overpopulation. Each of the global problems we face today is the result of too many people using too much of our planet's finite, non-renewable resources. . . . The true danger posed by our exploding population is not our absolute numbers but the inability of our environment to cope with so many of us doing what we do.

Population and Clean Water/Sanitation

Of the conflicts between population and resources, the one that will emerge the soonest and perhaps most dramatically will involve clean drinking water and a scarcity of water for sanitation, agriculture, and other uses. In the most tragic of circumstances, humans can survive in war zones and through natural disasters, they can bear disease and live marginally without shelter. Even a lack of adequate food does not mean a quick death. But humans can survive a lack of potable water for only a few days at most.

The United Nations has stated that more than 2.7 billion people will face severe water shortages by 2025 if world consumption of water continues at current rates, and another 2.5 billion will live in areas where it will be difficult to find sufficient fresh water to meet their needs. However, the UN also predicts consumption rates will increase by up to 12 percent per decade until 2025.

The head of the UN agency tasked with promoting socially and environmentally sustainable housing has warned that water will become the dominant issue of this century and its availability could threaten the world's social stability. Indeed, the UN Development Programme made the issue of water scarcity the subject of its 2006 Human Development Report. . . .

International development funding has not responded to this rising need and may not always reach those who need it most. The share of water as part of total official development assistance has remained at about 5 percent, while spending for education, health, and emergency aid has risen sharply. In addition, between 1990 and 2004, 60 percent of development assistance for water went to 20 countries and is still being distributed unequally between countries, according to a World Water Council report.

The implications of water needs and population growth are troubling. Of the top 20 recipient nations for water sector funding, 11 are in the top 20 overall in terms of world population rankings. However, only seven are rated by the UN as being least developed or other low income countries. According to the World Water Council, the three predominant factors when it comes to receiving aid are being demographically small, politically stable, and geopolitically "visible."

Populous and poor states not among the top 20 recipient will need to address their water risks without the bulk of international support. Family planning would be a very effective component in helping them manage the future. . . .

Population and Food Security

Food security is closely tied in many ways to climate change and water scarcity. Several additional factors affect the dynamic, however, including global food production (and the uncertainty over shifts from harvesting corn to producing more corn for ethanol), domestic subsidies, food aid, world prices for fertilizers and pesticides, and genetically modified crops.

In an interesting twist that clearly outlines the complex and troubling interrelationship between population growth, agriculture and climate change, while agriculture is a victim of climate change, it is also part of the problem. Livestock accounts for 18 percent of global greenhouse gas emissions, while forestry and deforestation is responsible for 18 percent of carbon dioxide emissions. Rice production is perhaps the main source of anthropogenic methane, emitting some 50 to 100 million metric tons per year.

Growing populations in states with at-risk agricultural production will only exacerbate the potential for both internal and cross-border conflicts. Lester R. Brown, president of the Earth Policy Institute, writes ". . . achieving an acceptable worldwide balance between food and people may now depend on stabilizing population as soon as possible, reducing the unhealthily high consumption of livestock products in industrial countries, and restricting the conversion of food crops to automotive fuels. . . ."

Population and Global Security

Population growth was an underlying if not a primary cause of the largest conflict in human history, the Second World War. In Germany, Adolf Hitler's principle of *lebensraum*, or "living space" for the growing German population, was a central component of his justification for the Nazi invasions into neighboring countries.

In Japan, an island nation with high population density in many areas, the need for resources for a growing population and economy was a part of the drive to invade Manchuria and other parts of China, as well as much of the rest of the Pacific region, beginning in the 1930s. Public policy researcher Jack Goldstone notes that population-related conflicts have been going on for centuries.

Growing populations in areas of dwindling resources have caused or intensified conflicts in many corners of the world. The situation in Sudan's Darfur region is one of the better-known of these. According to Kenyan environmentalist Wangari Maathai, 2004 Nobel Peace Prize recipient, "Darfur is an example of a situation where a dire scarcity of natural resources is manipulated by politicians . . . At its roots it is a struggle over controlling an environment that can no longer support all the people who must live on it."

Another key issue in conflict is rapid urbanization and the "youth bulge" in many countries. A spike in the numbers of young people can create strains on public services, such as education and health, and other resources, exacerbated by a lack of jobs, leading to increased poverty, overcrowding, frustration, alienation and unrest. Alternatively, as the proportion of young adults decreases, so does political instability, for example in Japan, South Korea, Thailand, and Sri Lanka.

Along these same lines, researchers have demonstrated that in countries with low birth rates and low infant mortality, the likelihood of civil conflict is less than in those with high birth rates and high infant mortality. As birth rates and infant mortality increase, the likelihood of civil conflict increases in a clear progression.

Population researcher Katherine Weiland has argued: "Family planning programs should be implemented as an essential component of national security for developing as well as developed countries. Achieving global security requires a worldwide commitment, through global cooperation, to attacking the social and economic problems that lead to insecurity." This cooperation and commitment is critical because,

> In today's interconnected world, conflict in less developed countries affects not only one country or region but has dangerous implications for global security. Globalization has created a world where stable countries are no longer isolated from their unstable neighbors and civil strife can easily move across borders and erupt into war.

Demographers and both social scientists and military experts have linked global security and population, which was regarded as a non-traditional security issue just a decade ago.

These include the promotion of a demographic transition of populations from high to low rates of birth and death; ensuring easily accessible reproductive health services for refugees, civilians in post-conflict environments, and all military personnel; and supporting improvements in the legal, educational and economic status of women to reach a "security demographic," a distinctive range of population structures and dynamics that make civil conflict less likely.

According to Goldstone, there are six major population trends that are likely to pose significant security challenges to developed nations by 2025, among them being the rapid growth and predominant role of urban populations in developing countries, shrinking populations in Europe, opposing age shifts between aging developed and youthful developing countries, and increasing migration from developing to developed countries. . . .

Population and Other Issues

The convergence of the concerns described through this paper will, of course, have a shock wave effect on several other associated issues, such as migration, refugees, poverty, health, and education.

To touch briefly on one of these, scientists are already issuing alarms related to increased risks from disease as populations rise. For example, countries with high population growth will experience the most severe increases in diarrheal and infectious diseases caused by climate change. WHO has tied rising global population to an unprecedented number (39 in all) of emerging new diseases, including AIDS, Ebola, SARS, and bird flu.

The many factors at the interface of human population growth and disease were explored in a 2007 paper in *Human Ecology,* and included health hazards such as poor vector control and sanitation, water and food contamination, air pollution, natural disasters, and chemical pollution.

Thus, the impact of population growth goes far beyond the issues covered here. But again, population is the root from which all issues and concerns are developed, and represents the obvious starting point in addressing realistic and practical resolutions.

Summary

The purpose of this paper has been to show the connections between population growth and several key, broad-ranging topical issues, whether meeting the Millennium Development Goals, resolving issues of climate change, addressing shortages of water and food, or examining aspects of global security. These connections are at times understood to various degrees by decision-makers, while at other times population has been overlooked or ignored.

A focus on population growth and international family planning programming, including commodities, distribution, and education, should be a part of any resolutions discussed for the myriad problems reviewed in this report. Family planning is one of the most proven and most cost-effective components for reaching real solutions to many of the world's more pressing problems.

It is recognized that reproductive health and family planning issues are complex and involve history, politics, local agendas, ethics, cultural norms and values, power relations, health, women's and human rights, economics, poverty, education and myriad other components and realities. All are urgent, and effective programs must include a comprehensive understanding of all issues.

Sexual and reproductive health, particularly family planning, is not a panacea in stabilizing global pressures. It also does not operate in a vacuum, any more than the other issues described. The potential solutions to each are also inextricably bound to each other. But as a component, population stability is a necessary and critical step in the effort to secure a positive future for all the earth's citizens; moreover, it is the key theme that binds them all.

There is reason for hope. Countries in which family planning is a routine part of health care have stabilized their populations, seen economic growth and political stability, and have provided education and health care for a greater share of their population. Tunisia, Egypt, Indonesia, and Mexico are just a few success stories for international family planning efforts.

Ultimately, the decisions of individual women will determine population growth. Given modern family planning knowledge, options, and access, women limit the size and spacing of their families. How well the world responds in providing information, education and supplies to those in need will be the key to managing the numerous, potential threats of the modern era.

Michael J. Miller   ➔ **NO**

The Under-Population Problem: An Interview with Steven W. Mosher on the Demographic Consequences of Birth Control Policies

Miller: *Dire scenarios about imminent overpopulation, from Malthus to Paul Ehrlich's* The Population Bomb, *have not materialized. Where are the mistakes in their calculations?*

Steven Mosher: In some cases they were deliberately exaggerated, even fabricated, in an attempt to frighten individuals into having not more than one or two children, and legislatures into funding population control programs.

Assuming that the alarmists really believed those projections, I think that their principal error came in the 1960s when they assumed that Third World countries would have to reach Western standards of living before birth rates decreased. They supposed that only affluence would convince people in Nigeria, China, or Peru to have fewer children.

Of course, population control programs played a role in limiting fertility. But the principal reason why almost all Latin American countries today are at or near replacement-rate fertility levels is that the death rate among infants and children went down, and therefore couples voluntarily stopped having large families. They're still relatively poor, yet they began limiting the number of children. Reduce the mortality rate and population growth ceases.

Miller: *Even if projections about limited resources are wrong, what's the harm in a little "under-population?" Isn't a nation with negative population growth like a factory that sells its unused CO_2 allowances to less environmentally friendly businesses?*

Mosher: A free-market economy is constantly looking for new markets for goods and services. The size of those markets is driven in large part by the size of the population. As a population grows, the demand for cars, houses, and other goods increases. As a population shrinks, this process works in reverse.

I think, though, that the dangers of population decline are even more serious than this would suggest, because a decline in absolute numbers of people is always preceded by population aging. The population gets out of balance: too few young people get married, have children and buy houses; and the population ages, which puts increasing demands on retirement and healthcare programs.

You might say, "Yes, but a growing population with lots of children has a bad worker-to-dependent ratio as well," but children don't require nearly as much health care as the elderly do, children don't consume as many resources, and children live with their parents, so there are economies of scale.

Europe, for example, is going to see tax rates go through the roof in order to support growing populations of the elderly. Who's going to be taxed? Working people in their 20s and 30s. When you tax that segment of the population you impoverish it and make it less likely that they will have children at all, much less large families. And so you eat your seed corn. You put so much economic pressure on the young and reproductive that they stop having children.

Birth rates in Catholic Spain and Italy are down to 1.1 children per couple. We've done some back-of-the-envelope calculations, and in Italy every young couple would have to have four children in order to stop the population decline that's currently underway. No combination of incentives in the world could turn this thing around. So Italians have no choice but to accept large numbers of immigrants, mostly Muslims from Albania, North Africa, and the Middle East. This creates the additional problem of integrating people from very different cultural, religious, and social backgrounds into Italian society.

Miller: *You observed the effects of the one-child policy imposed in Communist China in the early 1980s. How could such a radical population-control program be implemented in the world's most populous nation?*

Mosher: It's hard for Americans to imagine how any government could control over a billion people. Chinese law allows one child per couple in the cities; two in the countryside. How does Beijing enforce the rules?

People need to understand that there is a Communist Party presence in every village, hamlet, and neighborhood throughout the country. There are 60 million Chinese Communist Party members, roughly 5 percent of the population, and they're everywhere. Their job is to see that government policies are not just adhered to, but that they are popular and accepted by the people. The CCP works hard to quell dissent over the one-child policy.

There is a parallel organization for women called the Women's Federation, again with tens of millions of members. Their job since 1970 has been to enforce compliance with the one-child policy. What do they do? They keep extensive records on the rest of the female population and track menstrual cycles. They ensure that women who have not yet been sterilized are contracepting. They assist the sterilization teams that perform tubal ligations on women who have had two children. Then there are the family planning officials themselves, who run the whole operation.

It is a huge and costly effort. But mass mobilization campaigns are the kind of thing that the Chinese Communist Party is very good at. It is an Orwellian organization that is used to intrude into the most intimate decisions that people make.

There is dissent, of course. There are women who conceal their pregnancies and run away and go into hiding when they're discovered. We are able to help a few of these women through our Safe House program. But by and large the policy is effective.

Miller: *The last half-century saw the end of colonialism and also the worldwide spread of population control programs funded by the West. Have any Third World nations successfully resisted the "incentives" to start such programs?*

Mosher: In the book I quote African leaders who denounce this kind of new imperialism. To understand how intrusive it is, imagine the outcry if the Chinese government funded a program to reduce the American birthrate and paid workers to go door-to-door with contraceptives, insisting that American women use them. Yet that is what we, the United States, do around the world. It is not surprising that these programs are resented.

In the book I describe at length the enormous pressures that are brought to bear on governments around the world. Do you want short-term, long-term loans from the World Bank or the International Monetary Fund? You must have a family planning program in place. Do you want money from the US Agency for International Development (USAID)? You must distribute contraceptives to your women; we'll send you the pills. Many countries resisted these kinds of pressure for a time, but most have caved in.

There's another force at work here: many needy countries in Africa especially, are governed by corrupt dictators. How convenient for them to have a prestigious foreign theory on which to blame their countries' problems! "Our country is impoverished because there are too many people," the dictator can say, "not because my bureaucracy is hopelessly inept, lazy, and corrupt." The theory of overpopulation gives them an excuse for the results of their own misrule.

Miller: *How did the United States government get into the business of distributing contraceptives?*

Mosher: At the end of World War II the United States was engaged militarily around the world, and Americans learned where Burma, Singapore, and Papua New Guinea were. Since Japan and Europe [were] devastated, half the world's goods and services were produced in the United States. Being a generous people, we decided to fund foreign aid programs. We went in to improve living conditions around the world and succeeded in lowering infant mortality rates in a number of countries by providing modern medical care.

World population began to increase rapidly. Here is the origin of the notion that there is a "population bomb." If the population kept doubling every 30 years, the alarmists said, there would soon be tens of billions of people on the planet; unsustainable growth would eventually cause economic, environmental, and societal collapse.

The hysteria about "overpopulation" translated into a stampede to include family planning in our foreign aid program. Laws were passed stating that population stabilization was an official goal of US foreign policy, and that every foreign program had to have a family planning component.

The whole movement gained strength from both the left and the right. The liberal argument was that too many people would devastate the environment. The radical feminist argument was that women in Third World countries were being forced to breed because they didn't have access to modern contraceptives.

The conservative argument—it's really a national security argument—was that growing populations in Africa, Latin America, and Asia would destabilize the political situation in those regions and lead to Communist insurrection. The other "conservative" argument was that if Third World populations grew too rapidly, the Asians and the Africans and the Latin Americans might want to consume their minerals and resources instead of selling them to us at cheap prices.

Miller: *You write that "when the population controllers move into a poor country like Kenya or Peru, primary health care invariably suffers." Please explain.*

Mosher: Imagine that you're the minister of health in Peru and you have a fixed budget to pay a certain number of doctors and nurses in public clinics nationwide to provide medical care for the poor. Part of that budget comes from government revenues; it's a poor country, however, and much of your funding comes from foreign aid. Your principal source, the United States, announces that it wants you to make population control a priority of your medical care program. Not just one of 10 goals, along with combating malaria and providing vaccinations. "Unless you make it the number-one priority, we will stop our foreign aid; if you do, we will increase it."

You won't want to forfeit half your budget. In the case of Peru, the government actually launched a sterilization campaign. That country's doctors and nurses, who had been administering vaccinations, begin inserting IUDs and distributing birth control pills. Many surgeons who had been performing emergency surgery and appendectomies and setting broken bones were organized into mobile surgical teams to travel around doing nothing but tubal ligations.

We know from Dr. Carbone, the Peruvian minister of health who served after the sterilization campaign, that rates of infectious diseases skyrocketed in Peru during the height of the sterilization campaign.

In every country where pride of place is given to family planning, resources are taken away from other forms of healthcare. Death rates go up as people die of preventable diseases or from accidents because the medical system has other priorities—preventing pregnancies.

Miller: *Bishop Oscar Andres Rodriguez, then president of the Latin American Catholic bishops' conference, condemned a 1995 USAID report warning about "dangerous" population growth rates in Honduras. Are you aware of any attempt by the United States bishops to criticize USAID policies at the source?*

Mosher: No, I am not. The Respect Life Office of the US bishops' conference has been a very stout defender of the Mexico City Policy, which denies US family planning funding to any organization that does not specifically commit to eschew promoting or performing abortions or lobbying for the legalization of abortion. They have been helpful in getting laws passed like the Tiahrt Amendment, which defines voluntarism in family planning programs, mandates informed consent, and rules out targets and quotas or the use of experimental methods on women. They have also been helpful in pointing out abuses in these programs.

But what is needed is a full-scale frontal assault on the whole population-control enterprise. It needs to be defunded. We need to go turn out the lights at the United Nations Fund for Population Activities (UNFPA). If there was any reason for such an organization to exist in the 1960s, that reason no longer exists today.

Miller: *The encyclical Humanae Vitae turns 40 this summer. In your opinion, does the experience of recent decades corroborate the teaching of Paul VI about the social effects of contraception?*

Mosher: Absolutely. I think that it's one of the most prophetic documents ever penned by a pope. I think that Pope Paul VI was right not only in his general argument, but in his specific arguments about the rise in divorce rates, the rise in the abortion rate, the devaluing of children. On all of these points he was tremendously prescient. I think that we need to continue to read and study this document and subsequent documents like *Evangelium Vitae* (*The Gospel of Life*), which point out the dangers of going any farther down the road of devaluing and instrumentalizing human life.

Miller: *Do you think that there's any chance of mobilizing human rights groups to demand greater accountability from international organizations that promote population control?*

Mosher: Well, this was my great hope back in the 80s when I was doing my initial research on China. I went to Amnesty International, Human Rights Watch, and the major human rights organizations. I found the assistant secretary of state for human rights under the Reagan administration very sympathetic. For the first time in the state department's annual human rights report it mentioned, in the context of China, forced abortions and forced sterilizations. That was a victory.

The other human rights organizations were very reluctant to get involved because of their ideological commitment to abortion. It took several years, but in the late 1980s and early 1990s Amnesty International finally began to refer to forced abortion as a violation of human rights. Now, I'm afraid, Amnesty International has taken the former position that abortion is a human right, and it condemns countries that do not allow abortion on demand.

Miller: *What advice would you give to pro-life activists and legislators in Western nations who would like to defund population control programs?*

Mosher: We need a family-friendly foreign policy. Pro-life and pro-family groups have to learn a little bit about what's happening overseas and tell their congressmen that they think that our policies are fundamentally wrongheaded. In a world of falling birthrates we need pro-natal policies.

One US congressman expressed frustration to me not long ago. He said that when he voted against international population control funding, he got a half a dozen angry letters from his district. He said, "Can't anybody write me and tell me that I did the right thing? The other side can set people to writing or calling at a moment's notice." Well, we need to be doing that. Politicians are politicians. Even the best ones need to be encouraged. To know that where they lead, we're following.

EXPLORING THE ISSUE

Should the International Community Continue to Focus on Programs to Help Developing Countries Curb Population Growth?

Critical Thinking and Reflection

1. How does the demographic transition in the developed world differ from that in the developing world?
2. What are the implications for this difference?
3. What are the implications of the fact that the international community placed population growth on its agenda and considered the issue several times in the past 40 years?
4. Is population growth really a problem today?
5. What business does the international community have in trying to affect family planning choices throughout the world?

Is There Common Ground?

Clearly, there is an international consensus that individual family planning decisions have long-term national consequences. There is also agreement that although the international community ought not to get in the business of telling citizens how to behave demographically, individual nations may adopt policies to that effect. There is even a growing consensus that a changing focus from limiting population to creating better reproductive services for mothers is a laudable strategy.

Additional Resources

Christensen, David E., *Two Elephants in the Room: Overpopulation and Opportunities We Overlook at Our Peril* (Outskirts Press, 2010)

This book examines six possible solutions to world overpopulation.

Eager, Paige Whaley, *Global Population Policy: From Population Control to Reproductive Rights* (Ashgate Publishing, 2004)

This book describes how the global community's concern with high growth rates has been replaced with a focus on women's reproductive health. It also describes the role national governments in the developed countries and the United Nations would play in global population policy making.

Munz, Rainer and Reiterer, Albert F., *Overcrowded World: Global Population and International Migration* (Haus Publishing, 2010)

This book presents the basics of population growth and the effect of an aging population in the Western world.

Robinson, Warren C. and Ross, John A., *The Global Family Planning Revolution: Three Decades of Population Policies and Programs* (World Bank Publication, 2007)

This book describes the history of the global community's (national governments, private organizations, and international organizations) attempt to address ballooning population throughout the developing world after World War II.

Tobias, Michael et al., *NO VACANCY: Global Responses to the Human Population Explosion* (Hope Publishing House, 2006)

This book presents an optimistic view of the ability of the human race to cope with the expected population level at the end of the century.

ISSUE 2

Is Global Aging a Major Problem?

YES: Neil Howe and Richard Jackson, from "Global Aging and the Crisis of the 2020s," *Current History* (January 2011)

NO: Mark L. Haas, from "Pax Americana Geriatrica," *Miller-McCune* (July 14, 2008)

Learning Outcomes

After reading this issue, you should be able to:

- Gain an understanding of why the 2020s are said to be an upcoming decade of global population aging and population decline.
- Appreciate how a global aging and declining population will affect economic growth, living standards, and the shape of the world order.
- Understand how future demographic conditions will negatively influence developing societies differently.
- Discuss the need for national planners to consider future population trends in planning national strategy.
- Appreciate why the United States may be better able to cope with the effects of population aging and decline better than its Western counterparts.

ISSUE SUMMARY

YES: Neil Howe and Richard Jackson of the Center for Strategic and International Studies argue that global population aging is likely to have a profound and negative effect on global economic growth, living standards and conditions, and "the shape of the world order," particularly affecting China, Russia, Pakistan, Iran, and countries of the West.

NO: Mark L. Haas, Duquesne University professor, suggests that global aging will likely have a positive effect on the United States as its chief competitors will have a far more difficult time coping with their aging populations.

By 2030, one in eight inhabitants of this planet will be 65 years or older. The developed world is now faced with an aging population brought on by declining birth rates and an increasing life expectancy, and it will soon be followed by the developing world. The phenomenon first appeared during the last quarter of the previous century with the demographic transition from high birth and death rates to lower rates. The drop in death rates in these countries was a function of two basic factors: (1) the dramatic decline in both infant mortality (within the first year of birth) and child mortality (within the first five years) due to women being healthier during pregnancy and nursing periods, and due to the virtually universal inoculation of children against principal childhood diseases and (2) longer life spans, once people reach adulthood, in large part because of medical advances against key adult illnesses, such as cancer and heart disease.

Declining mortality rates yield an aging population in need of a variety of services—heath care, housing, and guards against inflation, for example—provided, in large part, by the tax dollars of the younger, producing sector of society. As the "gray" numbers of society grow, the labor force is increasingly called upon to provide more help for this class.

Declining birth and death rates mean that significantly more services will be needed to provide for the aging populations of the industrialized world, while at the same time, fewer individuals will be joining the workforce to provide the resources to pay for these services. However, some experts say that the new work force will be able to take advantage of the skills of the more aged, unlike previous eras. In order for national economies to grow in the information age, an expanding workforce may not be as important a prerequisite as it once was. Expanding minds, not bodies, may be the key to expanding economies and increased abilities to provide public services.

However, the elderly and the young are not randomly distributed throughout society, which is likely to create a growing set of regional problems. In the United States, for example, the educated young are likely to leave the "gray belt" of the north for the Sun Belt of the south, southwest, and west. Who will be left in the older, established sectors of the country that were originally at the forefront of the industrial age to care for the disproportionately elderly population? Peter G. Peterson introduces the phrase "the Floridization of the developed world," where retirees continue to flock in unprecedented numbers in order to capture the essence of the problems associated with the changing age composition in industrial societies. What will happen 30–40 years from now, when the respective sizes of the young and the elderly populations throughout the developed world will yield a much larger population at the twilight of their existence? Although the trend is most evident in the richer part of the globe, people are also living longer in the developing world, primarily because of the diffusion of modern medical practices. But unless society can accommodate their skills of later years, they may become an even bigger burden in the future for their national governments.

A 2001 report, *Preparing for an Aging World: The Case for Cross-National Research* (National Academy of Sciences), identified a number of areas in which policymakers need a better understanding of the consequences of aging and resultant appropriate policy responses. Unless national governments of the developed world can effectively respond to these issues, the economic and social consequences can have a significant negative impact in the aging population cohort as well as throughout the entire society. This theme was reiterated in a major report of The Population Reference Bureau in March 2005 (*Global Aging: The Challenge of Success*), suggesting three major challenges of an aging population: (1) economic development issues, (2) health and well-being issues, and (3) the challenge of enabling and supportive environments.

The issue of the changing age composition in the developed world was foreseen a few decades ago but its heightened visibility is relatively recent. This visibility culminated in a UN-sponsored conference on aging in Madrid in April 2002. Its plan of action commits governments to address the problem of aging and provides them with a set of 117 specific recommendations covering three basic areas: older individuals and development, advancing health and well-being into old age, and ensuring enabling and supportive environments.

With the successful demographic transition in the industrial world, the percentage of those older than 60 years is on the rise, whereas the labor force percentage is decreasing. In 1998, 19 percent of the first world population fell into the post-60 category (10 percent worldwide). Children younger than 15 years also make up 19 percent of the developed world's population, whereas the labor force is at 62 percent. With birth rates hovering around 1 percent or less, and life expectancy increasing, the percentages will likely continue to grow toward the upper end of the scale.

Paul Peterson has argued that the costs of global aging will outweigh the benefits, and the capacity of the developed world to pay for these costs is questionable at best. He suggests that the economic burden on the labor force will be "unprecedented" and offers a number of solutions ("Gray Dawn: The Global Aging Crisis" in *Foreign Affairs*, January/February 1999).

A U.S. Department of Commerce study, *An Aging World: 2008*, suggests nine trends that will likely present aging challenges throughout the globe. (1) The population is aging, as people 65 years and older will outnumber those younger than 5 years. (2) Life expectancy is increasing, raising questions about human lifespan. (3) The number of the oldest, those older than 80 years, is rising, and will more than double within 30 years. (4) Some countries are experiencing aging populations while their total populations decline. (5) Noncommunicable diseases are becoming an increasing burden as they now are the major cause of death among old people. (6) Because of longer lifespans and fewer children, family structures are changing and care options for the elderly may change. (7) There are shrinking ratios of workers to pensioners, as people live longer in retirement, taxing health and pension systems. (8) Social insurance systems are becoming less sustainable. (9) Population aging is having huge effects on social entitlement programs.

A World Bank study (Ronald Lee et al., *Some Economic Consequences of Global Aging*, December 2010) outlines concerns about the effects of aging on societies: slower economic growth, poverty among the elderly, generational equity, inadequate investment in physical and human capital, inefficiency in labor markets, suboptimal consumption profiles, and unsustainable public transfer systems.

The authors of one of this issue's readings, Neil Howe and Richard Jackson, describe the geopolitical implications of global aging for the highly developed societies in *The Graying of the Great Powers* (Center for Strategic and International Studies, 2008). The first is that both the population and the GDP of the developed world will decline as a percentage of global totals, thus leading to a loss of influence. Within the developed world, though, the U.S. share will rise, leading to increased influence. Most nations in sub-Saharan Africa and those in the Muslim world will experience large youth bulges, leading to a chronically unstable situation until at least the 2030s. Many nations in North Africa, the Middle East, South and East Asia, and the former Soviet bloc are experiencing rapid demographic change that could lead to either civil collapse or a reactive neo-authoritarianism. The threat of ethnic and religious conflict will continue as a security challenge throughout the world. The 2020s will be a decade of maximum political danger. The aging developed world will have shortages of young-adult man power. And finally, this world may struggle to remain culturally attractive and politically relevant to younger peoples.

Alternatively, some analysts are looking at an aging population from a lens that is not half empty but that has some positive aspects to it. One such positive possibility is a decrease in military conflict throughout the globe as societies face manpower shortages while dealing with social services for the elderly. Another approach is to observe how the experience of age is brought to bear in a productive way in modern societies that can reap the benefits of productive labor achieved through brains rather than brawn.

The YES selection by Neil Howe and Richard Jackson of the Center for Strategic and International Studies argues that global population aging is likely to have a profound and negative effect on global economic growth, living standards and conditions, and "the shape of the world order," particularly affecting China, Russia, Pakistan, Iran, and countries of the West. For them, the critical decade is the 2020s, when the ability of the developed world to maintain global security will be brought into question. In the NO selection, Mark L. Haas, Duquesne University professor, suggests that global aging will likely have a positive effect on the United States as its chief competitors will have a far greater challenge coping with their aging populations.

YES ↩

Neil Howe and
Richard Jackson

Global Aging and the Crisis of the 2020s

From the fall of the Roman and the Mayan empires to the Black Death to the colonization of the New World and the youth-driven revolutions of the twentieth century, demographic trends have played a decisive role in many of the great invasions, political upheavals, migrations, and environmental catastrophes of history. By the 2020s, an ominous new conjuncture of demographic trends may once again threaten widespread disruption. We are talking about global aging, which is likely to have a profound effect on economic growth, living standards, and the shape of the world order.

For the world's wealthy nations, the 2020s are set to be a decade of rapid population aging and population decline. The developed world has been aging for decades, due to falling birthrates and rising life expectancy. But in the 2020s, this aging will get an extra kick as large postwar baby boom generations move fully into retirement. According to the United Nations Population Division (whose projections are cited throughout this article), the median ages of Western Europe and Japan, which were 34 and 33 respectively as recently as 1980, will soar to 47 and 52 by 2030, assuming no increase in fertility. In Italy, Spain, and Japan, more than half of all adults will be older than the official retirement age—and there will be more people in their 70s than in their 20s.

Falling birthrates are not only transforming traditional population pyramids, leaving them top-heavy with elders, but are also ushering in a new era of workforce and population decline. The working-age population has already begun to contract in several large developed countries, including Germany and Japan. By 2030, it will be stagnant or contracting in nearly all developed countries, the only major exception being the United States. In a growing number of nations, total population will begin a gathering decline as well. Unless immigration or birthrates surge, Japan and some European nations are on track to lose nearly one-half of their total current populations by the end of the century.

These trends threaten to undermine the ability of today's developed countries to maintain global security. To begin with, they directly affect population size and GDP size, and hence the manpower and economic resources that nations can deploy. This is what RAND scholar Brian Nichiporuk calls "the bucket of capabilities" perspective. But population aging and decline can also indirectly affect capabilities—or even alter national goals themselves.

From *Current History,* January 2011, pp. 20–25. Copyright © 2011 by Current History, Inc. Reprinted by permission.

Rising pension and health care costs will place intense pressure on government budgets, potentially crowding out spending on other priorities, including national defense and foreign assistance. Economic performance may suffer as workforces gray and rates of savings and investment decline. As societies and electorates age, growing risk aversion and shorter time horizons may weaken not just the ability of the developed countries to play a major geopolitical role, but also their will.

The weakening of the developed countries might not be a cause for concern if we knew that the world as a whole were likely to become more pacific. But unfortunately, just the opposite may be the case. During the 2020s, the developing world will be buffeted by its own potentially destabilizing demographic storms. China will face a massive age wave that could slow economic growth and precipitate political crisis just as that country is overtaking America as the world's leading economic power. Russia will be in the midst of the steepest and most protracted population implosion of any major power since the plague-ridden Middle Ages. Meanwhile, many other developing countries, especially in the Muslim world, will experience a sudden new resurgence of youth whose aspirations they are unlikely to be able to meet.

The risk of social and political upheaval could grow throughout the developing world—even as the developed world's capacity to deal with such threats declines. Yet, if the developed world seems destined to see its geopolitical stature diminish, there is one partial but important exception to the trend: the United States. While it is fashionable to argue that US power has peaked, demography suggests America will play as important a role in shaping the world order in this century as it did in the last.

Graying Economies

Although population size alone does not confer geopolitical stature, no one disputes that population size and economic size together constitute a potent double engine of national power. A larger population allows greater numbers of young adults to serve in war and to occupy and pacify territory. A larger economy allows more spending on the hard power of national defense and the semi-hard power of foreign assistance. It can also enhance what political scientist Joseph Nye calls "soft power" by promoting business dominance, leverage with nongovernmental organizations and philanthropies, social envy and emulation, and cultural clout in the global media and popular culture.

The expectation that global aging will diminish the geopolitical stature of the developed world is thus based in part on simple arithmetic. By the 2020s and 2030s, the working-age population of Japan and many European countries will be contracting by between 0.5 and 1.5 percent per year. Even at full employment, growth in real GDP could stagnate or decline, since the number of workers may be falling faster than productivity is rising. Unless economic performance improves, some countries could face a future of secular economic stagnation—in other words, of zero real GDP growth from peak to peak of the business cycle.

Economic performance, in fact, is more likely to deteriorate than improve. Workforces in most developed countries will not only be stagnating or contracting, but also graying. A vast literature in the social and behavioral sciences establishes that worker productivity typically declines at older ages, especially in eras of rapid technological and market change.

Economies with graying workforces are also likely to be less entrepreneurial. According to the Global Entrepreneurship Monitor's 2007 survey of 53 countries, new business start-ups in high-income countries are heavily tilted toward the young. Of all "new entrepreneurs" in the survey (defined as owners of a business founded within the past three and one-half years), 40 percent were under age 35 and 69 percent under age 45. Only 9 percent were 55 or older.

At the same time, savings rates in the developed world will decline as a larger share of the population moves into the retirement years. If savings fall more than investment demand, as much macroeconomic modeling suggests is likely, either businesses will starve for investment funds or the developed economies' dependence on capital from higher-saving emerging markets will grow. In the first case, the penalty will be lower output. In the second, it will be higher debt service costs and the loss of political leverage, which history teaches is always ceded to creditor nations.

Even as economic growth slows, the developed countries will have to transfer a rising share of society's economic resources from working-age adults to nonworking elders. Graying means paying—more for pensions, more for health care, more for nursing homes for the frail elderly. According to projections by the Center for Strategic and International Studies, the cost of maintaining the current generosity of today's public old-age benefit systems would, on average across the developed countries, add an extra 7 percent of GDP to government budgets by 2030.

Yet the old-age benefit systems of most developed countries are already pushing the limits of fiscal and economic affordability. By the 2020s, political conflict over deep benefit cuts seems unavoidable. On one side will be young adults who face stagnant or declining after-tax earnings. On the other side will be retirees, who are often wholly dependent on pay-as-you-go public plans. In the 2020s, young people in developed countries will have the future on their side. Elders will have the votes on theirs.

Faced with the choice between economically ruinous tax hikes and politically impossible benefit cuts, many governments will choose a third option: cannibalizing other spending on everything from education and the environment to foreign assistance and national defense. As time goes by, the fiscal squeeze will make it progressively more difficult to pursue the obvious response to military manpower shortages—investing massively in military technology, and thereby substituting capital for labor.

Diminished Stature

The impact of global aging on the collective temperament of the developed countries is more difficult to quantify than its impact on their economies, but the consequences could be just as important—or even more so. With the size of domestic markets fixed or shrinking in many countries, businesses and unions may lobby for anticompetitive changes in the economy. We may see growing cartel behavior to protect market share and more restrictive rules on hiring and firing to protect jobs.

We may also see increasing pressure on governments to block foreign competition. Historically, eras of stagnant population and market growth—think of the 1930s—have been characterized by rising tariff barriers, autarky, corporatism, and other anticompetitive policies that tend to shut the door on free trade and free markets.

This shift in business psychology could be mirrored by a broader shift in social mood. Psychologically, older societies are likely to become more conservative in outlook and possibly more risk-averse in electoral and leadership behavior. Elder-dominated electorates may tend to lock in current public spending commitments at the expense of new priorities and shun decisive confrontations in favor of ad hoc settlements. Smaller families may be less willing to risk scarce youth in war.

We know that extremely youthful societies are in some ways dysfunctional—prone to violence, instability, and state failure. But extremely aged societies may also prove dysfunctional in some ways, favoring consumption over investment, the past over the future, and the old over the young.

Meanwhile, the rapid growth in ethnic and religious minority populations, due to ongoing immigration and higher-than-average minority fertility, could strain civic cohesion and foster a new diaspora politics. With the demand for low-wage labor rising, immigration (at its current rate) is on track by 2030 to double the percentage of Muslims in France and triple it in Germany. Some large European cities, including Amsterdam, Marseille, Birmingham, and Cologne, may be majority Muslim.

In Europe, the demographic ebb tide may deepen the crisis of confidence that is reflected in such best-selling books as *France Is Falling* by Nicolas Baverez, *Can Germany Be Saved?* by Hans-Werner Sinn, and *The Last Days of Europe* by Walter Laqueur. The media in Europe are already rife with dolorous stories about the closing of schools and maternity wards, the abandonment of rural towns, and the lawlessness of immigrant youths in large cities. In Japan, the government has half-seriously projected the date at which only one Japanese citizen will be left alive.

Over the next few decades, the outlook in the United States will increasingly diverge from that in the rest of the developed world. Yes, America is also graying, but to a lesser extent. Aside from Israel and Iceland, the United States is the only developed nation where fertility is at or above the replacement rate of 2.1 average lifetime births per woman. By 2030, its median age, now 37, will rise to only 39. Its working-age population, according to both US Census Bureau and UN projections, will also continue to grow through the 2020s and beyond, both because of its higher fertility rate and because of substantial net immigration, which America assimilates better than most other developed countries.

The United States faces serious structural challenges, including a bloated health care sector, a chronically low savings rate, and a political system that has difficulty making meaningful trade-offs among competing priorities. All of these problems threaten to become growing handicaps as the country's population ages. Yet, unlike Europe and Japan, the United States will still have the youth and the economic resources to play a major geopolitical role. The real challenge facing America by the 2020s may not be so much its inability to lead the developed world as the inability of the other developed nations to lend much assistance.

Perilous Transitions

Although the world's wealthy nations are leading the way into humanity's graying future, aging is a global phenomenon. Most of the developing world is also progressing through the so-called demographic transition—the shift from high mortality and high fertility to low mortality and low fertility that inevitably accompanies development and modernization. Since 1975, the average fertility rate in the developing world has dropped from 5.1 to 2.7 children per woman, the rate of population growth has decelerated from 2.2 to 1.3 percent per year, and the median age has risen from 21 to 28.

The demographic outlook in the developing world, however, is shaping up to be one of extraordinary diversity. In many of the poorest and least stable countries (especially in sub-Saharan Africa), the demographic transition has failed to gain traction, leaving countries burdened with large youth bulges. By contrast, in many of the most rapidly modernizing countries (especially in East Asia), the population shift from young and growing to old and stagnant or declining is occurring at a breathtaking pace—far more rapidly than it did in any of today's developed countries.

Notwithstanding this diversity, some demographers and political scientists believe that the unfolding of the transition is ushering in a new era in which demographic trends will promote global stability. This "demographic peace" thesis, as we dub it, begins with the observation that societies with rapidly growing populations and young age structures are often mired in poverty and prone to civil violence and state failure, while those with no or slow population growth and older age structures tend to be more affluent and stable. As the demographic transition progresses—and population growth slows, median ages rise, and child dependency burdens fall—the demographic peace thesis predicts that economic growth and social and political stability will follow.

We believe this thesis is deeply flawed. It fails to take into account the huge variation in the timing and pace of the demographic transition in the developing world. It tends to focus exclusively on the threat of state failure, which indeed is closely and negatively correlated with the degree of demographic transition, while ignoring the threat of "neo-authoritarian" state success, which is more likely to occur in societies in which the transition is well under way. We are, in other words, not talking just about a hostile version of the Somalia model, but also about a potentially hostile version of the China or Russia model, which appears to enjoy growing appeal among political leaders in many developing countries.

More fundamentally, the demographic peace thesis lacks any realistic sense of historical process. It is possible (though by no means assured) that the global security environment that emerges after the demographic transition has run its course will be safer than today's. It is very unlikely, however, that the transition will make the security environment progressively safer along the way. Journeys can be more dangerous than destinations.

Economists, sociologists, and historians who have studied the development process agree that societies, as they move from the traditional to the modern, are buffeted by powerful and disorienting social, cultural, and economic crosswinds. As countries are integrated into the global marketplace and global culture, traditional economic and social structures are overturned and traditional value systems are challenged.

Along with the economic benefits of rising living standards, development also brings the social costs of rapid urbanization, growing income inequality, and environmental degradation. When plotted against development, these stresses exhibit a hump-shaped or inverted-U pattern, meaning that they become most acute midway through the demographic transition.

The demographic transition can trigger a rise in extremism. Religious and cultural revitalization movements may seek to reaffirm traditional identities that are threatened by modernization and try to fill the void left when development uproots communities and fragments extended families. It is well documented that international terrorism, among the developing countries, is positively correlated with income, education, and urbanization. States that sponsor terrorism are rarely among the youngest and poorest countries; nor do the terrorists themselves usually originate in the youngest and poorest countries. Indeed, they are often disaffected members of the middle class in middle-income countries that are midway through the demographic transition.

Ethnic tensions can also grow. In many societies, some ethnic groups are more successful in the marketplace than others—which means that, as development accelerates and the market economy grows, rising inequality often falls along ethnic lines. The sociologist Amy Chua documents how the concentration of wealth among "market-dominant minorities" has triggered violent backlashes by majority populations in many developing countries, from Indonesia, Malaysia, and the Philippines (against the Chinese) to Sierra Leone (against the Lebanese) to the former Yugoslavia (against the Croats and Slovenes).

We have in fact only one historical example of a large group of countries that has completed the entire demographic transition—today's (mostly Western) developed nations. And their experience during that transition, from the late 1700s to the late 1900s, was filled with the most destructive revolutions, civil wars, and total wars in the history of civilization. The nations that engaged in World War II had a higher median age and a lower fertility rate—and thus were situated at a later stage of the transition—than most of today's developing world is projected to have over the next 20 years. Even if global aging breeds peace, in other words, we are not out of the woods yet.

Storms Ahead

A number of demographic storms are now brewing in different parts of the developing world. The moment of maximum risk still lies ahead—just a decade away, in the 2020s. Ominously, this is the same decade when the developed world will itself be experiencing its moment of greatest demographic stress.

Consider China, which may be the first country to grow old before it grows rich. For the past quarter-century, China has been "peacefully rising," thanks in part to a one-child-per-couple policy that has lowered dependency burdens and allowed both parents to work and contribute to China's boom. By the 2020s, however, the huge Red Guard generation, which was born before the country's fertility decline, will move into retirement, heavily taxing the resources of their children and the state.

China's coming age wave—by 2030 it will be an older country than the United States—may weaken the two pillars of the current regime's legitimacy: rapidly rising GDP and social stability. Imagine workforce growth slowing to zero while tens of millions of elders sink into indigence without pensions, without health care, and without large extended families to support them. China could careen toward social collapse—or, in reaction, toward an authoritarian clampdown. The arrival of China's age wave, and the turmoil it may bring, will coincide with its expected displacement of the United States as the world's largest economy in the 2020s. According to "power transition" theories of global conflict, this moment could be quite perilous.

By the 2020s, Russia, along with the rest of Eastern Europe, will be in the midst of an extended population decline as steep or steeper than any in the developed world. The Russian fertility rate has plunged far beneath the replacement level even as life expectancy has collapsed amid a widening health crisis. Russian men today can expect to live to 60—16 years less than American men and marginally less than their Red Army grandfathers at the end of World War II. By 2050, Russia is due to fall to 16th place in world population rankings, down from 4th place in 1950 (or third place, if we include all the territories of the former Soviet Union).

Prime Minister Vladimir Putin flatly calls Russia's demographic implosion "the most acute problem facing our country today." If the problem is not solved, Russia will weaken progressively, raising the nightmarish specter of a failing or failed state with nuclear weapons. Or this cornered bear may lash out in revanchist fury rather than meekly accept its demographic fate.

Of course, some regions of the developing world will remain extremely young in the 2020s. Sub-Saharan Africa, which is burdened by the world's highest fertility rates and is also ravaged by AIDS, will still be racked by large youth bulges. So will a scattering of impoverished and chronically unstable Muslim-majority countries, including Afghanistan, the Palestinian territories, Somalia, Sudan, and Yemen. If the correlation between extreme youth and violence endures, chronic unrest and state failure could persist in much of sub-Saharan Africa and parts of the Muslim world through the 2020s, or even longer if fertility rates fail to drop.

Meanwhile, many fast-modernizing countries where fertility has fallen very recently and very steeply will experience a sudden resurgence of youth in the 2020s. It is a law of demography that, when a population boom is followed by a bust, it causes a ripple effect, with a gradually fading cycle of echo booms and busts. In the 2010s, a bust generation will be coming of age in much of Latin America, South Asia, and the Muslim world. But by the 2020s, an echo boom will follow—dashing economic expectations and perhaps fueling political violence, religious extremism, and ethnic strife.

These echo booms will be especially large in Pakistan and Iran. In Pakistan, the decade-over-decade percentage growth in the number of people in the volatile 15- to 24-year-old age bracket is projected to drop from 32 percent in the 2000s to just 10 percent in the 2010s, but then leap upward again to 19 percent in the 2020s. In Iran, the swing in the size of the youth bulge population is projected to be even larger: minus 33 percent in the 2010s and plus 23 percent in the 2020s. These echo booms will be occurring in countries whose social fabric is already strained by rapid development. One country teeters on the brink of chaos, while the other aspires to regional hegemony. One already has nuclear weapons, while the other seems likely to obtain them.

Pax Americana Redux?

The demographer Nicholas Eberstadt has warned that demographic change may be "even more menacing to the security prospects of the Western alliance than was the cold war for the past generation." Although it would be fair to point out that such change usually presents opportunities as well as dangers, his basic point is incontestable: Planning national strategy for the next several decades with no regard for population projections is like setting sail without a map or a compass. It is likely to be an ill-fated voyage. In this sense, demography is the geopolitical cartography of the twenty-first century.

Although tomorrow's geopolitical map will surely be shaped in important ways by political choices yet to be made, the basic contours are already emerging. During the era of the Industrial Revolution, the population of what we now call the developed world grew faster than the rest of the world's population, peaking at 25 percent of the world total in 1930. Since then, its share has declined. By 2010, it stood at just 13 percent, and it is projected to decline still further, to 10 percent by 2050.

The collective GDP of the developed countries will also decline as a share of the world total—and much more steeply. According to new projections by the Carnegie Endowment for International Peace, the Group of 7 industrialized nations' share of the Group of 20 leading economies' total GDP will fall from 72 percent in 2009 to 40 percent in 2050. Driving this decline will be not just the slower growth of the developed world, as workforces age and stagnate or contract, but also the expansion of large, newly market-oriented economies, especially in East and South Asia.

Again, there is only one large country in the developed world that does not face a future of stunning relative demographic and economic decline:

the United States. Thanks to its relatively high fertility rate and substantial net immigration, its current global population share will remain virtually unchanged in the coming decades. According to the Carnegie projections, the US share of total G-20 GDP will drop significantly, from 34 percent in 2009 to 24 percent in 2050. The combined share of Canada, France, Germany, Italy, Japan, and the United Kingdom, however, will plunge from 38 percent to 16 percent.

By the middle of the twenty-first century, the dominant strength of the US economy within the developed world will have only one historical parallel: the immediate aftermath of World War II, exactly 100 years earlier, at the birth of the "Pax Americana."

The UN regularly publishes a table ranking the world's most populous countries over time. In 1950, six of the top twelve were developed countries. In 2000, only three were. By 2050, only one developed country will remain—the United States, still in third place. By then, it will be the only country among the top twelve committed since its founding to democracy, free markets, and civil liberties.

All told, population trends point inexorably toward a more dominant US role in a world that will need America more, not less.

Mark L. Haas   ➔ **NO**

Pax Americana Geriatrica

An unprecedented era of great-power aging makes it likely the 21st century will, again, be American.

Last year, Sergei Morozov, the governor of the Ulyanovsk region of central Russia, offered prizes to couples who agreed to take advantage of a "family contact day" and wound up producing babies nine months later, on June 12, Russia's national day. It was the third year running that Ulyanovsk had declared a "sex day" and offered prizes for babies born, according to the BBC. The 2007 grand prize (for conceptions in 2006, of course) was a sport utility vehicle.

The Ulyanovsk initiative is just a part of Russia's efforts to fight a looming demographic crisis that hovers over much of the world. Simply put, the world's great powers are growing old. Steep declines in birthrates over the last century and major increases in life expectancies have caused the populations of Britain, China, France, Germany, Japan, Russia and the United States to age at a substantial rate. In Russia, declining birthrates and other factors are not just aging the society but actually shrinking the country's population.

This phenomenon will have critical effects on America's international-security interests in coming decades. Most important, global aging will be a potent force for the continuation of American military and economic dominance. Aging populations are likely to result in the slowdown of states' economic growth at the same time that governments face pressure to pay for massive new expenditures for elderly care. This double economic dilemma will create such an austere fiscal environment that the other great powers will lack the resources necessary to overtake the United States' huge power lead. This analysis applies even to China, which most analysts point to as America's most likely future rival. China's aging problem will be particularly dramatic over the next 40 years, which will make it difficult for it to challenge American international supremacy.

Meanwhile, America also seems likely to face fewer threats from terrorism based in Islamic countries. If current demographic trends continue, many Islamic states—now in the throes of "youth bulges"—will be aging as societies in coming decades. As active and disaffected young people have aged in other parts of the world, they have become a source of political stability and economic development. There is reason to believe this pattern will

From *Miller-McCune,* July 14, 2008. Copyright © 2008 by Mark L. Haas. Reprinted by permission of the author. Mark L. Haas is Associate Professor of Political Science at Duquesne University in Pittsburgh. This article was originally published as the cover article in the August 2008 issue of Miller-McCune Magazine.

hold in Iraq, Pakistan, Saudi Arabia and other Muslim states as their youth slip into middle age.

Although the United States is also growing older, it is doing so to a lesser extent and less quickly than the other great powers. Consequently, the costs created by aging will be significantly lower for the United States than for potential competitors. Global aging is therefore likely not only to extend U.S. dominance (because the other major powers will lack the resources necessary to overtake the United States' economic and military power lead) but also to deepen it as these other states are likely to fall even farther behind the United States. By inhibiting the other powers from challenging American primacy, global aging increases the odds in favor of continued peaceful relations among these states. *Pax Americana* is therefore likely to extend well into the 21st century.

Although the United States is in better demographic shape than the other great powers, it, too, will confront massive new costs created by an aging population. The United States will be more secure from great-power rivalry than it is today, but it (and its allies) will be less able to realize other key international objectives, including preventing the proliferation of weapons of mass destruction, funding nation building and engaging in humanitarian interventions, among the many costly conflict-resolution and prevention efforts it now undertakes. To protect America's future international interests, it is vital that the country's current leaders adopt policies designed to strengthen its demographic advantages. In the future, America's ability to pay to care for its elderly citizens will become a matter not just of compassion but of national security.

Something New Under the Sun

The scope of the aging process in the great powers—a result of historically low fertility rates and expanding life expectancies—is unprecedented. By 2050, at least 20 percent of the citizens in Britain, China, France, Germany, Japan, Russia and the U.S. will be over 65, according to United Nations projections. In Japan, more than one of every three people will be over this age. In 2050, China will have more than 329 million people over 65, a total approximately equal to the entire current populations of France, Germany, Japan and the United Kingdom combined. As aging progresses over the next half-century, the populations in Germany, Japan and Russia are expected to shrink significantly. Russia's population is already decreasing by nearly 700,000 people per year, and Japan, too, is experiencing population decline. Russia's aging problem is so severe that, in 2006, *The New York Times* quoted President Vladimir Putin calling demography "Russia's most acute problem today."

The aging of the world's great powers is also happening quickly. It took France 115 years for the size of its 65-and-over age group to double from 7 to 14 percent of its population. The U.S. took 69 years to do so. China will experience this transformation in 27 years, or roughly one generation. China, in fact, will age at a pace and extent scarcely before witnessed in human history.

It is worth stressing that the predictions for global aging are very unlikely to be wrong. The reason for this certainty is simple: The elderly of the future are already born. Consequently, absent some global natural disaster, disease pandemic or other worldwide calamity (all extremely rare historically), the number of people in the world who are over 65 will increase dramatically in coming decades. Only major increases in immigration rates or fertility levels will prevent this inevitable rise in the number of elderly from resulting in significant increases in median ages in these states.

Such outcomes are unlikely. Over the next 50 years, immigration rates in the great powers would have to be orders of magnitude higher than historical levels to prevent population aging. Not only do the sheer numbers work against such an outcome, but some countries are becoming more hostile to immigration, despite its benefits for social aging. Both Japan and Russia passed laws in 2006 that will restrict immigration to these states, and right-wing parties have been on the rise across Europe since the 1990s, spurred largely by hostility toward immigrants.

Significant increases in fertility are also unlikely. Such an outcome would require a reversal of a centuries-long trend in the industrialized world, and one that has existed in many states despite the existence of pro-fertility governmental policies (perhaps the most direct of these being Russia's "sex days").

Aging in the most powerful actors in the international system is, in short, a virtual inevitability.

The Costs of Growing Old

In its most basic formulation, a state's gross domestic product is a product of the number of workers and overall productivity. When a country's work force shrinks as more people enter retirement than enter the labor market, so, too, will its GDP, unless productivity levels rise sufficiently to compensate for the loss. Japan's and Russia's working-age populations (ages 15 to 64) are expected to shrink by 34 percent by 2050, Germany's by 20 percent, France's by 6 percent and China's by 3 percent. To prevent these work force reductions from translating into overall GDP decline, states' productivity must increase proportionally. Although productivity will likely increase in most industrialized countries, work force contraction will still act as a substantial brake on economic growth in coming decades.

We are already witnessing this dynamic. Even though China is the youngest of the great powers, it is experiencing labor shortages that are threatening economic growth. These shortages are due in large part to the aging of China and reductions in the number of 15- to 35-year-olds there. Experts predict that shrinkage in China's working-age population will result in a loss of 1 percent per year from this state's GDP growth by the 2020s. The economic forecasts are even more dire for France, Germany and Japan, where massively contracting labor forces could result in *overall* annual GDP growth of roughly 1 percent in coming decades.

Significant societal aging may also limit productivity growth. The elderly are likely to be more conservative with their investments than younger people. The more risk averse a society's investment portfolio is, the less entrepreneurship will be funded and, thus, the lower the gains in productivity. National savings rates may also shrink in aging states as seniors spend down their savings. The Japanese government has already reported that national savings rates are down substantially due to social aging. Reduced savings may lead to rising interest rates and ultimately to reduced rates of productivity increases.

An even more important economic effect of societal aging is the strain that it places on governmental resources. All governments in the industrialized world have made commitments to pay for substantial portions of the retirement and health care costs of their elderly citizens. Social aging increases these obligations in two principal respects. First, the older a society is, the greater the number of retirees and senior citizens for which a particular government is responsible. Second, the elderly, on average, require significantly more resources than working-age adults. Studies have shown that seniors use three to five times more medical care than younger people, for example.

The pension systems across the industrialized world will be particularly taxing on governments' fiscal policies. The public pensions in all of the great powers are "pay as you go," meaning that current workers are taxed to support current retirees. This type of system does not place a significant strain on a state's economy as long as relatively high numbers of workers contribute to the system in relation to retirees. This will not be the case for much longer across the industrial world, and, in some cases, it is not true even today. France, Germany, Japan and Britain have roughly only four working-age adults per senior citizen. By 2050, only America among the great powers will have more than three working-age adults per elderly person.

The projected increases in governmental spending for the elderly in coming decades are sobering. Annual public pension and health care benefits to the elderly as a percentage of GDP are predicted to rise in 2040 by 15 percent in Japan (to an overall percentage of 27); by 13 percent in France (to an overall percentage of 29); by 11 percent in the United States (to an overall percentage of 20); by 10 percent in Germany (to an overall percentage of 26); and by 6 percent in Britain (to an overall percentage of 18).

These costs will be an increase of hundreds of billions of dollars to governments' annual expenditures for many decades. To give some perspective on their magnitude, consider the following: Roughly 35 years from now, the annual amount of money that the great powers will have to spend on elderly care is going to increase by many times what these states currently spend on their militaries, even after adjusting for inflation. By 2040, Germany will have to increase its annual spending on elderly care by more than seven times what it currently spends on defense. France will have to spend more than five times as much and Japan more than 15 times as much.

Pax Americana Geriatrica

Population aging in the great powers will help prolong U.S. power dominance in the 21st century for three primary reasons. First, the massive costs created by aging populations, especially in combination with probable slowdowns in economic growth, will inhibit other major powers from significantly increasing military expenditures; these factors are even likely to push many of these states to reduce military spending from current levels. Second, with aging populations and shrinking work forces, other great powers will be forced to decide whether to spend increasing percentages of their defense budgets on personnel costs and military pensions, at the expense of the most technologically sophisticated weaponry. The third factor reinforces both of the previous points: Although the U.S. population is aging, it is doing so to a lesser extent and less quickly than those of the other great powers. The pressures pushing for the crowding out of military spending in favor of elderly care and the increasing substitution of labor for capital within defense budgets will be considerably smaller for the U.S. than for potential great-power competitors. By inhibiting the other powers from challenging America's huge power lead, global aging will increase the likelihood of continued peaceful relations among these states.

We are, in fact, already witnessing in some states the crowding out of military spending for elderly care. Japan reduced military spending in the 2005 and 2006 budgets explicitly to pay for costs created by its rapidly aging population. The Japanese government has stated that over the next decade, general expenditures will have to be cut by 25 to 30 percent to address this problem. Similar pressure for cuts in defense spending to finance elderly-care costs is building in France and Germany.

The decision to cut military spending to pay elderly-care costs is likely to repeat itself in the state that is aging faster than any of the great powers: China. Rising longevity in China and the "one-child policy," which has helped lower dramatically China's fertility levels, have made China a rapidly aging society. By 2050, according to the U.N., China's median age is predicted to be nearly 45, one of the oldest in the world. (The oldest country in the world today, Japan, has a median age of just under 43). The ratio of working-age adults to elderly will shrink from just under 10 in 2000 to 2.5 by 2050. China today has roughly 100 million citizens over the age of 65. This number will double in 20 years. Roughly 30 years from now, it is expected to triple.

Despite the effects of the one-child policy on China's median age, China's leaders are unlikely to repeal it in the near future. *The New York Times* reports that the Chinese government significantly increased the fines this year for wealthy couples who violate the law and have more than one child. Although some Chinese officials talk about reconsidering this law, any changes that do occur will most likely be incremental. The longer the one-child policy stays in effect, the more quickly China will age.

China is particularly unprepared to pay for the costs of its rapidly aging population. China's elderly have very little savings. Nearly 80 percent of Chinese urban households with individuals aged 55 and over today have less than one year of income saved, and only 5 percent have more than two years of income in savings, according to Center for Strategic and International Studies and Asian Development Bank research. The Chinese government has also failed to set aside over the decades sufficient money to pay for elderly-care costs. Three-quarters of all Chinese workers are without any pension coverage, yet independent estimates have found a potential shortfall between China's governmental obligations to the elderly and saved assets to be as much as 150 percent of its GDP.

China will not be able to "grow" its way out of this dilemma. Despite China's very high levels of economic growth since the 1990s, it will become the first country to grow old before becoming an advanced industrial state. Even if China's economy continues to grow in coming decades at rates similar to those it has experienced in recent years, by 2035, its median age will reach the levels of France, Germany and Japan today but at GDP-per-capita levels significantly lower than these states currently possess.

China has traditionally relied on the family unit to provide for elderly care in lieu of adequate public and private resources. But as *The New York Times* has noted, increasing rates of divorce, urbanization (and related migration) and female work force participation will place significant strain on this tradition. Decreasing family size will prove especially problematic for preserving elderly welfare within the context of the family. Demographers refer to a rapidly growing "4-2-1" phenomenon in China, in which one child is responsible for caring for two parents and four grandparents.

Within 15 years, China's leaders will be faced with a difficult choice: Allow growing levels of poverty within an exploding elderly population, or provide the resources necessary to avoid this situation. The Chinese government's assumption since 2000 of unfunded pension liabilities of state-owned enterprises reveals the political and moral pressure working for the latter outcome. This pressure to significantly expand and deepen China's welfare system will only grow as its aging crisis becomes increasingly acute in the decades to come. In this context, the crowding out of military and other discretionary expenditures will be likely, to the great benefit of America's relative power position.

Aging is also likely to push militaries to spend more on personnel and less on other areas, including weapons development and procurement. This is important because no nation will be able to challenge U.S. military dominance without the ability to wage highly technologically sophisticated warfare. When states are forced to spend more of their military budgets on personnel than research, development and weapons procurement, the odds of continued U.S. military primacy increase substantially.

The oldest of the great powers are already devoting significantly more resources to military personnel than weapons purchases and research. Over the last 10 years, both France and Germany have dedicated nearly 60 percent of their military budgets to personnel. Germany spends nearly four times as much on personnel as weapons procurement; France, Japan and Russia roughly 2.5 times more. The United States, in contrast, dedicates only 1.15 times more money to personnel than weapons purchases.

Population aging is a key cause of increasing military personnel costs for two main reasons. First, as societies age, more people exit the work force than enter it. Increasing numbers of retirees in relation to new workers are likely to create labor shortages relative to previous levels of employment. The result will be increased competition among businesses and organizations—including the military—to hire workers. Consequently, if states' militaries want to be able to attract and keep the best employees in vital areas of operation—especially those in high-tech fields who usually have the most employment options and can command high salaries in the private sector—they are going to have to pay more to do so. If militaries do not increase their outlays for personnel, their effectiveness will diminish. A 2006 report endorsed by EU defense ministers made precisely these points, stating that the aging of Europe's people will "inevitably" lead to rising military personnel per capita costs if European forces are to remain effective.

Similarly, to keep military salaries on par with wages in its expanding economy, China—even though its armed forces are conscripted—has had to raise military wages sharply in recent years. According to the Chinese government, growing personnel expenses are the most important factor behind the growth of China's defense budget in the last decade.

The great powers' pension obligations to retired military personnel are also considerable. Russia spends significantly more on military retirees than on either weapons procurement or military research and development, according to its 2006 defense budget.

Pensions for military retirees are not one-time costs but go on for decades, doing nothing to increase states' power-projection capabilities. Every dollar spent on retirees is one less dollar that can be spent on weapons, research or active personnel. Consequently, every dollar spent in this area by the other great powers increases the likelihood of continued U.S. primacy.

U.S. Aging: Bad, But Better Than the Rest

At a gala event held at the National Press Club in Washington, D.C., on Oct. 15, 2007, Kathleen Casey-Kirschling, who was born one second after midnight on Jan. 1, 1946, became the first baby boomer to file for social security. Over the next 20 years, 76 million Americans from the age cohort born between 1946 and 1964 will join her.

The costs created by America's aging population are staggering. The Congressional Budget Office projects that by 2015, spending on the elderly will total almost $1.8 trillion, nearly half of the anticipated federal budget. Health care costs, in particular, are the United States' biggest problem regarding societal aging. The United States spends more than twice as much per capita in this area than any other industrial great power (though it ranks 48th in the world in life expectancy). According to conservative estimates—absent reforms—the costs of Medicare alone will be at least $2.6 trillion in 2050, after adjusting for inflation, which is roughly the size of the current U.S. federal budget.

Despite these expected cost increases, the United States is in significantly better shape to address the challenges created by its aging population than the other powers. The United States is the youngest of all the G-8 nations. Because it has the highest fertility and immigration rates of these countries, it will maintain, even strengthen, this position in coming decades. In 2050, the United States' median age will be the lowest of any of the great powers, in most cases by a substantial extent. (China's median age will surpass the United States' by 2020.) Perhaps most important, while the working-age populations in all the other great powers are predicted by 2050 to either decline (China, France, Germany, Japan and Russia) or increase modestly (Britain), this demographic group is expected to increase by 31 percent in the United States.

The United States' relatively youthful demographics will help greatly with the fiscal challenges created by aging. The growing U.S. labor force over the next 50 years will contribute to an expanding economy, thereby providing the government with additional revenue without it having to increase taxes, borrow more money or cut other spending. In addition, the United States has a relatively well-funded pension system (especially in relation to China, France, Germany and Russia); its public welfare commitments to the elderly are relatively modest compared with those of other industrialized powers; its citizens work many more hours per year and significantly later in life than the average individual in the other powers; and its tax burden is low compared with those of other powers.

American expectations are also comparatively favorable. In a 2008 Harris Interactive poll of citizens in the United States, Britain, France, Germany, Italy and Spain, Americans had the highest predictions of when they would retire (67.2 years old) and the lowest expectations—by far—regarding governmental support of their retirement. (Only 27 percent of Americans believed that the national government should bear most of their retirement costs; this percentage ranged from 45 to 72 in European countries.) These expectations reveal that U.S. citizens are much more amenable to entitlement reforms and benefit cuts than are most Europeans.

Again, the preceding facts do not mean that the United States will escape the fiscal burdens created by aging or that this phenomenon will not create negative ramifications for U.S. security. Rather, as burdensome as the public costs of aging will be for the United States, the public benefits owed to United States seniors as a percentage of GDP will likely remain substantially lower than in most of the other great powers. Moreover, the United States will be better positioned to pay for these costs than the other major actors. Global aging will therefore be a powerful force for the continuation of the relative power dominance of the United States.

Population Aging and the "War on Terrorism"

Numerous studies have shown that there is a strong, positive relationship between so-called youth bulges—a disproportionately high number of young people in a society—and political violence, including civil conflict and terrorism. Developing states' economies frequently have difficulty creating enough jobs to accommodate the exploding work forces in very young societies. Not surprisingly, the region that has the most youth bulges in the world—the Middle East and North Africa—also has, by far, the highest unemployment rates among young adults: 26 percent in 2006.

High levels of unemployment inevitably create strong grievances against existing political and economic policies, and, thus, a large pool of potential recruits for violent political change. The young tend to be particularly idealistic, which inclines members of this demographic group to believe that major political and social change can and should be made, even if this objective requires the use of force. The young are less likely to be married, have established careers or possess prominent positions in the community. As a result, young people, especially in the context of economic deprivation and political oppression, frequently feel that they have little to lose by engaging in violent acts designed to change the status quo.

Given the relationship between youth bulges and political violence and radicalism, it is no surprise that Islamic states in general—and Saudi Arabia,

Iraq, Palestine (aka the occupied territories), Afghanistan and Pakistan in particular—have been hotbeds for domestic violence and international terrorism in recent years. In 2000, at least 45 percent of all adults in these countries were in the 15-to-29 age range.

The potential good news for the U.S. is that population aging may help alleviate, albeit slowly, the deleterious effects of youth bulges in many Islamic states. If current trends in fertility rates continue, by 2030, the youth bulges in Iraq, Pakistan and Saudi Arabia will all have receded. Population aging and the diminishment of youth bulges have been a source of political stability and economic development in many other countries over the last half-century, including in East Asia and Europe. There is little reason to believe that this pattern will not hold true in Islamic states, even though the transformation will require several generations.

Demography may ultimately hold the key for winning the "war on terrorism."

The Bad News

Although global population aging is likely to create substantial security benefits for the United States in coming decades, the same phenomenon is also likely to threaten U.S. international interests in important ways.

First, the negative impact on the other great powers' economic growth and military spending is, in some respects, a double-edged sword. On the one hand, these outcomes will mean that no state will be able to overtake the United States' position of economic and military dominance. The same factor, though, will also reduce the amount of economic or military aid that other states will be able to contribute toward the realization of common international interests. Instead of increasing "burden sharing" with key allies, the United States will have to pay even more of the costs of its international goals than it does today.

Second, while the United States should expect less international aid from its allies, it, too, is likely to experience the slowing of economic growth and the crowding out of military expenditures for elderly care. America will in all likelihood have to scale back the scope of its international policies. The United States' current position of unprecedented power allows its leaders to pursue highly extensive global commitments. The United States has military personnel in more than 140 countries in the world, and over the last 15 years, the United States has engaged in nearly 50 military interventions, more than any other state, by far, in the system. The primary motivation in at least four of these operations—Somalia, Haiti, Bosnia and Kosovo—was humanitarian.

In the aftermath of many of these interventions, the United States devoted considerable resources to help create stable political and civil institutions (so-called nation building). America also plays the dominant role in facilitating international trade and has borne the primary costs in trying to prevent "rogue" states — including Iraq, Iran, North Korea and Libya—from acquiring weapons of mass destruction. The economic effects of an aging population will deny the United States the fiscal room necessary to maintain the extent of its current global position, let alone adopt major new international initiatives. In the face of the exploding costs for elderly care and retirement, the crowding out of other spending will occur even for the richest country in the history of the world, to the likely detriment of American security.

America's Golden Years?

The policy choices that flow from this article's analysis are clear. Internationally, America's long-term objective should be to help reduce fertility rates in developing countries. This outcome will likely reduce the problems created by youth bulges, including international terrorism. Policies that increase women's rights and educational and employment opportunities, as well as those that provide better access to birth control, are key means to this end. International development aid designed to increase states' GDP-per-capita levels should also be high among America's foreign-policy priorities. The United States, though, dedicates relatively few resources toward these goals. A December 2005 report issued by the Council on Foreign Relations with bipartisan leadership notes that demographics continued to be a neglected area of U.S. foreign policies. This important oversight needs to be corrected, and quickly.

In terms of domestic policies, U.S. leaders need to be proactive in maintaining America's enviable demographic position. Specifically, America should reduce Social Security and Medicare payments to wealthier citizens, maintain largely open immigration policies that help keep its median age relatively low and restrain the rising costs of its health care system.

Raising the retirement age to reduce the government's retirement obligations is a particularly effective—and logical—solution for the problems created by America's aging population. Social Security's original retirement age of 65 was set in 1935, when life expectancy was 63. Life expectancy today is 78. According to experts on this subject, a one-year increase in the retirement age would eliminate roughly one-third of Social Security's projected expenditures shortfall over the next 75 years. This calculation does not take into account the extra tax revenue the government would accrue from increased economic growth due to people working longer. Some predict that if seniors work an average of five years longer than they currently do, America's GDP in 2030 would be 7 to 8 percent larger than it otherwise would.

Although the need for reform on the aging issue is clear and compelling—and even though Americans appear amenable to adopting such reforms, as I discuss above—*U.S. politicians have failed to lead on this subject.* The immigration reform bill failed to pass Congress in 2007, major Social Security reform has not occurred since the 1980s and Medicare "reform" has mostly expanded obligations. The 2003 prescription drug benefits legislation, for example, increased the program's unfunded liability by $16.2 trillion, according to government projections.

The longer U.S. leaders delay in addressing the growing gap between elderly-care obligations and resources set aside to pay for them, the more painful such action will be when it comes. And delay in putting U.S. retirement and health care programs on sound financial footing may not only negate the otherwise substantial demographic advantages America enjoys but also reduce the support those advantages give to U.S. security in the 21st century.

EXPLORING THE ISSUE ↻

Is Global Aging a Major Problem?

Critical Thinking and Reflection

1. What do analysts really mean when they talk about a global aging population?
2. Why is the 2020s considered to be a decade of reckoning because of an aging global population?
3. What are differences and similarities regarding global aging between developed and developing societies?
4. Should national governments be concerned that their populations are about to go through a demographic transition that will lead to aging populations?
5. Are there positive consequences of an aging population?

Is There Common Ground?

There is now a consensus that demographic trends matter with respect to a wide range of public policy issues. There is also agreement on the nature of future trends, particularly as they relate to global aging. And societies are coming to agree on the economic implications of such aging.

Additional Resources

Jackson, Richard and Howe, Neil, *The Graying of the Great Powers* (Center for Strategic and International Studies, 2008)

This report describes global aging trends and geopolitical consequences.

Lee, Ronald D., *Global Population Aging and Its Economic Consequences* (AEI Press, 2007)

This book, first appearing as a lecture, describes how the risks of aging can be contained through foresight and public policy.

Lee, Ronald et al., *Some Economic Consequences of Global Aging* (The World Bank, December 2010)

As the title implies, this study spells out economic implications of global aging.

Magnus, George, *The Age of Aging: How Demographics Are Changing the Global Economy and Our World* (Wiley, 2008)

This book is an easily read analysis of basic demographic trends, particularly aging, and their consequences.

McMorrow, Kleran, *The Economic and Financial Market Consequences of Global Ageing* (Springer, 2010)

This book examines the effects of population changes on the size of the labor force and the broader financial implications.

National Institute on Aging, *Why Population Aging Matters: A Global Perspective* (Amazon Digital Services, 2007)

This book describes population trends, including known trends in global aging.

Robinson, Mary et al. (eds.), *Global Health and Global Aging* (Jossey-Bass, 2007)

This book describes the basic aspects of global aging, using real-world models from countries and regions that demonstrate best practices.

Uhlenberg, Peter, *International Handbook of Population Aging* (Springer, 2009)

This book examines research on various aspects of global aging, including how the world is changing as a consequence.

U.S. Department of Commerce, *An Aging World: 2008* (U.S. Census Bureau, 2008)

This comprehensive report describes global demographic trends and their implications, particularly as they relate to global aging.

ISSUE 3

Does Global Urbanization Lead Primarily to Undesirable Consequences?

YES: Divya Abhat, Shauna Dineen, Tamsyn Jones, Jim Motavalli, Rebecca Sanborn, and Kate Slomkowski, from "Cities of the Future: Today's 'Mega-Cities' Are Overcrowded and Environmentally Stressed," *E/The Environmental Magazine* (September/October 2005)

NO: UNFPA, from "People in Cities: Hope Countering Desolation," *UNFPA State of the World Population 2007: Unleashing the Potential of Urban Growth* (2007)

Learning Outcomes

After reading this issue, you should be able to:

- Describe urban/rural population growth patterns in both the developed and the developing worlds.
- Understand that increasing urbanization has both positive and negative effects on the environment and the economy.
- Understand the history of urban growth in both the developed and the developing worlds.
- Discuss how the world is transitioning from a rural to an urban predominance.
- Describe how cities have been a lure for rural poor to try to find better lives.
- Discuss how urbanization affects women's empowerment.

ISSUE SUMMARY

YES: Divya Abhat, editor of *E/The Environmental Magazine,* and colleagues suggest that the world's cities suffer from environmental ills, among them pollution, poverty, fresh water shortages, and disease.

NO: The UNFPA 2007 Report suggests that cities, in fact, facilitate a number of desirable conditions, such as gender-equitable change, more diverse employment possibilities, more economic well-being and security for women, women's empowerment, and access to better health care, among other positive changes.

Debates about the relative merits of urban and rural living have been with us for more than four decades. As urban population growth began in earnest to outstrip rural population growth, the debate became more pronounced, particularly in the past decade. The year 2007 witnessed a turning point in the history of the world's cities. For the first time, the world's urban and rural populations were equal. By 2009, the number of people living in urban areas had moved ahead of the number of those living in rural areas. Global urban population is expected to increase 84 percent by 2050, from 3.4 billion in 2009 to 6.3 billion. The global rural population is expected to reach a high of 3.5 billion in 2020, then slowly decline, reaching 2.9 billion in 2050. And the world urban population is not distributed evenly among cities of similar size. Rather, slightly more than half of urban dwellers live in cities with fewer than 5,000,000 inhabitants. Although cities with fewer than 100,000 people account for one-third of the global urban population, 21 megacities, each with at least 10 million people, account for about 10 percent of the global urban population. Until 1975, there were only three such megacities—New York, Tokyo, and Mexico City. Now most megacities are in the developing world. In 2009, half of the world's urban population resided in Asia. China and India top the list of Asian countries with large urban populations.

Percentages are different for the developed and developing worlds regarding the urban–rural split. In 1950, 55 percent of the population of the developed world resided in urban areas, compared with only 18 percent in the developing world. By 2000, 76 percent of those in the developed world were urbanized, and it is expected, according to the United Nations (UN) projections, to reach 82 percent by 2025. But because there will be low population growth throughout the developed world in the coming decades, the impact will not be substantial.

The story is different in the developing world. In 2000, the level of urbanization had risen to almost 40 percent. It will reach 50 percent by 2020 and is projected to be 54 percent in 2025. The percentages tell only part of the story, however, as they are not based on a stable national population level but will occur in the context of substantial increases in the national population level. To illustrate the dual implication of urban growth as the consequence of both migration to the cities and increased births on those already living in urban areas, the UN projects that the urban population in the developing world will more than double in size between 2000 and 2030, from just under 2 billion to almost 5 billion or nearly two-thirds of the world's population (UN-Habitat, *State of the World's Cities 2006/07,* Earthscan, 2007). Asia and Africa will experience the largest urban populations, but small and intermediate cities will absorb most of the urban growth. Tremendous inequality will exist in cities. One out of three city dwellers resides in an urban environment that qualifies as slum conditions, defined as a lack of durable housing, lack of sufficient living area, lack of access to improved water, lack of access to improved sanitation, and lack of secure land tenure.

There are two ways to examine rapid urbanization. One approach is to examine the adverse impacts of the urbanized area on the environment. Second, one can study the ability of society to provide services to the urban population. The best place to begin a discussion of urbanization's effects is found in "An Urbanizing World" (Martin P. Brockerhoff, *Population Bulletin,* Population Reference Bureau, 2000). According to Brockerhoff, increasing urbanization in the poor countries can be seen "as a welcome or as an alarming trend." He suggests that cities have been the "engines of economic development and the centers of industry and commerce." The diffusion of ideas is best found in cities around the world. And Brockerhoff observes the governmental cost savings of delivering goods and services to those in more densely populated environments.

The basic question of urbanization's goodness or badness relates to its impact on the poverty level of its inhabitants because poverty is at the heart of the ability of its owners to address ills caused by the social phenomenon, in this case, urbanization. The evidence is becoming clearer that poverty "is becoming more urban" (Gordon McGranahan and Edgar Pieterse, "Getting Urbanization Right: A Defining Development Challenge for the 21st Century"). These authors suggest that if present trends continue, about half of global citizens living on less than one dollar per day will be urban dwellers. The number of people living in urban slums—housing with serious deficiencies in water supplies and sanitary facilities and crowded conditions—is increasing.

Urban poverty, of course, has a direct impact in turn on urban health. Although rural health tends to be worse than urban health, the poverty, environmental degradation, and population demands of urbanization pose significant health risks. Melinda Moore and colleagues ("Global Urbanization and Impact on Health") suggest a range of health hazards and risks: "substandard housing, crowding, air pollution, insufficient or contaminated drinking water, inadequate sanitation and solid waste disposal services, vector-borne diseases, industrial waste, increased motor vehicle traffic, stress associated with poverty and unemployment, among others."

There is a more recent concern emerging among researchers about urbanization's impact—this time on biodiversity. One source has coined the phrase "heavy ecological footprints" ("Impact on the Environment," *Population Reports,* 2002) to describe the adverse effects. One study concludes, for example, that urban sprawl in the United States endangers more species than any other human behavior (Michael L. McKinney, "Urbanization, Biodiversity, and Conservation," *Bioscience,* 2002). A 2008 study by the Nature Conservancy and Harvard University concluded that failure to improve urban planning would lead to losing "some animals, plants and natural resources for good." The highest concentrations of endemic species are found in natural areas affected by urban growth. Eight percent of vertebrate species have been marked as endangered because of the impact of urban growth.

The current problem is not that cities of the developing world are growing but that they are expanding at a rapid pace. This calls into question the ability of both the government and the private sector to determine what is necessary for urbanites not only to survive but also to thrive. Many researchers believe that poverty and health problems (both physical and mental) are the consequences of urbanization. Brockerhoff also alludes to the potential for greater harm to residents of cities from natural disasters and environmental hazards.

This rapid growth is at the heart of the question of government's ability to provide necessary services to urban dwellers. Many observers call attention to the capacity of urban governments to take care of their urban inhabitants. The UN's 2007 report argued that attention must be paid to the challenges of urbanization in a preempted rather than reactionary manner. The report highlighted urbanization's advantages, foremost of which is the advantage of concentrating services to a concentrated population, as they allow for more effective and more inexpensive ways to provide social services, infrastructure, and amenities. And because a significant percentage of urban growth is occurring in medium-size cities rather than megacities, the United Nations Population Fund (UNFPA) argues that there is greater flexibility to expand correctly.

Although the literature calls attention to the adverse effect of urbanization on natural habitats, some suggest that concentrated urban growth actually minimizes such impact. Christopher Flavin of the Worldwatch Institute observes that cities are stepping up to the plate in combating climate change. Evidence suggests that urbanization has fueled the growth in religion throughout the world. And finally, a recent study suggests that contrary to popular belief, urbanization carries "significant health advantages especially in developing countries" (Clara K. Cohen et al., "Is Urbanization Good for a Nation's Health?").

An alternative way to look at urbanization is to move away from a focus on whether the urbanized government can provide necessary services to its citizens or whether urbanization has negative consequences for those urban dwellers. That is to consider the role urbanization plays in the country's total economic health. The World Bank's *Development Report 2009* makes the case for urbanization as a positive force. It suggests that urbanization helps the three spatial transformations that fuel economic growth: increasing density, reducing economic distance, and overcoming divisions. As Gordon McGranahan and Edgar Pieterse argue, more productive investment opportunities exist in urban areas, and thus economic growth will benefit from urban growth.

The two selections for this issue address the question of the consequences of urbanization. In the YES selection, Divya Abhat and colleagues argue that most urban dwellers in the developing world are already confronted by severe environmental problems that will only increase in nature as population continues to grow. In the NO selection, the UNFPA report advances the point that cities represent a better place to achieve a variety of positive goals, many relating to women's issues.

YES ↵

Divya Abhat et al.

Cities of the Future:
Today's "Mega-Cities"
Are Overcrowded and
Environmentally Stressed

We take big cities for granted today, but they are a relatively recent phenomenon. Most of human history concerns rural people making a living from the land. But the world is rapidly urbanizing, and it's not at all clear that our planet has the resources to cope with this relentless trend. And, unfortunately, most of the growth is occurring in urban centers ill-equipped for the pace of change. You've heard of the "birth dearth"? It's bypassing Dhaka, Mumbai, Mexico City and Lagos, cities that are adding population as many of their western counterparts contract.

The world's first cities grew up in what is now Iraq, on the plains of Mesopotamia near the banks of the Tigris and Euphrates Rivers. The first city in the world to have more than one million people was Rome at the height of its Empire in 5 A.D. At that time, world population was only 170 million. But Rome was something new in the world. It had developed its own sophisticated sanitation and traffic management systems, as well as aqueducts, multi-story low-income housing and even suburbs, but after it fell in 410 A.D. it would be 17 centuries before any metropolitan area had that many people.

The first large city in the modern era was Beijing, which surpassed one million population around 1800, followed soon after by New York and London. But at that time city life was the exception; only three percent of the world's population lived in urban areas in 1800.

The rise of manufacturing spurred relocation to urban centers from the 19th through the early 20th century. The cities had the jobs, and new arrivals from the countryside provided the factories with cheap, plentiful labor. But the cities were also unhealthy places to live because of crowded conditions, poor sanitation and the rapid transmission of infectious disease. As the Population Reference Bureau reports, deaths exceeded births in many large European cities until the middle of the 19th century. Populations grew, then, by continuing waves of migration from the countryside and from abroad.

From First World to Third

In the first half of the 20th century, the fastest urban growth was in western cities. New York, London and other First World capitals were magnets for immigration and job opportunity. In 1950, New York, London, Tokyo and Paris boasted of having the world's largest metropolitan populations. (Also in the top 10 were Moscow, Chicago, and the German city of Essen.) By then, New York had already become the first "mega-city," with more than 10 million people. It would not hold on to such exclusivity for long.

In the postwar period, many large American cities lost population as manufacturing fled overseas and returning soldiers taking advantage of the GI Bill fueled the process of suburbanization. Crime was also a factor. As an example, riot-torn Detroit lost 800,000 people between 1950 and 1996, and its population declined 33.9 percent between 1970 and 1996. Midwestern cities were particularly hard-hit. St. Louis, for instance, lost more than half its population in the same period, as did Pittsburgh. Cleveland precipitously declined, as did Buffalo, Cincinnati, Minneapolis and many other large cities, emerging as regional players rather than world leaders.

Meanwhile, while many American cities shrank, population around the world was growing dramatically. In the 20th century, world population increased from 1.65 billion to six billion. The highest rate of growth was in the late 1960s, when 80 million people were added every year.

According to the "World Population Data Sheet," global population will rise 46 percent between now and 2050 to about nine billion. While developed countries are losing population because of falling birth rates and carefully controlled immigration rates (only the United States reverses this trend, with 45 percent growth to 422 million predicted by 2050), population is exploding in the developing world.

India's population will likely grow 52 percent to 1.6 billion by 2050, when it will surpass China as the world's most populous country. The population in neighboring Pakistan will grow to 349 million, up 134 percent in 2050. Triple-digit growth rates also are forecast for Iraq, Afghanistan and Nepal.

Africa could double in population to 1.9 billion by 2050. These growth rates hold despite the world's highest rates of AIDS infection, and despite civil wars, famines and other factors. Despite strife in the Congo, it could triple to 181 million by 2050, while Nigeria doubles to 307 million.

Big Cities Get Bigger—and Poorer

According to a 1994 UN report, 1.7 billion of the world's 2.5 billion urban dwellers were then living in less-developed nations, which were also home to two-thirds of the world's mega-cities. The trend is rapidly accelerating. *People and the Planet* reports that by 2007, 3.2 billion people—a number larger than the entire global population of 1967—will live in cities. Developing countries will absorb nearly all of the world's population increases between today and 2030. The estimated urban growth rate of 1.8 percent for the period between

2000 and 2030 will double the number of city dwellers. Meanwhile, rural populations are growing scarcely at all.

Also by 2030, more than half of all Asians and Africans will live in urban areas. Latin America and the Caribbean will at that time be 84 percent urban, a level comparable to the United States. As urban population grows, rural populations will shrink. Asia is projected to lose 26 million rural dwellers between 2000 and 2030.

For many internal migrants, cities offer more hope of a job and better health care and educational opportunities. In many cases, they are home to an overwhelming percentage of a country's wealth. (Mexico City, for example, produces about 30 percent of Mexico's total Gross Domestic Product.) Marina Lupina, a Manila, Philippines, resident, told *People and the Planet* that she and her two children endure the conditions of city living (inhabiting a shack made from discarded wood and cardboard next to a fetid, refuse-choked canal) because she can earn $2 to $3 a day selling recycled cloth, compared to 50 cents as a farm laborer in the rural areas. "My girls will have a better life than I had," she says. "That's the main reason I came to Manila. We will stay no matter what."

Movement like this will lead to rapidly changing population levels in the world's cities, and emerging giants whose future preeminence can now only be guessed. "By 2050, an estimated two-thirds of the world's population will live in urban areas, imposing even more pressure on the space infrastructure and resources of cities, leading to social disintegration and horrific urban poverty," says Werner Fornos, president of the Washington-based Population Institute.

Today, the most populous city is Tokyo (26.5 million people in 2001), followed by Sao Paulo (18.3 million), Mexico City (18.3 million), New York (16.8 million) and Bombay/Mumbai (16.5 million). But by 2015 this list will change, with Tokyo remaining the largest city (then with 27.2 million), followed by Dhaka (Bangladesh), Mumbai, Sao Paulo, New Delhi and Mexico City (each with more than 20 million). New York will have moved down to seventh place, followed by Jakarta, Calcutta, Karachi and Lagos (all with more than 16 million).

The speed by which some mega-cities are growing has slowed. Thirty years ago, for instance, the UN projected Mexico City's population would grow beyond 30 million by 2000, but the actual figures are much lower. Other cities not growing as much as earlier seen are Rio de Janeiro, Calcutta, Cairo, and Seoul, Korea. But against this development is the very rapid growth of many other cities (in some cases, tenfold in 40 years) such as Amman (Jordan), Dar es Salaam (Tanzania), Lagos, and Nairobi.

The rise of mega-cities, comments the *Washington Post*, "poses formidable challenges in health care and the environment, in both the developed and developing world. The urban poor in developing countries live in squalor unlike anything they left behind . . . In Caracas, more than half the total housing stock is squatter housing. In Bangkok, the regional economy is 2.1 percent smaller than it otherwise would be because of time lost in traffic jams. The mega-cities of the future pose huge problems for waste management, water use and climate change."

In Cairo, Egypt, the rooftops of countless buildings are crowded with make-shift tents, shacks and mud shelters. It's not uncommon to see a family cooking their breakfast over an open fire while businesspeople work in their cubicles below. The city's housing shortage is so severe that thousands of Egyptians have moved into the massive historic cemetery known as the City of the Dead, where they hang clotheslines between tombs and sleep in mausoleums.

By 2015, there will be 33 mega-cities, 27 of them in the developing world. Although cities themselves occupy only two percent of the world's land, they have a major environmental impact on a much wider area. London, for example, requires roughly 60 times its own area to supply its nine million inhabitants with food and forest products. Mega-cities are likely to be a drain on the Earth's dwindling resources, while contributing mightily to environmental degradation themselves.

The Mega-City Environment

Mega-cities suffer from a catalog of environmental ills. A World Health Organization (WHO)/United Nations Environment Programme (UNEP) study found that seven of the cities—Mexico City, Beijing, Cairo, Jakarta, Los Angeles, Sao Paulo and Moscow—had three or more pollutants that exceeded the WHO health protection guidelines. All 20 of the cities studied by WHO/UNEP had at least one major pollutant that exceeded established health limits.

According to the World Resources Institute, "Millions of children living in the world's largest cities, particularly in developing countries, are exposed to life-threatening air pollution two to eight times above the maximum WHO guidelines. Indeed, more than 80 percent of all deaths in developing countries attributable to air pollution-induced lung infections are among children under five." In the big Asian mega-cities such as New Delhi, Beijing and Jakarta, approximately 20 to 30 percent of all respiratory disease stems from air pollution.

Almost all of the mega-cities face major fresh water challenges. Johannesburg, South Africa, is forced to draw water from highlands 370 miles away. In Bangkok, saltwater is making incursions into aquifers. Mexico City has a serious sinking problem because of excessive groundwater withdrawal.

More than a billion people, 20 percent of the world's population, live without regular access to clean running water. While poor people are forced to pay exorbitant fees for private water, many cities squander their resources through leakages and illegal drainage. "With the population of cities expected to increase to five billion by 2025," says Klaus Toepfer, executive director of the UNEP, "the urban demand for water is set to increase exponentially. This means that any solution to the water crisis is closely linked to the governance of cities."

Mega-city residents, crowded into unsanitary slums, are also subject to serious disease outbreaks. Lima, Peru (with population estimated at 9.4 million by 2015) suffered a cholera outbreak in the late 1990s partly because, as the *New York Times* reported, "Rural people new to Lima . . . live in houses without running water and use the outhouses that dot the hillsides above." Consumption of unsafe food and water subjects these people to life-threatening diarrhea and dehydration.

It's worth looking at some of these emerging mega-cities in detail, because daily life there is likely to be the pattern for a majority of the world's population. Most are already experiencing severe environmental problems that will only be exacerbated by rapid population increases. Our space-compromised list leaves out the largest European and American cities. These urban centers obviously face different challenges, among them high immigration rates.

Jakarta, Indonesia

A Yale University graduate student, who served as a college intern at the U.S. Embassy in Jakarta, brought back this account: "Directly adjacent to the Embassy's high-rise office building was a muddy, trash-filled canal that children bathed in every morning. The view from the top floors was unforgettable: a layer of brown sky rising up to meet the blue—a veritable pollution horizon. In the distance the tips of skyscrapers stretched up out of the atmospheric cesspool below, like giant corporate snorkels. Without fresh air to breathe, my days were characterized by nausea and constant low-grade headaches. I went to Indonesia wanting a career in government, and left determined to start a career working with the environment."

Jakarta is one of the world's fastest-growing cities. United Nations estimates put the city's 1995 population at 11.5 million, a dramatic increase from only 530,000 in 1930. Mohammad Dannisworo of the Bandung Institute of Technology (ITB) says 8.5 million people live within the city's boundaries at night and an additional 5.5 million migrate via 2.5 million private cars, 3.8 million motorcycles and 255,000 public transportation vehicles into the city during the day. This daily parade of combustion engines clogs the city streets and thickens the air, making Jakarta the world's third-most-polluted city after Bangkok and Mexico City.

Rapid growth has become one of the capital city's greatest challenges, as migrants continue to pour into Jakarta from the surrounding countryside in search of higher-paying jobs. An estimated 200,000 people come to the city looking for employment every year. In the face of such growth, the city has been unable to provide adequate housing, despite repeated attempts to launch urban improvement programs. The Kampung Improvement Program (KIP), established in the 1980s, was initially highly successful in boosting living conditions for more than 3.5 million established migrants, but it has been unable to accommodate the persistent migrant influx. There is an acute housing shortage, with a demand for 200,000 new units a year unfulfilled.

As Encarta describes it, "In the 1970s, efforts failed to control growth by prohibiting the entry of unemployed migrants. The current strategy emphasizes family planning, dispersing the population throughout the greater [metropolitan] region, and promoting transmigration (the voluntary movement of families to Indonesia's less-populated islands). Jakarta is a magnet for migrants . . . [During the late 1980s] most were between the ages of 15 and 39 years, many with six years of education or less."

The UN reports that the city's drinking water system is ineffective, leading 80 percent of Jakarta inhabitants to use underground water, which has become steadily depleted. In lowlying North Jakarta, groundwater depletion has caused serious land subsidence, making the area more vulnerable to flooding and allowing seawater from the Java Sea to seep into the coastal aquifers. According to Suyono Dikun, Deputy Minister for Infrastructure at the National Development Planning Board, more than 100 million people in Indonesia are living without proper access to clean water.

Jakarta's environment has been deteriorating rapidly, with serious air pollution and the lack of a waterborne sewer. Jakarta officials have only recently begun to acknowledge the source of over half of the city's air pollution, and have begun to take action against automobile congestion. The Blue Skies Program, founded in 1996, is dedicated to updating the city's public and private transportation technology. The project's successes to date include an increase in the percentage of vehicles meeting pollution standards, a near-complete phasing out of leaded gasoline, and an increase in the number of natural gas-fueled vehicles to 3,000 taxis, 500 passenger cars and 50 public buses.

The Blue Skies Project is pushing Jakarta toward a complete natural gas conversion and is working toward the installation of dedicated filling stations, establishing a fleet of natural gas-fueled passenger buses, supplying conversion kits for gasoline fueled cars, and creating adequate inspection and main tenance facilities.

Jakarta has acknowledged its traffic problems and undertaken both small and large scale projects to alleviate the stresses of pollution and congestion. The city has launched a "three-in-one" policy to encourage carpooling, demanding that every car on major thruways carry at least three passengers when passing through special zones from 4:30 P.M. to 7:30 P.M. The city has also undertaken the construction of a nearly 17-mile monorail system.

But if Jakarta really wants to alleviate its infrastructure problems, it has to work from within, says Gordon Feller of the California-based Urban Age Institute. "The mayor needs to create a partnership between the three sectors—the government, the local communities and the nongovernmental agencies. The job of the mayor is to empower the independent innovators, not to co-opt or block them."

Dhaka, Bangladesh

Dhaka had only 3.5 million people in 1951; now it has more than 13 million. The city has been gaining population at a rate of nearly seven percent a year since 1975, and it will be the world's second-largest city (after Tokyo) by 2015. According to a recent Japanese environmental report, "Dhaka city is beset with a number of socio-environmental problems. Traffic congestion, flooding, solid waste disposal, black smoke from vehicular and industrial emissions, air and noise pollution, and pollution of water bodies by industrial discharge. . . .

Black smoke coming out from the discharge is intolerable to breathe, burning eyes and throats. The city dwellers are being slowly poisoned by lead concentration in the city air 10 times higher than the government safety limit."

Because of a heavy concentration of cars burning leaded gasoline, Dhaka's children have one of the highest blood lead levels in the world. Almost 90 percent of primary school children tested had levels high enough to impair their developmental and learning abilities, according to a scientific study.

Water pollution is already rampant. According to the Japanese report, "The river Buriganga flows by the side of the densely populated area of the old city. Dumping of waste to the river by . . . industries is rather indiscriminate. . . . The indiscriminate discharge of domestic sewage, industrial effluents and open dumping of solid wastes are becoming a great concern from the point of water-environment degradation."

Nearly half of all Bangladeshis live below the poverty line, able only to glance at the gleaming new malls built in Dhaka. Urbanization and the pressures of poverty are severely stressing the country's once-abundant natural resources. According to U.S. Aid for International Development (USAID), "Pressures on Bangladesh's biological resources are intense and growing."

They include:

- Poor management of aquatic and terrestrial resources;
- Population growth;
- Overuse of resources;
- Unplanned building projects; and
- Expansion of agriculture onto less-productive lands, creating erosion and runoff, among other by-products.

Bangladesh's expanding population destroys critical habitats, reports USAID, causing a decrease in biodiversity. Most of Bangladesh's tropical forests and almost all of the freshwater floodplains have been negatively affected by human activities.

But despite all the negatives, there is a growing environmental movement in Bangladesh that is working to save Dhaka's natural resources. The Bangladesh Environmental Network (BEN), for instance, works on reducing the high level of arsenic in Bangladesh's water supply (more than 500 percent higher than World Health Organization standards), combats the country's severe flooding problem and tries to defeat India's River Linking Project, which could divert an estimated 10 to 20 percent of Bangladesh's water flow. Bangladesh Poribesh Andolon holds demonstrations and international action days to increase citizen awareness of endangered rivers.

International development projects are also addressing some of the country's environmental woes, including a $44 million arsenic mitigation project launched in 1998 and jointly financed by the World Bank and the Swiss Development and Cooperation Agency. The project is installing deep wells, installing hardware to capture rainwater, building sanitation plants, and expanding distribution systems. A $177 million World Bank project works with the government of Bangladesh to improve urban transportation in Dhaka. Private companies from Bangladesh and Pakistan recently announced a joint venture to construct a waste management plant that could handle 3,200 metric tons of solid waste per day, turning it into organic fertilizer.

Mexico City

Mexico City is like an anxious teenager, growing up faster than it probably should. That phenomenon manifests itself in awkward contrasts: Sports cars zipping down crowded streets, choked with air pollution; a Wal-Mart rising against a skyline of the ancient ruins of Teotihuacan; and trendy designer knock-off bags lining the walls of a grungy street stall.

The locale has long been a cultural hub—the ancient Aztec capital of Tenochtitlán, where Mexico City now stands, was the largest city in the Americas in the 14th century with a population of about 300,000. When the Spanish razed Tenochtitlán they erected Mexico City in its place, though a smallpox epidemic knocked the population back to 30,000. Mexico City served as the center of Spain's colonial empire during the 1500s, but the modern-day metropolis only began to materialize in the late 1930s when a combination of rapid economic growth, population growth, and a considerable rural migration filled the city with people.

The larger metropolitan area now engulfs once-distinct villages and population estimates range from 16 million to 30 million, depending on how the city's boundaries are drawn. Regardless, Mexico City is now widely considered the world's third-largest city, and still growing; birth rates are high and 1,100 new residents migrate to the capital each day.

With so many people crammed into a closed mountain valley, many environmental and social problems are bound to arise. Mexico City's air was ranked by WHO as the most contaminated in the world in 1992. By 1998, the Mexican capital had added the distinction of being "the world's most dangerous city for children." Twenty percent of the city's population lives in utter poverty, the Mega-Cities Project reports, 40 percent of the population lives in "informal settlements," and wealth is concentrated in very few hands.

A combination of population, geography and geology render air pollution one of the city's greatest problems. WHO studies have reported that it is unhealthy to breathe air with over 120 parts per billion of ozone contaminants more than one day a year, but residents breathe it more than 300 days a year. More than one million of the city's more than 18 million people suffer from permanent breathing problems.

According to the U.S. Energy Information Administration, "Exhaust fumes from Mexico City's approximately three million cars are the main source of air pollutants. Problems resulting from the high levels of exhaust are exacerbated by the fact that Mexico City is situated in a basin. The geography prevents winds from blowing away the pollution, trapping it above the city."

The International Development Research Center has observed that "despite more than a decade of stringent pollution control measures, a haze hangs over Mexico City most days, obscuring the surrounding snow-capped mountains and endangering the health of its inhabitants. Many factors have contributed to this situation: industrial growth, a population boom and the proliferation of vehicles." More than 30 percent of the city's vehicles are more than 20 years old.

Solid waste creates another major problem, and officials estimate that, of the 10,000 tons of waste generated each day, at least one-quarter is dumped illegally. The city also lacks an effective sanitation and water distribution system. According to the United Nations, "Urbanization has had a serious negative effect on the ecosystem of Mexico City. Although 80 percent of the population has piped inside plumbing, residents in the peripheral areas cannot access the sewage network and a great percentage of wastewater remains untreated as it passes to the north for use as irrigation water."

Perhaps three million residents at the edge of the city do not have access to sewers, says the Mega-Cities Project. Untreated waste from these locations is discharged directly into water bodies or into the ground, where it can contaminate ground water. Only 50 percent of residents in squatter settlements have access to plumbing, and these residents are more likely to suffer from health effects linked to inadequate sanitation. Furthermore, Mexico City is now relying on water pumped from lower elevations to quench an ever-deepening thirst; as the city continues to grow, the need for water and the politics surrounding that need are likely only to intensify.

Mexican industry is centered within the city and is primarily responsible for many of the city's environmental problems as well as for the prosperity that certain areas have achieved. Mexico City houses 80 percent of all the firms in the country, and 2.6 million cars and buses bring people to work and shop in them. Sandwiched in between slums and sewers are glitzy, luxurious neighborhoods and shopping centers, as chic as any in New York or Los Angeles.

The streets of the Zócalo, a central city plaza modeled after Spanish cities, serve as Mexico City's cultural hub. Unwittingly, the plaza has become one of the economic centers as well. Most job growth in Mexico occurs in the underground sector—in street stalls that cover every square inch of sidewalk space, women flipping tortillas curbside, and kids hawking phone cards or pirated CDs to passersby. Despite efforts to clean up activities that are illegal or considered eyesores, street vendors make up an enormous part of Mexico's job force and, according to the *Los Angeles Times,* are primarily responsible for keeping the official unemployment rate below that of the United States. . . .

➡ **NO**

People in Cities:
Hope Countering Desolation

The unprecedented urban growth taking place in developing countries reflects the hopes and aspirations of millions of new urbanites. Cities have enormous potential for improving people's lives, but inadequate urban management, often based on inaccurate perceptions and information, can turn opportunity into disaster.

Conscious of this gap, the Programme of Action of the International Conference on Population and Development recommended that: "Governments should increase the capacity and competence of city and municipal authorities to manage urban development, to safeguard the environment, to respond to the need of all citizens, including urban squatters, for personal safety, basic infrastructure and services, to eliminate health and social problems, including problems of drugs and criminality, and problems resulting from overcrowding and disasters, and to provide people with alternatives to living in areas prone to natural and man-made disasters.". . .

The Unseen Dramas of the Urban Poor

Until recently, rural settlements were the epicentre of poverty and human suffering. All measures of poverty, whether based on income, consumption or expenditure, showed that rural poverty was deeper and more widespread than in cities. Urban centres on the whole offered better access to health, education, basic infrastructure, information, knowledge and opportunity. Such findings were easy to understand in view of budgetary allocations, the concentration of services and the other intangible benefits of cities.

Poverty, however, is now increasing more rapidly in urban areas than in rural areas but has received far less attention. Aggregate statistics hide deep inequalities and gloss over concentrations of harsh poverty within cities. Most assessments actually underestimate the scale and depth of urban poverty. . . .

Urban mismanagement often squanders urban advantages and the urban potential for poverty reduction. Although urban poverty is growing faster than in rural areas, development agencies have only recently begun to appreciate that they need new interventions to attack its roots.

Slums: Unparalleled Concentration of Poverty . . .

Over 90 per cent of slum dwellers today are in the developing world. South Asia has the largest share, followed by Eastern Asia, sub-Saharan Africa and Latin America. China and India together have 37 per cent of the world's slums. In sub-Saharan Africa, urbanization has become virtually synonymous with slum growth; 72 per cent of the region's urban population lives under slum conditions, compared to 56 per cent in South Asia. The slum population of sub-Saharan Africa almost doubled in 15 years, reaching nearly 200 million in 2005.

The United Nations Millennium Declaration recognized the importance of addressing the situation of slum dwellers in reducing overall poverty and advancing human development. Despite the strength of this commitment, monitoring progress on the situation of slum dwellers has been a challenge. Proactive policy interventions are needed now if nations are to meet the spirit of Target 11 of the Millennium Development Goals and ameliorate the lives of millions of the urban poor.

The Persistent Disparities

Nowhere are the disadvantages of the urban poor compared with other city dwellers more marked than in the health area. Poor women are at a particular disadvantage. Although cash income is much more important in cities than in villages, income poverty is only one aspect of urban poverty. Others are poor-quality and overcrowded shelter, lack of public services and infrastructure such as piped water, sanitation facilities, garbage collection, drainage and roads, as well as insecure land tenure. . . . These disadvantages increase the health and work burdens of the urban poor and also increase their risks from environmental hazards and crime.

Poor people live in unhealthy environments. Health risks arise from poor sanitation, lack of clean water, overcrowded and poorly ventilated living and working environments and from air and industrial pollution. Inadequate diet reduces slum-dwellers' resistance to disease, especially because they live in the constant presence of pathogenic micro-organisms. . . .

The United Nations Development Programme's *Human Development Report* for 2006 provides an excellent overview and analysis of the relations between power, poverty and water. It highlights the fact that the stark realities of slum life defy statistical analysis. Frequently, many people live in compounds made up of several houses where one toilet serves all adults and children. Toilets may be reserved for adults, and children forced to go elsewhere in the compound or in the streets where they play. Sharing three toilets and one shower with 250 households in a community is not at all unusual in cities of sub-Saharan Africa. Conditions like these increase stress on all inhabitants, especially women who are also subject to greater risks of gender-based violence. In Latin America, only 33.6 per cent of the urban poor have access to flush toilets, compared to 63.7 per cent of their non-poor urban counterparts.

Water is a scarce and expensive resource for the urban poor, often obtained in small quantities from street vendors. Bought this way, unit costs can be much higher than for people who have running water in their homes. If there is a piped supply, obtaining it may involve long journeys to the neighbourhood water post, long waits, tiring trips back home with full jerry-cans, careful storage to minimize wastage and reusing the same water several times, increasing the risk of contamination.

Water chores take up a substantial part of women's and girls' time. A partial time-use study covering 10 sites in East Africa found that the waiting time for water increased from 28 minutes a day in 1967 to 92 minutes in 1997. The physical and time burdens come not so much from long distances from the source of supply, as in villages, but from the large numbers who have to use the same source. . . .

The association between poverty, environment and housing in urban areas is critical because it indicates a key area for intervention. Policies directed to improving shelter in urban areas can have huge impacts on poverty reduction and on environmental well-being. Advances in health and mortality indicators depend very much on urban water and sewage treatment. . . .

Women's Empowerment and Well-being: The Pillars of Sustainable Cities

As women are generally the poorest of the poor . . . eliminating social, cultural, political and economic discrimination against women is a prerequisite of eradicating poverty . . . in the context of sustainable development.

The social and physical amenities of cities facilitate gender-equitable change. Indeed, the concentration of population in urban areas opens many possibilities for women—whether migrants or natives—to meet, work, form social support networks, exchange information and organize around the things of greatest importance to them. Cities tend to favour greater cultural diversity and, as a corollary, more flexibility in the application of social norms that traditionally impinge on women's freedom of choice.

Compared with rural areas, cities offer women better educational facilities and more diverse employment options. They provide more opportunities for social and political participation, as well as access to media, information and technology. Cities offer many roads to decision-making power through community and political participation. Women can use urban space to project their voices, to participate in community politics and development and to influence social and political processes at all levels.

Women stand to benefit from the proximity and greater availability of urban services, such as water, sanitation, education, health and transportation facilities; all of these can reduce women's triple burden of reproductive, productive and community work and, in so doing, improve their health status and that of their children and families.

Education in Urban Settings: Closing the Gender Gap?

Urbanization increases girls' access to education and promotes cultural acceptance of their right to education. Primary, and especially secondary, education for girls has crucial multiplier effects that increase women's social and economic status and expand their freedom of choice. Educated women tend to marry later and have fewer and healthier children. In adulthood, they have greater employment potential, income-earning capacity and decision-making authority within the household. Other benefits include knowledge and capacities to maintain and protect their health, including preventing unwanted pregnancies and sexually transmitted infections (STIs), including HIV/AIDS. All of these are helpful in the fight against poverty. . . .

The Job Marketplace: A Way Out?

Employment possibilities are far more diverse in urban areas for both men and women. Urbanization has significantly boosted women's labour force participation. Paid employment for women not only increases household income but can trigger transformations in gender roles and elevate women's status in the family and society.

Worldwide, there has been a significant increase in women's non-agricultural wage employment during recent years. New opportunities have arisen, especially in tradable sectors and in home-based businesses linked to global production networks. For example, of the 50 million workers in export processing zones, 80 per cent are young women.

However, most growth of female employment is in the informal sector, which accounts for most new employment opportunities in the world, and where women are a large majority, especially in Africa and Asia. Informal employment is critical in enabling women to absorb the economic shocks that poor households experience. In this regard, women's employment, paid and unpaid, is of fundamental importance in keeping many households out of poverty. The downside is that much informal work is unstable, of poor quality and poorly paid.

The Long Road to Property Ownership for Women

Physical and financial assets offer women more than economic well-being and security. Legal property tenure increases women's opportunities to access credit, generate income and establish a cushion against poverty. It also empowers them in their relationships with their partners and their families, reduces vulnerability to gender-based violence and HIV/AIDS and provides a safety net for the elderly.

Women own less than 15 per cent of land world-wide. In some countries, women cannot legally own property separately from their husbands, particularly in parts of Asia and sub-Saharan Africa. Lacking legal title to land and property, women have virtually no collateral for obtaining loans and credit, thus limiting their economic options. In some settings, although women can legally own and inherit property, custom dictates that men control it and that it passes only to male heirs on a man's death. It is difficult or impossible in these circumstances for women to exercise their property rights in practice.

There is evidence that the difficulty of securing title to property in rural areas is prompting women to migrate to cities in hopes of securing property there, where prospects are assumed to be better. Women may also have better access to legal information and support in urban areas. Because of the greater social dynamism and range of economic possibilities open to women, cities are likely to offer more opportunities to acquire property in the long run.

Legal reforms are still necessary, however, to secure women's equal rights to own property. Where laws are in place, cities continue to need programmes and recourse mechanisms to tackle informal barriers such as customary practices, low awareness of rights, the high cost of land and housing and discriminatory lending and titling policies.

Property rights and access to credit are closely linked, so it is not surprising that women face difficulties in obtaining financial assets. Microcredit programmes have partially filled this need. Making its mark initially in rural settings, microcredit is also allowing poor urban women to leverage their capacities and improve their incomes.

Power Through Voice: Getting It Done Through Community Organizations

Decision-making power is one of the main indicators of women's empowerment. The prospects for women's formal participation in politics are improving, despite the many challenges they face, including gender discrimination and prejudice, multiple poorly-rewarded responsibilities and calls on their time and energy, lack of support in crucial areas such as reproductive health and lack of resources.

Some governments have enacted quotas or parity laws to address these barriers and ensure that women have a critical level of participation in city councils and local governments. Nevertheless, women make up only 16 per cent of members of national parliaments in Africa and Asia and 9 per cent in the Arab States. These percentages are well below what is believed to be a "critical mass" for women to influence policy and spending priorities.

Despite this bleak picture in the capitals of nations, women's participation in decentralized governance has increased. Local spheres of government offer greater opportunities for women's empowerment and political participation, a situation that reflects positively on women's prospects as urbanization increases. Moreover, countries with a higher percentage of women councillors are likely to have a higher number of women parliamentarians, which may, in turn, benefit women at the municipal level.

Urbanization can thus be a powerful factor in creating the conditions for women's empowerment. Turning this potential into reality is one of the most effective ways of promoting human rights, improving the living conditions of the poor and making the cities of developing countries better places in which to live.

Cities lend themselves to women's social and political participation at many levels. For poor women whose lives have been confined to home, family and work, the act of joining an organization immediately broadens their prospects. When women actively participate in an organization, or take on leadership roles, they gain self-confidence, new skills, knowledge and a greater understanding of the world. Organizing can address many of the limitations that poverty imposes on poor women; it can begin to counter the costs and risks of informal work. It can also help to reduce poor women's vulnerability, insecurity and dependence, including a lack of knowledge about the outside world and how it works.

Organizing also helps women who have few assets to pool resources, thereby increasing their economic power. Savings and credit groups may help the working poor access microfinance services, and producers with little capital may buy raw materials at wholesale prices by combining their resources.

Such advantages could be enhanced with more support. Poor women need a representative voice in the institutions and processes that establish social and economic policies in a global economy, in order to continue improving the living and working conditions of the poor. International, regional and national negotiations regarding free trade agreements, the Millennium Development Goals and poverty reduction strategies all need to include the voices and concerns of the urban poor and, in particular, informal workers, the majority of whom are women. Ensuring a voice for poor urban women at the highest level requires that government and international organizations support the growth of their organizations and build capacity for leadership.

Accessing Reproductive Health: It Should Be Much Better

Access to health care is particularly critical for women, because of their reproductive functions, because they are disproportionately burdened with providing care for the elderly and the sick and because they do more to relieve poverty at the community level. Better access to education and employment for women contributes to their overall empowerment, their capacity to exercise their right to health, including reproductive health, and, overall, improves their life chances.

These services and opportunities tend to be more readily available to women in urban than in rural areas. But for poor women, lack of time and money, as well as the lack of freedom to make household decisions, or even to move about the city, can negate these advantages. In urban areas, inclusive health policies and programmes, accompanied by better targeting of services and resources, could rapidly improve women's health, in particular their reproductive health.

Gender relations and poverty condition how couples and families approach sexual and reproductive behaviour. Poor urban women are exposed to higher levels of reproductive health risks than other urban women. They are also less likely to obtain good-quality services. They are more likely to face gender-based violence in the home and on the streets and continue to be subject to harmful traditional practices.

Total fertility rates are lower in urban than in rural areas throughout the world. But this does not mean that all urban women have the same access to reproductive health care, or even that they can all meet their needs for contraception. Poor women within cities are significantly less likely to use contraception and have higher fertility rates than their more affluent counterparts.

At times their reproductive health situation more closely resembles that of rural women. . . .

Unmet need for contraception among women predictably varies according to relative poverty. Surveys covering Asia, Latin America, North Africa and sub-Saharan Africa show generally higher levels of unmet need among the rural population when compared to the urban population, with poor urbanites midway between the rural and the urban population as a whole. In South-East Asia, for example, estimated unmet need is 23 per cent among the urban poor, compared to only 16 per cent among the urban non-poor.

Overall, poverty may be a better indicator of fertility patterns than rural or urban residence. For policymakers concerned with the rate of urban growth, it will thus be especially important to look at the interactions between population and poverty, and increasingly within urban settings. Prioritizing women's empowerment, augmenting their access to education and employment and providing good quality sexual and reproductive health information and services to both women and men leverages their choices and is conducive to smaller, healthier families. This helps meet the needs and rights of individuals, while simultaneously improving prospects for economic growth and human well-being. . . .

Maternal and Infant Mortality

Maternal mortality remains astoundingly high, at about 529,000 a year, more than 99 per cent in developing countries, and much of it readily preventable. Four out of five deaths are the direct result of obstetric complications, most of which could be averted through delivery with a skilled birth attendant and access to emergency obstetric services.

Skilled attendance and access to emergency care explain why maternal mortality is generally lower in urban areas, where women are three times more likely to deliver with skilled health personnel than women in rural areas. However, poor urban women are less likely to deliver with a skilled birth attendant. For example, only 10–20 per cent of women deliver with skilled health personnel in the slums of Kenya, Mali, Rwanda and Uganda, compared to between 68 and 86 per cent in non-slum urban areas.

There are a number of reasons why poor urban women do not seek maternal care. These include poverty and the more pressing demands of other household expenses, other demands on their time given their many other responsibilities and the absence of supporting infrastructure such as transport and childcare.

Shelter deprivation increases mortality rates for children under five. In Ethiopia, the mortality rate in slums (180 per 1,000 live births) is almost double that in non-slum housing (95). Similar differentials prevail in Guinea, Nigeria, Rwanda and the United Republic of Tanzania. Countries such as the Philippines and Uzbekistan, with much lower levels of child mortality, also show a relationship between shelter deprivation and child survival.

Although poor children born in cities are closer to hospitals and clinics, and their parents are generally better informed, they still die at rates comparable to rural children. Overcrowded and unhealthy living conditions, without adequate water and sanitation, provide a rich breeding ground for respiratory and intestinal diseases and increase mortality among malnourished urban children. . . .

HIV/AIDS in an Urban Context: New Risks, New Opportunities

In urban settings, the risk and prevalence of HIV/AIDS increases, but the longer-term possibilities of reducing the epidemic appear to be better there. Currently, the situation is bleak. Rural-to-urban migrants leave behind not only partners and family but often customary restrictions on sexual behaviour as well. Cash dependency, coupled with poverty and gender discrimination, may increase transactional sex; at the same time, it reduces opportunities for negotiating safe sex, especially for women and girls but also for younger men and boys. Injecting drug use tends to be higher in urban settings. Sexually transmitted infections and tuberculosis, which increase the acquisition and transmission of HIV, are also more common in urban areas.

Some rural people living with HIV migrate to cities for better treatment and care, including antiretroviral drugs. As a result, HIV prevalence is generally higher in urban than rural populations in sub-Saharan Africa, the epicentre of the AIDS epidemic. Botswana and South Africa both have high urbanization levels and extremely high HIV prevalence.

Urban poverty is linked to HIV transmission and reduces the likelihood of treatment. Street children, orphans, sex workers and poor women in urban areas are particularly vulnerable to HIV infection. Poor urban women are more likely to become victims of sexual violence or human trafficking, increasing their risk; moreover, they are less likely to know how to protect themselves. Women threatened with violence cannot negotiate safe sex.

There is, however, some good news. Recent evidence of a downturn in HIV prevalence in urban areas of some countries suggests that urbanization may have the potential to reduce the epidemic. Condoms—key for HIV prevention—and information about HIV transmission may be more readily available in urban areas. Stigma and discrimination may also be lower in urban areas, because of better education and more exposure to people living with HIV/AIDS.

Social Contradictions in Growing Cities: Dialogue and Discord

The Increasing Speed of Cultural Change

Since the 1950s, rapid urbanization has been a catalyst of cultural change. As globalization proceeds, the urban transition is having an enormous impact on ideas, values and beliefs. Such transformations have not been as uniform or seamless as social scientists predicted. The widening gaps between social groups make inequality more visible. In this atmosphere, large cities can generate creativity and solidarity, but also make conflicts more acute.

Rapidly growing cities, especially the larger ones, include various generations of migrants, each with a diversity of social and cultural backgrounds. Urban life thus exposes new arrivals to an assortment of cultural stimuli and presents them with new choices on a variety of issues, ranging from how their families are organized to what they do with their leisure time. In this sense, urbanization provides opportunities for broad cultural enrichment and is a prime mover of modernization. Through interaction of new urbanites with rural areas, it also accelerates social change across different regions.

At the same time, urbanites may lose contact with traditional norms and values. They may develop new aspirations, but not always the means to realize them. This, in turn, may lead to a sense of deracination and marginalization, accompanied by crises of identity, feelings of frustration and aggressive behaviour. Many people in developing countries also associate the processes of modernization and globalization with the imposition of Western values on their own cultures and resent them accordingly.

Urbanization and Religious Revival

The revival of religious adherence in its varied forms is one of the more noticeable cultural transformations accompanying urbanization. Rapid urbanization was expected to mean the triumph of rationality, secular values and the demystification of the world, as well as the relegation of religion to a secondary role. Instead, there has been a renewal in religious interest in many countries.

The growth of new religious movements is primarily an urban phenomenon, for example, radical Islam in the Arab region, Pentecostal Christianity in Latin America and parts of Africa and the cult of Shivaji in parts of India. In China, where cities are growing at a breakneck pace, religious movements are fast gaining adherents.

Increased urbanization, coupled with slow economic development and globalization, has helped to increase religious diversity as part of the multiplication of subcultures in cities. Rather than revivals of a tradition, the new religious movements can be seen as adaptations of religion to new circumstances.

Research has tended to focus on extreme religious responses—which have indeed gained numerous followers—hence the tendency to lump them all under the rubric of "fundamentalism." Yet religious revivalism has varied forms with different impacts, ranging from detached "new age" philosophy to immersion in the political process. Along this continuum, there are many manifestations of religious adherence. Together, they are rapidly changing political dynamics and the social identities of today's global citizens. . . .

The Changing Demographics of Growing Cities
Young People in Young Cities

A clear youth bulge marks the demographic profile of cities in developing countries; this bulge is particularly large in slum populations. The individual successes and failures of young people as they ride the wave of urban growth will be decisive for future development since these drastic demographic changes, combined with persistent poverty and unemployment, are a source of conflict in cities across developing countries. Yet political processes rarely reflect the priorities of youth, especially the hundreds of millions of urban children who live in poverty and in conditions that threaten their health, safety, education and prospects.

Young people are typically dynamic, resourceful and receptive to change: But if they are uncared for, unschooled, unguided and unemployed, their energy can turn in destructive, often self-destructive, directions. Investing in urban children and youth, helping them to integrate themselves fully into society, is a matter of human rights and social justice. It is also the key to releasing potential economic benefits and ensuring urban security.

It is estimated that as many as 60 per cent of all urban dwellers will be under the age of 18 by 2030. If urgent measures are not taken in terms of basic services, employment and housing, the youth bulge will grow up in poverty. The number of children born into slums in the developing world is increasing rapidly. . . . Slums generally have a much higher proportion of children. The health problems associated with such environments have already been described. . . .

Ageing and Urbanization

The number and proportion of older persons is increasing throughout the world. Urbanization in developing countries will concentrate an increasing proportion of the older population in urban areas. In Africa and Asia, older persons still live predominantly in rural areas, but it is expected that this situation will be reversed before 2020.

Given the context of limited access to social services, high incidence of poverty and low coverage of social security in many countries, this increase in the numbers of older people will challenge the capacity of national and local governments. In principle, urban areas offer more favourable conditions: better health facilities, home-nursing services and recreational facilities, as well as greater access to information and new technologies. Urban areas also favour the rise of associations of older persons, as well as the development of community-based services to support the sick and the frail. . . .

EXPLORING THE ISSUE

Does Global Urbanization Lead Primarily to Undesirable Consequences?

Critical Thinking and Reflection

1. Do there appear to be major differences between urban growth in megacities and medium-size cities?
2. Does poverty play the most important role in determining the urban condition throughout the world?
3. Are some, if not most, undesirable conditions of urban dwellers a function of factors other than their urban location?
4. Should the global community concentrate on using urban growth as fuel for economic growth rather than trying to find ways to slow down such growth?
5. Should the global community begin to look at urbanization as the glass half full rather than half empty?

Is There Common Ground?

One of the most studied global trends is that relating to demographic. The international community has commonly agreed upon information about present and future growth patterns, including data on urbanization. There is also much agreement regarding the impact of urbanization on natural habitats, although some are beginning to believe that there is a lessened impact in urban areas.

There is also agreement that although compact space leads to the potential for a more efficient and inexpensive way to address the adverse effects of urbanization on city dwellers, urban planners need new approaches in so doing. It appears self-evident that rapidly growing urbanized areas, particularly in the developing world, create special circumstances. Our visual image of such places accents this fact. First-world travelers, particularly to the developing world, are likely to take away from that experience a litany of pictures that paint a bleak image of life there. The critical question, though, is whether such environments really do create major problems for those who live within such areas and policy makers who must provide goods and services. Conventional wisdom that such problems must exist is found everywhere throughout the urbanization literature.

Additional Resources

Birth, Eugenie L. and Wachter, Susan M., eds., *Global Urbanization, The City in the Twenty-First Century* (University of Pennsylvania Press, 2011)

This book focuses on how the megacities of the world can address the range of problems confronting them.

Buckley, Robert, et al., eds., *Urbanization and Growth* (World Bank Publications, 2008)

This book focuses on the nexus between urbanization and economic growth.

Cordner, Gary, *Urbanization, Policing, and Security: Global Perspectives* (CRC, 2009)

This book presents a negative assessment of the conditions in urban areas around the globe.

Davis, Mike, *Planet of Slums* (Verso, 2007)

This book documents the great depth of urban poverty in the world.

Koonings, Kees, *Megacities: The Politics of Urban Exclusion and Violence in the Global South* (Zed Books, 2010)

This book describes the great deprivation associated with the rise of megacities throughout the world but particularly in the global south.

Martine, George, *The State of World Population 2007: Unleashing the Potential of Urban Growth* (UNFPA, 2007)

This book analyzes why such growth is occurring and what preparations need to take place to address the dramatic increases in urban growth forecasted for the first third of the twenty-first century.

Martine, George et al., eds., *The New Global Frontier: Urbanization, Poverty and Environment in the 21st Century* (Earthscan, 2008)

The book argues that global urbanization is the greatest priority of the twenty-first century.

Pomeroy, George, *Global Perspectives on Urbanization: Essays in Honor of Denath Mookherjee* (University Press of America, 2007)

This book examines a range of challenges related to urban poverty.

United Nations, *Global Report on Human Settlements 2009: Planning Sustainable Cities* (UN Human Settlements Program, 2009)

This UN report is a timely global assessment of conditions and trends of human settlements throughout the globe.

Vlahov, David et al., eds., *Urban Health: Global Perspectives* (Jossey-Bass, 2010)

This book focuses on the health consequences of modern changes on urban areas of the globe.

Internet References . . .

UNEP World Conservation Monitoring Centre

The United Nations Environment Programme's World Conservation Monitoring Centre Web site contains information on conservation and sustainable use of the globe's natural resources. The center provides information to policymakers concerning global trends in conservation, biodiversity, loss of species and habitats, and more. This site includes a list of publications and environmental links.

http://www.unep-wcmc.org

The International Institute for Sustainable Development

This nonprofit organization based in Canada provides a number of reporting services on a range of environmental issues, with special emphasis on policy initiatives associated with sustainable development.

http://www.iisd.ca

The Hunger Project

The Hunger Project is a nonprofit organization that is committed to the sustainable end of global hunger. This organization asserts that society-wide actions are needed to eliminate hunger and that global security depends on ensuring that everyone's basic needs are fulfilled. Included on this site is an outline of principles that guide the organization, information on why ending hunger is so important, and a list of programs sponsored by the Hunger Project in developing countries across South Asia, Latin America, and Africa.

http://www.thp.org

International Association for Environmental Hydrology

The International Association for Environmental Hydrology (IAEH) is a worldwide association of environmental hydrologists dedicated to the protection and cleanup of freshwater resources. The IAEH's mission is to provide a place to share technical information and exchange ideas and to provide a source of inexpensive tools for the environmental hydrologist, especially hydrologists and water resource engineers in developing countries.

http://www.hydroweb.com

United Nations Environment Programme (UNEP)

UNEP's general Web site provides a variety of information and links to other sources.

http://www.ourplanet.com

Global Resources and the Environment

*T*he availability of resources and the manner in which the planet's inhabitants use them characterize another major component of the global agenda. Many believe that environmentalists continue to be alarmists because of ideology, not science. Many others state that renewable resources are being consumed at a pace that is too fast to allow for replenishment, while nonrenewable resources are being consumed at a pace that is faster than our ability to find suitable replacements. Energy, water, and food continue to represent three important resources that occupy the minds of policymakers and consumers alike.

   The production, distribution, and consumption of these resources also leave their marks on the planet. A basic set of issues relates to whether these impacts are permanent, too degrading to the planet, too damaging to one's quality of life, or simply beyond a threshold of acceptability.

- Should Environmentalists Continue to Be Alarmists?

- Should the World Continue to Rely on Oil as the Major Source of Energy?

- Will the World Be Able to Feed Itself in the Foreseeable Future?

- Is the Threat of Global Warming Real?

- Can the Global Community Successfully Confront the Global Water Shortage?

ISSUE 4

Should Environmentalists Continue to Be Alarmists?

Yes: Paul B. Farrell, from "The Coming Population Wars: A 12-Bomb Equation," *MarketWatch* (September 29, 2009)

No: Ronald Bailey, from "Our Uncrowded Planet," *The American* (October 1, 2009)

Learning Outcomes

After reading this issue, you should be able to:

- Describe the 12 global time-bombs outlined in the YES article.
- Understand why some suggest that overpopulation and population per capita impacts are the triggers of the other 10 time-bombs.
- Discuss why long-term thinking is needed to address these time-bombs.
- Understand the counterarguments against the 12 time-bombs.
- Appreciate that there are two competing schools of thought concerning the globe's pending doom because of future trends across a number of important factors.

ISSUE SUMMARY

YES: Paul B. Farrell, an investing and personal finance columnist for *CBS MarketWatch*, describes 12 global time-bombs put forth by Jared Diamond, an environmental biologist. The two biggest are the overpopulation multiplier (population will increase 23 percent before it peaks) and the population impact monitor (third-world citizens will adopt much higher first-world consumption patterns).

NO: Ronald Bailey, *Reason* magazine's science correspondent, takes Farrell to task on each of his 12 time-bombs, arguing that current trends do not "portend a looming population apocalypse."

In January 2007, the Bulletin of Atomic Scientists added to their "doomsday clock," originally created to forecast nuclear annihilation, the new threat of environmental catastrophe to its predictions. This was the latest in the war of words between the doomsdayers and the environmental skeptics. For a few decades, the skeptics of the claims of many environmentalists that the world was in danger of ecological collapse and in the not-so-distant future looked to Julian Simon for guidance. And Simon did not disappoint, as he constantly questioned these researchers' motives and methodology—their models, data, and data analysis techniques. Two seminal works, *The Ultimate Resource* and *The Ultimate Resource 2,* in particular, attempted to demonstrate that much research was really bad science. Simon's popularity reached its height when he took on the leading spokesperson of pending environmental catastrophe, Paul Ehrlich, in the late 1970s. Ehrlich, a professor at Stanford, along with his wife Anne (also a Stanford professor), had been echoing "the sky is falling" message since the late 1960s. Simon challenged Ehrlich to a "forecasting duel," betting him $10,000 that the cost of five nongovernment raw materials (to be selected by Ehrlich) would fall by the end of the next decade (1990). Ehrlich lost the bet. With Simons' death in 1998, the critics of environmental doomsdayers lost their most effective voice and their central rallying cry.

Bjørn Lomborg, a young Danish political scientist, changed all of that with the 2001 publication of his *The Skeptical Environmentalist: Measuring the Real State of the World* (a take-off on the annual *State of the World Series* produced by Lester Brown and the Worldwatch Institute). Lomborg's central thesis is that statistical analyses of principal environmental indicators reveal that environmental problems have been overstated by most leading figures in the environmental movement. What distinguished Lomborg's book from the body of work that earned Simon the unofficial title of "doomsdayer" was that Lomborg received much greater and more widespread attention, both by the popular media and by those in academic and scientific circles. In effect, it has become the most popular anti-environmental book ever, prompting a huge backlash by those vested in the scientific community. Because the popular press appeared to accept Lomborg's assertions with an uncritical eye, the scientific community began a comprehensive counterattack against *The Skeptical Environmentalist. Scientific American,* in January 2002, published almost a dozen pages of critiques of the book by four experts and concluded that the book's purpose of showing the real state of the world was a failure.

The attention paid to Lomborg's book by *Scientific American* was typical of the responses found in every far corner of the scientific community. Not only were Lomborg's analyses attacked but his credentials were as well. Researchers scurried to discredit both him and his work, with a passion unseen heretofore in the debate over the potential for global environmental catastrophe. The Danish Committees on Scientific Dishonesty were called upon to investigate the work. The Danish Ministry of Science, Technology and Innovation found serious flaws in Lomborg's critique. One reviewer concluded by observing that he wished he could find that the book had some scientific merit but he could not. The British

Broadcasting Company (BBC) devoted a three-part series to Lomborg's claims. One critique was titled "No Friend of the Earth."

In the past decade, perhaps no better example of "the sky is falling" predictions followed by an onslaught of counter predictions is in the area of global warming. Google global warming or climate change and millions of citations appear. Go to amazon.com and you will find countless books, most with catchy titles as authors vie with one another for public attention. Phrases such as "Red Hot Lies," "Bad Science," "False Alarm," "Climate Cover-Up," "Naïve Politicians," "Climatism!: Science, Common Sense and the 21st Century's Hottest Topic (the obsession with global warming)" dot the landscape.

Similar public attention, through discourse and debate, has centered on health pandemics. The AIDS scare reached great heights in the 1990s as the world recognized that everyone was in danger of being infected, and there was a lack of consensus about how to avoid it. The 2009 HINI influenza scare caused a significant percentage of individuals to change behavior as fear swept over the global population. Currently, the world watches as Japan is confronted with the effects of a nuclear accident that threatens its population with both short-term and long-term medical consequences. And bioterrorism is on the radar screen of every government's foreign policy agenda. President George W. Bush took America to war with Iraq because of the fear of such disaster emanating from Saddam Hussein. And who can forget 9/11 when Americans watched in horror at the devastation that grew and grew right before our eyes on television. Fear about a future 9/11 was a driving force for the rest of the Bush presidency and continues today in dramatically increased government expenditures in combating a future 9/11. And the anthrax scare only contributed to our anxiety.

H.G. Wells captured the fear of global catastrophe in a 1903 London lecture: "It is impossible to show why certain things should not utterly destroy and end the human race and story; why night should not presently come down and make all our dreams and efforts vain." The source of this quote, *Global Catastrophic Risks* by Nick Bostrom and Milan Ćirković, details 554 pages of possible global disasters researched by scholars. Potential culprits range across long-term astrophysical processes; risks from nature (supervolcanism, comets and asteroids, supernovae, gamma-ray bursts, solar flares, and cosmic rays); risks from unintended consequences, such as climate change, plagues, and pandemics; risks from hostile acts (nuclear war, nuclear terrorism, and bioterrorism); and nanotechnology as risk.

These examples illustrate the debate put forth in this issue, namely, do environmentalists overstate the case for environmental decay and potential catastrophe? Ronald Bailey, probably the unofficial successor to Julian Simon's role as a principal critic of environmentalist ideology, provides one of the few positive critiques of *The Skeptical Environmentalist* in *Reason* magazine. His initial statement places the genesis of modern environmentalism in the radical movements of the 1960s, suggesting that their aim is to demonstrate that "the world is going to hell in a handbasket." Calling environmentalism an ideology, Bailey argues that like Marxists, environmentalists "have had to force the facts to fit their ideology." In sum, he suggests that the book deals a major blow to environmentalist ideology "by superbly documenting a response to environmental doomsaying."

An alternative approach to the question of whether environmentalists overstate the case for global catastrophe is found in the literature on fear. One such source is Marc Siegal's *False Alarm: The Truth About the Epidemic of Fear* (John Wiley & Sons, 2005). For Siegal, why is it that some societies have become desensitized to the chance of events like those mentioned earlier, while other societies function with the ever-present recognized fear of a pending disaster? What about the laws of probability, which dramatically favor virtually all of us in any given potentially dangerous situation?

The issue of whether science or ideology is at the heart of the environmental debate is a vexing one. The issue is framed by the juxtaposition of three groups. The first are those individuals, commonly called political or environmental activists, who emerged in the late 1960s and early 1970s following the success of the early civil rights movement. Taking its inspiration from the 1962 publication of Rachel Carson's *The Silent Spring*, which exposed the dangers of the pesticide DDT, many politically active individuals found a new cause. When the book received legitimacy because of President John Kennedy's order that his Science Advisory Committee address the issues raised therein, the environmental movement was underway. The second group, government policymakers, was then a part of the mix, and the third group, scientists, was soon to come on board.

Since the early 1970s through a variety of forums and arenas, the issue has been on the forefront of this global agenda. As with any issue where debates focus not only on how to address problems but also on whether, in fact, the problems really exist in the first place, many disparate formal and informal interest groups have become involved in all aspects of the debate—from trying to make the case that a problem exists and will ultimately have dire consequences if left unsolved to specific prescriptions for solving the issue. The intersection of science, public policy, and political activism then becomes like the center ring at a boxing match, where contenders vie for success. Objectivity clashes with passion as well-intentioned and not-so-well intentioned individuals attempt to influence the debate and the ultimate outcome. In many cases, the doomsdayers gain the upper hand as their commitment to change seems greater than those who urge caution until all the scientific evidence is in.

In the YES selection, Paul B. Farrell, an investing and personal finance columnist for *CBS MarketWatch*, describes 12 global time-bombs put forth by Jared Diamond, an environmental biologist. In the NO selection, Ronald Bailey, *Reason* magazine's science correspondent, takes Farrell to task on each of his 12 time-bombs, arguing that current trends do not "portend a looming population apocalypse."

YES ↵

Paul B. Farrell

The Coming Population Wars: A 12-Bomb Equation—Can Gates' Billionaires Club Stop These Inevitable Self-Destruct Triggers?

Arroyo Grande, Calif. (MarketWatch)—So what's the biggest time-bomb for Obama, America, capitalism, the world? No, not global warming. Not poverty. Not even peak oil. What is the absolute biggest, one like the trigger mechanism on a nuclear bomb, one that'll throw a wrench in global economic growth, ending capitalism, even destroying modern civilization?

The one that—if not solved soon—renders all efforts to solve all the other problems in the world, irrelevant, futile and virtually impossible?

News flash: the "Billionaires Club" knows: Bill Gates called billionaire philanthropists to a super-secret meeting in Manhattan last May. Included: Buffett, Rockefeller, Soros, Bloomberg, Turner, Oprah and others meeting at the "home of Sir Paul Nurse, a British Nobel prize biochemist and president of the private Rockefeller University, in Manhattan," reports John Harlow in the London TimesOnline. During an afternoon session each was "given 15 minutes to present their favorite cause. Over dinner they discussed how they might settle on an 'umbrella cause' that could harness their interests."

The world's biggest time-bomb? Overpopulation, say the billionaires.

And yet, global governments with their $50 trillion GDP, aren't even trying to solve the world's overpopulation problem. G-20 leaders ignore it. So by 2050 the Earth's population will explode by almost 50%, from 6.6 billion today to 9.3 billion says the United Nations.

And what about those billionaires and their billions? Can they stop the trend? Sadly no. Only a major crisis, a global catastrophe, a collapse beyond anything prior in world history will do it. Here's why.

Civilizations Collapse Fast, Crises Trigger, Leaders Clueless

"One of the disturbing facts of history is that so many civilizations collapse," warns Jared Diamond, an environmental biologist, Pulitzer prize winner and author of "Collapse: How Societies Choose to Fail or Succeed." Many "civilizations share a sharp curve of decline. Indeed, a society's demise may begin only a decade or two after it reaches its peak population, wealth and power."

Other voices are darker, shrill: "We're past the point of no return." "It's already too late." "The end is near." As with Rome's collapse, it happens fast. Clueless leaders are caught off-guard, like Greenspan, Bernanke and Paulson a couple years ago.

Call it "WWIII: The Population Wars." A few years ago *Fortune* analyzed a classified Pentagon report predicting that "climate could change radically and fast. That would be the mother of all national security issues." Population unrest would then create "massive droughts, turning farmland into dust bowls and forests to ashes." And "by 2020 there is little doubt that something drastic is happening . . . an old pattern could emerge; warfare defining human life." War will be the end-game: For capitalism, civilization, earth?

Diamond's 12-part equation is very simple, fits perfectly with a global warfare scenario: "More people require more food, space, water, energy, and other resources. . . . There is a long built-in momentum to human population growth called the 'demographic bulge' with a disproportionate number of children and young reproductive-age people." And if the "bulge" stops for any reason, game over. Economic "growth" ends, killing capitalism.

So look closely: Diamond's equation has 12 time-bombs. But note, the first two are the biggest triggers in the formula. The other 10 are derivative variables.

1. Overpopulation Multiplier: According to TimesOnline: A few months before the billionaires meeting Gates noted: "Official [U.N.] projections say the world's population will peak at 9.3 billion [up from 6.6 billion today] but with charitable initiatives, such as better reproductive health care, we think we can cap that at 8.3 billion." Still, that's 23% more than today's 6.6 billion.

Can it be stopped? In a recent special issue of Scientific American, population was called "the most overlooked and essential strategy for achieving long-term balance with the environment." Why? Population's the new "third-rail" for politicians. So they ignore it.

Yet, if all nations consumed resources at the same rate as America, we'd need six Earths to survive. Unfortunately that scenario is unstoppable. Because by 2050, while America's population grows from 300 million to a mere 400 million, the rest of the world will explode from 6.3 billion to 8.9 billion, with over 1.4 billion each in China and India.

2. Population Impact Multiplier: Diamond warns: "There are 'optimists' who argue that the world could support double its human population." But he adds, they "consider only the increase in human numbers and not average increase in per-capita impact. But I have not heard anyone who seriously argues that the world could support 12 times it's current impact." And yet, that's exactly what happens with "all third-world inhabitants adopting first-world standards."

Folks, we oversold the American dream. Now everyone wants it. Not just 300 million Americans, but 6.3 billion people worldwide are demanding more, more, more!

"What really counts," says Diamond, "is not the number of people alone, but their impact on the environment," the "per-capita impact." First-world citizens "consume 32 times more resources such as fossil fuels, and put out 32 times more waste, than do the inhabitants of the Third World." So the race is on: "Low impact people are becoming high-impact people" aspiring "to first-world living standards." The American dream is now the global dream.

Warning: The "Impact Multiplier" will drive the global "WWIII-Population Wars" equation even if there is zero population growth to 2050!

In Diamond's masterpiece, "Collapse," the two key variables are what we call the "Over-Population Multiplier" and "Population Impact Multiplier." Now let's closely examine Diamond's other 10 variables that are driving our "WWIII-Population Wars" equation:

3. Food: Two billion people, mostly poor, depend on fish and other wild foods for protein. They "have collapsed or are in steep decline" forcing use of more costly animal proteins. The U.N. calls the global food crisis a "silent tsunami." Food prices rise making it worse for the 2.7 billion living below poverty levels on two dollars a day.

In "The End of Plenty," National Geographic warns that even a new "green revolution" of "synthetic fertilizers, pesticides, and irrigation, supercharged by genetically engineered seeds" may fail. Why? A joint World Bank/U.N. study "concluded that the immense production increases brought about by science and technology the past 30 years have failed to improve food access for many of the world's poor."

Meanwhile, a Time cover story warns that America's "addiction to meat" has led to farming that's "destructive of the soil, the environment and us."

4. Water: Diamond warns: "Most of the world's fresh water in rivers and lakes is already being used for irrigation, domestic and industrial water," transportation, fisheries and recreation. Water problems destroyed many earlier civilizations: "Today over a million people lack access to reliable safe drinking water." British International Development Minister recently warned that two-thirds of the world will live in water-stressed countries by 2015.

Water will trade like oil futures as wars are fought over water and other basic essentials noted earlier in *Fortune*'s analysis of the Pentagon report predicting that warfare will define human life in this scenario of the near future.

5. Farmland: Crop soils are "being carried away by water and wind erosion at rates between 10 to 40 times the rates of soil formation," much higher in forests where the soil-erosion rate is "between 500 and 10,000 times" replacement rate. And this is increasing in today's new age of the 100,000-acre megafires.

6. Forests: We are destroying natural habitats and rain forests at an accelerating rate. Half the world's original forests have been converted to urban developments. A quarter of what remains will be converted in the next 50 years.

7. Toxic Chemicals: Often our solutions create more problems than they solve. For example, industries "manufacture or release into the air, soil, oceans, lakes, and rivers many toxic chemicals" that break down slowly or not at all. Consider the deadly impact of insecticides, pesticides, herbicides, detergents, plastics . . . the list is endless.

8. Energy Resources, Oil, Natural Gas and Coal: Pimco manages $747 billion: equity, bonds and commodity funds. Manager Bill Gross recently described a "significant break" in the world's "growth pattern." He's betting we're past the "peak oil" tipping point. Consumer shopping will continue declining as economies grow very slowly in the future and "corporate profits will be static."

A recent issue of Foreign Policy Journal warns of the "7 Myths About Alternative Energy." Are biofuels, solar and nuclear the "major ticket?" No, they're not, never will be.

9. Solar Energy: Sunlight is not unlimited. Diamond: We're already using "half of the Earth's photosynthetic capacity" and we will reach the max by mid-century. In "Plundering the Amazon," Bloomberg Markets magazine warned that Alcoa, Cargill and other companies "have bypassed laws designed to prevent destruction of the world's largest rain forest . . . robbing the earth of its best shield against global warming."

Free market capitalism may be the enemy of survival.

10. Ozone Layer: "Human activities produce gases that escape into the atmosphere" where they can destroy the protective ozone or absorb and reduce solar energy.

11. Diversity: "A significant fraction of wild species, populations and genetic diversity has been lost, and at present rates, a large percent of the rest will disappear in half century."

12. Alien Species: Transferring species to lands where they're not native can have unintended and catastrophic effects, "preying on, parasitizing, infecting or outcompeting" native animals and plants that lack evolutionary resistance.

In spite of the clear message in Diamond's 12 time-bombs, he still says he's a "cautious optimist." What fuels his hope? Our leaders need "the courage to practice long-term thinking, and to make bold, courageous, anticipatory decisions at a time when problems have become perceptible but before they reach crisis proportions."

Unfortunately, history tells us that cautious leaders are myopic, driven more by self-interest and nationalism than courage and long-term thinking. Eventually they're caught off guard and their worlds collapse, fast. They only respond to crises.

And, yes, out of crisis may come opportunity. As Nobel economist Milton Friedman put it in his classic, "Capitalism and Freedom:" "Only a crisis— actual or perceived—produces real change" because in the aftermath of crisis "the politically impossible becomes politically inevitable." Too many, how-ever, delay and respond to crises with too little, too late.

Bottom line: The betting odds are 100% that global leaders will wait for a Pentagon-style "black swan" crisis before acting. Unfortunately, that delay positions the "WWIII: The Population Wars" dead ahead.

Ronald Bailey → **NO**

Our Uncrowded Planet

Imminent doom has been declared again. But don't worry, neo-Malthusian predictions of overpopulation are wrong.

Every so often, the overpopulation meme erupts into public discourse and imminent doom is declared again. A particularly overwrought example of the overpopulation meme and its alleged problems appeared recently in the Wall Street Journal's MarketWatch in a piece by regular financial columnist Paul B. Farrell.

Farrell asserts that overpopulation is "the biggest time-bomb for Obama, America, capitalism, the world." Bigger than global warming, poverty, or peak oil. Overpopulation will end capitalism and maybe even destroy modern civilization. As evidence, Farrell cites what he calls neo-Malthusian biologist Jared Diamond's 12-factor equation of population doom.

It turns out that Farrell is wrong or misleading about the environmental and human effects of all 12 factors he cites. Let's take them one by one.

1. Overpopulation Multiplier: Looking at the most recent United Nations' population projections, it is likely that world population will peak somewhere between 8 and 9 billion near the middle of this century (current population is about 6.8 billion) and then begin declining back toward 6 billion by 2100. In addition, if lower fertility rates are the goal, promoting economic freedom is the way to achieve it. In 2002, Seth Norton, a business economics professor at Wheaton College in Illinois, published a remarkably interesting study on the inverse relationship between economic freedom and fertility. Norton found that the fertility rate in countries that ranked low on economic freedom averaged 4.27 children per woman while countries with high economic freedom rankings had an average fertility rate of 1.82 children per woman.

2. Population Impact Multiplier: Farrell mirrors Diamond's concern that the world's poor want to become rich. This means that they aim to consume more. Can the Earth sustain increased consumption? Yes, economic efficiency is dematerializing the economy and thus will spare more land and other resources for nature. As Jesse Ausubel, director of the human environment program at Rockefeller University, and colleagues have shown, although the average global consumer enjoyed 45 percent more affluence in 2006 than in 1980, each consumed only 22 percent more crops and 13 percent more energy.

See below for more information on positive trends in agriculture, water usage, and forest growth.

3. Food: Farrell says we are running out. It is true that far too many people are on the verge of starvation and the recent economic crisis has pushed even more in that direction. But Farrell and Diamond overlook the fact that crop yields have been increasing at a rate of about 2 percent per year for 100 years and now population is growing at 1 percent per year. Agronomist Paul Waggoner argued in his a 1996 article, "How Much Land Can Ten Billion People Spare for Nature?" published in the journal *Daedalus,* that "if during the next sixty to seventy years the world farmer reaches the average yield of today's U.S. corn grower, the 10 billion will need only half of today's cropland while they eat today's American calories." If Waggoner is right—and all signs are that he is—the future will be populated by fat people who will have plenty of wilderness in which to frolic.

4. Water: There is no doubt that a lot of fresh water is being wasted. However, we know how to solve that problem—create property rights and free markets for water. For example, water use per capita in the United States has been declining for two decades. Farrell and Diamond propagate the stale water wars meme. Transboundary water cooperation rather than conflict is the norm. "The simple explanation is that water is simply too important to fight over," notes Aaron Wolf, the Oregon State University professor who heads up the Program in Water Conflict Management. Wolf observes that history records that the last water war occurred 4500 years ago between Lagash and Umma over irrigation rights in what is now Iraq.

5. Farmland: First note that vast increases in agricultural productivity over the past half century spared an area about the size of South America from being plowed up to produce food for the current population. In a 2000 Science article, soil scientist Pierre Crosson and colleagues noted, "studies of the onfarm productivity effects based on 1982 N[ational] R[esource] I[nventory] cropland erosion indicated that if those rates continue for 100 years, crop yields (output per hectare) would be reduced only 2 to 4 percent. These results indicate that the productivity effects of soil erosion are not significant enough to justify increased federal outlays to reduce the erosion, but not all agree." In any case, soil erosion is a problem that is being addressed by modern high-tech no-till agriculture.

6. Forests: Farrell claims that forests are being destroyed at an accelerating rate. He is wrong. Forest regrowth is the actual trend in many places. A 2006 article on forest trends in the Proceedings of the National Academy of Sciences found "Among 50 nations with extensive forests reported in the Food and Agriculture Organization's comprehensive Global Forest Resources Assessment 2005, no nation where annual per capita gross domestic product exceeded $4,600 had a negative rate of growing stock change." In fact, leaving aside Brazil and Indonesia, globally the forests of the world increased by about

2 percent since 1990. And there is further good news—a quarter to a third of the tropical forests that have been cut down are now regenerating.

7. Toxic chemicals: Farrell writes, "Consider the deadly impact of insecticides, pesticides, herbicides, detergents, plastics . . . the list is endless." When one actually considers the impact on synthetic chemicals on people, it turns out that the more man-made chemicals, the higher do human life expectancies rise. Contrary to activist claims, trace amounts of synthetic chemicals are not producing a cancer epidemic. In fact, cancer incidence rates in the U.S. have been falling for nearly a decade.

8. Energy Resources, Oil, Natural Gas, and Coal: Farrell is just incoherent here. He hints at "peak oil," and supplies may become tight, but that would largely be a result of political factors, not the depletion of reserves. As for coal and natural gas supplies, no one is suggesting their imminent depletion.

9. Solar Energy: Farrell does not here mean photovoltaic power, but rather the Earth's "photosynthetic capacity," that is, the ability of plants to turn sunlight into food, fuel, and other useful products. Apparently, he thinks that humanity is using too much of it. To the extent this is a problem, biotech advances are already addressing it by researching ways to boost crop productivity by transforming plants from less efficient C3 photosynthesizers to the more efficient C4 pathway.

10. Ozone Layer: Farrell seems unaware of the fact that this problem has already largely been dealt with. To the extent this was a problem, the Montreal Protocol in 1987 that banned the refrigerants that were depleting the ozone layer has fixed it. This month, NASA reported a slightly positive trend of ozone increase of almost 1 percent per decade in the total ozone from the past 14 years.

11. Diversity: Biodiversity trends are notoriously difficult to predict. In 1979, Oxford University biologist Norman Myers suggested in his book *The Sinking Ark* that 40,000 species per year were going extinct and that 1 million species would be gone by the year 2000. Myers suggested that the world could "lose one-quarter of all species by the year 2000." At a 1979 symposium at Brigham Young University, Thomas Lovejoy, former president of The H. John Heinz III Center for Science, Economics, and the Environment announced that he had made "an estimate of extinctions that will take place between now and the end of the century. Attempting to be conservative wherever possible, I still came up with a reduction of global diversity between one-seventh and one-fifth." Lovejoy drew up the first projections of global extinction rates for the "Global 2000 Report to the President" in 1980. If Lovejoy had been right, between 15 and 20 percent of all species alive in 1980 would be extinct right now. No one believes that extinctions of this magnitude have occurred over the last three decades.

What happens to humanity if many species do go extinct? In a 2003 *Science* article called "Prospects for Biodiversity," Martin Jenkins, who works for the United Nations Environment Programme-World Conservation Monitoring Center, pointed out that even if the dire projections of extinction rates being made by conservation advocates are correct, they "will not, in themselves, threaten the survival of humans as a species." The Science article notes, "In truth, ecologists and conservationists have struggled to demonstrate the increased material benefits to humans of 'intact' wild systems over largely anthropogenic ones [like farms]. . . . Where increased benefits of natural systems have been shown, they are usually marginal and local."

12. Alien Species: Farrell claims, "transferring species to lands where they're not native can have unintended and catastrophic effects." Mostly not. Biologist Mark Davis chalks up most opposition to "alien" species to prejudice and muddy thinking, adding in the current issue of the *New Scientist* that "you may be surprised to learn that only a few per cent of introduced species are harmful. Most are relatively benign." As I pointed out nine years ago, the preference for native over non-native species is essentially a religious one. It has no warrant in biology.

While there certainly are environmental problems, current trends do not portend a looming population apocalypse. Instead, the 21st century will be more likely remembered as the century of ecological restoration.

EXPLORING THE ISSUE

Should Environmentalists Continue to Be Alarmists?

Critical Thinking and Reflection

1. What do you think about the heated attacks on people like Paul Ehrlich on the one side and Bjørn Lomborg on the other by writers who differ in their views?
2. Because the human race has been able to move bigger and bigger mountains, that is, affect greater change in the world because of increased technological capacity, does this raise the potential for larger and more frequent catastrophes?
3. Whenever you hear about a global disaster such as a health pandemic, do you immediately begin to show anxiety about the likelihood that you might contract the disease?
4. Of Paul Farrell's list of 12 time-bombs, which one or two frighten you the most and why?
5. Of Ronald Bailey's retort against Farrell, which of the 12 rationales appear most reasonable and why?

Is There Common Ground?

At first glance, it is difficult to find common ground between these two positions. But both do concede that the potential for far-reaching consequences as a result of some natural or human event is greater because of modernization, globalization, and the fact that everything is ultimately connected to everything else, as the ecosystem experts suggest. In the area of environmental health issues, there clearly is agreement on the greater dangers posed by the shrinking of the global frontiers, as people and diseases have the capacity to move around the earth at an increasingly greater speed, thus more easily affecting the far corners of the globe.

Additional Resources

Berlau, John, *Eco-Freaks: Environmentalism Is Hazardous to Your Health!* (Thomas Nelson, 2006)

>   This book takes a critical look at environmental "eco-extremists."

Cunningham, William, *Environmental Science: A Global Concern* (11th ed., McGraw-Hill, 2009)

>   This book is a general introduction to environmental science for non-science majors, giving a global theme to essential issues.

Lomborg, Bjørn, *Cool It: The Skeptical Environmentalist's Guide to Global Warming* (Vintage, 2008)

> This book by a controversial critic of those who argue that global warming is pervasive does not deny climate change but presents alternative solutions to the mainstream doomsdayers.

Moyers, Bill, *Welcome to Doomsday* (New York Review of Books, 2006)

> This book takes to task the disregard of the previous (Bush) administration's "disregard for science and environmental realities" and blames the influence of the Christian Right.

Murray, Iain, *The Really Inconvenient Truths: Seven Environmental Catastrophes Liberals Don't Want You to Know About—Because They Helped Cause Them* (Regnery, 2008)

> This is an especially intriguing book.

Shiva, Vandana, *Soil Not Oil: Environmental Justice in an Age of Climate Change* (South End Press, 2008)

> This book focuses on the link between industrial agriculture and climate change, arguing for the return of the small independent farm.

Siegal, Marc, *False Alarm: The Truth about the Epidemic of Fear* (Wiley, 2006)

> This book argues that many of the worst-case scenarios about global catastrophes will not happen. The author argues that the overarching fear of such events is unfounded.

Tol, Richard, ed., *Environmental Crises* (Springer, 2010)

> This book focuses on the art and science of predicting environmental change. Four major case studies—climate change, emissions of gasoline, fisheries policies, and marine oil pollution—are examined.

ISSUE 5

Should the World Continue to Rely on Oil as the Major Source of Energy?

YES: Nansen G. Saleri, from "The World Has Plenty of Oil," *Wall Street Journal Sunday* (March 4, 2008)

NO: Lester R. Brown, from "Is World Oil Production Peaking?" *Eco-Economy Update* (November 15, 2007)

Learning Outcomes
After reading this issue, you should be able to:
• Understand the argument that the world is nowhere near its peak in global oil supplies.
• Understand why some analysts believe that world oil production might be peaking.
• Describe the different ways of assessing how to measure the future prospects for oil production.
• Describe briefly the relationship between OPEC's changing production levels and the inability of national distribution systems to adjust to these changes.
• Describe the effect of modernizing oil extraction methods on the tipping point of peak oil.
• Discuss the effect of political unrest in the Middle East and North Africa on the price of oil.

ISSUE SUMMARY

YES: Nansen G. Saleri, president and CEO of Quantum Reservoir Input and the oil industry's preeminent authority on the issue, suggests that the world is "nowhere close to reaching a peak in global oil supplies." He argues that the future transition to oil alternatives will be the result of their superiority rather than the diminishing supply of oil.

NO: Lester R. Brown, founder and president of Earth Policy Institute, suggests that there has been a "pronounced loss of momentum" in the growth of oil production, a likely result of demand outpacing discoveries, leading to declining oil production prospects.

As 2010 arrived, gas prices passed the $3 a gallon level, with no end in sight. Within a year, the unthinkable occurred, as prices edged toward $4 a gallon. This sharp increase in the cost of oil coincided with a wave of political unrest sweeping the Middle East and North Africa. Observed first in Tunisia, it quickly spread to Yemen, Egypt, Bahrain, and eventually to Libya. Although these countries represent a small percentage of oil-exporting nations and although Saudi Arabia promised to make up the difference in oil production, the cost of a gallon of gas spiraled upward in conjunction with political turmoil. The cost of a gallon at the pump was also correlated with the rise in the price of a barrel of oil at the source. In early March 2010, the price of a barrel of oil was close to $120, about $25 more than it should have been based on simple supply and demand.

This was not the first crisis in recent times, however, as the beginning of the new millennium had witnessed an oil crisis almost immediately, the third major crisis in the last 30 years (1972–2002 and 1979 were the dates of earlier problems), and the fourth crisis appeared in 2008 as prices passed $3 a gallon for a while. The crisis of 2000 manifested itself in the United States via much higher gasoline prices and in Europe via both rising prices and shortages at the pump. Both were caused by the inability of national distribution systems to adjust to the Organization of Petroleum Exporting Countries' (OPEC's) changing production levels. The 2000 panic eventually subsided but reappeared in 2005 in the wake of the uncertainty surrounding the Iraqi war and the war on terrorism. Four major crises and a minor one in less than 40 years thus characterize the oil issue.

These earlier major fuel crises are discrete episodes in a much larger problem facing the human race, particularly the industrial world. That is, oil, the earth's current principal source of energy, is a finite resource that ultimately will be totally exhausted. And unlike earlier energy transitions, where a more attractive source invited a change (such as from wood to coal and from coal to oil), the next energy transition is being forced upon the human race in the absence of an attractive alternative. In short, we are being pushed out of our almost total reliance on oil toward a new system with a host of unknowns. What will the new fuel be? Will it be from a single source or some combination? Will it be a more attractive source? Will the source be readily available at a reasonable price, or will a new cartel emerge that controls much of the supply? Will its production and consumption lead to major new environmental consequences? Will it require major changes to our lifestyles and standards of living? When will we be forced to jump into using this new source?

The 2010 crisis is different from the earlier crises in the 1970s in one way in that the earlier crises had the imprint of OPEC vindictive behavior to the West on it. Today, Saudi Arabia has its own fear of domestic political unrest and thus wants to see as much stability as possible so as to help the Saudi leadership maintain its control over its population. But oil prices rose nonetheless as oil speculators cornered the market, forcing prices upward. The recent spike in the price at the pump is one example of the effect of such speculation.

But the 2010 crisis is also similar to other oil crises in that price increases do not reflect the simple supply and demand equation but, instead, are in part also a function of external unrelated forces, be they vindictive behavior of a cartel of nations or greedy behavior of individual investors. And for the latter, high oil prices is the goal, not certainty of supply. This is unfortunate for large Western consumers of oil as well as the largest producers such as Saudi Arabia. As long as consuming countries must rely on autocratic and sometimes unfriendly national regimes for their oil, fear, volatility, and uncertainly will characterize the scene.

Since these consumers cannot dramatically increase their own internal supply of oil under present technology, the answer may lie in alternative sources of energy. Before considering new sources of fuel, other questions need to be asked. Are the calls for a viable alternative to oil premature? Are we simply running scared without cause? Did we learn the wrong lessons from the earlier energy crises? More specifically, were these crises artificially created or a consequence of the actual physical unavailability of the energy source? Have these crises really been about running out of oil globally, or were they due to other phenomena at work, such as poor distribution planning by oil companies or the use of oil as a political weapon by oil-exporting countries?

For well over half a century now, Western oil-consuming countries have been predicting the end of oil. Using a model known as Hubbert's Curve (named after a U.S. geologist who designed it in the 1930s), policymakers have predicted that the world would run out of oil at various times; the most recent prediction is that oil will run out a couple of decades from now. Simply put, the model visualizes all known available resources and the patterns of consumption on a timeline until the wells run dry. Despite such prognostication, it was not until the crisis of the early 1970s that national governments began to consider ways of both prolonging the oil system and finding a suitable replacement. Prior to that time, governments as well as the private sector encouraged energy consumption. "The more, the merrier" was an oft-heard refrain. Increases in energy consumption were associated with economic growth. After Europe recovered from the devastation of World War II, for example, every 1 percent increase in energy consumption brought a similar growth in economic output. To the extent that governments engaged in energy policy making, it was designed solely to encourage increased production and consumption. Prices were kept low and the energy was readily available. Policies making energy distribution systems more efficient and consumption patterns both more efficient and lowered were almost nonexistent.

Yet, when one reads the UN assessment of foreseeable world energy supplies (Hisham Khatib et al., *World Energy Assessment: Energy and the Challenge of Sustainability* (United Nations Development Programme, 2002)), a sobering message appears. Do not panic just yet. The study reveals no serious energy shortage during the first half of the twenty-first century. In fact, the report suggests that oil supply conditions have actually improved since the crises of the

97

1970s and early 1980s. The report goes further in its assessment, concluding that fossil fuel reserves are "sufficient to cover global requirements throughout this century, even with a high-growth scenario." Another source suggesting no shortages for some time is *The Myth of the Oil Crisis: Overcoming the Challenges of depletion, Geopolitics, and Global Warming* (Robin M. Mills, Praeger, 2008). Francis R. Stabler argues in "The Pump Will Never Run Dry" (*The Futurist,* November 1998), that technology and free enterprise will combine to allow the human race to continue its reliance on oil far into the future. For Stabler, the title of his article tells the reader everything. The pump will not run dry!

To be sure, his view of the future availability of gas is a minority one. One supporter is Julian L. Simon who argues in his *The Ultimate Resource 2* (1996) that even God may not know exactly how much oil and gas are "out there." Chapter 11 of Simon's book is titled "When Will We Run Out of Oil? Never!" Another supporter of Stabler is Bjørn Lomborg in *The Skeptical Environmentalist: Measuring the Real State of the World* (Cambridge University Press, 2001). Arguing that the world seems to find more fossil energy than it consumes, he concludes that "we have oil for at least 40 years at present consumption, at least 60 years' worth of gas, and 230 years' worth of coal." Simon and Lomborg are joined by Michael C. Lynch in a published article on the Web under global oil supply (msn.com) titled "Crying Wolf: Warnings about Oil Supply."

Today, the search for an alternative to oil still continues. Nuclear energy, once thought to be the answer, may play a future role, but at a reduced level. Both water power and wind power remain possibilities, as do biomass, geothermal energy, and solar energy. Many also believe that the developed world is about to enter the hydrogen age to meet future energy needs. The question before us, therefore, is whether the international community has the luxury of some time before all deposits of oil are exhausted. The two selections for this issue suggest different answers to this last question. In the YES selection, Nansen G. Saleri, the oil industry's preeminent authority on the issue, suggests that the world was not even close to reaching a peak in supplies. In the NO selection, Lester R. Brown, no less an authority on the public interest side of the issue, argues that the world is already experiencing a loss of momentum in oil production growth, with future prospects declining.

YES ↵

The World Has Plenty of Oil

Many energy analysts view the ongoing waltz of crude prices with the mystical $100 mark—notwithstanding the dollar's anemia—as another sign of the beginning of the end for the oil era. "[A]t the furthest out, it will be a crisis in 2008 to 2012," declares Matthew Simmons, the most vocal voice among the "neo-peak-oil" club. Tempering this pessimism only slightly is the viewpoint gaining ground among many industry leaders, who argue that daily production by 2030 of 100 million barrels will be difficult.

In fact, we are nowhere close to reaching a peak in global oil supplies.

Given a set of assumptions, forecasting the peak-oil-point—defined as the onset of global production decline—is a relatively trivial problem. Four primary factors will pinpoint its exact timing. The trivial becomes far more complex because the four factors—resources in place (how many barrels initially underground), recovery efficiency (what percentage is ultimately recoverable), rate of consumption, and state of depletion at peak (how empty is the global tank when decline kicks in)—are inherently uncertain.

What Are the Global Resources in Place?

Estimates vary. But approximately six to eight trillion barrels each for conventional and unconventional oil resources (shale oil, tar sands, extra heavy oil) represent probable figures—inclusive of future discoveries. As a matter of context, the globe has consumed only one out of a grand total of 12 to 16 trillion barrels underground.

What Percentage of Global Resources Is Ultimately Recoverable?

The industry recovers an average of only one out of three barrels of conventional resources underground and considerably less for the unconventional.

This benchmark, established over the past century, is poised to change upward. Modern science and unfolding technologies will, in all likelihood, double recovery efficiencies. Even a 10% gain in extraction efficiency on a global scale will unlock 1.2 to 1.6 trillion barrels of extra resources—an additional 50-year supply at current consumption rates.

From *Wall Street Journal Sunday*, March 4, 2008. Copyright © 2008 by Nansen G. Saleri. Reprinted by permission of the author and Dow Jones & Company.

The impact of modern oil extraction techniques is already evident across the globe. Abqaiq and Ghawar, two of the flagship oil fields of Saudi Arabia, are well on their way to recover at least two out of three barrels underground—in the process raising recovery expectations for the remainder of the Kingdom's oil assets, which account for one-quarter of world reserves.

Are the lessons and successes of Ghawar transferable to the countless struggling fields around the world—most conspicuously in Venezuela, Mexico, Iran or the former Soviet Union—where irreversible declines in production are mistakenly accepted as the norm and in fact fuel the "neo-peak-oil" alarmism? The answer is a definitive yes.

Hundred-dollar oil will provide a clear incentive for reinvigorating fields and unlocking extra barrels through the use of new technologies. The consequences for emerging oil-rich regions such as Iraq can be far more rewarding. By 2040 the country's production and reserves might potentially rival those of Saudi Arabia.

Paradoxically, high crude prices may temporarily mask the inefficiencies of others, which may still remain profitable despite continuing to use 1960-vintage production methods. But modernism will inevitably prevail: The national oil companies that hold over 90% of the earth's conventional oil endowment will be pressed to adopt new and better technologies.

What Will Be the Average Rate of Crude Consumption Between Now and Peak Oil?

Current daily global consumption stands around 86 million barrels, with projected annual increases ranging from 0% to 2% depending on various economic outlooks. Thus average consumption levels ranging from 90 to 110 million barrels represent a reasonable bracket. Any economic slowdown—as intimated by the recent tremors in the global equity markets—will favor the lower end of this spectrum.

This is not to suggest that global supply capacity will grow steadily unimpeded by bottlenecks—manpower, access, resource nationalism, legacy issues, logistical constraints, etc.—within the energy equation. However, near-term obstacles do not determine the global supply ceiling at 2030 or 2050. Market forces, given the benefit of time and the burgeoning mobility of technology and innovation across borders, will tame transitional obstacles.

When Will Peak Oil Arrive?

This widely accepted tipping point—50% of ultimately recoverable resources consumed—is largely a tribute to King Hubbert, a distinguished Shell geologist who predicted the peak oil point for the U.S. lower 48 states. While his timing was very good (he forecast 1968 versus 1970 in fact), he underestimated peak daily production (9.5 million barrels actual versus 8 million estimated).

But modern extraction methods will undoubtedly stretch Hubbert's "50% assumption," which was based on Sputnik-era technologies. Even a modest shift—to 55% of recoverable resources consumed—will delay the onset by 20–25 years.

Where do reasonable assumptions surrounding peak oil lead us? My view, subjective and imprecise, points to a period between 2045 and 2067 as the most likely outcome.

Cambridge Energy Associates forecasts the global daily liquids production to rise to 115 million barrels by 2017 versus 86 million at present. Instead of a sharp peak per Hubbert's model, an undulating, multi-decade long plateau production era sets in—i.e., no sudden-death ending.

The world is not running out of oil anytime soon. A gradual transitioning on the global scale away from a fossil-based energy system may in fact happen during the 21st century. The root causes, however, will most likely have less to do with lack of supplies and far more with superior alternatives. The overused observation that "the Stone Age did not end due to a lack of stones" may in fact find its match.

The solutions to global energy needs require an intelligent integration of environmental, geopolitical and technical perspectives each with its own subsets of complexity. On one of these—the oil supply component—the news is positive. Sufficient liquid crude supplies do exist to sustain production rates at or near 100 million barrels per day almost to the end of this century.

Technology matters. The benefits of scientific advancement observable in the production of better mobile phones, TVs and life-extending pharmaceuticals will not, somehow, bypass the extraction of usable oil resources. To argue otherwise distracts from a focused debate on what the correct energy-policy priorities should be, both for the United States and the world community at large.

Lester R. Brown

↱ **NO**

Is World Oil Production Peaking?

Is world oil production peaking? Quite possibly. Data from the International Energy Agency (IEA) show a pronounced loss of momentum in the growth of oil production during the last few years. After climbing from 82.90 million barrels per day (mb/d) in 2004 to 84.15 mb/d in 2005, output only increased to 84.80 mb/d in 2006 and then declined to 84.62 mb/d during the first 10 months of 2007.

The combination of world production slowing down or starting to decline while demand continues to rise rapidly is putting strong upward pressure on prices. Over the past two years, oil prices have climbed from $50 to nearly $100 a barrel. If production growth continues to lag behind the increase in demand, how high will prices go?

There are many ways of assessing the oil production prospect. One is to look at the relationship between oil discoveries and production, a technique pioneered by the legendary U.S. geologist M. King Hubbert. Given the nature of oil production, Hubbert theorized that the time lag between the peaking of new discoveries and that of production was predictable. Noting that the discovery of new reserves in the United States peaked around 1930, he predicted in 1956 that U.S. oil output would peak in 1970. He hit it right on the head.

Globally, oil discoveries peaked in the 1960s. Each year since 1984, world oil production has exceeded new oil discoveries, and by a widening gap. In 2006, the 31 billion barrels of oil extracted far exceeded the discovery of 9 billion barrels.

The aging of oil fields also tells us something about the oil prospect. The world's 20 largest oil fields were all discovered between 1917 and 1979. . . . Sadad al-Husseini, former senior Saudi oil official, reports that the annual output from the world's aging fields is falling by 4 mb/d. Offsetting this decline with new discoveries or with more-advanced extraction technologies is becoming increasingly difficult.

Yet another way of assessing the oil prospect is to look separately at the leading oil-producing countries where production is falling, the ones where production is still rising, and those that appear to be on the verge of a downturn. Among the leading oil producers, output appears to have peaked and turned downward in a dozen or so and to still be rising in nine.

From *Eco-Economy Update*, November 15, 2007. Copyright © 2007 by Earth Policy Institute. Reprinted by permission.

Among the post-peak countries are the United States, which peaked at 9.6 mb/d in 1970, dropping to 5.1 mb/d in 2006; Venezuela, where output also peaked in 1970; and the two North Sea oil producers, the United Kingdom and Norway, which peaked in 1999 and 2000.

The pre-peak countries are dominated by Russia, now the world's leading oil producer, having eclipsed Saudi Arabia in 2006. Two other countries with substantial potential for increasing output are Canada, largely because of its tar sands, and Kazakhstan, which is developing the Kashagan oil field in the Caspian Sea, the only large find in recent decades. Other pre-peak countries include Algeria, Angola, Brazil, Nigeria, Qatar, and the United Arab Emirates.

Among the countries where production may be peaking are Saudi Arabia, Mexico, and China. The big question is Saudi Arabia. Saudi officials claim they can produce far more oil, but the giant Ghawar oil field—the world's largest by far and the one that has supplied half of Saudi oil output for decades—is 56 years old and in its declining years. Saudi oil production data for the first eight months of 2007 show output of 8.62 mb/d, a drop of 6 percent from the 9.15 mb/d of 2006. If Saudi Arabia cannot restore growth in its oil production, then peak oil is on our doorstep.

In Mexico, the second-ranking supplier to the United States after Canada, output apparently peaked in 2004 at 3.4 mb/d. U.S. geologist Walter Youngquist notes that Cantarell, the country's dominant oil field, is now in steep decline, and that Mexico could be an oil importer by 2015. Production in China, slightly higher than in Mexico, may also be about to peak.

A number of prominent geologists are convinced that global oil production has peaked or is about to do so. "The whole world has now been seismically searched and picked over," says independent geologist Colin Campbell. "Geological knowledge has improved enormously in the past 30 years and it is almost inconceivable now that major fields remain to be found."

Kenneth Deffeyes, a highly respected geologist, said in his 2005 book, *Beyond Oil,* "It is my opinion that the peak will occur in late 2005 or in the first few months of 2006." Youngquist and A. M. Samsam Bakhtiari of the Iranian National Oil Company each projected that production would peak in 2007.

The Energy Watch Group in Germany, which recently analyzed oil production data country by country, also concluded that world oil production has peaked. They project it will decline by 7 percent a year, falling to 58 mb/d in 2020. Bakhtiari projects a decline in oil production to 55 mb/d in 2020, slightly lower than the German group. In stark contrast, the IEA and the U.S. Department of Energy are each projecting world oil output in 2020 at 104 mb/d.

The peaking of world oil production will be a seismic event, marking one of the great fault lines in world economic history. When oil output is no longer expanding, no country can get more oil unless another gets less.

Oil-intensive industries will be hit hard. Cheap airfares will become history, for instance. The airline industry's projected growth of 5 percent a year over the next decade will evaporate. The food industry will be severely affected by rising oil prices, since both modern agriculture and food transport are oil-intensive. The automobile industry will suffer as well when demand for cars plummets. Pressures will intensify on the three or more major auto companies that are developing plug-in hybrid cars that run largely on electricity to bring them to market quickly.

Higher oil prices have long been needed both to more accurately reflect the indirect costs of burning oil, such as climate change, and to encourage more-efficient use of a resource that is fast being depleted. While higher prices are desirable, the rise should not be so abrupt that it leads to severe economic disruptions.

Some countries are much more vulnerable to an oil decline than others. For example, the United States—which has long neglected public transportation—is particularly vulnerable because 88 percent of the U.S. workforce travels to work by car.

Since options for expanding supply are limited, efforts to prevent oil prices from rising well beyond $100 per barrel in the years ahead depend on reducing demand, largely within the transportation sector. And since the United States consumes more gasoline than the next 20 countries combined, it must play a lead role in cutting oil use.

A campaign to reduce oil use rapidly might best be launched at an emergency meeting of the G-8, since its members dominate world oil consumption. If governments fail to act quickly and decisively to reduce oil use, oil prices could soar as demand outruns supply, leading to a global recession or—in a worst-case scenario—a 1930s-type global depression.

EXPLORING THE ISSUE

Should the World Continue to Rely on Oil as the Major Source of Energy?

Critical Thinking and Reflection

1. Can we accept with any level of confidence predictions of the date when peak oil is reached?
2. To what extent is the supply/demand equation becoming less important or even irrelevant to the potential for a global oil crisis?
3. Should the United States reconsider its support for people's movements in oil-exporting countries with autocratic governments in light of these movements' effects on oil prices?
4. What are the lessons from the recent nuclear energy disaster in Japan on the search for a viable energy alternative(s) to oil?
5. Does Organization of Petroleum Exporting Countries (OPEC) remain an important international actor in the global energy arena?

Is There Common Ground?

Since oil is a finite resource, the planet will obviously run out of the resource some day. No responsible analyst denies this scenario. There is also recognition by many in the field that one great unknown factor is the extent to which new future technologies will extend the life of oil as the dominant resource, and if so, for how long? Modern technologies have trumped earlier predictions several times and there is little reason to believe that they may not play a role in the future.

There is also strong consensus that no single alternative energy source is poised to replace oil yet. And the recent nuclear energy disaster in Japan only emphasizes this point.

Additional Resources

Crane, Hewitt, *A Cubic Mile of Oil: Realities and Options for Averting the Looming Global Energy Crisis* (Oxford University Press, 2010)

> This book conceptualizes future global energy use, introducing the concept of one cubic mile of oil (CMO) as a measure. It argues that annual consumption is currently 3.0 CMOs but by midcentury, it will be between 6 and 9 CMOs.

Gorelick, Steven M., *Oil Panic and the Global Crisis: Predictions and Myths* (Wiley-Blackwell, 2009)

> This book exposes the myths on both sides about global oil. It argues that although the supply of oil is not infinite, the ultimate size of oil reserves is poorly known.

Library of Congress, "U.S. and Global Oil Markets," from "U.S. Offshore Oil and Gas Resources: Prospects and Processes," *Congressional Research Service Report* (April 26, 2010)

> This article reveals trends in the U.S. oil demand and production for the 2000s.

Mills, Robin M., *The Myth of the Oil Crisis: Overcoming the Challenges of Depletion, Geopolitics, and Global Warming* (Praeger, 2008)

> This book by an oil insider purports to debunk myths about global oil, suggesting that enough oil exists for decades to come.

Rasizade, Alec, "The End of Cheap Oil," *Contemporary Review* (Autumn, 2008)

> This article examines the recent history of oil pricing, coming to the conclusion that the major oil and gas producers now dominate the global economic situation.

Ruppert, Michael, *Confronting Collapse: The Crisis of Energy and Money in a Post Peak Oil World* (Chelsea Green Publishing, 2009)

> This book describes the relationship of oil shortages and pricing. It suggests that the world is on the verge of collapse as a consequence. It then lays out a 25-point plan of action to avert it.

Whipple, Tom, "Peak Oil," *Bulletin of the Atomic Scientists* (November/December, 2008)

> This article addresses the debate over when oil production will begin to fall, thus forcing transition to other energy sources.

ISSUE 6

Will the World Be Able to Feed Itself in the Foreseeable Future?

YES: **Stephen Lendman**, from "Global Food Crisis: Hunger Plagues Haiti and the World," *Global Research* (April 21, 2008)

NO: **Lester Brown**, from "The Great Food Crisis of 2011: It's Real and It's Not Going Away Anytime Soon," *Foreign Policy* (January 10, 2011)

Learning Outcomes

After reading this issue, you should be able to:

- Gain an understanding of how the factors that contributed to a global food problem in the 1970s were different from those contributing to the food crisis of the 2000s.
- Understand the consequence of treating global food as a commodity rather than as a nutrient.
- Understand that the current global food problem is really a global food price problem.
- Discuss the factors on both the demand and supply sides of the food equation that adversely affect food prices.
- Describe how factors associated with climate change will likely affect national food security.

ISSUE SUMMARY

YES: Stephen Lendman, a research associate of the Centre for Research on Globalization in Montreal, argues that the global food crisis is related to rising prices in an economically troubled time rather than to a lack of food production.

NO: Lester Brown, founder and president of Earth Policy Institute, argues that unlike in the past when weather was the culprit, the spike in food prices is now caused by trends on both sides of the food supply/demand equation that are causing higher food prices.

The lead editorial in *The New York Times* on March 3, 2008 began with the sentence: "The world's food situation is bleak. . . ." The primary culprit, according to the editorial is the rising cost of wheat. The blame, in turn, was placed on the growing impact of biofuels. Others echoed the same message, adding climate change and the rising cost of shipping to the list of culprits. The UN Food and Agricultural Organization (FAO) also issued a series of warnings in late 2007 and early 2008 about the growing food crisis. Nine days later, United Nations Secretary-General Ban Ki Moon in *The Washington Post* also sound the global food alarm, alluding to high food costs and food insecurity.

Nineteen months later in October 2009, the UN FAO Director-General Jacques Diouf in a major speech suggested that agriculture would have to become more productive if the globe's growing population was to be fed. He suggested that future production growth would be found in increased yields and better crop intensity. Further, he argued that a major problem was that food was not being produced by 70 percent of the world's poor who worked in agriculture.

In November 2010, FAO issued its latest edition of *Food Outlook*. In it, the UN organization suggested that another food crisis was upon us, caused primarily by less than anticipated food production. At the same time, FAO also targeted higher grain prices. The International Food Policy Research Institute (IFPRI) echoed the need for more production, blaming growing world population and negative production results because of climate change and suggesting that rising food prices were simply a result of the increased demand.

These studies followed pre-2008 reports about food supply and demand. For example, the IFPRI 2007 report, *The World Food Situation: New Driving Forces and Required Actions,* found these "new driving forces" on both the supply and demand side. Rising incomes and urbanization led to the call for better food (meat and milk). On the supply side, increased food production–related energy prices and the large-scale diversion of corn from food to energy (ethanol) production as well as less than desirable weather all contribute to a lowered supply.

Private individuals share the same view, such as Robert G. Lewis, former U.S. government administer, who once oversaw farm price support programs. Lewis, writing in *World Policy Institute* (2008), suggests that despite short-term problems relating to pricing, the real enduring problem is that demand for more and better food is growing at a fast pace. And the demand is occurring in places whose population can less afford to purchase food. Of course, not everyone believed that for whatever the reason, food shortage was a myth despite the fact that one in six people are going hungry. One such individual is John McCabe, who makes his case on the blog, *Give It to Me Raw.*

Visualize two pictures. One is a group of people in Africa, including a significant number of small children, who show dramatic signs of advanced malnutrition and even starvation. The second picture shows an apparently wealthy couple finishing a meal at a rather expensive restaurant. The waiter removes their plates still half-full of food, and deposits them in the kitchen garbage can. These scenarios once highlighted a popular film about world hunger. The implication was quite clear. If only the wealthy would share their food with the poor, no one would go hungry. Today the simplicity of this image is obvious. And yet the crisis of 2008 said nothing about an inadequate or maldistributed supply of food.

This issue addresses the question of whether or not the world will be able to feed itself by the middle of the twenty-first century. A prior question, of course, is whether or not enough food is grown throughout the world today to handle current nutritional and caloric needs of all the planet's citizens. News accounts of chronic food shortages somewhere in the world seem to have been appearing with regularly consistency for close to 40 years. This time has witnessed graphic accounts in news specials about the consequences of insufficient food, usually somewhere in sub-Saharan Africa. Also, several national and international studies have been commissioned to address world hunger. An American study organized by President Carter, for example, concluded that the root cause of hunger was poverty.

One might deduce from all of this activity that population growth had outpaced food production and that the planet's agricultural capabilities are no longer sufficient, or that the poor have been priced out of the marketplace. Yet, the ability of most countries to grow enough food has not yet been challenged. During the 1970–2000 period, only one region of the globe, sub-Saharan Africa, was unable to have its own food production keep pace with population growth.

This is instructive because, beginning in the early 1970s, a number of factors conspired to lessen the likelihood that all humans would go to bed each night adequately nourished. Weather in major food-producing countries turned bad; a number of countries, most notably Japan and the Soviet Union, entered the world grain-importing business with a vengeance; the cost of energy used to enhance agricultural output rose dramatically; and less capital was available to poorer countries as loans or grants for purchasing agricultural inputs or the finished product (food) itself. Yet, the world has had little difficulty growing sufficient food, enough to provide every person with two loaves of bread per day as well as other commodities.

Why then did famine and other food-related maladies appear with increasing frequency? The simple answer is that food has been treated as a commodity, not a nutrient. Those who can afford to buy food or grow their own do not go hungry. However, the world's poor became increasingly unable to afford either to create their own successful agricultural ventures or to buy enough food.

The problem for the next half-century, then, has several facets to it. First, can the planet physically sustain increases in food production equal to or greater than the ability of the human race to reproduce itself? This question can only be answered by examining both factors in the comparison—likely future food production levels and future fertility scenarios. A second question relates to the economic dimension —will those poorer countries of the globe that are unable to grow their own food have sufficient assets to purchase it, or will the international community create a global distribution network that ignores a country's ability to pay? And third, will countries that want to grow their own food be given the opportunity to do so?

Three alternative perspectives are relevant to a discussion over the world's future ability to feed its population. The most basic alternative is the question of the target of international action. At its most basic, the root cause of hunger is poverty, first suggested by President Jimmy Carter's hunger commission. If the truth is in the ability to afford to pay for food, why not simply focus on eliminating poverty, hence solving the food problem?

Two other alternative perspectives are found in the literature. One is a report by the Rabobank group, "Sustainability and Security of the Global Food Supply Chain" (undated). Although it concludes that there is sufficient global potential to produce the 70 percent more food needed for 2050, the key factor is the global food system, a long supply chain that "encompasses different countries and numerous participants and stakeholders." To this group, less important are balancing food shortages across regions/countries and changing dietary habits and needs.

A very different alternative approach has recently been advanced by the Worldwatch Institute (*The State of the World 2011*). Instead of growing more food, the key to addressing the food crisis is to "encourage self-sufficiency and waste reduction." That is, the emphasis should not be on the food production side of the equation but, rather, on the food consumption side. This was earlier seen in the energy issue where attention away from production to consumption changed the entire global mindset in the mid-1970s. This view is shared by Julian Cribb, award-winning journalist, who suggests that rarely have we been advised "of the true ecological costs of eating" (*The Coming Famine*, 2010). He argues the need for a world diet that "is sparing of energy, water, land, and other inputs and has minimal impact on the eider environment." He adds other "big-picture solutions": curbing waste, sharing knowledge, recarbonizing, and movement toward a world farm.

The selections for this issue address the specific question of the planet's continuing ability to grow sufficient food for its growing population. In the YES selection, Stephen Lendman suggests that rising prices in an economically troubled time makes it extremely difficult for the world to be adequately fed. In the NO selection, Lester Brown blames the food crisis on a number of factors on both sides of the supply/demand equation.

YES ↲

Global Food Crisis: Hunger Plagues Haiti and the World

Consumers in rich countries feel it in supermarkets but in the world's poorest ones people are starving. The reason—soaring food prices, and it's triggered riots around the world in places like Mexico, Indonesia, Yemen, the Philippines, Cambodia, Morocco, Senegal, Uzbekistan, Guinea, Mauritania, Egypt, Cameroon, Bangladesh, Burkina Faso, Ivory Coast, Peru, Bolivia and Haiti that was once nearly food self-sufficient but now relies on imports for most of its supply and (like other food-importing countries) is at the mercy of agribusiness.

Wheat shortages in Peru are acute enough to have the military make bread with potato flour (a native crop). In Pakistan, thousands of troops guard trucks carrying wheat and flour. In Thailand, rice farmers take shifts staying awake nights guarding their fields from thieves. The crop's price has about doubled in recent months; it's the staple for half or more of the world's population, but rising prices and fearing scarcity have prompted some of the world's largest producers to export less—Thailand (the world's largest exporter), Vietnam, India, Egypt, Cambodia with others likely to follow as world output lags demand. Producers of other grains are doing the same like Argentina, Kazakhstan and China. The less they export, the higher prices go.

Other factors are high oil prices and transportation costs, growing demand, commodity speculation, pests in southeast Asia, a 10-year Australian drought, floods in Bangladesh and elsewhere, a 45-day cold snap in China, and other natural but mostly manipulated factors like crop diversion for biofuels; these have combined to create a growing world crisis, with more on this below. It's at the same time millions of Chinese and Indians have higher incomes, are changing their eating habits, and are consuming more meat, chicken and other animal products that place huge demands on grains to produce.

Here's a UK April 8 *Times* online snapshot of the situation in parts of Asia:

— Filipino farmers caught hoarding rice risk a life in jail sentence for "economic sabotage;"
— thousands of (Jakarta) Indonesian soya bean cake makers are striking against the destruction of their livelihood;
— once food self-sufficient countries like Japan and South Korea are reacting "bitterly (as) the world's food stocks-to-consumption ratio plunges to an all-time low;"

From GlobalResearch.ca, April 21, 2008. Copyright © 2008 by Center for Research on Globalization (CRG). Reprinted by permission.

— India no longer can export millions of tons of rice; instead it's forced to have a "special strategic food reserve on top of its existing wheat and rice stockpiles;"
— Thailand is the world's largest rice producer; its price rose 50% in the past month;
— countries like the Philippines and Sri Lanka are scrambling for secure rice supplies; they and other Asian countries are struggling to cope with soaring prices and insufficient supply;
— overall, rice is the staple food for three billion people; one-third of them survive on less than $1 a day and are "food insecure;" it means they may starve to death without aid.

The UN Food and Agricultural Organization (FAO) reported that world-wide food costs rose almost 40% in 2007 while grains spiked 42% and dairy prices nearly 80%. The World Bank said food prices are up 83% since 2005. As of December, this caused 37 countries to face food crises and 20 to impose price controls in response.

It also affected aid agencies like the UN's World Food Program (WFP). Because of soaring food and energy costs, the WFP sent an urgent appeal to donors on March 20 to help fill a $500 million resource gap for its work. Since then, food prices increased another 20% and show no signs of abating. For the world's poor, like the people of Haiti, things are desperate, people can't afford food, they scratch by any way they can, but many are starving and don't make it. . . .

World Hunger—A Growing Problem for All Nations

The situation is so dire, protests may erupt anywhere, any time, and rich countries aren't immune, including America. Poverty in the world's richest country is growing, and organizations like the Center for Economic Policy Research (CEPR) and Economic Policy Institute (EPI) document it. They report on a permanent (and growing) underclass of over 37 million people earning poverty-level wages and say that official statistics understate the problem. They note an unprecedented wealth gap between rich and poor, a dying middle class, and growing millions in extreme poverty.

It affects the unemployed as well in times of economic distress, but official government data conceals to what extent. If employment calculations were made as originally mandated, the true rate would be around 13% instead of the Department of Labor's 5.1%. The same is true for inflation that's around 12% at the retail level instead of the official 4% that's hooey.

Under conditions of duress, hunger is the clearest symptom; it's rising, and current food inflation threatens to spiral it out of control if nothing is done to address it. It's the highest in decades with 2007 signaling what's ahead—eggs up 25% last year; milk 17%; rice, bread and pasta 12%, and look at prices on the Chicago Board of Trade (CBOT):

— grains and soy prices are at multi-year highs;
— wheat hit an all-time high above $12 a bushel with little relief ahead in spite of a temporary pullback in price; the US Department of Agriculture

forecasts that global wheat stocks this year will fall to a 30 year low of 109.7 million metric tons; USDA also projected US wheat stocks by year end 2008 at 272 million bushels—the lowest level since 1948;
— corn and soybeans are also at record levels; soybeans are at over $15 a bushel; corn prices shot above $6 a bushel as demand for this and other crops soar in spite of US farmers planting as much of them as possible to cash in on high prices.

Growing demand, a weak dollar, but mostly another factor to be discussed below is responsible—the increased use of corn for ethanol production with farmers diverting more of their acreage from other crops to plant more of what's most in demand. Forty-three per cent of corn production is for livestock feed, but around one-fifth is for biofuels according to the National Corn Growers Association (NCGA). Other estimates are as high as 25–30% compared to 14% two years ago, and NCGA estimates one-third of the crop in 2009 will be for ethanol, not food. It's fueling US and world food inflation with five year forecasts of it rising even faster.

In the world's poorest countries, people starve. Here, they go on food stamps with a projected unprecedented 28 million Americans getting them this year as joblessness increases in a weak economy. However, many millions in need aren't eligible as social services are cut to finance foreign wars and tax cuts for the rich, with poor folks at home losing out as a result. A family of four only qualifies now if its net monthly income is at or below $1721 or $20,652 a year. Even then, it gets the same $542 monthly amount recipients received in 1996 to cover today's much higher prices or around $1 dollar a meal per person and falling.

This is the UN's World Food Program (WFP)'s dilemma worldwide at a time donations coming in are inadequate. Its Executive Director, Josette Sheeran, said "Our ability to reach people is going down just as needs go up. . . . We are seeing a new face of hunger in which people (can't afford to buy food). . . . Situations that were previously not urgent" are now desperate. WFP's funding needs keep rising. It estimates them at $3.5 billion, they'll likely go higher, and they're for approved projects to feed 73 million people in 78 counties worldwide. WFP foresees much greater potential needs for unseen emergencies and for far greater numbers of people in need.

People (who aren't poor) in rich countries can manage with food accounting for about 10% of consumption. In ones like China, it's around 30%, but in sub-Saharan Africa and the poor in Latin America and Asia it's about 60% (or even 80%) and rising. It means food aid is vital, and without it people will starve. But as food prices rise, the amount forthcoming (when it's most needed) falls because not enough money is available and too few donors offer help.

Agencies that can are doing less with ones like USAID saying it's cutting the amount of food aid it provides but won't say why. It's mission is to help the rich, not the poor, or as it states on its web site: as a US government agency, it "receives (its) overall foreign policy guidance from the Secretary of State (and its mission is to) further America's foreign policy interests (in the areas of) economic growth, agriculture and trade. . . ." That leaves out the poor.

Oxfam worries about what USAID ignores. It called for immediate action by donors and governments to protect the world's poor against rising food prices. One spokesperson said: "Global economic uncertainty, high food prices, drought (and other factors) all pose a serious threat to (the) vulnerable." Another added: "More and more people are going to be facing food shortages in the future. (Because of) rising food prices we need to think (of its) impact on (the world's poor) who are spending up to 80% of their incomes on food."

The UN Special Rapporteur on the Right to Food, Jean Ziegler, also expressed alarm. In comments to the French daily Liberation he said: "We are heading for a very long period of rioting, conflicts (and) waves of uncontrollable regional instability marked by the despair of the most vulnerable populations." He noted that even under normal circumstances hunger plagues the world and claims the life of a child under age 10 every five seconds. Because of the present crisis, we now face "an imminent massacre."

Besides the usual factors cited, it's vital to ask why, but don't expect Brazil's Lula to explain. Biofuel production is the main culprit, but not according to him. Brazil is a major biofuels producer. Last year it signed an R&D "Ethanol Pact" with Washington to develop "next generation" technologies for even more production.

In an April 16 Reuters report, the former union leader was dismissive about the current crisis and rejected criticisms that biofuels are at fault. In spite of protests at home and around the world, he told reporters: "Don't tell me. . . . that food is expensive because of biodiesel. (It's) expensive because" peoples' economic situation has improved and they're eating more. It's true in parts of China and India, but not in most other countries where incomes haven't kept pace with inflation.

Biofuels—A Scourge of Our Times

The idea of combustible fuels from organic material has been around since the early auto age, but only recently took off. Because they're from plant-based or animal byproduct (renewable) sources, bio or agrofuels are (falsely) touted as a solution to a growing world energy shortage with a huge claimed added benefit—the nonsensical notion that they're clean and green without all the troublesome issues connected to fossil fuels.

Biofuel is a general term to describe all fuels from organic matter. The two most common kinds are bioethanol as a substitute for gasoline, and biodiesel that serves the same purpose for that type fuel.

Bioethanol is produced from sugar-rich crops like corn, wheat and sugar cane. Most cars can burn a petroleum fuel blend with up to 10% bioethanol without any engine modifications. Some newer cars can run on pure bioethanol.

Biodiesel is produced from a variety of vegetable oils, including soybean, palm and rapeseed (canola), plus animal fats. This fuel can replace regular diesel with no engine modifications required.

Cellulosic ethanol is another variety and is made by breaking down fiber from grasses or most other kinds of plants. Biofuels of all types are renewable since crops are grown in season, harvested, then replanted for more output repeatedly.

In George Bush's 2007 State of the Union address, he announced, "It's in our vital interest to diversify America's energy supply [and we] must continue investing in new methods of producing ethanol [to] reduce gasoline usage in the United States by 20% in the next 10 years. [To do it] we must [set] a mandatory fuels [target of] 35 billion gallons of renewable and alternative fuels in 2017 [to] reduce our dependence on foreign oil."

Congress earlier passed the Energy Policy Act of 2005 that mandated ethanol fuel production rise to 4 billion gallons in 2006 and 7.5 billion by 2012. It already reached 6.5 billion barrels last year and is heading for 9 billion this year.

The 2007 Energy Independence and Security Act gave added impetus to the Bush administration scheme with plenty of agribusiness subsidies backing it. Its final version sailed through both Houses in December, and George Bush made it official on December 19. It upped the stakes over 2005 with one of its provisions calling for 36 billion gallons of renewable fuels by 2022 to replace 15% of their equivalent in oil. It represents a nearly fivefold increase from current levels, and new goals ahead may set it higher as rising oil prices (topping $117 a barrel April 21) make a case for cheaper alternatives, and some in the environmental community claim biofuels are eco-friendly.

Hold the applause, and look at the facts. In a nutshell, organic fuels trash rainforests, deplete water reserves, kill off species, and increase greenhouse emissions when the full effects of producing them are included. At least that's what *Science* magazine says on the latter point. It reviewed studies that examined how destruction of natural ecosystems (such as tropical rain forests and South American grasslands) not only releases greenhouse gases when they're burned and plowed but also deprives the planet of natural sponges to absorb carbon emissions. Cropland also absorbs less carbon than rain forests or even the scrubland it replaces.

Nature Conservancy scientist Joseph Fargione (lead author of one study) concluded that grassland clearance releases 93 times the greenhouse gases that would be saved by fuel made annually on that land. For scientists and others concerned about global warming, the research indicated that biofuel production exacerbates the problem and thus should be reconsidered. Others disagree and so far the trend continues with Europe and America both setting ambitious goals that pay little attention to the consequences they ignore.

Eric Holt-Gimenez, executive director of the Food First/Institute for Food and Development Policy, pays close attention and wrote about it in an article published last June by Agencia Latinoamericana de Informacion (ALAI) and thereafter widely distributed. It's headlined "Biofuels: The Five Myths of the Agro-fuels Transition." As he puts it: "The mythic baggage of the agro-fuels transition needs to be publicly unpacked."

1. Agrofuels aren't clean and green. As cited above, they produce far greater greenhouse gas emissions than they save and also require large amounts of oil-based fertilizers that contribute even more.

2. Agrofuel production will be hugely destructive to forests in countries like Brazil where vast Amazon devastation is well documented and is currently increasing at nearly 325,000 hectares a year. By 2020 in Indonesia, "palm oil plantations for bio-diesel [will continue to be] the primary cause of forest loss [in a] country with one of the highest deforestation rates in the world."

3. Agrofuels will destroy rural development. Small farmers will be forced off their land and so will many thousands of others in communities to make way for Big Oil, Agribusiness, and Agribiotech to move in and take over for the huge profits to be extracted in the multi-billions.

4. Agrofuels increase hunger. The poor are always hurt most, the topic is covered above, and Holt-Gimenez quotes another forecast. It's the International Food Policy Research Institute's estimate that basic food staple prices will rise 30–33% by 2010, but that figure already undershoots based on current data. FPRI also sees the rise continuing to 2020 by another 26 to 135% that will be catastrophic for the world's poor who can't afford today's prices and are ill-equipped to raise their incomes more than marginally if at all.

5. Better "second-generation" argofuels aren't around the corner. Examples touted are eco-friendly fast-growing trees and switchgrass (a dominant warm season central North American tallgrass prairie species). Holt-Gimenez calls the argument a "bait and switch-grass shell game" to make the case for first generation production now ongoing. The same environmental problems exists, and they'll be hugely exacerbated by more extensive GMO crop plantings.

Holt-Gimenez sees agrofuels as a "genetic Trojan horse" that's letting agribusiness giants like Monsanto "colonize both our fuel and food system," do little to offset a growing demand for oil, reap huge profits from the scheme, get them at taxpayers' expense, and that's exactly what's happening with Big Oil in on it, too, as a way to diversify through large biofuel investments. More on this below.

The Ghost of Henry Kissinger

Kissinger made a chilling 1970 comment that explains a lot about what's happening now—"Control oil and you control nations; control food and you control the people." Combine it with unchallengeable military power and you control everything, and Kissinger likely said that, too.

He said plenty more in his classified 1974 memo on a secret project called National Security Study Memorandum 200 (NSSM 200) for a "world population plan of action" for drastic global population control. He meant reducing it by hundreds of millions, using food as a weapon, and overall reorganizing the global food market to destroy family farms and replace them with [agribusiness-run] factory ones. It's been ongoing for decades, backed since January 1995 by WTO muscle, and characterized now by huge agribusiness giants with monstrous vertically integrated powers over the food we eat—from research labs to plantings to processing to the supermarket and other food outlet shelves around the world.

But it's even worse than that. Today, five agribusiness behemoths, with little fanfare and enormous government backing, plan big at our expense—to control the world's food supply by making it all genetically engineered with biofuels one part of a larger scheme.

By diverting crops for fuel, prices have exploded, and five "Ag biotech" giants are exploiting it—Monsanto, DuPont, Dow Agrisciences, Syngenta and Bayer CropScience AG. Their solution—make all crops GMO, tout it as a way to increase output and reduce costs, and claim it's the solution to today's soaring prices and world hunger.

In fact, agribusiness power raises prices, controls output to keep them high, and the main factor behind today's situation is the conversion of US farmland to biofuel factories. With less crop output for food and world demand for it growing, prices are rising, and rampant commodity speculation exacerbates the problem with traders profiting hugely and loving it. It's another part of the multi-decade wealth transfer scheme from the world's majority to the elite few. While the trend continues, its momentum is self-sustaining, and it works because governments back it. They subsidize the problem, keep regulations loose, give business free reign, and maintain that markets work best so let them.

As mentioned above, about 43% of US corn output goes for animal feed, but growing amounts are for biofuels—now possibly 25–30% of production compared to around 14% two years ago, up 300% since 2001, and today the total exceeds what's earmarked for export, with no slowing down of this trend in sight. The result, of course, is world grain reserves are falling, prices soaring, millions starving, governments permitting it, and it's only the early innings of a long-term horrifying trend—radically transforming agriculture in humanly destructive ways:

— letting agribusiness and Big Oil giants control it for profit at the expense of consumer health and well-being;
— making it all genetically engineered and inflicting great potential harm to human health; and
— producing reduced crop amounts for food, diverting greater quantities for fuel, allowing prices to soar, making food as dear as oil, ending government's responsibility for food security, and tolerating the unthinkable—putting hundreds of millions of poor around the world in jeopardy and letting them starve to death for profit.

This is the brave new world neoliberal schemers have in mind. They're well along with their plans, marginally diverted by today's economic distress, well aware that growing world protests could prove hugely disruptive, but very focused, nonetheless, on finding clever ways to push ahead with what's worked pretty well for them so far, so they're not about to let human misery jeopardize big profits.

If they won't reform, people have to do it for them, and throughout history that's how it's always worked. Over time, the stakes keep rising as the threats become greater, and today they may be as great as they've ever been.

What better time for a new social movement like those in the past that were pivotal forces for change. Famed community organizer Saul Alinsky knew the way to beat organized money is with organized people. In combination, they've succeeded by taking to the streets, striking, boycotting, challenging authority, disrupting business, paying with their lives and ultimately prevailing by knowing change never comes from the top down. It's always from the grassroots, from the bottom up, and what better time for it than now. It's high time democracy worked for everyone, [so] that destructive GMO and biofuels schemes won't be tolerated, and "America the Beautiful" won't any longer just be for elites and no one else.

Lester Brown → **NO**

The Great Food Crisis of 2011: It's Real and It's Not Going Away Anytime Soon

As the new year begins, the price of wheat is setting an all-time high in the United Kingdom. Food riots are spreading across Algeria. Russia is importing grain to sustain its cattle herds until spring grazing begins. India is wrestling with an 18-percent annual food inflation rate, sparking protests. China is looking abroad for potentially massive quantities of wheat and corn. The Mexican government is buying corn futures to avoid unmanageable tortilla price rises. And on January 5, the U.N. Food and Agricultural organization announced that its food price index for December hit an all-time high.

But whereas in years past, it's been weather that has caused a spike in commodities prices, now it's trends on both sides of the food supply/demand equation that are driving up prices. On the demand side, the culprits are population growth, rising affluence, and the use of grain to fuel cars. On the supply side: soil erosion, aquifer depletion, the loss of cropland to nonfarm uses, the diversion of irrigation water to cities, the plateauing of crop yields in agriculturally advanced countries, and—due to climate change—crop-withering heat waves and melting mountain glaciers and ice sheets. These climate-related trends seem destined to take a far greater toll in the future.

There's at least a glimmer of good news on the demand side: World population growth, which peaked at 2 percent per year around 1970, dropped below 1.2 percent per year in 2010. But because the world population has nearly doubled since 1970, we are still adding 80 million people each year. Tonight, there will be 219,000 additional mouths to feed at the dinner table, and many of them will be greeted with empty plates. Another 219,000 will join us tomorrow night. At some point, this relentless growth begins to tax both the skills of farmers and the limits of the earth's land and water resources.

Beyond population growth, there are now some 3 billion people moving up the food chain, eating greater quantities of grain-intensive livestock and poultry products. The rise in meat, milk, and egg consumption in fast-growing developing countries has no precedent. Total meat consumption in China today is already nearly double that in the United States.

The third major source of demand growth is the use of crops to produce fuel for cars. In the United States, which harvested 416 million tons of grain in 2009, 119 million tons went to ethanol distilleries to produce fuel for cars. That's enough to feed 350 million people for a year. The massive U.S. investment in ethanol distilleries sets the stage for direct competition between cars and people for the world grain harvest. In Europe, where much of the auto fleet runs on diesel fuel, there is growing demand for plant-based diesel oil, principally from rapeseed and palm oil. This demand for oil-bearing crops is not only reducing the land available to produce food crops in Europe, it is also driving the clearing of rainforests in Indonesia and Malaysia for palm oil plantations.

The combined effect of these three growing demands is stunning: a doubling in the annual growth in world grain consumption from an average of 21 million tons per year in 1990–2005 to 41 million tons per year in 2005–2010. Most of this huge jump is attributable to the **orgy of investment** in ethanol distilleries in the United States in 2006–2008.

While the annual demand growth for grain was doubling, new constraints were emerging on the supply side, even as longstanding ones such as soil erosion intensified. An estimated one third of the world's cropland is losing topsoil faster than new soil is forming through natural processes—and thus is losing its inherent productivity. Two huge dust bowls are forming, one across northwest China, western Mongolia, and central Asia; the other in central Africa. Each of these dwarfs the U.S. dust bowl of the 1930s.

Satellite images show a steady flow of dust storms leaving these regions, each one typically carrying millions of tons of precious topsoil. In North China, some 24,000 rural villages have been abandoned or partly depopulated as grasslands have been destroyed by overgrazing and as croplands have been inundated by migrating sand dunes.

In countries with severe soil erosion, such as Mongolia and Lesotho, grain harvests are shrinking as erosion lowers yields and eventually leads to cropland abandonment. The result is spreading hunger and growing dependence on imports. Haiti and North Korea, two countries with severely eroded soils, are chronically dependent on food aid from abroad.

Meanwhile, aquifer depletion is fast shrinking the amount of irrigated area in many parts of the world; this relatively recent phenomenon is driven by the large-scale use of mechanical pumps to exploit underground water. Today, half the world's people live in countries where water tables are falling as overpumping depletes aquifers. Once an aquifer is depleted, pumping is necessarily reduced to the rate of recharge unless it is a fossil (nonreplenishable) aquifer, in which case pumping ends altogether. But sooner or later, falling water tables translate into rising food prices.

Irrigated area is shrinking in the Middle East, notably in Saudi Arabia, Syria, Iraq, and possibly Yemen. In Saudi Arabia, which was totally dependent on a now-depleted fossil aquifer for its wheat self-sufficiency, production is in a freefall. From 2007 to 2010, Saudi wheat production fell by more than two thirds. By 2012, wheat production will likely end entirely, leaving the country totally dependent on imported grain.

The Arab Middle East is the first geographic region where spreading water shortages are shrinking the grain harvest. But the really big water deficits are in India, where the World Bank numbers indicate that 175 million people are being fed with grain that is produced by overpumping. In China, over-pumping provides food for some 130 million people. In the United States, the world's other leading grain producer, irrigated area is shrinking in key agricultural states such as California and Texas.

The last decade has witnessed the emergence of yet another constraint on growth in global agricultural productivity: the shrinking backlog of untapped technologies. In some agriculturally advanced countries, farmers are using all available technologies to raise yields. In Japan, the first country to see a sustained rise in grain yield per acre, rice yields have been flat now for 14 years. Rice yields in South Korea and China are now approaching those in Japan. Assuming that farmers in these two countries will face the same constraints as those in Japan, more than a third of the world rice harvest will soon be produced in countries with little potential for further raising rice yields.

A similar situation is emerging with wheat yields in Europe. In France, Germany, and the United Kingdom, wheat yields are no longer rising at all. These three countries together account for roughly one-eighth of the world wheat harvest. Another trend slowing the growth in the world grain harvest is the conversion of cropland to nonfarm uses. Suburban sprawl, industrial construction, and the paving of land for roads, highways, and parking lots are claiming cropland in the Central Valley of California, the Nile River basin in Egypt, and in densely populated countries that are rapidly industrializing, such as China and India. In 2011, new car sales in China are projected to reach 20 million—a record for any country. The U.S. rule of thumb is that for every 5 million cars added to a country's fleet, roughly 1 million acres must be paved to accommodate them. And cropland is often the loser.

Fast-growing cities are also competing with farmers for irrigation water. In areas where all water is being spoken for, such as most countries in the Middle East, northern China, the southwestern United States, and most of India, diverting water to cities means less irrigation water available for food production. California has lost perhaps a million acres of irrigated land in recent years as farmers have sold huge amounts of water to the thirsty millions in Los Angeles and San Diego.

The rising temperature is also making it more difficult to expand the world grain harvest fast enough to keep up with the record pace of demand. Crop ecologists have their own rule of thumb: For each 1 degree Celsius rise in temperature above the optimum during the growing season, we can expect a 10 percent decline in grain yields. This temperature effect on yields was all too visible in western Russia during the summer of 2010 as the harvest was decimated when temperatures soared far above the norm.

Another emerging trend that threatens food security is the melting of mountain glaciers. This is of particular concern in the Himalayas and on the Tibetan plateau, where the ice melt from glaciers helps sustain not only the major rivers of Asia during the dry season, such as the Indus, Ganges, Mekong, Yangtze, and Yellow rivers, but also the irrigation systems dependent on these rivers. Without this ice melt, the grain harvest would drop precipitously and prices would rise accordingly.

And finally, over the longer term, melting ice sheets in Greenland and West Antarctica, combined with thermal expansion of the oceans, threaten to raise the sea level by up to six feet during this century. Even a three-foot rise would inundate half of the riceland in Bangladesh. It would also put under water much of the Mekong Delta that produces half the rice in Vietnam, the world's number two rice exporter. Altogether there are some 19 other rice-growing river deltas in Asia where harvests would be substantially reduced by a rising sea level.

The current surge in world grain and soybean prices, and in food prices more broadly, is not a temporary phenomenon. We can no longer expect that things will soon return to normal, because in a world with a rapidly changing climate system there is no norm to return to.

The unrest of these past few weeks is just the beginning. It is no longer conflict between heavily armed superpowers, but rather spreading food shortages and rising food prices—and the political turmoil this would lead to—that threatens our global future. Unless governments quickly redefine security and shift expenditures from military uses to investing in climate change mitigation, water efficiency, soil conservation, and population stabilization, the world will in all likelihood be facing a future with both more climate instability and food price volatility. If business as usual continues, food prices will only trend upward.

EXPLORING THE ISSUE

Will the World Be Able to Feed Itself in the Foreseeable Future?

Critical Thinking and Reflection

1. Are the factors leading to the first global food crisis in the early 1970s still relevant today?
2. Does the picture of overfed people in the developed world juxtaposed against starving individuals in the developing world capture the essence of the food problem or is it misleading in any way(s)?
3. Is the recent global food crisis really a global food costs crisis?
4. What effect will economic development in the poorer regions of the globe have on the capacity of the future world to feed itself?
5. Is it realistic to think that people will unilaterally choose to become self-sufficient (grow their own food) and practice better food anti-waste patterns of behavior?

Is There Common Ground?

Analysts are in agreement that increased population and increased affluence among the currently less-affluent peoples of the world will increase the demand for food in the next 50 years. There is also significant agreement that enough food is currently produced but that the distribution system is flawed for whatever reason. Although most allude to the effect of high food prices, there is more disagreement on the cause(s) of the higher prices.

Additional Resources

Bread for the World Institute, *Hunger 2009: Global Development Charting a New Course, 19th Annual Report on the State of the World* (Bread for the World Institute, 2009)

> This report presents a somewhat optimistic viewpoint about future food prospects.

Clapp, Jennifer (ed.), *Global Food Crisis: The Governance Challenges and Opportunities* (Wilfrid Laurier University Press, 2009)

> Policymakers and scholars examine the causes and consequences of the recent food price crisis, looking at governance challenges and opportunities.

Cribb, Julian, *The Coming Famine: The Global Food Crisis and What We Can Do to Avoid It* (University of California Press, 2010)

> The author describes the confluence of a number of shortages—water, land, energy, technology, and knowledge—that will constrain the world's ability to address future increased demand for food.

Food and Agricultural Organization, "The State of Food Security in the World 2006," (United Nations, 2006)

> This report lays out an argument for a more optimistic scenario for the twenty-first century. The report suggests that future demand will be met in three ways: (1) tapping into adequate potential farmland, (2) increasing the rate of irrigation, and (3) acquiring higher yield levels due to improved technology.

Fraser, Evan D. G. and Rimas, Andrew, *Empires of Food: Feast, Famine, and the Rise and Fall of Civilizations* (Free Press, 2010)

> This book describes the history of food's role in the rise and fall of civilizations. It emphasizes today's negative impact of climate change, rising fuel costs, and a shrinking agricultural frontier on food availability, and argues the importance of global food systems.

Headley, Derek, *Reflections on the Global Food Crisis: How Did It Happen? How Has It Hurt? And How Can We Prevent the Next One?* (International Food Policy Research Institute, 2010)

> This book examines the 2008 food crisis, blaming it on rising energy prices, growing demand for biofuels, the U.S. dollar depreciation, and various trade stocks.

Himmelgreen, David, *NAPA Bulletin, Number 32, The Global Food Crisis: New Insights into an Age-Old Problem* (Wiley-Blackwell, 2010)

> The book focuses on ways in which anthropology can be used to address the global food crisis.

Holt-Gimenez, Eric and Patel, Raj, *Food Rebellions!: Forging Food Sovereignty to Solve the Global Food Crisis* (Pambazuka Press, 2009)

> This study of the global food crisis focuses on the underdeveloped world and underserved communities in the developed world. It argues that the erosion of local control over food systems has made countries dependent on the "volatile global market."

Karrer, Linda, *Global Food Crisis: A Critical Analysis* (VDM Verlag, 2010)

> This book describes the 2008 food crisis, the short-term policies to address this crisis, and longer term policy recommendations. The essential argument is that the global food crisis is really a global food price crisis.

Patel, Raj, *Stuffed and Starved: The Hidden Battle for the World Food System* (Melville House, 2008)

> The author describes the imbalance of the world food situation, with an epidemic of obesity in some parts and starvation in other areas.

Roberts, Paul, *The End of Food* (Houghton Mifflin Harcourt, 2008)

> The book uses a variety of interesting case narratives to describe flaws in the global food system.

Rosin, Christopher et al., *Food Systems Failure: The Global Food Crisis and the Future of Agriculture* (Earthscan, 2011)

> This book describes the current food crisis, focusing on contradictions in policy and practice that prevent solutions.

Is the Threat of Global Warming Real?

YES: Bill McKibben, from "Think Again: Climate Change," *Foreign Policy* (January/February 2009)

NO: Richard Lindzen, from "A Case Against Precipitous Climate Action," *Global Warming Foundation* (January 15, 2011)

Learning Outcomes

After reading this issue, you should be able to:

- Gain an understanding of the extent to which scientists are divided on the issue of global warming.
- Describe the debate over the extent to which the globe is currently becoming warmer.
- Describe why some believe that global warming alarmists have agendas to exploit the issue.
- Understand the argument that climate change helps as many as it hurts.
- Understand the position that climate change is really much more than an environmental problem for countries trying to deal with its potential consequences.

ISSUE SUMMARY

YES: Bill McKibben, author of numerous books on ecological issues, addresses seven myths about climate change, arguing that the global community must act now if it is to save the earth from a climate catastrophe.

NO: Richard Lindzen, Alfred P. Sloan professor of meteorology at MIT, cautions us not to act too hastily in addressing assumed climate change as the evidence does not support such a conclusion or the need for hysteria.

The issue of global warming is to the current era what acid rain was to the 1970s. Just as the blighted trees and polluted lakes of Scandinavia captured the hearts of the then newly emerging group of environmentalists, the issue of global warming has been front page news for more than a decade and fodder for environmentalists and policymakers everywhere. Library citations abound, making it the most often written about global issue today. Web sites pop up, public interest groups emerge, and scientists and nonscientists pick up the rallying cry for one side or another. "Googling" the words "global warming" on the Internet yields many millions in responses.

Both sides of the issue can find a substantial number of scientists, measured in the thousands, to support their case that the Earth is or is not warming. Both sides can find hundreds of experts who will attest that the warming is either a cyclical phenomenon or the consequence of human behavior. Both sides can find a substantial number of policymakers and policy observers who will say that the Kyoto Treaty is humankind's best hope to reverse the global warming trend or that the treaty is seriously flawed with substantial negative consequences for the United States. It is an issue whose debate heats up on occasion as the international community grapples with answers to the various disagreements summarized previously. Finally, it is an issue whose potential solutions on the table will impact different sectors of the economy and different countries differently.

In December 2007, the Intergovernmental Panel on Climate Change (IPCC), and former U.S. vice president Al Gore were jointly awarded the Nobel Peace Prize for their work "to build up and disseminate greater knowledge about man-made climate change, and to lay the foundations for measures" to counteract such change. Critics of global warming were quick to respond, accusing the Nobel peace committee of having a liberal bias. This award was the culmination of a story that began 15 years earlier at the UN-sponsored Earth Summit in Rio de Janeiro in 1992, when a global climate treaty was signed. According to S. Fred Singer, in *Hot Talks, Cold Science: Global Warming's Unfinished Debate* (Independent Institute, 1998), the treaty rested on three basic assumptions. First, global warming has been detected in the records of climate of the last 100 years. Second, a substantial warming in the future will produce catastrophic consequences— droughts, floods, storms, a rapid and significant rise in sea level, agricultural collapse, and the spread of tropical disease. And third, the scientific and policy-making communities know (1) which atmospheric concentrations of greenhouse gases are dangerous and which ones are not, (2) that drastic reductions of carbon dioxide (CO_2) emissions as well as energy use in general by industrialized countries will stabilize CO_2 concentrations at close to current levels, and (3) that such economically damaging measures can be justified politically despite no significant scientific support for global warming as a threat.

Since the Earth Summit, it appears that scientists have opted for placement into one of the three camps. The first camp buys into the three assumptions outlined previously. In late 1995, 2500 leading climate scientists announced in the first IPCC report that the planet was warming due to coal and gas emissions.

Scientists in a second camp suggest that although global warming has occurred and continues at the present, the source of such temperature rise cannot be ascertained yet. The conclusions of the Earth Summit were misunderstood by many in the scientific community, the second camp would suggest. For these scientists, computer models, the basis of much evidence for the first group, have not yet linked global warming to human activities.

A third group of scientists, representing a minority, argues that we cannot be certain that global warming is taking place, yet alone determine its cause. They present a number of arguments in support of their position. Among them is the contention that presatellite data (pre-1979) showing a century-long pattern of warming is an illusion because satellite data (post-1979) reveal no such warming. Furthermore, when warming was present, it did not occur at the same time as a rise in greenhouse gases. Scientists in the third camp are also skeptical of studying global warming in the laboratory. They suggest, moreover, that most of the scientists who have opted for one of the first two camps have done so as a consequence of laboratory experiments, rather than of evidence from the real world.

Despite what some believe to be wide differences in scientific thinking about the existence of global warming and its origins, the global community has moved forward with attempts to achieve consensus among the nations of the world for taking appropriate action to curtail human activities thought to affect warming. A 1997 international meeting in Kyoto, Japan, concluded with an agreement for reaching goals established at the earlier Earth Summit. Thirty-eight industrialized countries, including the United States, agreed to reduction levels outlined in the treaty. However, the U.S. Senate never ratified the treaty, and the Bush Administration decided not to support it. Nonetheless, the two basic criteria for going into effect—the required number of countries (55) with the required levels of carbon dioxide's emissions (55 percent of CO_2 emissions from developed countries) must sign the treaty—were met when Russia ratified the treaty on November 18, 2004. The treaty went into effect on February 19, 2005. In the 2007 IPCC report (fourth in the series of IPCC reports), more than 2500 scientists reaffirmed the existence of global warming. The report suggests that among the risks are warming temperatures, heat waves, heavy rains, drought, stronger storms, decreased biodiversity, and sea level rise.

And yet, there are loud voices in the scientific community and the media against the two basic premises about global warming or, more recently, climate change as most are now beginning to call the phenomenon associated with changing global temperatures. On the one hand are scientists who eagerly seek various forums to articulate their dissenting minority voice against what appears to be a larger consensus. One particular scientific voice is Richard Lindzen, MIT-endowed professor of meteorology and contributor of the NO article in this issue. Contributing by printed word, in speech in public gatherings, and in testimony before the American government, Lindzen has painstakingly provided evidence in support of his claims. A second type of voice is found among conservative politicians who argue against government expenditures for combating the climate phenomena. The current attempt of American conservative legislators to defund the Environmental Protection Agency is an example of this second type of activist. Finally, there are the public print media who use their forum, Internet or print journalism, to argue against rushing to judgment on the global warming issue. The literature is replete with individuals who use public modes of communication to fight who they believe to be global warming alarmists.

A typical example is Paul MacRae, a Canadian journalist who is now a professor at the University of Victoria. His book, *False Alarm: Global Warming— Facts Versus Fears* (Spring Bay Press, 2010), contains the following eye-catching phrase across the cover: "Why Almost Everything We've Been Told About Global Warming is Misleading, Exaggerated, or Just Plain Wrong." The back cover outlines some of the book's contents, using an alarmists' claim versus fact point/counterpoint. For example, alarmists claim the planet is warming, but MacRae counters with "The planet hasn't warmed since the late 1990s." Or, alarmists claim that today's warming is unprecedented but MacRae counters with "The planet has been warmer at least four times in the past 7,000 years." Alarmists claim that higher temperatures and CO_2 levels will cause oblivion, but MacRae counters with for "90% of the past 600 million years, temperatures and CO_2 levels have been higher than today's and sometimes much higher." Alarmists claim that more carbon omissions will accelerate global warming, but MacRae counters that "The more CO_2 in the air, the less warming effect it has per unit." And finally, alarmists claim that human carbon emissions will cause the oceans to rise at least 20 feet, but MacRae counters that "During previous interglacials sea levels also rose this high and even higher . . . and [it] is natural and will occur no matter what humans do or don't do."

On the other side are equally strong statements about global warming. A recent National Oceanic and Atmospheric Administration (NOAA) report revealed that data on 10 key climate indicators all lead to the same conclusion: "the scientific evidence that our world is warming is unmistakable." More than 300 scientists from 160 research groups in 48 countries participated in the study. The report indicates that for the first time in history, human society will function under a new set of climate conditions taking shape. Seven of the 10 indicators are rising: "air temperatures over land, sea-surface temperature, air temperature over oceans, sea level, ocean heat, humidity and troposphere temperature in the 'active-weather' layer of the atmosphere closest to the Earth's surface. Three indicators are declining: Arctic sea ice, glaciers and spring snow cover in the Northern hemisphere."

Although the debate has centered around the existence of global warming, an alternative argument is the debate over the role humans have played in his process. This is equally important in influencing the decision of government to get involved and in what fashion.

The YES selection by Bill McKibben attacks seven myths about global warming and argues for immediate government action if the planet is to be saved. In the NO selection, Richard Lindzen continues his anti–global warming message with the thought that serious leaders "need to courageously resist hysteria."

YES ↵   **Bill McKibben**

Think Again: Climate Change

"Scientists Are Divided"

No, they're not. In the early years of the global warming debate, there was great controversy over whether the planet was warming, whether humans were the cause, and whether it would be a significant problem. That debate is long since over. Although the details of future forecasts remain unclear, there's no serious question about the general shape of what's to come.

Every national academy of science, long lists of Nobel laureates, and in recent years even the science advisors of President George W. Bush have agreed that we are heating the planet. Indeed, there is a more thorough scientific process here than on almost any other issue: Two decades ago, the United Nations formed the Intergovernmental Panel on Climate Change (IPCC) and charged its scientists with synthesizing the peer-reviewed science and developing broad-based conclusions. The reports have found since 1995 that warming is dangerous and caused by humans. The panel's most recent report, in November 2007, found it is "very likely" (defined as more than 90 percent certain, or about as certain as science gets) that heat-trapping emissions from human activities have caused "most of the observed increase in global average temperatures since the mid-20th century."

If anything, many scientists now think that the IPCC has been too conservative—both because member countries must sign off on the conclusions and because there's a time lag. Its last report synthesized data from the early part of the decade, not the latest scary results, such as what we're now seeing in the Arctic.

In the summer of 2007, ice in the Arctic Ocean melted. It melts a little every summer, of course, but this time was different—by late September, there was 25 percent less ice than ever measured before. And it wasn't a one-time accident. By the end of the summer season in 2008, so much ice had melted that both the Northwest and Northeast passages were open. In other words, you could circumnavigate the Arctic on open water. The computer models, which are just a few years old, said this shouldn't have happened until sometime late in the 21st century. Even skeptics can't dispute such alarming events.

"We Have Time"

Wrong. Time might be the toughest part of the equation. That melting Arctic ice is unsettling not only because it proves the planet is warming rapidly, but also because it will help speed up the warming. That old white ice reflected 80 percent of incoming solar radiation back to space; the new blue water left behind absorbs 80 percent of that sunshine. The process amps up. And there are many other such feedback loops. Another occurs as northern permafrost thaws. Huge amounts of methane long trapped below the ice begin to escape into the atmosphere; methane is an even more potent greenhouse gas than carbon dioxide.

Such examples are the biggest reason why many experts are now fast-forwarding their estimates of how quickly we must shift away from fossil fuel. Indian economist Rajendra Pachauri, who accepted the 2007 Nobel Peace Prize alongside Al Gore on behalf of the IPCC, said recently that we must begin to make fundamental reforms by 2012 or watch the climate system spin out of control; NASA scientist James Hansen, who was the first to blow the whistle on climate change in the late 1980s, has said that we must stop burning coal by 2030. Period.

All of which makes the Copenhagen climate change talks that are set to take place in December 2009 more urgent than they appeared a few years ago. At issue is a seemingly small number: the level of carbon dioxide in the air. Hansen argues that 350 parts per million is the highest level we can maintain "if humanity wishes to preserve a planet similar to that on which civilization developed and to which life on Earth is adapted." But because we're already past that mark—the air outside is currently about 387 parts per million and growing by about 2 parts annually—global warming suddenly feels less like a huge problem, and more like an Oh-My-God Emergency.

"Climate Change Will Help as Many Places as It Hurts"

Wishful thinking. For a long time, the winners-and-losers calculus was pretty standard: Though climate change will cause some parts of the planet to flood or shrivel up, other frigid, rainy regions would at least get some warmer days every year. Or so the thinking went. But more recently, models have begun to show that after a certain point almost everyone on the planet will suffer. Crops might be easier to grow in some places for a few decades as the danger of frost recedes, but over time the threat of heat stress and drought will almost certainly be stronger.

A 2003 report commissioned by the Pentagon forecasts the possibility of violent storms across Europe, megadroughts across the Southwest United States and Mexico, and unpredictable monsoons causing food shortages in China. "Envision Pakistan, India, and China—all armed with nuclear weapons—skirmishing at their borders over refugees, access to shared rivers, and arable land," the report warned. Or Spain and Portugal "fighting over fishing rights—leading to conflicts at sea."

Of course, there are a few places we used to think of as possible winners—mostly the far north, where Canada and Russia could theoretically produce more grain with longer growing seasons, or perhaps explore for oil beneath the newly melted Arctic ice cap. But even those places will have to deal with expensive consequences—a real military race across the high Arctic, for instance.

Want more bad news? Here's how that Pentagon report's scenario played out: As the planet's carrying capacity shrinks, an ancient pattern of desperate, all-out wars over food, water, and energy supplies would reemerge. The report refers to the work of Harvard archaeologist Steven LeBlanc, who notes that wars over resources were the norm until about three centuries ago. When such conflicts broke out, 25 percent of a population's adult males usually died. As abrupt climate change hits home, warfare may again come to define human life. Set against that bleak backdrop, the potential upside of a few longer growing seasons in Vladivostok doesn't seem like an even trade.

"It's China's Fault"

Not so much. China is an easy target to blame for the climate crisis. In the midst of its industrial revolution, China has overtaken the United States as the world's biggest carbon dioxide producer. And everyone has read about the one-a-week pace of power plant construction there. But those numbers are misleading, and not just because a lot of that carbon dioxide was emitted to build products for the West to consume. Rather, it's because China has four times the population of the United States, and per capita is really the only way to think about these emissions. And by that standard, each Chinese person now emits just over a quarter of the carbon dioxide that each American does. Not only that, but carbon dioxide lives in the atmosphere for more than a century. China has been at it in a big way less than 20 years, so it will be many, many years before the Chinese are as responsible for global warming as Americans.

What's more, unlike many of their counterparts in the United States, Chinese officials have begun a concerted effort to reduce emissions in the midst of their country's staggering growth. China now leads the world in the deployment of renewable energy, and there's barely a car made in the United States that can meet China's much tougher fuel-economy standards.

For its part, the United States must develop a plan to cut emissions—something that has eluded Americans for the entire two-decade history of the problem. Although the U.S. Senate voted down the last such attempt, Barack Obama has promised that it will be a priority in his administration. He favors some variation of a "cap and trade" plan that would limit the total amount of carbon dioxide the United States could release, thus putting a price on what has until now been free.

Despite the rapid industrialization of countries such as China and India, and the careless neglect of rich ones such as the United States, climate change is neither any one country's fault, nor any one country's responsibility. It will require sacrifice from everyone. Just as the Chinese might have to use somewhat more expensive power to protect the global environment, Americans will have to pay some of the difference in price, even if just in technology.

Call it a Marshall Plan for the environment. Such a plan makes eminent moral and practical sense and could probably be structured so as to bolster emerging green energy industries in the West. But asking Americans to pay to put up windmills in China will be a hard political sell in a country that already thinks China is prospering at its expense. It could be the biggest test of the country's political maturity in many years.

"Climate Change Is an Environmental Problem"

Not really. Environmentalists were the first to sound the alarm. But carbon dioxide is not like traditional pollution. There's no Clean Air Act that can solve it. We must make a fundamental transformation in the most important part of our economies, shifting away from fossil fuels and on to something else. That means, for the United States, it's at least as much a problem for the Commerce and Treasury departments as it is for the Environmental Protection Agency.

And because every country on Earth will have to coordinate, it's far and away the biggest foreign-policy issue we face. (You were thinking terrorism? It's hard to figure out a scenario in which Osama bin Laden destroys Western civilization. It's easy to figure out how it happens with a rising sea level and a wrecked hydrological cycle.)

Expecting the environmental movement to lead this fight is like asking the USDA to wage the war in Iraq. It's not equipped for this kind of battle. It may be ready to save Alaska's Arctic National Wildlife Refuge, which is a noble undertaking but on a far smaller scale. Unless climate change is quickly de-ghettoized, the chances of making a real difference are small.

"Solving It Will Be Painful"

It depends. What's your definition of painful? On the one hand, you're talking about transforming the backbone of the world's industrial and consumer system. That's certainly expensive. On the other hand, say you manage to convert a lot of it to solar or wind power—think of the money you'd save on fuel.

And then there's the growing realization that we don't have many other possible sources for the economic growth we'll need to pull ourselves out of our current economic crisis. Luckily, green energy should be bigger than IT and biotech combined.

Almost from the moment scientists began studying the problem of climate change, people have been trying to estimate the costs of solving it. The real answer, though, is that it's such a huge transformation that no one really knows for sure. The bottom line is, the growth rate in energy use worldwide could be cut in half during the next 15 years and the steps would, net, save more money than they cost. The IPCC included a cost estimate in its latest five-year update on climate change and looked a little further into the future. It found that an attempt to keep carbon levels below about 500 parts per million would shave a little bit off the world's economic growth—but only a little. As in, the world would have to wait until Thanksgiving 2030 to be as rich as it would have been on January 1 of that year. And in return, it would have a much-transformed energy system.

Unfortunately though, those estimates are probably too optimistic. For one thing, in the years since they were published, the science has grown darker. Deeper and quicker cuts now seem mandatory.

But so far we've just been counting the costs of fixing the system. What about the cost of doing nothing? Nicholas Stern, a renowned economist commissioned by the British government to study the question, concluded that the costs of climate change could eventually reach the combined costs of both world wars and the Great Depression. In 2003, Swiss Re, the world's biggest reinsurance company, and Harvard Medical School explained why global warming would be so expensive. It's not just the infrastructure, such as sea walls against rising oceans, for example. It's also that the increased costs of natural disasters begin to compound. The diminishing time between monster storms in places such as the U.S. Gulf Coast could eventually mean that parts of "developed countries would experience developing nation conditions for prolonged periods." Quite simply, we've already done too much damage and waited too long to have any easy options left.

"We Can Reverse Climate Change"

If only. Solving this crisis is no longer an option. Human beings have already raised the temperature of the planet about a degree Fahrenheit. When people first began to focus on global warming (which is, remember, only 20 years ago), the general consensus was that at this point we'd just be standing on the threshold of realizing its consequences—that the big changes would be a degree or two and hence several decades down the road. But scientists seem to have systematically underestimated just how delicate the balance of the planet's physical systems really is.

The warming is happening faster than we expected, and the results are more widespread and more disturbing. Even that rise of 1 degree has seriously perturbed hydrological cycles: Because warm air holds more water vapor than cold air does, both droughts and floods are increasing dramatically. Just look at the record levels of insurance payouts, for instance. Mosquitoes, able to survive in new places, are spreading more malaria and dengue. Coral reefs are dying, and so are vast stretches of forest.

None of that is going to stop, even if we do everything right from here on out. Given the time lag between when we emit carbon and when the air heats up, we're already guaranteed at least another degree of warming.

The only question now is whether we're going to hold off catastrophe. It won't be easy, because the scientific consensus calls for roughly 5 degrees more warming this century unless we do just about everything right. And if our behavior up until now is any indication, we won't.

Richard Lindzen ⟶ **NO**

A Case Against Precipitous Climate Action

The notion of a static, unchanging climate is foreign to the history of the earth or any other planet with a fluid envelope. The fact that the developed world went into hysterics over changes in global mean temperature anomaly of a few tenths of a degree will astound future generations. Such hysteria simply represents the scientific illiteracy of much of the public, the susceptibility of the public to the substitution of repetition for truth, and the exploitation of these weaknesses by politicians, environmental promoters, and, after 20 years of media drum beating, many others as well. Climate is always changing. We have had ice ages and warmer periods when alligators were found in Spitzbergen. Ice ages have occurred in a hundred thousand year cycle for the last 700 thousand years, and there have been previous periods that appear to have been warmer than the present despite CO_2 levels being lower than they are now. More recently, we have had the medieval warm period and the little ice age. During the latter, alpine glaciers advanced to the chagrin of overrun villages. Since the beginning of the 19th century these glaciers have been retreating. Frankly, we don't fully understand either the advance or the retreat.

For small changes in climate associated with tenths of a degree, there is no need for any external cause. The earth is never exactly in equilibrium. The motions of the massive oceans where heat is moved between deep layers and the surface provides variability on time scales from years to centuries. Recent work (Tsonis et al., 2007), suggests that this variability is enough to account for all climate change since the 19th century.

For warming since 1979, there is a further problem. The dominant role of cumulus convection in the tropics requires that temperature approximately follow what is called a moist adiabatic profile. This requires that warming in the tropical upper troposphere be 2–3 times greater than at the surface. Indeed, all models do show this, but the data doesn't and this means that something is wrong with the data. It is well known that above about 2 km altitude, the tropical temperatures are pretty homogeneous in the horizontal so that sampling is not a problem. Below two km (roughly the height of what is referred to as the trade wind inversion), there is much more horizontal variability, and, therefore, there is a profound sampling problem. Under the circumstances, it is reasonable to conclude that the problem resides in the surface data, and that the actual trend at the surface is about 60% too large. Even the claimed trend is larger than what models would have projected but for the inclusion of an arbitrary fudge factor due to aerosol cooling. The discrepancy was reported by Lindzen (2007) and by Douglass et al. (2007). Inevitably in climate science, when data conflicts with models, a small coterie of scientists can be counted upon to modify the data. Thus, Santer et al. (2008), argue that stretching uncertainties in observations and models might marginally eliminate the inconsistency. That the data should always need correcting to agree with models is totally implausible and indicative of a certain corruption within the climate science community.

It turns out that there is a much more fundamental and unambiguous check of the role of feedbacks in enhancing greenhouse warming that also shows that all models are greatly exaggerating climate sensitivity. Here, it must be noted that the greenhouse effect operates by inhibiting the cooling of the climate by reducing net outgoing radiation. However, the contribution of increasing CO_2 alone does not, in fact, lead to much warming (approximately 1 deg. C for each doubling of CO_2).

The larger predictions from climate models are due to the fact that, within these models, the more important greenhouse substances, water vapor and clouds, act to greatly amplify whatever CO_2 does. This is referred to as a positive feedback. It means that increases in surface temperature are accompanied by reductions in the net outgoing radiation—thus enhancing the greenhouse warming. All climate models show such changes when forced by observed surface temperatures. Satellite observations of the earth's radiation budget al.low us to determine whether such a reduction does, in fact, accompany increases in surface temperature in nature. As it turns out, the satellite data from the ERBE instrument (Barkstrom, 1984, Wong et al., 2006) shows that the feedback in nature is strongly negative—strongly reducing the direct effect of CO_2 (Lindzen and Choi, 2009) in profound contrast to the model behavior. This analysis makes clear that even when all models agree, they can all be wrong, and that this is the situation for the all important question of climate sensitivity. Unfortunately, Lindzen and Choi (2009) contained a number of errors; however, as shown in a paper currently under review, these errors were not relevant to the main conclusion.

According to the UN's Intergovernmental Panel on Climate Change, the greenhouse forcing from man made greenhouse gases is already about 86% of what one expects from a doubling of CO_2 (with about half coming from methane, nitrous oxide, freons and ozone), and alarming predictions depend on models for which the sensitivity to a doubling for CO_2 is greater than 2C which implies that we should already have seen much more warming than we have seen thus far, even if all the warming we have seen so far were due to man. This contradiction is rendered more acute by the fact that there has been no statistically significant net global warming for the last fourteen years. Modelers defend this situation, as we have already noted, by arguing that aerosols have cancelled much of the warming (viz Schwartz et al., 2010), and that models adequately account for natural unforced internal variability. However, a recent paper (Ramanathan, 2007) points out that aerosols can warm as well as cool, while scientists at the UK's Hadley Centre for Climate Research recently noted that their model did not appropriately deal with natural internal variability thus demolishing the basis for the IPCC's iconic attribution (Smith et al., 2007). Interestingly (though not unexpectedly), the British paper did not stress this. Rather, they speculated that natural internal variability might step aside in 2009, allowing warming to resume. Resume? Thus, the fact that warming has ceased for the past fourteen years is acknowledged. It should be noted that, more recently, German modelers have moved the date for 'resumption' up to 2015 (Keenlyside et al., 2008).

Climate alarmists respond that some of the hottest years on record have occurred during the past decade. Given that we are in a relatively warm period, this is not surprising, but it says nothing about trends.

Given that the evidence (and I have noted only a few of many pieces of evidence) strongly implies that anthropogenic warming has been greatly exaggerated, the basis for alarm due to such warming is similarly diminished. However, a really important point is that the case for alarm would still be weak even if anthropogenic global warming were significant. Polar bears, arctic summer sea ice, regional droughts and floods, coral bleaching, hurricanes, alpine glaciers, malaria, etc. all depend not on some global average of surface temperature anomaly, but on a huge number of regional variables including temperature, humidity, cloud cover, precipitation, and direction and magnitude of wind. The state of the ocean is also often crucial. Our ability to forecast any of these over periods beyond a few days is minimal (a leading modeler refers to it as essentially guesswork). Yet, each catastrophic forecast depends on each of these being in a specific range. The odds of any specific catastrophe actually occurring are almost zero. This was equally true for earlier forecasts of famine for the 1980's, global cooling in the 1970's, Y2K and many others. Regionally, year to year fluctuations in temperature are over four times larger than fluctuations in the global mean. Much of this variation has to be independent of the global mean; otherwise the global mean would vary much more. This is simply to note that factors other than global warming are more important to any specific situation. This is not to say that disasters will not occur; they always have occurred and this will not change in the future. Fighting global warming with symbolic gestures will certainly not change this. However, history tells us that greater wealth and development can profoundly increase our resilience.

In view of the above, one may reasonably ask why there is the current alarm, and, in particular, why the astounding upsurge in alarmism of the past 4 years. When an issue like global warming is around for over twenty years, numerous agendas are developed to exploit the issue. The interests of the environmental movement in acquiring more power, influence, and donations are reasonably clear. So too are the interests of bureaucrats for whom control of CO_2 is a dream-come-true. After all, CO_2 is a product of breathing itself. Politicians can see the possibility of taxation that will be cheerfully accepted because it is necessary for 'saving' the earth. Nations have seen how to exploit this issue in order to gain competitive advantages. But, by now, things have gone much further. The case of ENRON (a now bankrupt Texas energy firm) is illustrative in this respect. Before disintegrating in a pyrotechnic display of unscrupulous manipulation, ENRON had been one of the most intense lobbyists for Kyoto. It had hoped to become a trading firm dealing in carbon emission rights. This was no small hope. These rights are likely to amount to over a trillion dollars, and the commissions will run into many billions. Hedge funds are actively examining the possibilities; so was the late Lehman Brothers. Goldman Sachs has lobbied extensively for the 'cap and trade' bill, and is well positioned to make billions. It is probably no accident that Gore, himself, is associated with such activities. The sale of indulgences is already in full swing with organizations selling offsets to one's carbon footprint while sometimes acknowledging that the offsets are irrelevant. The possibilities for corruption are immense. Archer Daniels Midland (America's largest agribusiness) has successfully lobbied for ethanol requirements for gasoline, and the resulting demand for ethanol may already be contributing to large increases in corn prices and associated hardship in the developing world (not to mention poorer car performance). And finally, there are the numerous well meaning individuals who have allowed propagandists to convince them that in accepting the alarmist view of anthropogenic climate change, they are displaying intelligence and virtue. For them, their psychic welfare is at stake.

With all this at stake, one can readily suspect that there might be a sense of urgency provoked by the possibility that warming may have ceased and that the case for such warming as was seen being due in significant measure to man, disintegrating. For those committed to the more venal agendas, the need to act soon, before the public appreciates the situation, is real indeed. However, for more serious leaders, the need to courageously resist hysteria is clear. Wasting resources on symbolically fighting ever present climate change is no substitute for prudence. Nor is the assumption that the earth's climate reached a point of perfection in the middle of the twentieth century a sign of intelligence.

References

Barkstrom, B.R., 1984: The Earth Radiation Budget Experiment (ERBE), Bull. Amer. Meteor. Soc., 65, 1170–1185)

Douglass, D.H., J.R. Christy, B.D. Pearsona and S. F. Singer, 2007: A comparison of tropical temperature trends with model predictions, Int. J. Climatol., DOI: 10.1002/joc.1651

Keenlyside, N.S., M. Lateef, et al., 2008: Advancing decadal-scale climate prediction in the North Atlantic sector, Nature, 453, 84–88.

Lindzen, R.S. and Y.-S. Choi, 2009: On the determination of climate feedbacks from ERBE data, accepted Geophys. Res. Ltrs.

Lindzen, R.S., 2007: Taking greenhouse warming seriously. Energy & Environment, 18, 937–950.

Ramanathan, V., M.V. Ramana, et al., 2007: Warming trends in Asia amplified by brown cloud solar absorption, Nature, 448, 575–578.

Santer, B. D., P. W. Thorne, L. Haimberger, K. E. Taylor, T. M. L. Wigley, J. R. Lanzante, S. Solomon, M. Free, P. J. Gleckler, P. D. Jones, T. R. Karl, S. A. Klein,

C. Mears, D. Nychka, G. A. Schmidt, S. C. Sherwood, and F. J. Wentz, 2008: Consistency of modelled and observed temperature trends in the tropical troposphere, Intl. J. of Climatology, 28, 1703–1722.

Schwartz, S.E., R.J. Charlson, R.A. Kahn, J.A. Ogren, and H. Rodhe, 2010: Why hasn't the Earth warmed as much as expected?, J. Climate, 23, 2453–2464.

Smith, D.M., S. Cusack, A.W. Colman, C.K. Folland, G.R. Harris, J.M. Murphy, 2007: Improved Surface Temperature Prediction for the Coming Decade from a Global Climate Model, Science, 317, 796–799.

Tsonis, A. A., K. Swanson, and S. Kravtsov, 2007: A new dynamical mechanism for major climate shifts, Geophys. Res. Ltrs., 34, L13705, doi:10.1029/2007GL030288

Wong, T., B. A. Wielicki, et al., 2006: Reexamination of the observed decadal variability of the earth radiation budget using altitude-corrected ERBE/ERBS nonscanner WFOV Data, J. Climate, 19, 4028–4040.

EXPLORING THE ISSUE

Is the Threat of Global Warming Real?

Critical Thinking and Reflection

1. Is the evidence strong enough to conclude that global warming has been occurring for a period of time?
2. Is there compelling evidence that catastrophic consequences will occur unless global warming stops?
3. Is there compelling evidence that today's global warming is caused in large part by human action?
4. What can you conclude from the fact that there are many reputable scientists on each side of the global warming issue?
5. Does the global community have enough compelling evidence that governments ought to spend enormous amount of public funds to lessen and/or eliminate presumed causes of global warming?

Is There Common Ground?

Assessing the existence of common ground on the issue of global warming or the broader issue of climate change is difficult. While the scientific community and the general public agree on the fact that the global climate is changing, they disagree on the role that humans play in that process. A higher percentage of scientists compared to the general public place significant blame on humans for these changes. A vast majority of members within the scientific community also accept the views found in the various reports of the Intergovernmental panel on Climate Change (IPCC) concerning the current state of climate change, and its causes and consequences. Reading the research findings of most members of the scientific community would lead one to believe that disagreements of an earlier day regarding the basic questions associated with climate change have been settled. But nonetheless, within the scientific community one finds a handful of scientists who, along with popular non-scientific writers, have cornered the market on books with sensational titles that enjoy wide circulation among the general public. Thus, it is not surprising that one finds a larger lack of consensus among the general public, as well as among politicians, regarding the basic questions associated with climate change.

Additional Resources

Alexander, Ralph B., *Global Warming False Alarm: The Bad Science Behind the United Nations' Assertion that Man-Made CO_2 Causes Global Warming* (Canterbury Publishing, 2009)

The book focuses on the "flawed science" behind the UN's Intergovernmental Panel on Climate Change's position that recent climate change is the result of human activity.

Al Gore, *An Inconvenient Truth* (both in DVD and print, 2006)

This has become the poster source for those who support the link between human behavior and rises in global temperature.

Booker, Christopher, *The Real Global Warming Disaster: Is the Obsession with "Climate Change" Turning Out to Be the Most Costly Scientific Blunder in History?* (Continuum, 2009)

This book argues that the planet is not warming, and efforts to address this "imaginary problem" will have global economic disaster.

Climate Action Network (www.climatenetwork.org)

This is a Web site for a worldwide network of more than 430 non-governmental organizations, termed the Climate Action Network or CAN.

Glover, Peter C. and Economides, Michael J., *Energy and Climate Wars: How Naïve Politicians, Green Ideologies, and Media Elites Are Undermining the Truth About Energy and Climate* (Continuum, 2010)

These authors focus on exposing "energy and climate myths" at the heart of today's public debate.

Goreham, Steve, *Climatism!: Science, Common Sense, and the 21st Century's Hottest Topic* (New Lenox Books, 2010)

This well-researched book focuses on the science and politics of global warming, arguing that climate change is a function of natural causes and not man-made.

Hoggan, James and Littlemore, Richard, *Climate Cover-Up: The Crusade to Deny Global Warming* (Greystone Books, 2009)

The book focuses on how the linkages between self-interested business organizations and conservative think tanks have campaigned to question global warming.

Horner, Christopher C., *Red Hot Lies: How Global Warming Alarmists Use Threats, Fraud, and Deception to Keep You Misinformed* (Regnery Publishing, 2008)

This book is a frontal attack on those who support the idea of global warming, arguing that the global warming lobby uses a variety of questionable tactics to perpetuate the idea of its existence.

Lomberg, Bjorn (ed.), *Smart Solutions to Climate Change: Comparing Costs and Benefits* (Cambridge University Press, 2010)

This collection of essays focuses on likely costs and benefits of a range of policy options to global warming.

MacRae, Paul, *False Alarm: Global Warming—Facts Versus Fears* (Spring Bay Press, 2010)

This book focuses on the shortcomings of the global warming scare, including the hypothesis that the planet is not warming now and has not been since the late 1990s.

The Heartland Institute (www.heartland.org/studies/ieguide.htm)

This Web site suggests "seven facts" to counteract observations such as those of the recent and earlier IPCC studies. First, "most scientists do not believe human activities threaten to disrupt the earth's climate." Second, "the most reliable temperature data show no global warming trend." Third, "global computer models are too crude to predict future climate changes." Fourth, "the IPCC did not prove that human activities are causing global warming" (a reference to the 1995 study). Fifth, "a modest amount of global warming, should it occur, would be beneficial to the natural world and to human civilization." Sixth, "reducing our greenhouse gas emissions would be costly and would not stop global warming." And seventh, "the best strategy to pursue is one of 'no regrets'." The latter refers to the idea that it is it is not better to be safe than sorry (suggested by the other side), as immediate action will not make us safer, just poorer.

U.S. government Web site on global warming (www.epa.gov/climatechange/index.html)

This is the official U.S. government Web site on global warming.

ISSUE 8

Can the Global Community Successfully Confront the Global Water Shortage?

YES: Peter Rogers, from "Facing the Freshwater Crisis," *Scientific American* (August 2008)

NO: Mark Clayton, from "Is Water Becoming 'the New Oil'?" *Christian Science Monitor* (May 29, 2008)

Learning Outcomes

After reading this issue, you should be able to:

- Gain an understanding of the role played by increasing population size and affluence in global water scarcity.
- Describe the role played by other factors beyond population size and affluence in global water scarcity.
- Discuss ways to eliminate global water waste.
- Describe a range of existing technologies for averting a global water crisis.
- Understand the term "peak water" and its implications for the global water crisis.

ISSUE SUMMARY

YES: Peter Rogers, professor of environmental engineering at Harvard University, suggests that existing technologies exist for averting a global water crisis, but the global community must act soon.

NO: Mark Clayton, staff writer for *The Christian Science Monitor*, suggests that changes in population, pollution, and climate are creating water shortages around the globe, leading private companies to take advantage of the increased demand for clean water while governments are slow to act.

As the World Water Council suggests, the times of "easy water" are long gone. Water shortages and other water problems are occurring with greater frequency, particularly in large cities. Some observers have speculated that the situation is reminiscent of the fate that befell ancient glorious cities like Rome. Recognition that the supply of water is a growing problem is not new. As early as 1964, the United Nations Environmental Programme (UNEP) revealed that close to a billion people were at risk from desertification. At the Earth Summit in Rio de Janeiro in 1992, world leaders reaffirmed that desertification was of serious concern.

Moreover, since these early warnings about global water, in conference after conference and study after study, increasing population growth and declining water supplies and quality are being linked together, as is the relationship between the planet's ability to meet its growing food needs and available water. Lester R. Brown, in "Water Deficits Growing in Many Countries: Water Shortages May Cause Food Shortages," *Eco-Economy Update 2002–11* (August 6, 2002), sums up the problem this way: "The world is incurring a vast water deficit. It is largely invisible, historically recent, and growing fast." The World Water Council's study, "World Water Actions Report, Third Draft" (October 31, 2002), describes the problem in much the same way: "Water is no longer taken for granted as a plentiful resource that will always be available when we need it." The report continued with the observation that increasing numbers of people in more and more countries are discovering that water is a "limited resource that must be managed for the benefit of people and the environment, in the present and in the future." In short, water is fast becoming both a food-related issue and a health-related problem. Some scholars are now arguing that water shortage is likely to become the twenty-first century's analog to the oil crisis of the last half of the previous century. The one major difference, as scholars are quick to point out, is that water is not like oil; there is no substitute.

Proclamations of impending water problems abound. Peter Gleick, in *The World's Water 1998–99: The Biennial Report on Freshwater Resources* (Island Press, 1998), reports that the demand for freshwater increased sixfold between 1900 and 1995, twice the rate of population growth. The UN study *United Nations Comprehensive Assessment of Freshwater Resources of the World* (1997) suggested that one-third of the world's population lives in countries having medium to high water stress. One 2001 headline reporting the release of a new study proclaimed that "Global thirst 'will turn millions into water refugees'" (*The Independent,* 1999). News reports released by the UN Food and Agricultural Organization in conjunction with World Food Day 2002 asserted that water scarcity could result in millions of people having inadequate access to clean water or sufficient food. And the World Meteorological Organization predicts that two out of every three people will live in water-stressed conditions by 2050 if consumption patterns remain the same.

Sandra Postel, in *Pillar of Sand: Can the Irrigation Miracle Last?* (W.W. Norton, 1999), suggests another variant of the water problem. For her, the time-tested method of maximizing water usage in the past, irrigation, may not be feasible as world population marches toward 7 billion. She points to the inadequacy of surface water supplies, increasing depletion of groundwater supplies, the salinization of the land, and the conversion of traditional agricultural land to other uses as reasons for the likely inability of irrigation to be a continuing panacea. Yet, the 1997 UN study concluded that annual irrigation use would need to increase 30 percent for annual food production to double, necessary for meeting food demands of 2025.

The issue of water quality is also in the news. The World Health Organization reports that in some parts of the world, up to 80 percent of all transmittable diseases are attributable to the consumption of contaminated water. Also, a UNEP-sponsored study, *Global Environment Outlook 2000*, reported that 200 scientists from 50 countries pointed to the shortage of clean water as one of the most pressing global issues.

More recent studies bring the same message. The UN's *World Water Development Report 2009* lays out the problems and the challenges of global water, and suggests that current decision-making processes are not up to the challenge of addressing these problems. The report outlines major issues in the areas of access to drinking water infrastructure, sanitation infrastructure, effects of population growth, agriculture and livestock, energy, sanitation treatment of waste water, climate change, and migration issues related to water scarcity.

In 2010, the World Water Council, an international water think tank sponsored by the World Bank and the UN, also sounded the alarm, suggesting that more than one out of six humans lack access to safe drinking water, while more than two out of six lack adequate sanitation. The council suggests that during the next 50 years, population growth coupled with industrialization and urbanization will dramatically increase the demand for safe water.

Water.org cites a variety of official UN and other international governmental organization studies to reveal bullet points relating to the statistics of the global water problems. A sampling of its information includes the following:

- 3.575 million people die each year from water-related diseases.
- People living in slums pay 5–10 times more per liter of water than the rich in the same city.
- An American taking a 5-minute shower uses more water than a developing world person uses in a day.
- Lack of sanitation is the world's biggest cause of infection.
- Diarrhea remains the second leading cause of death for children under five.
- Every 20 seconds, a child dies from a water-related disease.
- Children in poor environments often carry 1000 parasitic worms in their bodies at any given moment.
- In any one day, more than 200 million hours are spent collecting water for domestic use.
- At any given moment, half of the world's hospital beds are occupied by people with water-related diseases.
- Less than 1 percent of the world's fresh water is readily accessible for direct human usage.
- By 2025, 48 countries will face freshwater stress or scarcity.

The World Water Council recently suggested a comprehensive plan of action that focused on four major initiatives: supporting political action to improve water and sanitation services and water management, deepening the involvement of major water users, strengthening regional cooperation to achieve water security and economic development, and mobilizing citizens and consumers to address the global water crisis.

Although most allude to a current water shortage that will only worsen, a few analysts suggest otherwise. Bjørn Lomborg, the "skeptical scientist," has taken this issue in *The Skeptical Environment: Measuring the Real State of the World* (2002) with the opposing view in the global water debate. His argument can be summed up in his simple quote: "Basically we have sufficient water." Lomborg maintains that water supplies rose during the twentieth century and that we have gained access to more water through technology. Benjamin Radford suggests that when one distills the evidence behind the dire headlines, there is "one little fact. There is no water shortage."

Although most of the discussion and debate center on either the dwindling fresh water supply or unequal access thereto, an alternative view suggests that the real issue may be corporate control of water. Maude Barlow in *Blue Covenant* (2007), makes the case that it is privatization of fresh water and other corporate behavior that contribute significantly to the global water crisis. From putting massive amounts of water into bottles for sale to individuals to controlling large amounts of water used in industry to controlling the world water trade, for-profit private corporations have used supply/demand and other economic principles to undercut the global community to address the global water crisis.

But there is hope, as the YES selection from Peter Rogers suggests, that existing technologies exist that can avert a global water crisis. The NO selection by Mark Clayton is more pessimistic.

YES ↵

Peter Rogers

Facing the Freshwater Crisis

A friend of mine lives in a middle-class neighborhood of New Delhi, one of the richest cities in India. Although the area gets a fair amount of rain every year, he wakes in the morning to the blare of a megaphone announcing that freshwater will be available only for the next hour. He rushes to fill the bathtub and other receptacles to last the day. New Delhi's endemic shortfalls occur largely because water managers decided some years back to divert large amounts from upstream rivers and reservoirs to irrigate crops.

My son, who lives in arid Phoenix, arises to the low, schussing sounds of sprinklers watering verdant suburban lawns and golf courses. Although Phoenix sits amid the Sonoran Desert, he enjoys a virtually unlimited water supply. Politicians there have allowed irrigation water to be shifted away from farming operations to cities and suburbs, while permitting recycled wastewater to be employed for landscaping and other nonpotable applications.

As in New Delhi and Phoenix, policymakers worldwide wield great power over how water resources are managed. Wise use of such power will become increasingly important as the years go by because the world's demand for freshwater is currently overtaking its ready supply in many places, and this situation shows no sign of abating. That the problem is well-known makes it no less disturbing: today one out of six people, more than a billion, suffer inadequate access to safe freshwater. By 2025, according to data released by the United Nations, the freshwater resources of more than half the countries across the globe will undergo either stress—for example, when people increasingly demand more water than is available or safe for use—or outright shortages. By midcentury as much as three quarters of the earth's population could face scarcities of freshwater.

Scientists expect water scarcity to become more common in large part because the world's population is rising and many people are getting richer (thus expanding demand) and because global climate change is exacerbating aridity and reducing supply in many regions. What is more, many water sources are threatened by faulty waste disposal, releases of industrial pollutants, fertilizer runoff and coastal influxes of saltwater into aquifers as groundwater is depleted. Because lack of access to water can lead to starvation, disease, political instability and even armed conflict, failure to take action can have broad and grave consequences.

Fortunately, to a great extent, the technologies and policy tools required to conserve existing freshwater and to secure more of it are known; I will discuss several that seem particularly effective. What is needed now is action. Governments and authorities at every level have to formulate and execute concrete plans for implementing the political, economic and technological measures that can ensure water security now and in the coming decades.

Sources of Shortages

Solving the world's water problems requires, as a start, an understanding of how much freshwater each person requires, along with knowledge of the factors that impede supply and increase demand in different parts of the world. Malin Falkenmark of the Stockholm International Water Institute and other experts estimate that, on average, each person on the earth needs a minimum of 1,000 cubic meters (m3) of water per year—equivalent to two fifths of the volume of an Olympic-size swimming pool—for drinking, hygiene and growing food for sustenance. Whether people get enough depends greatly on where they live, because the distribution of global water resources varies widely.

Providing adequate water is especially challenging in drier, underdeveloped and developing nations with large populations, because demand in those areas is high and supply is low. Rivers such as the Nile, the Jordan, the Yangtze and the Ganges are not only overtaxed, they also now regularly peter out for long periods during the year. And the levels of the underground aquifers below New Delhi, Beijing and many other burgeoning urban areas are falling.

Shortages of freshwater are meanwhile growing more common in developed countries as well. Severe droughts in the U.S., for instance, have recently left many cities and towns in the northern part of Georgia and large swaths of the Southwest scrambling for water. Emblematic of the problem are the man-made lakes Mead and Powell, both of which are fed by the overstressed Colorado River. Every year the lakes record their ongoing decline with successive, chalky high-water marks left on their tall canyon walls like so many bathtub rings.

Golden Rule

Location, of course, does not wholly determine the availability of water in a given place: the ability to pay plays a major role. People in the American West have an old saying: "Water usually runs downhill, but it always runs uphill to money." In other words, when supplies are deficient, the powers that be typically divert them to higher-revenue-generating activities at the expense of lower-revenue-generating ones. So those with the money get water, while others do not.

Such arrangements often leave poor people and nonhuman consumers of water—the flora and fauna of the adjacent ecosystems—with insufficient allocations. And even the best intentions can be distorted by the economic realities described by that Western aphorism.

A case in point occurred in one of the best-managed watersheds (or catchments) in the world, the Murray-Darling River Basin in southeast Australia. Decades ago the agriculturalists and the government there divided up the waters among the human users—grape growers, wheat farmers and sheep ranchers—in a sophisticated way based on equity and economics. The regional water-planning agreement allowed the participants to trade water and market water rights. It even reserved a significant part of the aqueous resource for the associated ecosystems and their natural inhabitants, key "users" that are often ignored even though their health in large measure underlies the well-being of their entire region. Water and marsh plants, both macro and micro, for example, often do much to remove human-derived waste from the water that passes through the ecosystems in which they live.

It turns out, however, that the quantities of water that the planners had set aside to sustain the local environment were inadequate—an underestimation that became apparent during periodic droughts—in particular, the one that has wrought havoc in the area for the last half a dozen years. The territory surrounding the Murray-Darling Basin area dried out and then burned away in tremendous wildfires in recent years.

The economic actors had all taken their share reasonably enough; they just did not consider the needs of the natural environment, which suffered greatly when its inadequate supply was reduced to critical levels by drought. The members of the Murray-Darling Basin Commission are now frantically trying to extricate themselves from the disastrous results of their misallocation of the total water resource.

Given the difficulties of sensibly apportioning the water supply within a single nation, imagine the complexities of doing so for international river basins such as that of the Jordan River, which borders on Lebanon, Syria, Israel, the Palestinian areas and Jordan, all of which have claims to the shared, but limited, supply in an extremely parched region. The struggle for freshwater has contributed to civil and military disputes in the area. Only continuing negotiations and compromise have kept this tense situation under control.

Determining Demand

Like supply, demand for water varies from place to place. Not only does demand rise with population size and growth rate, it also tends to go up with income level: richer groups generally consume more water, especially in urban and industrial areas. The affluent also insist on services such as wastewater treatment and intensive farm irrigation. In many cities, and in particular in the more densely populated territories of Asia and Africa, water demands are growing rapidly.

In addition to income levels, water prices help to set the extent of demand. For example, in the late 1990s, when my colleagues and I simulated global water use from 2000 until 2050, we found that worldwide water requirements would rise from 3,350 cubic kilometers (km^3)—roughly equal to the volume of Lake Huron—to 4,900 km^3 if income and prices remained as they were in 1998. (A cubic kilometer of water is equivalent to the volume of 400,000 Olympic swimming pools.) But the demand would grow almost threefold (to 9,250 km^3) if the incomes of the poorest nations were to continue to climb to levels equivalent to those of middle-income countries today and if the governments of those nations were to pursue no special policies to restrict water use. This increased requirement would greatly intensify the pressure on water supplies, a result that agrees fairly well with forecasts made by the International Water Management Institute (IWMI) when it considered a "business-as-usual," or "do-nothing-different," scenario in the 2007 study *Water for Food, Water for Life.*

Ways to Limit Waste

Given the importance of economics and income in water matters, it is clear that reasonable pricing policies that promote greater conservation by domestic and industrial users are worth adopting. In the past the cost of freshwater in the U.S. and other economic powers has been too low to encourage users to save water: as often happens when people exploit a natural resource, few worry about waste if a commodity is so cheap that it seems almost free.

Setting higher prices for water where possible is therefore near the top of my prescription list. It makes a lot of sense in developed nations, particularly in large cities and industrial areas, and more and more in developing ones as well. Higher water prices can, for instance, spur the adoption of measures such as the systematic reuse of used water (so-called gray water) for nonpotable applications. It can also encourage water agencies to build recycling and reclamation systems.

Raising prices can in addition convince municipalities and others to reduce water losses by improving maintenance of water-delivery systems. One of the major consequences of pricing water too low is that insufficient funds are generated for future development and preventive upkeep. In 2002 the U.S. Government Accountability Office reported that many domestic water utilities defer infrastructure maintenance so that they can remain within their limited operating budgets. Rather than avoiding major failures by detecting leaks early on, they usually wait until water mains break before fixing them.

The cost of repairing and modernizing the water infrastructures of the U.S. and Canada to reduce losses and ensure continued operation will be high, however. The consulting firm Booz Allen Hamilton has projected that the two countries will need to spend $3.6 trillion combined on their water systems over the next 25 years.

When the goal is to save water, another key strategy should be to focus on the largest consumers. That approach places irrigated agriculture in the bull's-eye: compared with any other single activity, conserving irrigation flows would conserve dramatically more freshwater. To meet world food requirements in 2050 without any technological improvements to irrigated agriculture methods, farmers will need a substantial rise in irrigation water supplies (an increase from the current 2,700 to 4,000 km^3), according to the IWMI study.

On the other hand, even a modest 10 percent rise in irrigation efficiency would free up more water than is evaporated off by all other users. This goal could be achieved by stopping up leaks in the water-delivery infrastructure and by implementing low-loss storage of water as well as more efficient application of water to farm crops.

An agreement between municipal water suppliers in southern California and nearby irrigators in the Imperial Irrigation District illustrates one creative conservation effort. The municipal group is paying to line leaky irrigation canals with waterproof materials, and the water that is saved will go to municipal needs.

An additional approach to saving irrigation water involves channeling water that is eventually intended for crop fields to underground storage in the nongrowing season. In most parts of the world, rainfall and snow accumulation—and runoff to rivers—peak during the nongrowing seasons of the year, when demand for irrigation water is lowest. The fundamental task for managers is therefore to transfer water from the high-supply season to the high-demand season when farmers need to irrigate crops.

The most common solution is to hold surface water behind dams until the growing season, but the exposure evaporates much of this supply. Underground storage would limit evaporation loss. For such storage to be feasible, engineers would first have to find large subsurface reservoirs that can be recharged readily by surface supplies and that can easily return their contents aboveground when needed for irrigation. Such "water banks" are currently operating in Arizona, California and elsewhere.

More extensive use of drip-irrigation systems, which minimize consumption by allowing water to seep in slowly either from the soil surface or directly into the root zone, would also do much to stem demand for irrigation water. Investments in new crop varieties that can tolerate low water levels and drought, as well as brackish and even saline water, could also help reduce requirements for irrigation water.

Given the rising demand for agricultural products as populations and incomes grow, it is unlikely that water managers can significantly lower the quantity of water now dedicated to irrigated agriculture. But improvements in irrigation efficiency as well as crop yields can help hold any increases to reasonable levels.

More Steps to Take

Keeping the demand for irrigation water in arid and semiarid areas down while still meeting the world's future food requirements can be supported by supplying "virtual water" to those places. The term relates to the amount of water expended in producing food or commercial goods. If such products are exported to a dry region, then that area will not have to use its own water to create them. Hence, the items represent a transfer of water to the recipient locale and supply them with so-called virtual water.

The notion of virtual water may sound initially like a mere accounting device, but provision of goods—and the virtual-water content of those goods—is helping many dry countries avoid using their own water supplies for growing crops, thus freeing up large quantities for other applications. The virtual-water concept and expanded trade have also led to the resolution of many international disputes caused by water scarcity. Imports of virtual water in products by Jordan have reduced the chance of water-based conflict with its neighbor Israel, for example.

The magnitude of annual global trade in virtual water exceeds 800 billion m^3 of water a year; the equivalent of 10 Nile Rivers. Liberalizing trade of farm products and reducing tariff restrictions that now deter the flow of foodstuffs would significantly enhance global virtual-water flows. Truly free farm trade, for instance, would double the current annual total delivery of virtual water to more than 1.7 trillion m^3.

Whatever benefits the world may accrue from virtual-water transfers, the populations of growing cities need real, flowing water to drink, as well as for hygiene and sanitation. The ever expanding demand for urban, water-based sanitation services can be reduced by adopting dry, or low-water-use, devices such as dry composting toilets with urine separation systems. These technologies divert urine for reuse in agriculture and convert the remaining waste on-site into an organic compost that can enrich soil. Operating basically like garden compost heaps, these units employ aerobic microbes to break down human waste into a nontoxic, nutrient-rich substance. Farmers can exploit the resulting composted organic matter as crop fertilizer. These techniques can be used safely, even in fairly dense urban settings, as exemplified by installations at the Gebers Housing Project in a suburb of Stockholm and many other pilot projects.

Essentially, civil engineers can employ this technology to decouple water supplies from sanitation systems, a move that could save significant amounts of freshwater if it were more widely employed. Moreover, recycled waste could cut the use of fertilizer derived from fossil fuels.

Beyond constraining demand for freshwater, the opposite approach, increasing its supply, will be a critical component of the solution to water shortages. Some 3 percent of all the water on the earth is fresh; all the rest is salty. But desalination tools are poised to exploit that huge source of salty water. A recent, substantial reduction in the costs for the most energy-efficient desalination technology—membrane reverse-osmosis systems—means that many coastal cities can now secure new sources of potable water.

During reverse osmosis, salty water flows into the first of two chambers that are separated by a semipermeable (water-passing) membrane. The second chamber contains freshwater. Then a substantial amount of pressure is applied to the chamber with the salt solution in it. Over time the pressure forces the water molecules through the membrane to the freshwater side.

Engineers have achieved cost savings by implementing a variety of upgrades, including better membranes that require less pressure, and therefore energy, to filter water and system modularization, which makes construction easier. Large-scale desalination plants using the new, more economical technology have been built in Singapore and Tampa Bay, Fla.

Scientists are now working on reverse-osmosis filters composed of carbon nanotubes that offer better separation efficiencies and the potential of lowering desalination costs by an additional 30 percent. This technology, which has been demonstrated in prototypes, is steadily approaching commercial use. Despite the improvements in energy efficiency, however, the applicability of reverse osmosis is to some degree limited by the fact that the technology is still energy-intensive, so the availability of affordable power is important to significantly expanding its application.

A Return on Investment

Not surprisingly, staving off future water shortages means spending money—a lot of it. Analysts at Booz Allen Hamilton have estimated that to provide water needed for all uses through 2030, the world will need to invest as much as $1 trillion a year on applying existing technologies for conserving water, maintaining and replacing infrastructure, and constructing sanitation systems. This is a daunting figure to be sure, but perhaps not so huge when put in perspective. The required sum turns out to be about 1.5 percent of today's annual global gross domestic product, or about $120 per capita, a seemingly achievable expenditure.

Unfortunately, investment in water facilities as a percentage of gross domestic product has dropped by half in most countries since the late 1990s. If a crisis arises in the coming decades, it will not be for lack of know-how; it will come from a lack of foresight and from an unwillingness to spend the needed money.

There is, however, at least one cause for optimism: the most populous countries with the largest water infrastructure needs—India and China—are precisely those that are experiencing rapid economic growth. The part of the globe that is most likely to continue suffering from inadequate water access—Africa and its one billion inhabitants—spends the least on water infrastructure and cannot afford to spend much; it is crucial, therefore, that wealthier nations provide more funds to assist the effort.

The international community can reduce the chances of a global water crisis if it puts its collective mind to the challenge. We do not have to invent new technologies; we must simply accelerate the adoption of existing techniques to conserve and enhance the water supply. Solving the water problem will not be easy, but we can succeed if we start right away and stick to it. Otherwise, much of the world will go thirsty.

Mark Clayton ➜ **NO**

Is Water Becoming the New Oil?

Public fountains are dry in Barcelona, Spain, a city so parched there's a €9,000 ($13,000) fine if you're caught watering your flowers. A tanker ship docked there this month carrying 5 million gallons of precious fresh water—and officials are scrambling to line up more such shipments to slake public thirst.

Barcelona is not alone. Cyprus will ferry water from Greece this summer. Australian cities are buying water from that nation's farmers and building desalination plants. Thirsty China plans to divert Himalayan water. And 18 million southern Californians are bracing for their first water-rationing in years.

"Water," Dow Chemical Chairman Andrew Liveris told the World Economic Forum in February, "is the oil of this century." Developed nations have taken cheap, abundant fresh water largely for granted. Now global population growth, pollution, and climate change are shaping a new view of water as "blue gold."

Water's hot-commodity status has snared the attention of big equipment suppliers like General Electric as well as big private water companies that buy or manage municipal supplies—notably France-based Suez and Aqua America, the largest US-based private water company.

Global water markets, including drinking water distribution, management, waste treatment, and agriculture, are a nearly $500 billion market and growing fast, says a 2007 global investment report.

But governments pushing to privatize costly-to-maintain public water systems are colliding with a global "water is a human right" movement. Because water is essential for human life, its distribution is best left to more publicly accountable government authorities to distribute at prices the poorest can afford, those water warriors say.

"We're at a transition point where fundamental decisions need to be made by societies about how this basic human need—water—is going to be provided," says Christopher Kilian, clean-water program director for the Boston-based Conservation Law Foundation. "The profit motive and basic human need [for water] are just inherently in conflict."

Will "peak water" displace "peak oil" as the central resource question? Some see such a scenario rising.

"What's different now is that it's increasingly obvious that we're running up against limits to new [fresh water] supplies," says Peter Gleick, a water expert and president of the Pacific Institute for Studies in Development, Environment, and Security, a nonpartisan think tank in Oakland, Calif. "It's no longer cheap and easy to drill another well or dam another river."

The idea of "peak water" is an imperfect analogy, he says. Unlike oil, water is not used up but only changes forms. The world still has the same 326 quintillion gallons, NASA estimates.

But some 97 percent of it is salty. The world's remaining accessible fresh-water supplies are divided among industry (20 percent), agriculture (70 percent), and domestic use (10 percent), according to the United Nations.

Meanwhile, fresh-water consumption worldwide has more than doubled since World War II, to nearly 4,000 cubic kilometers annually, and set to rise another 25 percent by 2030, says a 2007 report by the Zurich-based Sustainable Asset Management (SAM) group investment firm.

Up to triple that is available for human use, so there should be plenty, the report says. But waste, climate change, and pollution have left clean water supplies running short.

"We have ignored demand for decades, just assuming supplies of water would be there," Dr. Gleick says. "Now we have to learn to manage water demand and—on top of that—deal with climate change, too."

Population and economic growth across Asia and the rest of the developing world is a major factor driving fresh-water scarcity. The earth's human population is predicted to rise from 6 billion to about 9 billion by 2050, the UN reports. Feeding them will mean more irrigation for crops.

Increasing attention is also being paid to the global "virtual water" trade. It appears in food or other products that require water to produce, products that are then exported to another nation. The US may consume even more water—virtual water—by importing goods that require lots of water to make. At the same time, the US exports virtual water through goods it sells abroad.

As scarcity drives up the cost of fresh water, more efficient use of water will play a huge role, experts say, including:

- Superefficient drip irrigation is far more frugal than "flood" irrigation. But water's low cost in the US provides little incentive to build new irrigation systems.
- Aging, leaking water pipes waste billions of gallons daily. The cost to fix them could be $500 billion over the next 30 years, the federal government estimates.
- Desalination. Dozens of plants are in planning stages or under construction in the US and abroad, reports say.
- Privatization. When private for-profit companies sell at a price based on what it costs to produce water, that higher price curbs water waste and water consumption, economists say.

In the US today, about 33.5 million Americans get their drinking water from privately owned utilities that make up about 16 percent of the nation's community water systems, according to the National Association of Water Companies, a trade association.

"While water is essential to life, and we believe everyone deserves the right of access to water, that doesn't mean water is free or should be provided free," says Peter Cook, executive director of the NAWC. "Water should be priced at the cost to provide it—and subsidized for those who can't afford it."

But private companies' promises of efficient, cost-effective water delivery have not always come true. Bolivia ejected giant engineering firm Bechtel in 2000, unhappy over the spiking cost of water for the city of Cochabamba. Last year Bolivia's president publicly celebrated the departure of French water company Suez, which had held a 30-year contract to supply La Paz.

In her book *Blue Covenant,* Maude Barlow—one of the leaders of the fledgling "water justice" movement—sees a dark future if private monopolies control access to fresh water. She sees this happening when, instead of curbing pollution and increasing conservation, governments throw up their hands and sell public water companies to the private sector or contract with private desalination companies.

"Water is a public resource and a human right that should be available to all," she says. "All these companies are doing is recycling dirty water, selling it back to utilities and us at a huge price. But they haven't been as successful as they want to be. People are concerned about their drinking water and they've met resistance."

Private-water industry officials say those pushing to make water a "human right" are ideologues struggling to preserve inefficient public water authorities that sell water below the cost to produce it and so cheaply it is wasted—doing little to extend service to the poor.

"There are three basic things in life: food, water, and air," says Paul Marin, who three years ago led a successful door-to-door campaign to keep the town council of Emmaus, Pa., from selling its local water company. "In this country, we have privatized our food. Now there's a lot of interest in water on Wall Street. . . . But I can tell you it's putting the fox in charge of the henhouse to privatize water. It's a mistake."

Water and War: Will Scarcity Lead to Conflict?

Cherrapunjee, a town in eastern India, once held bragging rights as the "wettest place on earth," and still gets nearly 40 feet of rain a year. Ironically, officials recently brought in Israeli water-management experts to help manage and retain water that today sluices off the area's deforested landscape so that the area can get by in months when no rain falls.

"Global warming isn't going to change the amount of water, but some places used to getting it won't, and others that don't, will get more," says Dan Nees, a water-trading analyst with the World Resources Institute. "Water scarcity may be one of the most underappreciated global political and environmental challenges of our time." Water woes could have an impact on global peace and stability.

In January, United Nations Secretary-General Ban Ki Moon cited a report by International Alert, a self-described peacebuilding organization based in

London. The report identified 46 countries with a combined population of 2.7 billion people where contention over water has created "a high risk of violent conflict" by 2025.

In the developing world—particularly in China, India, and other parts of Asia—rising economic success means a rising demand for clean water and an increased potential for conflict. China is one of the world's fastest-growing nations, but its lakes, rivers, and groundwater are badly polluted because of the widespread dumping of industrial wastes. Tibet has huge fresh water reserves.

While news reports have generally cited Tibetans' concerns over exploitation of their natural resources by China, little has been reported about China's keen interest in Tibet's Himalayan water supplies, locked up in rapidly melting glaciers.

"It's clear that one of the key reasons that China is interested in Tibet is its water," Dr. Gleick says. "They don't want to risk any loss of control over these water resources."

The Times (London) reported in 2006 that China is proceeding with plans for nearly 200 miles of canals to divert water from the Himalayan plateau to China's parched Yellow River. China's water plans are a major problem for the Dalai Lama's government in exile, says a report released this month by Circle of Blue, a branch of the Pacific Institute, a nonpartisan think tank.

Himalayan water is particularly sensitive because it supplies the rivers that bring water to more than half a dozen Asian countries. Plans to divert water could cause intense debate.

"Once this issue of water resources comes up," wrote Elizabeth Economy, director of Asia Studies at the Council on Foreign Affairs, to Circle of Blue researchers in a report earlier this month, "and it seems inevitable at this point that it will—it also raises emerging conflicts with India and Southeast Asia."

Tibet is not the only water-rich country wary of a water-poor neighbor. Canada, which has immense fresh-water resources, is wary of its water-thirsty superpower neighbor to the south, observers say. With Lake Mead low in the US Southwest, and now Florida and Georgia squabbling over water, the US could certainly use a sip (or gulp) of Canada's supplies. (Canada has 20 percent of the world's fresh water.)

But don't look for a water pipeline from Canada's northern reaches to the US southwest anytime soon. Water raises national fervor in Canada, and Canadians are reluctant to share their birthright with a United States that has mismanaged—in Canada's eyes—its own supplies. Indeed, the prospect of losing control of its water under free-trade or other agreements is something Canadians seem to worry about constantly.

A year ago, Canada's House of Commons voted 134 to 108 in favor of a motion to recommend that its federal government "begin talks with its American and Mexican counterparts to exclude water from the scope of NAFTA." . . .

EXPLORING THE ISSUE

Can the Global Community Successfully Confront the Global Water Shortage?

Critical Thinking and Reflection

1. To what extent do you think that projections of insufficient quantities of fresh water are accurate?
2. Do you believe that the real culprit is the distribution of global water rather than the total amount of water?
3. To what effect do you believe that the privatization of global fresh water is at the heart of the global water issue?
4. Can the global community prevent corporations from controlling fresh water as they have oil?
5. Is the water crisis really a function of three basic factors: total supply versus demand, unequal distribution, and corporate privatization of fresh water?

Is There Common Ground?

Although many analysts differ over whether a global water *crisis* is already here, there is an overwhelming consensus that given population growth and the growth of affluence, future generations will face a water crisis. There is also an emerging belief among many that if the international community is willing to act, technologies are or will be there that will allow the world to do so. The lessons from another diminishing resource, oil, should be instructive here.

Additional Resources

Barlow, Maude, *Blue Covenant: The Global Water Crisis and the Coming Battle for the Right to Water* (New Press, 2009)

> This activist pushes in this book for a blue covenant to make global water a human right and a public trust rather than a commercial product.

Caldecott, Julian, *Water: The Causes, Costs, and Failure of a Global Crisis* (Virgin Books, 2010)

> The author spells out the history, science, economics, and politics behind the global water crisis.

Hoffmann, Steve, *Planet Water: Investing in the World's Most Valuable Resource* (Wiley, 2009)

> The author lays out the basic issues of global water and makes the case that water will rival oil as a scarce commodity.

Jones, J. Anthony et al. (eds.), *Threats to Global Water Security* (Springer, 2009)

> This book focuses on threats to the global water supply, both direct and indirect man-made.

Rogers, Peter and Leal, Susan, *Running Out of Water: The Looming Crisis and Solutions to Conserve Our Most Precious Resource* (Palgrave Macmillan, 2010)

> This book lays out the growing global water crisis. It describes how the renewable nature of water lulls humans into a belief that they will be able to produce enough.

"Whose Water Is It Anyway? The Global Water Crisis & How We Can Help Solve It," *E—The Environmental Magazine* (March–April 2010)

> This issue of E—*The Environmental Magazine* examines the broad aspects of the global water crisis and how it can be successfully addressed.

Internet References . . .

United Nations Office on Drugs and Crime

Established in 1997, this UN organization assists members in their struggle against illicit drugs and human trafficking. It focuses on research, assistance with treaties, and field-based technical assistance. It is headquartered in Vienna with 21 field offices.

http://www.unodc.org

World Health Organization

This international organization's Web site provides substantial information about current and potential pandemics as well as other Web site links. See also http://www.globalhealthreporting.org and http://www.globalhealthfacts.org for additional information.

http://www.who.int/en/

Council of Europe

The Council of Europe established a campaign in 2006 to combat trafficking of human beings. It focuses on creating awareness among governments, NGOs, and civil society about the problem, as well as promoting global public policy to combat the problem.

http://www.coe.int

Global Policy Forum

This Web site lists numerous globalization Web sites as well as other sources on globalization.

http://www.globalpolicy.org

Globalization: Threat or Opportunity?

This Web site contains the article "Globalization: Threat or Opportunity?" by the staff of the International Monetary Fund (IMF). This article discusses such aspects of globalization as current trends, positive and negative outcomes, and the role of institutions and organizations. The site also contains numerous articles on globalization.

http://www.imf.org/external/np/exr/ib/2000/041200.htm

About.com Web Search

Search "natural disasters" for a long list of Web sites.

http://www.websearch.about.com

Expanding Global Forces and Movements

*O*ur ability to travel from one part of the globe to another in a short amount of time has expanded dramatically since the Wright brothers first lifted an airplane off the sand dunes of North Carolina's Outer Banks. The decline of national borders has also been made possible by the explosion of global technology. This technological explosion has not only increased the speed of information dissemination but has also expanded its reach and impact, making any individual with Internet access a global actor in every sense of the term.

Many consequences flow from this realization, including the expansion of the drug war and the global spread of health pandemics along with the trafficking in human beings against their will or larger impacts of natural disasters. In addition, flow of money, information, and ideas that connect people around the world also create fissures of conflict that heighten anxieties and cause increased tensions between rich and poor, connected and disconnected, and cultures and regimes. The impact of these new and emerging patterns of access is yet to be fully calculated or realized, but we do know that billions are feeling their impact, and the result is both exhilarating and frightening.

- Can the Global Community "Win" the Drug War?

- Is the International Community Adequately Prepared to Address Global Health Pandemics?

- Do Adequate Strategies Exist to Combat Human Trafficking?

- Is the International Community Making Progress in Addressing Natural Disasters?

- Is the Global Economic Crisis a Failure of Capitalism?

- Is Social Media Becoming the Most Powerful Force in Global Politics?

ISSUE 9

Can the Global Community "Win" the Drug War?

YES: United Nations Office on Drugs and Crime, from *World Drug Report 2010* (United Nations Publications, 2010)

NO: Mike Trace, from *Drug Policy—Lessons Learnt, and Options for the Future* (Global Commission on Drug Policies, 2010)

Learning Outcomes

After reading this issue, you should be able to:

- Gain an understanding of positive global developments in illicit drug production, trafficking, and consumption.
- Understand that in spite of possible developments, the stockpiling of existing stocks of opium suggests the ability to supply users for an extended period.
- Describe the international drug control regime (framework) and the logic behind it.
- Describe why some believe that the idea of a drug-free world is as far away as ever.
- Discuss the negative side effects of the implementation of the current drug control strategy.

ISSUE SUMMARY

YES: This 2010 report by the United Nations Office on Drugs and Crime suggests that "drug control has matured" and efforts are paying off as the world's supply of the two main problem drugs, opiates and cocaine, has been declining over the past 2 years since the previous UN report.

NO: According to Mike Trace, Chairman of the International Drug Policy Consortium and former British drug czar, the objective of a drug-free world is "as far away as ever," suggesting the effects of badly conceived and implemented drug policies as well as political and institutional barriers.

The *World Drug Report 2010* concluded that the United Nations General Assembly's 1998 call for the elimination or significant reduction of illicit production and abuse by 2008 was not successful. So a new target date, 2019, was selected. Two major lessons were learned, according to the report. First, "the mere sum of uncoordinated national and sectoral efforts, even successful ones, cannot result in a global success." The second lesson is that "countries with limited means cannot resist, and counter the impact of, powerful transnational trafficking flows on their own." The study concluded with the charge to the international community to "interweave drug supply and demand reduction interventions and integrate strategies on the scale of the drug markets."

In 1999, the United Nations (UN) pegged the world illicit drug trade at $400 billion, about the size of the Spanish economy. Such activity takes place as part of a global supply chain that "uses everything from passenger jets that can carry shipments of cocaine worth $500 million in a single trip to custom-built submarines that ply the waters between Colombia and Puerto Rico." *The UN 2010 World Drug Report* suggested the global drug control had "matured" and a more balanced approach to reduce supply and demand as well as disrupting illicit flows "is paying off." Global supply of the two main problem drugs, opiates and cocaine, has been in decline for the past 2 years. The area under cultivation throughout the globe has dropped by 23 percent across the planet. Opium production is experiencing a global problem since a blight might destroy a quarter of Afghanistan's production. Coca production has also declined by 28 percent in the past 10 years. Heroin and cocaine markets "are stable in the developed world" and the U.S. consumption of cocaine has actually declined by about two-thirds in the 1990s and another quarter in the past decade.

It is a different story in the poorer sectors of the world, so bad that the 2010 report concludes that there is a "risk of a public health disaster" in the third world. Booming heroin consumption in Eastern Africa, surging cocaine usage in West Africa and South America, and increased production and abuse of synthetic drugs in the Middle East and Southeast Asia characterize the developing world landscape.

Let us consider more closely the global drug system of production, distribution, and consumption. With respect to production, opium poppy area cultivation declined by 15 percent in 2009 and 23 percent since 2007. This resulted in a 13 percent drop in global opium production and a 9 percent decline in heroin production. Global coca area cultivation declined by 13 percent since 2007 and by 28 percent since 2000. This resulted in a 16 percent drop in global cocaine production. Regarding distribution or the trafficking of illicit drugs, most transfers involve cocaine and heroin, with some cannabis resin and ecstasy smuggled as well. Global cocaine seizures "have stabilized over the last few years," while opiate (both opium and heroin) seizures are increasing. Cannabis herb seizures have increased 23 percent in a 3-year period.

With respect to consumption, the report revealed that between 155 and 250 million people between the ages 15 and 64 used illicit substances at least once in 2008. This is 3.5–5.7 percent of the population. Cannabis use involves the larger group of users, 129–190 million people. Amphetamine users are the next highest group, followed by cocaine and opiates users. It is important to distinguish between one-time or very casual users and the "problem users"— those who inject drugs and/or are considered dependent on the drugs. Global estimates include between 16 and 38 million problem users, or 10–15 percent of all users. An overwhelming majority of problem users received no treatment. Cannabis remains the most widely consumed illicit drug throughout the world. Cocaine users represent the next highest group, followed by opiates. Finally, the misuse of legal prescription drugs is not part of these data.

The report followed good news relating to government action in the 2004 and 2007 reports. Especially important was the emergence of a consensus among governments and global public opinion that the current levels of illegal drug use is unacceptable. In two drug-producing regions, declines in production actually occurred. In Southeast Asia, opium poppy cultivation continues to drop in Myanmar and Laos. In the Andean region, coca cultivation has declined for four straight years in the three leading producing countries (Colombia, Peru, and Bolivia).

The illegal movement of drugs across national borders is accompanied by the same kind of movement for illegal weapons. They go hand in hand with one another. It was estimated by the UN in its 2004 report that only 3 percent of such weapons (18 million of a total of 550 million in circulation) are used by government, the military, or police.

This increase in drug use has occurred despite a rather long history of government attempts to control the illegal international drug trade. Beginning in 1961, such efforts have been part of governments' worldwide social policies. Precisely because drug policy crosses over into social policy, policymakers and scholars have been at odds over how best to deal with this ever growing problem, whether talking about national policy or international policy. Simply stated, the debate has centered on legalization versus prohibition and treatment versus prevention.

Policies of the United States have always had the goal of drug use reduction and punishment for abusers, resulting in less attention to treatment. This includes a number of important elements, as outlined in a Congressional Research Service Brief for Congress (2003): "(1) eradication of narcotic crops, (2) interdiction and law enforcement activities in drug-producing and drug-transmitting countries, (3) international cooperation, (4) sanctions/economic assistance, and (5) institution development." Many have charged the United States and those other countries that share its fundamental philosophy of drug wars of using the issue to expand its national power in other domains. On the other hand, other countries, particularly those in Western Europe, have been shifting attention for some time away from "repressive policies" and toward those associated with harm reduction and treatment.

Despite rhetoric from a variety of governmental reports extolling the successes of various governmental actions, there is an increasing outcry by many, including leaders in the field about the long futility of such efforts. Many of them point to the fact that the war on drugs was now 40 years old when

President Richard Nixon declared drug abuse as "public enemy No. 1." Ethan Nadelmann (*The Disastrous War on Drugs Turns 40: 5 Ways to Stop the Madness,* February 11, 2011) has been especially hard on American policy, arguing that the illegal operators are winning and in the process creating crime, violence, and corruption along the way. For Nadelmann, five themes have emerged.

1. Marijuana legalization will happen as it is now only a question of when and how.
2. "Over-incarceration is the problem, not the solution."
3. The drug war has become "the new Jim Crow" as racial minorities suffer disproportionately.
4. "Politics must no longer be allowed to trump science—and compassion, common sense, and fiscal prudence—in dealing with illegal drugs."
5. And the question of legalization should be on the table.

The late American diplomat Richard Holbrooke earlier declared that the war on drugs in Afghanistan was a failure, not to mention some negative side effects associated with the failed war. And U.S. drug czar Gil Kerlikowske has stated that the 40-year war costing $1 trillion and hundreds of thousands of lives has resulted in a larger and more intense problem. President Obama has increased spending, with two-thirds of it going to interdiction and law enforcement.

The principal alternative approach is to lessen the emphasis on addressing the supply and distribution of illicit drugs. Instead, the focus would be on the consumption side of the global illicit drug system. And whatever focus on the consumer exists, it should not emphasize punishment but should, instead, focus on both treatment and on lowering the demand for such drugs.

The two selections in this section contribute to the debate over the proper approach to "winning" the drug war. The UN's 2010 report presents an optimistic picture of the effects of governmental action in the war on drugs, with strong language used to paint the picture. The NO selection by Mike Trace, chairman of the International Drug Policy Consortium and former British drug czar, states the objective of a drug free world is "as far away as ever," suggesting the effects of badly conceived and implemented drug policies as well as political and institutional barriers.

YES ↵

**United Nations Office
on Drugs and Crime**

World Drug Report 2010

Foreword

In the past decade, drug control has matured. Policy has become more responsive to the needs of those most seriously affected, along the whole chain of the
drug industry—from poor farmers who cultivate it, to desperate addicts who
consume it, as well as those caught in the cross-fire of the traffickers. Countries
are learning from each others' experiences, and drawing on expertise from the
international community.

Drug control is also increasingly taking a more balanced approach,
focussed on development, security, justice and health to reduce supply and
demand, and disrupting illicit flows. There is an understanding that in regions
where illicit crops are grown, it is vital to eradicate poverty, not just drugs.
There is a realization that underdevelopment makes countries vulnerable to
drug trafficking, and other forms of organized crime: therefore development is
part of drug control, and vice versa.

Most importantly, we have returned to the roots of drug control, placing health at the core of drug policy. By recognizing that drug addiction is a
treatable health condition, we have developed scientific, yet compassionate,
new ways to help those affected. Slowly, people are starting to realize that drug
addicts should be sent to treatment, not to jail. And drug treatment is becoming part of mainstream healthcare.

Beware [of] the Side Effects of Complacency

This approach is paying off. The world's supply of the two main problem
drugs—opiates and cocaine—has been declining over the last two years. The
global area under opium cultivation has dropped by almost a quarter (23%)
in the past two years, and opium production looks set to fall steeply this year
due to a blight that could wipe out a quarter of Afghanistan's production. Coca
cultivation is down by 28% in the past decade. Heroin and cocaine markets
are stable in the developed world. Indeed, cocaine consumption has fallen significantly in the United States in the past few years. The retail value of the US
cocaine market has declined by about two thirds in the 1990s, and by about
one quarter in the past decade. One reason behind the violence in Mexico is
that drug traffickers are fighting over a shrinking market.

Shifting the Problem to the Developing World

Most worrisome are recent developments in the third world. Market forces have already shaped the asymmetric dimensions of the drug economy; the world's biggest consumers of the poison (the rich countries) have imposed upon the poor (the main locations of supply and trafficking) the greatest damage.

But poor countries have other priorities and fewer resources. They are not in a position to absorb the consequences of increased drug use. As a result, there is now the risk of a public health disaster in developing countries that would enslave masses of humanity to the misery of drug dependence—another drama in lands already ravaged by so many tragedies. The warning lights are already flashing. Look at the boom in heroin consumption in Eastern Africa, or the explosion of cocaine use in West Africa or South America, or the surge in the production and abuse of synthetic drugs in the Middle East and South East Asia. We will not solve the world drugs problem by shifting consumption from the developed to the developing world.

Changing to Other Drugs

Furthermore, stabilization of the cocaine and heroin markets masks a growing problem of the misuse of prescription drugs in many parts of the world. And the global number of people using amphetamine-type stimulants (ATS) is likely to exceed the number of opiate and cocaine users combined. The ATS market is harder to track because of short trafficking routes (manufacturing usually takes place close to main consumer markets), and the fact that many of the raw materials are both legal and readily available. Furthermore, manufacturers are quick to market new products (like ketamine, Mephedrone and Spice) and exploit new markets. We will not solve the world drugs problem if addiction simply shifts from cocaine and heroin to other addictive substances.

What do we propose, at UNODC? We champion placing drug policy at the intersection of health, security, development and justice. Let me explain.

The Right to Health

(a) Universal access to drug therapy. At the United Nations, we are working with the World Health Organization, and advocate universal access to drug treatment. We work with UNAIDS to prevent an HIV epidemic among injecting addicts. I appreciate the support that is coming from the community level for these initiatives.

(b) Universal access to therapy by means of drugs. We should not only stop the harm caused by drugs: we should unleash the capacity of drugs to do good. What do I mean? Recall that the Preamble of the Single Convention (from 1961) recognizes that ". . . *the medical use of narcotic drugs is indispensible for the relief of pain, . . . and adequate provision must be made to ensure their availability* . . . Although there is an over-supply of opium in the world, many people who suffer major illnesses have no access to palliative care. Why should a Nigerian consumed by AIDS or a Mexican cancer patient, be denied medication offered to their Swedish or American counterparts? Help us overcome cultural, professional, administrative and socio-economic factors that conspire to deny people the opium-based relief (morphine) they need.

The Right to Development

While the pendulum of drug control is swinging back towards the right to health and human rights, we must not neglect development.

As illustrated in various recent UNODC reports, including this one, drug production and trafficking are both causes and consequences of poverty. Indeed, 22 of the 34 countries least likely to achieve the Millennium Development Goals are in the midst—or emerging from—conflicts, located in regions that are magnets for drug cultivation and trafficking. More development means less crime and less conflict. That is why UNODC is working with governments, regional organizations and development banks to promote drug control policy as ways to foster development, and vice-versa—for example in the Balkans, Central and West Asia, Mesoamerica, West and East Africa.

The Right to Security

Yet, the stakes are high and getting higher. Drug-trafficking has become the main source of revenue for organized crime, as well as to terrorists and insurgents: in other words, drug-related illegality has become a threat to nations in so many theatres around the world. Recent developments in West Africa, the Sahel, and parts of Central America show the very real dangers of narcotrafficking to security, even the sovereignty of states.

So grave is the danger that the issue is now periodically on the agenda of the Security Council. Unless we deal effectively with the threat posed by organized crime, our societies will be held hostage—and drug control will be jeopardized, by renewed calls to dump the three UN drug conventions that critics say are the cause of crime and instability. This would undo the progress that has been made in drug control over the past decade, and unleash a public health disaster.

Human Rights

Above all, we must move human rights into the mainstream of drug control. Around the world, millions of people (including children) caught taking drugs are sent to jail, not to treatment. In some countries, what is supposed to be drug treatment amounts to cruel, inhuman or degrading punishment—the equivalent of torture. In several Member States, people are executed for drug-related offences. In others, drug traffickers are gunned down by extra-judicial hit squads. As human beings, we have a shared responsibility to ensure that this comes to an end. Just because people take drugs, or are behind bars, this doesn't abolish their right to be a person protected by the law—domestic and international.

The Global Perspective Offered by the *World Drug Report 2010*

In conclusion, this *World Drug Report* shows the various components of the drug market, and explains the dynamics that drive them. It confirms that drug policy must stay the course we have promoted at UNODC over the past years, focussed on the four basic rights of health, development, security and human rights.

Antonio Maria Costa
Executive Director
United Nations Office on Drugs and Crime

Executive Summary

In 1998, a special session of the UN General Assembly decided to work towards the "elimination or significant reduction" of illicit drug production and abuse by 2008, and adopted a series of sectoral plans to reach that objective. Gathered at the end of the 10-year period, Member States were not satisfied with the results and declared that they were still "gravely concerned about the growing threat posed by the world drug problem." The decision was taken to continue the effort over the following decade.

Can overall drug supply and demand be "eliminated or significantly reduced" by 2019, as called for by the Member States? At the national level, one can hope that many countries will be able to significantly improve their drug control situation within a decade. Will these local successes translate into an overall improvement at the global level?

A clear lesson from the history of drug control is that the mere sum of uncoordinated national and sectoral efforts, even successful ones, cannot result in a global success. Another lesson is that countries with limited means cannot resist, and counter the impact of, powerful transnational trafficking flows on their own.

To achieve the 2019 objectives, the international community needs to interweave drug supply and demand reduction interventions and integrate national efforts in the framework of renewed international strategies on the scale of the drug markets. To do so, it is urgent to improve our understanding of how illicit transnational drug economies operate. This *World Drug Report* is a contribution toward this objective. . . .

Global Developments in Illicit Drug Production, Trafficking and Consumption

Production

There have been a number of encouraging developments in global cocaine and heroin markets recently:

- The global area under opium poppy cultivation declined to 181,400 hectares (ha) in 2009 (15%) or by 23% since 2007.

- In line with declines in the area under cultivation, global opium production fell from 8,890 metric tons (mt) in 2007 to 7,754 mt in 2009 (−13%), and potential heroin production declined from 757 mt in 2007 to 657 mt in 2009.
- The global area under coca cultivation declined to 158,800 ha in 2009 (5%), by 13% since 2007 or by 28% since 2000.
- The estimated global cocaine production fell from 1,024 mt in 2007 to 865 mt in 2008 (−16%). Global fresh coca leaf production fell by 4% in 2009 (by 14% between 2007 and 2009).

The recent successes, however, must be considered in the context of the long-term challenge. Since 1998, the year of the last UN General Assembly Special Session (UNGASS) devoted to the drug problem, global potential opium production has increased by 78%, from 4,346 mt to 7,754 mt in 2009. Fortunately, these production increases do not correspond to consumption increases, as it appears that large amounts of opium have been stockpiled in recent years. This means, however, that even if production were completely eliminated today, existing stocks could supply users for at least two years.

The increase in global potential cocaine production over the 1998–2008 period seems to have been more moderate (5%), from 825 mt to 865 mt, although there remain uncertainties around coca yields and production efficiency. Nonetheless, available data are sufficiently robust to state that global cocaine production has declined significantly in recent years (2004–2009).

In contrast to heroin and cocaine, only very broad production estimates can be given for cannabis and amphetamine-type stimulants (ATS). Due to the decentralization of production, it is difficult to track global trends in either of these markets. Between 13,000 and 66,100 mt of herbal cannabis were produced in 2008, as were 2,200 to 9,900 mt of cannabis resin. Manufacture of the amphetamines-group of ATS (amphetamine, methamphetamine, methcathinone and related substances) was in the range of 161 to 588 mt in 2008. Manufacture of drugs marketed as 'ecstasy' ranged from 55 to 133 mt.

Trafficking
Most of the long-distance trafficking involves cocaine and heroin, although some cannabis resin and ecstasy are also smuggled between regions. Much of the cannabis herb, methamphetamine and amphetamine consumed in the world is produced locally.

Global cocaine seizures have stabilized over the last few years. Seizures have declined in North America and Europe, but have risen in South and Central America. Trafficking through West Africa, which increased rapidly between 2004 and 2007, appears to have declined in 2008 and 2009, but this situation may change and needs to be monitored carefully.

Opiate seizures continue to increase. This applies to both opium and heroin seizures. Morphine[1] seizures, in contrast, declined in 2008. The largest seizures continue to be reported from the countries neighbouring Afghanistan, notably the Islamic Republic of Iran and Pakistan.

Tracking global ATS seizures is more complicated, because there are several products involved that appeal to different markets, including amphetamine, methamphetamine and 'ecstasy.' After tripling in the early years of this decade, ATS seizures have remained stable since 2006. Ecstasy seizures showed a marked decline in 2008 compared to a year earlier. Global seizures of amphetamine and methamphetamine remained largely stable at very high levels in 2008.

Global cannabis herb seizures increased over the 2006–2008 period (+23%), especially in South America, reaching levels last reported in 2004. Global cannabis resin seizures increased markedly over the 2006–2008 period (+62%) and clearly exceeded the previous peak of 2004. Large increases in cannabis resin seizures in 2008 were reported from the Near and Middle East region, as well as from Europe and Africa.

Consumption

Globally, UNODC estimates that between 155 and 250 million people (3.5% to 5.7% of the population aged 15–64) used illicit substances at least once in 2008. Globally, cannabis users comprise the largest number of illicit drug users (129–190 million people). Amphetamine-group substances rank as the second most commonly used drug, followed by cocaine and opiates.

At the core of drug consumption lie the 'problem drug users': those who inject drugs and/or are considered dependent, facing serious social and health consequences as a result. Based on the global estimates of the number of cannabis, opiate, cocaine and ATS users, it is estimated that there were between 16 and 38 million problem drug users in the world in 2008. This represents 10% to 15% of all people who used drugs that year. It can be estimated that in 2008, globally, between 12% and 30% of problem drug users had received treatment in the past year, which means that between 11 and 33.5 million problem drug users did not receive treatment that year.

The lack of data in many countries still limits the understanding of the drug use problem in many countries, particularly in Africa, some parts of Asia and the Pacific Islands. The broad range of the estimates reflects the uncertainties in the available global data.

Data on the delivery of treatment services for problem drug users can provide valuable information on variations in drug use problems across regions. The share of treatment services delivered to users of different drugs varies markedly in different regions of the world. In Europe and Asia, most of the treatment demand is for opiates. In the Americas, it is cocaine, and in Africa and Oceania, it is cannabis. These ratios have changed over time. As compared to a decade ago, treatments related to cannabis have increased in Europe, South America and Oceania, suggesting that an increased proportion of cannabis use can become problematic. Over the same period of time, cocaine treatment demand has been declining in the Americas, especially in North America, while it has increased in Europe. The relative importance of opiates for drug treatment, on the other hand, has declined in Europe, Asia and (in particular) Oceania, while it rose in Africa. ATS are commanding a growing share of treatment services globally.

Estimates of the sizes of the user populations in various parts of the world are derived from household and school surveys and indirect methods. Unfortunately, population-based surveys are conducted very irregularly in most countries, so there remain significant gaps in the knowledge of the extent of drug use in some parts of the world.

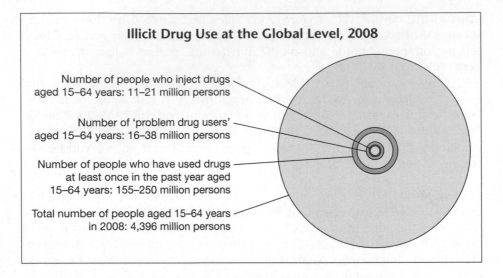

Illicit Drug Use at the Global Level, 2008

Number of people who inject drugs aged 15–64 years: 11–21 million persons

Number of 'problem drug users' aged 15–64 years: 16–38 million persons

Number of people who have used drugs at least once in the past year aged 15–64 years: 155–250 million persons

Total number of people aged 15–64 years in 2008: 4,396 million persons

Cannabis remains the most widely consumed drug worldwide. Global annual cannabis use prevalence is estimated between 2.9% and 4.3% of the population aged 15–64. The highest is in Oceania (9.3% to 14.8%), followed by the Americas (6.3% to 6.6%). There are an estimated 15–19.3 million annual cocaine users (annual prevalence of 0.3% to 0.4%) in the world. North America (2%), Oceania (1.4% to 1.7%) and West Europe (1.5%) are the regions with the highest prevalence rates. Between 12.8 and 21.8 million people (0.3% to 0.5% of the world population aged 15–64) used opiates in 2008. More than half of the world's opiate users are in Asia. UNODC estimates that between 13.7 and 52.9 million people aged 15 to 64 had used an amphetamine-type substance in the past year (0.3% to 1.2% of the population), including 10.5 to 25.8 million ecstasy users (0.2% to 0.6% of the population). Oceania, East and South-East Asia, North America, and West and Central Europe are the regions with the highest prevalence rates of ATS use.

In addition to the drugs mentioned above, the misuse of prescription drugs, such as synthetic opioids, benzodiazepines or synthetic prescription stimulants, is a growing health problem in a number of developed and developing countries.

The Main Drug Markets
The global illicit opiate and cocaine markets represent two of the biggest transnational drugs and crime threats of our time. They appear at the same time as persistent problems from a previous era of drug control, priorities for interventions due to the severity of their impacts on affected societies and good candidates for a global solution within a reasonable time frame. Since they are both sourced from relatively concentrated production areas, most of their components are directly or indirectly linked to one another.

In addition, ATS have gained a large share of the global drug market over the last two decades and have come to represent a major and evolving threat for present and future drug control efforts. Since 1990, there has been a spread in ATS manufacture with more than a third of Member States having reported ATS-related manufacture activity to date. Moreover, the global number of ATS users is likely to exceed the number of opiate and cocaine users combined.

Cocaine   The global area under coca cultivation decreased by 5% last year, from 167,600 ha in 2008 to 158,800 ha in 2009. This change is mainly due to a significant decrease in Colombia, not offset by increases in Peru and the Plurinational State of Bolivia. The global area under coca cultivation declined by 28% over the 2000–2009 period. In 2009, Colombia represented about 43% of global cultivation, with Peru contributing 38% and the Plurinational State of Bolivia 19%. . . .

In 2008, the potential production of pure cocaine amounted to some 865 mt. This is considerably less than four years previously, when almost 1,050 mt were generated. Most of these drugs are destined for consumers in North America (6.2 million users in 2008) and Europe (4 to 5 million users). These two regions, with 70% of the demand and 85% of the total value, play the main role in shaping the evolution of the global cocaine market. Another 2.7 million users are found in South America, Central America and the Caribbean.

The Largest Cocaine Market: North America   North America is the largest regional cocaine market, with close to 40% of the global cocaine-using popula-tion. In 2008, it appears that 196 mt of pure cocaine were required to satisfy North American demand. To get this amount to the consumer (accounting for seizures, consumption in transit countries and purity), about 309 mt must have left the Andean region toward the north in 2008. This would represent about half the cocaine that leaves this region, a smaller share than in the recent past. Based on forensic testing of cocaine seized in the United States, most of the cocaine consumed in North America was produced in Colombia.

The North American cocaine market appears to be in decline. Household surveys, school surveys, forensic testing and law enforcement observation all con-firm that fewer people in North America as a whole are consuming cocaine than in the past. Cocaine use in the United States has been declining for some time. The decline has been particularly pronounced since 2006, likely due to pressure on supply related to law enforcement interventions in Colombia and Mexico.

If there was a supply shortage for the United States market, this would be expected to generate an increase in cocaine prices. Street prices have not risen much, but purity has dropped greatly. When purity is taken into consideration, the cost of a gram of pure cocaine on the US market has indeed increased dra-matically. Dealers in the United States apparently prefer to cut quality rather than increase price, and the result appears to have helped reduce demand.

As a whole, the retail value of the United States cocaine market declined by about two thirds in the 1990s, and by about another quarter in the last dec-ade. About 70% of the profits made off the cocaine trade in the United States accrue between mid-level dealers and the consumer. Farmers and traffickers in Colombia keep less than 3% of the retail sales value of the cocaine they produce.

The Second Largest Cocaine Market: Europe   The world's second largest flow of cocaine is directed towards Europe, and this flow has been growing rapidly.

The largest national cocaine market within Europe is the United Kingdom, followed by Spain, Italy, Germany and France. Cocaine use prevalence levels are higher in the United Kingdom and Spain than in the United States.

Recent data suggest that the rapid growth of the European cocaine market is beginning to level off in some of the biggest national markets such as Italy, Spain and Germany. Consumption is still growing in the United Kingdom and in some of the smaller European markets, however. In 2008, an estimated 124 mt of cocaine were consumed in Europe. To supply this demand, an esti-mated 212 mt departed South America toward Europe, about one quarter of total production. A greater share of this quantity comes from Peru and the Plurinational State of Bolivia than in the case of the United States.

The primary countries of entry to the European market are Spain and the Netherlands. Most of the trafficking is maritime. Significant transit routes flow from former colonies or overseas territories of the European nations to their counterparts on the continent. Flows through West Africa appear to have declined since 2007, bur could resume in the near future.

While the volumes are lower, the value of the European cocaine market (US$34 billion) is almost as high as in the case of the North American market (US$37 billion), because purity-adjusted cocaine retail prices are higher in Europe. European street prices in 2008 are about half what they were in 1990, but purity has declined and the dollar has weakened against the euro. In dollar terms, the purity-adjusted price of cocaine in Europe has increased since 2002.

As in the North American market, only a fraction of the retail value goes to those who produce the drug. The intercontinental traffickers receive a larger share than in the North American case, but more than half of the retail value still accrues ro wholesalers and retailers within Europe.

Heroin

Heroin is the most widely consumed illicit opiate in the world. It is derived from opium, which itself can have an illicit use. Of the opium that is not con-verted into heroin, two thirds is consumed in just five countries: the Islamic Republic of Iran (42%), Afghanistan (7%), Pakistan (7%), India (6%) and the Russian Federation (5%). Other opiates are also abused, including various poppy straw concoctions and prescription opiods, but heroin remains the most problematic opiate internationally.

With the exception of 2001, when there was hardly any opium poppy cultivation in Afghanistan, global opium production expanded remarkably in the first decade of the twenty-first century until 2007, apparently with no com-mensurate expansion in demand. Opium production subsequently declined over the 2007–2009 period (from 8,890 to 7,754 mt), though remaining significantly above estimated global demand (some 5,000 mt for consumption and seizures). The declining farm-gate price of opium in Afghanistan in recent years has been more pronounced than the decline in heroin prices. This may reflect a number of factors, including rising prices for heroin precursors (particularly acetic anhydride) in that country and a build-up of stocks of opium not processed into heroin.

Although Afghanistan is the source of most of the world's illicit opiates (6,900 mt of opium or 89% of the world total in 2009), significant quantities are also produced in Myanmar (330 mt) and Latin America (notably in Mexico and Colombia). Since 2003, Mexico has been the world's third largest source of opium, and the quantities produced in 2008 (325 mt) came close to the quantities produced in Myanmar in 2009.

There are indications that the downward trend in global opium production over the 2007–2009 period will continue in 2010. Early indications for 2010 (as revealed in UNODC's *Afghanistan Opium Winter Rapid Assessment*) suggested that area under opium cultivation in Afghanistan could remain basically stable, but yields will likely decline due to a blight.

Both opium and heroin seizures continued to increase in 2008. Morphine seizures, however, continued the declining trend started in 2007. Although heroin seizures have followed a generally increasing trend since 2002, they have been outpaced by the growth in global opium seizures, possibly reflecting difficulties faced by Afghan laboratory operators to obtain sufficient precursor chemicals to transform the large quantities of harvested opium into heroin. Most of the opium seizures continue to be made in the Islamic Republic of Iran, neighbouring Afghanistan. The global rise in opium seizures thus largely reflected the growing opium seizures made by the authorities in the Islamic Republic of Iran.

The world's two largest markets for Afghan opiates are the Russian Federation and West Europe, which together consume almost half the heroin produced in the world. About 340 mt of heroin is estimated to have been consumed globally in 2008. To meet this demand, accounting for seizures, some 430 mt would have had to be produced. UNODC estimates suggest that about 380 mt were produced out of Afghan opium that year, supplying the bulk of global demand.

The Largest Heroin Market: West Europe   The world's largest heroin market is West Europe, and about half of this market is contained in just three countries: the United Kingdom, Italy and France. Heroin use appears to be decreasing in most West European countries, although the harms associated with heroin use seem to be increasing, as reflected in heroin-induced deaths. . . .

The Second Largest Heroin Market: The Russian Federation   Some 25% of all Afghan heroin (95 mt) is trafficked each year from Afghanistan into Central Asia to meet a demand of some 70 mt in the Russian Federation, along the 'Northern Route'. The number of opiate users in the Russian Federation is estimated at between 1.6 and 1.8 million people, equivalent to a prevalence rate of 1.6% of the population aged 15–64. There is a very high prevalence of HIV among drug users (some 37%). . . .

Note

1. Morphine represents an intermediate step in the processing of opium to heroin, and is rarely consumed as a drug in its own right.

➡ **NO**

Drug Policy—Lessons Learnt, and Options for the Future

What Is the 'Logical Framework' Behind the Current International Drug Control Regime? What Objectives Does It Set Out to Achieve, and What Assumptions Have Been Made About How to Best Meet These Objectives?

The international community has experienced almost 100 years of international drug control agreements since The Hague Convention was adopted in 1912. The current United Nations comprehensive framework for the control of psychoactive drugs—represented by the 1961 Single Convention on Narcotic Drugs—is almost 50 years old. While the nature of the markets and patterns of use of the various substances controlled under these agreements have changed significantly since 1961, it is useful to start an analysis of future policy options by returning to the original purpose and assumptions behind the Single Convention.

First, it is important to remember that the experts drafting the Single Convention, and the diplomats negotiating its passage, were operating in a very different political and social environment than today. Drug use was much less widespread, and illegal drug markets were more geographically confined, and less diverse. The phenomenon of international organised crime deriving most of its income from drug markets had not yet arisen, the widespread use of cocaine and other stimulants was not a significant consideration, and no one could have predicted the arrival of HIV, and its widespread transmission through injecting drug use.

Nonetheless, the political will at that time was sufficient to create a unified framework for the control of a wide range of psychoactive substances, using a twin track approach—the creation of a supervised global system for the production, distribution and use of psychoactive substances for medical and research purposes; and the prohibition of the production, distribution and possession of those substances for any other purpose. The preamble to the Single Convention[1] makes it absolutely clear that the ultimate aim of the drug control system is the improvement of the 'health and welfare of mankind,' but the design of the system, and the focus of implementation since its adoption by member states, betrays a number of assumptions on how best to achieve this objective, that have since been shown to be questionable at best, and in some cases clearly flawed.

A paper prepared for the Commission by Martin Jelsma will give more detail on the experience of the UN system, but this paper will focus on four key assumptions implicit within the creation of that system:

- That it is possible to suppress the wholesale illicit supply of controlled substances by removing sources of production, and preventing their distribution across borders.
- That it is possible to suppress illicit retail distribution of controlled substances, thereby preventing access to those substances by potential users, either physically or economically (i.e. by raising the price).
- That it is possible to suppress demand for the recreational use of controlled substances through a mixture of education and information on their risks, and deterrence through detection and punishment of users.
- That, through successes in each of the above areas, the phenomenon of illicit drug use would gradually be reduced in scale, which in turn would lead to the desired objective of maximised human health and welfare.

This set of assumptions is based on a wider belief that there was a simple linear relationship between the scale of the drug market, and the level of harm to human health and welfare (i.e. the smaller the market, the fewer the harms), so the singular focus of the system has been on reducing the scale of the illegal drug market, with the eventual aim of a 'drug free world'. The experience of the last 50 years shows that the relationship between scale and harms is much more complex, with different drug market dynamics and patterns of consumption leading to different levels of problems, for example:

- A cannabis market in which the product is grown near the point of consumption, and distributed through small scale friendship networks produces much lower social and criminal problems than a cannabis market involving the control by organised gangs of production and distribution across long distances.[2]
- The injection of street heroin of unpredictable purity, and the lifestyle associated with obtaining and using the drug through illicit channels, creates much higher levels of health and social harms than the oral ingestion of other forms of opiate (particularly if supplied or administered under medical supervision), even if the overall number of users is the same.[3]

As a result, many governments have started to move the focus of their drug policy away from a singular drive (usually referred to rhetorically as a 'war on drugs') to reduce the scale of their drug markets, towards greater attention and resources being applied to tackling specific market or consumption related problems, such as HIV/AIDS or petty crime. The speed and extent to which this change of focus should be followed remains hugely controversial, with many governments and institutions fighting to retain the simplicity of the original model.

To What Extent Have the Objectives of the System Been Achieved Over the Past 50 Years?

Much of the political debate between 'tough' (i.e. enforcement focus) and 'soft' (i.e. health and social focus) approaches to drug policy is based on moral and ideological beliefs. While this position may have an attractive clarity and simplicity, policymakers have a duty to understand and act on the evidence of effectiveness or otherwise, and to pursue policies and public investments that maximise the health and welfare of their citizens. Fortunately, the evidence and understanding of how drug policies and strategies impact on drug use and markets has increased markedly in the 50 years since the system was created. Unfortunately, the gaps in the evidence base, and complexity of the issues, mean that there can be no universally 'correct' policy deduced from what we currently know.

Therefore, we need to critically examine the extent to which current policies and strategies are achieving the objectives set out for them, and apply the lessons to the development of future policy. This section reviews progress and lessons against the assumptions articulated in [the first section] above.

Suppressing Wholesale Supply

Strategies in this regard have been in place for the full century of drug control, and have received unequivocal political support, and massive financial investment. Unfortunately, all this effort has not achieved the desired control and constriction of wholesale markets. The scale of global markets in the main plant based psychoactive products—heroin, cocaine and cannabis—is now significantly larger than when the Single Convention was adopted. While there have been some signs of stabilisation in recent years at an overall global level, this masks significant increases in new markets and distribution routes for these substances (particularly in developing countries), and the parallel growth in markets for a wide range of synthetically produced alternatives.

Tactics designed to reduce wholesale supply have had very limited impact—action in source countries has been expensive and complicated, and even when implemented, serves only to drive cultivation and production to new areas (this is referred to as the 'balloon effect'):

- Decades of careful eradication and alternative development work in the opium growing areas of the golden triangle of Laos, Myanmar (then Burma) and Thailand eventually had an impact, but the focus of production then moved to Afghanistan, with consequences that still haunt the international community.
- Extensive (and expensive—US$ 7.3 billion have been spent by the USA on Plan Colombia alone since 2000)[4] military interventions and eradication programmes in the Andean coca growing region over the past 30 years have only served to move the concentration

of cultivation within and between the countries of Peru, Bolivia and Colombia, with no reduction of overall production, and no sustained impact on wholesale or retail prices or availability.

• While much more widely grown, and therefore less subject to source country action, cannabis retail markets in Europe have increasingly been served by production close to the point of consumption, as opposed to the previous pattern of large scale cultivation in North Africa, and distribution by organised crime.

Suppressing Retail Markets

Efforts to stifle the flow of drugs from points of production to retail markets (generally described as interdiction), have also met with fundamental problems. Even the largest seizures of drugs en route to consumer markets have failed to make a sustained impact on price, availability or purity. This is due to a mixture of practical and economic considerations—in a globalised world, the opportunities and methods for moving consignments of compact commodities are just too diverse, and the resources and ingenuity of traffickers too great, for law enforcement authorities to prevail. Furthermore, the level of seizures required to make a meaningful impact on the consumer market are beyond the capacity of even the most well resourced state agencies—the UK government commissioned an economic analysis on this question that concluded that it would be necessary to seize 60 to 80% of plant-based drugs coming in to the country to make a measurable impact on price and availability, while the best estimate of the proportion actually seized per year has never exceeded 20%.[5] [NB—While this analysis has certainly been true historically, there are signs of significant upheavals in the UK heroin market in early 2011. The reasons and impacts are not yet understood, but may give us further insights into the relationship between enforcement and price. IDPC will produce a briefing paper on this issue later in the year].

This depressing picture of supply reduction failures is actually compounded by analysis of what happens on the rare occasions when the strategy succeeds in creating a sustained shortage of a particular substance. A series of successful operations by Australian law enforcement agencies, allied with shifting priorities of Asian trafficking organisations, led to a 2-year heroin shortage in Australia in the early part of this century. While this phenomenon did result in a significant downturn in heroin use in that country (leading to reduced injecting and overdose deaths), users tended to switch to other drugs such as cocaine and methamphetamine, rather than to give up or seek treatment, leading to an upsurge in the problems associated with those substances (mainly an increase in mental disorders and street violence).[6]

Reducing Demand

In parallel with these supply reduction efforts, demand reduction strategies have attempted to reduce the number of people wanting to use drugs, primarily through two mechanisms—education and deterrence. Both strategies have, in general, had little impact on overall population rates of drug use.

Large scale education and prevention programmes aimed at the whole population have been tried in most countries in some form or other. The idea is that potential drug users will be less likely to initiate or continue drug use if they are presented with warnings of the health and social risks of such use. Many of these campaigns have exaggerated the risks in an attempt to maximise the impact. Where long term evaluations of whole population education campaigns have been carried out, they have found that, at best, these programmes have had only marginal and short lived impacts on overall levels of drug use. Initiation into drug use generally occurs amongst the young, who have a high tolerance of risk taking, and low levels of trust in official information, particularly when it is exaggerated and inconsistent with their own experience.[7] More promising results have been achieved by targeted and community based prevention projects, where more tailored approaches are delivered to smaller sub-populations at risk (for example children in care, or those in trouble at school). Some of these have been shown to divert a proportion of the target population away from a drug using lifestyle but, by their 'micro' nature, do not impact on the 'macro' whole population prevalence.

Beyond education and information, governments have used more direct forms of deterrence—primarily the threat of arrest and punishment under the criminal law, but also mechanisms for detection and punishment in schools, work places, and clubs and associations. Drug testing programmes, allied with punishments such as exclusion from school or other institutions, sacking or other disciplinary actions at work, or denial of access to benefits such as university grants, have all been tried. Once again, we find that the results in terms of deterring initiation and continuing use are limited.[8] Surveys of drug users show that the reasons behind their decisions are primarily driven by personal social and emotional factors, peer pressure, and fashion.[9] The risk of being caught and the nature of associated punishment played little part. All countries have enacted laws against possession of controlled drugs, and to varying extents hoped that the enforcement of these laws will deter potential users. Some countries have consciously tried to raise the level of detection and punishment to a point that every potential user is in constant fear of being caught. The USA has gone furthest down this road, with a peak of 1.66 million drug-related offences in 2009 (and among these, 1.35 million for drug possession alone), and the implementation of mandatory minimum prison terms.[10] Despite this massive political and financial investment, levels of drug use in the USA have for decades remained consistently higher than almost any other country in the world.[11] Even at this high level of arrests, it has been calculated that the average drug user in the USA has a miniscule chance of detection on each occasion of use—hardly the level of risk that is going to alter their behaviour.[12]

Some countries have tried to reduce drug dependence by pursuing treatment models that punish and humiliate users. This philosophy was behind some of the early therapeutic communities developed in the USA and Europe in the 1960 and 1970s, and has more recently been employed in a range of 'forced treatment' facilities that have been developed in many south-east Asian countries in recent years. These facilities have corralled large numbers of drug users, often without due process or any assessment of treatment need, in conditions that breach international human rights standards.[13] Unsurprisingly, these facilities have had very little success in rehabilitating users, and have attracted widespread condemnation.

Impact on the Overall Scale of the Market

Various mixtures of these strategies and tactics have been implemented around the world over the last 50 years, but there is no evidence that any national government has been able to achieve anything like the objective of a controlled and diminished drug market, let alone a drug free world. There are some countries that have never experienced the same growth of drug markets as neighbouring countries (e.g. Japan), and a very small number that have managed to limit an already established drug market—claims are often made that Sweden has achieved this turnaround through a mixture of strong enforcement, and consistent prevention and social messaging. While it seems true that Sweden has kept overall population rates of drug use relatively low by European standards, their rates are no lower than countries with liberal policies (such as Portugal and the Netherlands), and some of the related problems such as market related violence, and HIV and overdose rates, are no lower in Sweden than comparable countries.[14] While there is no conclusive research on this issue, it seems likely that the comparative wealth and social cohesion of countries like Sweden and Japan, together with their strong public commitment to an anti-drug philosophy (conditions that are hard to replicate through policy decisions) are significant factors in their relatively low prevalence, but these countries do continue to experience significant levels of drug use and problems.

At a global level, the picture is clearer. Although figures are not available for the early 1960s, it is universally acknowledged that the scale of drug use and drug markets have grown exponentially over the period of implementation of a global control regime that had reduction and eradication as its objectives.[15] In countries where time series data are available (Europe, North America and Australasia), there is a documented steady growth of the use of the three main plant based drugs (heroin, cocaine and cannabis) throughout the 1970s, 1980s and 1990s and, when there were some signs of stabilisation in these markets in the last 10 years, a corresponding growth in the use of a bewildering variety of synthetically produced stimulants and hallucinogens.[16] This diversification of substances, production and consumption patterns moves much faster than the ability of lawmakers, educators and enforcement agencies to respond.

Defenders of the current system (most notably, the former head of the United Nations Office on Drugs and Crime—UNODC, Antonio Costa) have argued that the implementation of strong prevention and enforcement policies have 'contained' the problem at a lower level than, for example, alcohol or tobacco. Also, using the example of pre-revolutionary China, that unfettered trade in narcotics would lead to massive rates of addiction and social upheaval.[17] While both of these contentions have little historic evidence to back them up,[18] and can to some extent be put down to the 'wishful thinking' of the man responsible for claiming success of existing policies, it is important that any proposal to take more liberal approaches addresses the question of what impact it will have on the overall scale of the market.

What Are the Negative Side Effects of the Implementation of the Drug Control System?

The primary strategies and tactics, in which the authors of the drug control regime have put so much faith, have failed to deliver a significant and sustained reduction in the scale of supply or demand for any of the main types of drug, over a 50 year period in which the international community has shown unequivocal political and financial commitment. When viewed from the perspective of the fundamental objective of the system—to maximise human health and welfare—we also need to consider the negative side-effects (what the UN describes as 'unintended consequences') of the implementation of the system on the health and welfare of individuals and communities.

The UNODC (the agency charged with overseeing the implementation of the conventions) itself acknowledges significant negative consequences of the drug control regime, some of which can be summarised as [follows].[19]

An Increase in the Power and Reach of Organized Crime

One of the most significant 'unintended consequences' of the international drug control regime has been the growth in the power and wealth of a global web of organised crime networks. These groups operate in a transnational and transcontinental market through which they link the producers and consumers of illicit drugs; they are also deeply involved in the manufacture of synthetic drugs, and the movement of precursor chemicals. With widespread corruption and (often) high levels of violence, they control and operate a vast global market whose overall worth is the subject of controversy, but certainly runs into the 100s of billions of US dollars,[20] the high end estimate being in the region of $400 billion.[21] While the social impact of this increased wealth is hard to measure, it is certain to increase the crime and corruption challenges faced by legitimate authority in many parts of the world.

The Stigmatisation and Marginalisation of Large Numbers of Citizens

It is well documented that harsh living conditions, trauma and emotional difficulties are major factors leading to drug use. It is therefore unsurprising that drug dependence remains concentrated among the most marginalised groups in society. Whereas much of the work of social affairs and development agencies at the national and international level have focused on improving the living conditions of poor and marginalised groups, and on promoting their social and economical integration in society, many aspects of drug control policies have had the opposite effect. Programmes focusing on widespread arrests and harsh sanctions towards drug users have [led] to further marginalisation and stigmatisation, pushing them away from jobs, education and other health and social services, and driving them into more risky behaviours.[22] This process of criminalisation and marginalisation is acknowledged by the United Nations as a major barrier to the global challenges of tackling HIV/AIDS, and of promoting social and economic development.[23]

Misdirected Expenditure

Over the past decades, the vast majority of financial resources allocated by governments and the international community has targeted the illicit market.[24] At global, regional and national levels, resources have been committed to reducing the size of drug markets, primarily through law enforcement activities. Public health, treatment and harm reduction measures have suffered accordingly, the support they have received being more rhetorical than substantial. Instead of the most dangerous and influential criminals within the illicit market, it is street dealers and mules—those most easily replaced in the drug trade—that have made up prosecution statistics. This strategy has produced little impact on the overall scale of the market, while the socio-economic poverty that often underpins problematic use in consumer countries and illicit crop growing in production zones has lacked adequate, sustained and properly sequenced funding.

Human Rights Violations

Many human rights abuses have resulted from the implementation of drug control strategies, including excessive use of force and extra-judicial killings; the destruction of the main means of subsistence of many farmers and environmental destruction due to crop eradication campaigns; ill-treatment of drug users in the name of drug treatment; violations to the right to health because of the failure to provide drug users with adequate drug dependence treatment and lack of access to essential medicines for pain relief; the implementation of discriminatory policies towards drug users, minorities, women and children; and the imposition of disproportionate punishments, including the death penalty and life imprisonment, for drug-related offences.[25]

Why Do Policymakers Remain Attracted to 'War on Drugs' Approaches in the Face of These Problems?

Given the ever-growing body of evidence demonstrating the lack of impact of current drug policies and strategies on the overall scale of illegal drug markets, and the growing awareness of the negative side effects of these strategies on health and social welfare, it could be seen as surprising that most policymakers continue to support the current approach. In western democracies with decades of experience in drug policy design and review, most political rhetoric continues to focus on the need to maintain resolve, or to strengthen commitment, or to clamp down on some new drug or pattern of use or supply.

In developing countries, where drug problems are a newer challenge, the initial impulse of political leaders is invariably to respond to new concerns with calls for a fight against the 'scourge' of drugs. It is hard to think of another area of social policy where such a clear lack of progress maintains such widespread political support, so we need to understand why this is so. I would suggest that there are four inter-related reasons:

- The main political attraction of war on drugs rhetoric, and the policies that follow, is that they allow the government to look tough and active on a problem that the public cares about. The picture in the public's mind, built up over decades of news coverage and cop shows, is of all drug traffickers as ruthless criminals, and all drug users as morally suspect. While there are, of course, real life examples that fit these caricatures, we now know that most drug producers are some of the world's most marginalised rural poor; that many traffickers are couriers (or 'mules') coerced into transporting drugs across borders; and most drug users are indistinguishable from other citizens, apart from their choice of substance. Policymakers can therefore use a very effective rhetorical symbolism, by promising to tackle the drug problem through tough enforcement, and can demonstrate their commitment by pushing through tougher laws, publicising big seizures, and arresting more users. These have been largely effective political strategies, as the awkward reality that the underlying drug related problems remain unresolved receives little attention.
- The political alternative—that of questioning the 'tough on drugs' orthodoxy, of promoting policies that are more tolerant of drug use, or that reduce enforcement or punishment—represents a high risk strategy for any politician. As the former Prime Minister of Luxembourg, Jean-Claude Juncker, has succinctly put it: 'We know what to do, but we don't know how to get re-elected once we have done it.' Drug policy is often referred to as a 'third rail' issue—a railway metaphor that loosely means that if you touch it, you are going to be electrocuted. In the bear pit of local and national politics, any leader who questions traditional policies, or promotes alternatives, is easily caricatured by media and political opponents as 'soft on drugs,' weak on law and order, or in favour of greater drug use. It is perhaps therefore not surprising that a large number of policymakers at all levels privately hold views on the best direction for drug policies and strategies that they are unwilling to express in the public arena.
- These political dynamics are underpinned by some real conceptual and intellectual problems regarding the case for drug policy reform. The first of these is how to address the contention—often stated, and currently the position of the UNODC—that, although enforcement based policies have not reduced the scale of the drug problem, they have at least contained what otherwise would be an 'epidemic' or 'flood' of increased drug markets and use, with all the related problems increasing accordingly. This once again has a seductive political message— that the government and law enforcement authorities are protecting society from social and moral breakdown. It is also a contention that cannot be disproved until alternative models are implemented, and the impact on levels of use and problems fully tested. However, a

political leader considering alternative approaches will surely be criticised for taking great risks with a 'leap into the unknown.' In fact, there
are some policy lessons we have learnt regarding the impact of more
tolerant policies on the level and nature of drug use and markets—
broadly, in countries and states where laws or enforcement practices
have been liberalised, there seems to have been a minimal impact on
overall levels of use, and broadly positive impacts on related health
and social problems, and costs to the taxpayer. Similarly, simple com-
parisons between countries with high or low levels of enforcement
and punishment show no correlation between tough approaches and
lower levels of use. Certainly, there has been no sign (in places like The
Netherlands, Switzerland, Portugal and Australia) of the explosion of
drug use and addiction that has often been feared. Levels of drug use
in a given society seem to be largely a function of the innate proper-
ties of the substance (i.e. do people like its effects or not), fashion, the
nature of that society—levels of inequality, social cohesion or trauma,
and the availability and price of particular substances. What remains
unknown, of course, is what would be the impact on these market
dynamics of the full legalisation of drugs—and, within such a system
of regulation, the impact of the involvement (in marketing and political lobbying terms) of legitimate commercial businesses, such as is
currently the case with the alcohol or tobacco companies.

- The second problem facing the reform-minded policymaker is that the
issue is so complex, that trying to replace a simple and seductive political
message with one that acknowledges such complexity, and recognises
that the government cannot in fact 'solve' the drug problem entirely,
is a high-risk political strategy. Most policymakers who have tried this
approach, have been criticised as giving in to the drug barons, or for
not showing enough bravery for the fight. These particular dynamics
have improved in recent years—to a varying extent in different political
cultures—but the reasons for reform are still difficult to synthesise into
an effective political message. A number of difficult propositions have
to be sold to the public—that the current system (that we have all supported politically and financially) is not working; that a better approach
involves the management of drug markets and drug use, because they
will never be completely eradicated; and that this approach involves
being more tolerant of the behaviour of a proportion of drug producers,
distributors and users. Support for these propositions requires the audience to accept and understand the complexity of the policy challenge,
while there will always be other voices reiterating the simple message 'if
we get tougher we will eventually win.'

Therefore, considering the political dynamics surrounding this issue, it is perhaps not so surprising that so few policymakers have openly questioned the
status quo, or pushed for reform. However, these political realities seem to
be changing quickly in many parts of the world—there are increasingly clear
challenges to the idea that harsh enforcement leads to reduced health and
social harms, so that claims for success based on seizures or arrests are greeted
with scepticism; most electorates now have a broad view that the war on
drugs is not working; increasing numbers of citizens know friends and family

who are drug users, or who have developed drug problems, so are less likely to accept the stigma and condemnation; and a rapidly increasing number of political leaders are 'coming out' to acknowledge that we need to think about new approaches, which gives legitimacy and profile to a more sophisticated debate.

What Are the Budgetary and Institutional Impediments to Review and Reform of Drug Policies?

In addition to the difficult political dynamics around drug policy issues, we need to be aware of the institutional and budgetary dynamics as well. In any field of national and international government activity that has received unequivocal political and financial support over decades, there will inevitably be a significant and established network of institutions and agencies that have been built up on the back of a particular view of policy and strategy. In the drug control field, these institutions owe their budgets and power to the war on drugs, and will be resistant to policies or initiatives that question their value, or threaten their financial and political pre-eminence. As drug control has been seen for 100 years as primarily a crime and law enforcement issue, the dominant institutions at national and international level are rooted in that sector.

At national level, the budgets and power of law enforcement agencies in many countries have been built up to a large degree on the contention that their activities are essential to achieving victory in the war on drugs. This is particularly true of those institutions specifically created for drug control purposes, such as the Drug Enforcement Administration in the USA (annual budget $2.6 billion), which is typical in that it has become a significant political force in US national debates, and atypical in that it also exerts significant influence in other countries. While the DEA is the largest and best known of the national drug control agencies, there are structures in most countries that only exist to design and implement drug control strategies. While some of these structures have included health and social programmes in their work more recently, they still tend to be dominated culturally and financially by law enforcement imperatives. They have a significant institutional investment, therefore, in the continuation of existing patterns of resource allocation.

Law enforcement agencies that have more generic responsibilities have also expanded and benefited from drug control policies—police services at all levels, together with court and prison administrations, customs agencies, and even the military, have used the drugs issue to expand their budgets and influence in good times, and to defend against cuts in the bad times. In the drug policy debate around the world, representatives of these institutions can be strong and effective advocates for a continuation of law enforcement investment, a message that usually finds a receptive ear in the corridors of power. The publication in early 2010 of the Obama administration's first drug control budget was expected to represent a reversal of the trend of ever-increasing budgets for the DEA and other law enforcement institutions and initiatives. In the event, and despite the avowed intention of the new administration to subject the value for money of these investments to close scrutiny in an era of fiscal restraint, the new budget has maintained the same pattern and level of funding.

Internationally, the institutions developed to oversee and implement the UN agreements on controlled drugs have similarly been built on the assumption that strong prohibition strategies, and a law enforcement focus, were the best way to achieve the objectives of the control system. All three of the main institutions have been slow to react to the limited success of 'Plan A', and the increasing need for balance in policy and programming:

- The UNODC is the Vienna-based UN executive agency that oversees the shared work of the international community to implement the drug control treaties. With an annual budget of US$250 million,[26] and around 1,500 staff based around the world, much of its early work was focused on encouraging member states to sign and ratify the drug control conventions, and supporting them to enact strong domestic drug laws, and establish strategies and institutions to implement them. The agency has therefore developed on the basis of a strong vested interest in the success and continuation of member state commitment to these activities. It is a relatively small executive agency, but has been successful in maintaining a high level of ratification for the 3 conventions it oversees[27] and no member state has followed procedures to pull out of any of the agreements. Operationally, the agency has been less successful—it receives a very small allocation of general funds from UN headquarters, so is heavily reliant on voluntary donations from member states. The majority of these donations have traditionally come from countries (particularly the US) who have at times used them as a lever to ensure that the UNODC maintains a strong 'war on drugs' line. These dynamics have, however, changed in recent years, with a greater proportion of funds coming from the EU and its member states, and more of it being directed towards health and social programmes. It is probably no coincidence, therefore, that the policy positions of the UNODC have become more balanced over this period. However, the extent to which the management of the agency can reform its operations is limited by an ever present financial crisis, allied to the need to maintain existing funding streams. This does not create helpful conditions for strategic thinking, or planned reforms.
- Another reason for the inability of the UNODC to adapt quickly to changing circumstances is the fact that its governing body, the Commission on Narcotic Drugs (CND), has inbuilt mechanisms that block reform. Although the CND officially consists of just 53 member states, there is a longstanding convention that all member states present at its annual meetings (held in Vienna in March of each year) should agree by consensus to any key policy decision. The budget, key operations, and policy positions of the agency are therefore decided through CND resolutions that are negotiated in minute detail, resulting in confused and often surreal mandates being handed down to the executive. In a situation where at least some member states—for many years led by

the US, but now led by other influential countries such as Russia and Japan—have been committed to the global strengthening of the war on drugs at all costs, those member states that have wanted to modernise and achieve more health and development based policies have found it almost impossible to advance their cause through the CND. One particularly absurd example is that it is still impossible to use the words 'harm reduction' in any CND resolution, despite the fact that harm reduction strategies have been the accepted UN and WHO approach to HIV prevention amongst drug users for many years. This bias against reform and in favour of law enforcement is underpinned by the fact that the vast majority of member state delegations to the CND are made up of senior law enforcement officials.

- There is a third body within the UN drug control architecture that has become an even more strident opponent of drug policy reform. In addition to the responsibility for operating the system set up to manage the legal production, distribution and use of controlled substances for medical and scientific purposes, the International Narcotics Control Board (INCB) was established by the 1961 Convention to act as a watchdog of the conventions: helping member states to find the right balance between control and health responsibilities, pointing out where member states were failing to comply with the obligations that they had signed up to, and working with them to address these concerns. The Board consists of 13 members who are meant to be appointed for their legal and medical expertise, and act independently of the political interests of member states and UN agencies. It has a secretariat based within the UNODC. The culture and methods of operation of the Board have fluctuated since its inception but, at least for the last 25 years, it has acted more as a guardian of the traditional view of global drug control—promoting strong laws and enforcement practices, and being quick to criticise any perceived liberal initiative. Member states have colluded with this one-eyed approach, voting members on to the board who are politically motivated rather than technical experts, and failing to demand changes in the Board's methods of operation. It is becoming clearer however, that the work of the INCB is out of step with the norms and standards of the UN system, and the enthusiasm amongst member states for reforming their role is increasing.

Finally, the fact that drug control debates within the multilateral system have been entirely channelled through the Vienna based crime and enforcement structures is itself a major impediment to a co-ordinated and coherent international system. Most national governments, recognising that the drugs phenomenon is multi-faceted (requiring a balance between health, criminal justice, education, security and social policies), have established co-ordinating mechanisms to manage these inter-relationships, but the UN system continues to leave the issue to its law enforcement agencies. Much larger multilateral bodies—such as the World Health Organisation, UNAIDS, the UN Development Programme and the Human Rights treaty bodies—struggle to have their voices heard in Vienna. This must change if the UN is to give coherent global leadership on this issue.

Therefore, at the national and international level, strong institutional interests mitigate against objective strategic review, and the implementation of the necessary modernising reforms. While there are signs that all of these structures are adjusting their rhetoric and positions in reaction to changing circumstances—realities on the ground, changing public opinion, and the work of NGOs and academic analysts—it is disappointing that the biggest governmental organisations act as a brake on these debates, rather than their leaders. Any proposals for reform will therefore need to recognise these realities, and include strategies for convincing the leaders of these institutions to accept the need for change.

Conclusion

Policymakers have discovered that the achievement of drug control objectives is a much more difficult and complex task than was ever conceived of by the architects of the global system. What is now common knowledge—that prohibition and harsh enforcement cannot control the basic human impulse to use psychoactive substances, and the immutable rules of commodity markets—was hypothesised by a small number of voices through the 20th century, and has been repeatedly indicated by all respectable academic and policy analysis conducted in recent years.[28] The appropriate political and strategic debate in reaction to this learning has for decades been hampered by the willingness of policymakers and the responsible institutions to use drug policy as a symbolic issue, rather than as a search for practical responses to wider health, social and crime problems. Now that this trick is becoming more exposed, and therefore less viable, governments have broadly four options of how to react to the current impasse:

- Pursue policies and investments that ramp up enforcement activities and punishments to a level that actually succeeds in stifling the flow of controlled substances around the world, and in deterring a large proportion of the population from deciding to use them. Despite the rhetoric, this approach is not currently being implemented in any part of the world.
- Continue with policies that try to show that enforcement and deterrence are the priority, while offering minority support to health and social programmes in the name of balance, and defending limited impact with promises of new crackdowns and initiatives. This is the current political strategy of most governments around the world.
- Refocus drug policies and programmes explicitly away from attempts to reduce the scale of the market, and on to reducing the specific harms arising from drug use and markets, such as HIV/AIDS, addiction, or violence and corruption. While many countries have introduced aspects of a targeted problem solving approach within their strategies, none have explicitly made this the guiding principle of their policy, and openly articulated to the electorate that market reduction is not the main goal.
- Conclude that greater control of supply, demand and related problems can be achieved through moving to a regulated system of

distribution—i.e. legalisation. This change of paradigm has not been implemented anywhere in the world, and any country wishing to do so would need to withdraw from the UN conventions.[29] Notwithstanding this, a policy option that was difficult to discuss seriously as recently as 2009, is now being given close attention at all levels, with the strong showing for California's 'Proposition 19,' and public support from an increasing number of high profile public figures.

The final issue to consider is the level of hunger for change amongst the public and policymakers. For various reasons, there are stronger pressures for reform in some countries (for example in North and Latin America, or South-East Asia) where the issues are at the top of the political agenda, than others (for example much of Europe) where the issue has less immediacy. The proposals for reform that the Commission wishes to bring forward will therefore be received with differing levels of enthusiasm, depending on the level of comfort and complacency on this issue amongst governments and institutions, and the citizens that support them.

References

1. The Single Convention on Narcotic Drugs of 1961, http://www.unodc.org/pdf/convention_1961_en.pdf

2. Feilding, A., Room, R., Fischer, B., Hall, W., Lenton, S. & Reuter, P. (2008), *The Global Cannabis Commission report—cannabis policy: moving beyond stalemate,* http://www.beckleyfoundation.org/pdf/BF_Cannabis_Commission_ Report.pdf

3. See, for example, Fischer B, Rehm J, Kirst M, et al. (2002), 'Heroin-assisted treatment as a response to the public health problem of opiate dependence.' *Eur J Public Health* 12:228–234.

4. Washington Office on Latin America (14 July 2010), *Don't call it a mode.,* http://justf.org/files/pubs/notmodel.pdf

5. UK Cabinet Office (12 May 2003), *Strategy Unit Drugs report—Phase one: understanding the issues,* http://www.cabinetoffice.gov.uk/media/cabinetoffice/strategy/assets/drugs_report.pdf

6. Bush, W., Roberts, M., Trace, M. (2004), *Upheavals in the Australian drug market: heroin drought, stimulant flood* (The Beckley Foundation Drug policy Programme), http://www.beckleyfoundation.org/pdf/paper_04.pdf

7. See for example: Plant, E. & Plant, M. (1999), 'Primary prevention for young children: a comment on the UK government's 10 year drug strategy.' *International Journal of Drug Policy* 10(5): 385–401. http://www.ijdp.org/article/S0955-3959(99)00019-5/abstract; Lynam, D.R., et al. (1999), 'Project DARE: no effects at 10-year follow-up.' *Journal of Consulting and Clinical Psychology* 67(4): 590–593.

8. Roche, A.M., Pidd, K., Bywood, P., Duraisingam, V., Steenson, T., Freeman, T. & Nicholas, R. (2007), *Drug testing in schools—Evidence, impacts and alternatives* (Australian National Council on Drugs: Camberra), http://drugaids.socialnet.org.hk/Documents/australia_drug_testing_in_schools%20(1).pdf

9. Gorsuch, R.L. & Butler M.C. (1976), 'Initial drug abuse: a review of predisposing social psychological factors,' *Psychological Bulletin* **83**(1): 120–137, http://www.sciencedirect.com/science?_ob=ArticleURL&_udi=B6WY5-4NP4KW6-7&_user=10&_coverDate=01%2F31%2F1976&_rdoc=1&_fmt=high&_orig=search&_origin=search&_sort=d&_docanchor=&view=c&_searchStrId=1494646275&_rerunOrigin=scholar.google&_acct=C000050221&_version=1&_urlVersion=0&_userid=10&md5=bfb28ae51b54f3778ac9537770972d54&searchtype=a

10. Department of Justice, Federal Bureau of Investigation (2010), 'Arrests,' *Preliminary uniform crime report 2009,* http://www.fbi.gov/about-us/cjis/ucr/crime-in-the-u.s/2009

11. See Bewley-Taylor, D., Hallam, C. & Allan, R. (March 2009), *The incarceration of drug offenders: an overview,* Beckley Foundation Drug Policy Programme and International Centre for Prison Studies, King's College London, University of London, Report Sixteen. http://www.beckleyfoundation.org/pdf/BF_Report_16.pdf

12. Mark A. R. Kleiman, *Against excess: drug policy for results* (New York: Basic Books, 1992), http://www.sppsr.ucla.edu/faculty/kleiman/book/

13. UNODC (March 2010), *Discussion paper—From coercion to cohesion: treating drug dependence trhough healthcare, not punishment* (DRAFT). http://www.idpc.net/sites/default/files/library/Coercion%20FULL%20doc%20(2).pdf

14. Hallam, C. (January 2010), *Briefing paper 20—What can we learn from Sweden's drug policy experience?* (The Beckley Foundation Drug Policy Programme), http://www.idpc.net/sites/default/files/library/Sweden%20Briefing%20Paper%20final.pdf

15. According to the UNODC, "Until the mid-1960s, global cocaine seizures were measured in the tens of kilograms annually. In recent years, they have been in the hundreds of tons," *In* UNODC (2010), *2010 World Drug Report,* http://www.unodc.org/documents/wdr/WDR_2010/World_Drug_Report_2010_lo-res.pdf

16. UNODC (2009), *Trends and patterns of amphetamine-type stimulant and other drugs in East and South-East Asia (and neighbouring regions),* http://www.unodc.org/documents/eastasiaandpacific//2009/11/ats-report/2009_Patterns_and_Trends.pdf. In his *Foreword* to the World Drug Report 2010, Antonio Costa observes that, 'the global number of people using amphetamine-type stimulants (ATS) is likely to exceed the number of opiate and cocaine users combined.' p. 4

17. Commission on Narcotic Drugs 52nd session 11–20 March 2009 and Commission on Crime Prevention and Criminal Justice (22 January 2009), *Activities of the United Nations Office on Drugs and Crime, report of the Executive Director,* E/CN.7/2009/3-E/CN.15/2009/3, http://www.unodc.org/documents/commissions/CND-Uploads/CND-52-RelatedFiles/CND-52-Documents/CND52-ECN72009-03+ECN152009-03-E.pdf

18. See: Transnational Institute (June 2008), *Rewriting History: A Response to the 2008 World Drug Report.* http://www.idpc.net/php-bin/documents/TNI_RewritingHistory_2008_EN.pdf; International Drug Policy Consortium (September 2008), *The 2008 World Drug Report: A Response from the International Drug Policy Consortium,* pp. 2–7; International Drug Policy Consortium (September 2006), *IDPC Briefing Paper 2—The 2006 World Drug Report: winning the war on drugs?* pp. 5–6. http://www.idpc.net/sites/default/files/library/IDPC_BP_02_WorldDrugReport2006_EN.pdf

19. Commission on Narcotic Drugs (7 March 2008), *Making drug control 'fit for purpose': building on the UNGASS decade—Report by the Executive Director of the United Nations Office on Drugs and Crime as a contribution to the review of the twentieth special session of the General Assembly* (E/CN.7/2008/CRP.17), http://www.unodc.org/documents/commissions/CND-Session51/CND-UNGASS-CRPs/ECN72008CRP17.pdf

20. Francisco E. Thoumi, PhD (Winter 2005), 'The numbers game: let's all guess the size of the illegal drug industry!' *Journal of Drug Issues* 35(1).

21. UNODC: World Drug Report 1997 http://www.unodc.org/unodc/en/data-and-analysis/WDR.html

22. International Drug Policy Consortium (2010), 'Chapter 1: core principles,' *IDPC Drug Policy Guide,* http://www.idpc.net/sites/default/files/library/IDPC%20Drug%20Policy%20Guide_Version%201.pdf

23. United Nations Secretary General (26 June 2010), *Message for International Day Against Drug Abuse and Illicit Trafficking.* http://www.idpc.net/sites/default/files/alerts/Secretary%20General%20Message%2026%20June%202010-%20english%20(2).pdf

24. UNODC: Fit for Purpose: Building on the UNGASS Decade http://www.idpc.net/publications/building-on-ungass-decade

25. The Beckley Foundation Drug Policy Programme (March 2010), *Report No. 13—Recalibrating the regime: the need for a human rights-based approach to international drug policy,* http://idpc.net/sites/default/files/library/Recalibrating%20the%20regime.pdf; International Drug Policy Consortium (2010), 'Chapter 1: core principles', *IDPC Drug Policy Guide.* http://www.idpc.net/sites/default/files/library/IDPC%20Drug%20Policy%20Guide_Version%201.pdf

26. The UNODC budget for drugs and crime for the biennium 2008–2009 amounted to US$504.7 million. See: UNODC website: http://www.unodc.org/unodc/en/donors/index.html?ref=menutop

27. The 1971 Convention on Psychotropic Substances was ratified by 183 states, while the 1988 Convention against Illicit Traffic in Narcotic Drugs and Psychotropic Substances and the 1961 Single Convention on Narcotic Drugs was ratified by 184 states.

28. European Commission, Trimbos Instituut & Rand Europe (2009), *A report on global illicit drug markets 1998–2007* (Editors: Peter Reuter & Franz Trautmann). http://www.idpc.net/php-bin/documents/EU_Markets_Study_EN0409.pdf

29. 'Chapter VI—Beyond the current drug conventions,' *In* Feilding, A., Room, R., Fischer, B., Hall, W., Lenton, S. & Reuter, P. (2008), *The Global Cannabis Commission Report—Cannabis policy: moving beyond stalemate,* pp. 151–168. http://www.beckleyfoundation.org/pdf/BF_Cannabis_Commission_Report.pdf

EXPLORING THE ISSUE

Can the Global Community "Win" the Drug War?

Critical Thinking and Reflection

1. What general conclusions do you draw from the information on current production, distribution, and consumption levels of illicit drugs?
2. Do you believe that the American focus on drug use reduction and punishment for abusers rather than treatment for users has been a good idea?
3. What do you make of the extreme attacks by individuals who have been part of the war on drug enforcement teams?
4. Will legalization of most illicit drugs lead to less associated crime and violence?
5. Should the United States concentrate on influencing the demand for illicit drugs rather than continuing to focus on lowering and/or eliminating their supply?

Is There Common Ground?

There is one major area of agreement among drug war a majority of policy makers as well as global public opinion. Both believe that current levels of illegal drug use are unacceptable.

Additional Resources

Andreas, Peter and Greenhill, Kelly M., *Sex, Drugs and Body Counts: The Politics of Numbers in Global Crime and Conflict* (Cornell University Press, 2010)

> This book takes to task gross figures thrown around in print and in the media regarding the number of people affected by various global crimes, including drugs.

Bull, Melissa, *Governing the Heroin Trade* (Ashgate, 2008)

> The author examines the history, economics, and politics of the prohibition of certain drugs. It addresses the failures, unintended consequences, and other difficulties of global efforts to combat illegal drugs.

Buxton, Julia, *The Political Economy of Narcotics: Production, Consumption and Global Markets* (Zed books, 2006)

> This book examines the entire global drug world. It argues that prohibition has been a failed policy. Instead, it argues for a framework

that addresses current incentives for growers, sellers, and consumers of narcotics.

Christine Jojarth, *Crime, War, and Global Trafficking: Designing International Cooperation* (Cambridge University Press, 2009)

This book is critical of efforts of international institutions in the war on drugs.

Fukumi, Sayaka, *Cocaine Trafficking in Latin America* (Ashgate, 2008)

This book focuses on the different approaches taken by the United States and the European Union for dealing with the problem of cocaine trafficking.

Garry Leech, *Beyond Bogota: Diary of a Drug War Journalist in Colombia* (Beacon Press, 2009)

This book is an insider's look at the drug situation in Colombia.

Gootenberg, Paul, *Andean Cocaine: The Making of a Global Drug* (The University of North Carolina Press, 2009)

This book examines the history of cocaine since the nineteenth century as background to an analysis of the twentieth-century cocaine epidemic.

Jojarth, Christine, *Crime, War, and Global Trafficking: Designing International Cooperation* (Cambridge University Press, 2009)

This book argues that only international institutions with strong compliance mechanisms can successfully address the lucrative opportunities for traffickers of drugs and other desired products.

Keefer, Philip and Loayza, Norman, *Innocent Bystanders: Developing Countries and the War on Drugs* (World Bank Publications, 2010)

This book addresses the international consequences of alternative drug policies, criticizing specifically the policy pursued by the United States and other developed countries.

Marcy, William, *The Politics of Cocaine: How U.S. Foreign Policy Has Created a Thriving Drug Industry in Central and South America* (Lawrence Hill Books, 2010)

The author addresses why South American drug trafficking remains strong despite billions of dollars poured into fighting it. He argues that there are no simple solutions.

ISSUE 10

Is the International Community Adequately Prepared to Address Global Health Pandemics?

YES: Global Influenza Programme, from "Responding to the Avian Influenza Pandemic Threat," *Communicable Disease Surveillance and Response* (World Health Organization, 2005)

NO: Heath A. Kelly et al., from "We Should Not Be Complacent About Our Population-Based Public Health Response to the First Influenza Pandemic of the 21st Century," *BMC Public Health* (vol. 11, no. 78, 2011)

Learning Outcomes

After reading this issue, you should be able to:

- Contrast the world of 500 or 100 years ago with today's world in terms of the likelihood of widespread devastating pandemics.
- Describe steps that individual countries, the international community, and the World Health Organization can undertake to prepare the world for the next influenza pandemic.
- Describe the case study of the global response to the 2009 H1N1 virus pandemic.
- Describe lessons to be learned from the 2009 H1N1 pandemic.
- Discuss potential solutions to future pandemics by the authors of the H1N1 case study.

ISSUE SUMMARY

YES: The document from the World Health Organization lays out a comprehensive program of action for individual countries, the international community, and WHO to address the next influenza pandemic.

NO: Heath Kelly and colleagues, at the Victorian Infectious Diseases Reference Laboratory in Melbourne, suggest that the lessons of the global community's dealing with the H1N1 virus in 2009 show that its strategies "could not control the spread" of the virus.

Hear the words "global pandemics" and one thinks of the bubonic plague or Black Death of the Middle Ages where an estimated 30 percent of Europe's population died, or the influenza epidemic of 1918 that killed upward of 40 million or one in 20 people worldwide and fully a third of the human race were afflicted. Both seem like stories from a bygone era when modern medicine was unknown, where people were simply at the mercy of the spreading tendencies of the virulent diseases, and where the international community had yet to begin to cooperate to address such outbreaks. The latter did not begin to happen until the 1830s when a board was established in Egypt to track diseases throughout the Mediterranean region. In 1851, European governments gathered formally for the first time in Paris to discuss sanitary matters in light of persistent cholera epidemics plaguing Europe. And the first permanent health organization was founded in 1902 in the Western Hemisphere.

The world of medicine is different today, which leads many to assume that somewhere on the shelves of the local pharmacy or the Centers for Disease Control and Prevention in Atlanta lies a counteragent to whatever killer lurks out there. In 2009, however, the world watched in much the same way as it did 750 years ago or 93 years ago. The reason was the culprit H1N1 swine flu. In April 2009, it was reported that a Mexican boy had flu caused by a mosaic of swine/bird/human flu known as H1N1. On the other side of the ocean in Cairo, the Egyptian government ordered the killing of 300,000 animals as a precaution. Soon in every corner of the planet, officials began to take precautions and deaths began to mount. This 2009 scare followed on the heels of a global scare two decades earlier as a virulent disease of another type, AIDS, began to sweep across Africa to all other sectors of the globe.

The world is far different from that of the fourteenth century or even 1918. Globalization is with us. The world has shrunk, literally and figuratively, as the human race's ability to move people, money, goods, information, and also unwanted agents across national boundaries and to the far corners of the globe has increased exponentially. Viruses, germs, parasites, and other virulent disease agents can and do move much more easily than at any time in recorded history. Today's airplane is much faster than yesterday's ship.

The word "pandemic" is derived from two Greek words *pan* meaning "all" and *demos* meaning "people." Thus, a global pandemic is an epidemic of some infectious disease that can and is spreading at a rapid rate throughout the world. Officially, the World Health Organization (WHO) labels a disease outbreak a pandemic if community-level outbreaks of a disease are occurring in more than one country in a WHO region of the globe and one additional country in a different WHO region. Throughout history, humankind has fallen victim to many such killers. As early as the Peloponnesian War in fifth-century B.C. Greece, typhoid fever was responsible for the deaths of upward of 25 percent of combatants and civilians alike, necessitating major changes in military tactics. Imperial Rome felt the wrath of a plague thought to be smallpox, as did the eastern Mediterranean during its political height several centuries later. In the past 100 years, influenza (1918, 1957, and 1968), typhoid, and cholera were major killers. In recent years, other infectious diseases have made front page news: HIV, Ebola virus, SARS, and most recently, avian or bird flu. For a while, the latter flu struck tremendous fear in the hearts of global travelers and governmental policymakers everywhere.

WHO Europe predicted that as many as 175–360 million people could fall victim if the 2009 outbreak was severe enough. The bird flu was front page news because more than 150 million birds had died worldwide from one of its earlier strains, H5N1. This strain was first found in humans in 1997, and WHO estimated that the human fatality rate has been 50 percent, with 69 deaths occurring as of December 2005. One might be prompted to ask: what was the "big deal, only 134 confirmed cases?" It is not quite so simple. Unlike previous pandemics that hit suddenly and without little or any warning, the avian flu gave us a clear warning. The loss in poultry had been enormous. And with the jump to humans, with an initial high mortality rate, our senses had been awakened to the potential for global human disaster.

But there was good news as well. There was time to prepare for the worst-case scenario and diminish its likelihood. The flu had the attention of all relevant world health agencies and most national agencies, and steps were undertaken to find a way to combat this contagious disease. Whether global preparedness or simply the natural evolution of this particular strain of influenza, the 2009 global scare was not matched by reality, as the resultant mortality rates were not much different from those of the annual flu outbreaks.

WHO, created by the United Nations following World War II, became the first modern international organization in the fight against widespread diseases and it continues to play a leading role against both epidemics and pandemics. It is now joined by a complex network of international governmental and nongovernmental organizations and private foundations. This network has enjoyed great successes in several areas: smallpox, polio, and measles. And it has also proven to becoming effective in more recent challenges of SARS and AIDS.

One of the reasons for success has been the recognition by WHO that successful response to an emerging pandemic not only depends on the cooperation among health professionals and organizations throughout the world but also what WHO calls "the whole of society." The latter include all governments, businesses, and civil society who work to "sustain essential infrastructure and mitigate impacts on the economy and the functioning of society." WHO has spelled out its master plan for a total societal response in *Whole-of Society Pandemic Readiness: WHO Guidelines for Pandemic Preparedness and Response in the Non-Health Sector* (July 2009). This plan encompasses five basic principles: a whole-of-society approach, preparedness at all levels, attention to critical interdependencies, a scenario-based response, and respect for ethical norms. Each sector of society must have a flexible response plan in place. National and local governments must provide leadership while local governments stand ready to undertake specific actions. Standard operating principles and detailed communication strategies must be developed by governments. All relevant executive branches, from defense to finance, must be involved. Each provider of essential services, such as water and energy, must know the critical linkages and interdependencies among all providers. Plans for different scenarios, from mild to severe, must be developed. And finally, preparedness and response must be consistent with ethical norms and human rights considerations, with special attention to vulnerable peoples throughout the globe. The latter include people who have no access to health systems, estimated at one billion throughout the globe.

The issue of especially vulnerable people suggests an alternative way to view pandemics. The pandemics in our lifetimes have originated in the developing world. As the developing world lacked the appropriate health infrastructure, these diseases took hold and spread, eventually crossing national boundaries and making their way to the far corners of the earth. Had the diseases been confronted with an adequate health infrastructure with a detailed plan of action and the resources to implement it, the diseases might have been contained within one country. Toba Bryant and Dennis Raphael so suggest in the title of an article on the subject, "The Real Epidemic is Inequality" (2010). The essential thesis of their work is that (1) health inequalities growing out of social inequalities represent the primary health issue in the world and (2) the pace and scope of epidemics and pandemics are influenced by a function, in part, of these inequalities, particularly in the developing world.

Although this global issue addresses pandemics in general, we have selected avian flu as a case study of world pandemics and global responses because of its recent notoriety with the media and policymakers alike. In the YES selection, the WHO lays out a comprehensive program of action for individual countries, the international community, and WHO to address the next influenza pandemic. In the NO selection, Heath Kelly and colleagues, at the Victorian Infectious Diseases Reference Laboratory in Melbourne, suggest that the lessons of the global community's dealing with the H1N1 virus in 2009 show that its strategies "could not control the spread" of the virus, a conclusion shared by the head of WHO's global influenza program. The authors suggest that this was even more surprising, given that the pandemic was far less severe than originally anticipated.

YES ↵ Global Influenza Programme

Responding to the Avian Influenza Pandemic Threat

Purpose

This document sets out activities that can be undertaken by individual countries, the international community, and WHO to prepare the world for the next influenza pandemic and mitigate its impact once international spread has begun. Recommended activities are specific to the threat posed by the continuing spread of the H5N1 virus. Addressed to policy-makers, the document also describes issues that can guide policy choices in a situation characterized by both urgency and uncertainty. Recommendations are phase-wise in their approach, with levels of alert, and corresponding activities, changing according to epidemiological indicators of increased threat.

In view of the immediacy of the threat, WHO recommends that all countries undertake urgent action to prepare for a pandemic. Advice on doing so is contained in the recently revised *WHO global influenza preparedness plan* and a new *WHO checklist for influenza pandemic preparedness planning*. To further assist in preparedness planning, WHO is developing a model country plan that will give many developing countries a head start in assessing their status of preparedness and identifying priority needs. Support for rehearsing these plans during simulation exercises will also be provided.

Opportunities to Intervene

As the present situation continues to evolve towards a pandemic, countries, the international community, and WHO have several phase-wise opportunities to intervene, moving from a pre-pandemic situation, through emergence of a pandemic virus, to declaration of a pandemic and its subsequent spread. During the present pre-pandemic phase, interventions aim to reduce the risk that a pandemic virus will emerge and gather better disease intelligence, particularly concerning changes in the behaviour of the virus that signal improved transmissibility. The second opportunity to intervene occurs coincident with the first signal that the virus has improved its transmissibility, and aims to change the early history of the pandemic. The final opportunity occurs after a pandemic has begun. Interventions at this point aim to reduce morbidity, mortality, and social disruption.

From *Communicable Disease Surveillance and Response,* Global Influenza Programme, 2005, pp. 1–4, 6–7, 9–10, 12, 14–15. Copyright © 2005 by World Health Organization. Reprinted by permission of WHO Press.

Objectives

The objectives of the strategic actions correspond to the principal opportunities to intervene and are likewise phase-wise.

Phase: pre-pandemic
1. Reduce opportunities for human infection
2. Strengthen the early warning system
Phase: emergence of a pandemic virus
3. Contain or delay spread at the source
Phase: pandemic declared and spreading internationally
4. Reduce morbidity, mortality, and social disruption
5. Conduct research to guide response measures

Strategic Actions

The document describes strategic actions that can be undertaken to capitalize on each opportunity to intervene. Given the many uncertainties about the evolution of the pandemic threat, including the amount of time left to prepare, a wise approach involves a mix of measures that immediately address critical problems with longer-term measures that sustainably improve the world's capacity to protect itself against the recurring pandemic threat.

Background

Influenza pandemics have historically taken the world by surprise, giving health services little time to prepare for the abrupt increases in cases and deaths that characterize these events and make them so disruptive. Vaccines—the most important intervention for reducing morbidity and mortality—were available for the 1957 and 1968 pandemic viruses, but arrived too late to have an impact. As a result, great social and economic disruption, as well as loss of life, accompanied the three pandemics of the previous century.

The present situation is markedly different for several reasons. First, the world has been warned in advance. For more than a year, conditions favouring another pandemic have been unfolding in parts of Asia. Warnings that a pandemic may be imminent have come from both changes in the epidemiology of human and animal disease and an expanding geographical presence of the virus, creating further opportunities for human exposure. While neither the timing nor the severity of the next pandemic can be predicted, evidence that the virus is now endemic in bird populations means that the present level of risk will not be easily diminished.

Second, this advance warning has brought an unprecedented opportunity to prepare for a pandemic and develop ways to mitigate its effects. To date, the main preparedness activities undertaken by countries have concentrated on preparing and rehearsing response plans, developing a pandemic vaccine, and securing supplies of antiviral drugs. Because these activities are costly, wealthy countries are presently the best prepared; countries where H5N1 is endemic—and where a pandemic virus is most likely to emerge—lag far behind. More countries now have pandemic preparedness plans: around one-fifth of the world's countries have some form of a response plan, but these vary greatly in comprehensiveness and stage of completion. Access to antiviral drugs and, more importantly, to vaccines remains a major problem because of finite manufacturing capacity as well as costs. Some 23 countries have ordered antiviral drugs for national stockpiles, but the principal manufacturer will not be able to fill all orders for at least another year. Fewer than 10 countries have domestic vaccine companies engaged in work on a pandemic vaccine. A November 2004 WHO consultation reached the stark conclusion that, on present trends, the majority of developing countries would have no access to a vaccine during the first wave of a pandemic and possibly throughout its duration.

Apart from stimulating national preparedness activities, the present situation has opened an unprecedented opportunity for international intervention aimed at delaying the emergence of a pandemic virus or forestalling its international spread. Doing so is in the self-interest of all nations, as such a strategy could gain time to augment vaccine supplies. At present capacity, each day of manufacturing gained can mean an additional 5 million doses of vaccine. International support can also strengthen the early warning system in endemic countries, again benefiting preparedness planning and priority setting in all nations. Finally, international support is needed to ensure that large parts of the world do not experience a pandemic without the protection of a vaccine.

Pandemics are remarkable events in that they affect all parts of the world, regardless of socioeconomic status or standards of health care, hygiene and sanitation. Once international spread begins, each government will understandably make protection of its own population the first priority. The best opportunity for international collaboration—in the interest of all countries—is now, before a pandemic begins.

Situation Assessment

1. The risk of a pandemic is great.

Since late 2003, the world has moved closer to a pandemic than at any time since 1968, when the last of the previous century's three pandemics occurred. All prerequisites for the start of a pandemic have now been met save one: the establishment of efficient human-to-human transmission. During 2005, ominous changes have been observed in the epidemiology of the disease in animals. Human cases are continuing to occur, and the virus has expanded its geographical range to include new countries, thus increasing the size of the population at risk. Each new human case gives the virus an opportunity to evolve towards a fully transmissible pandemic strain.

2. The risk will persist.

Evidence shows that the H5N1 virus is now endemic in parts of Asia, having established an ecological niche in poultry. The risk of further human cases will persist, as will opportunities for a pandemic virus to emerge. Outbreaks have recurred despite aggressive control measures, including the culling of more than 140 million poultry. Wild migratory birds—historically the host reservoir of all influenza A viruses—are now dying in large numbers from highly pathogenic H5N1. Domestic ducks can excrete large quantities of highly pathogenic virus without showing signs of illness. Their silent role in maintaining transmission further complicates control in poultry and makes human avoidance of risky behaviours more difficult.

3. Evolution of the threat cannot be predicted.

Given the constantly changing nature of influenza viruses, the timing and severity of the next pandemic cannot be predicted. The final step—improved transmissibility among humans—can take place via two principal mechanisms: a reassortment event, in which genetic material is exchanged between human and avian viruses during co-infection of a human or pig, and a more gradual process of adaptive mutation, whereby the capability of these viruses to bind to human cells would increase during subsequent infections of humans. Reassortment could result in a fully transmissible pandemic virus, announced by a sudden surge of cases with explosive spread. Adaptive mutation, expressed initially as small clusters of human cases with evidence of limited transmission, will probably give the world some time to take defensive action. Again, whether such a "grace period" will be granted is unknown.

4. The early warning system is weak.

As the evolution of the threat cannot be predicted, a sensitive early warning system is needed to detect the first sign of changes in the behaviour of the virus. In risk-prone countries, disease information systems and health, veterinary, and laboratory capacities are weak. Most affected countries cannot adequately compensate farmers for culled poultry, thus discouraging the reporting of outbreaks in the rural areas where the vast majority of human cases have occurred. Veterinary extension services frequently fail to reach these areas. Rural poverty perpetuates high-risk behaviours, including the traditional home-slaughter and consumption of diseased birds. Detection of human cases is impeded by patchy surveillance in these areas. Diagnosis of human cases is impeded by weak laboratory support and the complexity and high costs of testing. Few affected countries have the staff and resources needed to thoroughly investigate human cases and, most importantly, to detect and investigate clusters of cases—an essential warning signal. In virtually all affected countries, antiviral drugs are in very short supply.

The dilemma of preparing for a potentially catastrophic but unpredictable event is great for all countries, but most especially so for countries affected by H5N1 outbreaks in animals and humans. These countries, in which rural subsistence farming is a backbone of economic life, have experienced direct and enormous agricultural losses, presently estimated at more than US$10 billion. They are being asked to sustain—if not intensify—resource-intensive activities needed to safeguard international public health while struggling to cope with many other competing health and infectious disease priorities.

5. Preventive intervention is possible, but untested.

Should a pandemic virus begin to emerge through the more gradual process of adaptive mutation, early intervention with antiviral drugs, supported by other public health measures, could theoretically prevent the virus from further improving its transmissibility, thus either preventing a pandemic or delaying its international spread. While this strategy has been proposed by many influenza experts, it remains untested; no effort has ever been made to alter the natural course of a pandemic at its source.

6. Reduction of morbidity and mortality during a pandemic will be impeded by inadequate medical supplies.

Vaccination and the use of antiviral drugs are two of the most important response measures for reducing morbidity and mortality during a pandemic. On present trends, neither of these interventions will be available in adequate quantities or equitably distributed at the start of a pandemic and for many months thereafter.

1. Reduce Opportunities for Human Infection
Strategic Actions

- **Support the FAO/OIE control strategy**

  The FAO/OIE technical recommendations describe specific control measures and explain how they should be implemented. The global strategy, developed in collaboration with WHO, takes its urgency from the risk to human health, including that arising from a pandemic, posed by the continuing circulation of the virus in animals. The strategy adopts a progressive approach, with different control options presented in line with different disease profiles, including such factors as poultry densities, farming systems, and whether infections have occurred in commercial farms or small rural holdings. The proposed initial focus is on Viet Nam, Thailand, Cambodia, and Indonesia, the four countries where human cases of infection with H5N1 avian influenza have been detected.

Clear and workable measures are proposed for different countries and situations within countries. Vaccination is being recommended as an appropriate control measure in some, but not all, epidemiological situations. Other measures set out in the strategy include strict biosecurity at commercial farms, use of compartmentalization and zoning concepts, control of animal and product movements, and a restructuring of the poultry industry in some countries. The strategy notes strong political will to tackle the problem. Nonetheless, time-frames for reaching control objectives are now being measured in years.

In July 2005, OIE member countries approved new standards, recognized by the World Trade Organization, specific to avian influenza and aimed at improving the safety of international trade of poultry and poultry products. The new standards cover methods of surveillance, compulsory international notification of low- and highly-pathogenic strains of avian influenza, the use of vaccination, and food safety of poultry products. Compliance with these standards should be given priority in efforts to strengthen early detection, reporting, and response in countries currently affected by outbreaks of H5N1 avian influenza.

- **Intensify collaboration between the animal and public health sectors**

WHO will appoint dedicated staff to increase the present exchange of information between agricultural and health sectors at the international level. Increased collaboration between the two sectors serves three main purposes: to pinpoint areas of disease activity in animals where vigilance for human cases should be intensified, to ensure that measures for controlling the disease in animals are compatible with reduced opportunities for human exposure, and to ensure that advice to rural communities on protective measures remains in line with the evolving nature of the disease in animals.

WHO will undertake joint action with FAO and OIE to understand the evolution of H5N1 viruses in Asia. Achieving this objective requires acquisition and sharing of a full inventory of H5N1 viruses, from humans, poultry, wild birds, and other animals, and sequences.

WHO will stress the importance of controlling the disease in rural areas. Measures to control the disease in animals of necessity consider how best to regain agricultural productivity and international trade, and this objective is reflected in the FAO/OIE strategy. While elimination of the virus from the commercial poultry sector alone will aid agricultural recovery, it may not significantly reduce opportunities for human exposure, as the vast majority of cases to date have been associated with exposure to small rural flocks. No case has yet been detected among workers in the commercial poultry sector. The FAO/OIE strategy fully recognizes that control of disease in rural "backyard" flocks will be the most difficult challenge; strong support from the health sector, as expressed by WHO, helps gather the political will to meet this challenge. In addition, it is imperative that measures for controlling disease in rural flocks are accompanied by risk communication to farmers and their families.

A joint FAO/OIE/WHO meeting, held in Malaysia in July 2005, addressed the links between animal disease and risks of human exposures and infections, and defined preventive measures that should be jointly introduced by the animal and public health sectors. Priority was given to interventions in the backyard rural farming system and in so-called wet markets where live poultry are sold under crowded and often unsanitary conditions.

WHO, FAO, and OIE have jointly established a Global Early Warning and Response System (GLEWS) for transboundary animal diseases. The new mechanism combines the existing outbreak alert, verification, and response capacities of the three agencies and helps ensure that disease tracking at WHO benefits from the latest information on relevant animal diseases. The system formalizes the sharing of epidemiological information and provides the operational framework for joint field missions to affected areas.

- **Strengthen risk communication to rural residents**

  WHO will, through its research networks and in collaboration with FAO and OIE, improve understanding of the links between animal disease, human behaviours, and the risk of acquiring H5N1 infection. This information will be used as the basis for risk communication to rural residents.

  Well-known and avoidable behaviours with a high risk of infection continue to occur in rural areas. Ongoing risk communication is needed to alert rural residents to these risks and explain how to avoid them. Better knowledge about the relationship between animal and human disease, obtained by WHO in collaboration with FAO/OIE, can be used to make present risk communication more precise and thus better able to prevent risky behaviours.

- **Improve approaches to environmental detection of the virus**

  WHO, FAO, and OIE will facilitate, through their research networks, the rapid development of new methods for detecting the virus in environmental samples. The purpose of these methods is to gain a better understanding of conditions that increase the risk of human infection and therefore favour emergence of a pandemic virus. Such knowledge underpins the success of primary prevention of a pandemic through disease control in animals. It also underpins advice to rural residents on behaviours to avoid. Reliance on routine veterinary surveillance, which is weak in most risk-prone countries, has not produced an adequate understanding of the relationship between animal and human disease. For example, in some cases, outbreaks in poultry are detected only after a human case has been confirmed. In other cases, investigation of human cases has failed to find a link with disease in animals.

2. Strengthen the Early Warning System

Strategic Actions

- **Improve the detection of human cases**

  WHO will provide the training, diagnostic reagents, and administrative support for external verification needed to improve the speed and reliability of case detection. To date, the vast majority of cases have been detected following hospitalization for respiratory illness. Hospitals in affected countries need support in case detection, laboratory confirmation, and reporting. Apart from its role in an early warning system, rapid laboratory confirmation signals the need to isolate patients and manage them according to strict procedures of infection control, and can thus help prevent further cases.

Diagnostic support continues to be provided by laboratories in the WHO network. However, because the initial symptoms of H5N1 infection mimic those of many diseases common in these countries, accurate case detection requires the testing of large numbers of samples. Improved local capacity is therefore a more rational solution.

Because of its high pathogenicity, H5N1 can be handled safely only by specially trained staff working in specially equipped laboratories operating at a high level of biosecurity. These facilities do not presently exist in the majority of affected countries. As an alternative, laboratory capacity can be enhanced by strengthening the existing system of national influenza centres or by providing mobile high-containment laboratories. Supportive activities include training in laboratory methods needed for H5N1 diagnosis, distribution of up-to-date diagnostic reagents, and coordination of work between national laboratories and epidemiological institutions.

An infrastructure needs to be developed to complement national testing with rapid international verification in WHO certified laboratories, especially as each confirmed human case yields information essential to risk assessment. The capacity to do so already exists. WHO offers countries rapid administrative support to ship samples outside affected countries. Such forms of assistance become especially critical when clusters of cases occur and require investigation.

- **Combine detection of new outbreaks in animals with active searches for human cases**

Using epidemiologists in its country offices and, when necessary, external partners, WHO will ensure that detection of new outbreaks of highly pathogenic H5N1 in poultry is accompanied by active searches for human cases. Surveillance in several countries where H5N1 is considered endemic in birds is inadequate and suspicions are strong that human cases have been missed. Cambodia's four human cases were detected only after patients sought treatment in neighbouring Viet Nam, where physicians are on high alert for cases and familiar with the clinical presentation.

- **Support epidemiological investigation**

Reliable risk assessment depends on thorough investigation of sporadic human cases and clusters of cases. Guidelines for outbreak investigation, specific to H5N1 and to the epidemiological situation in different countries, are being developed on an urgent basis for use in training national teams. These guidelines give particular emphasis to the investigation of clusters of cases and determination of whether human-to-human transmission has occurred. Teams assembled from institutions in the WHO Global Outbreak Alert and Response Network (GOARN) can be deployed for rapid on-site investigative support.

- **Coordinate clinical research in Asia**

  Clinical data on human cases need to be compiled and compared in order to elucidate modes of transmission, identify groups at risk, and find better treatments. Work has begun to establish a network of hospitals, modelled on the WHO global influenza surveillance network, engaged in clinical research on human disease. The network will link together the principal hospitals in Asia that are treating H5N1 patients and conducting clinical research. Technical support will allow rapid exchange of information and sharing of specimens and research results, and encourage the use of standardized protocols for treatment and standardized sampling procedures for investigation.

  Identification of risk groups guides preventive measures and early interventions. Provision of high-quality data on clinical course, outcome, and treatment efficacy meets an obvious and immediate need in countries with human cases. Answers to some key questions—the efficacy of antiviral drugs, optimum dose, and prescribing schedules—could benefit health services elsewhere once a pandemic is under way.

- **Strengthen risk assessment**

  WHO's daily operations need to be strengthened to ensure constant collection and verification of epidemiological and virological information essential for risk assessment. Ministries of health and research institutions in affected countries need to be more fully engaged in the collection and verification of data. Ministries and institutions in non-affected countries should help assess the significance of these data, and the results should be issued rapidly. These activities, currently coordinated by WHO, need to escalate; influenza viruses can evolve rapidly and in unexpected ways that alter risk assessment, as evidenced by the recent detection of highly pathogenic H5N1 viruses in migratory birds. Functions of the WHO network of laboratories with expertise in the analysis of H5N1 viruses can be improved through tools, such as a genetic database, and a strong collaboration with veterinary laboratory networks to ensure that animal as well as human viruses are kept under constant surveillance.

- **Strengthen existing national influenza centres throughout the risk-prone region**

  Many existing national influenza centres, designated by WHO, already possess considerable infrastructure in the form of equipment and trained personnel. Additional support, particularly in the form of diagnostic reagents, could help strengthen the early warning system in risk-prone countries and their neighbours.

- **Give risk-prone countries an incentive to collaborate internationally**

  The promise of assistance is a strong motivation to report cases and share clinical specimens internationally. A high-level meeting should be convened so that heads of state in industrialized countries and in risk-prone countries can seek solutions and reach agreement on the kinds of support considered most desirable by individual countries.

3. Contain or Delay Spread at the Source

Strategic Actions

- **Establish an international stockpile of antiviral drugs**

  WHO will establish an international stockpile of antiviral drugs for rapid response at the start of a pandemic. The stockpile is a strategic option that serves the interests of the international community as well as those of the initially affected populations. Issues that need to be addressed include logistics associated with deployment and administration, and licensing for use in individual countries. Mechanisms for using an international stockpile need to be defined more precisely in terms of epidemiological triggers for deploying the stockpile and time-frames for emergency delivery and administration. WHO is working closely with groups engaged in mathematical modelling and others to guide the development of early containment strategies.

  While pursuit of this option thus has no guarantee of success, it nonetheless needs to be undertaken as it represents one of the few preventive options for an event with predictably severe consequences for every country in the world. It is also the best guarantee that populations initially affected will have access to drugs for treatment. Should early containment fail to completely halt spread of the virus, a delay in wide international spread would gain time to intensify preparedness. It can be expected that most governments will begin introducing emergency measures only when the threat of a pandemic is certain and immediate. A lead time for doing so of one month or more could allow many health services to build surge capacity and make the necessary conversion from routine to emergency services.

- **Develop mass delivery mechanisms for antiviral drugs**

  Several WHO programmes, such as those for the emergency response to outbreaks of poliomyelitis, measles, epidemic-prone meningitis, and yellow fever, have acquired considerable experience in the urgent mass delivery of vaccines in developing countries. Less experience exists for the mass delivery of antiviral drugs, where administration is complicated by the need for drugs to be taken over several days and the need for different dosing schedules according to therapeutic or prophylactic use. WHO will develop and pilot test delivery mechanisms for antiviral drugs in collaboration with national health authorities and industry. Studies will assess coverage rates that could be achieved, taking into account compliance rates, and ways to support this intervention with other measures, such as area quarantine.

- **Conduct surveillance of antiviral susceptibility**

Using its existing network of influenza laboratories, WHO will establish a surveillance programme for antiviral susceptibility testing, modelled on a similar programme for anti-tuberculosis drugs. Use of an international stockpile to attempt to halt an outbreak will involve administration of drugs to large numbers of people for several weeks. A mechanism must be in place to monitor any resulting changes in virus susceptibility to these drugs. The development of drug resistance would threaten the effectiveness of national stockpiles of antiviral drugs established for domestic use. The work of WHO collaborating centres for influenza and reference laboratories for H5N1 analysis can be coordinated to include anti-viral susceptibility testing.

4. Reduce Morbidity, Mortality, and Social Disruption
Strategic Actions

- **Monitor the evolving pandemic in real time**

Many characteristics of a pandemic that will guide the selection of response measures will become apparent only after the new virus has emerged and begun to cause large numbers of cases. WHO, assisted by virtual networks of experts, will monitor the unfolding epidemiological and clinical behaviour of the new virus in real time. This monitoring will give health authorities answers to key questions about age groups at greatest risk, infectivity of the virus, severity of the disease, attack rates, risk to health care workers, and mortality rates. Such monitoring can also help determine whether severe illness and deaths are caused by primary viral pneumonia or secondary bacterial pneumonia, which responds to antibiotics, and thus guide the emergency provision of supplies. Experts in mathematical modelling will be included in the earliest field assessment teams to make the forecasting of trends as reliable as possible.

- **Introduce non-pharmaceutical interventions**

Answers to these questions will help officials select measures—closing of schools, quarantine, a ban on mass gatherings, travel restrictions—that match the behaviour of the virus and thus have the greatest chance of reducing the number of cases and delaying geographical spread. WHO has produced guidance on the use of such measures at different stages at the start of a pandemic and after its international spread.

- **Use antiviral drugs to protect priority groups**

WHO recommends that countries with sufficient resources invest in a stockpile of antiviral drugs for domestic use, particularly at the start of a pandemic when mass vaccination is not an option and priority groups, such as frontline workers, need to be protected.

- **Augment vaccine supplies**

  WHO, in collaboration with industry and regulatory authorities, has introduced fast-track procedures for the development and licensing of a pandemic vaccine. Strategies have also been developed that make the most of scarce vaccine antigen and thus allow more quantities of vaccine to be produced despite the limits of existing plant capacity. Once a pandemic is declared, all manufacturers will switch from production of seasonal vaccines to production of a pandemic vaccine. Countries need to address liability issues that could arise following mass administration of a pandemic vaccine and ensure adequate warehousing, logistics, and complementary supplies, such as syringes.

- **Ensure equitable access to vaccines**

  The present strong interdependence of commerce and trade means that the international community cannot afford to allow large parts of the world to experience a pandemic unprotected by a vaccine. The humanitarian and ethical arguments for providing such protection are readily apparent. As a matter of urgency, WHO must build a political process aimed at finding ways to further augment production capacity dramatically and make vaccines affordable and accessible in the developing world. WHO will also work with donor agencies on the latter issue.

- **Communicate risks to the public**

  As soon as a pandemic is declared, health authorities will need to start a continuous process of risk communication to the public. Many difficult issues—the inevitable spread to all countries, the shortage of vaccines and antiviral drugs, justification for the selection of priority groups for protection—will need to be addressed. Effective risk communication, supported by confidence in government authorities and the reliability of their information, may help mitigate some of the social and economic disruption attributed to an anxious public. Countries are advised to plan in advance. A communication strategy for a pandemic situation should include training in outbreak communication and integration of communicators in senior management teams.

5. Conduct Research to Guide Response Measures
Strategic Actions

- **Assess the epidemiological characteristics of an emerging pandemic**

  At the start of a pandemic, policy-makers will face an immediate need for epidemiological data on the principal age groups affected, modes of transmission, and pathogenicity. Such data will support urgent decisions about target groups for vaccination and receipt of antiviral drugs. They can also be used to support forecasts on local and global patterns of spread as an early warning that helps national authorities intensify preparedness measures. WHO will identify epidemiological centres for collecting these data and establish standardized research protocols.

- **Monitor the effectiveness of health interventions**

  Several non-pharmaceutical interventions have been recommended to reduce local and international spread of a pandemic and lower the rate of transmission. While many of these interventions have proved useful in the prevention and control of other infectious diseases, their effectiveness during a pandemic has never been comprehensively evaluated. More information is needed on their feasibility, effectiveness, and acceptability to populations. WHO will establish study sites and develop study protocols to evaluate these interventions at local, national, and international levels. Comparative data on the effectiveness of different interventions are also important, as several measures are associated with very high levels of social disruption.

- **Evaluate the medical and economic consequences**

  WHO will establish study sites and develop protocols for prospective evaluation of the medical and economic consequences of the pandemic so that future health interventions can be adjusted accordingly. In the past, such evaluations have been conducted only after a pandemic had ended. Their value as a policy guide for the allocation of resources has been flawed because of inadequate data.

Heath A. Kelly et al.　　　　　　　　　　　　　　　　**NO**

We Should Not Be Complacent About Our Population-Based Public Health Response to the First Influenza Pandemic of the 21st Century

Background and Discussion

The World Health Organization (WHO) declared that spread of the newly recognised quadruple reassortant influenza A H1N1 virus satisfied the criteria for a pandemic on June 11, 2009, [1] although technically conditions for declaring a pandemic had been met some weeks earlier. The virus, generally referred to as pandemic influenza H1N1 2009 (pH1N1), had first been recognised in Mexico and the United States in late April 2009. More than a year later, WHO has declared the pandemic to be over and early assessments of the global response have commenced [2].

When the pandemic was declared, Dr Margaret Chan, the Director of WHO, advised member states to implement their pandemic plans [1] and health agencies, other government agencies and businesses worked hard to do this. In most countries it may be correct to conclude, as did an evaluation of the UK response, that the "pandemic and the response it generated have provided confirmation of the value of planning and preparedness" [3]. It is also true that the apparent success of the response in 2009 must not lead to complacency. We now know that the relatively low virulence of pH1N1 meant we did not need to have implemented effective responses to get a good outcome.

The response to the pandemic included clinical and public health measures. In developed countries, such as Australia, the clinical response was effective for those whose illnesses were serious [4]. Clinical care will very likely have reduced the number of deaths due to pandemic influenza [5], although the use of extra-corporeal membrane oxygenation was seen as a last resort and was not supported by the conclusions of a systematic review [6]. In developed and developing countries, the public health response focused on both the individual and the population. Individual responses promoted attention to personal hygiene, with an emphasis on cough hygiene and hand washing, which may not have been optimal [7], and the use of personal protective equipment for those considered to be at increased risk of infection [8]. Population-based public health responses to the pandemic focused on two major elements: non-pharmaceutical and pharmaceutical interventions. The former comprised border control and various elements of social distancing, while the latter focused on anti-viral medication for treatment and/or prophylaxis, and the development of a strain-specific vaccine.

Australia used the pharmaceutical and non-pharmaceutical interventions detailed in its pandemic plan [9] in an effort to *delay* entry of the virus into the country, *contain* the virus to limited areas once it had entered the country, *sustain* a response when widespread community transmission had been established and to *protect* the vulnerable [10]—the latter being a new response phase formulated once it was realised that the pandemic was not associated with the high case fatality ratios that had been anticipated [11]. We use Australia's experience to draw attention to issues related to the public health population-based pandemic response. The scope of this perspective does not allow us to consider other categories of response.

Now is the time to acknowledge that a number of the strategies used in response to the 2009 pandemic could not control the spread of a novel influenza virus and their place in future pandemic response plans needs to be reconsidered in light of emerging new evidence. We examine four critical cornerstones of Australia's public health population-based response, namely border control, school closure (as an example of social distancing), the use of anti-viral medication and the development and use of a pandemic vaccine. We provide evidence from the pandemic experience in other countries to support our arguments.

Border Control

In a very different world, Australia successfully applied maritime quarantine to delay the entry of a pandemic H1N1 virus into the country in 1918 and 1919. This was in contrast to many of Australia's Pacific neighbours. For instance, the virus reached New Zealand in October 1918 but did not enter Australia until January of the following year. Estimated death rates in countries where the entry of the virus had been delayed were lower than rates where earlier entry was documented [12].

Prior to the 2009 pandemic, modelling studies had suggested a very limited role for border screening, providing an estimated delay of only 1–2 weeks without draconian measures that would be economically unacceptable in most countries [13]. A review of border control in Australia following the SARS epidemic pointed out the opportunity cost of screening. No case was identified despite 1.8 million passengers being screened, 794 referred for further evaluation and four identified as possible cases [14]. A similar lack of success was suggested in a review of the likely success of border control for influenza in other countries [15]. Indeed, it can be argued that prior to the pandemic there was only very limited scientific evidence for border control as an effective intervention. Despite this in 2009, as an island nation with history on its side, Australia, like many other (non-island) countries, embraced the concept.

Australia implemented a combination of approaches in an attempt to detect infected arriving passengers at international airports. These comprised notification of health status of passengers by airline staff (the pilot or crew identified passengers with respiratory symptoms), thermal scanning (infrared cameras were installed in airport terminals), health declaration cards (the passenger reported current symptoms) and nurses at border entry points reviewed and tested passengers detected by one of these screening tools. In the Australian state of Queensland, although the number of passengers screened was not reported, and was likely to have been many tens of thousands, only four cases of confirmed pandemic influenza were found from 780 passengers identified by one or more of these border screening measures [16]. No cases were detected by similar screening at the busy international airport in Perth, Western Australia (unpublished data).

It has been suggested that Australia did well in its response to managing the pandemic, specifically in delaying establishment of community transmission [17]. During this time preparations were made to respond to a pandemic that was anticipated to result in many deaths. However, based on epidemiological and modelling evidence, we have demonstrated that community transmission was almost certainly established in the state of Victoria around the time the virus was first recognised in North and Central America in late April 2009 [18]. This followed one or more unrecognised silent importations, and spread of the virus in Australia came substantially from within its borders rather than from overseas. We now know that this is an entirely plausible scenario, given that a significant proportion of pH1N1 infections were afebrile [19] or entirely asymptomatic [20] and therefore impossible to detect at the border—or anywhere else.

This should not be surprising, as the finding that a high proportion of influenza infections are asymptomatic or afebrile was not new. Published experimental data from volunteer studies had previously shown that 33% of proven seasonal influenza infections were asymptomatic, but this varied by influenza type and subtype [21]. In particular, as few as 37% of experimental infections with influenza A(H1N1) were associated with fever recorded as >37.8°C, while 30% were completely asymptomatic [21]. Moreover, viral shedding in the pre-symptomatic phase of influenza infection has recently been confirmed to occur in approximately 1–8% of naturally acquired infections, in a study in which 14% of all influenza infections were asymptomatic and 31% of infections with influenza A (H1N1 or H3N2) did not have fever at the onset of other symptoms [22].

Prodromal, asymptomatic and afebrile infections cannot be detected by temperature measurement, one of the main components of border control, whether by thermal scanning or by core temperature measurement of symptomatic travellers [23]. Moreover, the proportion of afebrile or asymptomatic people is likely to be higher in infected travellers, as more severely unwell people will be less likely to travel. Thermal imaging is therefore even less likely to have been effective at the borders than in other places where more severely ill patients are seen [24]. Indeed, China used intensive thermal screening for pH1N1 at airports and had a positive detection rate of only 14 cases per million passengers screened [25].

The use of border control was evidently not based on a current understanding of influenza epidemiology and was not supported by modelling studies. In particular one modelling study, published two years before the identification of the current pandemic virus, showed that past pandemic patterns could not be adequately modelled without inclusion of asymptomatic infection (as well as varying degrees of pre-existing immunity) [26].

Nonetheless, an early evaluation of the 2009 pandemic, with limitations acknowledged by its authors, suggested that border screening may have led to delays of 7 to 12 days in the establishment of local transmission [27]. We accept that border screening will have detected a limited number of influenza cases, but suggest that many more cases will have been missed than were detected. In Australia, at least, it is likely that border screening was implemented after the virus had entered the country [18]. On balance, we conclude that border screening was as ineffective as it should have been expected to be.

School Closure

It is generally accepted that children, especially children of school age, are responsible for amplification of influenza epidemics [28]. An intervention targeting schools could therefore theoretically be effective in interrupting an epidemic. This assumption is supported by modelling studies, but only when all schools are closed early and remain closed for an unrealistically long period, upto the duration of the pandemic [29]. Modelling also shows that delay in closing schools, or partial closure of schools, are less effective interventions, [29] although, if school closures are timely, they may delay the peak and decrease the peak incidence of the epidemic [30].

As expected, the pH1N1 infection rate was high among school aged children [20,31]. Of the first 997 cases of confirmed pH1N1 infection in the state of Victoria in Australia, 67% were aged 5–17 years [32]. In Australia, school closure was intended to be associated with voluntary home quarantine. When a school—or class within a school—was closed, members of the class were asked to voluntarily quarantine themselves at home. This meant that parents of young children were frequently required to take time off work to care for children who would otherwise have been at school. Home quarantine has its own risks. We have recently shown that when an entire family was quarantined, the risk of secondary spread within households was increased by approximately 2.5-fold [33].

Moreover, compliance with other social distancing measures needed to have been effective for school closures themselves to have been effective. A survey in Western Australia of parents of school children whose schools were closed at some stage during the pandemic indicated that 74% of home-quarantined children participated in outside activities at least once during the nominal quarantine period, recording an average of 3.7 activities per child. Most commonly reported were attendances at sporting events, parks, beaches and stores, places where it is likely other children would be exposed [34]. Public documentation of school closure during the pH1N1 epidemic in Australia is minimal, but the policy in the early phase of the pH1N1 response was to close only those classes with confirmed cases, escalating to whole schools where multiple classes across different age groups were affected. In the state of Queensland only 2.8% of all schools were closed for short periods [16]. In Western Australia school closures were only for one week and sometimes involved only closure of specific classes [34]. Too limited in scope and time, these strategies could not have been effective in interrupting the spread of the pandemic.

On the other hand, experience in Japan confirmed the conclusions from modelling [30]. Early widespread school closures in a defined area were successful in delaying pandemic spread in that area, but when the schools were re-opened, pandemic spread resumed [35]. In Hong Kong closure of kindergartens, pre-schools and primary schools appeared to decrease the attack rate in children aged less than 12 years for the weeks of closure [36] but the effect on the final attack rate in school children is yet to be evaluated. Indeed, it has been argued that the potential benefit of closing schools during a pandemic must be balanced against the enormous social disruption that ensues [37]. Only where schools were closed early and remained closed would there have been any significant interruption of the spread of the pandemic.

Neuraminidase Inhibitors for Treatment and Prophylaxis

Countries around the world adopted different approaches to the use of neuraminidase inhibitors (NAIs) in their pandemic plans. In addition to treatment provisions, Australia opted for a stockpile of approximately 10 million courses of NAIs with the intention of implementing widespread prophylaxis, which has been shown in trials to be 58–84% effective in preventing laboratory proven influenza infection if given early following exposure [38]. However, even in the early phases of the response, when numbers of suspected and confirmed pH1N1 cases were low, those with responsibility for contact tracing were rapidly overwhelmed. The logistical difficulties of timely delivery of NAIs to those eligible for treatment or prophylaxis were such that it was likely only a minority received their medication in time for it to be effective. Lateness of NAI availability has been confirmed in a Victorian study of treatment doses. Oseltamivir was prescribed for only 207 (21%) of the first 1,000 confirmed cases. Of 690 cases confirmed not to have received oselatamivir,670 were not eligible because more than 48 hours had elapsed since symptom onset (Unpublished data, James Fielding, epidemiologist, Victorian Infectious Diseases Reference Laboratory).

Other approaches to NAI distribution were used around the world, with varying effectiveness. For example, the UK National Health Service implemented an electronic checklist to allow patients rapid access to NAIs. Bypassing doctors and laboratory testing, this system aimed to speed up NAI availability. However, only 1932/16,560 (17%) of people who received NAIs using the electronic checklist subsequently tested positive for pH1N1 [39].

On the other hand, in four outbreaks in Singapore military camps, when NAIs were able to be delivered effectively in conjunction with isolation of confirmed cases and quarantine of contacts, a beneficial effect could be demonstrated. These measures, which included ring prophylaxis with oseltamivir, resulted in a reduction of the infection rate in the outbreaks from 6.4% to 0.6% [40]. This study demonstrates the potential benefit of NAIs if available early in outbreaks, and when combined with social distancing. However extension of this strategy to large heterogeneous populations remains unproven and it may be feasible only in closed communities, such as boarding schools, military barracks and residential care facilities.

Another important consideration in setting out to provide mass treatment and prophylaxis with NAIs is the possibility of development of resistant strains. Surveillance studies during the first wave of the pandemic demonstrated a low frequency of resistance to oseltamivir and no reported resistance to zanamivir. Prior to 2007, it was rare to detect oseltamivir-resistant influenza strains in untreated patients, due to the compromised infectivity and transmissibility of many of the resistant mutants in the absence of drug pressure. But in 2007/2008 an oseltamivir resistant seasonal A(H1N1) variant emerged that demonstrated viral fitness at least equivalent to the oseltamivir-susceptible strain. The resistant strain spread rapidly around the world and by 2009 had completely replaced the susceptible strain [41]. An oseltamivir-resistant pH1N1 virus might also retain viral fitness and subsequently spread throughout the community. Fortunately, to date, only a low frequency of oseltamivir-resistant pH1N1 strains have been identified [42].

An anti-viral stockpile without a well-developed logistic strategy and resourcing for effective early delivery for treatment of cases and prophylaxis of contacts is not an adequate plan for successful limitation of viral spread in a population, especially considering that the high proportion of cases with asymptomatic and mild infections will not be identified. Moreover, as we have seen with seasonal H1N1 viruses, resistance may develop to NAIs and a resistant virus may retain viral fitness allowing it to become widespread. This would render stockpiles useless. Revised pandemic plans should therefore consider limiting the use of NAIs to treatment of those with more severe influenza infection or medical conditions that make them more vulnerable to complications. Dependent on the availability of NAIs and access to appropriate medical care, treatment should be commenced early in the course of the illness. In Germany the median delay between symptom onset and antiviral treatment was significantly longer in fatal cases than non-fatal cases [43]. Prophylaxis should probably be reserved for closed communities, with any plan for wide-scale use of prophylactic NAIs dependent on a large workforce able to perform contact tracing and a detailed logistics plan for early delivery.

A Pandemic Strain Specific Influenza Vaccine

After China, Australia was the second country in the world to roll out a population-based pandemic vaccine program, with monovalent pandemic vaccine available by 30 September 2009 [44]. The first wave of the pandemic in Australia had ended by this date. It was not expected that the vaccine would have been available in time to modify the first pandemic wave anywhere in the world. However, even in Australia, it was a case of 'too much too late'. An early estimate of 18% was made for population wide coverage for the vaccine [45].

Most pandemic vaccines in Australia were formulated as multi-dose vials. Given recommendations that the vial contents should be used or discarded within 24 hours of first use, wastage was expected with this formulation. It has been estimated that around 40% of pH1N1 vaccine doses delivered to Australian general practices may have been wasted [46]. There was also concern among some immunisation providers, and within the general community, that the multi-dose vials contained the preservative thiomersal, which had been phased out of paediatric vaccines, and that use of the vials potentially increased the risk of contamination, including with blood-borne viruses [47]. Such concerns, whether ill-founded or not, were likely to have impacted adversely on vaccine uptake, even in identified high risk groups [48]. While it may be reasonable to assume that vaccine uptake would have been higher if the disease had indeed been more severe, future pandemic plans need to include greater flexibility in vaccine purchasing and contracting arrangements, and refinement of vaccine delivery protocols and public messaging, in order to minimise wastage and optimise uptake [49].

The 21st century marks the first time pandemic-specific vaccines have been manufactured on a large scale. A preliminary report from Germany using the screening method estimated pandemic vaccine effectiveness for an adjuvanted pandemic vaccine of 97% in people aged 14–59 years [50]. A similar high level of protection has been reported for children in Canada [51], although a more modest effectiveness of 72% has subsequently been reported from a pooled case control analysis from a number of European countries [52]. While vaccines were effective in protecting individuals, population coverage in Australia and other countries was unlikely to have been sufficient for the vaccine to have modulated the spread of the pandemic virus. However some European countries, such as Germany, experienced a very modest first pandemic wave [43] and, had they achieved high coverage with pandemic vaccine, may have been able to modify pandemic virus transmission in the next influenza season. Nonetheless, the experience with pH1N1suggests that a pandemic vaccine will always be too late, at least for one hemisphere, using current vaccine manufacturing technology.

Summary

Control of pandemic influenza is a critical issue and one on which the world has already spent billions of dollars, both in planning and during the recent response to pH1N1. There are obvious lessons to be learnt from the first pandemic of the 21st century, a pandemic which was much less severe than many plans had anticipated [53]. If we think our response to this pandemic was adequate, we may be falsely reassured. A more severe pandemic may find us wanting. A mild pandemic may find us over reacting. However, with appropriate collection and analysis of data it should be possible to identify the severity of future pandemics early and to make a measured response [54]. The World

Health Organization, governments and other agencies around the world are currently involved in reviews of the management of the pandemic [55]. It is vital that these reviews, while not diminishing the commitment and hard work of those who implemented the response plans in 2009, carefully assess the evidence base for those plans.

In addition, the widespread implications of the response to the pandemic—for policy makers, health professionals and the public—make it important for these reviews to be in the public domain. In Australia, where pandemic reviews are not yet in the public domain, there were examples where messages appeared to be mixed, and which confused both the public and healthcare professionals [56]. Partially closing some schools for short periods and not implementing other social distancing measures, such as cancelling public gatherings, is just one example.

Although we have provided examples from Australia, we believe our arguments will have relevance for many other countries. 'One size fits all', where authorities have only one response strategy for viruses with different infection rates and case fatality ratios, is not an appropriate response to pandemic preparedness. Revised pandemic plans should include different responses for different pandemic severities [57]. All areas of pandemic planning need to be re-examined, but perhaps by alternative processes to those that led to current plans. Certainly, new evidence about the practical difficulties and/or ineffectiveness of control measures, such as border control and school closures, needs to be considered seriously. The inadequacy of many plans has recently been publicly acknowledged by the head of the WHO's global influenza programme. Speaking at a United Kingdom Health Protection Agency conference on the international response to the H1N1 pandemic, Dr Sylvie Briand is reported to have said that the containment strategy during the last pandemic was 'not feasible' and that guidelines might have to be overhauled [58]. We believe this is sound advice.

References

1. Chan M: World now at the start of an influenza pandemic. [http://www.who .int/mediacentre/news/statements/2009/h1n1_pandemic_phase6_20090611/en/ index.html].

2. Wise J: UK response to H1N1 pandemic was highly satisfactory, independent review says. *BMJ* 2010, 341:c3569.

3. Hine Dame D: The 2009 Influenza Pandemic. An independent review of the UK response to the 2009 influenza pandemic. London: Cabinet Office; 2010.

4. Webb SA, Pettila V, Seppelt I, Bellomo R, Bailey M, Cooper DJ, Cretikos M, Davies AR, Finfer S, Harrigan PW, *et al:* Critical care services and 2009 H1N1 influenza in Australia and New Zealand. *N Engl J Med* 2009, 361:1925–1934.

5. Davies A, Jones D, Bailey M, Beca J, Bellomo R, Blackwell N, Forrest P, Gattas D, Granger E, Herkes R, *et al:* Extracorporeal Membrane Oxygenation for 2009 Influenza A(H1N1) Acute Respiratory Distress Syndrome. *JAMA* 2009, 302:1888–1895.

6. Mitchell MD, Mikkelsen ME, Umscheid CA, Lee I, Fuchs BD, Halpern SD: A systematic review to inform institutional decisions about the use of extracorporeal membrane oxygenation during the H1N1 influenza pandemic. *Crit Care Med* 2010, 38:1398–1404.

7. Murray R, Chandler C, Clarkson Y, Wilson N, Baker M, Cunningham R: Suboptimal hand sanitiser usage in a hospital entrance during an influenza pandemic, New Zealand, August 2009. *Euro Surveill* 2009, 14:19331.

8. Queensland Government State Health Emergency Coordination Centre: Pandemic (H1N1) 2009: Advice for the wearing of personal protective equipment for "frontline" staff. [http://newsletters.gpqld.com.au/content/Document/H1N1/13%20August%2009/08%20CHOO27CMEAG-Frontline%20PPE%20-%20 28%20July%2009%20Published.pdf].

9. Australian Government Department of Health and Ageing: Australian Health Management Plan for Pandemic Influenza. [http://www.flupandemic .gov.au/internet/panflu/publishing.nsf/Content/ahmppi-2009].

10. Australian Government Department of Health and Ageing: Australian Health Management Plan for Pandemic Influenza, Protect Phase Annex. [http:// www.flupandemic.gov.au/internet/panflu/publishing.nsf/Content/protect- annex].

11. Baker M, Kelly H, Wilson N: Pandemic H1N1 influenza lessons from the southern hemisphere. *Euro Surveill* 2009, 14:19370.

12. McLeod MA, Baker M, Wilson N, Kelly H, Kiedrzynski T, Kool JL: Protective effect of maritime quarantine in South Pacific jurisdictions, 1918-19 influenza pandemic. *Emerg Infect Dis* 2008, 14:468–470.

13. Ferguson NM, Cummings DA, Fraser C, Cajka JC, Cooley PC, Burke DS: Strategies for mitigating an influenza pandemic. *Nature* 2006, 442:448–452.

14. Samaan G, Patel M, Spencer J, Roberts L: Border screening for SARS in Australia: what has been learnt? *Med J Aust* 2004, 180:220–223.

15. Bell DM: Non-pharmaceutical interventions for pandemic influenza, national and community measures. *Emerg Infect Dis* 2006, 12:88–94.

16. Appuhamy RD, Beard FH, Phung HN, Selvey CE, Birrell FA, Culleton TH: The changing phases of pandemic (H1N1) 2009 in Queensland: an overview of public health actions and epidemiology. *Med J Aust* 2010, 192:94–97.

17. Bishop JF, Murnane MP, Owen R: Australia's winter with the 2009 pandemic influenza A (H1N1) virus. *N Engl J Med* 2009, 361:2591–2594.

18. Kelly H, Mercer GN, Fielding JE, Dowse GK, Glass K, Carcione D, Grant KA, Effler PV, Lester RA: Community circulation of pandemic influenza H1N1 was established in one Australian state at the same time the virus was first recognised in North America. *PLoS One* 2010, 5:e11341.

19. Gerrard J, Keijzers G, Zhang P, Vossen C, Macbeth D: Clinical diagnostic criteria for isolating patients admitted to hospital with suspected pandemic influenza. *Lancet* 2009, 374:1673.

20. Miller E, Hoschler K, Hardelid P, Stanford E, Andrews N, Zambon M: Incidence of 2009 pandemic influenza A H1N1 infection in England: a cross-sectional serological study. *Lancet* 2010, 375:1100–1108.

21. Carrat F, Vergu E, Ferguson NM, Lemaitre M, Cauchemez S, Leach S, Valleron AJ: Time lines of infection and disease in human influenza: a review of volunteer challenge studies. *Am J Epidemiol* 2008, 167:775–785.

22. Lau LL, Cowling BJ, Fang VJ, Chan KH, Lau EH, Lipsitch M, Cheng CK, Houck PM, Uyeki TM, Peiris JS, Leung GM: Viral shedding and clinical illness in naturally acquired influenza virus infections. *J Infect Dis* 2010, 201:1509–1516.

23. Duncan AR, Priest PC, Jennings LC, Brunton CR, Baker MG: Screening for influenza infection in international airline travelers. *Am J Public Health* 2009, 99(Suppl 2):S360-362.

24. Hausfater P, Zhao Y, Defrenne S, Bonnet P, Riou B: Cutaneous infrared thermometry for detecting febrile patients. *Emerging Infectious Diseases* 2008, 14:1255–1258.

25. Cao B, Li XW, Mao Y, Wang J, Lu HZ, Chen YS, Liang ZA, Liang L, Zhang SJ, Zhang B, *et al:* Clinical features of the initial cases of 2009 pandemic influenza A (H1N1) virus infection in China. *N Engl J Med* 2009, 361:2507–2517.

26. Mathews JD, McCaw CT, McVernon J, McBryde ES, McCaw JM: A biological model for influenza transmission: pandemic planning implications of asymptomatic infection and immunity. *PLoS One* 2007, 2:e1220.

27. Cowling BJ, Lau LL, Wu P, Wong IIW, Fang VJ, Riley S, Nishiura H: Entry screening to delay local transmission of 2009 pandemic influenza A (H1N1). *BMC Infect Dis* 2010, 10:82.

28. Committee on Infectious Diseases: Policy statement—Prevention of influenza: recommendations for influenza immunization of children, 2007–2008. *Pediatrics* 2008, 121:e1016-e1031.

29. Milne GJ, Kelso JK, Kelly HA, Huband ST, McVernon J: A small community model for the transmission of infectious diseases: comparison of school closure as an intervention in individual-based models of an influenza pandemic. *PLoS One* 2008, 3:e4005.

30. Cauchemez S, Valleron AJ, Boelle PY, Flahault A, Ferguson NM: Estimating the impact of school closure on influenza transmission from Sentinel data. *Nature* 2008, 452:750–754.

31. New South Wales public health network: Progression and impact of the first winter wave of the 2009 pandemic H1N1 influenza in New South Wales, Australia. *Euro Surveill* 2009, 14(42):pii=19365.

32. Fielding J, Higgins N, Gregory J, Grant K, Catton M, Bergeri I, Lester R, Kelly H: Pandemic H1N1 influenza surveillance in Victoria, Australia, April—September, 2009. *Euro Surveill* 2009, 14:19368.

33. Looker C, Carville K, Grant K, Kelly H: Influenza A (H1N1) in Victoria, Australia: a community case series and analysis of household transmission. PLoS One 2010, 5:e13702.

34. Effler PV, Carcione D, Giele C, Dowse GK, Goggin L, Mak DB: Household responses to pandemic (H1N1) 2009-related school closures, Perth, Western Australia. *Emerg Infect Dis* 2010, 16:205–211.

35. Nishiura H, Chowell G, Safan M, Castillo-Chavez C: Pros and cons of estimating the reproduction number from early epidemic growth rate of influenza A (H1N1). *Theor Biol Med Model* 2009, 7:1.

36. Wu JT, Cowling BJ, Lau EH, Ip DK, Ho LM, Tsang T, Chuang SK, Leung PY, Lo SV, Liu SH, Riley S: School closure and mitigation of pandemic (H1N1) 2009, Hong Kong. *Emerg Infect Dis* 2010, 16:538–541.

37. Cauchemez S, Ferguson NM, Wachtel C, Tegnell A, Saour G, Duncan B, Nicoll A: Closure of schools during an influenza pandemic. *Lancet Infect Dis* 2009, 9:473–481.

38. Jefferson T, Jones M, Doshi P, Del Mar C: Neuraminidase inhibitors for preventing and treating influenza in healthy adults: systematic review and meta-analysis. *BMJ* 2009, 339:b5106.

39. Triggle N: Swine flu drug hand-out service raises concern. [http://news.bbc.co.uk/2/hi/health/10491328.stm].

40. Lee VJ, Yap J, Cook AR, Chen MI, Tay JK, Tan BH, Loh JP, Chew SW, Koh WH, Lin R, *et al:* Oseltamivir ring prophylaxis for containment of 2009 H1N1 influenza outbreaks. *N Engl J Med* 2010, 362:2166–2174.

41. Hurt AC, Ernest J, Deng YM, Iannello P, Besselaar TG, Birch C, Buchy P, Chittaganpitch M, Chiu SC, Dwyer D, *et al:* Emergence and spread of oseltamivir-resistant A(H1N1) influenza viruses in Oceania, South East Asia and South Africa. *Antiviral Res* 2009, 83:90–93.

42. World Health Organization: Weekly update on oseltamivir resistance to pandemic influenza A (H1N1) 2009 viruses. [http://www.who.int/entity/csr/disease/influenza/2011_01_28_weekly_web_update_oseltamivir_resistance.pdf].

43. Wilking H, Buda S, von der Lippe E, Altmann D, Krause G, Eckmanns T, Haas W: Mortality of 2009 pandemic influenza A(H1N1) in Germany. *Euro Surveill* 2010, 15(49):pii=19741.

44. Australian Government Department of Health and Ageing: Free Pandemic Flu Vaccine Available For All. [http://www.health.gov.au/internet/ministers/publishing.nsf/Content/907DAC8DDA4756C6CA25764100112643/SFile/nr167.pdf].

45. Australian Government Australian Institute of Health and Welfare: 2010 Pandemic Vaccination Survey: Summary results. *Cat no PHE* 128 2010.

46. Turnour CE, Conaty SJ, Cretikos MA: An audit of pandemic (H1N1) 2009 influenza vaccine wastage in general practice. *Med J Aust* 2010, 192:541.

47. Drain PK, Nelson CM, Lloyd JS: Single-dose versus multi-dose vaccine vials for immunization programmes in developing countries. *Bull World Health Organ* 2003, 81:726–731.

48. Mak DB, Daly AM, Armstrong PK, Effler PV: Pandemic (H1N1) 2009 influenza vaccination coverage in Western Australia. *Med J Aust* 2010, 193:401–404.

49. Harris KM, Maurer J, Kellermann AL: Influenza vaccine–safe, effective, and mistrusted. *N Engl J Med* 2010, 363:2183–2185.

50. Wichmann O, Stocker P, Poggensee G, Altmann D, Walter D, Hellenbrand W, Krause G, Eckmanns T: Pandemic influenza A(H1N1) 2009 breakthrough infections and estimates of vaccine effectiveness in Germany 2009–2010. *Euro Surveill* 2010, 15(18):pii=19561.

51. Van Buynder PG, Dhaliwal JK, Van Buynder JL, Couturier C, Minville-Leblanc M, Garceau R, Tremblay FW: Protective effect of single-dose

adjuvanted pandemic influenza vaccine in children. *Influenza Other Respi Viruses* 2010, 4:171–178.

52. Valenciano M, Kissling E, Cohen JM, Oroszi B, A B, Rizzo C, Nunes B, Pitigoi D, Amparro LC, Mosnier A, *et al:* Estimates of pandemic influenza vaccine effectiveness in Europe, 2009–2010: Results of influenza monitoring vaccine effectiveness in Europe (I-MOVE) multicentre case-control study. *Plos Med* 2010, 9(1):e1000388.

53. Centers for Disease Control and Prevention: Pandemic severity index. [http://www.flu.gov/professional/community/commitigation.html#XVI].

54. Van Kerkhove MD, Asikainen T, Becker NG, Bjorge S, Desenclos JC, dos Santos T, Fraser C, Leung GM, Lipsitch M, Longini IM Jr, *et al:* Studies needed to address public health challenges of the 2009 H1N1 influenza pandemic: Insights from modeling. *PLoS Med* 2010, 7:e1000275.

55. Godlee F: Conflicts of interest and pandemic flu. *BMJ* 2010, 340:c2947.

56. Kotsimbos T, Waterer G, Jenkins C, Kelly PM, Cheng A, Hancox RJ, Holmes M, Wood-Baker R, Bowler S, Irving L, Thompson P: Influenza A/H1N1_09: Australia and New Zealand's winter of discontent. *Am J Respir Crit Care Med* 2010, 181:300–306.

57. Doshi P: Pandemic influenza: severity must be taken into account. *J Infect Dis* 2010, 201:1444–1445.

58. Briand S: Challenges of pandemic influenza nationally and internationally. [http://www.hpa-events.org.uk/hpa/frontend/reg/titem.csp?pageID=51531&eventID=110&eventID=11].

EXPLORING THE ISSUE ⟳

Is the International Community Adequately Prepared to Address Global Health Pandemics?

Critical Thinking and Reflection

1. Does the WHO plan in the first reading represent a sound comprehensive plan of action or a fanciful idea not grounded in reality?
2. Was the lack of a full-blown global H1N1 flu pandemic in 2009 a function of the global community's response or simply good luck?
3. Is the developing world at greater risk against global pandemics than the developed world?
4. Is the world better off today as opposed to 100 years ago in its capacity to prevent the global spread of an epidemic into a pandemic?
5. Do you believe that the developed world's governments have taken notice of the nature and scope of pandemics and have begun to act to address the issue?

Is There Common Ground?

There is much common ground on the issue of global pandemics. The global community is in agreement about the need for comprehensive planning among all governments if not all segments of society. And increasingly, the developed world now understands the inequalities existing in the developing world and that these lead to greater probability of the rise and spread of pandemics originating in these poorer countries.

Additional Resources

Beck, Eduard J., Mays, Nicholas and Whiteside, Alan W. (eds.), *The HIV Pandemic: Local and Global Implications*, Oxford University Press (2008).

This is a historical overview of the HIV pandemic.

Condon, Barry and Sinha, Tapen, *Global Lessons from the AIDS Pandemic: Economic, Financial, Legal and Political Implications* (Springer, 2010)

This book uses a multidisciplinary approach to address the AIDS issue, examining specific countries and regions. It reveals lesson highlights in the global fight against AIDS.

Dorrance, John M. (ed.), *Global Time Bomb: Surviving the H1N1 Swine Flu Pandemic and Other Global Health Threats* (Madrona Books, 2009)

> This book focuses primarily on how to survive the H1N1 flu pandemic, but it also provides information about other global health threats.

Dry, Sarah and Leach, Melissa, *Epidemics: Science, Governance and Social Justice* (Earthscan, 2010)

> This book focuses on the causes and responses to various epidemics, contrasting between short-term emergency-type responses and longer term approaches to diseases.

Enserink, Martin, "New Study Casts Doubt on Plans for Pandemic Containment," *Science* (February 24, 2006)

> This study cautions the reader about the 2005 WHO report listed in this Additional Resources section.

Kilbourne, Edwin D., "Influenza Pandemics of the 20th Century," *Emerging Infectious Diseases* (January 2006)

> This article suggests that the keystone of influenza prevention is vaccination, not simply hand washing, hand wringing, public education, or gauze masks.

World Health Organization, *Avian Influenza: Assessing the Pandemic Threat* (2005)

> This publication traces the evolution of the outbreaks of the H5N1 avian influenza, lessons from past pandemics, its origins in poultry, and future actions "in the face of an uncertain threat."

Youngerman, Barry, *Pandemics and Global Health* (Checkmark Books, 2008)

> This book is a comprehensive introduction to the history and current situation regarding global pandemics.

ISSUE 11

Do Adequate Strategies Exist to Combat Human Trafficking?

YES: **Luis CdeBaca**, from "A Decade in Review, A Decade Before Us: Celebrating Successes and Developing New Strategies at the 10th Anniversary of the Trafficking Victims Protection Act," speech at 2010 Freedom Network Conference, Washington, DC (U.S. Department of State, March 18, 2008)

NO: **United Nations Office on Drugs and Crime**, from *Human Trafficking: An Overview* (United Nations Publications, 2008)

Learning Outcomes

After reading this issue, you should be able to:

- Gain an understanding of the nature of human trafficking and its underlying conditions.
- Discuss what is meant by a victim-centered approach to dealing with human traffic.
- Discuss the meaning of the three "Ps" in addressing the issue of human trafficking.
- Describe the 10 objectives of the United Nations in dealing with human trafficking.
- Describe the positive steps taken by the international community since 2000 in understanding human trafficking.

ISSUE SUMMARY

YES: Luis CdeBaca, ambassador-at-large for the U.S. Department of State, reported in a speech at the Freedom Network Conference that "appreciable progress" has been made in understanding the issue of human trafficking and thus the global community is in "the early stages of positive change" in addressing the issue.

NO: This 2008 UN report suggests that despite increased international attention and national responses to the problem of human trafficking, it is still "a very tragic reality" as even if traffickers come under investigation, they still face little risk of convictions.

Human trafficking is defined by the United Nations (UN) as "the recruitment, transportation, transfer, harbouring or receipt of persons, by means of the threat or use of force or other forms of coercion, of abduction, of fraud, of deception, of the abuse of power or of a position of vulnerability or of the giving or receiving of payments or benefits to achieve the consent of a person having control over another person, for the purpose of exploitation" (*Trafficking in Persons—Global Patterns,* United Nations, Office on Drug and Crime, April 2006). Exploitation may take any one of several forms: prostitution, forced labor, slavery, or other forms of servitude. Although slavery has been with us since ancient times, the existence of human trafficking across national borders, particularly involving major distances, is a relatively new escalation of a problem that in the past was addressed as a domestic issue, if addressed at all. The first evidence of modern international slavery occurred in 1877 at a meeting of the International Abolitionist Federation at Geneva. There, a report discussed dozens of women being sent to Austria and Hungary under the pretext of work as governesses for work in brothels. A decade later, the issue arose in London through a newspaper account, leading to a public outcry. In 1899, the first international congress to address the issue of white slave traffic was held, with 120 nations represented. International legislation soon followed. With the creation of the United Nations after World War II, the UN took responsibility for enforcing the agreement. But the issue does not appear to be high on the radar screen of either the UN or its member states for much of the rest of the twentieth century.

It is not until a dramatic expansion occurred as communism was falling throughout the latter half of the 1980s that the issue began to garner public attention. Louise Shelley (*Human Trafficking: A Global Perspective,* Cambridge University Press, 2010) suggests that this expansion was related to globalization, with its emphasis on "free markets, free trade, greater economic competition, and a decline in state intervention in the economy." The end of the cold war also played a major role as organized crime in the former Soviet republics and former East European communist countries discovered how lucrative human trafficking could be. Loosened controls in these countries led to exploitation of national legal systems as criminals operated across national boundaries with relative impunity. Added to this mix was the absence of a coordinated international attempt to combat the issue. Finally, there is the increased demand in both the labor and the sex areas. And the easy movement across national boundaries only exacerbates the problem.

Shelley sees globalization as the instrument through which human trafficking flourishes. The increased volume of international cargo means that inspections often go wanting, allowing smuggled individuals to easily cross national boundaries. Modern communication has been a major contributor, as Web sites blatantly advertise sex tourism, arranged relationships, and pornography, and e-mails and cell phones are standard operating procedures. Globalization has also meant decreased border controls throughout the developed world. Economic factors have played a role. First, it was the difficult transition from communism to capitalism that led the losers in this process to find other means of employment, with human trafficking as a likely result. Then, it was the downturn in the global economy in 2008 that played a strong role. Shelley also points to the dramatic increase on "grand corruption," building on decades of small-scale corruption throughout the world. Finally, political factors have been major contributors to human trafficking. The end of the cold war not only loosened state control over every human activity, it also led to a dramatic increase in local conflicts, creating more victims who tried to flee the violence. In turn, this has led to a global condition of statelessness, as increasingly people are citizens of no country and live in limbo, with difficulty in finding employment and with no legal protection of a national government. Add the dramatic population increase in poorer countries and increased urbanization, and you find a large number of individuals, especially women, desperately searching for a better life.

People are abducted or "recruited" in the country of origin, transferred through a standard network to another region of the globe, and then exploited in the destination country. If at any point exploitation is interrupted or ceases, victims can be rescued and might receive support from the country of destination. Victims might be repatriated to their country of origin or, less likely, relocated to a third country. Too often, victims are treated as illegal migrants and treated accordingly. The UN estimates that 127 countries act as countries of origin, whereas 137 countries serve as countries of destination. Profits are estimated by the UN to be $7 billion per year, with between 700,000 and 4 million new victims annually.

When one hears of human trafficking, one usually thinks of sexual exploitation rather than of forced labor. This is not surprising as not only are individual victim stories more compelling, the former type of exploitation represents the more frequent topic of dialogue among policymakers and is also the more frequent occurrence as reported to the UN by a three-to-one margin. With respect to victims, 77 percent are women, 33 percent children, 48 percent girls, 12 percent boys, and 9 percent males (the sum of percentages is more than 100 because one source can indicate more than one victim profile). It is not surprising that most women and female children are exploited sexually, while most male adults and children are subjected to forced labor. Sexual exploitation is more typically found in Central and Southeastern Europe. Former Soviet republics serve as a huge source of origin. Africa ranks high as a region of victim origin as well, although most end up in forced labor rather than in sexual exploitation. Asia is a region of both origin and destination. Countries at the top of the list include Thailand, Japan, India, Taiwan, and Pakistan. The same UN study found that nationals of Asia and Europe represent the bulk of traffickers. And most traffickers who are arrested are nationals of the country where the arrest occurred.

Human trafficking has been part of the global landscape for centuries. What is different today is the magnitude and scope of the trafficking and the extent to which organized crime is involved in facilitating such nefarious activity. And yet the global community is still only in the position of trying to identify the nature and extent of the problem, let alone ascertaining how to deal with it. In April 2006, the United Nations Office on Drugs and Crime released its most recent report on the human trafficking problem. Titled *Trafficking in Persons: Global Patterns* (United Nations Office on Drugs and Crime, April 2006); its message was clear. The starting point for addressing the problem is the implementation of the Protocol to Prevent, Suppress and Punish Trafficking in Persons, Especially Women and Children. National governments are called upon to take a leading role in (1) the prevention of trafficking, (2) prosecution of violators, and (3) protection of victims.

Consider the task of prevention. Nations are expected to establish comprehensive policies and programs to prevent and combat trafficking, including research, information, and media campaigns. Nations must attempt to alleviate the vulnerability of people, especially women and children. They must create steps to discourage demand for victims. Nations must also prevent transportation opportunities for traffickers. Finally, they must exchange information and increase cooperation among border control agencies. The UN report also suggests several steps with respect to prosecution. The first step is to "ensure the integrity and security of travel and identity documents" and thus prevent their misuse. Domestic laws must be enacted making human trafficking a criminal offense, and these laws must apply to victims of both genders and all ages. Penalties must be adequate to the crime. Finally, victims must be protected and possibly compensated.

The third role, clearly an alternative approach, outlined in the UN report, focuses on protection of victims. This represents an alternative to the previous international focus, which essentially ignored the plight of the victims. Specifically, victims must be able to achieve "physical, psychological and social recovery." The physical safety of victims is also paramount. The final step relates to the future home of victims, whether they want to remain in the location where found or whether they wish to return home.

In the YES selection, Luis CdeBaca of the U.S. Department of State states that "appreciable progress" is being made in grasping an understanding of human trafficking. In the NO selection, the UN report emphasizes that little convictions of traffickers still characterize the issue.

YES ↵

Luis CdeBaca

A Decade in Review, A Decade Before Us: Celebrating Successes and Developing New Strategies at the 10th Anniversary of the Trafficking Victims Protection Act

Thank you for the invitation to address you today as we discuss where to go next and what strategies will best serve those of you on the front lines against trafficking. The last time I had the honor to address you was when I was a prosecutor at the Department of Justice. Today, I am humbled to be here with my friends in a new capacity. A broader capacity. With broader responsibilities. And with a broader vision of how to combat trafficking worldwide. I wanted to talk with you today about how far we have come, where we are, and where I hope we can go, together.

Recently, the Secretary General of the United Nations, Ban Ki-Moon, said, "Slavery is [even] re-emerging in new forms, including the sale of children, debt bondage and human trafficking. Its roots lie in ignorance, intolerance and greed. We must confront these in every way we can. We must create a climate in which such unthinking abuse and cruelty are inconceivable."

Modern history has witnessed as many manifestations of enslavement as there are attempts to define and respond to it in the international community. Ten years ago, the United Nations made yet another attempt, yet this time there was a marked difference. Instead of focusing on one form of compelled service over another—forced labor, bonded labor, slavery, slavery-like practices—there was an effort to put forward the concept that *all* forms should be criminalized, victims of *all* forms deserved protection, and prevention of *all* forms was a worthwhile endeavor to attack the problem at its core. This concept captured in the Palermo Protocol is what we now know by the umbrella term "trafficking in persons" and respond to through the overarching response of the "three Ps." But whatever the particular euphemism we see used, as Secretary Clinton recently said to the Cabinet, "Let's call it what it is, a modern form of slavery."

In the year 2000, there was a considerable focus on women and children. At the time, the most visible form of trafficking was women and girls from the former Soviet Union being duped by false advertisements for work in Western

From 2010 Freedom Network Conference, March 18, 2008.

Europe only to find themselves trapped in brothels and strip clubs. The image of the helpless vulnerable victim, reminiscent of anachronistic approaches to this problem back in the 1800s garnered worldwide attention, but also demonstrated the weaknesses of that old legal regime. It became clear that a holistic approach was needed, one that focused more on the exploitation than merely on the movement of people for immoral purposes. That year, the international community and the United States adopted instruments embodying the "three Ps," which included a strong law enforcement approach that captured the true harm: enslavement in all its forms.

This year, we celebrate the 10-year anniversary of the Palermo Protocol and the 137 countries that have adopted it, as well as the 10-year anniversary of the Trafficking Victims Protection Act (TVPA) signed into law under the Clinton Administration. Thousands of victims have been helped; thousands of traffickers have been arrested and prosecuted, neither of which would have come about without the legal and policy achievements of the last decade.

Over 10 years, we have made appreciable progress in understanding human trafficking:

- people are enslaved in every country;
- it is a fluid phenomenon, responding to market demands, vulnerabilities in laws, weak penalties, and economic instability;
- more people are trafficked for forced labor than commercial sex;
- there is less duping and kidnapping of naïve victims than there is coercion of people who initially agreed to do the work; movement is not required;
- men comprise a significant number of trafficking victims; and
- traffickers use rape as a weapon against women, whether in a field, factory, brothel, or suburban home.

No country has attained a sophisticated or truly comprehensive response to this massive, ever increasing, ever changing crime. Ten years of focused efforts is the mere infancy of a movement; thus, every country is still learning what trafficking is and what works in response to it, and every country must do more to fulfill the promise of the Palermo Protocol as the vast majority of millions enslaved today have yet to feel any progress.

The Obama Administration response builds upon 10 years of the "three Ps" in practice, which has illuminated a new path for the future.

We know human trafficking is: a human rights abuse; a byproduct of conflict; a threat to national security, public health and democracy; a labor and migration issue; and a growing global phenomenon. It is also a crime: a crime akin to murder and rape and kidnapping. And so the Palermo Protocol mandates criminalization of trafficking in persons, and the TVPA is law enforcement driven, because a policy solution to a heinous crime problem must involve freeing the victims and punishing their tormentors.

As long as there are about 5,000 prosecutions worldwide every year, governments send a message that the injustice suffered by victims is not a national or an international priority. Too often the victims of this crime are perceived to be throwaways—runaways, poor, prostitutes, or illegals. Some are still clinging to the image of the "white slavery" victim. These biases and mis-conceptions of victims impact whether they are identified and whether their traffickers are brought to justice. A narrow focus hinders a robust law enforce-ment response and allows traffickers to operate with impunity. Moreover, it diminishes the promise of equal protection under the law, undermining basic rule of law principles. Traffickers should not be assessed by who their victims are, but by the heinous crimes they commit. Otherwise, we are sending a mes-sage that the traffickers are not hurting people who matter. *All* victims have a right to see their traffickers brought to justice and to be heard through the legal process. Compassionate and smart prosecution is thus the foundation of a victim-centered approach.

And yet, prosecution alone cannot provide victims with the compassion and patience that meets their immediate needs and long-term potential alike. The "three Ps" serve as an interlocking paradigm; no single "P" can work inde-pendently of another. Therefore, it is not enough to prosecute traffickers if we do not also provide assistance to the survivors and work to ensure that no one else is victimized.

A victim-centered approach does not mean helping a trafficked person long enough to obtain the testimony; it means obligations that extend well beyond the confines of a criminal case. It means partnerships between law enforcement and service providers, not just to win the case, but as colleagues sharing the responsibility of letting the survivors' voices be heard.

Protection means policies with the best interest of the victim in mind. Like counseling, legal services, educational and economic opportunities and all of the good work that the Freedom Network is known to perform so well. It means the conception of a system and process that recognizes and reinstates the power of the survivor. We can and must assess how better to allow you as service providers to do your jobs, including ways in which legal service provid-ers can keep their doors open. As I work with countries around the world, I see too many who condition any relief on not just willingness to cooperate as here in the United States, but on actual testimony and even winning the case. And in many countries, even that will only delay the inevitable detention and deportation. We need to constantly assess how we can do better. Protection must be viewed and implemented as a responsibility to restore the dignity of a person whose rights were violated just as we view other victims of crime.

Similarly, every trafficker put in prison leads to the prevention of traf-ficking of future victims by that trafficker. The Palermo Protocol describes prevention as creating public awareness campaigns, addressing root causes, and conducting law enforcement-related activities. But these strategies alone cannot be the sum of our prevention efforts. A decade later, governments are expanding their understanding of prevention to include policies and practices that cut off modern slavery at the source. This includes initiatives in which government, corporations, and consumers come together to ensure that free trade means free labor rather than labor for free.

Prevention at its best targets key vulnerabilities in legal systems, policies and implementation, which allows trafficking to occur such as unregistered births, tolerance within government procurement and contracting, unchecked labor recruiting companies, restrictive visas that can be used as coercive tools, or lax labor law enforcement. It lies in targeted initiatives to protect the rights of marginalized, low-income workers including domestic servants, farm workers, miners, and garment workers who are subject to offenses on a continuum of labor exploitation including trafficking.

Again, we must remind ourselves of the victim. Do we value cheap lettuce more than we value the hands that picked it? We must still criminalize the trafficker and protect the victims while also devising laws, policies and partnerships that allow us to attack the problem at its source.

Prevention can and should also be an effort in harnessing the economic impetus for this crime in order to fight it by increasing criminal and civil penalties for companies that do not adequately police their supply chains and granting preferences to those that do.

This vision of the "three Ps" I believe is more nuanced and better understood than it has been at any point in our 10 years working together. But it won't be realized unless we all hold one another accountable to it. The TVPA helps us do so with important new tools that stand for the proposition that ignorance is not an excuse. The strip club owner, who looks the other way as so-called talent agents enslave women, is no longer just a bystander; he is an accomplice. So too for the grower who looks the other way as farm labor contractors use force and threats to get in the crops. To those who have turned a willfully blind eye to the exploitation in front of them, the new law puts down a marker: whether you partake or profit, you're accountable. Period.

And in that spirit, we need to hold ourselves accountable as well. To hold countries, including our own, accountable for policies and practices that either create or further endanger populations vulnerable to trafficking. This year, we will rank the United States in the annual Trafficking Report for the first time because, as Secretary Clinton said, "I believe when you shine a bright light you need to shine it on everyone, and we will rank ourselves." Last week, the State Department posted a federal register notice inviting your submissions in reporting on the degree to which the United States complies with the minimum standards for the elimination of trafficking in persons. I am hoping that you will help us present an accurate picture of the successes and challenges the United States faces in combating trafficking, particularly with what is happening at the state and local level.

A year ago, when President Obama took office, people around the globe were hopeful for a new day where America would lead the world through positive change. Today, we have seen the early stages of positive change take place on a range of issues, including human trafficking.

The United States continues to be a global leader on this issue. I am mindful that the world is not only watching, but also replicating what we do. And by "we," I mean everyone in this room. I have seen how our good work at home becomes the international standard to which other countries are held. I am proud in my role as Ambassador to hold up the Freedom Network's standard of care and partnership as true models for others to follow. You know all too well that our strength is in a collective, collaborative approach because when it is fragmented or partial the victims continue to suffer. Together we bring to bear amazing energy, talent and resources and I think we need to think of ways to capitalize on them.

And so together, let's agree to spread some core messages:

- That we are here to assist *all* trafficked persons whom we encounter, be they foreign born or U.S. citizens or found in labor or sex trafficking;
- That we will engage in partnerships with the private sector to have companies offer jobs to trafficked persons and who are willing to be accountable for their supply chains;
- That we will work to identify the weaknesses in our laws and our implementation to provide a better system of enforcement and services;
- That we will challenge people to think about their slavery footprint and consider where their food, clothing and manufactured goods come from;
- That we will force what has largely been a federal effort down to the state and local level as well;
- That we will overcome barriers to identification and services, continuing a victim-centered approach and focusing on populations at greatest risk; and
- That we keep our doors open to continue the discussion.

In this year of anniversaries, we now find ourselves in an era of new partnerships and new possibilities. We can capitalize on this moment through your leadership, your hard work, and a renewed commitment to work in partnership. There is so much energy and goodwill in this room that, together, I believe we can start to dismantle modern slavery as it exists today in bold new ways.

Human Trafficking: An Overview

Despite increasing global attention and significant, if fractured, national responses, human trafficking is, today, a very tragic reality. While the majority of Member States have ratified the Protocol to Prevent, Suppress and Punish Trafficking in Persons, Especially Women and Children, and other international instruments, human trafficking still remains a crime with low risks and high profit. The United Nations Global Initiative to Fight Human Trafficking (UN.GIFT) provides a much-needed boost to enhance global efforts of all stakeholders: to tackle the crime; to examine the countermeasures taken; and to identify shortcomings.

In order to take the right steps to combat human trafficking, we need to improve our knowledge of its nature, the underlying conditions, as well as the profiles of traffickers and victims. Lack of data on the nature and severity of the problem remains a problem. Available information is often based on estimates with little explanation on how figures were calculated.

Some basic patterns and trends are apparent. Human trafficking is a process, with people being abducted or recruited in the country of origin, transferred through transit regions and then exploited in the country of destination. In the case of internal trafficking, all three stages would occur within the borders of a single country. Coercive or deceptive recruitment methods vary, as do transport modes. Further, the forms of exploitation differ, although for several years the focus has been on sexual exploitation rather than on forced labour and other forms of exploitation.

Inadequate knowledge of this crime is often a consequence of failure to identify victims as such. Among those who are identified, adult women are most frequently reported to be trafficked, followed by children. The factors that make people vulnerable to trafficking and exploitation are complex and determined, in part, by the stage of the trafficking process the victim is in. There are vulnerabilities related to the conditions in the country of origin. Also the transport itself makes people vulnerable, as they may not have proper documents or financial means and, therefore, depend on traffickers. The exploitation phase produces some additional vulnerabilities, as, for example, when victims have illegal status in the country or are physically isolated. Far less information on offenders is available than on their victims. Traffickers can be involved in various functions—as, for example, recruiters, transporters or exploiters—and various activities during different stages of the trafficking process, including forging documents, corruption and the withholding of their victims' documents. Organized criminal groups can be heavily involved in human trafficking, at different operational levels.

One clear conclusion is that traffickers still face little risk. Even where trafficking is criminalized in a State, investigations most often do not result in convictions or, where they do, in appropriate punishment of the offenders.

It is imperative that Governments ratify and implement the Trafficking Protocol, the first international instrument to address this crime.

The challenges to eradicate human trafficking are significant, but are known and can be addressed. They include:

- Lack of knowledge
- Lack of a national legal framework
- Lack of policy and capacity to respond
- Limited protection of and assistance to victims
- Limited international cooperation

I. Why UN.GIFT

. . . Trafficking in persons was a violation against humanity 200 years ago, as it still is today. It has also continued to be an international issue. Virtually every country in the world is affected by trafficking for sexual exploitation or forced labour. Reliable global data are limited, but the number of victims is believed to be reaching epidemic proportions. Data taken from the United Nations Office on Drugs and Crime (UNODC) report on trafficking in persons[1] document the trafficking of human beings from 127 countries to be exploited in 137 countries.

While there is clearly support to eradicate trafficking in persons, the challenges are immense. While the majority of United Nations Member States have ratified the Protocol to Prevent, Suppress and Punish Trafficking in Persons, Especially Women and Children, supplementing the United Nations Convention against Transnational Organized Crime,[2] lack of action to implement it remains a problem. Many trafficking victims still go through the tribulation without anyone identifying them. Confusion between trafficking in persons and smuggling of migrants prevents victims from receiving protection and support as their fundamental right. The conviction rate of traffickers remains very low and punishments do not reflect the seriousness of the crime. Human trafficking remains a crime with low risks and high profits and it violates the basic human rights of victims.

Against this background of both progress and challenges, UNODC, in partnership with the International Labour Organization (ILO), the International Organization for Migration (IOM), the United Nations Children's Fund (UNICEF), the Office of the United Nations High Commissioner for Human Rights (UNHCHR) and the Organization for Security and Cooperation in Europe (OSCE), launched the Global Initiative to Fight Human Trafficking (UN.GIFT) in March 2007.

UN.GIFT has 10 objectives:

1. **Awareness**—demonstrate to the world that human trafficking exists and mobilize people to stop it.
2. **Strengthen prevention**—to inform vulnerable groups and alleviate the factors that make people vulnerable to trafficking.
3. **Demand**—to attack the problem at its source by lowering incentives to trade and lowering demand for the products and services of exploited people.
4. **Support and protection of victims**—to ensure medical, psychological and material assistance, keeping in mind the special needs of women and children and people at risk, such as those in refugee camps and conflict zones.
5. **Law enforcement**—to improve information exchange on trafficking routes, trafficker profiles and victim identification in order to dismantle criminal groups, convict more traffickers and ensure that the punishment fits the crime.
6. **International commitments**—to ensure that international commitments are turned into national laws targeting technical and legal assistance to countries in greatest need and to monitor implementation.
7. **Data**—to deepen global understanding of the scope and nature of trafficking in persons by more data collection and analysis, better data-sharing, joint research initiatives and evidence-based reports on global trafficking trends.
8. **Partnership**—to build up regional and thematic networks involving civil society, intergovernmental organizations and the private sector.
9. **Resources**—to attract and leverage resources for the sustainable funding of projects around the world committed to ending human trafficking.
10. **Member States' participation**—to give Member States a strong sense of ownership in the process and create long-term momentum.

II. The Severity and Nature of a Crime That Shames Us All

. . . Trafficking in persons is dynamic, adaptable, opportunistic and, like many other forms of criminal activity, it takes advantage of conflicts, humanitarian disasters and the vulnerability of people in situations of crisis. It is multidisciplinary and involves a wide range of actors. To combat the crime, it is essential to understand the nature of human trafficking and its underlying conditions, as well as the profiles of traffickers and victims.

A. Severity

Several estimates on the size of the problem have been released recently. Also, different sources have provided estimates on the revenue that organized criminal groups raise from trafficking. To date, however, there is no broad agreement regarding the methodology that should be used to calculate such numbers—as a result, figures quoted often contradict each other.[3] At the global level, four organizations have databases on trafficking in persons: the United States Government, ILO, IOM and UNODC. Only the United States Government and ILO estimate the global number of victims, while IOM collects data on assisted victims and UNODC traces the major international trafficking routes of the victims (see table below).[4]

ILO has estimated that the minimum number of persons in forced labour, including sexual exploitation, as a result of trafficking at any given time is 2.5 million. Of these, 1.4 million are in Asia and the Pacific, 270,000 in industrialized countries, 250,000 in Latin America and the Caribbean, 230,000 in the Middle East and Northern Africa, 200,000 in countries with economies in transition and 130,000 in sub-Saharan countries.[5]

According to United States Government–sponsored research completed in 2006, approximately 800,000 people are trafficked across national borders annually, which does not include the millions trafficked within their own countries.[6]

A non-governmental organization (NGO), Free the Slaves, estimates that there are 27 million slaves in the world today. According to their estimates, more than 1.3 million people are enslaved in Latin America and the Caribbean, nearly 1 million in Africa and the Middle East and 24 million in Asia.[7] A joint study published in 2002 by ILO and the International Institute of Tropical Agriculture found that an estimated 284,000 children on cocoa farms in Western Africa were either involved in hazardous work, were unprotected or enslaved, or had been trafficked.[8]

According to ILO,[9] the annual profits made from the exploitation of all trafficked forced labour are as follows:

	Millions of United States dollars
At the global level	31.7
Industrialized economies	15.5
Countries with economies in transition	3.4
Asia and the Pacific	9.7
Latin America and the Caribbean	1.3
Sub-Saharan Africa	1.6
Middle East and North America	1.5

1. Latin America[10]

Even though the countries in the region of Latin America and the Caribbean are primarily source countries for trafficking victims,[11] there has been an intensification of inter- and intraregional movement, causing growing needs for integrated public policies that focus on these places as transit and destination countries.

According to a 2005 IOM report, trafficking in women and girls for purposes of sexual exploitation has become a $16-billion-a-year business in Latin America. Some estimates have suggested that this figure represents almost half of what is generated worldwide as trafficking profits. The United States State Department estimates that tens of thousands of Latin American women and children are trafficked for sexual exploitation each year. And although it tends to be underreported, trafficking for forced labour is generally perceived to be a major and growing problem, as workers are being exploited for slave labour within the region and, increasingly, are also ending up in situations of forced labour after migrating to European countries and the United States.

2. Western and Central Africa[12]

Traffickers pocket substantial criminal proceeds from various forms of exploitation of victims. In Western and Central Africa, these victims are predominantly women and children who live in the harshest conditions of vulnerability. Armed conflict, socio-political instability, bad governance, environmental stress and disaster drastically increase the vulnerability of children to trafficking for a variety of exploitative purposes, including their recruitment and abuse in situations of armed conflict and war.

When looking at the entire region, three major trafficking trends, two of which are transnational, can be identified:

- Children who are trafficked within the region for the purpose of labour exploitation
- Women and girls who are trafficked both within and out of the region for sexual exploitation
- Large-scale internal trafficking, which takes place within the borders of a State

Several countries in the region are both origin and destination countries for women and girls who are trafficked for sexual exploitation. The main destinations outside the region are in Western Europe, Southern Africa and the Middle East.

Patterns of internal trafficking within the region often remain hidden behind the issues of transnational trafficking. Conflict, poverty, and HIV/AIDS leave adults and especially children vulnerable to trafficking within their own national borders. General trends within the Economic Community of West African States (ECOWAS) include trafficking from rural to urban and industrial areas for employment and sexual exploitation. Larger farming and fishing communities in fertile lands and along coastal areas also receive large numbers of internally trafficked persons for labour.

3. South Asia[13]

In South Asia, there are many countries used as origin, transit and destination countries for trafficking. Victims are sent to other countries in the region and to other parts of the world. Even more prevalent is the movement of persons within the countries for exploitation in various forms. Even though there are no definite numbers of victims, it is estimated that 150,000 victims are trafficked from the region annually.[14] Many studies have revealed that trafficking in women and children is on the rise in Asia.

Trafficking for commercial sexual exploitation is the most virulent form of trafficking in the region. The movement of young girls from South Asian countries to brothels is common, taking place either between countries or within countries. There is further movement to the Middle East as well as other destinations. Internal displacement due to conflict in some countries, poverty and lack of employment opportunities increase the vulnerability to being trafficked.

South Asia is also home to one of the largest concentrations of people living with HIV/AIDS. Women involved in the sex business—as a group—are an important driver of the epidemic. Recent research involving repatriated women who worked at commercial sex markets in Nepal show that many of those who have been trafficked are at significantly higher risk of contracting HIV than are non-trafficked women.

4. East Asia and the Pacific

The UNODC publication on trafficking patterns shows that trafficking in Asian victims to other countries within Asia is frequently reported. In particular, South-East Asia is often reported to be an origin region for trafficking into Asian countries.[15]

Though trafficking in persons is not considered to be as imminent a threat to border integrity as migrant smuggling, several countries in the Pacific have acknowledged that people have been trafficked across their borders. There are also indications that the number of people trafficked from, to and through the region will increase and that the primary purpose will be for the purpose of sexual exploitation.[16]

5. Eastern Africa[17]

Trafficking in persons is an ongoing phenomenon within the region of Eastern Africa. The phenomenon is present not only in transnational trafficking; internal trafficking is endemic. Children, women and, to a lesser extent, men are victims of trafficking in, from and to the region.

Girls are trafficked for exploitation in domestic labour, forced prostitution and forced marriage. Trafficked boys are also exploited in areas such as farming, livestock, plantation work and fishing. Women are trafficked for domestic labour, forced prostitution and the hospitality industry, and men are trafficked mainly for manual and agriculture labour, construction work and criminal activities.

Internal trafficking in children and women from rural and urban areas is mainly for exploitative domestic work and commercial sex work. However, transnational trafficking of women to other African countries, Europe and the Middle East is mainly for sexual exploitation and domestic work.

Statistics from a study on child trafficking in Eastern African countries show that the majority of the trafficked children are those who have either completed primary or secondary education and have nothing to do. Moreover, most of the children are trafficked by people they know (in some cases, by relatives). The most vulnerable age is 13–18 years. HIV/AIDS has also contributed to the trafficking phenomenon; the majority of trafficked children are orphans. African society is a changing society; traditional fostering practices have led to the abuse of fostered children, who are often sold for profit.

It is estimated that 25,000–30,000 girls and boys have been abducted and recruited into armed ranks by rebel forces. In the last 20 years, some of the children abducted have ended up in other African countries while others have been taken to the Middle East, Europe and America.

According to a study conducted by UNICEF, child sex tourism and sexual exploitation of children in Eastern Africa have reached alarmingly high levels. About 15,000 children, or 30 per cent of girls aged 12–18, in tourist districts along the Eastern African coast engage in the practice of exchanging casual sex for cash. A related study by the Federation of Kenya Employers indicates that the majority of these children are victims of internal trafficking from other provinces. According to the media reports children are also trafficked for domestic work—this is internal trafficking that entails the movement of the victims from rural areas to urban and periurban areas to work in homes.

B. Nature

Even though all human trafficking cases have their individual characteristics, most follow the same pattern: people are abducted or recruited in the country of origin, transferred through transit regions and then exploited in the country of destination. If, at some stage, the exploitation of the victims is interrupted or ended, they can be rescued as victims of trafficking and they may receive support in the country of destination. Victims may be repatriated to their country of origin; in some cases, relocated in a third country; or, as unfortunately still happens all too often, deported from countries of destination or transit as illegal migrants.

1. Trends

Based on the UNODC report on human trafficking,[18] the regions of the Commonwealth of Independent States, Central and South-Eastern Europe, Western Africa and South-East Asia are most commonly reported as being regions of origin for human trafficking. Countries in Western Europe, North America and Asia, in particular in West Asia, are reported more frequently as countries of destination. Countries of Central and South-Eastern Europe and Western Europe are highly reported as transit regions. Outside of Europe, South-East Asia, Central America and Western Africa are also frequently reported as transit subregions.

2. Process

For trafficking to work, the traffickers have either to force or to convince their victims to leave their familiar surroundings and to travel with them. This can be achieved in a number of ways.

Based on the IOM Counter-Trafficking Database,[19] which includes information on victims who have been assisted by IOM projects in 78 countries, most recruitment occurs through personal contacts. According to the database, 46 per cent of victims knew their recruiter and 54 per cent were recruited by strangers. In addition, 52 per cent of recruiters were men and 42 per cent women, and in 6 per cent of recruitments both men and women were involved as recruiters.

Transportation routes and methods depend upon geographical conditions. Victims are trafficked by aircraft, boat, rail, ferry and road or simply on foot in order to reach the country of destination. The route may include a transit country or it may be direct between the origin and destination locations. The crossing of borders may be done overtly or covertly, legally or illegally. Related criminal offences include abuses of immigration and border control laws, corruption of officials, forgery of documents, acts of coercion against the victim, unlawful confinement and the withholding of identity papers and other documents.[20]

In the Trafficking Protocol, the purpose of exploitation, includes, at a minimum, the exploitation of the prostitution of others or other forms of sexual exploitation, forced labour or services, slavery or practices similar to slavery, servitude or the removal of organs.[21] Based on several studies, the purpose of human trafficking is reported to be mainly sexual exploitation.

For several years, human trafficking for sexual exploitation has dominated discussions on the issue, while trafficking in persons for forced labour has not been viewed as a major problem in many countries. The identification of trafficking victims who are exploited through forced labour has in addition been even less successful than in the case of sexual exploitation.[22]

Victims of trafficking very often suffer threats and violence when they are exploited. In the case of both labour and sexual exploitation, traffickers use threats and actual violence to maintain control over their victims and to prevent them from escaping.

3. Victims

Identification and rescue of victims may take place during different phases of the trafficking in persons process: potential victims may be identified, for example, when crossing borders or at any other point of the transportation stage. Identification is probably most common when victims are exploited in the country of destination. In some cases, a particular effort is made to identify victims returning to their home countries.

Adult women are most frequently reported to be victims of trafficking, followed by children who have been trafficked.

According to the IOM database, the biggest age group receiving assistance is that from 18 to 24. Many trafficking victims have at least middle-level education.

There are several factors that make potential victims vulnerable to trafficking. It is a complex issue and there is no single categorization of vulnerability to human trafficking. A review of trafficking reports, however, reveals some of the contributing factors, while also showing how little we actually know about the issue of vulnerability to human trafficking. Potential and actual victims can be vulnerable to victimization throughout the trafficking process.

Factors affecting vulnerability in the countries of origin include age, gender and poverty. Children are vulnerable to the demands and expectations of those in authority, including their parents, extended family and teachers.

Women are vulnerable to trafficking because they are often excluded from employment, higher education and legal as well as political parity. Many forms of gender-based violations, such as rape, domestic violence and harmful traditional practices, are linked to social and cultural situations that contribute to the vulnerability of women to being trafficked.[23]

In a study on physical and mental health consequences of human trafficking in Europe it was found that 60 per cent of victims had experienced physical or sexual violence before they were trafficked.[24]

Vulnerabilities may contribute to the victimization of a person at the beginning of the trafficking process. However, they are not identical to root causes, which are determined by domestic policy decisions and social, cultural and religious practices.[25]

The link between poverty and human trafficking is complex. Poor people are vulnerable to trafficking by virtue of exerting little social power and having few income options. They often do not challenge social superiors in relation to migrant contracts and working conditions. However, it is not necessarily the poorest of the poor who become victims of trafficking, although in many cases victims are poor, especially victims in developing countries.

When the countries reported most frequently as countries of origin and destination[26] are compared against the United Nations Human Development Index,[27] it can be seen that, while the top countries of destination are rated highly in terms of human development, most of the top countries of origin are at the middle human development level. Thus, it can be concluded that those targeted as victims of trafficking are not the poorest of the poor, but rather people with at least some resources.

Often moving from one country to another or even moving within a country makes people vulnerable. Travellers may not have proper travel documents so they may be in a country illegally. They may not know the local language, they may not have any social network to assist them or they may be totally dependent on members of their own ethnic group receiving them in the destination country. Often foreigners do not have access to any national health care or social support system.

Once they are in the country of destination, traffickers may confiscate the victim's documents, creating a situation where victims are made to believe that they are in the country illegally. Traffickers can then use this vulnerability of non-documented victims as a control mechanism. Unfortunately, sometimes authorities reinforce the vulnerability by failing to identify victims, which then results in their immediate deportation.

Sometimes service providers may also increase the vulnerability to re-trafficking. In some countries, shelters for victims of domestic violence are also used to protect and support victims of human trafficking. This may lead to a situation where foreign victims are discriminated against. In addition, receiving support may be dependent on a number of conditions, which may lead victims to decide not to use the services.

The return process should ensure the safe and dignified return of each individual victim. It should involve a risk assessment of the country to which the victim is going to return, coordination between countries of origin and destination, a supported transportation and travel process, reception and referral upon arrival and transportation within the home country. Unfortunately, many return processes are not carried out in an ideal way and may themselves pose risks to victims, making them vulnerable to re-trafficking.[28]

4. Offenders

Traffickers can operate as recruiters, transporters or exploiters or they can be involved in trafficking through forgery of documents, corruption, money-laundering or other criminal activity. Several crimes can be connected to human trafficking.

In several countries, the majority of offenders are nationals of the same country in which the trafficking case is investigated.[29] Traffickers can be men or women, and in some criminal groups women indeed play a significant role in the trafficking process. For example, trafficking in women from Nigeria to Italy is managed mainly by women, with men relegated to largely secondary functions.[30] According to the German Criminal Police (BKA), more than 20 per cent of suspects in German human trafficking cases are women.[31]

Relatively few offenders in human trafficking cases are prosecuted successfully, resulting in a very small number of convictions of traffickers. In recent years, many countries have revised their legislation in order to comply with the requirements of the Trafficking Protocol. However, the implementation of this legislation is still pending in many countries.

Organized criminal groups can be heavily involved in human trafficking. According to the United Nations Convention against Transnational Organized Crime, an organized criminal group:[32]

- Is a structured group of three or more persons existing for a period of time
- Acts in concert with the aim of committing one or more serious crimes or offences
- Obtains, directly or indirectly, a financial or other material benefit

In Europe, groups operating in the field of human trafficking are mainly loose networks rather than mafia-type, hierarchical organizations. They include different nationals operating in their area of competence and, while they specialize in human trafficking, they also operate in related crimes such as pimping, forgery of documents, smuggling of migrants and money-laundering.

Notes

1. United Nations Office on Drugs and Crime, Trafficking in Persons: Global Patterns (Vienna, 2006). . . .

2. The Protocol was adopted by the General Assembly in its resolution 55/25 of 15 November 2000 and entered into force on 25 December 2003. The Protocol's ratification status can be consulted at . . .

3. *A recent expert panel convened by the Government Accountability Office of the United States of America stated that the severity of trafficking in persons*

should be measured by using qualitative and quantitative indicators (Human Trafficking: Monitoring and Evaluation of International Projects Are Limited, but Experts Suggest Improvements, GAO report GAO-07-1034 (Washington, D.C., July 2007)).

4. United States of America, Government Accountability Office, *Human Trafficking: Better Data, Strategy, and Reporting Needed to Enhance U.S. Anti-trafficking Efforts Abroad,* GAO report GAO-06-825 (Washington, D.C., July 2006).

5. International Labour Organization, *A Global Alliance against Forced Labour* (Geneva, International Labour Office, 2005).

6. United States of America, Department of State, *Trafficking in Persons Report 2007. . . .*

7. Free the Slaves, Map of Slavery Worldwide. . . .

8. United States of America, Department of State, *Trafficking in Persons Report 2006. . . .*

9. Patrick Belser, *Forced Labour and Human Trafficking: Estimating the Profits,* working paper (Geneva, International Labour Office, 2005), p. 17.

10. Challenges to the Implementation of the National Plan of Action against Trafficking in Persons, Brasilia, 2–4 October 2007, report of the UN.GIFT regional event for Latin America and the Caribbean.

11. United Nations Office on Drugs and Crime, *Trafficking in Persons. . . .*

12. "Trafficking in children for their use in armed conflict," report of the UN.GIFT regional event for West and Central Africa, Côte d'Ivoire, 26–28 November 2007.

13. *Responding to Trafficking for Sexual Exploitation in South Asia, New Delhi, 10–11 October 2007,* report of the UN.GIFT regional event for South Asia (Vienna, 2008).

14. Congressional Research Service, *Trafficking in Women and Children: the U.S. and International Response* (Washington, D.C., United States Library of Congress, 2001).

15. United Nations Office on Drugs and Crime, *Trafficking in Persons . . . ,* p. 88.

16. Marika McAdam, "Transnational organized crime in the Pacific: acting regionally for human security," *Eastern Horizons* (Bangkok), autumn/winter 2006, p. 7.

17. "Vulnerabilities of conflict and post-conflict countries," report of the UN.GIFT regional event for Eastern Africa, Uganda, 19–22 June 2007.

18. United Nations Office on Drugs and Crime, *Trafficking in Persons. . . .*

19. International Organization for Migration, Counter-Trafficking Database, 78 Countries, 1999–2006 (1999).

20. United Nations Office on Drugs and Crime, *Trafficking in Persons. . . .*

21. The full text of the Trafficking Protocol is included as annex II to General Assembly resolution 55/25. . . .

22. Michèle A. Clark, "Vulnerability, prevention and human trafficking: the need for a new paradigm," background paper, Vienna Forum to Fight Human Trafficking, 2007.

23. Cathy Zimmermann and others, *Stolen Smiles: a Summary Report on the Physical and Psychological Health Consequences of Women and Adolescents Trafficked in Europe* (London, London School of Medicine and Tropical Medicine, 2006). . . .

24. United Nations Office on Drugs and Crime, *Trafficking in Persons.* . . .

25. See the website of the United Nations Development Programme (UNDP). . . .

26. International Centre for Migration Policy Development, *Listening to Victims.* . . .

27. United Nations Office on Drugs and Crime, *Trafficking in Persons.* . . .

28. United Nations Interregional Crime and Justice Research Institute, *Trafficking of Nigerian Girls to Italy* (2004), p. 222.

29. Germany, *Bundeslagebild Menschenhandel 2005* (Bundeskriminalamt, 2006).

30. Article 2, subparagraph (a). The Convention was adopted by the General Assembly in its resolution 55/25 of 15 November 2000 and entered into force on 29 September 2003. The Convention's ratification status can be consulted at . . .

EXPLORING THE ISSUE

Do Adequate Strategies Exist to Combat Human Trafficking?

Critical Thinking and Reflection

1. Why is greater attention now being paid to human trafficking?
2. What affects have changes in the global environment in the past 25 years had on human trafficking?
3. Can anything be done to lower the demand for human traffic services?
4. Do you believe that governments are serious about combating human trafficking?
5. Are victims ignored in government strategies for dealing with human trafficking?

Is There Common Ground?

The major area of agreement is on the recognition by governments throughout the world that there has been a major increase in human trafficking as a consequence of the end of the cold war and the rise of globalization. There is also agreement that coordinated efforts among governments at all levels—local, national, and global—are critical to successfully addressing the issue.

Additional Resources

Aronowitz, Alexis A., *Human trafficking, Human Misery: The Global Trade in Human Beings* (Praeger, 2009)

> This book is a concise introduction the human trafficking.

Batstone, David, *Not for Sale: the Return of the Global Slave Trade—and How We Can Fight It* (HarperOne, 2010)

> This book describes those individuals and groups that are fighting against human trafficking.

Cameron, Sally, and Newman, Edward (eds.), *Trafficking in Humans: Social, Cultural and Political Dimensions* (UNU Press, 2008)

> The book presents a broad look at human trafficking, including a discussion of the link between trafficking and larger issues such as human rights and migration.

DeStefano, Anthony M., *The War on Human Trafficking: U.S. Policy Assessed* (Rutgers University Press, 2008)

> This book focuses on efforts to combat human trafficking.

Lee, Maggy, *Trafficking and Global Crime Control* (Sage, 2010)

> The author addresses major trends and future directions on sex and labor trafficking.

McCabe, Kimberly A., *Sex Trafficking: A Global Perspective* (Lexington Books, 2010)

> This book examines geographic region characteristics of human trafficking.

Savona, Ernesto and Stefanizzi, Sonia (eds.), *Measuring Human Trafficking: Complexitites and Pitfalls* (Springer, 2010)

> This book argues for a system to provide current qualitative and quantitative data on human trafficking for those who are fighting the problem.

Shelley, Louise, *Human Trafficking: A Global Perspective* (Cambridge University Press, 2010)

> The author focuses on all types of human trafficking, with emphasis on the operations of the business and the nature of the traffickers themselves.

Skinner, E. Benjamin, *A Crime So Monstrous: Face-to-Face with Modern-Day Slavery* (Free Press, 2008)

> The author presents an impassioned look at human trafficking, particularly in Haiti, Sudan, Romania, and India. He also reveals the inner-workings of the U.S. State Department's effort against trafficking.

Wyler, Llana Sun, and Siskin, Alison, *Trafficking in Persons: U.S. Policy and Issues for Congress* (BiblioGov, 2010)

> This book examines the extent of global human trafficking, and both the international and the U.S. response.

Wylie, Gillian, and McRedmond, Penelope (eds.), *Human Trafficking in Europe: Character, Causes and Consequences* (Palgrave Macmillan, 2010)

> The book focuses on human trafficking in Europe, with attention paid to causes, migration policies, and gender inequality.

ISSUE 12

Is the International Community Making Progress in Addressing Natural Disasters?

YES: United Nations, from "Risk and Poverty in a Changing Climate: Invest Today for a Safer Tomorrow," *Summary and Recommendations: 2009 Global Assessment Report on Disaster Risk Reduction* (United Nations Publications, 2009)

NO: David Rothkopf, from "Averting Disaster: Calamities Like the Haiti Quake Aren't Just Predictable—They're Preventable," *Newsweek* (January 25, 2010)

Learning Outcomes

After reading this issue, you should be able to:

- Describe the main features of the *Hyogo Framework for Action 2005–2015: Building the Resilience of Nations and Communities in Disasters*.
- Discuss why the 2009 UN report suggests that countries are making significant progress in strengthening their capacities to address past deficiencies and gaps in their disaster preparedness.
- Gain an understanding of why the UN report also believes that there is an imperative for urgent action to address disaster risk.
- Discuss why David Rothkopf believes that disasters like the earthquake in Haiti are preventable.
- Discuss why many believe that the potential for megadisasters will likely only increase.

ISSUE SUMMARY

YES: The International Strategy for Disaster Reduction Secretariat, a unit within the United Nations, suggests that countries are making "significant progress" in strengthening their capacities to address past deficiencies and gaps in their disaster preparedness and response. At the center of progress is the plan, *Hyogo Framework for Action 2005–2015,* which is aimed at reducing human and nonhuman disaster losses.

NO: David Rothkopf, president of Garten Rothkopf (an international consulting agency) and a member of former president Bill Clinton's international trade team, argues that the efforts of international organizations to prevent natural disasters from escalating into megadisasters "have fallen short of what is required."

In the first two months of 2010, the world witnessed two high-impact, high-publicity earthquakes, when Haiti and Chile were dramatically victimized by the changing forces of nature. The death toll in impoverished Haiti reached a quarter of a million people and the level of property damage was unparalleled in recent memory. Although Chile sustained far less loss of human life, the devastation was far-reaching despite the government's prolonged attempts to earthquake-proof its major cities. Following on the heels of these two 2010 disasters was the 2011 massive earthquake in Japan followed by the devastating tsunami, which in turn destroyed cities, left thousands killed in its wake, and unleashed a nuclear crisis that currently rivals that of Chernobyl. Its long-term impact on human and nonhuman life is still being calculated as the international community and Japan are trying to deal with the short-term effects while assessing the long-term damage to Japan and beyond.

Although these three traumatic events captured the attention of news makers and the public the world over, there is an enormous number of smaller disasters in a given year that taken together produce a significant amount of human and nonhuman loss. Bill McGuire (*Global Catastrophes,* Oxford University Press, 2002) provides a picture of disaster activity and potential. He estimates that Earth's tectonic plates move at the same rate as fingernail growth, and 1400 earthquakes occur every day somewhere on the planet. Fifty volcanoes erupt each year among the 3000 possibilities, while around 40 hurricanes, typhoons, and cyclones batter the Earth. McGuire estimates that 15 million people have died in the past millennium, virtually all in the developing world.

And the number of natural disasters and the level of damages caused therein have been growing for decades. Thirty-five years ago, the global costs of weather-related disasters, for example, totaled about $9 billion, whereas 15 years ago, the amount had risen to about $45 billion, and costs continue to soar today with each passing year. The United Nations (UN) has estimated that although 2009 had fewer natural disasters than usual, there were still 245 events that affected 58 million people worldwide. Others have suggested that over the past two decades, an average of 200,000 individuals have been affected by such events each year. The International Federation of Red Cross and Red Crescent Societies has estimated that if present trends continue, global natural disaster costs will reach $300 billion annually by midcentury.

Challenges associated with global disasters have increased significantly in recent times, as suggested in the "2009 Global Assessment Report." And the risk of substantial loss of property and life is concentrated in a very small portion of the Earth's surfaces as well as in a very small number of disasters. Data in the "2009 Global Assessment Report" show that between 1975 and 2008, 8866 disasters resulted in 2,283,767 deaths. Of these, 23 megadisasters were responsible for 1,786,084 deaths, or to put it another way, 0.26% of the calamities resulted in 78.2% of the mortality. And just 25 megadisasters (0.28%) accounted for 40% of the economic losses.

Risk is also not evenly divided, as poorer countries appear to have a disproportionately high share of the risk and also experience greater economic losses. Of equal concern is the fact that global disaster risk is increasing, particularly in those countries that are below the median income levels. And these latter countries are precisely the least resilient ones, in the words of the report. Underlying risk drivers affect both the incidence and the severity of natural disasters. Poor urban governance, vulnerable rural livelihoods, declining ecosystems, and global climate change are all pinpointed as culprits in the ongoing disaster sagas.

McGuire paints a gloomy long-term future. For him, the planet is well on its way into "a cycle of warming that is certain to lead to dramatic geophysical, social, and economic changes during the next hundred years that will impinge—almost entirely detrimentally—on everyone." He also believes that the earth is on the verge of a new Ice Age that will happen within 10,000 years or sooner with global warming. And McGuire also sees asteroids capable of killing a quarter of the planet's population continue to hurtle across our path. And given the boom in population and its location, a giant tsunami or volcanic eruption will result in tremendous destruction and disruption. Species extinction represents another major catastrophe, as between 3000 and 30,000 species from a total of 10 million are wiped from the planet each year.

Thinking even much further into the future, the literature is replete with grave warnings. In a collection of essays (*Global Catastrophic Risks,* 2008), editors Nick Bostrom and Milan Ćirković provide several statements of doom. "Our particular world is thus likely to end its life in fire. . . . Ashes to ashes, dust to dust, particles to particles—such is the ultimate fate of our universe." The editors suggest that the most global catastrophe will occur from human activities, particularly "industrial civilization and advance technologies." Currently, they argue, the risk of infectious pandemic disease is the biggest worry. Nuclear war, biotechnology, and nuclear terrorism are more likely possibilities.

Although many believe that natural disasters are random phenomena, it is clear that the consequences per calamity continue to magnify because of human action. This is not surprising, as the International Federation of Red Cross and Red Crescent Societies has suggested. For this organization, earlier disasters that were more locally confined with fewer people affected are now more likely to yield consequences that ignore national boundaries in their increasing geographical scope or impact far greater numbers of more heavily concentrated populations. The increased global risk is due, the organization suggests, to "population growth, unplanned urbanization, environmental degradation, technological and socio-economic conditions including conflicts and competition for scarce resources, climate change, disease epidemics, poverty and pressure from development within high risk zones."

International attention to the impact of natural disasters is not new. In December 1989, the UN designated the 1990s as the International Decade for Natural Disaster Reduction (IDNDR) with the objective of using cooperative global efforts to reduce loss and disruption of life brought on by natural disasters. This, in turn, led to the first World Conference on Disaster Reduction, held in Yokohama, Japan in 1994. The plan of action focused on recommendations for addressing the prevention, preparedness, and mitigation of disaster risk.

The international community reconvened in Kobe, Japan in early 2005 for the purpose of "taking stock" of the previous decade's efforts to address natural disasters. The conference acknowledged that disaster loss was on the rise with increasingly global consequences. Additionally, it stated that accelerated cooperative steps must be undertaken to build the necessary capacities to "manage and reduce risk." Its action plan, the *Hyogo Framework for Action 2005–2015: Building the Resilience of Nations and Communities to Disasters*, emphasized five major priorities for action: (1) "Ensure that disaster risk reduction is a national and a local priority with a strong institutional basis for implementation"; (2) "identify, assess, and monitor disaster risks and enhance early warning"; (3) "use knowledge, innovation and education to build a culture of safety and resilience at all levels"; (4) "reduce the underlying risk factors"; and (5) "strengthen disaster preparedness for effective response at all levels." The important role played by early warning systems, whether with respect to tsunamis, volcanoes, or every kind of disaster in between, has been particularly emphasized in virtually every meeting and every document relating to natural disasters since then.

One alternative way to look at the potential for natural disaster is to focus on global warming as a culprit. For some time, conventional wisdom suggested the link. But recently, The Intergovernmental Panel on Climate Change (IPCC) has been forced to backtrack. A second alternative approach is to ignore those events that will be likely Earth-shattering but for which there is a very low level of probability of happening, such as a major asteroid.

In the YES selection, the "2009 Global Assessment Report" concludes that countries are "making significant progress" in overcoming deficiencies in the area of disaster preparedness and response, despite increases in disaster risk. Enhanced early warning capabilities have appeared throughout the globe. In the NO selection, David Rothkopf argues that the most shocking part of the Haiti disaster was that the "damage was so predictable." He suggests that the number of megadisasters such as Haiti will only increase unless the international community commits the billions of dollars necessary to really address disaster prevention and risk reduction.

YES ↵

Risk and Poverty in a Changing Climate: Invest Today for a Safer Tomorrow
Summary and Recommendations: 2009 Global Assessment Report on Disaster Risk Reduction

Key Findings and Recommendations

- Global disaster risk is highly concentrated in poorer countries with weaker governance. Particularly in low and low-middle income countries with rapid economic growth, the exposure of people and assets to natural hazards is growing at a faster rate than risk-reducing capacities are being strengthened, leading to increasing disaster risk.
- Countries with small and vulnerable economies, such as many small-island developing states (SIDS) and land-locked developing countries (LLDCs), have the highest economic vulnerability to natural hazards. Many also have extreme trade limitations.
- Most disaster mortality and asset destruction is intensively concentrated in very small areas exposed to infrequent but extreme hazards. However, low-intensity damage to housing, local infrastructure, crops and livestock, which interrupts and erodes livelihoods, is extensively spread within many countries and occurs very frequently. Such damage represents a significant and largely unaccounted for facet of disaster impacts.
- Poorer communities suffer a disproportionate share of disaster loss. Poor households are usually less resilient to loss and are rarely covered by insurance or social protection. Disaster impacts lead to income and consumption shortfalls and negatively affect welfare and human development, often over the long term.
- Weather-related disaster risk is expanding rapidly both in terms of the territories affected, the losses reported and the frequency of events. This expansive tendency cannot be explained by improved disaster reporting alone. In countries with weaker risk-reducing capacities, underlying risk drivers such as poor urban governance, vulnerable rural livelihoods and ecosystem decline underpin this rapid expansion of weather-related disaster risk.

- Climate change is already changing the geographic distribution, frequency and intensity of weather-related hazards and threatens to undermine the resilience of poorer countries and their citizens to absorb loss and recover from disaster impacts. This combination of increasing hazard and decreasing resilience makes climate change a global driver of disaster risk. Climate change will magnify the uneven distribution of risk skewing disaster impacts even further towards poor communities in developing countries.
- Progress towards reducing disaster risk is still mixed. In general terms, countries are making significant progress in strengthening capacities, institutional systems and legislation to address deficiencies in disaster preparedness and response. Good progress is also being made in other areas, such as the enhancement of early warning. In contrast, countries report little progress in mainstreaming disaster risk reduction considerations into social, economic, urban, environmental and infrastructural planning and development.
- The governance arrangements for disaster risk reduction in many countries do not facilitate the integration of risk considerations into development. In general, the institutional and legislative arrangements for disaster risk reduction are weakly connected to development sectors.
- The policy and institutional frameworks for climate change adaptation and poverty reduction are only weakly connected to those for disaster risk reduction, at both the national and international levels. Countries have difficulty addressing underlying risk drivers such as poor urban and local governance, vulnerable rural livelihoods and ecosystem decline in a way that leads to a reduction in the risk of damages and economic loss.
- Documented experience in upgrading squatter settlements, providing access to land and infrastructure for the urban poor, strengthening rural livelihoods, protecting ecosystems, and using microfinance, microinsurance and index-based insurance to strengthen resilience shows that it is possible to address the underlying drivers of disaster risk. However, in most countries these experiences are not integrated into the policy mainstream.
- A failure to address the underlying risk drivers will result in dramatic increases in disaster risk and associated poverty outcomes. In contrast, if addressing these drivers is given priority, risk can be reduced, human development protected and adaptation to climate change facilitated. Rather than a cost, this should be seen as an investment in building a more secure, stable, sustainable and equitable future. Given the urgency posed by climate change, decisive action needs to be taken now. . . .

Global Disaster Risk: The Challenge
Risk Is Intensively Concentrated

The risk of both mortality and economic loss in disasters is highly concentrated in a very small portion of the Earth's surface. Countries with large populations exposed to severe natural hazards account for a very large proportion of global disaster risk. For example, 75% of global flood mortality risk is concentrated in only three countries: Bangladesh, China and India.

Similarly mortality and economic loss are concentrated in a very small number of disasters. Between 1975 and 2008, EMDAT[1] recorded 8,866 disasters killing 2,283,767 people. Of these 23 megadisasters killed 1,786,084 people, meaning that 0.26% of the events accounted for 78.2% of the mortality.[2] In the same period internationally recorded economic losses were US$ 1,527.6 billion. Just 25 megadisasters, representing 0.28% of the events, accounted for 40% of the loss.

However, small island developing states (SIDS) and other small countries have far higher levels of relative risk with respect to the size of their populations and economies. For example, in the case of tropical cyclones, Vanuatu has the highest mortality risk per million inhabitants in the world, with St. Kitts and Nevis in third place.

Risk Is Unevenly Distributed

Disaster risk is not evenly distributed. Developing countries concentrate a hugely disproportionate share of the risk. For example, both Japan and the Philippines are exposed to frequent tropical cyclones. In Japan, approximately 22.5 million people are exposed annually, compared to 16 million people in the Philippines. However, the estimated annual death toll from cyclones in the Philippines is almost 17 times greater than that of Japan.

This uneven distribution of risk is also true for groups of countries. For the same number of people exposed to tropical cyclones, mortality risk in low-income countries is approximately 200 times higher than in OECD countries.

Poorer countries also experience higher economic losses in relation to the size of their economies. OECD countries, including Australia, Japan and the United States of America, account for almost 70% of estimated global annual economic losses to tropical cyclones—approximately 90 times more than the losses in exposed countries in sub-Saharan Africa. However, when looked at in terms of economic loss relative to exposed GDP, sub-Saharan African countries experience almost three and a half times more economic loss; Latin America and the Caribbean over six times more; and in the case of floods South Asia experiences approximately 15 times more economic loss than OECD countries.

These examples show that disaster risk is not just a consequence of hazard severity and exposure. Risk is configured by a range of other drivers related to a country's economic and social development. These include not only income and economic strength but also governance factors such as the quality of institutions, transparency and accountability. Wealthier countries tend to have better institutions, more effective early warning, disaster preparedness and response systems, and more open government that tends to be more supportive of disaster risk reduction. Well-governed countries with higher human development indicators generally have lower levels of risk than countries with weaker governance.

Risk Is Increasing

While wealthier countries are usually less risk prone than poorer countries, economic development must be accompanied by the strengthening of governance capacities if disaster risk is to be reduced. Rapid economic and urban development can lead to a growing concentration of people and economic assets in hazard prone cities, fertile river valleys and coastal areas. Disaster risk increases if the exposure of people and assets to natural hazards increases faster than countries can strengthen their risk-reducing capacities by putting policy, institutions, legislation, planning and regulatory frameworks in place.

In absolute terms, and assuming constant hazard levels, global disaster risk increased between 1990 and 2007. In the case of floods, mortality risk increased by 13% from 1990 to 2007. Over the same period flood economic loss risk increased by 35%. These increases in disaster risk are primarily driven by the growing exposure of people and economic assets. The number of people exposed to floods increased by 28% over the same period, while exposed GDP increased by 98%. Most flood risk is concentrated in Asian countries, such as China and India. While global GDP increased by 64%, China and India increased their GDP by 420% and 185%, respectively. Over the same period, vulnerability declined; in the case of flood mortality risk by 11%, and flood economic loss risk by 32%. But this reduction in vulnerability was insufficient to compensate for the increase in exposure.

This suggests that disaster risk is increasing fastest in low- and lower-middle income countries with rapidly growing economies. These countries have rapidly increasing exposure but relatively weak institutions. While they are making improvements in risk-reducing capacities these have yet to catch up with rising exposure. In contrast, most high-income countries experience more moderate increases in exposure and have already reduced a significant part of their vulnerability.

Relative to the size of the global population and GDP, risk may actually be falling. For example, when recorded economic losses are adjusted for inflation and expressed as a proportion of global GDP they are fairly stable.

Small and Vulnerable Economies Are Least Resilient

Countries with small and vulnerable economies, such as many SIDS and landlocked developing countries (LLDCs), have seen their economic development set back decades by disaster impacts. The countries with the highest ratio of economic losses in disasters, with respect to their capital stock are all SIDS and LLDCs, such as Samoa and St. Lucia. Madagascar shows a different pattern but a clear impact of disaster loss on cumulative net capital formation.

In contrast, the impact of major disasters on high-income countries such as the United States of America is imperceptible, even though that country has experienced huge economic losses, for example the US$ 125 billion associated with Hurricane Katrina in 2005. Similarly, there is no marked effect in large low-income countries such as India or middle-income countries such as Colombia. The implications are that disasters do not have a significant impact on capital accumulation in countries with large economies, but a devastating impact on those with small economies.

The countries with the highest economic vulnerability are those with the highest ratio of economic losses to capital stock and the lowest economic resilience to shocks, indicated by very low national savings. Many of these countries also have extreme limitations to their ability to benefit from international trade, characterized by a very low participation in world export markets (less than 0.1%) and low export diversification. SIDS and LLDCs together constitute 60% of the countries with high, and 67% with very high, economic vulnerability to disasters, as measured by the above variables, and comprise about two thirds of all countries affected by extreme trade limitations in the same groups. . . .

The Underlying Risk Drivers

Poor Urban Governance

By 2008, over half the world's population was living in urban areas and by 2010 it is projected that 73% of the world's urban population and most of its largest cities will be in developing countries. . . .

Evidence from cities in Africa, Asia and Latin America, shows that the expansion of informal settlements is closely associated with the rapid increase in weather-related disaster reports in urban areas. . . . The centrifugal expansion of reported floods has mirrored the expansion of informal settlements in the city.

Urbanization per se tends to increase the intensity of run-off during storms and heavy rains. Instead of being absorbed into the ground, greater volumes of rainwater are channelled into drains, culverts and streams. Informal settlements typically occupy land deemed unsuitable for residential or commercial use, located in low lying flood prone areas, on landslide prone hillsides or in ravines, exposing people to hazard. Houses are built and modified without reference to hazard resistant building standards. In many cities there has been an underinvestment in building drains and in maintaining those that exist, particularly in informal settlements. Many floods are caused as much by deficient or non-existent drainage as by the intensity of rainfall.

Vulnerable Rural Livelihoods

Livelihood vulnerability is an underlying driver of disaster risk and poverty in many areas. Approximately 75% of the people living below the international poverty line (US$ 1.25 per day) live and work in rural areas:[3] 268 million in sub-Saharan Africa; 223 million in East Asia and the Pacific; and 394 million in South Asia. Even in countries experiencing rapid economic development, such as China, there are 175 million rural dwellers below this poverty line. Disaster losses affect huge numbers in poor rural areas. In sub-Saharan Africa, during the 2001–2003 drought, an estimated 206 million people, or 32% of the region's population, were undernourished, a number only slightly less than the total 268 million rural poor[4]. . . .

The high structural vulnerability of housing, schools, infrastructure and other assets in poor rural areas exposed to floods, tropical cyclones and earthquakes also leads to major mortality in disasters. Rural housing is usually built with local materials and labour and without hazard resistant building techniques. The collapse of heavy earth walls led to the destruction of 329,579 houses in the 2005 Kashmir earthquake. The lack of protection offered by wattle and daub, and thatch houses in Myanmar contributed to the deaths of 140,000 people in the 2008 cyclone. The isolation of many poor rural areas, combined with under investment by government in infrastructure and in disaster preparedness and response capacities, further increases asset and mortality risk.

Declining Ecosystems

People receive substantial benefits or services from ecosystems. These include provisioning services which provide energy, water, food and fibre for both urban and rural households, as well as regulating services, such as the mitigation of floods and storm surges. Most ecosystems have been intentionally or unintentionally modified to increase the supply of certain categories of services and institutions have been developed to govern access and use of these services. However, because ecosystems produce many services simultaneously, an increase in the supply of one service, such as food, can frequently lead to declines in other services, such as flood regulation.

The Millennium Assessment found that the supply of approximately 60% of the ecosystem services evaluated (15 of 24) were in decline.[5] At the same time, consumption of more than 80% of the services was found to be increasing. In other words, the flow of most ecosystem services is increasing at the same time as the total stock is decreasing. In particular, the Millennium Assessment identified that while people have modified ecosystems to increase provisioning services, these modifications have led to the decline of regulating ecosystem services, including those responsible for mitigating hazards, such as fires and floods. . . .

Global Climate Change

Changes in Means and Extremes Lead to Increasing Hazard and Declining Resilience

Climate change is probably the greatest global outcome of environmental inequity. It is driven by greenhouse gas emissions that have brought benefits to affluent societies and individuals, yet most of the burdens fall on developing countries and their poorest citizens. . . .

There is already evidence that some kinds of weather-related hazard are increasing. . . . The average annual number of cyclones has been fairly stable, (between 54.9 and 58.1 per year) since 1976, regardless of sea surface temperature (SST). However, in warmer years there are more Category 3 and 4 (i.e. more intense) cyclones and fewer in Categories 1 and 2. In particular, compared to the period between 1976 and 1984, when there were no data on SST, there are now significantly more category 4 and 5 cyclones. This is in line with the findings of the IPCC Fourth Assessment Report and recent research that has estimated that a 1°C increase in SST would lead to a 31% increase in the global frequency of Category 4 and 5 cyclones per year.

Climate Change Magnifies the Uneven Distribution of Disaster Risk

By increasing hazard at the same time as it erodes resilience, climate change has a magnifying effect on disaster risk. In particular, climate change will magnify the uneven distribution of risk, skewing disaster impacts even further towards poor communities in developing countries. . . .

Ninety-seven percent of the documented local-level loss reports are weather-related. This means that a very significant part of emerging disaster risk in developing countries is highly sensitive to any increase in hazard intensity and frequency due to climate change. It is likely that climate change is already contributing to the rapid increase in the number of weather-related loss reports since 1980, although at present it is not possible to calculate by how much. . . .

Progress in Addressing Disaster Risk
The Hyogo Framework for Action

In 2005, 168 countries adopted the Hyogo Framework of Action (HFA), a comprehensive set of five priorities that aim to achieve a substantial reduction in disaster losses, in terms of lives and social, economic and environmental assets of communities and countries by 2015.

A recent review by 62 countries[6] indicates that progress towards this objective is still mixed. In general terms, countries are making significant progress in strengthening capacities, institutional systems and legislation to address deficiencies in disaster preparedness and response. Good progress is also being made in other areas, such as the enhancement of early warning. As a result, some lower-income countries, such as Bangladesh and Cuba, have already made dramatic strides in reducing mortality risk in the face of hazards such as tropical cyclones and floods, which are sensitive to improvements in early warning, preparedness and response. For example, despite being hit by five successive hurricanes in 2008, only 7 deaths were reported in Cuba.

In contrast, countries report little progress in mainstreaming disaster risk reduction considerations into social, economic, urban, environmental and infrastructural planning and development. Early warning and preparedness can help to evacuate people in the case of a cyclone. But housing, schools and infrastructure cannot be evacuated and, if not structurally resistant, they are damaged or destroyed.

Across all five HFA Priorities for Action, high-income countries outperform low- and middle-income countries. In these high-income countries, the adoption of hazard resistant building standards, planning and environmental regulations as well as a web of institutions and systems that protect citizens when disasters occur, have enabled a substantial reduction in vulnerability.

In the case of the least-developed countries, some lack the basic technical, human, institutional and financial capacities to address even the most basic aspects of disaster risk reduction.

Between these two poles, many middle- and low-income countries have made major strides towards developing national policies, institutional systems and legislation for disaster risk reduction. Unfortunately this has not been translated into reductions in disaster risk in the principal development sectors. It would appear that countries have difficulty addressing underlying risk drivers such as poor urban and local governance, vulnerable rural livelihoods and ecosystem decline in a way that leads to a reduction in the risk of damage and economic loss. At the same time, the governance arrangements for disaster risk reduction in many countries do not facilitate the integration of risk considerations into development. In general, the institutional and legislative arrangements for disaster risk reduction are weakly connected to development sectors. Mainstreaming is challenged by a range of factors that include difficulties in compiling comprehensive information on disaster risks, weak engagement by the development sectors and major difficulties in ensuring implementation, enforcement and accountability.

Climate Change Adaptation

Many countries are also developing plans and strategies to adapt to climate change, for example through National Adaptation Programmes of Action (NAPAs). In principle, given that increased risk from weather-related hazards is a manifestation of climate change, adaptation could and should reinforce disaster risk reduction efforts. The Report has not comprehensively reviewed progress in adaptation. However, there is evidence to show that progress in implementation is still slow and adaptation policy and institutional frameworks are largely disconnected from those created to reduce disaster risk, at both the national and international levels. Adaptation faces similar challenges to disaster risk reduction, in particular a governance framework that can allow risk in the development sectors to be addressed.

Poverty Reduction

Large numbers of Poverty Reduction Strategy Papers (PRSPs) explicitly recognize the poverty outcomes associated with disaster impacts and some include sections on disaster risk reduction. In principle, poverty reduction efforts in both rural and urban areas have a considerable potential to address the underlying risk drivers if they are clearly focused. In most countries, however, poverty reduction has only weak functional connections to the policy and institutional frameworks for disaster risk reduction. Unless disaster risk considerations are factored into poverty-reducing development, the result may be increased risk, as the collapse of schools in earthquakes so poignantly illustrates. At the same time, the inclusion of disaster risk reduction in PRSPs is often limited to disaster preparedness and response aspects. Therefore, the potential of PRSPs to address the underlying risk drivers is still not fully exploited.

Conclusions
The Imperative for Urgent Action

Current progress under the HFA and in related areas of poverty reduction and climate change adaptation is not leading to a reduction in disaster risk. The Report highlights that risk is continuing to increase, even assuming constant hazard levels, and that any further increase will disproportionately affect poor communities in developing countries. Climate change magnifies the uneven distribution of risk, increasing both disaster risk and poverty outcomes in these communities. Unless this trend is reversed it will be impossible to achieve the HFA and progress towards the Millennium Development Goals (MDGs) will be compromised.

The evidence provided in the Report underlines the urgency of avoiding dangerous climate change. Greater urgency in efforts to reduce global greenhouse gas emissions and reduce energy consumption are required if a potentially catastrophic increase in disaster risk is to be avoided, the impacts of which will be largely concentrated in developing countries.

Action in other policy areas is also required. The countries with the highest relative risk and the lowest resilience to disaster impacts are those with small and vulnerable economies, such as many SIDS and LLDCs. The low resilience of these countries is associated with extreme limitations in their ability to participate in global trade. Efforts are therefore required to coordinate policies on trade and productive sector development in these countries.

Unfortunately, the world is committed to significant climate change, even if rapid progress is achieved towards a low-carbon economy. Therefore, disaster prone countries will only be able to avoid further increases in disaster impacts and poverty outcomes by taking decisive action to address the underlying drivers that are responsible for the concentration and expansion of risk. The Report highlights the need to strengthen capacities to address three key drivers: poor urban governance, vulnerable rural livelihoods and ecosystem decline. Weak social protection is a fourth driver, which, while not examined in depth in the Report, is also important.

A failure to address these drivers will result in dramatic increases in disaster risk and associated poverty outcomes. In contrast, if addressing these drivers is given priority, risk can be reduced, human development protected and adaptation to climate change facilitated. Rather than a cost, this should be seen as an investment in building a more secure, stable, sustainable and equitable future. Given the urgency posed by climate change, decisive action needs to be taken now.

A Policy Framework for Risk-Reducing Development

It is possible to address the underlying drivers of disaster risk. In all regions of the world, documented experience in upgrading squatter settlements, providing access to land and infrastructure for the urban poor, strengthening rural livelihoods, protecting ecosystems, and using microfinance, microinsurance and index-based insurance to strengthen resilience show that it can be done.

The most successful of these experiences have emerged in the context of innovative partnerships between national and local governments and civil society and are leading to a sustainable reduction in risks.

These experiences demonstrate that the underlying risk drivers can be addressed, and that the tools, methods and approaches necessary to do so already exist. However, they must still be integrated into the policy mainstream. Most countries still lack a determined and focused high-level development policy framework that addresses these drivers and is supportive of such innovative approaches. Without such central support, ongoing efforts in disaster risk reduction and climate change adaptation cannot gain traction.

The need to strengthen capacities to develop and implement such a policy framework is particularly urgent in those low- and middle-income countries where hazard exposure is growing most rapidly, where risks are concentrated, and where the magnifying effects of climate change will be most felt. Risk-reducing development is essential if disaster risk reduction is to be mainstreamed into development and if development is to be adapted to climate change.

The adoption of such an overarching policy framework would allow the different plans, programmes and projects in poverty reduction, climate change adaptation and disaster risk reduction—as well as in sustainable development in general—to become better aligned in order to address the underlying drivers of disaster risk. These plans and programmes include PRSPs, NAPAs, United Nations Development Assistance Frameworks and nationally specific programming instruments. To be relevant and successful such a policy framework must be at the centre of the political agenda, backed by dedicated resources in the national budget, and should have leadership at the highest levels of government.

If a policy framework for risk-reducing development is to be actionable a different culture of implementation will be required, one that builds on government-civil society partnerships and cooperation. Such partnerships can dramatically reduce the costs of risk reduction, ensure local acceptance, and help to build social capital, which reduces long-term vulnerability.

Effective Risk Reduction Governance

In addition to a policy framework that prioritizes risk-reducing development, a set of governance arrangements is needed for disaster risk reduction, poverty reduction and climate change adaptation that is capable of ensuring that risk considerations are factored into all development investments. Improvements to risk reduction governance are critical, in order to provide a vehicle for policy and a systematic approach to planning, financing and monitoring investment in all sectors.

In particular, the existing institutional and governance arrangements for disaster risk reduction and climate change adaptation need to be harmonized, building on existing systems of public administration. The development of a single governance framework for risk reduction would seem to offer opportunities for more effective policy implementation and for avoiding duplication and lack of coordination. The harmonization of international frameworks and requirements for planning and reporting would be supportive of better integration at the country level.

The institutional and administrative responsibility for risk reduction has to be vested at the highest possible level in government, in order to have the necessary political authority and resources to influence development policy. If risk reduction can be included explicitly in national development plans and budgets, all parts of government are then able to programme risk reduction actions and investments.

Fortunately, many countries are already putting into place innovative mechanisms that enable this mainstreaming and harmonization to occur. These include factoring disaster risk reduction into national development plans and budgets; development of new institutional structures for hazard monitoring and risk assessment that integrate existing scientific and technical institutions; the inclusion of cost–benefit analysis into public investment systems; the involvement of the national audit or controller's office in supporting implementation, enforcement and accountability in all sectors and at all levels of government; improvements in early warning systems; and the application of innovative mechanisms for risk transfer.

Disaster Risk Reduction
Is an Investment Not a Cost

To seriously address the underlying risk factors on the scale necessary requires major investment. It is difficult to provide an accurate global estimate of this cost but the calculations developed by the Millennium Project serve to give an idea of the magnitude. These costs can be significantly reduced through adopting participatory approaches, but it is clear that several hundred billion dollars are required. This figure is coherent with estimates regarding the cost of climate change adaptation. An increase in the resources available for climate change adaptation will be required, as well as those pledged for the MDGs. In the context of the global economic crisis, investments in infrastructure and employment creation can provide opportunities to address the underlying risk drivers, for example through investments to improve drainage in flood prone areas.

Disaster risk reduction is usually conceptualized as an additional cost. In fact one of the principal arguments used to justify a lack of progress in disaster risk reduction is that developing countries have other priorities, such as reducing poverty, and cannot afford the additional costs of disaster risk reduction. The Report puts forward a contrasting view. Investment in disaster risk reduction generally represents a large saving in terms of avoided losses and reconstruction costs and is thus a way of lowering the costs of poverty reduction and of addressing the underlying risk factors. This means that the real cost of addressing the underlying risk drivers is actually lower if disaster risk reduction is included.

In conclusion, the key requirements are to help countries strengthen governance arrangements and improve management of investments for addressing the underlying risk factors, and to ensure disaster risk reduction is incorporated into those investments. Without strengthening these arrangements and capacities, even large investments in development may have little tangible effect or be counter-productive. If governance arrangements and capacities for risk reduction can be strengthened, small investments can produce huge benefits. Investing today to strengthen capacities is essential if future generations are to enjoy a safer tomorrow.

Notes

1. The Office for US Foreign Disaster Assistance/Centre for Research on the Epidemiology of Disasters (OFDA/CRED) International Disaster Database: . . .

2. EMDAT does not register reports of small-scale disasters below its threshold of 10 deaths, 100 people affected or a call for international assistance.

3. Ravaillon, C. (2008) *The Developing World Is Poorer Than We Thought but No Less Successful in the Fight Against Poverty.* Washington DC. World Bank.

4. FAO (Food and Agriculture Organization of the United Nations) (2006) *The State of Food Insecurity in the World.* Rome. FAO.

5. Millennium Ecosystem Assessment (2005) *Ecosystems and Human Well-Being: Current State and Trends: Findings of the Condition and Trends Working Group.* Washington DC. Island Press.

6. The number of countries that had prepared interim HFA progress reports by the end of February, 2009.

David Rothkopf ➡ **NO**

Averting Disaster: Calamities Like the Haiti Quake Aren't Just Predictable—They're Preventable

The most shocking thing about the disaster in Haiti was not that it was so sudden, violent, and horrific in its human toll. It's that the damage was so predictable. Seismologists warned that the country was at risk as recently as two years ago. Haiti is also the latest in a string of nearly annual megadisasters extending back through the past decade, calamities claiming tens of thousands of lives more because poverty and the forces of nature met with foreseeably tragic consequences.

During the Clinton administration, I helped lead an interagency effort to assist the country after our intervention there in 1994. Our reasons for wanting to help were not, of course, entirely or even primarily charitable. While we acted out of a sincere commitment on the part of a president who is now the U.N. special envoy to that battered country, we naturally also worried that further social disintegration would result in waves of unwanted immigrants arriving on our shores. Viewing tiny Haiti primarily as a source of problems for America has been—after neglect—the single most important driver of U.S. policies toward that country since its independence.

Traveling regularly to Port-au-Prince, I could not help but be struck by Haiti's vibrancy or its largely untapped promise. Nor, sadly, could I ignore the deprivation or the petty infighting among the island's elites that blocked Haitians from the few opportunities at progress that ever wafted across their shores. We tried to help, to organize business missions, to mobilize funding of local projects, to apply comparatively low-voltage policy paddles to the heart of a nearly lifeless economic victim. But given the island's manifold, often heartbreaking, problems—weak governance, feeble infrastructure, illiteracy—it was clear that our efforts would likely be only palliative.

And it was also clear that America's interest would wane and Haiti would remain on life support. Year to year, such countries receive just enough aid for them to fade from our consciousness and consciences. Development dollars seem to have two purposes: buying friends we may need to advance specific national interests and renting a little peace of mind by postponing calamity. But inevitably the money is too little, and countries like Haiti come crashing into our lives with the next crisis—almost invariably a crisis that is more costly in human and financial terms than the steps we might have taken to prevent or mitigate it in the first place.

Weep as one might at the pictures now streaming out of Port-au-Prince, what is sadder still is that it is just the latest example of a blight to which the international community has devoted too little attention and too few resources. Take every terror attack in the past 20 years. Add every airline crash. Add SARS or H1N1. Add many of the diseases whose causes are championed by high-profile telethons and gala fundraisers. The total death toll pales when compared with what might be called the world's megadisasters. Before Haiti, an estimated 70,000 people perished in 2008's earthquake in Sichuan, China. Before that almost 150,000 died when the cyclone Nargis struck Burma. In 2005, the death toll from an earthquake in the mountains of Kashmir approached 90,000. The year before, in the greatest such recent disaster, the Indian Ocean tsunami killed perhaps 230,000.

While the events seem disparate, in each case telltale traits recur. Fragile communities of the world's most vulnerable people were forced by circumstance to root themselves in treacherous soil—near shorelines but below or too near sea level, on mountainsides, and in cities along fault lines. As in the case of Haiti, scientists warned that the situations were precarious. As in the case of Haiti, local governments failed—often due to lack of resources—to establish or enforce minimum building codes or to put in place the infrastructure that could make warning, escape, or rescue likely.

These stunning calamities are almost inevitably reported as "out of the blue" events, "acts of God," proof of fate's fickleness. But in fact they are a class of global threat as real and as manageable as pandemics or many of the other problems with which the international community grapples. We could take several more meaningful steps to prevent natural disasters from becoming megadisasters: establishing and effectively promoting best practices for building, safety inspection, and remedial construction that can work in impoverished settings; sharing technical know-how; providing early-warning technologies; better training societies and preparing the international community to respond; providing essential infrastructure; and where necessary relocating communities or providing needed sea walls, retaining walls, structural supports, survivable power, water systems, and first-response capacity.

Organizations like the United Nations have made earnest and periodic efforts to address these concerns. But the results have clearly fallen far short of what is required. Would it be expensive to promote these changes more fully? By what measure? Tens of billions? Yes. Hundreds of billions? Perhaps. But compared to the cost of the war in Iraq or the Wall Street bailout? Just a fraction. To the human cost of the disasters themselves? Incalculably less.

Current trends—from rising seas and the changing severe weather patterns associated with global warming to the rapid, often poorly planned urbanization of the developing world—mean megadisasters will only become more likely. Wouldn't it be fitting—and a sign that we appreciated the true costs of what has happened in tragic Haiti—if the rebuilding there became a case study in how the international community can work together to develop new standards, new designs, and a genuine commitment to reducing the risk of such calamities in the future? A reborn Port-au-Prince could be a showcase for ideas about affordable, durable housing, for enhanced regional cooperation—and for how we can apply lessons that have been learned at an unfathomably great cost.

EXPLORING THE ISSUE

Is the International Community Making Progress in Addressing Natural Disasters?

Critical Thinking and Reflection

1. How comfortable are you about the positive picture about disaster preparedness and response painted in the 2009 UN global assessment report?
2. Should countries in the richer parts of the world believe that they are at less risk of potential devastating consequences of a natural disaster?
3. What are the lessons to be learned from the recent massive earthquake and resultant tsunami in Japan?
4. Is Rothkopf being too critical when he suggests that the damage from the 2010 earthquake in Haiti was so predictable?
5. Do the potential disaster possibilities outlined in the Böstrom/Ćirković volume give you cause for concern?

Is There Common Ground?

There is now a common recognition that natural disasters are occurring with increasing frequency. There is also agreement that global consequences of such events are becoming more far reaching. Finally, the international community now understands the importance of disaster preparedness and response. The number of international governmental and nongovernmental organizations addressing some aspect of the problem is truly impressive. Twenty-one specialized UN agencies and other related organizations are involved in the assault on natural disasters and numerous other UN agencies also play a role. As a consequence, it is evident that there has been major attention paid to natural disasters by both international organizations and national governments over the past 30 years, and this attention is increasing, not diminishing.

Additional Resources

Bostrom, Nick and Ćirković, Milan (eds.), *Global Catastrophic Risks* (Oxford University Press, 2008)

> This book of readings examines the range of large-scale catastrophic risks confronting the planet in both the short run and far into the future.

Haque, C. Emdad, *Mitigation of Natural Hazards and Disasters: International Perspectives* (Springer, 2010)

This book focuses on the prevention, mitigation, and management of international hazards and disasters.

International Federation of Red Cross and Red Crescent Societies, *World Disasters Report 2009—Focus on Early Warning, Early Action* (2009)

This important nongovernmental organization publication spells out where the international community is with respect to early warning systems.

International Strategy for Disaster Reduction, *Hyogo Framework for Action 2005–2015: Building the Resilience of Nations and Communities to Disasters* (2006)

This report provides comprehensive information about the World Conference on Disaster Reduction in Kobe, Japan in early 2005. The report spells out lessons learned and gaps identified in the Yokohama strategy and describes the priorities for 2005–2015.

Karen, Pradyumna P. and Subbiah, Shanmugam P. (eds.), *The Indian Ocean Tsunami: The Global Response to a Natural Disaster* (The University Press of Kentucky, 2010)

This book is the first comprehensive account of the international response and recovery effort of this tsunami.

McGuire, Bill, *Global Catastrophes: A Very Short Introduction* (Oxford University Press, 2009)

The author focuses on the many potential catastrophes facing the planet, examining the probability of the events happening and human survival.

Officer, Charles and Page, Jake, *When the Planet Rages: Natural Disasters, Global Warming . . . and the Future of the Earth* (Oxford University Press, 2009)

This book describes numerous geological hazards around the world. Attention is paid to hurricane Katrina and the Indian Ocean tsunami of 2004.

Smil, Vaclav, *Global Catastrophes and Trends: The Next Fifty Years* (The MIT Press, 2008)

The author examines both rare catastrophes as well as global trends that unfold over time. The author does not argue for or against a doomsday scenario for various issues. Instead, he suggests that the global community must understand change if it is to address these possible events.

United Nations, *Five Years After the Tsunami in the Indian Ocean* (2009)

This study focuses on early warning systems for tsunamis and other ocean hazards.

ISSUE 13

Is the Global Economic Crisis a Failure of Capitalism?

YES: Katsuhito Iwai, from "Global Financial Crisis Shows Inherent Instability of Capitalism," *The Tokyo Foundation* (December 8, 2008)

NO: Dani Rodrik, from "Coming Soon: Capitalism 3.0," *The Taipei Times* (February 11, 2009)

Learning Outcomes

After reading this issue, you should be able to:

- Understand the current global financial crisis in a historical perspective.
- Grasp the broad parameters of why this crisis occurred.
- Understand how globalization has reshaped some of the rules of capitalism.
- Realize that technology has accelerated the pace of financial exchange with both positive and negative consequences.

ISSUE SUMMARY

YES: Katsuhito Iwai, professor of economics at the University of Tokyo, argues that the current economic collapse is a sign of the inherent instability of global capitalism. He argues that capitalism's failure in this crisis is inherent because capitalism is based on speculation and therefore belief or faith in the strength of the system and its various parts.

NO: Dani Rodrik, professor of international political economy at Harvard University's John F. Kennedy School of Government, contends that the current economic downturn is not a sign of capitalism's failure but rather its need for reinvention and adaptation. Rodrik argues that this is precisely why capitalism will survive and thrive because it is so changeable based on new trends and conditions.

The past three years saw one of the most monumental economic shifts in modern times. In what some are now calling "The Great Recession," the world's economy watched tens of trillions of dollars of value lost and entire fortunes disappear in a shrinking stock market. Currencies plummeted, land values around the globe fell, and major economic giants seemingly collapsed overnight (Lehman Brothers, AIG, GM, Chrysler). The sheer shock of the collapse and the magnitude of the crisis have left millions around the world wondering not only what happened but also what comes next. And despite signs of recovery and growth in the United States, Europe, China, and Latin America, the periodic insolvency of countries like Greece, Portugal, Ireland, and Spain and the growing instability in the Middle East have only added to this crisis.

This is not the first such collapse, nor is it necessarily the worst; recall the economic shocks of 1873 and 1929 as examples. But this crisis is marked by some unique dimensions that have given all cause for pause and uncertainty. First, the sheer speed of the collapse was unprecedented. The evolution of communication technology and the way that technology can facilitate economic transaction and money transfers has made economic changes, wealth creation, and diminution nearly instantaneous. Thus, the ripple effects of economic loss or even a lack of confidence are rapid and devastating. The contagion effect that takes hold when rumors of or actual collapses takes place creates an almost tsunami-like impact on the global economy and on people's basic confidence in it. All of this is a direct result of technological advancement.

Second, the centrality of money not productivity in the global economy is a unique phenomenon in global history. For example, in the United States the total GDP of products made is roughly 4.5 trillion dollars while the monetary economy is roughly 14.7 trillion. As a result, those who buy and sell money, derivatives, and the like represent a far greater share of the world economy than product creators and manufacturers and as such have a far greater impact on the economy for good or ill. And since that money is not "real" in the sense that actual dollars are not being traded but rather speculative value is what makes that huge portion of the global economy tenuous and subject to the vagaries of confidence and speculation by people and companies that most people never have heard of or seen.

The third element is that when these economies spiral as a result of risky monetary leveraging by banks and hedge fund managers, the only entities large enough to intercede are governments. The efforts such as the bailouts in the United States, Europe, and elsewhere create enormous budget and debt pressures on those societies that have enormous consequences for human services and other necessities affecting virtually every social strata of society. The ripple effects of government intervention to stabilize the economy are profound, extensive, and touch every municipality and every home in one way or another. The overall impact will be felt for years to come.

Amidst this tumult, the analysis of this economic collapse is in full swing and many point to an inflated housing market, deregulation, excess greed, and a failure of economic leadership or all of the above as reasons for the collapse. Mostly this analysis comes from those who see the system as fixable. They argue that the fundamentals are still there but mechanisms need adjustment and government intervention is needed. This view is probably shared by most of the political parties that occupy the right and center of the political spectrum in democracies of the world today.

Others, however, have speculated that this collapse is part of a larger historical trend that calls into question the vitality of capitalism itself and thus means we need to critically analyze the system and reform it significantly or risk future and more devastating changes. This view is shared by a variety of factions on the left but also among libertarians and others in various societies. They argue that the collapse represents basic flaws in capitalism tied to credit, speculation, regulations, and the like ultimately requiring a complete overhaul of if not scrapping of the capitalist system.

Still others principally among communists and socialists argue that this event has opened up the realities of a global capitalist system and thus demands its scrapping to be replaced by a communist-socialist system of one form or another. These analysts see the simple fact of private economic control as the central problem with the global economy and thus the quickest and surest way to "fix" it.

In this section, two authors address the issue of what this collapse means for capitalism as a system. Iwai contends that this crisis illuminates fundamental issues with capitalism that reflects its inherent instability. He argues that if these issues are not addressed then capitalism as we know it will not and probably cannot survive. Rodrik takes a more optimistic view. He views capitalism as a highly flexible system able to adapt to waves of technological and social changes to meet current and future demands and thus views this crisis as part of a longer line of such events and not as some might argue, the death knell of capitalism.

YES ↵

Katsuhito Iwai

Global Financial Crisis Shows Inherent Instability of Capitalism

The Great Depression set off by the US stock market crash in 1929 dragged on through the 1930s. I doubt anyone will deny that the current financial crisis is the biggest in scale that the world has experienced since then. Unlike at the time of the Great Depression, when governments were slow to take countermeasures, the financial authorities of Japan, the United States, and Europe have been coordinating their response to provide financial institutions with infusions of public funds. This seems to have worked for now, causing the situation to become somewhat calmer. The chances of another 1930s-style Great Depression are small. But stock prices continue to move up and down violently, and the world is at the brink of falling into a "lost decade" if matters are mishandled in the period lying ahead.

I am surprised that such a major financial panic has occurred during my own lifetime. Timing aside, however, the occurrence itself does not surprise me. I have always maintained that capitalism is inherently unstable, and so this development was theoretically predictable.

John Maynard Keynes believed that the market economy was unstable and that it was necessary to use monetary and fiscal policy to tame its instability. This thinking became the pillar of government policy after the Great Depression, particularly in the United States, and it proved successful. But this successful approach ended up being carried too far, with the result that the institutions of the state for countercyclical economic policy measures became overgrown and highly wasteful.

From the 1960s on, the neoclassical economics propounded by Milton Friedman and others came to the fore in Britain, the United States, and elsewhere. According to this theory, the market economy should be kept as free as possible of government intervention and regulation; the purer it is allowed to be, the more efficient and stable it will become. Neoclassical economics provided the theoretical underpinnings of the policies adopted by the Thatcher administration in Britain and the Reagan administration in the United States during the 1980s, and it has established itself as the orthodox form of economic thinking.[1]

This thinking has been carried to the extreme by the current Bush administration, which has sought to do away with regulations, allow the securitization

As seen on www.tokyofoundation.org, December 8, 2008. Originally appeared in *Asahi Shimbun*, October 17, 2008. Copyright © 2008 by Katsuhito Iwai. Reprinted by permission of Asahi Shimbun and the author.

of debts and everything else imaginable, and spread the workings of the market to every corner of the world.

It is fair to consider what we have been witnessing in recent years to have been a grand experiment of global scale aimed at the creation of the laissez-faire utopia conceived by the neoclassical school. The experiment's success came under test from around the time of the East Asian currency crisis in the late 1990s, and it had begun to show signs of unraveling, but the current crisis has brought its collapse. An inconvenient truth about capitalism is that efficiency and stability cannot be achieved simultaneously.

Even Money Is Purely Speculative

Why is capitalism unstable? Because it is fundamentally based on speculation. Consider carmakers, for example. They build automobiles not for themselves but in the expectation that others will buy them to ride in. There is an element of speculation in this process.

Milton Friedman and his followers in mainstream economics, however, claim that speculation leads to stability. Those investors who buy high and sell low, they argue, are irrational and will promptly fall by the wayside. Only the rational investors who buy low and sell high will survive; this will cause markets to be stable.

What they assert may apply to an idyllic market where investors mediate between producers and consumers. But, the activity in financial markets, including markets for stocks, bonds, foreign currency and their derivatives, is of [an] entirely different nature. It is professional investors and investment funds that dominate the markets and compete with each other. They buy and sell based not on their forecasts of long-term demand/supply conditions but on their observations of each other's movements and readings of each other's intentions. When a price is expected to rise or fall, it is not irrational to buy or sell more and move the price further up or down, leading to speculative bubbles and panics.

The more fundamental reason I believe that capitalism as a whole is speculative and inherently unstable is that the money on which it is based is itself speculative. Money has made the economy much more efficient by making it possible to conduct transactions without the trouble of exchanging on a barter basis. But money has no intrinsic value. People are willing to hold it only because they expect other people to accept it in exchange for something else, with the people who accept it expecting that yet other people will accept it in turn.

To hold money is, in other words, the purest form of speculation, and trust in it is based on circular, bootstrap logic: Everybody uses money as money merely because everybody believes everybody else uses it as money.

In this light, we can see that money has two faces: It brings greater efficiency, but at the same time it has the potential of causing great instability. In a capitalist economy supported by money, it is impossible for efficiency and stability to coexist as claimed by the neoclassical economists.

This bootstrap logic of money also underlies the present financial crisis. The subprime loans that set off the crisis are extremely risky loans to people with low creditworthiness. Because the risk of default on such loans is so high, a single subprime loan by itself is unattractive as a financial product. But bundling many such loans together and securitizing them made the risks seem diluted, and as a result of further bundling with numerous other financial instruments into big packages that were then dispersed around the globe, the risks became invisible from the surface.

As the financial products created in this way were traded more and more steadily among numerous parties, they began to be considered readily convertible to cash and other safe assets. They came to be seen as being like the money in which people place supreme trust. Here again we see the workings of bootstrap logic: Everybody trusted the products as safe merely because everybody believed everybody else trusted them as safe. But when the subprime loans whose risks were concealed therein went bad, trust in all financial products toppled like a row of dominoes. This is the essence of the current financial crisis.

A major difference between this and the Asian currency crisis and other financial crises that preceded it is that the value of the US dollar, the key currency of the international monetary system, may be severely shaken. The instability of money as a purely speculative construct—a problem that has been concealed up to now—may come to the surface henceforth in the form of the crisis in the key currency. I do not have space to discuss this problem here, however.

Aim for Second Best

What should we do next? The capitalist world is inherently unstable. So, contrary to the assertions of the neoclassical school, there is no ideal state that we can seek to achieve; all we can do is aim for second best. Capitalism has to be freed from the capitalistic ideology of laissez-faire, and we have to reassert the old-fashioned idea of the necessity of governmental controls on financial institutions to curb their high leverage and excessive speculation. And whenever a crisis strikes, we just have to deal with it using a patchwork of rescue measures, such as buying up of bad loans and infusions of public funds.

This outlook may seem bleak, but if we look back over history, we see that economies have repeatedly experienced the formation of bubbles followed by their collapse, but meanwhile, they have steadily grown more efficient over the course of time. Our only option is eternal pragmatism in search of a better second best.

Like Adam and Eve, we have tasted the forbidden fruit. In our case it is the freedom that capitalism has given us. The sweet fruit of freedom carries its own "original sin," namely the knowledge that capitalism is inherently unstable. But this freedom is not something we should—or can—give up.

Note

1. In Japan's case, neoclassical economic thinking informed the structural reform program of Prime Minister Jun'ichiro Koizumi's administration (2001–6), which sought to achieve an economic recovery led by the private sector, eschewing the previous reliance on fiscal pump priming. . . .

Dani Rodrik **⤷ NO**

Coming Soon: Capitalism 3.0

Capitalism is in the throes of its most severe crisis in many decades. A combination of deep recession, global economic dislocations and effective nationalisation of large swathes of the financial sector in the world's advanced economies has deeply unsettled the balance between markets and states. Where the new balance will be struck is anybody's guess.

Those who predict capitalism's demise have to contend with one important historical fact: capitalism has an almost unlimited capacity to reinvent itself. Indeed, its malleability is the reason it has overcome periodic crises over the centuries and outlived critics from Karl Marx on. The real question is not whether capitalism can survive—it can—but whether world leaders will demonstrate the leadership needed to take it to its next phase as we emerge from our current predicament.

Capitalism has no equal when it comes to unleashing the collective economic energies of human societies. That is why all prosperous societies are capitalistic in the broad sense of the term: they are organized around private property and allow markets to play a large role in allocating resources and determining economic rewards. The catch is that neither property rights nor markets can function on their own. They require other social institutions to support them.

So property rights rely on courts and legal enforcement, and markets depend on regulators to rein in abuse and fix market failures. At the political level, capitalism requires compensation and transfer mechanisms to render its outcomes acceptable. As the current crisis has demonstrated yet again, capitalism needs stabilising arrangements such as a lender of last resort and a counter-cyclical fiscal policy. In other words, capitalism is not self-creating, self-sustaining, self-regulating or self-stabilising.

The history of capitalism has been a process of learning and re-learning these lessons. Adam Smith's idealised market society required little more than a 'night-watchman state.' All that governments needed to do to ensure the division of labour was to enforce property rights, keep the peace and collect a few taxes to pay for a limited range of public goods.

Through the early part of the twentieth century, capitalism was governed by a narrow vision of the public institutions needed to uphold it. In practice, the state's reach often went beyond this conception (as, say, in the case of Bismarck's introduction of old-age pensions in Germany in 1889). But governments continued to see their economic roles in restricted terms.

This began to change as societies became more democratic and labour unions and other groups mobilised against capitalism's perceived abuses. Anti-trust policies were spearheaded in the Unites States. The usefulness of activist monetary and fiscal policies became widely accepted in the aftermath of the Great Depression.

The share of public spending in national income rose rapidly in today's industrialised countries, from below 10 per cent on average at the end of the nineteenth century to more than 20 per cent just before World War II. And, in the wake of WWII, most countries erected elaborate social-welfare states in which the public sector expanded to more than 40 per cent of national income on average.

This 'mixed-economy' model was the crowning achievement of the twentieth century. The new balance that it established between state and market set the stage for an unprecedented period of social cohesion, stability and prosperity in the advanced economies that lasted until the mid-1970s.

This model became frayed from the 1980s on, and now appears to have broken down. The reason can be expressed in one word: globalization.

The postwar mixed economy was built for and operated at the level of nation-states and required keeping the international economy at bay. The Bretton Woods-GATT regime entailed a 'shallow' form of international economic integration that implied controls on international capital flows, which Keynes and his contemporaries had viewed as crucial for domestic economic management. Countries were required to undertake only limited trade liberalisation, with plenty of exceptions for socially sensitive sectors (agriculture, textiles, services). This left them free to build their own versions of national capitalism, as long as they obeyed a few simple international rules.

The current crisis shows how far we have come from that model. Financial globalisation, in particular, played havoc with the old rules. When Chinese-style capitalism met American-style capitalism, with few safety valves in place, it gave rise to an explosive mix. There were no protective mechanisms to prevent a global liquidity glut from developing and then, in combination with US regulatory failings, from producing a spectacular housing boom and crash. Nor were there any international roadblocks to prevent the crisis from spreading from its epicentre.

The lesson is not that capitalism is dead. It is that we need to reinvent it for a new century in which the forces of economic globalisation are much more powerful than before. Just as Smith's minimal capitalism was transformed into Keynes' mixed economy, we need to contemplate a transition from the national version of the mixed economy to its global counterpart.

This means imagining a better balance between markets and their supporting institutions at the global level. Sometimes, this will require extending institutions outward from nation-states and strengthening global governance. At other times, it will mean preventing markets from expanding beyond the reach of institutions that must remain national. The right approach will differ across country groupings and among issue areas.

Designing the next capitalism will not be easy. But we do have history on our side: capitalism's saving grace is that it is almost infinitely malleable.

EXPLORING THE ISSUE

Is the Global Economic Crisis a Failure of Capitalism?

Critical Thinking and Reflection

1. Can the capitalist system be managed and regulated to prevent future crises?
2. Should the system be managed or regulated?
3. What role does the public and private sector play in a globalized economic system?
4. Can people's interests be protected in such a system?
5. How can future technological advancement help or hinder the global economy?

Is There Common Ground?

The need to understand the global economic crisis is strong on all sides of this issue. That analysis however will take years to sort through. Currently, there does seem to be consensus on two important baseline assumptions. The first is that technology has changed the nature of economic exchange and it must be understood and mastered. Second, we live in a globalizing world economy where competition is global and thus the expectations of individuals and groups must be understood through a global and not just national perspective.

Additional Resources

Morris, Charles R., *The Trillion Dollar Meltdown: High Rollers, Easy Money and the Great Credit Crash* (PublicAffairs, 2009)

> According to Morris, the astronomical leverage at investment banks and their hedge fund and private equity clients virtually guarantees massive disruption in global markets. The crash, when it comes, will have no firebreaks.

Sen, Amartya, "Capitalism Beyond the Crisis," *New York Times Review of Books* (March, 2009)

> The present economic crises do not call for a "new capitalism," but they do demand a new understanding of older ideas, such as those of Adam Smith and Arthur Pigou—many of which have been sadly neglected, argues Amartya Sen.

Woodhill, Louis R., "Sorry but Capitalism Did Not Fail," *Real Clear Markets* (March, 2009)

> Woodhill writes on the current world-wide economic and financial crisis and contends that the crisis does not represent a failure of capitalism, but is a result of mistakes made by the U.S. Federal Reserve, aided by Congress and the Administration.

"Capitalism on Trial," *SocialistWorkers.org* (September, 2008)

ISSUE 14

Is Social Media Becoming the Most Powerful Force in Global Politics?

YES: Clay Shirky, "The Net Advantage," *Prospect* (December 11, 2009)

NO: Evgeny Morozov, "How Dictators Watch Us on the Web" *Prospect* (November 18, 2009)

Learning Outcomes

After reading this issue, you should be able to:

- Understand what social media is in a political and economic context.
- Grasp why it is so powerful.
- Understand how it has impacted politics and commerce over the past decade.
- Appreciate the speed of its dissemination.
- Speculate as to what its impact may be in just a few short years.

ISSUE SUMMARY

YES: Clay Shirky argues that social media has and will empower individuals and groups in profound ways giving political movements power, reach, and access. He contends that it will change the power dynamic between these groups and the state (often the object if not adversary of political action) and make insurrection and revolution more likely to occur and potentially to succeed.

NO: Evgeny Morozov contends that the social media revolution cuts both ways. He argues that rather than social media being a tool for overcoming oppression and empowering groups, it has and will be a mechanism for regimes to exercise greater control and dominance. He argues that rather than a panacea, it is a multiedged sword whose full impact, wielded by whom, is yet to be determined.

Over the past decade, coming on the heels of the Internet revolution, a new force has emerged in the global landscape. That force is social media. The marriage of Google and Facebook and thousands of other social networking sites with mobile computer/phone technologies have created a network proliferating at a rate unheard of just five years before. It is safe to argue that social media and its manifestations have impacted economics, human interaction, privacy, politics, conflict, and how we as humans see ourselves in the global context. And because it has happened so quickly, no one has written the definitive analysis of its rise or impact, yet.

The data on the rise of social media are staggering. For example, if Facebook were a country it would be the fourth largest in the world. Three hundred million distinct people a month log into Facebook. YouTube has produced more video content in the last six months than all of the film content in the first 50 years of television. It took radio 38 years to reach 50 million listeners, TV took 13 years, the Internet 4 years, and Facebook adds 50 million people every nine months. Eighty percent of people under the age of 35 in the West have mobile access 24 hours a day. Today there are 200 million blogs on every subject, movement, and philosophy. One could fill a book with such facts about social media.

The proliferation of the mobile computer and other such devices and the rapidity with which varying generations of said technology develop means that the demand for such technology and more importantly meaningful content is growing exponentially. Connectivity, access, choice, and content is driving every group, subgroup, and individual to demand more and as such the power of these connections is expanding at a rate beyond our immediate ability to fully understand it.

As discussed in Issue 13, the technology does not dictate the growth of the money economy beyond states to impact it, it just facilitates that growth. This is also true in social media. Some argue that social media like Facebook is corporate and therefore infringes on privacy and freedom by using personal data to manage personnel behavior for profit. Whether that argument is true is not the issue. What is clear is that Facebook's expansion has simply outstripped most who try to anticipate and analyze its impact. One example is of course in facilitating human relationships. One of every eight marriages today is the result of social networking. Meeting people online is now the preferred method of making initial contact, gathering information about someone you met, and determining whether you have "a connection." Why? Because connecting in that way is perceived to be safe, inclusive, and empowering.

In terms of media reporting, the line between news reporting and blogging and layperson observations is now thoroughly blurred. Thus, "stories" are just as likely to have been created by bloggers as reporters and although some are often lies or inaccurate some are actually quite on target. The first real reports on the capture and killing of Osama bin Laden were from a neighbor in Abbottabad who heard the helicopters and tweeted that it was odd to hear them so late at night. The world got its first inkling that something was afoot before any news or announcement. Further, previously isolated groups and individuals can be connected to like-minded people through social media. This has a positive impact for those seeking solace, counsel, or support for shared grief or interests but for those espousing philosophies of hatred and violence it is empowering and motivating, for example, Major Hasan.

Fundamentally, social media allows people to connect and communicate feelings, ideas, and perceptions in real time and thus creation-directed action. What we are currently seeing in the Middle East is a direct manifestation of that power and effect. Literally millions of people across several states are sharing their frustrations and views in cyberspace and turning that into active opposition to governments that they perceive as responsible for failed aspirations. Through that communication and its speed, those millions can be activated to act on behalf of a cause or issue and thus bring pressure to bear where traditionally little could be brought. Further, social media can move faster than regimes and thus take advantage of changing conditions and situations. No longer are arms the only measure of whether protest can be successful.

In the YES selection, Shirky contends that the force of social media can bring about monumental change in the global political space. He argues that if political and social groups utilize this mechanism, they can attain change and social and political justice on a scale heretofore not imagined by traditional scholars. Morozov is a bit more cynical and contends that the Internet and social media can be used just as effectively by governments and entities to maintain control, collect information, and keep their positions from being challenged. He resists the idea that it is a force for good but rather sees it as a force to be used by all for whatever their motivations.

Other views tend to slide along this spectrum but I think few would argue that social media is still evolving and mutating and that its ultimate impact is yet to be even envisioned let along evaluated.

YES ↵

Clay Shirky

The Net Advantage

In Prospect's December cover story, "How dictators watch us on the web," Evgeny Morozov criticises my views on the impact of social media on political unrest. Indeed, he even says I am "the man most responsible for the intellectual confusion over the political role of the internet." In part, I would like to agree with some of his criticisms, while partially disputing some of his assertions too.

Let me start with a basic statement of belief: because civic life is not just created by the actions of individuals, but by the actions of groups, the spread of mobile phones and internet connectivity will reshape that civic life, changing the ways members of the public interact with one another.

Though germane, this argument says little to nothing about the tempo, mode, or ultimate shape such a transformation will take. There are a number of possible scenarios for changed interaction between the public and the state, some rosy, others distinctly less so. Crucially however, Morozov's reading is in response to a specific strain of internet utopianism—let's call it the "just-add-internet" hypothesis. In this model, the effect of social media on the lives of citizens in authoritarian regimes will be swift, unstoppable, and positive—a kind of digitised 1989. And it will lead us to expect the prominence of social media in any society's rapid democratisation.

While this argument is overtly simplistic, I have nonetheless helped fuel it by discussing mechanisms through which citizens can coordinate group action, while failing to note the ways that visible public action also provides new counter-moves to repressive regimes. Morozov is right to criticise me for this imbalance, and for the resulting (and undue) optimism it engenders about social media as a democratising force; I stand corrected.

Nevertheless, I want to defend the notion—which Morozov goes after in the "man most responsible for intellectual confusion" section of his essay— that social media improves political information cascades, as outlined by the political scientist Susanne Lohmann. It also represents a new dynamic within political protest, which will alter the struggle between insurrectionists and the state, even if the state wins in any given clash. Where this will lead to a net advantage for popular uprisings in authoritarian regimes is an open question— and a point on which Morozov and I still disagree on—but the new circumstances of coordinated public action, I believe, marks an essential change in the civilian part of the "arms race."

Lohmann's mechanism for how information cascades operate is simple: when a small group is willing to take public action against a regime, and the

regime's reaction is muted, it provides information about the value of participation to the group of citizens who opted not to participate. Some members of
this group will then join in the next round of protests.

In turn, further non-reaction by the regime will provide additional information to the next group of "fence-sitters," thereby increasing participation.
Consequently, strong reaction by the regime can be effective in putting down
insurrection, but at the same time risks constraining and, in extreme cases,
delegitimising the regime itself. If the regime acts late, it can thus lose in one
of two ways: the insurrections can win, or the state can win, but at Pyrrhic
costs. Between those two cases, the state can also succeed in putting down the
insurrection at low cost to itself.

Prior to the spread of social media, a typical classic case of late and failed
reaction by the regime to an information cascade is the one documented by
Lohmann, around the collapse of communism in eastern Europe. The classic
case of late and successful reaction by a regime is Tiananmen Square and, even
there, the subsequent alteration of the Chinese state continues to be driven in
part by the recognition that without continued economic improvement, the
same forces that drove insurrection might return. Though the regime always
holds most of the power, insurrections that take advantage of the dynamics of
information cascades thus offer protesters both offensive and defensive capabilities that they wouldn't otherwise have.

But both these examples took place prior to the invention of the internet and widespread use of mobile phones. The question, today, is what the
increased ability on the part of citizens armed with those tools can do to
achieve shared public knowledge and coordinated action.

Morozov introduces both the Belarusian and Iranian protests as examples of places where this struggle can be seen. The October Square protests in
Minsk in 2006 did not, however, destabilise the Lukashenko government, and
surveillance of the mob on LiveJournal helped limit use of flash mob techniques by protesters. The flash mob participants were not able to use either the
offensive or defensive capabilities of social media to permanent advantage—
there is not enough discontent in the rest of the population to cause them to
join in, the government's reaction was sufficiently swift and harsh, and documentation of those events did not resonate outside the country.

Sadly for residents of Belarus, leaders of countries with low geopolitical
importance will always find it easier to deflect democratic movements, social
media or no, than leaders in more strategically vital countries. The case of
Belarus is therefore one in which protesters have been given new capabilities
for organising, but where the state's reaction has remained effective. In the
arms race in Minsk, the tools have changed, but the end result resembles the
old equilibrium state. This is the kind of outcome whose strategic ramifications Morozov has highlighted better than anyone.

The Iranian situation, which Morozov also mentions, is much more
complex: the government relies more on its perceived legitimacy, both democratic and theocratic, than Belarus. Moreover, Iran's geopolitical importance is
paramount on many fronts at once. Clearly, the protests following the 12th
June elections were aided by social media. Although Twitter got top billing in

western accounts, the most important tools during the Tehran protests were mobile phones, whether to send text messages, photos, or videos. Twitter, predominantly, was a gateway to western attention.

By the time the regime managed to shut down the various modes of communication available to the Tehran protesters, they were retiring to rooftops and shouting slogans into the night. Although this act of coordination did not use technology per se, it was made possible by the visible evidence provided by users documenting and broadcasting the earlier solidarity of the street protests. This is why figures showing how few people use social media for political change are red herrings. Insurrections, even pro-democracy insurrections, always begin as minority affairs, driven by a small, young, and well-educated population before they expand more widely. In the Iranian case, once the information about general discontent had successfully cascaded, the coordination among the populace remained intact, even when the tools which helped disseminate that information were shut down.

This makes the situation in Tehran a key test. As usual, the state has more power than the insurgents, but the insurgency has nevertheless achieved the transition from distributed but uncoordinated discontent to being an actual protest movement, and part of that transition was achieved with these tools. Mousavi, and other opposition figures, now know that when they speak out, they do so representing a public, rather than an aggregate of discontented individuals. And when mass action does become possible, it again unleashes protests, as seen in the incredible outpouring of anti-Khamenei sentiment on 13 Aban (4th November), usually a day of anti-American protest—an outpouring documented hundreds of times via videos posted to YouTube.

It is impossible to know how the next few months in Iran will unfold, but the use of social media has already passed several tests: it has enabled citizens to coordinate with one another better than previously, to broadcast events like Basij violence or the killing of Neda Aga Soltan to the rest of the world, and, by forcing the regime to shut down communications apparatus, the protesters have infected Iran with a kind of technological auto-immune disease. However great the regime's short-term desire to keep the protesters from communicating with one another, a modern economy simply cannot function if people can't use their phones. The regime may yet crush protests, but even if they do, the events of June to November this year will still have broken the old illusion of a happy balance between democratic, theocratic, and military power in Iran.

I accept Morozov's criticism of *Here Comes Everybody*. That book was about social media rather than politics—it was an imbalanced account of the arms race between citizens and their governments. However, even within the logic of the arms race, the easier the assembly of citizens, the more ubiquitous the ability to document atrocities. And the more the self-damaging measures which states take—like shutting down mobile phones networks—will resolve themselves as a net advantage for insurrection within authoritarian regimes. Net advantage, in some cases, is a far cry from the "just-add-internet" hypothesis, but it is a view that is considerably more optimistic about the balance of power between citizens and the state than Morozov's.

Evgeny Morozov ➡ **NO**

How Dictators
Watch Us on the Web

My homeland of Belarus is an unlikely place for an internet revolution. The country, controlled by authoritarian President Alexander Lukashenko since 1994, was once described by Condoleezza Rice as "the last outpost of tyranny in Europe."

Its last presidential election in March 2006 was followed by a short-lived and unsuccessful revolution. The initial protests were brutally suppressed. But where public rallies couldn't succeed, protesters turned to more creative forms of insurgency: flash mobs. In a flash mob, social media or email is used to assemble a group of people in a public place, who then perform together a brief, often surreal action. Some young Belarusians used the blogging service LiveJournal to organise a series of events in Minsk with subtle anti-government messages. In a typical flash mob, the youngsters smiled, read newspapers or ate ice-cream. There was nothing openly political but the subtext was: "It's better to lick ice-cream than the president's ass!" The security services made many arrests, but their actions were captured in photos that were posted on LiveJournal and on photo-sharing websites like Flickr. Western bloggers and then traditional media picked up the news, drawing attention to the harsh crackdown.

Details of this rebellion have since been celebrated by a cadre of mostly western thinkers who believe that digital activism can help to topple authoritarian regimes. Belarusian flash mobs are invoked to illustrate how a new generation of decentralised protesters, armed only with technology, can oppose the state in ways unthought of in 1968 or 1989. But these digital enthusiasts rarely tell you what happened next.

Enthusiasm for the idea of digital revolution abounds. In October, I was invited to testify to the Commission on Security and Cooperation in Europe in Washington DC—a hotchpotch of US congressmen, diplomats and military officials. The group was holding a hearing titled: "Twitter Against Tyrants: New Media in Authoritarian Regimes." I would once have happily accepted the premise, but recently my thinking has changed. From 2006–08 I worked on western-funded internet projects in the former Soviet Union—most with a "let's-promote-democracy-through-blogs" angle. But last year I quit. Our mission to use the internet to nudge citizens of authoritarian regimes to challenge the status quo had so many unexpected consequences that, at times, it seemed to be hurting the very causes we were trying to promote.

At the hearing, I was the lonely voice of dissent in a sea of optimism. In one speech, Senator Sam Brownback, a Republican known for his conservative Christian views, implored us to "tear down the new walls of the 21st century, the cyber-walls and electronic censorship technology used by tyrants."

Jon Stewart, host of the satirical programme The Daily Show, recently poked fun at a similar suggestion from a congressman that the web was freeing the peoples of Iraq, Afghanistan and Iran: "What, we could have liberated them over the internet? Why did we send an army when we could do it the same way we buy shoes?" Unfortunately, critical voices like his are rare. The majority of the media, so cranky when reporting the internet's impact on their industry, keep producing tear-jerking examples of the marriage of political protest and social media. And what a list it is: Burmese monks defying an evil junta with digital cameras; Filipino teenagers using SMS to create a "textual revolution"; Egyptian activists using encryption to hide from the all-seeing-eye of the Mukhabarat; even Brazilian ecologists using Google maps to show deforestation in the Amazon delta. And did I mention Moldova, China and Iran? These cyber-dissidents, we are told, now take their struggles online, swapping leaflets for Twitter updates and ditching fax machines for iPhones.

But that isn't what happened in Belarus. After the first flash mob, the authorities began monitoring By_mob, the LiveJournal community where the activities were announced. The police started to show up at the events, often before the flashmobbers did. Not only did they detain participants, but they too took photos. These—along with the protesters' own online images—were used to identify troublemakers, many of whom were then interrogated by the KGB, threatened with suspension from university, or worse. This intimidation didn't go unnoticed. Soon, only hardcore activists would show up. Social media created a digital panopticon that thwarted the revolution: its networks, transmitting public fear, were infiltrated and hopelessly outgunned by the power of the state.

The Belarusian government shows no sign of being embarrassed by the fact it arrested people for eating ice-cream. Despite what digital enthusiasts tell you, the emergence of new digital spaces for dissent also lead to new ways of tracking it. Analogue activism was pretty safe: if one node in a protest network got busted, the rest of the group was probably OK. But getting access to an activist's inbox puts all their interlocutors in the frame, too. The result is a cat-and-mouse game in which protesters try to hide from the authorities by carving out unconventional niches. In Iran, dissidents used to be active on Goodreads, an international social networking website for book-lovers. Here they quietly engaged in conversations about politics and culture, unseen by the censors—that is, until the Los Angeles Times helpfully published an article about what was going on, tipping the authorities off.

Social networking, then, has inadvertently made it easier to gather intelligence about activist networks. Even a tiny security flaw in the settings of one Facebook profile can compromise the security of many others. A study by two MIT students, reported in September, showed it is possible to predict a person's sexual orientation by analysing their Facebook friends; bad news for those in regions where homosexuality carries the threat of beatings and prison. And many authoritarian regimes are turning to data-mining companies to help them identify troublemakers. TRS Technologies in China is one such company. It boasts that "thanks to our technology, the work of ten internet cops can now be done by just one."

***

This does not mean that cyber dissent is an illusion. There are three main strands to the "democracy by tweets" theory. First, despite my caveats, the internet can if used properly give dissidents secure and cheap tools of communication. Russian activists can use hard-to-tap Skype in place of insecure phone lines, for example. Dissidents can encrypt emails, distribute antigovernment materials without leaving a paper trail, and use clever tools to bypass internet filters. It's now easier to be a "one-man NGO": with Google Docs, you can do your own printing, lowering the risk of leaks. Second, new technology makes bloody crackdowns riskier, as police are surrounded by digital cameras and pictures can quickly be sent to western news agencies. Some governments, like Burma and North Korea, don't care about looking brutal, but many others do. Third, technology reduces the marginal cost of protest, helping to turn "fence-sitters" into protesters at critical moments. An apolitical Iranian student, for instance, might find that all her Facebook friends are protesting and decide to take part.

This third point, however, needs careful examination. The argument goes like this. Thanks to the internet, governments have lost their monopoly on controlling information, while citizens have acquired access to other sources of knowledge and the ability to organise more safely. Many people will use this access to learn more about democracy, which will unshackle them from government propaganda. They will use this new power to push the government on accountability (as has happened to a limited extent in China, where online campaigners have had corrupt local officials sacked). When the next crisis strikes—such as the flawed Iranian election in 2009, or high fuel prices in Burma in 2007—citizens will turn to the internet to see how unpopular the regime has become. Discovering others of like mind, they will see the protests and, if the regime hasn't responded with violence, join to create a "snowball" capable of crushing the most rigid authoritarian structure.

Social scientists have named these snowballs "information cascades." They explain why, when most citizens may believe that a revolution will not succeed, they will still pour into the streets if everyone else is protesting; so many people can't be wrong. Perhaps the most famous example is described in a 1994 paper by UCLA political scientist Susanne Lohmann. She sought to explain the sudden appeal of the "Monday demonstrations" in the East German town of Leipzig, which began in September 1989. Lohmann argues that the East German fence-sitters watched the protests unfold and, noting the lack of government retaliation, decided to join in. In the circumstances, it was the most rational thing for them to do.

It's not hard to see how the internet might amplify information cascades and so strengthen the position of activists. The point is made most famously by the American web guru Clay Shirky. He is a darling of the social media world, a consultant for government, corporate and philanthropic bodies, and a source for reporters seeking quotes on how the internet is changing protest. He is also the man most responsible for the intellectual confusion over the political role of the internet. Shirky adapted Lohmann's theories for the age of MySpace in his bestseller *Here Comes Everybody* (2008). The major lesson he drew from Leipzig is that people should "protest in ways that the state was unlikely to interfere with, and distribute evidence of their actions widely." Why? Protesters are in a win-win situation: "If the state didn't react, the documentation would serve as evidence that the protesting was safe. If the state did react, then the documentation of the crackdown could be used to spur an international outcry."

But the truth is often different. In Belarus, most fence-sitters watched the state's response and, acting rationally, went searching for higher fences. In Iran this year, the famous photograph of Neda Agha-Soltan, murdered in the streets, went viral and became a symbol of the "green revolution." Whether it encouraged any fence-sitters is much less obvious.

Information cascades often fail to translate into crowds, even without state fear-mongering. Last year's anti-Farc protests in Colombia—aided by Facebook—attracted huge crowds. But this year's anti-Chávez protests did not, although they were organised by the same group using the same methods. The aim was for 50m people to rally worldwide but only a few thousand turned up. The same has been true when people have tried to organise protests in Azerbaijan and Russia.

Yet even if the internet doesn't always bring people out onto the streets, its adherents have another, subtler argument. For democracy to succeed, they say, you need civil movements to help make protests more intense, frequent and well-attended. A vibrant civil society can challenge those in power by documenting corruption or uncovering activities like the murder of political enemies. In democracies, this function is mostly performed by the media, NGOs or opposition parties. In authoritarian states—or so the story goes—it is largely up to lone individuals, who often get locked up as a result. Yet if citizens can form ad-hoc groups, gain access to unbiased information and connect with each other, challenges to the state become more likely. And social theorists like Robert Putnam argue that the emergence of such groups increases social capital and trust among citizens.

It is true that the internet is building what I call "digital civic infrastructure"—new ways to access data and networks to distribute it. This logic underlies many western efforts to reshape cyberspace in authoritarian states. The British foreign secretary David Miliband has enthused about the potential of the communications revolution to "fuel the drive for social justice." "If it's true that there are more bloggers per head of population in Iran than in any other country, this makes me optimistic," he has also said. In early November, US secretary of state Hillary Clinton announced Civil Society 2.0, a project to help grassroots organisations around the world use digital technology, which will include tuition in online campaigning and how to leverage social networks.

But the emergence of this seemingly benign infrastructure can backfire on western governments. The first snag is that turning the internet into a new platform for civic participation requires certainty that only pro-western and pro-democracy forces will participate. Most authoritarian societies, however, defy easy classification into the "good guys vs bad guys" paradigms of the Bush era. In Egypt, for example, the extremist Muslim Brotherhood is a political force—albeit mostly missing from the Egyptian parliament—that can teach Hosni Mubarak a lesson about civic participation. It has an enviable digital presence and a sophisticated internet strategy: for example, campaigning online to get activists released from prison. Western governments shouldn't be surprised when groups like this become the loudest voices in new digital spaces: they are hugely popular and are commonly denied a place in the heavily policed traditional public sphere.

Similarly, the smartest and most active user of new media in Lebanon is not the western-backed government of Saad Hariri, but the fundamentalist troublemakers of Hizbullah, whose suave manipulation of cyberspace was on display during the 2006 war with Israel. In Russia, the internet has given a boost to extreme right-wing groups like the Movement Against Illegal Immigration, which has been using Google Maps to visualise the location of ethnic minorities in Russian cities and encouraging its members to hound them out. Criminal gangs in Mexico are fond of YouTube, where they flaunt their power by uploading videos of their graphic killings. Generally, in the absence of strong democratic norms and institutions, the internet has fuelled a drive for vigilante justice rather than the social variety Miliband was expecting.

And it gets worse. Ultra-loyalist groups supporting Thailand's monarchy were active during both the September 2006 coup and more recent street protests, finding anti-monarchy material that needed to be censored via a website called Protecttheking.net. In this, they are essentially doing the job usually reserved for the secret police. In much the same way, the Iranian revolutionary guards posted online photos of the most ardent protesters at the June 2009 rallies, asking pro-Ahmadinejad Iranians to identify them. And in August 2009 religious fundamentalists in Saudi Arabia launched a campaign to identify YouTube videos they found offensive and pressure the company to delete them—a form of digital "hacktivism" which must be delighting the official censors.

And it doesn't help that anyone with a computer and an internet connection can launch a cyber-attack on a sovereign nation. Last year I took part in one—purely for the sake of experiment—on the websites of the Georgian government. As the Russian tanks were marching into South Ossetia, I was sitting in a cafe in Berlin with a laptop and instructions culled from Russian nationalist blogs. All I had to do was to input the targets provided—the URLs of hostile Georgian institutions (curiously, the British embassy in Tbilisi was on that list)—click "Start" and sit back. I did it out of curiosity; thousands of Russians did it out of patriotism. And the Russian government turned a blind eye. The results of the attack were unclear. For a brief period some government emails and a few dozen websites were either slow or unavailable; some Georgian banks couldn't offer online services for a short period.

Yet while the internet may take the power away from an authoritarian (or any other) state or institution, that power is not necessarily transferred to pro-democracy groups. Instead it often flows to groups who, if anything, are nastier than the regime. Social media's greatest assets—anonymity, "virality," interconnectedness—are also its main weaknesses.

***

So how do repressive governments use the internet? As we have seen, the security services can turn technology against the logistics of protest. But the advent of blogging and social networking has also made it easier for the state to plant and promote its own messages, spinning and neutralising online discussions before they translate into offline action. The "great firewall of China," which supposedly keeps the Chinese in the dark, is legendary. In truth, such methods of internet censorship no longer work. They might stop the man on the street, but a half determined activist can find a way round. And more often than not, official attempts to delete a post by an anti-government blogger will backfire, as the blogger's allies take on the task of distributing it through their own networks. Governments have long lost absolute control over how the information spreads online, and extirpating it from blogs is no longer a viable option. Instead, they fight back. It is no trouble to dispatch commentators to accuse a dissident of being an infidel, a sexual deviant, a criminal, or worst of all a CIA stooge.

Moreover, the distracting noise of the internet—the gossip, pornography, and conspiracy theories—can act as a de-politicising factor. Providing unfettered access to information is not by itself going to push citizens of authoritarian states to learn about their government's crimes. Political scientists talk about the preference for non-political information as "rational ignorance." It's a fancy way of saying that most people, whether in democracies or not, prefer to read about trivia and what's useful in daily life—restaurant and film reviews and so on—than about the tedious business of governance.

One study from early 2007, by a Saudi academic, showed that 70 per cent of all content swapped by Saudi teenagers via Bluetooth was pornographic. Authoritarian governments know that the internet could be a new opium for the masses. They are tolerant of rampant internet piracy, as in China. In many cases, they push the cyber-hedonistic pursuits of their youth. Government-controlled internet providers in Belarus, for example, run dedicated servers full of pirated digital goodies for their clients to download for free. Under this new social contract, internet users are allowed plenty of autonomy online—just so long as they don't venture into politics.

***

We shouldn't kid ourselves. Nobody knows how to create sustainable digital public spheres capable of promoting democracy. Western interventions can even thwart the natural development of such spaces. Governments usually give cash to a favoured NGO—often based outside the authoritarian state in question—which has the job of creating new social media infrastructure: group blogs, social networks, search engines and other services that we take for granted in the west. The NGOs then hire local talent to work on a Belarusian Twitter or an Egyptian version of the blog-search platform Technorati.

Yet these services work because they are born in entrepreneurial cultures where they can be speedily built and adapted to local needs. The stodgy form-filling process of angling for the next juicy grant, which in truth drives nearly all NGOs, is a world away from a freewheeling Palo Alto start-up. The result is a clumsy arrangement in which NGOs toil away on lengthy, expensive and unnecessary projects instead of ditching them when it becomes apparent they won't work and moving on to the next idea. Despite millions of dollars poured into the former Soviet Union, NGO-funded new media projects that are alive and kicking a year after the original grant has ended can be counted on the fingers of one hand.

So should we stop funding projects that use the internet to promote democracy? Of course not. Even a sceptic like me can see the upside. Western governments and NGOs shouldn't abandon their digital democracy push, they should just improve it. One way would be to invest in tools that help make digital civic spaces less susceptible to government spin. There are some interesting prototypes—particularly based around Wikipedia edits—that supply readers with visual hints that some contributors may not be trustworthy. As Twitter and Facebook emerge as platforms for cyber-activism in authoritarian states, it is essential they are aware of their new global obligations, including the need to protect the data entrusted to them by activists. Elsewhere, cyber-attacks on NGOs are poised to intensify. We in the west should be prepared to step in and help the dissenting voices, providing free and prompt assistance to get back online as soon as possible.

Some consistency in dealing with cyber-attacks is also needed. If we treat cyber-attacks that Russian nationalists launch on Estonian or Georgian targets as crimes, we cannot approve when our own "hacktivists" launch similar attacks on Iranian government websites. And western governments should refrain from confirming paranoid autocrats' theories about a Twitter revolution, thus necessitating a crackdown. During the Iran protests this year, the US state department called Twitter executives and asked them to delay maintenance of the site so Iranians could continue using it to protest. There was no better way to confirm Iranian suspicions that the US government was somehow behind the protest.

One final idea. Let us in future be a bit more sceptical about the need to recreate the protest wheel. In almost all countries run by authoritarian regimes there is an untapped mass of activists, dissidents, and anti-government intellectuals who have barely heard of Facebook. Reaching out to these offline but effective networks will yield more value than trying to badger bloggers to take up political activities. Western embassies working on the ground in authoritarian states often excel at identifying and empowering such networks and new media literacy should become part of diplomatic training. After all, these old-school types are the people who brought democracy to central and eastern Europe. And it will probably be them who win freedom for China and Iran too.

EXPLORING THE ISSUE

Is Social Media Becoming the Most Powerful Force in Global Politics?

Critical Thinking and Reflection

1. How powerful can social media become in global politics?
2. Who if anyone will control or manage it?
3. Will the private corporate sector be in control, or states or private individuals?
4. Will it be manipulated for democratic ends, anarchistic designs, or more state control?

Is There Common Ground?

The only consensus on the impact of social media is that it is monumental. All agree that Facebook, YouTube, and the like, combined with faster and faster waves of technological change as the generations speed by mean that the space of social media will only expand in scope and impact. Analysts agree that we have only scratched the surface of its reach. That is why there is a good deal of optimism combined with anxiety about its direction.

As long as the stakes are political power and billions of dollars, the true impact of social media will be caused by the varying motivations of those who attempt to harness its reach.

Additional Resources

Aaker, Jennifer et al., *The Dragonfly Effect* (John Wiley and Sons, 2010)

This book outlines powerful ways to use social media to drive social change.

Shirky, Clay, *Here Comes Everybody: The Power of Organizing Without Organizations* (The Penguin Press, 2008)

Shirky evaluates the effect of the Internet on modern group dynamics.

Smith, Jackie, *Social Media for Global Democracy* (Johns Hopkins University Press, 2008)

This selection sheds new light on the struggle to define the course of globalization.

Qualman, Erik, *Socialnomics: How Social Media Transforms the Way We Do Business* (John Wiley and Sons, 2011)

This book takes a look at the business implications of social media, and tap its considerable power to increase sales, cut marketing costs, and communicate directly with consumers.

Internet References . . .

Nuclear Terrorism: How to Prevent It

This site of the Nuclear Control Institute discusses nuclear terrorism, such as the possibility of another nuclear 9/11 and how best to prevent it. Topics include terrorists' ability to build nuclear weapons, the threat of "dirty bombs," and whether nuclear reactors are adequately protected against attack.

http://www.nci.org/nuketerror.htm

Center for Defense Information

The Center provides expert analysis on 48 different topic areas in the U.S. national and international security.

http://www.cdi.org

Public Broadcasting System (PBS)

Use the key phrase "religious extremism" on this site to locate a variety of sources relating to religious and cultural extremism and their contemporary consequences.

http://www.pbs.org

Exploring Global Conflict: An Internet Guide to the Study of Conflict

This Internet resource is designed to provide understanding of global conflict. Information related to specific conflicts in areas such as Northern Ireland, the Middle East, the Great Lakes region in Africa, and the former Yugoslavia.

http://www.uwm.edu/Dept/CIS/conflict/congeneral.html

Central Intelligence Agency

The U.S. government agency provides substantial information on its Web site regarding U.S. issues abroad.

http://www.cia.gov/terrorism/

The Cato Institute

This U.S. public organization conducts research on a wide range of public policy issues. It subscribes to what it terms "basic American principles."

http://cato.org/current/civil-liberties/

Center for Strategic and International Studies (CSIS)

CSIS provides information on terrorism in the aftermath of 9/11, and the threats from Iran and China. The URL noted here leads directly to its thinking on the issue of homeland defense.

http://www.csis.org/homeland

The New Global Security Dilemma

*W*ith the end of the cold war, the concept of security was freed from the constraints of bipolar power politics. No longer were issues framed simply in terms of United States–Soviet conflict (Vietnam, Afghanistan, the Middle East), but rather seen in more complex terms related to issues of ethnicity, fundamentalism and cultural division, nuclear proliferation, and new forms of conflict. These concerns were always there but were always muted by the apparent "larger" issues of superpower rivalry. Whether this was largely a Soviet and U.S. construct or not is for historians to decide. What is clear is that these issues have taken center stage in terms of security threats to the stability of the global community.

These include concerns over nuclear proliferation, religious and cultural extremism, terrorism, and the reemergence of great power politics in the form of Russian–Chinese rivalry and the democracy movements sweeping through the Middle East.

This section examines some of the key issues shaping the security dilemma of the twenty-first century.

- Are We Headed for a Nuclear 9/11?

- Is Religious and Cultural Extremism a Global Security Threat?

- Is a Nuclear Iran a Global Security Threat?

- Will China Be the Next Superpower?

- Has Al-Qaeda and Its Jihad Against the United States Been Defeated?

- Is the Middle East Undergoing a Democratic Revolution?

ISSUE 15

Are We Headed for a Nuclear 9/11?

YES: Brian Michael Jenkins, from "Terrorists Can Think Strategically: Lessons Learned from the Mumbai Attacks," Rand Corporation (January 2009)

NO: Graham Allison, from "Time to Bury a Dangerous Legacy— Part I," *Yale Global Online* (March 14, 2008)

Learning Outcomes
After reading this issue, you should be able to:
• Understand the rationale for threat of a nuclear 9/11.
• Grasp where such threats come from and how they can be neutralized.
• Appreciate the complexity of such a threat.
• Understand whether such a threat is probable or highly unlikely.

ISSUE SUMMARY

YES: Brian Michael Jenkins, senior advisor to the President of the Rand Corporation, in testimony before the U.S. Senate Committee on Homeland Security and Governmental Affairs, posited that a team of terrorists could be inserted into the United States and carry out a Mumbai-style attack as terrorism has "increasingly become an effective strategic weapon."

NO: Graham Allison, Harvard professor and director of the Belfer Center for Science and International Affairs, affirms that we are not likely to experience a nuclear 9/11 because "nuclear terrorism is preventable by a feasible, affordable agenda of actions that . . . would shrink the risk of nuclear terrorism to nearly zero."

Since the terrorist attacks of September 11, 2001, much has been written about the specter of nuclear terrorism in the form of either a thermonuclear device or the releasing of a dirty bomb (one loaded with radioactive material) in an urban/civilian setting. The events of September 11 have all but ensured the world's preoccupation with such an event for the foreseeable future. Indeed, the 2009 arrest of a U.S. man with dirty bomb materials indicates that such plans may indeed be in the works between Al-Qaeda and other terrorist cells. When this horror is combined with the availability of elements of nuclear-related material in places like the states of the former Soviet Union, Pakistan, India, Iran, North Korea, and many other states, one can envision a variety of sobering scenarios.

Hollywood feeds these views with such films as *The Sum of All Fears* and *The Peacemaker*, in which nuclear terrorism is portrayed as all too easy to carry out and likely to occur. It is difficult in such environments to separate fact from fiction and to ascertain objectively the probabilities of such events. So many factors go into a successful initiative in this area. One must find a committed cadre of terrorists, sufficient financial backing, technological know-how, intense security and secrecy, the means of delivery, and many other variables, including luck. In truth, such acts may have already been planned and tried by terrorists only to be thwarted by governments, security services, or terrorist mistakes and incompetence. We do not know, and we may never know.

In addition, the United States and other Western states have greatly enhanced their nuclear/radioactive detection techniques over the past 10 years. Satellite technology, drone monitoring, and other forms of intelligence make communication via any technological form subject to interception and analysis, thus revealing more of what terrorist or other groups may be planning. Also, partnerships between the United States, Russia, China, and other states have made such events not impossible but certainly less likely to occur over the past 10 years.

Despite these enhanced security measures, regional and ethnic conflicts of a particularly savage nature in places like Chechnya, Kashmir, Colombia, and Afghanistan help to fuel fears that adequately financed zealots will see in nuclear weapons a swift and catastrophic answer to their demands and angers. Osama bin Laden's contribution to worldwide terrorism has been the success of money over security and the realization that particularly destructive acts with high levels of coordination can be "successful." Despite his recent death at the hands of U.S. Navy Seals, others with similar ambitions will undoubtedly continue their plans against real or perceived enemies.

In addition, the fact that Pakistan currently possesses nuclear weapons but is facing increased instability and challenges from external and internal fundamentalist forces raises other concerns in this area. What if such forces are able to co-opt the Pakistani military and take power? With nuclear weapons at their disposal could they not supply terrorist groups surreptitiously and thus make such a nuclear 9/11 more likely.

Conversely, many argue that fear of the terrorist threat has left us imagining that which is not likely. They point to a myriad of roadblocks to terrorist groups' obtaining all of the elements necessary for a nuclear or dirty bomb. They cite technological impediments, monetary issues, lack of sophistication, and inability to deliver. They also cite governments' universal desire to prevent such actions. Even critics of Iran and North Korea have argued that even if these countries have nuclear weapons they would not deliver them to terrorist groups, nor would they use them except in the direst of circumstances, such as regime survival. They argue that the threat is overblown and, in some cases, merely used to justify increased security and the restriction of civil liberties.

Still others contend that the principles of deterrence that were omnipresent and applicable during the cold war would simply reemerge within a more proliferated global society. Simply put, terrorist groups bent on using such a device if they could acquire it would risk total annihilation should they go that route. The United States and other nuclear states would simply obliterate them and the safe havens from which they would operate.

The following selections reflect the debate about a nuclear 9/11. In the YES selection, Brian Michael Jenkins focuses on the ability and resourcefulness of the terrorists and argues that recent events indicate a real ability to carry out such an attack. In the NO selection, Graham Allison focuses on the targets, the United States and the West, and insists that a coordinated strategy can stop such an event.

YES ↵   Brian Michael Jenkins

Terrorists Can Think Strategically

Lessons Learned From the Mumbai Attacks

Mr. Chairman and Members of the Committee, it is an honor to appear before you today. The Mumbai attack was still ongoing when RAND initiated an analysis to determine what lessons might be learned from it. This analysis, part of RAND's continuing research on terrorism and homeland security, was documented in a report I co-authored along with other RAND analysts. Specifically, I contributed the sections on the terrorists' strategic motives and the execution of the attack.

We relied on both informed official sources and media reporting. My analysis benefited greatly from the detailed descriptions of the attack provided by officers from the New York Police Department, who were on the scene and whose reports were shared with law enforcement and others in the United States.

Copies of our report have been made available to members of the Committee. Additional copies are available here, and the report is also on RAND's website. For convenience, I have appended the key findings to my testimony. The following observations derive from this report and other relevant research.

Terrorism has increasingly become an effective strategic weapon. Earlier generations of terrorists seldom thought beyond the barrels of their guns. In contrast, the masterminds of the Mumbai terrorist attacks displayed sophisticated strategic thinking in their choice of targets and their efforts to achieve multiple objectives. They were able to capture and hold international attention. They sought to exacerbate communal tensions in India and provoke a crisis between India and Pakistan, thereby persuading Pakistan to redeploy troops to its frontier with India, which in turn would take pressure off of the Taliban, al Qaeda, and other groups operating along the Afghan frontier. All terrorist attacks are recruiting posters. The Mumbai attackers established their terrorist credentials and now rival al Qaeda in reputation.

Al Qaeda is not the only galaxy in the jihadist universe—new contenders that have signed on to al Qaeda's ideology of global terror. Even as we have degraded al Qaeda's operational capabilities, the idea of a violent global jihad has spread from North Africa to South Asia. The Mumbai attack

From *Testimony Series*, January 2009, pp. 1–4. Copyright © 2009 by Rand Corporation. Reprinted by permission via Copyright Clearance Center.

foreshadows a continuing terrorist campaign in India. More broadly, it suggests that the global struggle against the jihadists is far from over.

Terrorists can innovate tactically to obviate existing security measures and confuse authorities. Authorities are obliged to prevent the recurrence of the most recent attack, while knowing that other terrorists will analyze the security in place, devise new tactics, and do the unexpected. The Mumbai attackers did not plant bombs in crowded train coaches, as in the 2006 Mumbai terrorist attack. Instead, gunmen attacked the train station. They did not detonate car bombs as in the 1993 Mumbai attacks or the more recent terrorist attacks on hotels in Indonesia, Egypt, Jordan and Pakistan. They seized control of hotels where they started fires. Multiple attacks at different locations prevented authorities from developing an overall assessment of the situation.

Once again, terrorists have demonstrated that with simple tactics and low-tech weapons, they can produce vastly disproportionate results. The Mumbai attack was sequential, highly mobile, and a departure from the now common suicide bombings, but the tactics were simple—armed assaults, carjackings, drive-by shootings, building takeovers, barricade and hostage situations. The attack was carried out by ten men armed with easily obtained assault weapons, semi-automatic pistols, hand grenades, and simple improvised explosive devices—little more than the arsenal of an infantryman in the 1940s—along with 21st century cell phones, BlackBerries, and GPS locators.

Terrorists will continue to focus on soft targets that offer high body counts and that have iconic value. Nationally and internationally recognized venues that offer ease of access, certainty of tactical success, and the opportunity to kill in quantity will guide target selection. Public spaces are inherently difficult to protect. Major investments in target hardening make sense for government only when these provide a net security benefit, that is, when they do not merely displace the risk to another equally lucrative and accessible target.

Terrorists view public surface transportation as a killing field. One of the two-man terrorist teams went to Mumbai's main train station and opened fire on commuters. While the attacks on the other targets were theoretically aimed at killing foreigners, the attack at the train station was aimed solely at slaughter. It accounted for more than a third of the total deaths.

This underscores a trend that should be a priority issue in the United States. Public surface transportation offers terrorists easily accessible, dense populations in confined environments—ideal killing zones for gunmen or improvised explosive devices, which remain the most common form of attack. According to analysis by the Mineta Transportation Institute's National Transportation Security Center, two-thirds of all terrorist attacks on surface transportation were intended to kill; 37 percent resulted in fatalities (compared with between 20 and 25 percent of terrorist attacks overall); 75 percent of the fatal attacks involved multiple fatalities; and 28 percent of those involved 10 or more fatalities.

Terrorist attacks on flagship hotels are increasing in number, in total casualties, and in casualties per incident.   This trend places increasing demands on hotel security. However, while terrorist attacks are spectacular, they are statistically rare in comparison to ordinary violent crime. In the past forty years, fewer than five hundred hotel guests in the entire world have been killed by terrorists, out of a total global hotel guest population at any time of nearly ten million.

Pakistan's principal defense against external pressure is not its nuclear arsenal, but its own political fragility—its government's less-than-full cooperation is preferable to the country's collapse and descent into chaos.   Pakistan continues to play a prominent and problematic role in the overlapping armed conflicts and terrorist campaigns in India, Afghanistan, and Pakistan itself. Al Qaeda, the Taliban, Lashkar-e-Taiba and other insurgent and terrorist groups find sanctuary in Pakistan's turbulent tribal areas. Historically, some of them have drawn on support from the Pakistan government itself. While the Government of Pakistan has been helpful in capturing some key terrorist operatives, Pakistan is accused of protecting others. And it has been understandably reluctant to use military force against its own citizens in the remote tribal areas where these groups reside. When it has used military force, government forces have not fared well. Public sentiment imposes further constraints. Many Pakistanis regard India and the United States, not al Qaeda or the Taliban, as greater threats to Pakistan's national security. This was perceived as an obstacle to U.S. counterterrorist efforts even before 9/11.

The success of the Mumbai attackers in paralyzing a large city and commanding the attention of the world's news media for nearly three days will encourage similar operations in the future.   Terrorists will continue to effectively embed themselves among civilians, taking hostages and using them as human shields to impede responders and maximize collateral casualties. We should expect to see more of this tactic.

Could a Mumbai-style attack happen in the United States?   It could. The difference lies in planning and scale. Assembling and training a ten-man team of suicidal attackers seems far beyond the capabilities of the conspirators identified in any of the local terrorist plots discovered in this country since 9/11. We have no evidence of that level of dedication or planning skills.

However, we have seen lone gunmen and pairs of shooters, motivated by mental illness or political cause, run amok, determined to kill in quantity. The Long Island Railroad, Empire State Building, LAX, Virginia Tech, and Columbine cases come to mind. In 1955, four Puerto Rican separatists opened fire in a then unguarded Capitol Building, wounding five members of Congress. Firearms are readily available in the United States. And some of the perpetrators of the attacks mentioned above planned for their attacks for months, while building their arsenals. Therefore, an attack on the ground, carried out by a small number of self-radicalized, homegrown terrorists armed with readily available weapons, perhaps causing scores of casualties, while still far beyond what we have seen in the terrorist plots uncovered thus far, is not inconceivable.

Could a team of terrorists, recruited and trained abroad as the Mumbai attackers were, be inserted into the United States, perhaps on a U.S.-registered fishing vessel or pleasure boat, to carry out a Mumbai-style attack? Although our intelligence has greatly improved, the answer again must be a qualified yes. It could conceivably happen here, although I would expect our police response to be much swifter and more effective than we saw in Mumbai.

Graham Allison　　　　　　　　　　　　　　　　　　➤ **NO**

Time to Bury a Dangerous Legacy–Part I

One month after the terrorist assault on the World Trade Center and the Pentagon, on October 11, 2001, President George W. Bush faced a more terrifying prospect. At that morning's presidential daily intelligence briefing, George Tenet, the director of central intelligence, informed the president that a CIA agent codenamed "Dragonfire" had reported that Al Qaeda terrorists possessed a 10-kiloton nuclear bomb, evidently stolen from the Russian arsenal. According to Dragonfire, this nuclear weapon was in New York City.

The government dispatched a top-secret nuclear emergency support team to the city. Under a cloak of secrecy that excluded even Mayor Rudolph Giuliani, these nuclear ninjas searched for the bomb. On a normal workday, half a million people crowd the area within a half-mile radius of Times Square. A noon detonation in Midtown Manhattan would kill them all instantly. Hundreds of thousands of others would die from collapsing buildings, fire and fallout in the hours thereafter. The electromagnetic pulse generated by the blast would fry cell phones and other electronic communication. The wounded would overwhelm hospitals and emergency services. Firemen would fight an uncontrolled ring of fires for days afterward.

In the hours that followed, Condoleezza Rice, then national security adviser, analyzed what strategists call the "problem from hell." Unlike the Cold War, when the US and the Soviet Union knew that an attack against the other would elicit a retaliatory strike or greater measure, Al Qaeda—with no return address—had no such fear of reprisal. Even if the president were prepared to negotiate, Al Qaeda has no phone number to call.

Concerned that Al Qaeda could have smuggled a nuclear weapon into Washington as well, the president ordered Vice President Dick Cheney to leave the capital for an "undisclosed location," where he would remain for weeks to follow—standard procedure to ensure "continuity of government" in case of a decapitation strike against US political leadership. Several hundred federal employees from more than a dozen government agencies joined the vice president at this secret site, the core of an alternative government that would seek to cope in the aftermath of a nuclear explosion that destroyed Washington.

Six months earlier the CIA's Counterterrorism Center had picked up chatter in Al Qaeda channels about an "American Hiroshima." The CIA knew that Osama bin Laden's fascination with nuclear weapons went back at least to 1992, when he attempted to buy highly enriched uranium from South Africa. Al Qaeda operatives were alleged to have negotiated with Chechen separatists in Russia to buy a nuclear warhead, which the Chechen warlord Shamil Basayev claimed to have acquired from Russian arsenals. The CIA's special task force on Al Qaeda had noted the terrorist group's emphasis on thorough planning, intensive training and repetition of successful tactics. The task force highlighted Al Qaeda's preference for symbolic targets and spectacular attacks.

As CIA analysts examined Dragonfire's report and compared it with other bits of information, they noted that the September attack on the World Trade Center had set the bar higher for future terrorist attacks. Psychologically, a nuclear attack would stagger the world's imagination. New York was, in the jargon of national-security experts, "target rich."

As it turned out, Dragonfire's report proved to be a false alarm. But the central takeaway from the case is this: The US government had no grounds in science or logic to dismiss this possibility, nor could it do so today.

There's no established methodology for assessing the probability of an unprecedented event that could have such catastrophic consequences. Nonetheless, in "Nuclear Terrorism" I state my considered judgment that if the US and other governments just keep doing what they are doing today, a nuclear terrorist attack in a major city is more likely than not by 2014.

Richard Garwin, a designer of the hydrogen bomb whom Enrico Fermi once called, "the only true genius I had ever met," told Congress in March 2007 that he estimated a "20 percent per year probability of a nuclear explosion with American cities and European cities included." My Harvard colleague Matthew Bunn has created a model that estimates the probability of a nuclear terrorist attack over a 10-year period to be 29 percent—identical to the average estimate from a poll of security experts commissioned by Senator Richard Lugar in 2005.

Former Secretary of Defense William Perry has expressed his own view that my work may underestimate the risk. Warren Buffet, the world's most successful investor and legendary odds-maker in pricing insurance policies for unlikely but catastrophic events, concluded that nuclear terrorism is "inevitable." As he has stated: "I don't see any way that it won't happen."

The good news is that nuclear terrorism is preventable by a feasible, affordable agenda of actions that, if taken, would shrink the risk of nuclear terrorism to nearly zero. A global strategy to prevent this ultimate catastrophe can be organized under a Doctrine of Three No's: No loose nukes, no new nascent nukes, no new nuclear weapons. The first requires securing all nuclear weapons and weapons-usable material, on the fastest possible timetable, to a new "gold standard." The second does not allow for any new national capabilities to enrich uranium or reprocess plutonium. The third draws a line under the current eight and a half nuclear powers—the five members of the Security Council and India, Israel, Pakistan and North Korea—and says unambiguously: "Stop. No More."

The US cannot unilaterally sustain a successful strategy to prevent nuclear terrorism. Nor can the necessary actions simply be commanded, compelled or coerced. Instead, they require deep and steady international cooperation rooted in the recognition that nations share a common threat that requires a common strategy. A Global Alliance Against Nuclear Terrorism is therefore in order. The mission of this alliance should be to minimize the risk of nuclear terrorism by taking every action physically, technically and diplomatically possible to prevent nuclear weapons or materials from falling into the hands of terrorists.

Constructing such an alliance will require the US and other nuclear-weapons states to confront the question of a "fourth no": no nuclear weapons. While US or Russian possession of nuclear arsenals is not a major driver of Iran's nuclear ambitions, and while Osama bin Laden would not be less interested in acquiring a nuclear weapon if the US eliminated its current arsenals, the proposition that nuclear weapons are necessary for the security of US and Russia but intolerably dangerous if acquired by Iran or South Africa is difficult to sell to nuclear have-nots.

The question of a categorical "fourth no" has come to the fore with the January 2007 opinion piece in the *Wall Street Journal* by George P. Shultz, William J. Perry, Henry A. Kissinger and Sam Nunn, calling upon the US and other states to act to realize their Non-Proliferation Treaty commitment and President Reagan's vision of "a world free of nuclear weapons." Towards that goal, the immediate agenda should be to devalue nuclear weapons and minimize their role in international affairs. This should begin with nuclear-weapons states pledging to the following principles: no new national enrichment, no nuclear tests, no first use of a nuclear bomb and no new nuclear weapons.

Faced with the possibility of an American Hiroshima, many are paralyzed by a combination of denial and fatalism. This is unwarranted. Through a combination of imagination, a clear agenda for action and fierce determination to pursue it, the countdown to a nuclear 9/11 can be stopped.

EXPLORING THE ISSUE

Are We Headed for a Nuclear 9/11?

Critical Thinking and Reflection

1. How much preparation can any society engage in to prevent such an attack?
2. Is there a way to build an antinuclear terror regime among states?
3. What would the response be to such an attack?
4. What does this threat, no matter how large or small, say about intelligence and counterterrorism?

Is There Common Ground?

There are many arguments to support the contention that nuclear and dirty bombs are hard to obtain, difficult to move and assemble, and even harder to deliver. There is also ample evidence to suggest that most, if not all, of the U.S. government's work is in one way or another designed to thwart such actions because of the enormous consequences were such acts to be carried out. These facts should make Americans rest easier and allay fears if only for reasons of probability.

However, Allison's contention that failure to assume the worst may prevent the thwarting of such terrorist designs is persuasive. Since September 11, it is clear that the world has entered a new phase of terrorist action and a new level of funding, sophistication, and motivation. The attitude that because something is difficult it is unlikely to take place may be too dangerous to possess.

Overall, we can all agree on two elements. First is that many different states have a vested interest in thwarting such an act and second is that mutual interest should fuel effective nonproliferation movements across the globe.

Additional Resources

Allison, Graham, *Nuclear Terrorism: The Ultimate Preventable Catastrophe* (Times Books, 2004)

Brzezinski, Zbigniew, *The Choice: Global Domination or Global Leadership* (Basic Books, 2005)

Landau, Elaine, *Osama bin Laden: A War Against the West* (Twenty-First Century Books, 2002)

Lodal, Jan, *The Price of Dominance: The New Weapons of Mass Destruction and Their Challenge to American Leadership* (Council on Foreign Relations Press, 2001)

Stern, Jessica, *The Ultimate Terrorists* (Harvard University Press, 1999)

ISSUE 16

Is Religious and Cultural Extremism a Global Security Threat?

YES: Hussein Solomon, from "Global Security in the Age of Religious Extremism," *PRISM* (August 2006)

NO: Shibley Telhami, from "Testimony Before the House Armed Services Committee: Between Terrorism and Religious Extremism" (November 3, 2005)

Learning Outcomes

After reading this issue, you should be able to:

- Understand the nature of religious and cultural extremism in a global context.
- Understand its interaction with new violent tactics.
- Grasp its impact on the world in an age of terrorism.
- Appreciate that such extremism is contextually and culturally defined.
- Understand that it is a sensitive issue for many around the world.

ISSUE SUMMARY

YES: Hussein Solomon argues that when religious extremism, which is a security threat in and of itself, is merged with state power, the threat to global security is potentially catastrophic and must be met with clear and uncompromising policies. He contends that this is present across all religions, and he uses both a born-again George Bush and a fundamentalist Mahmoud Ahmadinejad as his examples.

NO: Shibley Telhami, on the other hand, does not argue that religious extremism is the threat, but rather that global security threats are from political groups with political agendas and not extremism as such.

Religious and cultural extremism has been a part of the global landscape for millennia. Since the dawn of civilization, groups of people have defined themselves by their language, religious beliefs, race, and other factors distinguishing their culture from "the other." Once this occurred, conflicts over resources, land, and allegiances began and have continued to varying degrees. Religion as a catalyst for this conflict has always been present, particularly in Europe, the Middle East, and Asia, throughout the Greek–Roman and Middle Ages periods.

Although religious and cultural extremism is not a new force, the methods of idea dissemination and the speed with which groups can connect certainly are. Today in the age of globalization, religious extremism has a variety of mediums through which it can transmit its messages and as such appears, on the surface, to be a very potent force. This is certainly true in the Islamic world. Fundamentalist Islam has seized the mantle of religious extremism even though there are such extremists among all major religious groups. The increasing radicalism of the Palestinian movement combined with the high-profile acts of Al-Qaeda has underscored this perception. The concept of martyrdom has now permeated the extremist culture such that suicide attacks, be they in a Jerusalem school or at the World Trade Center, are offered as pure manifestations of allegiance to one's faith. Although it is often difficult to extract the political and economic motivations of these groups from their religious zealotry, one dimension is clear. Whatever the real political motives of the leaders of these groups may be, the rank and file truly believe that they are martyrs in a cause ordained and blessed by their God.

Such extremism is not confined to any one religion or culture, however. There are numerous examples among Christian sects, Jewish denominations, and among most cultures around the world. Whether it is xenophobia present in some cultures, or fear of being together exploited by religious or political leaders, almost every society has faced forms of extremism that have resulted in violence. Such examples just in the past 20 years at varying scales include the Rwandan genocide, the Bosnian-Serbian-Croatian conflict, and the fundamentalist violence in the United States aimed at abortion clinics and doctors.

The globalization of media in all of its forms has transformed more localized fundamentalist extremism into global movements with reach through every computer terminal and into the home of every disgruntled believer. As such, extremist cells have emerged throughout the world with a small but highly motivated minority of believers committed to violence as their only means of political and social expression. Although the highest profile acts appear to be committed by Islamic fundamentalists, all faiths possess such zealotry and have examples of violence in the name of "pure belief."

What is also new and ominous is the connection through the Internet between such extremist movements and social loners. The case of Major Hasan and the attack in Waco at Fort Hood is an example. One's computer terminal and the Internet become a kind of activating devices for social loners and misfits looking for someone to blame and a cause to belong to. Earlier they used to have to actually read, go to rallies, or join some organizations, now they can merely log on and find solace in the extremist teachings of some faith or culture and even become motivated to act. This development means fanatical groups can exert outreach to a far greater extent than ever before.

Combined with this reality comes the prevalence and proliferation of weaponry be it biological, chemical, or nuclear that can transform an extremist act from local to global in seconds. Thus, smaller extremist groups can have great geopolitical and psychological impact, making them large state international actors well beyond their actual size, influence, or following. When one or two fanatics are able to attain a sizeable audience for their extremism through violence, all of the other social loners with other deep-seeded psychological issues seeking recognition now have an example to follow.

In the following section, two noted scholars argue whether it is religious extremism or simply political goals that are the security threat. In the YES selection, Hussein Soloman contends that when religious extremism is combined with state power in any system, violence, conflict, and death will follow. He makes the controversial argument that George Bush with his fundamentalist Christian beliefs and Mahmoud Ahmadinejad with his Islamic fundamentalism present global security threats. He contends that their fundamentalism when merged with instruments of state power leads to abuses, conflict, and death for their own citizens and innocents in arenas of conflict.

In the NO selection, Shibley Telhami presents the case that states and interests compete and extremism in and of itself is not the culprit. He argues that the extremism of the Iranian regime or Al-Qaeda is not what makes them a threat but rather the anti-Western sentiment that they have tapped into. Their goals and interests combined with a willingness to engage in violent terrorism constitute the security threat and not the fact that they have a religious base.

YES

Hussein Solomon

Global Security in the Age of Religious Extremism

A World Caught between Hope and Despair

We live in a world fecund with both hope and despair. Images of hope are aplenty. From Ireland, comes the story of the Irish Republican Army (IRA) formally giving up its armed struggle. From the Gaza strip, we see Israel's evacuation of Jewish settlers from occupied Palestinian land; and from Kashmir we witness rapprochement and reconciliation overcoming the enmity and quest for vengeance of the past. At the same time there is despair; which emanates from the fact that religion, which brings meaning to one's life and preaches peace, love and generosity has morphed into something ugly and violent. In Japan, we have seen Aum Shinrikyo (the Supreme Truth) cult release sarin gas in Tokyo's subways. From India's Gujarat State, we saw Hindu fundamentalists kill hundreds of their fellow Muslim citizens. In northern Uganda, Joseph Kony and his Christian fundamentalist Lord's Resistance Army aim to overthrow the secular government of Yoweri Museveni and to replace it with a government observant of the biblical Ten Commandments. In the process, the commandment "Thou Shall Not Kill" has been violated thousands of times. From the United States, we see people motivated by strong Christian principles bombing abortion clinics or federal buildings as in the case of Timothy McVeigh—the infamous Oklahoma bomber. The world has also witnessed Jewish fundamentalism in the form of Yigal Amir's assassination of former Israeli Prime Minister Yitzhak Rabin after he signed the Oslo Peace Accords. The rise of a violent Islamic fundamentalism was vividly illustrated by the tragic events of 9/11 in New York and Washington and by the atrocities committed more recently in Amman, Jordan.

While the violent religious fundamentalism of these non-state actors constitute a grave threat to national, regional and international security—this article will focus rather on the threat posed by state-sanctioned religious fundamentalism. The underlying premise here is that when religious extremists capture state power, the threat posed to international security is infinitely worse than that posed by non-state actors given the control that they can now exercise over the resources of the state. Two cases illustrate the point well: the United States under George W. Bush and Iran under Mahmoud Ahmadinejad.

George W. Bush Finds God

In 1985 George W. Bush found God by way of a Bible study group and studied the scriptures intensely for the next two years. In the process he developed an ideology, which dovetailed neatly with the mentality of the conservative evangelicals in the US. Later when he decided to run for public office, his political strategist Karl Rove drew the link between Bush's Christian beliefs and the evangelical sector. This proved to be an immensely successful strategy given the evangelical voting bloc—one in three American Christians call themselves evangelical. To put it another way, there are 80 million born-again Christians of voting age in the United States—George W. Bush is one of them. As he prepared for elections first as Governor and later for the presidency, whilst others candidates spoke about their political platform, Bush spoke about his faith. Thus when a reporter asked him who his favourite philosopher was, Bush replied: *"Christ, because he changed my heart."* Using religion to get elected, however, was one thing; acting on those strong Christian beliefs as president is quite another. Yet this is exactly what the Christian right sought to achieve—after all, their man occupied the White House. Their efforts ranged across the social spectrum from the issue of euthanasia to same sex marriage to the teaching of intelligent design (another term for creationism) as opposed to evolution in school textbooks.

However, it is perhaps in the realm of foreign policy that the religious views of George Bush hold the greatest menace. For one thing, he subscribes to Manichaeism that divides reality into Absolute Good and Absolute Evil. Juan Stam notes that the Christian Church rejected this as heretical many centuries ago. Yet, time and time again George W. Bush uses this rather simple dichotomy of good versus evil. The U.S. and its allies are good and have been "called" by God to serve as his instrument against the evildoers. On the other hand— the other side is described as the "Axis of Evil." Such a simplistic dichotomy is extremely problematic. First, do Iran and North Korea really have so much in common with one another that one lumps them together? Second, using phrases like "Axis of Evil" suggest that a regime, a country, or a set of countries are merely evil but does not point to the level of factionalism occurring inside a country or how one might capitalise on it to serve one's own national interest. To sum up then, "Axis of Evil" is a primitive and simple term for a complex world that is characterised less by black and white and more by shades of grey.

Beyond the terminology, however, there are even more serious problems with George W. Bush occupying the Oval Office and these relate to the idea that God speaks to him. Arnon Regular writing in Israel's *Haaretz* newspaper reported that when George Bush met with then Palestinian Prime Minister Abbas in Aqaba he said: *"God told me to strike at Al-Qaeda and I struck them and then He instructed me to strike at Saddam, which I did, and now I am determined to solve the problem in the Middle East."* Such statements do irreparable harm to US policy in the Middle East. How does one promote secular democracies in the Middle East when the President of the United States is himself undermining the First Amendment as it relates to the separation of Church and State?

Meanwhile Ira Chernus raised other objections against such a statement: *"If he truly believes that he hears the voice of God, there is no telling what God might say tomorrow. This is a man who can launch the world's biggest arsenal of weapons of mass destruction—biological, chemical, and nuclear at any moment. . . . When the President lets God tell him what to do, it violates the spirit of democracy. In a democracy, it is the people, not God, who make the decisions. The president is supposed to represent the will of the people. Yes, he must seek the best advice he can get and use his own best judgment. That means relying on facts, intelligent analysis, and rational thought—not divine inspiration. Once the President lets God's voice replace the human mind, we are back in the Middle Ages, back in the very situation our revolution was supposed to get us out of."*

Professor Ira Chernus' perspective was echoed almost fifty years previously by that formidable First Lady, Eleanor Roosevelt: *"Anyone who knows history, particularly the history of Europe, will, I think, recognize that the domination of education or of government by any one particular religious faith is never a good arrangement for the people."*

Throughout the Afghan and Iraqi wars, President Bush did not shy away from identifying God with his own project. Thus when he appeared in his flight suit on the aircraft carrier Abraham Lincoln, he said to US troops: *"And wherever you go, you carry a message of hope—a message that is ancient and ever new. In the words of the prophet Isaiah, 'To the captives, come out! To those who are in darkness, be free!'"* It should be noted that Bush's use of God and the Bible is unprecedented in US political history and stands in sharp contrast to, for instance, President Abraham Lincoln. During the American Civil War, Lincoln did not claim that God was on his side. Indeed in his famous second inaugural address, he said that the war was a curse on both armies.

Mahmoud Ahmadinejad and the Mahdi

June 2005 witnessed the election of Mahmoud Ahmadinejad as President of the Islamic Republic of Iran. Amongst the people voting for him some cited his anti-corruption stance, others his desire to better the lot of the common Iranian man and woman, and still others his piety. Few could have guessed where this piety was to lead him and Iran as soon as he assumed the presidency. For one thing, the delicate balance between conservatives and reformists that the regime sought to preserve has been destroyed with Ahmadinejad's election. Before the June elections, Iran's supreme leader Ayatollah Ali Khamenei, stated that ". . . *the existence of two factions [conservative and reformist] serves the regime, like the two wings of a bird.*" But Ahmadinejad has been removing reformists as well as those conservatives allied to his political rivals from positions of power and has been replacing them with incompetent cronies who share his ideological vision. The political establishment in Tehran is bound to experience further shocks following the announcement by Ahmadinejad's spiritual advisor, the extremist Ayatollah Mohammed Taqi Mesbah-Yazdi, that ". . . *with a true Islamic government at hand, Iran has no need for future elections.*" The delicate balance that Ayatollah Khamenei has sought to preserve has been utterly destroyed.

At this point it might be useful to ask what this pious ideological vision that Ahmadinejad subscribes to is. Much of his vision relates to his devotion to the 12th Imam, also known as the Mahdi, who vanished in 941. According to Shiite Muslims this Imam will return at the end of time to lead an era of Islamic justice. The fact that Ahmadinejad fervently believes in this should not be viewed as a problem. The fact that President Ahmadinejad is prepared to act out on this belief as Iranian President should be cause for alarm. As mayor of Tehran, Ahmadinejad refurbished a major boulevard on the grounds that the Mahdi was to travel along it upon his return. Similarly, soon after winning the presidency, Ahmadinejad allocated the equivalent of 12 million British pounds of government funds to enlarge the shrine and mosque of the Mahdi. Diverting public funds in this manner, from pressing social needs towards the "imminent" return of an Imam who has not made his appearance in eleven centuries, borders on either the criminal or the insane.

However, it is not only at the level of social expenditure that the Mahdi intrudes on Ahmadinejad's thoughts. Indeed, Ahmadinejad believes in reorienting the country's economic, cultural and political policies based on the Mahdi's return and judgment day. Moreover, the urgency to reorient the country's policies emanates from Ahmadinejad's belief that the Hidden Imam will appear in two years. How he knows that the Mahdi will appear in two years' time is anyone's guess, though some supporters of the Iranian President suggest that he must have heard it from the Mahdi himself. Ahmadinejad was also quite prepared to share his penetrating insights with the world when he addressed the United Nations in September, calling for the reappearance of the Imam.

Nevertheless, Ahmadinejad's address to the UN General Assembly was memorable for other reasons as well. When recounting his address to Ayatollah Javadi Amoli, one of Iran's leading clerics, Ahmadinejad stated that he felt that there was a light around him during his entire address at the podium "*during which time the world leaders did not blink. They were astonished as if a hand held them there and made them sit. It had opened their eyes and ears for the message of the Islamic Republic.*" Some commentators have taken this mysticism of the Iranian President seriously and wonder if his saying these things serves a political purpose—transforming Ahmadinejad into the instrument of the Mahdi, thereby placing him above political reproach. In that case, the comment by Ayatollah Mesbah-Yazdi on there not being a need for future elections does fit into this broader political strategy.

Ahmadinejad's strong belief in the imminent return of the Mahdi does hold grave foreign policy implications. The fact that the Mahdi will only return at the End Times—a period characterised by intense international turmoil, is in itself instructive and may help to explain Ahmadinejad's foreign policy. Some analysts commented on how unfazed he was following the tremendous international outcry after he stated that Israel should be wiped off the map. However, from his ideological position both his statement and the reaction to it only contributed to the intense international turmoil that is a necessary precondition for the reappearance of the Mahdi. In that sense any punitive measures embarked upon by the international community would, rather than prompting a moderation of Tehran's current bellicose foreign policy, prompt the hawks around Ahmadinejad to congratulate themselves on a job well done. Moreover, such punitive measures may also serve to push moderates in Iran into the camp of Ahmadinejad, not because they share his ideology, but in order to provide a united front in defence of the national interest.

The Response

So how does one defeat the religious fundamentalists occupying high office? The first thing to realise is that, whilst both Bush and Ahmadinejad need to be neutralised in that as presidents of their respective countries they have tremendous power in order to engage in their religious fantasies, we should not personalise the issue either. Both Bush and Ahmadinejad head up powerful constituencies who share the beliefs of their president. The Reverend Pat Robertson's calling for the removal of Venezuelan President Hugo Chavez illustrates the point well. Thus the ideology of the movement that has brought them into high office needs to be delegitimised by their co-religionists. This is already happening in both the US and Iran.

In the US, clerics like Fritz Ritsch, Presbyterian minister in Bethesda, Maryland are deeply offended by Bush's simple dichotomy of good and evil and the characterisation that the US is on the side of angels. As he stated: "*It is by no means certain that we are as pure as the driven snow or that our international policy is so pure.*" Indeed nearly all the mainstream churches, including Bush's own United Methodists are opposed to the war in Iraq. Meanwhile, academics, journalists, and various civil society groupings in the US have started opposing various aspects of the agenda of the Christian right. Amongst the most prominent of these has been former US President Jimmy Carter. In his latest book entitled *Our Endangered Values: America's Moral Crisis*, Carter, a devout Southern Baptist, raised serious concerns about the religious right's openly political agenda. He also argues that their open hostility to a range of sinners from homosexuals to the federal judiciary run counter to America's democratic freedom. Finally he calls for a clear separation of Church and State.

In Iran, too, the religious, academic, and political establishments have taken on Ahmadinejad in a dramatic way. Akbar Alami, an Iranian legislator, has questioned the President's claims of being surrounded by an aura of light, noting that not even Islam's holiest figures have made such claims. Ayatollah Mohammed Ali Abtahi, a former vice president, expressed his concern with the use of religious slogans and Ayatollah Yusuf Saanei urged: "*We should rule the country according to Islamic law, but we should not use religious ideas in politics. Even Ayatollah Khomeini did not believe we should do this.*" Professor Hamid Reza Jalaipour at Tehran University also casts doubt on the broader politico-religious project of the President: "*The question is, can his reliance on Imam Mahdi be turned into a political ideology? I don't think so. Even the leading theologians in Qum do not take these allusions seriously.*"

The second aspect of a response relates to neutralising the incumbent politically. In the US, this process is well advanced and George W. Bush has been transformed into a lame-duck president. What is interesting is that Republicans have also turned against their president as they vote with the Democrats. From Plamegate and Scooter Libby to the spiralling deficit, to the war in Iraq, and to the issue of illegal wiretaps, the Bush Administration is under extreme pressure. In recent weeks, the Administration suffered two humiliating setbacks. The first relates to it accepting the anti-torture amendment proposed by Republican Senator John McCain after initially making clear its objection to it. This underscores the weakness of the Bush Administration at this moment. Second, Bush and his fellow hawks had to fight tooth and nail to get the Patriot Act renewed. In the process major concessions were made on the part of the Administration.

In Iran, too, the process of vigorously neutralising President Ahmadinejad has begun. Inside the country, Ahmadinejad has been criticised for his seeming lack of tact and his confrontational style. For instance, shortly after Ahmadinejad's statement that Israel should be wiped off the map, Ali Akbar Rafsanjani, a former Iranian President and currently a major ally of Ayatollah Khamenei, stated at Friday prayers in Tehran: "*We have no problems with the Jews and highly respect Judaism as a holy religion.*" Those opposed to Ahmadinejad's bellicose foreign policy have also established discreet back-channel contacts with the Americans over Iran's nuclear programme.

The Iranian Parliament has also moved to politically neutralise Ahmadinejad in two ways, firstly, by undermining his populist political programme. In this regard it has already dismantled the centrepiece of Ahmadinejad's populist programme the Imam Reza Care Fund that sought to provide interest-free loans for young people to marry as well as various employment programmes. Second, parliament has sought to weaken the President and strengthen the hand of Ayatollah Khamenei. For instance, the Speaker of Parliament, Gholamali Haddad-Adel, urged support for the concept of *Velayat-e-Faqih* (leadership of the supreme jurisprudent), introduced by Ayatollah Khomeini. However Ayatollah Khamenei is also taking active measures to weaken Ahmadinejad. Recently he gave the Expediency Council, a 32-member non-elected political arbitration body, sweeping new powers to supervise parliament, the judiciary, and the executive. This body is headed up by Rafsanjani. More ominously for Ahmadinejad, the Expediency Council's secretary, Mohsen Razaie, announced: "*The adjudication of the Expediency Council is the final word. And even if other state actors do not agree with it, it is still the final word and they have to accept that.*" Here it is interesting to note that Razaie used to be the commander of the Islamic Revolutionary Guard Corps (IRGC). This has led some commentators to believe that the senior echelons of the Revolutionary Guards may still be loyal to Ayatollah Khamenei as opposed to Ahmadinejad.

The third response has been to capitalise on the failure of the incumbent, thereby neutralising him further. Iraq has been such a failure for the Bush Administration. According to US statistics, 2,071 US soldiers have lost their lives and 16,000 others were wounded. Moreover, 39 percent of soldiers returning from Iraq are suffering from psychological trauma. In addition to the human costs, the Iraq and Afghanistan wars have already cost the American taxpayer $300 billion. Seen in the light of the US budget deficit, these economic costs are staggering. Opponents of the Bush Administration—Republican and Democrat—have been quick to attack and they have pressed Bush for a timetable for the withdrawal of US troops from Iraq. The senior military echelons have also voiced their concern on the sustainability of current troop levels in Iraq vis-à-vis securing other US interests. Failure in Iraq has certainly tempered the messianic zeal of Bush's foreign policy hawks. Thus their approach to the nuclear programme of Tehran and the already nuclear-armed Pyongyang regime has been radically different from that of Baghdad under Saddam Hussein when they refused to give Hans Blix and his nuclear weapons inspectors more time.

Whilst it is still early days for the Ahmadinejad administration, it is equally clear that a strategy of setting the incumbent up for failure that would then be used against him is being pursued. Consider the way the Iranian parliament has been dismantling aspects of Ahmadinejad's populist programme as described above. Whilst Ayatollah Khamenei's supporters may hope that this might undermine Ahmadinejad in the eyes of his supporters in that he will be unable to make good on his promises, it is equally clear that such a strategy is a high risk one. Ahmadinejad might well fail in his social programme and this might well anger his support base. However, Ahmadinejad could also direct this popular anger towards parliament, towards Ayatollah Khamenei and Rafsanjani. In the process, he could become stronger.

We also need to realise that Ahmadinejad is not simply passively allowing these machinations against him to take place. He has also gone on the offensive against his political rivals. For instance, he has recently purged the upper echelons of Iran's diplomatic corps. According to some reports, these may number as many as 40 of Iran's senior diplomats. These were inevitably allies of Rafsanjani or others who were appointed by the reformist Ayatollah Mohammed Khatami, Ahmadinejad's predecessor. Even more disconcerting is the fact that amongst those purged were Iran's ambassadors to London, Paris, Geneva, Berlin and Kuala Lumpur. This has resulted in Ed Blanche speculating on whether the purge of these particular diplomats was also an attempt on the part of Ahmadinejad to close the back-channel contacts existing between Tehran and Washington.

Conclusion

As this titanic power struggle continues in Tehran, there are deeper questions that need to be posed in the short-to-medium term. In the medium term, we do believe that the political power of the religious right-wing in the US will weaken as developments deteriorate in Iraq, Afghanistan and elsewhere, such as Latin America where we have seen the roll-back of American influence most dramatically in Evo Morales' Bolivia and Hugo Chavez's Venezuela. Indeed some pollsters are comparing George Bush's low popularity ratings with those of President Nixon at the time of the Watergate scandal. More importantly, the United States was established as a secular state and increasingly we see prominent individuals like President Carter as well as a plethora of civil society groups fighting back for the secular state promised in the US Constitution and the Bill of Rights. They seem to be winning the battle.

It is a very different situation in Iran. The 1979 Iranian revolution established a theocratic state that, in its current composition, cannot be secular. Nor, indeed can it be democratic. To understand this, we need to understand the fundamental split between Shiites and Sunnis in Islam. The democratic tradition is strong in Islam. Concepts such as freedom (*hurriyyah*), equality (*musawat*) and justice (*'adl*) are all intrinsic to the Qur'an. The fact that the first caliph after Prophet Muhammad's death in 632 C.E. was elected by majority consensus by a council of various Muslim tribes is ample proof of the democratic credentials of Islam. But this very election of the first Caliph saw the split between Sunnis and Shiites. Shiites broke away from mainstream Muslims after the election of the first Caliph since they wanted Imam Ali who was the cousin and son-in-law of Prophet Muhammad to succeed as Caliph. The majority (Sunnis) did not vote for Ali on the basis of his youth and inexperience. Thus the very origins of Shi'ism as a political doctrine lay in its anti-democratic foundations.

These anti-democratic foundations have been built upon by Ayatollah Khomeini, the founder of the Islamic Republic in 1979 when he established such concepts as the *Velayat-e-Faqih* or Leadership of the Supreme Jurisprudent. This concept has more in common with Plato's Philosopher-King and the Divine Right of Kings in the Middle Ages than with Islamic political thought and serves no other purpose than to consolidate the power of the ruling mullahs over a hapless population. It is important to understand this structure of the Iranian state in order to understand the limitation of reform of the state itself. This limitation was patently obvious during the presidency of Ahmadinejad's predecessor, Ayatollah Khatami. Despite him stressing moderation and a dialogue of civilizations as opposed to clash of civilizations, the reform movement foundered on the bedrock of a totalitarian theocratic state. One should also bear in mind that even without Ahmadinejad, the Iranian state will continue to be a source of insecurity to its own people as well as to the region—notice here Tehran's support for Hamas and Hezbollah.

In the short-term the most troubling aspect relates to Iran's nuclear programme. Whilst the Iranian regime stresses that their nuclear programme is for civilian purposes, as Mohammed El-Khawas notes the problem is that much of the technology used for civilian power generation could also be used for weapons as well. However, the problem goes beyond merely dual use technology in that the Iranian government did conceal its nuclear programme for eighteen years. It should be noted here that failure to notify the International Atomic Energy Agency (IAEA) is a clear breach of Iran's nuclear obligations under the Nuclear Non-Proliferation Treaty (NPT). Iran also failed to disclose to the IAEA all its uranium enrichment facilities. Other worrying indicators that Tehran may not be interested in nuclear energy for purely civilian purposes are the fact that "... *IAEA inspectors discovered traces of highly enriched uranium far above the levels needed for civilian use.*" Moreover, El-Khawas also notes that Iran is building the infrastructure for nuclear weapons production like the heavy-water reactor at Arak that can produce plutonium.

Still another reason to hold a somewhat sceptical stance towards the Iranian regime lies in the cat-and-mouse game it has been playing with the IAEA. In November 2004, for instance, Tehran agreed in Paris to freeze its entire uranium enrichment programme until a long-term agreement was reached. Some weeks later, however, when UN inspectors tried to confirm

Iran's compliance with the suspension, they were not permitted to put UN seals on some enrichment equipment at Natanz. These developments clearly do not inspire confidence in the regime. In the final instance, the international community cannot allow President Ahmadinejad's bellicose regime to possess nuclear weapons. More so, the international community cannot allow a man who believes in the return of the Mahdi and with him the End Times in two years time. The international community cannot allow a man who believes that a halo of light surrounds him to have his finger on a nuclear button.

Shibley Telhami → **NO**

Testimony Before the House Armed Services Committee Between Terrorism and Religious Extremism

Let me say at the outset that the gravest threat to the United States today is neither Islamic groups nor Islamic fundamentalism as such. The central threat facing the United States of America is the threat of catastrophic terror by al-Qaeda and its allies. The nature of this threat justifies the allocation of significant resources to counter the threat and defeat al-Qaeda and its allies. But we must be very careful in identifying who the core enemy is and not waste resources and energies on strategies that do not confront the primary threat, and worse yet, could backfire.

First, while we must oppose all terrorism, and we have many local enemies in various parts of the world, most such enemies do not pose the kind of catastrophic threat that al-Qaeda does, and thus do not warrant the kind of resources that could take away from our effort to directly confront the primary threat.

Second, although religious extremism is something most of us would oppose, we have to be very careful not to jump to the conclusion that the threat to the United States stems from religious extremism as such. We have extremists all over the world, as we do in our own country, but most of them do not seek to cause catastrophic harm to us and most do not have the capacity or the support to do so even if they wanted to.

Third, al-Qaeda presents such a high threat to the United States primarily for three reasons: Unlike most local extremist groups around the world, it has a demonstrated capacity to organize on a global scale and a demonstrated global reach. As a non-state actor, it is not sensitive to deterrence and thus is capable of being maximally reckless in its operations and thus poses the potential for catastrophic attacks that are limited only by its capabilities. And while it may care about local issues in the Muslim world, in the end its agenda is broader and more dangerous and could thus not be realistically satisfied by political means. In the end, it is reasonable to conclude that al-Qaeda does aim to overthrow the existing political order in the Muslim world and replace it with a Taliban-like fanatical order, and it sees the United States as the anchor of the existing order.

U.S. House of Representatives, November 3, 2005.

But it is wrong and even dangerous to assume that this aim of al-Qaeda is their primary strength, or that it is the primary reason some in the Muslim countries have expressed sympathy with it. It is also wrong to assume that most Muslim groups, including local extremist groups, share its objectives. We must differentiate above all what we see as pervasive unfavorable views in the Muslim world from the views of al-Qaeda and like-minded groups. We must also differentiate between the causes of anti-Americanism and the causes of al-Qaeda terrorism. If we don't, we risk helping push vastly diverse groups together in a way that undermines our effort to defeat al-Qaeda.

It is no secret that the United States has faced significant resentment in the past few years in Muslim countries. Is this a consequence of a rising clash of values that plays into the strengths of al-Qaeda? Most public opinion surveys in Arab and Muslim countries indicate otherwise. In my most recent survey completed October 24th, 2005, (with Zogby International) among 3900 Arabs in Saudi Arabia, Egypt, the United Arab Emirates, Jordan, Lebanon, and Morocco, 78 percent say that they base their views on American policies and only 12 percent say they base them on values. When given a number of Western, Muslim, and other non-Western countries to choose from as possible places to live or send family members to study, most of them name Western European countries or the US and those who name the other countries, including Muslim Pakistan, are in the single digit.

More importantly the cause of the sympathy that some have for al-Qaeda is vastly different from al-Qaeda's own aims: When asked what aspects of al-Qaeda, if any, they sympathize with most, only six percent said they sympathize with the aim of establishing a Taliban-like state, and only seven percent sympathized with al-Qaeda's methods. On the other hand, 35 percent said they sympathize with its standing up to the US and another 19 percent said they sympathize with its stand on behalf of Muslim causes such as the issue of Palestine. Twenty-six percent said "none."

These results are bolstered by other findings. Contrary to the Taliban world view, the vast majority of Arabs (88 percent), including in Saudi Arabia, want women to have the right to work outside the home either always or when economically necessary. That is precisely why al-Qaeda primarily highlights issues that resonate with the public in its recruitment tapes and strategies, such as Iraq, Palestine, and authoritarianism. Even those who oppose the US presence in Iraq and want to see the US defeated do not wish to have Abu Musaab al-Zarqawi as their ruler. That is not what they wish for their own children.

It is dangerous to have a high level of resentment of the United States, whatever its sources, not only because it may increase the ability of al-Qaeda and its allies to recruit, but also because people's incentives to help the United States to effectively combat the threat of al-Qaeda diminishes. If they resent us more than they fear al-Qaeda, our challenge increases dramatically. If they start believing, as most have, that one of our real aims is to weaken the Muslim world, not just to defeat al-Qaeda, al-Qaeda gains by default.

What are the issues for most Muslims in their attitudes toward the U.S.? What makes a difference in bridging the gap? Before I make some ending remarks on this issue, allow me to note that the Muslim world is not the only place where resentment of the United States runs high today, so some of the answers are not particular to the Muslim world and may have to do with the role of the United States in the current international system. But in the Arab and Muslim world there are some specific issues that we can identify.

From the public opinion surveys that I have conducted in the Middle East, the single most important demographic variable in the Arab world explaining unfavorable views of the United States was income. It speaks volumes about the rampant poverty and unemployment, linked to poor education, which must be confronted.

Second, regional issues are paramount. Iraq is certainly central, but the Palestinian-Israeli conflict remains the "prism of pain" through which Arabs see the United States. This speaks to the need for active American diplomacy to resolve regional conflict.

Third, Zogby International polls have shown clearly that those who have visited the United States or studied here, and those who have had other encounters with Americans in the region, were far more disposed to having a favorable opinion of the United States than those who didn't. This speaks to the need for major public diplomacy programs to encourage interactions.

In the end, we must define the central enemy correctly. It is primarily al-Qaeda and its allies as organizations that must be defeated. It is not terrorism broadly and it is not Islamism broadly. Terrorism is not an ideology, and al-Qaeda's ideology of seeking a Taliban-like world order is its source of weakness in the Muslim world, not its source of strength. Our strategy must isolate it by addressing the issues that most Muslims care about—not blur the distinction between the vast majorities with whom we have no principled quarrel and those few whose aims can never be reconciled with America's.

Allow me to end on a cautionary note. In broadly defining the threat as "Islamic extremism" without specifying what we mean exactly, we risk much. In fighting serious threats like that posed by al-Qaeda there is certainly a need to rely in part on significant covert operations as well as overt ones. But, there have recently been reports of the possible broadening of such operations to include extremist groups, leaders, and clergy. My worry is that we do not have, and probably never will, the kind of expertise that allows us to determine who's a friend and who's an enemy simply on the basis of utterances. One could end up targeting as suspects millions of people in a world of 1.2 billion Muslims. Given the deficient expertise in our bureaucracies in the languages, religions, and cultures of the Muslim world, we risk the chance of mistakes that could backfire, relying on locals who have their own agendas, and wasting precious resources. The strategy in the first place must remain focused on the operational and the logistical, not on what people say.

EXPLORING THE ISSUE

Is Religious and Cultural Extremism a Global Security Threat?

Critical Thinking and Reflection

1. Is religious and cultural extremism on the rise or merely amplified by technology?
2. Are states and other actors equipped to confront such extremism?
3. What mechanisms exist for the international community to combat this violent behavior?
4. Can such extremism be defeated with violence and reprisals?
5. What is the role of philosophers and theologians in this struggle?

Is There Common Ground?

Most people in the world are not extremists given to violence in defense of religious or cultural goals. The vast majority of people view that behavior as abhorrent. This simple fact makes crafting a strategy to confront such behavior easily conceived. It does however require those who would exploit such behavior for crass political ends to be identified and sanctioned if that behavior is to be mitigated.

Scholars have been researching cultural and religious extremism for decades. The work is usually cyclical and results from the ebbs and flows of violence perpetrated by such groups.

Ultimately the question of whether religious or cultural extremism is a global security threat rests not with how we define such extremism or who believes what. It may simply be a function of two objective dimensions of a globalizing society. One is the ability of extremist groups to have global projection through technology and thus activate like-minded souls, and second is the prevalence of weapons of mass destruction that, if allowed to fall into extremist hands, will most definitely pose a grave threat to global security.

Additional Resources

Harris, Sam, *The End of Faith: Religion, Terror and the Future of Reason* (W.W. Norton & Company, 2004)

> This is a book on the controversial argument regarding religion and terror.

Hitchens, Christopher, *God Is Not Great: How Religion Poisons Everything* (Warner Books, 2007)

> Hitchens contends that organised religion is "violent, irrational, intolerant, allied to *racism, tribalism,* and *bigotry,* invested in *ignorance* and hostile to *free inquiry,* contemptuous of women and *coercive* toward children," and that accordingly it "ought to have a great deal on its conscience."

Juergensmeyer, Mark, *Terror in the Mind of God: The Global Rise of Religious Violence* (University of California Press, 2003)

> In this book, Juergensmeyer explores the 1993 World Trade Center explosion, Hamas suicide bombings, the Tokyo subway nerve gas attack, and the killing of abortion clinic doctors in the United States.

Larsson, J.P., *Understanding Religious Violence: Thinking Outside the Box on Terrorism* (Ashgate Publishing, 2004)

> In this book, Larsson investigates religious violence, terrorism and armed conflict in order to deliver the understanding required for a more peaceful world and to allow for a framework of conflict transformation.

ISSUE 17

Is a Nuclear Iran a Global Security Threat?

YES: Dore Gold, from "The Rise of Nuclear Iran: How Tehran Defies the West," *The Henry Jackson Society* (October 12, 2009)

NO: Scott Horton, from "Reality Check: Iran Is Not a Nuclear Threat," *The Christian Science Monitor* (September 17, 2010)

Learning Outcomes

After reading this issue, you should be able to:

- Have a clearer sense of Iran's potential to build and deliver a nuclear bomb.
- Understand the states and interests impacted by such a development.
- Appreciate what the options are for preventing such an occurrence.
- Grasp the regional implications for surrounding states including Israel and the United States.

ISSUE SUMMARY

YES: Dore Gold contends that a nuclear Iran is a global security threat because of the nature of the fundamentalist regime, its antipathy for both Israel and the United States, and its clear support for international terrorism. He argues that evidence clearly indicates that it is developing a bomb and its past behavior means it will be likely to use it.

NO: Scott Horton contends that through media misrepresentation, governmental propaganda, and outright falsehoods, the myth has been created that a nuclear Iran is a global security threat. Horton argues that Iran has acted within its rights and treaty obligations and as such presents no more a threat than any other country that may or may not develop nuclear weapons.

The issue of nuclear proliferation has been a global concern since the first atomic explosion at Alamogordo, New Mexico, in 1945. That event ushered in a new era in weaponry, war, strategy, and tactics that still resonates today. Each successive nuclear power of the proclaimed (United States, Russia, China, Great Britain, France, India, and Pakistan) and unproclaimed (Israel and South Africa) nuclear club of states has been deeply aware of the issue of proliferation. In fact, all of these states to one degree or another have largely agreed on the need to maintain the exclusivity of the nuclear club.

The fall of the Soviet Union did much to change the terrain of nuclear proliferation policy. For decades, the United States and the Soviet Union agreed on the need for a nonproliferation regime and worked, cajoled, and threatened allies and others not to develop nuclear weapons. This often had the desired effect of limiting the size of the nuclear club and, in particular, incentivizing those states that could develop weapons (e.g., Italy, Spain, Turkey, East Germany, and North Korea) to keep from doing so.

Now with only one remaining superpower, many states view their security as dependent upon their own forces and less on their ability to develop a strong relationship with one superpower over another. This is certainly true for states that had traditionally opposed U.S. policy and sought support from the Soviet Union.

Essentially, many regional states with interests opposed to the United States now see no countervailing superpower to protect their interests and thus face a bandwagon or balancing dilemma. Do we move toward the United States as the preeminent power to satisfy our interests or balance against it by developing our own regional weapons deterrent to U.S. hegemony? States across the globe chose either of these approaches and acted accordingly. Since many states such as Brazil, Italy, Spain, France, Britain, and China among others had developed weapons production capacities, states such as North Korea, Iran, Syria, Libya, and Iraq among others began pursuing technologies and delivery systems (missiles) that could expand their own deterrent capability. Some vigorously pursued the nuclear option.

Iran is an example of one state that in rhetoric and actions has chosen the path of balancing against U.S. policy interests in a myriad of ways. They have supported groups opposed to U.S. policy interests, funded terrorism against Israel and the United States, and of course to some degree pursued nuclear technology with the assistance of the French, Chinese, and Russians among others. The Arab states in the region along with Israel and the states of the Indian subcontinent all view this possible development with concern. Each actor has different but intermingled reasons for fearing an Iranian fundamentalist government with a nuclear option.

There are others, however, who view the acquisition of nuclear weapons by Iran as merely an evolution of proliferation with no more destabilizing an effect as Israel, Pakistan, or India's acquisition. They contend that Iran has security and political interests like any other state and when or if they develop such weapons will utilize their presence as a deterrent to attack rather than a wedge to threaten and intimidate their neighbors and adversaries.

In the following selections, the authors reflect two competing views of the Iranian threat. Gold articulates a commonly held view within the media and within U.S. and Israeli policy circles that Iran's effort at nuclear acquisition is an existential threat to western interests and represents a fundamental shift in the balance of power in the Middle East. By implication Gold suggest that any policy aimed at thwarting this effort is justified. Horton takes the view that Iran's ambitions like that of Pakistan and India before it does not constitute a shift in power but rather a defensive posture in reaction to the U.S. invasion of Iraq and western presence in the Arab gulf states.

Although both analyses agree that Iran pursues interests antithetical to U.S. policy, they have different conclusions regarding Iran's current level of security threat and future scenarios.

Whatever one's perspective, one fact is certainly clear: States like Iran, Saudi Arabia, North Korea, Syria, and others will get closer to having the ability to produce nuclear technology and weaponry. The current proliferation regime can mitigate these developments but probably not stop them. Thus, the world community will have to deal with nuclear proliferation and the "threats," real or perceived, that these weapons create. The result will be a greater probability of a regional nuclear war.

YES

The Rise of Nuclear Iran: How Tehran Defies the West

*B*y kind invitation of Patrick Mercer MP, Dore Gold, Israel's former UN Ambassador and special advisor to Prime Minister Netanyahu, spoke of the very real threat posed to global security by Iran's nuclear ambitions. He explained how a nuclear armed Iran poses a very different threat to other nuclear armed states. The world's biggest sponsor of international terrorism, a nuclear armed Iran would provide an umbrella of protection to numerous terrorist organisations, greatly reducing the ability of states to deal with these threats effectively. The meeting was held at the Houses of Parliament on 12 October 2009.

This subject, the rise of nuclear Iran, relates to the security of all of us. Iran's ambitions, Iran's missile programme, Iran's nuclear programme, relate to the security not just of Israel but of the entire Middle East and I would say the world.

Let me begin with a fundamental question: Why do we suspect Iran? Why do we think Iran is developing nuclear weapons? When the October talks in Geneva were about to begin there were Western diplomats who were still saying, "Let Iran convince us that this is a civilian nuclear programme."

Why is it that I don't buy that Iran's nuclear programme is purely civil? The easiest answer to that is the fact that Iran today has the third largest reserves of oil in the world and the second largest reserves of natural gas in the world, so why the desire to develop nuclear power to provide electricity?

Nonetheless, I'm going to accept half the Iranian argument because in 2006, the Iranian energy minister noted that Iran is not investing sufficiently in the maintenance of its oil fields, and a lot of that has to do with Western sanctions on Iran. As a result, he predicted that by 2015 the decline of the Iranian oil fields will lead to a situation where Iran no longer exports oil and all production will be solely for internal purposes. So if we take his argument, one could understand that maybe they have to turn to nuclear energy. It also turns out that Iran has domestic uranium ore that they can mine, so if they were seeking a nuclear alternative to petroleum, they would have uranium as a source of electricity.

Why, even if we accept the argument that their oil fields are declining, is that still a phoney argument? Because it turns out that if you look at the size of the uranium deposits in Iran, they aren't that great. Those working in the US state department have estimated that if Iranians built six reactors for domestic

From *The Henry Jackson Society,* October 12, 2009.

production, their uranium reserves would be sufficient to run those reactors for just 12 years. You don't build a whole industry if all you're going to get is 12 years out of it.

So my argument is that the uranium in Iran may not be sufficient for producing electricity, but it is certainly sufficient for manufacturing of atomic bombs.

Let me add one other element. The concern of the international community since the disclosure of the first uranium enrichment plant in 2002 at Natanz, has been the question of why Iran has to enrich uranium domestically. Most countries with civilian nuclear programmes don't enrich their own uranium, they import enriched uranium; Spain and Sweden for example. Indeed, if all its stock is sufficient for just 12 years with six reactors, they're going to have to import anyway, so why go through this expensive process now of building enrichment reactors? Again, all this points to a different intent. It has to do with developing an atomic weapons programme.

A number of other pieces of information have come together that should cause a great deal of alarm in people who follow this subject. First of all the quantities of uranium that have already been enriched. At the time of US elections in 2008, the IAEA said Iran had produced 839 kg of low-enriched uranium. By August 2009, that number had reached 1,508 kg. What you need for an atomic bomb is 700 kg of low-enriched uranium which you put back into modified centrifuges to reach the higher-enriched weapons grade uranium. That 700 kg of low-enriched uranium will yield about 20–25 kg of weapons-grade uranium, meaning that Iran can now produce two atomic bombs.

The second element that has us concerned has to do with the sensitive information the IAEA has been disclosing, provided to it by various Western intelligence agencies. For instance, the CIA laptop containing detailed drawings of how to build a nuclear warhead and optimum altitudes for flight. You can say that's information the CIA put forward for its own reasons, but the IAEA, in 2008, lectured to ambassadors about that information and other information it received. Some of you may have heard of the secret annex to that report that was not disclosed to the public. I can only read a few lines:

"The agency has information, known as the 'alleged studies,' that the Ministry of Defence of Iran has conducted, and may still be conducting a comprehensive programme aimed at the development of a nuclear payload, to be delivered using the Shahab 3 missile system."

The Shahab 3 is a 1,300 km-range missile with the capacity to hit Saudi Arabia and Israel and here the IAEA is saying that Iranians seem to be designing how to outfit the warhead of that missile with nuclear weapons. We are also seeing in Iran the development of a robust ballistic missile system that goes far beyond what many people believe.

When you put these elements together, it all points to a full-blown nuclear weapons programme, and nothing else. I think what's also a concern is the fact that Iran is not a "status-quo" country. There are countries in the world that are happy with what they have, that aren't interested in expansion or intruding on their neighbours and basically just want to be left on their own. Then there are states that are active, that are actively intervening in the affairs of their neighbours and have interests well beyond their own borders and Iran is really in that latter category. It is Iran that is engaged in the insurgency in Afghanistan, providing the Taleban, who were their enemies 10 years ago with weaponry and other forms of assistance to fight US and UK forces in that country. It is Iran that has been engaged in Iraq, particularly through the Shiite militias in southern Iraq. It is Iran which declared, earlier this year that Bahrain, an independent kingdom, is a province of Iran. And that came from individuals very close to the supreme leader, Ayatollah Khameini. Iran is active in Lebanon; it created and sustains Hezbollah. It's involved in the Gaza Strip, in Egypt, Sudan and Yemen.

So if you take the fact that Iran is one of the largest supporters of international terrorism today, and you team that up with the nuclear capabilities that I've been describing, you have a security situation which the West has not yet seen. This is an entirely new situation that we have to anticipate and understand. And it makes the handling of the Iranian issue all the more urgent.

What makes the problem all the more difficult is that we have been facing in the last few years a number of influential organisations and individuals who have been purposefully understating the problem. First and foremost among these is the US National Intelligence Estimate (NIE) from December 2007.

It stated, "We assess with high confidence that until the fall of 2003, Iran was working to develop nuclear weapons, but we judge that in the fall of 2003, Tehran halted its nuclear weapons programme."

When the US NIE says the programme's been halted, most people think that's the problem solved. The problem with the report is that it deals only with certain aspects of the programme. Now with hindsight, looking at recent reports of a secret uranium enrichment site constructed near Qom, these words should be outrageous to us. When President Obama disclosed this new facility, senior members of his administration gave a briefing that they put on the website saying, "We have known about this secret facility for several years."

That takes us back to 2007 at least, and yet the NIE said that uranium enrichment work had halted. In other words, the US probably knew about the Qom facility, and yet chose to pretend it was finished.

This is just one example of how this whole problem has not been properly dealt with. We were even told that the supreme leader had issued a fatwa declaring the acquisition of nuclear weapons to be immoral. So the message was, be calm and don't worry. Yet there is no nuclear fatwa. I asked a top Iranian scholar in the US, and he could not find the fatwa. This is a falsehood, but it's another example of the falsehoods that have been misleading people on this issue.

I want to ask you the following question: What does it mean to have an Iran with nuclear missiles? Most people think of it like Russia and the US having nuclear weapons. You press a button to launch; they work as a deterrent and so on. I have a different, more realistic scenario. I think we have the problem that the world's biggest supporter of international terrorism is about to get a nuclear umbrella, and that means that terrorist groups will have a protective umbrella over them.

The whole point of George W. Bush's decision to remove the Taliban after 9/11 was to send a very clear message: "You attack the American homeland and we will take down your regime."

This is probably why the US is so determined to stay in Afghanistan in spite of all the difficulties. But fast forward to 2012. Iran has operational nuclear weapons that can strike deep into Europe, and eventually towards the Eastern seaboard of the US. Will the US, UK and NATO as a whole have the same freedom of manoeuvre to say to states that support terrorism, "We will take you down if you attack us?" Will, the US Congress authorise sending forces abroad against a state armed with nuclear weapons? In other words the entire balance in the War on Terror shifts, because the state that is the largest global sponsor of terrorism today now has nuclear capabilities.

One further, crucial mistake people make is to believe that Iran's protective umbrella will only extend to Shiite terror groups. But Iran supports the Taliban in Afghanistan. When Al-Qaeda had to find new sanctuary after the 2001 invasion, it went to two places immediately: Pakistan and Iran, and there was a huge al-Qaeda presence in Iran, and there is still an al-Qaeda presence today.

In Azerbaijan, which is a Shiite state, there's a Sunni insurgency fighting the Shiite regime, but for reasons of geopolitics, Iran supports the Sunni insurgency against the Shiite government of Azerbaijan because it's pro-American.

What I am trying to suggest is that this nuclear umbrella of Iran will unfurl and will be able to provide protection, not just to Shiite Hezbollah, but to Sunni organisations such as al-Qaeda and Hamas.

In terms of how this threat is viewed not just in the West, but in the Arab world, for instance Saudi Arabia, I have no doubt that if the doors were closed, the Saudis would agree with most of what I have just said. People forget that in 1996, there was an organisation called Hezbollah al-Hejaz, or "Saudi Hezbollah" operating inside Saudi territory, which killed 19 US airmen helping train the Saudi air force, and a number of Saudis in an attack.

I believe there is a lot of common interest in the Middle East to see Iran halted. I personally believe this is best facilitated through discussion with Israelis and regional security forces, but we shouldn't make this all very public. It should be handled quietly.

In fact, a major problem comes from Europe in the form of EU funding for NGOs that are involved in the Arab-Israeli conflict, but which pursue agendas which are incompatible with member state policies. I like transparency, but there is an extensive amount of EU intervention in our conflict that is incompatible with the security of Israel.

As for Russia, for its own commercial reasons, it has decided to complete the shared reactor at Bushir that was begun with the Germans during the time of the Shah. The Russians claim they have an arrangement with the Iranians to supply them with uranium and to take out the used fuel rods from that reactor so they cannot be reprocessed to produce plutonium. I simply would not rely on Iran to be honest on this.

If the international community doesn't act, could Israel act alone, without the US? I will say that Israel has been thinking about this problem for a very long time. A country does not develop advanced satellite technology if it's just concerned with monitoring Hezbollah operatives across the border. The Israeli air force has been training for action and all options are on the table, but I would say the official position is that there is hope, even at this late date, that the key players in the international community will take action. This is not just a security interest for Israel, but the Arab states and I would say Europe as well.

So how can we stop Iran without military force? Iran is dependent upon imports for 40 per cent of its consumption. If the EU and US said, "You cannot do business in the EU and US if you sell gasoline to Iran," that would drastically reduce the gasoline supply, push up the prices internally and destabalise the regime. That's effective action that doesn't require a Security Council resolution; that doesn't require Russian acquiescence and that doesn't require the firing of a single shot. What it requires is the political will.

I will finish by asking you to remember North Korea. In 2002, it suddenly made a decision to evict the IAEA nuclear monitors and tear the seals off their nuclear reactors. By 2006, it conducted its first nuclear test and in 2009 we saw the second. In other words, North Korea succeeded in breaking out of the IAEA's limitations and conducting tests.

Iran followed all this closely and unfortunately, what they are internalising today is that the West has little will. In July, the G8 declared Iran had until September to put forward a serious proposal on their nuclear programme. The Iranians sent a five-page memo which frankly was mostly drivel. Now the deadline has passed and nothing has happened. The next thing that has happened has been the disclosure of the secret nuclear facility at Qom. So what have the Iranians learned? They have learned that they can break every deadline and every barrier and nothing happens.

You might think that Iran's behaviour at present is brazen and risky. It looks much less brazen and risky if you recall how often Iran has already defied the West and got away with it. It is my belief that Iran is now not far from the short sprint to developing weapons-grade uranium.

Scott Horton ➡ **NO**

Reality Check: Iran Is Not a Nuclear Threat

Forget the neoconservative hype. The facts show Iran is not and has not been a nuclear threat to either the United States or Israel

Politicians, lobbyists, and propagandists have spent nearly two decades pushing the lie that Iran poses a nuclear weapons threat to the United States and Israel. After a brief respite in the intensity of the wolf cries over the past two years, the neoconservative movement has decided to relaunch the "Must Bomb Iran" brand.

The fact that Iran is not and has not been a nuclear threat to either nation is rendered irrelevant by a narrative of universal "concern" about its nuclear program.

US Media Distortions

In mid-August, for example, after *The New York Times* quite uncharacteristically ran a piece diminishing the supposed danger of Iranian nukes, the story was misrepresented in newspapers and on TV stations across the country in the most frightening terms. As MSNBC's news reader put it that afternoon: "Intelligence sources say Iran is only one year away from a nuclear bomb!"

On August 13, on Fox News, former US ambassador to the UN John Bolton implicitly urged Israel to attack Iran's new light-water reactor at Bushehr before it began "functioning," the implication being that the reactor represented some sort of dire threat. But the facts are not on Mr. Bolton's side. The Bushehr reactor is not useful for producing weapons-grade plutonium, and the Russians have a deal to keep all the waste themselves.

On September 6, the International Atomic Energy Agency (IAEA) released a new paper on the implementation of Iran's Safeguards Agreement which reported that the agency has "continued to verify the non-diversion of declared nuclear material in Iran to any military or other special purpose."

Yet despite the IAEA report and clear assertions to the contrary, news articles that followed were dishonest to the extreme, interpreting this clean bill of health as just another wisp of smoke indicating nuclear fire in a horrifying near-future.

From *The Christian Science Monitor* by Scott Horton, September 17, 2010. Copyright © 2010 by Scott Horton. Reprinted by permission of the author.

A *Washington Post* article published the very same day led the way with the aggressive and misleading headline "UN Report: Iran stockpiling nuclear materials," "shorthanding" the facts right out of the narrative. The facts are that Iran's terrifying nuclear "stockpile" is a small amount of uranium enriched to industrial grade levels for use in its domestic energy and medical isotope programs, all of it "safeguarded" by the IAEA.

More Sensational Claims

If the smokescreen wasn't thick enough, late last week a group of Marxist holy warrior exiles called the Mujahadeen-e-Khalq, working with the very same neoconservatives who sponsored Ahmad Chalabi's Iraqi National Congress—which manufactured so much of the propaganda that convinced the American people to support the invasion of that country—accused the Iranian government of building a secret nuclear enrichment facility buried deep in tunnels near Qazvin.

Headlines once again blared in total negligence and without verification that here indeed was, an official told Fox News, proof that Iran has a "hidden, secret nuclear weapons program." TV news anchors on every channel furiously mopped sweat from their brows, hearts-a-tremor. When will the forces of good rise to stop this evil?!

Yet even US officials quickly admitted that they've known about these tunnels for years. "[T]here's no reason at this point to think it's nuclear," one US official said—a quote that appeared in Fox's article, but only after five paragraphs of breathless allegations. All day long, top-of-the-hour news updates on TV and radio let the false impression stand.

IAEA inspectors have had open access to the gas conversion facility at Isfahan, the enrichment facility at Natanz, and the new lightwater reactor at Bushehr, as well as the secondary enrichment facility under construction at Qom.

An Ignored Clean Bill of Health

The September 6 IAEA report confirming for the zillionth time the non-diversion of nuclear material should be the last word on the subject until the next time they say the same thing: Iran, a long-time signatory of the Nuclear Non-Proliferation Treaty (NPT), is not in violation of its Safeguards Agreement.

So what's all the hubbub about Iran's "nuclear defiance" and "danger"?

The IAEA's latest report does note that Iran has "not provided the necessary cooperation to permit the Agency to confirm that all nuclear material in Iran is in peaceful activities." Indeed, the agency's frequent mentions of Iran's "lack of full cooperation" is a big reason why US media reports portray Iran in ominous terms.

But here, too, US media frequently miss the point. Never mind that 118 nations around the world have signed a statement criticizing the IAEA's "peaceful activities" conclusion as a departure from standard verification language. More broadly, Iran's "lack of full cooperation" by itself is an outcome of Western bullying and propaganda.

Real Reason for Lack of Cooperation

The US and the UN, acting upon no legitimate authority whatsoever, have demanded that Iran submit to an Additional Protocol to the Safeguards Agreement, which would allow endless inspections on issues not directly related to Iran's use of nuclear materials. They have also demanded that Iran cease all uranium enrichment and submit to an endless regime of questions based mostly on the "alleged studies" documents, which several sources have said are forgeries posing as a pilfered laptop of a dead Iranian nuclear scientist. [**Editor's note:** *The original version of this article misstated an implication of the Additional Protocol.*]

These separate, UN Security Council-mandated investigations have even demanded blueprints for Shahab 3 missiles—a subject far removed from hexafluoride gas or any legitimate IAEA function. In 2003, Iran voluntarily agreed to the extra burden of the unratified Additional Protocol during "good faith negotiations" with the so-called "E-3," Britain, France, and Germany, acting on behalf of the US. When those negotiations broke down, Iran withdrew in 2006.

With these details left out of the discussion, the impression is left that Iran is refusing to abide by international law, when in fact, it is completely within its NPT obligations.

An Outrageous Standard

Meanwhile, Washington continues to apply to Iran the outrageous standard it used in the run-up to the Iraq war: an unfriendly nation must "prove" it doesn't have dangerous weapons or a secret program to make them—or potentially face military action.

"Proving a negative" is, to say the least, a difficult obligation to meet: You say you haven't read Webster's Dictionary cover to cover? Prove it!

The bottom line is that Iran is still within its unalienable rights to peaceful nuclear technology under the NPT and the Safeguards Agreement—a point even Tehran's fiercest critics (grudgingly) acknowledge. The only issues it is defying are the illegitimate sanctions and demands of the US and UN, which themselves defy logic and sense.

Journalists' Ethical Obligation

It is far past time for the members of the American media to get their act together and begin asking serious follow-up questions of the politicians, "experts," and lobbyists they interview on the subject of Iran's nuclear program.

Many of these same journalists still have the blood of hundreds of thousands of innocent Iraqis on their hands from the months they spent continuously and uncritically parroting the lies, half-truths, and distortions of agenda-driven Iraqi dissidents and their neocon champions who pushed us into the Iraq war.

Perhaps this is their shot at redemption.

EXPLORING THE ISSUE

Is a Nuclear Iran a Global Security Threat?

Critical Thinking and Reflection

1. Is Iran different than other states that have pursued nuclear weapons?
2. Has Iran done anything to indicate that it would use nuclear weapons, for example, against Israel, were it to acquire them?
3. Can a nonproliferation regime survive Iran's acquisition of nuclear weapons?
4. What is the likelihood of preemption by either Israel or the Unites States should Iran develop such weaponry?
5. Can a coalition be fashioned to prevent such acquisition?

Is There Common Ground?

The nuclear proliferation issue is a constant source of anxiety for nuclear and nonnuclear states alike. Who will join the club next? Are they a stable regime? What are their interests and goals and would they be predisposed to using nuclear weapons to achieve their regional interests? Views about these issues are divergent and reflect the differences that exist in the global community. Most people believe that more nuclear powers mean the greater chance for a nuclear exchange. Most also believe that the control of nuclear weaponry by a few means that those states posses the upper hand on the adjudication of global issues and interests.

In the Middle East and Persian Gulf, the stakes are even higher. Global oil supplies, the Israeli-Palestinian enmity, terrorism, Islamic fundamentalism, and U.S. geopolitical interests combine to make for a volatile and unstable mix. The only nuclear powers in the region are Israel, India, and Pakistan. If we exclude India and Pakistan for a moment, we see that a nuclear fundamentalist Iran forces the world community to examine several important questions. Would a nuclear Iran change the balance of power between Israel and its Arab neighbors? Would Israel allow such a development or preempt as they did in Osirak, Iraq, in 1979? Would Iran be predisposed to distributing nuclear technology to terrorist groups they support, like the Hezbollah of Lebanon?

The only area of consensus is that the more nuclear weapons technology spreads the greater its likelihood of use. Thus, whether one believes in the peacefulness of the Iranian regime or not, the spread of nuclear weapons only increases the likelihood of another Hiroshima or Nagasaki.

Additional Resources

Evans, Michael and Corsi, Jerome, *Showdown with Nuclear Iran: Radical Islam's Messianic Mission to Destroy Israel and Cripple the United States* (Thomas Nelson, 2006)

> This accuont is an examination of how Iran's president (a radical Shiite zealot) believes he has a "divine mission" to usher in the apocalypse and thereby herald the second coming of a Shia Muslim messiah-and how he is trying to achieve this by building his arsenal and threatening to cripple America and destroy Israel in a nuclear holocaust.

Jafarzadeh, Alireza, *The Iran Threat: President Ahmadinejad and the Coming Nuclear Crisis* (Palgrave Macmillan, 2007)

> This book outlines the inner workings and plans of Iran's mullahs. With access to dissident groups inside Iran, Alireza Jafarzadeh traces President Ahmadinejad's radical roots and involvement in terror attacks to his impact on Iran's weapons program.

Ritter, Scott, *Target Iran: The Truth About the White House's Plans for Regime Change* (Nation Books, 2006)

> Ritter claims that Iraq had been effectively disarmed were ignored by both the Bush administration and the mainstream media. In the wake of the debacle, Ritter has been vindicated. Now Ritter, a former UN weapons inspector, has set his sights on the White House's hyping of Iran's alleged nuclear weapons program.

Venter, A.J., *Iran's Nuclear Option* (Casemate, 2005)

> This book details the extent to which Iran's weapons program has developed, and the clandestine manner in which its nuclear technology has been acquired.

ISSUE 18

Will China Be the Next Superpower?

YES: Shujie Yao, from "Can China Really Become the Next Superpower?" *China Policy Institute* (April 2007)

NO: Minxin Pei, from "China's Not a Superpower," *The Diplomat* (2010)

Learning Outcomes

After reading this issue, you should be able to:

- Understand the strengths and weaknesses of the Chinese political and economic situation.
- Grasp the challenges it faces amidst its current economic growth and expansion.
- Understand how its political culture impacts its global role.
- Appreciate the complexity of such rapid development and how the United States and the rest of the world views China's rise to prominence.

ISSUE SUMMARY

YES: Shujie Yao analyzes the current state of the Chinese economy and policy and postulates several possible scenarios for development. Ultimately, he surmises that China will develop as the next superpower by the mid-twenty-first century.

NO: Minxin Pei argues that the political and economic situation in China is not as stable and robust as we believe. He contends that there are structural economic concerns and growing political unrest that will mitigate China's ascension to superpower status and for the foreseeable future.

In 1979, four years after the death of Mao and the reign of the Gang of Four, Deng Xiaoping emerged as the supreme leader of the Chinese Communist Party. At that moment, he set China on a course of largely managed capitalist economic growth and expansion, military modernization and reform, and consequently profound social and political change. This was all engineered from the center of the political system and under the control of the Communist party. The impact of this change in Chinese policy has been monumental. China now is one of the fastest growing economies on earth, producing goods and services at a rate of sustained growth unseen in the global economy. Its share of the export/import market has grown exponentially such that little is consumed or used that does not have a China link. With 1.3 billion people, China now has multiple economies where some 300 million live much as people in the United States and West do, while some 800,000 million live in agrarian poverty and subsistence levels.

With this growth have come infrastructure development, urban expansion, monetary wealth creation, and profound societal change. Although the Chinese communist party maintains tight control, the society and economy continue to revolutionize themselves. Scholars and policymakers marvel at this change while trying to analyze its short- and long-term impact. Opinions vary as to how sustainable this growth is and whether it be managed and controlled by an authoritarian regime. Further, there is wide disagreement as to whether China's resurgence is creating a superpower or paper tiger and how strong the educational, social, and political foundation on which this growth is based really is.

China faces profound challenges with this growth. How does it maintain political control and keep true democratic reforms at bay? How does it maintain economic growth as China becomes even more tied to the global economy with its vast nuances and competing trends? How does it modernize its military and technologies to adapt to China's growing status and how does it exercise that status in the world of global diplomatic relations where its presence has not been strong?

Over the past 30 years, China has overcome its Maoist experiment and earlier colonial history to emerge as a vibrant growing economy. GDP growth rates alone have been between 8% and 15% per year for several years. The ingenuity, hard work, and vast resources of China have been unleashed in a mixed economic set of policies and the result has been vast increases in production, huge amounts of foreign investment, and vast wealth creation that is transforming China. On these points all scholars agree.

China's 1.3 billion people also are subjected to immense poverty in the countryside and in selected urban areas. They have significant infrastructure issues left over from the communist era and the political system leaves little room for expression and community empowerment for literally billions. China is in many ways the best global example of a dramatic play with important and broadly defined characters acting out on a global stage and it is unclear as to where the story will go.

Several key variables will determine China's ultimate direction. First, China is in the midst of a strong growth and investment phase that is directly tied to this era of globalization. In fact, it would have been impossible for China to have grown so quickly in the last 15 years without the presence of globalization. This means that many factors outside of China's control will impact its development including the direction of the U.S., European, and other economies and the ability of China to embrace technological changes.

Second, the enormous growth of a strong middle class in China raises questions as to political expression for these tens of millions and what values this middle class will embrace. Will they be content with an authoritarian model or will they demand greater forms of expression that tear at the foundational fabric of the political system.

Third, can current labor supply in China and costs be maintained amidst a growing and interdependent global economy? Already, there are signs of breaks in the China advantage in this area as other regions of the world compete for manufacturing jobs based on cheap labor costs.

Fourth, will China be able to translate economic growth into political influence and power in places like the Middle East, Africa, and Latin America? Superpower status is in part a function of global influence and reach, and China has yet to show the will to exercise that reach and influence. Can China develop the military force structure for such power projection and what drain will this place on the civilian economy. It remains an open question as to whether it aspires to such a role.

In the following selections, two authors explore a question that will be of primary focus for global scholars for the next decade. Will China be the next superpower? In the YES selection, Shujie Yao summarizes his analysis determining that the probability of China's emergence as a superpower is great given the presence of certain key variables. These include prudent and careful management of a mixed economy, available labor pool, access to resources, and of course the capacity to innovate. Minxin Pei points to structural defects in the Chinese (and Indian) economies and systems that preclude superpower status. These include income inequality, infrastructure obstacles, bureaucratic inefficiencies, and a less than sophisticated notion of capital accumulation and reinvestment.

Fundamentally, both analyses agree that the potential for China's rise to superpower status is there, yet both see different scenarios as to how and in what form that potential will be realized.

YES ↙

Shujie Yao

Can China Really Become
the Next Superpower?

This paper aims to answer the question whether China can really become the next superpower through assessing China's economic performance in the past three decades and evaluating the key constraints on China's future development. It presents a few possible scenarios to sketch how likely it is that China will become the next superpower towards the middle of the 21st century.

Introduction

China has been successful in the last three decades under economic reform and a policy of openness. The economic miracle has been due to Deng Xiaoping's gradualism and pragmatism in economic reforms and social changes, the smooth transformation to a mixed economy and the shift of development strategy from closed-door to openness.

China's fast growth has been accompanied by many difficult social, political and environmental problems. Rising inequality, persistence of absolute poverty, environmental degradation, corruption, and declining standards of traditional Chinese moral and social values are key constraints and challenges to China's further growth. China's future depends on its ability to solve these problems.

The most pessimistic scenario is that China is unable to face up to those challenges and constraints, rendering the country vulnerable to polarisation, corruption and financial/material crises with little hope of becoming a real superpower. The most optimistic scenario is that China is able to maintain high economic growth, to reduce inequality and poverty, to improve the natural environment, and to overcome the potential problems of energy and material shortage. In this scenario, China will overtake Japan by 2017 and the US by 2037. China will also become a world leader of science and technology, possessing the world's most advanced space, nuclear, computer, biological, medical, energy and military technologies.

What Constitutes a Superpower

The US and the former USSR are two examples of superpowers. The US has been the most powerful country in all aspects: the size of its economy, per capita gross domestic product (GDP), military strength, science and technologies, and international influence. The former USSR used to have huge military capability and influence over the world order. It was the only country able to challenge the US before the end of the cold war. Its economic strength was by no means comparable to that of the US. The key question is whether there will be another superpower in the next few decades, and if yes, which country? Russia, India, Japan or Germany is unlikely to become the next superpower for various reasons. Hence, one likely candidate must be China.

However, even if China can become the world's largest economy, it does not mean that China will automatically become a superpower. There are some other conditions for China to be a real superpower. Such conditions should include the level of per capita income, social justice and income equality, the ability to become a world leader of science and technology, and the ability to influence regional and global peace and order.

China's Rise and Its Significance in the World Economy

China's economic reform is the largest project in human history because it has affected a population 16 times that of the four Asian Tigers (South Korea, Taiwan, Singapore and Hong Kong) combined, and more than 10 times that of Japan.

During 1978–2006, China achieved an average annual growth of 9.6% in real GDP. Two different ways are currently used to measure GDP: in nominal dollars using official exchange rates and in [the purchasing power in American dollars of other currencies—in this case, the Chinese currency] dollars using the actual buying power of currencies. Measured in PPP dollars, China's GDP in 2006 was $10.5 trillion, compared with $12.9 trillion for the US, $13.0 trillion for the EU, $4.1 trillion for Japan, $3.9 trillion for India, $2.6 trillion for Germany and $1.9 trillion for the UK. China is the third largest economic bloc after the EU and the US and the second largest economy after the US. PPP dollars tend to overstate the level of GDP for poor countries like China and India. Measured in nominal dollars, China was the fourth largest economy after the US, Japan, and Germany, with a total GDP of $2.72 trillion (20.94 trillion [the official Chinese currency]) in 2006. China will overtake Germany to become the third largest economy in 2007 or 2008.

In the last thirty years, China's real GDP increased 13 fold, real per capita GDP over nine fold, and real per capita consumption more than six fold. Many consumer goods and services that were virtually unknown in 1978 have become daily necessities in Chinese households today, including colour TVs, telephones, motor cycles and computers. In 1978, China ranked number 23 in world trade. By 2006, China was the third largest trading nation in both imports and exports, with a total trade volume of $1.8 trillion, generating a surplus of $177.8 billion. China had little foreign direct investment (FDI) before 1992 but has been competing with the US in recent years as the world's largest host of foreign capital.

China is the world's largest producer and consumer of many key industrial and agricultural products, including steel, cement, coal, fertilizers, colour TVs, cloth, cereals, meat, fish, vegetables, fruits, cotton and rapeseeds. By 2006, China had constructed 3.48 million km of highways and 45,460 km of motorways, or five times the total length of motorways in the UK. China is currently constructing the same length of the entire UK motorway system every two years. In 1978, China had only 598 universities recruiting 0.4 million students; by 2006, it had 1,800 universities recruiting over 5 million students and sending another 120,000 students abroad.

High and sustained economic growth has led to rapid industrialisation and urbanization. During 1978–2006, agriculture's share in national GDP declined from 28% to 11%, agricultural employment in national employment from 71% to 45%, rural population in national population from 82% to 57%.

Why China Succeeds

China's economic miracle can be attributed to its institutional reforms, transforming the former plan system to a mixed plan and market system. The approach of reform is gradual, guided by Deng's theory of 'Crossing the River by Feeling the Stones.' The reform was carefully managed with appropriate experimentation, accurate timing, correct sequence and manageable scale. Reforms progressed from agriculture and the countryside to the urban economy and state-owned enterprises, from the real economic sectors to the banking and other financial sectors, and from prices to the labour and capital markets, etc.

Adopting appropriate development strategies is another reason for China's success. Development strategies are shifted from import substitution to export-push and from closed-door to openness and globalisation.

China's reforms have been guided by some important development theories unavailable from existing economics text books. One such theory is 'Spots to Lead Areas' development, which is featured with some growing centres propelling the growth in the surrounding areas and then remote regions through the transmission of growth momentum incubated in the growth centres. In the early 1980s, China established the special economic zones and open coastal cities to be the country's growth centres.

Another theory is 'Walking with Two Legs' development to improve China's capability in science, technology and innovation. China has relied heavily on foreign technologies through direct purchase or indirectly through FDI to improve productivity. It has also invested heavily to improve its ability in technological innovation and knowledge creation at home.

Constraints and Challenges

Although China has made tremendous progress in the last thirty years, it is now faced with many challenges and constraints. The most important problems include high and rising inequality, corruption and persistency of poverty, environmental pollution, and over-dependency on non-renewable resources. All these problems could loom so large that China may become vulnerable to various crises. China's GDP is about 5% (14% in PPP terms) of the world total but it consumes more than one-third of the world's outputs of coal, steel and cement. China's past pattern of industrial growth is unlikely to be sustainable in the future.

Rising inequality and corruption are two major social and political issues which can render China vulnerable to social and political unrest, causing unwanted disruption to its economic progress.

Current Policies and Possible Scenarios

The government is aware of China's development constraints and challenges. Some policies have been implemented to resolve these problems through building a harmonious society and reducing income inequality. In agriculture, more land will be converted into forest and grass. Agricultural production will become more efficient and less dependent on chemical fertilisers and pesticides. More investments will be made in the rural areas to improve farm incomes and reduce urban-rural and inter-regional inequality. More effective measures are being adopted to combat corruption and strengthen the leadership of the Communist Party. Huge investments have been planned for the next 30 years to greatly improve the country's human capital, research and innovation capability in the strategic areas of space, energy, environment, computer and internet, biology and medicine, military affairs and defence, transportation and telecommunications, etc.

If the current policies are ineffective, China's growth can slow down, leading to higher unemployment and more poverty. In this scenario, the chance of China becoming a superpower will be small. If all policies are effectively implemented, China will be able to maintain high growth, to reduce inequality, poverty, and corruption, to improve production efficiency and the environment. In this scenario, China will overtake Japan to become the second largest economy by 2017 and the US by 2037, and will become another superpower. This prediction is based on the assumption that all countries continue to grow in the next 30 years following their own growth trends in the past three decades and that GDP is measured in nominal dollars, not in PPP dollars. By 2037, China will also become a world leader of science and technology and have sufficient military and/or diplomatic capability to compete with the US in maintaining regional and global peace and order.

Further Readings

Hu, Angang (2007), *'Five Major Scale Effects of China's Rise on the World,'* paper presented to the 18th Annual Conference of Chinese Economic Association (UK), April, University of Nottingham.

Hu, Angang (2007), 'National Life Cycle and the Rise of China,' paper presented to the 18th Annual Conference of Chinese Economic Association (UK), April, University of Nottingham.

Yao, Shujie (2005), *Economic Growth, Income Distribution and Poverty Reduction in China under Economic Reforms,* RoutledgeCurzon, ISBN 0-415-33196-X.

Yao, Shujie and Kailei, Wei (2007), 'Economic Growth in the Present of FDI from a Newly Industrializing Economy's Perspective,' *Journal of Comparative Economics,* 35(1), 211–234.

Yao, Shujie, L. Hanmer, and Zhongyi, Zhang (2004), 'The Implications of Growing Inequality on Poverty Peduction in China,' *China Economic Review,* 15, 145–163.

Minxin Pei ➡ **NO**

China's Not a Superpower

. . . and won't be anytime soon, according to *Minxin Pei*, who says its political and economic situation is more precarious than it looks.

With the United States apparently in terminal decline as the world's sole superpower, the fashionable question to ask is which country will be the new superpower? The near-unanimous answer, it seems, is China. Poised to overtake Japan as the world's 2nd largest economy in 2010, the Middle Kingdom has all the requisite elements of power—an extensive industrial base, a strong state, a nuclear-armed military, a continental-sized territory, a permanent seat on the United Nations Security Council and a large population base—to be considered as Uncle Sam's most eligible and logical equal. Indeed, the perception that China has already become the world's second superpower has grown so strong that some in the West have proposed a G2—the United States and China—as a new partnership to address the world's most pressing problems.

To be sure, the perception of China as the next superpower is grounded, at least in part, in the country's amazing rise over the last three decades. Powered by near-double digit economic growth since 1979, China has transformed itself from an isolated, impoverished and demoralized society into a confident, prospering global trading power. With a GDP of $4.4 trillion and total foreign trade of $2.6 trillion in 2008, China has firmly established itself as a premier world economic powerhouse.

Yet, despite such undeniable achievements, it may be too soon to regard China as the world's next superpower. Without doubt, China has already become a great power, a status given to countries that not only effectively defend their sovereignty, but also wield significant influence worldwide on economic and security issues. But a great power is not necessarily a superpower. In world history, only one country—the United States—has truly acquired all the capabilities of a superpower: a technologically advanced economy, a hitech military, a fully integrated nation, insuperable military and economic advantages vis-à-vis potential competitors, capacity to provide global public goods and an appealing ideology. Even in its heydays, the former Soviet Union was, at best, a one-dimensional superpower—capable of competing against the United States militarily, but lacking all the other crucial instruments of national power.

Meanwhile, the challenges China faces in becoming the next superpower are truly daunting. Even as its economic output is expected to exceed $5 trillion in 2010, per capita income in China will remain under $4000, roughly one-tenth of the level of the United States and Japan. More than half of the Chinese population still live in villages, most without access to safe drinking water, basic healthcare, or decent education. With urbanization growing at about 1 percent a year, it will take another three decades for China to reduce the size of its peasantry to a quarter of the population. As long as China has an oversized peasantry, with hundreds of millions of low-income rural residents surviving on the margins of modernity, it is unlikely to become a real superpower.

To believe that China is the next superpower, it's also necessary to assume that China's super-charged economic growth will continue. Unfortunately, relying on any country's past performance to predict its future prospects is a risky proposition. China's stunning economic growth performance since 1979 notwithstanding, its ability to sustain the same level of growth is by no means assured. In fact, the likelihood that China's growth will slow down significantly in the next two decades is real and even substantial. Several favourable structural factors, such as the demographic dividend (derived from a relatively younger population), virtually unlimited access to the global markets, high savings rates and discounted environmental costs, will gradually disappear. Like Japan, China is becoming an ageing society, due in no small part to the effectiveness of the government's stringent one-child policy (which limits urban families to a single child). The share of the population 60 years and above will be 17 percent by 2020, and this ageing will increase healthcare and pension costs while reducing savings and investments. Although the exact magnitude of the reduction in the savings and the increase in healthcare and pension spending is uncertain, their combined negative effects on economic growth could be substantial.

Another obstacle to China's future growth lies in the country's export-led growth model. As a middle-income country with limited domestic demand, China has relied on exports to increase its growth. While this strategy, which has been employed successfully in East Asia, has served China well for the past two decades, its future viability is now deeply in doubt. As the world's second largest exporter (although China is expected to surpass Germany as the world's largest exporter in 2010), China is encountering protectionist resistance in its major markets (the United States and Europe). In particular, China's policy of maintaining an under-valued currency to keep its exports competitive is now being blamed for worsening global imbalances and weakening the economies of its trading partners.

Unlike its East Asian neighbours, which are relatively small trading powers, China's sheer size means it has the capacity to cause severe economic disruptions to its trading partners. Unless the Chinese government abandons its mercantilist strategy, a global backlash against Chinese exports can't be ruled out. Because net export growth has provided China at least an extra two percentage points growth over the past five years, a slowdown in China's exports in the future will mean an overall lower rate of growth. To be sure, China can compensate for the loss of its external demand by increasing domestic consumption. But this process requires a complete overhaul of China's growth strategy, a politically difficult and painful step the incumbent government has been unable to take.

A third constraint on China's future growth is environmental degradation. Over the past three decades, China has neglected its environment for the sake of economic growth, with disastrous consequences. Today, air and water pollution kills about 750,000 people a year. The aggregate costs of pollution are roughly 8 percent of the GDP. Official estimates suggest that mitigating environmental degradation requires an investment of an additional 1.5 percent of GDP each year. Climate change will severely affect China's water supplies and exacerbate the drought in the north. China's business-as-usual approach to growth, which relies on cheap energy and no-cost pollution, will no longer be sustainable.

Uncertain economic prospects aside, China's rise to superpower status will also be constrained by a host of political factors. First and foremost, Chinese leaders will find themselves in search of a global vision and a political mission. Countries don't become superpowers merely because they have acquired hard power. The exercise of power must be informed by ideas and visions that have universal appeal. The United States did not become a true superpower until it entered the Second World War, even though it had attained all the requisite elements of a superpower long before Pearl Harbor. The political challenge for China in the future is whether it will be able to find the political ideals and visions to guide the use of its power. At the moment, China is economically prosperous but ideologically bankrupt. It believes in neither communism nor liberal democracy. Besides depriving China of a source of soft power, the lack of appealing ideals and visions for the world is also responsible for the inward-looking mindset of the Chinese leadership, which has so far paid only lip service to calls for China to assume greater international responsibility.

Unlike the United States, China will find its capacity to exercise power abroad greatly constrained by the lack of political integration at home. The Chinese Communist Party may have defied the doomsayers who repeatedly exaggerated its demise in the past. But the party's political monopoly is by no means secure. It holds on to its power by both delivering satisfactory economic performance and repressing challengers to its authority. As Chinese society grows more sophisticated and autonomous, the party will find it increasingly difficult to deny the rights of political participation to the urban middle-class. As a one-party regime, the Communist Party has also fallen victim to internal corruption. The combination of political challenge from the rising middle-class and progressive internal decay will increase the probability of a regime change in the future, a process that's likely to be disruptive, even cataclysmic.

A possible democratic transition is not the only thing feared by the Chinese ruling elites—ethnic secessionism may be even more threatening. For all intents and purposes, China is not a nation-state, but a multi-national empire with huge chunks of its territory (Tibet and Xinjiang) inhabited by secessionist-minded minority groups. The risks of internal fragmentation, on top of the perennial Taiwan problem, will mean that China will have to devote enormous military and security resources to defending its territorial integrity. This structural weakness makes China less able to project power abroad and more vulnerable to the machinations of its competitors, who could exploit China's ethnic tensions to tie Beijing's hands.

Geopolitically, the limits on Chinese power will be equally severe. While the United States is blessed by weak neighbours, China has to contend with strong regional rivals—India, Japan, and Russia. Even China's middle-sized neighbours, South Korea, Indonesia, and Vietnam, are no pushovers. China's rise has already triggered a regional geopolitical realignment aimed at checking Beijing's ambitions and reach. For example, the United States has greatly expanded its strategic cooperation with India so that New Delhi will be able to stand up to Beijing. Japan has also increased its economic aid to India for the same strategic purpose. Even Russia, China's partner of convenience for the moment, remains guarded about China. Moscow has refused to sell Beijing top-line weaponry and limited its energy supplies to China. For all its anti-American rhetoric, South Korea still counts on the United States for its economic prosperity and security. As for Vietnam and Indonesia, the two Southeast Asian countries most sceptical about China's future intentions, they are hedging their bets carefully. While trying not to offend China openly, they have significantly improved their ties with the United States and Japan, China's implicit regional rivals.

As a result of such geopolitical counter-balancing, China will be unable to become a hegemon in Asia—a power with complete dominance over its regional rivals. By definition, a country cannot become a global superpower unless it is also a regional hegemon, such as the United States. As a great power hemmed in by powerful and vigilant neighbours, China must constantly watch its back while trying to project power and influence on the global stage.

Such a status—a globally influential great power, but not a dominant superpower—is something nobody should dismiss lightly. Pax Americana is an accident of history that cannot be copied by another country. For the world, it should not be obsessed by the fear that China will become another superpower. Instead, it should learn to live with China as a great power.

The question is: what kind of great power is China?

Ironically, while the rest of the world has taken China's future as a superpower for granted, Chinese leaders themselves are more aware of the inherent limits of the country's strength. As a result, Beijing exercises its newly acquired clout with extreme caution, eschewing external entanglements, frowning upon direct military presence abroad, avoiding costly international obligations and living with the international economic and security order established and dominated by the United States. Of course, China guards its national interests, particularly its sovereignty, jealously. On matters of its territorial integrity and economic well-being, Beijing seldom hesitates to flex its muscles. But it draws the line on empire-building overseas via the extension of its military power.

So for the foreseeable future, China will be, at best, only an economic superpower by virtue of its role as one of the world's greatest trading powers (in this sense, both Germany and Japan should be considered economic superpowers as well). Its geopolitical and military influence, meanwhile, will remain constrained by internal fragilities and external rivalry.

While China will always have a seat at the table on the global stage, its willingness and capacity to exercise leadership will most likely disappoint those who expect Beijing to behave like a superpower. It's not that China doesn't want to be a superpower. The simple truth is that it is not, and will not be one.

EXPLORING THE ISSUE

Will China Be the Next Superpower?

Critical Thinking and Reflection

1. Can China maintain its growth and expansion without political reform?
2. Does China want to exercise more global influence?
3. What is the nature of China's relationship with the United States and does it necessarily mean rivalry or cooperation?
4. Does China have global ambitions?

Is There Common Ground?

Certainly, China has the potential to be the next superpower and it also has a well-thought-out plan for growth and modernization. Can China pull it off? Even the most generous analysis of the rise of the United State to superpower status admits that it was a process that took generations to come to fruition. The explosion of the atomic bomb was merely the culmination of a long path of industrialization, military expansion, and developing internationalism among the political elite. China seems to be on the path but whether it can sustain it and continue to embrace it remains an open question.

Additional Resources

Bergsten, C. Fred, Gill, Bates, Lardy, Nicholas, Mitchell, Derek, *China the Balance Sheet: What the World Needs to Know About the Emerging Superpower* (Public Affairs, 2006)

> This book provides an indispensable survey of China, the world's largest country—a vast land with 1.4 billion people and the world's most dynamic economy.

Fishman, Ted C., *China Inc.: How the Rise of the Next Superpower Challenges America and the World* (Scribner, 2006)

> A lively, fact-packed account of China's spectacular, 30-year transformation from economic shambles following Mao's Cultural Revolution to burgeoning market superpower, this book offers a torrent of statistics, case studies and anecdotes to tell a by now familiar but still worrisome story succinctly.

Jacques, Martin, *When China Rules the World: The End of the Western World and the Birth of a New Global Order* (Penguin Press HC, 2009)

> A convincing economic, political and cultural analysis of waning Western dominance and the rise of China and a new paradigm of modernity.

Shirk, Susan, *China: Fragile Superpower: How China's Internal Politics Could Derail Its Peaceful Rise* (Oxford University press, 2007)

> In this book, Shirk opens up the black box of Chinese politics and finds that the real danger lies elsewhere—not in China's astonishing growth, but in the deep insecurity of its leaders.

ISSUE 19

Have Al-Qaeda and Its Jihad Against the United States Been Defeated?

YES: Fareed Zakaria, from "The Jihad Against the Jihadis: How Moderate Muslim Leaders Waged War on Extremists—and Won," *Newsweek* (February 22, 2010)

NO: Scott Stewart, from "Jihadism in 2010: The Threat Continues," *STRATFOR* (January 6, 2010)

Learning Outcomes

After reading this issue, you should be able to:

- Evaluate the relative strength of Al-Qaeda vis-a-vis the U.S. war on terror.
- Define and understand what such a movement seeks and what are its strengths and weaknesses.
- Understand why Al-Qaeda and the United States are at war and understand the challenges the United States faces in combating them.
- Grasp the complexity and difficult nature of the struggle.

ISSUE SUMMARY

YES: Fareed Zakaria argues through the acts of moderate Muslims across the Islamic world, "We have turned the corner on the war between extremism and the West and . . . now we are in a new phase of clean up and rebuilding of relationships." His argument rests on the actions of Muslim regimes in Saudi Arabia, Pakistan, and Indonesia who are fighting back against jihadism, engaging in military and political policies that are marginalizing extremists and consequently winning the war.

NO: Scott Stewart contends that despite Western victories against Al-Qaeda based in the Afghan–Pakistan border region, regional groups and cells have taken up the slack and the threat of extremism and jihad is still strong and ominous. He focuses on the work of these groups in Somalia, Yemen, and North Africa to illustrate this continued fight.

9/11 was not the beginning of the enmity between Islamic fundamentalism and the United States and its allies but it certainly was the explosion that turned the conflict into a full-fledged war. For close to 10 years, the United States has been at war with fundamentalist terrorist groups and in particular Al-Qaeda led by Osama bin Laden. The United States' invasion of Afghanistan, its later invasion of Iraq, and its support for regimes from Pakistan, Indonesia, Saudi Arabia, and Morocco are predicated in part on their shared opposition to Al-Qaeda.

Al-Qaeda and its allies around the Muslim world have identified the United States as one of several threats to the purity of Islam and the primacy of Muslims in what they consider Muslim lands. Along with secular and/or corrupt Arab regimes and of course Israel, Al-Qaeda has launched a jihad against these forces and is using terrorism as its main weapon.

The tenor of the conflicts around the world has grown increasingly bitter and the casualties continue to mount. There are ebbs and flows to this conflict in the various theatres of battle. For example, since 9/11 several efforts at likeminded attacks have been thwarted, most recently the "underwear bomber" over Detroit. However, other bombings in Bali, London, and Moscow have been successful. In Afghanistan and the border regions of Pakistan, the battle rages with renewed U.S. troop levels, allied assistance, and increasing attacks from Al-Qaeda and its Taliban allies.

Amidst the military struggle, there is a political, philosophical battle ensuing between these sides for essentially the hearts and minds of the Muslim world. That battle is waged over the airwaves and through the Internet. Al-Qaeda is a tiny minority to be sure but they along with the United States and others are waging a propaganda battle for the sympathy, support, and active involvement of the so-called Muslim street, those hundreds of millions of Muslims who watch and evaluate their position in the struggle. Lately, there has been much talk and writing about victory or at least turning the corner in the struggle. Analysts have speculated about whether Al-Qaeda is on the run, on its last legs, or near collapse. Others have argued that this is a long struggle and while there will be victories and defeats, one cannot defeat this enemy until other changes occur in the Muslim world that are more socioeconomic and thus systemic.

There is a revolution in the Muslim world. It has been developing and evolving throughout most of the twentieth century. In the wake of World War I and British and French colonialism, Islamic fundamentalist thought grew in Egypt among what would become the Muslim Brotherhood and it spread throughout the Arab world and then into non-Arab Islam. The genesis of this thought was the need for the Islamic world to rediscover its roots, reject much of the influences of non-Muslim peoples and places, and develop conceptions of governance fused with Islam and not separate from it.

The forms that this movement has taken among both Shiite and Sunni Muslims have been numerous. The most dramatic examples of its success are of course in Iran, Afghanistan under the Taliban, Algeria, and in other places. As this movement has encountered resistance from secular Muslim regimes, kingdoms, and authoritarian dictatorships and from the West, it has increasingly seen itself as downtrodden, thwarted, and under attack. These feelings and beliefs have led to its further radicalization and the growing adoption of terrorism as it weapon of resistance.

Thus, the war between the United States and Al-Qaeda, between fundamentalist Islam and the West has a long genesis. Its most recent phase in the post-9/11 period has been marked by violence and war across several states in South Asia and the Middle East, Europe, and here in the United States.

Consequently, it is difficult to divorce the rise of extreme fundamentalist thought in the Muslim world from violence against those who it believes oppose it. The fundamentalist revolution in the Muslim world must run its course principally among Muslims. In that sense, Fareed Zakaria is right. Only Muslims can defeat Muslims in the greater battle for the hearts and minds of Muslim thought. Whether that battle is military, political, socioeconomic, or philosophical, that is where the ultimate success of Al-Qaeda will be determined.

Whether jihad has been defeated by the United States and West is more than likely an open question. Ups and downs in that battle will likely continue as long as extreme fundamentalism has a voice and converts those who see the United States as the primary enemy to their interests and ambitions. Religious extremism and zealotry is and has been a part of every great faith. How it is dealt with is usually determined not by those who believe in something different but those who believe in the same things.

The authors of the YES and NO selections represent two perspectives on this issue. In the YES selection, Fareed Zakaria contends that through a series of events and actions, moderate Muslims have made their choice and are actively fighting Al-Qaeda and such extremism and thus are winning the conflict. In fact he argues that the battle is essentially over and now all that is left is to mop up the remaining zealots and holdouts.

In the NO selection, Scott Stewart of STRATFOR argues that the Al-Qaeda threat and jihad remain. They are just changing character and tactics to adapt to the changing force structure. He argues that they are becoming more decentralized and localized and thus represent a strong threat. The battle is not over, just entering a new phase.

YES ↵

Fareed Zakaria

The Jihad Against the Jihadis: How Moderate Muslim Leaders Waged War on Extremists—and Won

September 11, 2001, was gruesome enough on its own terms, but for many of us, the real fear was of what might follow. Not only had al-Qaeda shown it was capable of sophisticated and ruthless attacks, but a far greater concern was that the group had or could establish a powerful hold on the hearts and minds of Muslims. And if Muslims sympathized with al-Qaeda's cause, we were in for a herculean struggle. There are more than 1.5 billion Muslims living in more than 150 countries across the world. If jihadist ideology became attractive to a significant part of this population, the West faced a clash of civilizations without end, one marked by blood and tears.

These fears were well founded. The 9/11 attacks opened the curtain on a world of radical and violent Islam that had been festering in the Arab lands and had been exported across the globe, from London to Jakarta. Polls all over the Muslim world revealed deep anger against America and the West and a surprising degree of support for Osama bin Laden. Governments in most of these countries were ambivalent about this phenomenon, assuming that the Islamists' wrath would focus on the United States and not themselves. Large, important countries like Saudi Arabia and Indonesia seemed vulnerable.

More than eight eventful years have passed, but in some ways it still feels like 2001. Republicans have clearly decided that fanning the public's fears of rampant jihadism continues to be a winning strategy. Commentators furnish examples of backwardness and brutality from various parts of the Muslim world—and there are many—to highlight the grave threat we face.

But, in fact, the entire terrain of the war on terror has evolved dramatically. Put simply, the moderates are fighting back and the tide is turning. We no longer fear the possibility of a major country succumbing to jihadist ideology. In most Muslim nations, mainstream rulers have stabilized their regimes and their societies, and extremists have been isolated. This has not led to the flowering of Jeffersonian democracy or liberalism. But modern, somewhat secular forces are clearly in control and widely supported across the Muslim world. Polls, elections, and in-depth studies all confirm this trend.

The focus of our concern now is not a broad political movement but a handful of fanatics scattered across the globe. Yet Washington's vast nation-building machinery continues to spend tens of billions of dollars in Iraq and Afghanistan, and there are calls to do more in Yemen and Somalia. What we have to ask ourselves is whether any of that really will deter these small bands of extremists. Some of them come out of the established democracies of the West, hardly places where nation building will help. We have to understand the changes in the landscape of Islam if we are going to effectively fight the enemy on the ground, rather than the enemy in our minds.

Once, no country was more worrying than bin Laden's homeland. The Kingdom of Saudi Arabia, steward of the holy cities of Mecca and Medina, had surpassed Egypt as the de facto leader of the Arab world because of the vast sums of money it doled out to Islamic causes—usually those consonant with its puritanical Wahhabi doctrines. Since 1979 the Saudi regime had openly appeased its home-grown Islamists, handing over key ministries and funds to reactionary mullahs. Visitors to Saudi Arabia after 9/11 were shocked by what they heard there. Educated Saudis—including senior members of the government—publicly endorsed wild conspiracy theories and denied that any Saudis had been involved in the 9/11 attacks. Even those who accepted reality argued that the fury of some Arabs was inevitable, given America's one-sided foreign policy on the Arab–Israeli issue.

America's initial reaction to 9/11 was to focus on al-Qaeda. The group was driven out of its base in Afghanistan and was pursued wherever it went. Its money was tracked and blocked, its fighters arrested and killed. Many other nations joined in, from France to Malaysia. After all, no government wanted to let terrorists run loose in its land.

But a broader conversation also began, one that asked, "Why is this happening, and what can we do about it?" The most influential statement on Islam to come out of the post-9/11 era was not a presidential speech or an intellectual's essay. It was, believe it or not, a United Nations report. In 2002 the U.N. Development Program published a detailed study of the Arab world. The paper made plain that in an era of globalization, openness, diversity, and tolerance, the Arabs were the world's great laggards. Using hard data, the report painted a picture of political, social, and intellectual stagnation in countries from the Maghreb to the Gulf. And it was written by a team of Arab scholars. This was not paternalism or imperialism. It was truth.

The report, and many essays and speeches by political figures and intellectuals in the West, launched a process of reflection in the Arab world. The debate did not take the form that many in the West wanted—no one said, "You're right, we are backward." But still, leaders in Arab countries were forced to advocate modernity and moderation openly rather than hoping that they could quietly reap its fruits by day while palling around with the mullahs at night. The Bush administration launched a series of programs across the Muslim world to strengthen moderates, shore up civil society, and build forces of tolerance and pluralism. All this has had an effect. From Dubai to Amman to Cairo, in some form or another, authorities have begun opening up economic and political systems that had been tightly closed. The changes have sometimes been small, but the arrows are finally moving in the right direction.

Ultimately, the catalyst for change was something more lethal than a report. After 9/11, al-Qaeda was full of bluster: recall the videotapes of bin Laden and his deputy, Ayman al-Zawahiri, boasting of their plans. Yet they confronted a far less permissive environment. Moving money, people, and materials had all become much more difficult. So they, and local groups inspired by them, began attacking where they could—striking local targets rather than global ones, including a nightclub and hotel in Indonesia, a wedding party in Jordan, cafés in Casablanca and Istanbul, and resorts in Egypt. They threatened the regimes that, either by accident or design, had allowed them to live and breathe.

Over the course of 2003 and 2004, Saudi Arabia was rocked by a series of such terrorist attacks, some directed against foreigners, but others at the heart of the Saudi regime—the Ministry of the Interior and compounds within the oil industry. The monarchy recognized that it had spawned dark forces that were now endangering its very existence. In 2005 a man of wisdom and moderation, King Abdullah, formally ascended to the throne and inaugurated a large-scale political and intellectual effort aimed at discrediting the ideology of jihadism. Mullahs were ordered to denounce suicide bombings and violence more generally. Education was pried out of the hands of the clerics. Terrorists and terror suspects were "rehabilitated" through extensive programs of education, job training, and counseling. Central Command chief Gen. David Petraeus said to me, "The Saudi role in taking on al-Qaeda, both by force but also using political, social, religious, and educational tools, is one of the most important, least reported positive developments in the war on terror."

Perhaps the most successful country to combat jihadism has been the world's most populous Muslim nation, Indonesia. In 2002 that country seemed destined for a long and painful struggle with the forces of radical Islam. The nation was rocked by terror attacks, and a local Qaeda affiliate, Jemaah Islamiah, appeared to be gaining strength. But eight years later, JI has been marginalized and mainstream political parties have gained ground, all while a young democracy has flowered after the collapse of the Suharto dictatorship.

Magnus Ranstorp of Stockholm's Center for Asymmetric Threat Studies recently published a careful study examining Indonesia's success in beating back extremism. The main lesson, he writes, is to involve not just government but civil society as a whole, including media and cultural figures who can act as counterforces to terrorism. (That approach obviously has greater potential in regions and countries with open and vibrant political systems—Southeast Asia, Turkey, and India—than in the Arab world.)

Iraq occupies an odd place in this narrative. While the invasion of Iraq inflamed the Muslim world and the series of blunders during the initial occupation period created dangerous chaos at the heart of the Middle East, Iraq also became a stage on which al-Qaeda played a deadly hand, and lost. As al-Qaeda in Iraq gained militarily, it began losing politically. It turned from its broader global ideology to focus on a narrow sectarian agenda, killing Shias and fueling a Sunni–Shia civil war. In doing so, the group also employed a level of brutality and violence that shocked most Iraqis. Where the group gained control, even pious people were repulsed by its reactionary behavior. In Anbar province, the heart of the Sunni insurgency, al-Qaeda in Iraq would routinely cut off the fingers of smokers. Even those Sunnis who feared the new Iraq began to prefer Shia rule to such medievalism.

Since 9/11, Western commentators have been calling on moderate Muslim leaders to condemn jihadist ideology, issue *fatwas* against suicide bombing, and denounce al-Qaeda. Since about 2006, they've begun to do so in significant numbers. In 2007 one of bin Laden's most prominent Saudi mentors, the preacher and scholar Salman al-Odah, wrote an open letter criticizing him for "fostering a culture of suicide bombings that has caused bloodshed and suffering, and brought ruin to entire Muslim communities and families." That same year Abdulaziz al ash-Sheikh, the grand mufti of Saudi Arabia, issued a *fatwa* prohibiting Saudis from engaging in jihad abroad and accused both bin Laden and Arab regimes of "transforming our youth into walking bombs to accomplish their own political and military aims." One of al-Qaeda's own top theorists, Abdul-Aziz el-Sherif, renounced its extremism, including the killing of civilians and the choosing of targets based on religion and nationality. Sherif—a longtime associate of Zawahiri who crafted what became known as al-Qaeda's guide to jihad—has called on militants to desist from terrorism, and authored a rebuttal of his former cohorts.

Al-Azhar University in Cairo, the oldest and most prestigious school of Islamic learning, now routinely condemns jihadism. The Darul Uloom Deoband movement in India, home to the original radicalism that influenced al-Qaeda, has inveighed against suicide bombing since 2008. None of these groups or people have become pro-American or liberal, but they have become anti-jihadist.

This might seem like an esoteric debate. But consider: the most important moderates to denounce militants have been the families of radicals. In the case of both the five young American Muslims from Virginia arrested in Pakistan last year and Christmas bomber Umar Farouk Abdulmutallab, parents were the ones to report their worries about their own children to the U.S. government—an act so stunning that it requires far more examination, and praise, than it has gotten. This is where soft power becomes critical. Were the fathers of these boys convinced that the United States would torture, maim, and execute their children without any sense of justice, they would not have come forward. I doubt that any Chechen father has turned his child over to Vladimir Putin's regime.

The data on public opinion in the Muslim world are now overwhelming. London School of Economics professor Fawaz Gerges has analyzed polls from dozens of Muslim countries over the past few years. He notes that in a range of places—Jordan, Pakistan, Indonesia, Lebanon, and Bangladesh—there have been substantial declines in the number of people who say suicide bombing and other forms of violence against civilian targets can be justified to defend Islam. Wide majorities say such attacks are, at most, rarely acceptable.

The shift has been especially dramatic in Jordan, where only 12 percent of Jordanians view suicide attacks as "often or sometimes justified" (down from 57 percent in 2005). In Indonesia, 85 percent of respondents agree that terrorist attacks are "rarely/never justified" (in 2002, by contrast, only 70 percent opposed such attacks). In Pakistan, that figure is 90 percent, up from 43 percent in 2002.

Gerges points out that, by comparison, only 46 percent of Americans say that "bombing and other attacks intentionally aimed at civilians" are "never justified," while 24 percent believe these attacks are "often or sometimes justified."

This shift does not reflect a turn away from religiosity or even from a backward conception of Islam. That ideological struggle persists and will take decades, not years, to resolve itself. But the battle against jihadism has fared much better, much sooner, than anyone could have imagined.

The exceptions to this picture readily spring to mind—Afghanistan, Pakistan, Yemen. But consider the conditions in those countries. In Afghanistan, jihadist ideology has wrapped itself around a genuine ethnic struggle in which Pashtuns feel that they are being dispossessed by rival groups. In Pakistan, the regime is still where Saudi Arabia was in 2003 and 2004: slowly coming to realize that the extremism it had fostered has now become a threat to its own survival. In Yemen, the state simply lacks the basic capacity to fight back. So the rule might simply be that in those places where a government lacks the desire, will, or capacity to fight jihadism, al-Qaeda can continue to thrive.

But the nature of the enemy is now quite different. It is not a movement capable of winning over the Arab street. Its political appeal does not make rulers tremble. The video messages of bin Laden and Zawahiri once unsettled moderate regimes. Now they are mostly dismissed as almost comical attempts to find popular causes to latch onto. (After the financial crash, bin Laden tried his hand at bashing greedy bankers.)

This is not an argument to relax our efforts to hunt down militants. Al-Qaeda remains a group of relentless, ruthless killers who are trying to recruit other fanatics to carry out hideous attacks that would do terrible damage to civilized society. But the group's aura is gone, its political influence limited. Its few remaining fighters are spread thinly throughout the world and face hostile environments almost everywhere.

America is no longer engaged in a civilizational struggle throughout the Muslim world, but a military and intelligence campaign in a set of discrete places. Now, that latter struggle might well require politics, diplomacy, and development assistance—in the manner that good foreign policy always does (Petraeus calls this a "whole-of-government strategy"). We have allies; we need to support them. But the target is only a handful of extremist organizations that have found a small group of fanatics to carry out their plans. To put it another way, even if the United States pursues a broad and successful effort at nation building in Afghanistan and Yemen, does anyone really think that will deter the next Nigerian misfit—or fanatic from Detroit—from getting on a plane with chemicals in his underwear? Such people cannot be won over. They cannot be reasoned with; they can only be captured or killed.

The enemy is not vast; the swamp is being drained. Al-Qaeda has already lost in the realm of ideology. What remains is the battle to defeat it in the nooks, crannies, and crevices of the real world.

→ **NO**

Jihadism in 2010: The Threat Continues

For the past several years, STRATFOR has published an annual forecast on al-Qaeda and the jihadist movement. Since our first jihadist forecast in January 2006, we have focused heavily on the devolution of jihadism from a phenomenon primarily involving the core al-Qaeda group to one based mainly on the wider jihadist movement and the devolving, decentralized threat it poses.

The central theme of last year's forecast was that al-Qaeda was an important force on the ideological battlefield, but that the efforts of the United States and its allies had marginalized the group on the physical battlefield and kept it bottled up in a limited geographic area. Because of this, we forecast that the most significant threat in terms of physical attacks stemmed from regional jihadist franchises and grassroots operatives and not the al Qaeda core. We also wrote that we believed the threat posed by such attacks would remain tactical and not rise to the level of a strategic threat. To reflect this reality, we even dropped al-Qaeda from the title of our annual forecast and simply named it Jihadism in 2009: The Trends Continue.

The past year proved to be very busy in terms of attacks and thwarted plots emanating from jihadist actors. But, as forecast, the primary militants involved in carrying out these terrorist plots were almost exclusively from regional jihadist groups and grassroots operatives, and not militants dispatched by the al-Qaeda core. We anticipate that this dynamic will continue, and if anything, the trend will be for some regional franchise groups to become even more involved in transnational attacks, thus further usurping the position of al-Qaeda prime at the vanguard of jihadism on the physical battlefield.

A Note on "Al-Qaeda"

As a quick reminder, STRATFOR views what most people refer to as "al-Qaeda" as a global jihadist network rather than a monolithic entity. This network consists of three distinct entities. The first is a core vanguard organization, which we frequently refer to as al-Qaeda prime or the al-Qaeda core. The al-Qaeda core is comprised of Osama bin Laden and his small circle of close, trusted associates, such as Ayman al-Zawahiri. Due to intense pressure by the U.S.

government and its allies, this core group has been reduced in size since 9/11 and remains relatively small because of operational security concerns. This insular group is laying low in Pakistan near the Afghan border and comprises only a small portion of the larger jihadist universe.

The second layer of the network is composed of local or regional terrorist or insurgent groups that have adopted jihadist ideology. Some of these groups have publicly claimed allegiance to bin Laden and the al-Qaeda core and become what we refer to as franchise groups, like al-Qaeda in the Islamic Maghreb (AQIM) or al-Qaeda in the Arabian Peninsula (AQAP). Other groups may adopt some or all of al-Qaeda's jihadist ideology and cooperate with the core group, but they will maintain their independence for a variety of reasons. Such groups include the Tehrik-i-Taliban Pakistan (TTP), Lashkar-e-Taiba (LeT) and Harkat-ul-Jihad e-Islami (HUJI). Indeed, in the case of some larger organizations such as LeT, some of the group's factions may actually oppose close cooperation with al-Qaeda.

The third and broadest layer of the network is the grassroots jihadist movement, that is, people inspired by the al-Qaeda core and the franchise groups but who may have little or no actual connection to these groups.

As we move down this hierarchy, we also move down in operational capability and expertise in what we call terrorist tradecraft—the set of skills required to conduct a terrorist attack. The operatives belonging to the al-Qaeda core are generally better trained than their regional counterparts, and both of these layers tend to be far better trained than the grassroots operatives. Indeed, many grassroots operatives travel to places like Pakistan and Yemen in order to seek training from these other groups.

The Internet has long proved to be an important tool for these groups to reach out to potential grassroots operatives. Jihadist chat rooms and Web sites provide indoctrination in jihadist ideology and also serve as a means for aspiring jihadists to make contact with like-minded individuals and even the jihadist groups themselves.

2009 Forecast Review

Overall, our 2009 forecast was fairly accurate. As noted above, we wrote that the United States would continue its operations to decapitate the al-Qaeda core and that this would cause the group to be marginalized from the physical jihad, and that has happened.

While we missed forecasting the resurgence of jihadist militant groups in Yemen and Somalia in 2008, in our 2009 forecast we covered these two countries carefully. We wrote that the al-Qaeda franchises in Yemen had taken a hit in 2008 but that they could recover in 2009 given the opportunity. Indeed, the groups received a significant boost when they merged into a single group that also incorporated the remnants of al-Qaeda in Saudi Arabia, which had been forced by Saudi security to flee the country. We closely followed this new group, which named itself al-Qaeda in the Arabian Peninsula (AQAP), and STRATFOR was the first organization we know of to discuss the threat AQAP posed to civil aviation when we raised this subject on Sept. 2 and elaborated on it Sept. 16, in an analysis titled Convergence: The Challenge of Aviation Security. That threat manifested itself in the attempt to destroy an airliner traveling from Amsterdam to Detroit on Christmas Day 2009—an operation that very nearly succeeded.

Regarding Somalia, we have also been closely following al Shabaab and the other jihadist groups there, such as Hizbul Islam. Al Shabaab publicly pledged allegiance to Osama bin Laden in September 2009 and therefore has formally joined the ranks of al-Qaeda's regional franchise groups. However, as we forecast last January, while the instability present in Somalia provides al Shabaab the opportunity to flourish, the factionalization of the country (including the jihadist groups operating there) has also served to keep al Shabaab from dominating the other actors and assuming control of the country.

We also forecast that, while Iraq had been relatively quiet in 2008, the level of violence there could surge in 2009 due to the Awakening Councils being taken off the U.S. payroll and having their control transferred to the Shiite-dominated Iraqi government, which might not pay them and integrate them into the armed forces. Indeed, since August, we have seen three waves of major coordinated attacks against Iraqi ministry buildings in Baghdad linked to the al-Qaeda affiliate in Iraq, the Islamic State of Iraq. Since this violence is tied to the political situation in Iraq, and there is a clear correlation between the funds being cut to the Awakening Councils and these attacks, we anticipate that this violence will continue through the parliamentary elections in March. The attacks could even continue after that, if the Sunni powers in Iraq deem that their interests are not being addressed appropriately.

As in 2008, we paid close attention in 2009 to the situation in Pakistan. This not only was because Pakistan is the home of the al-Qaeda core's leadership but also because of the threat that the TTP and the other jihadist groups in the country posed to the stability of the nuclear-armed state. As we watched Pakistan for signs that it was becoming a failed state, we noted that the government was actually making considerable headway in its fight against its jihadist insurgency. Indeed, by late in the year, the Pakistanis had launched not only a successful offensive in Swat and the adjacent districts but also an offensive into South Waziristan, the heart of the TTP's territory.

We also forecast that the bulk of the attacks worldwide in 2009 would be conducted by regional jihadist franchise groups and, to a lesser extent, grassroots jihadists, rather than the al-Qaeda core, which was correct.

In relation to attacks against the United States, we wrote that we did not see a strategic threat to the United States from the jihadists, but that the threat of simple attacks against soft targets remained in 2009. We said we had been surprised that there were no such attacks in 2008 but that, given the vulnerabilities that existed and the ease with which such attacks could be conducted, we believed they were certainly possible. During 2009, we did see simple attacks by grassroots operatives in Little Rock, Arkansas, and at Fort Hood, Texas, along with several other grassroots plots thwarted by authorities.

Forecast for 2010

In the coming year we believe that, globally, we will see many of the trends continue from last year. We believe that the al-Qaeda core will continue to be marginalized on the physical battlefield and struggle to remain relevant on the ideological battlefield. The regional jihadist franchise groups will continue to be at the vanguard of the physical battle, and the grassroots operatives will remain a persistent, though lower-level, threat.

One thing we noticed in recent months was that the regional groups were becoming more transnational in their attacks, with AQAP involved in the attack on Saudi Deputy Interior Minister Prince Mohammed bin Nayef in Saudi Arabia as well as the trans-Atlantic airliner bombing plot on Christmas Day. Additionally, we saw HUJI planning an attack against the Jyllands-Posten newspaper and cartoonist Kurt Westergaard in Denmark, and on Jan. 1, 2010, a Somali man reportedly associated with al Shabaab broke into Westergaard's home armed with an axe and knife and allegedly tried to kill him. We believe that in 2010 we will see more examples of regional groups like al Shabaab and AQAP reaching out to become more transnational, perhaps even conducting attacks in the United States and Europe.

We also believe that, due to the open nature of the U.S. and European societies and the ease of conducting attacks against them, we will see more grassroots plots, if not successful attacks, in the United States and Europe in the coming year. The concept behind AQAP leader Nasir al-Wahayshi's article calling for jihadists to conduct simple attacks against a variety of targets may be gaining popularity among grassroots jihadists. Certainly, the above-mentioned attack in Denmark involving an axe and knife was simple in nature. It could also have been deadly had the cartoonist not had a panic room within his residence. We will be watching for more simple attacks.

As far as targets, we believe that they will remain largely the same for 2010. Soft targets such as hotels will continue to be popular, since most jihadists lack the ability to attack hard targets outside of conflict zones. However, jihadists have demonstrated a continuing fixation on attacking commercial aviation targets, and we can anticipate additional plots and attacks focusing on aircraft.

Regionally, we will be watching for the following:

- **Pakistan:** Can the United States find and kill the al-Qaeda core's leadership? A Pakistani official told the Chinese Xinhua news agency on Jan. 4 that terrorism will come to an end in Pakistan in 2010, but we are not nearly so optimistic. Even though the military has made good progress in its South Waziristan offensive, most of the militants moved to other areas of Pakistan rather than engage in frontal combat with Pakistan's army. The area along the border with Pakistan is rugged and has proved hard to pacify for hundreds of years. We don't think the Pakistanis will be able to bring the area under control in only one year. Clearly, the Pakistanis have made progress, but they are not out of the woods. The TTP has launched a number of attacks in the Punjabi core of Pakistan (and in Karachi) and we see no end to this violence in 2010.

- **Afghanistan:** We will continue to closely monitor jihadist actors in this war-torn country. Our forecast for this conflict is included in our Annual Forecast 2010, published on Jan. 4.
- **Yemen:** We will be watching closely to see if AQAP will follow the normal jihadist group lifespan of making a big splash, coming to the notice of the world and then being hit heavily by the host government with U.S. support. This pattern was exhibited a few years back by AQAP's Saudi al-Qaeda brethren, and judging by the operations in Yemen over the past month, it looks like 2010 might be a tough year for the group. It is important to note that the strikes against the group on Dec. 17 and Dec. 24 predated the Christmas bombing attempt, and the pressure on them will undoubtedly be ratcheted up considerably in the wake of that attack. Even as the memory of the Christmas Day attack begins to fade in the media and political circles, the focus on Yemen will continue in the counterterrorism community.
- **Indonesia:** Can Tanzim Qaedat al-Jihad find an effective leader to guide it back from the edge of destruction after the death of Noordin Mohammad Top and the deaths or captures of several of his top lieutenants? Or will the Indonesians be able to enjoy further success against the group's surviving members?
- **North Africa:** Will AQIM continue to shy away from the al-Qaeda core's targeting philosophy and essentially function as the Salafist Group for Preaching and Combat with a different name in Algeria? Or will AQIM shift back toward al-Qaeda's philosophy of attacking the far enemy and using suicide bombers and large vehicle bombs? In Mauritania, Niger and Mali, will the AQIM-affiliated cells there be able to progress beyond amateurish attacks and petty banditry to become a credible militant organization?
- **Somalia:** We believe the factionalism in Somalia and within the jihadist community there will continue to hamper al Shabaab. The questions we will be looking to answer are: Will al Shabaab be able to gain significant control of areas of the country that can be used to harbor and train foreign militants? And, will the group decide to use its contacts within the Somali diaspora to conduct attacks in East Africa, South Africa, Australia, Europe and the United States? We believe that al Shabaab is on its way to becoming a transnational player and that 2010 may well be the year that it breaks out and then draws international attention like AQAP has done in recent months.
- **India:** We anticipate that Kashmiri jihadist groups will continue to plan attacks against India in an effort to stir-up communal violence in that country and stoke tensions between India and Pakistan—and provide a breather to the jihadist groups being pressured by the government of Pakistan.

As long as the ideology of jihadism survives, the jihadists will be able to recruit new militants and their war against the world will continue. The battle will oscillate between periods of high and low intensity as regional groups rise in power and are taken down. We don't believe jihadists pose a strategic geopolitical threat on a global, or even regional, scale, but they will certainly continue to launch attacks and kill people in 2010.

EXPLORING THE ISSUE

Have Al-Qaeda and Its Jihad Against the United States Been Defeated?

Critical Thinking and Reflection

1. Can a group like Al-Qaeda be defeated or neutralized?
2. Does the killing of Osama bin Laden by the United States mean the demise of Al-Qaeda?
3. If not, what constitute victory against such an enemy?
4. Is the United States using the right tactic to win or should it change its approach?
5. Is the "Arab Spring" a sign of the eventual death of Al-Qaeda?

Is There Common Ground?

Overall, issues of economic development, political enfranchisement, and the Israeli-Palestinian issue will determine the long-term prospects of jihadism and radical fundamentalism in the Muslim world. As the recent "Arab Spring" seems to indicate, issues of economic opportunity and freedom of thought and action seem to be primary drivers of disenchantment with existing regimes, particularly among the youth. Whatever one's political views, most analysts agree that economic opportunity for young people and political engagement will lead to less of a radicalized Muslim world and as such, less of a jihadist spirit that is the fuel for groups like Al-Qaeda and others.

Additional Resources

Halper, Daniel, "Osama bin Laden's Death and the Future of al Qaeda," *The Weekly Standard* (May 4, 2011)

Khalaf, Roula, "Al Qaeda Sidelined by the Rise of Peaceful Protest," *The Financial Times* (May 2, 2011)

McGirk, Tim, "Could Bin Laden's Death Bankrupt al Qaeda?" *TIME* (May 3, 2011)

Murphy, Dan, "Bin Laden's Death Puts Exclamation Point on al Qaeda's Demise," *The Christian Science Monitor* (May 3, 2011)

ISSUE 20

Is the Middle East Undergoing a Democratic Revolution?

YES: Fareed Zakaria, from "How Democracy Can Work in the Middle East," *TIME* (February 3, 2011)

NO: Adam Shatz, from "After Mubarak," *The London Review of Books* (February 17, 2011)

Learning Outcomes

After reading this issue, you should be able to:

- Understand the monumental nature of the antigovernmental movements under way across the Middle East.
- Appreciate the fragility of those regimes and the uncertainty of the result as this revolution takes form.
- Recognize the limits of outside states' ability to impact these movements.
- Understand the role of social media and the youth in these movements.
- Appreciate the uncertainty of what the results will be in both the short and long terms.

ISSUE SUMMARY

YES: Fareed Zakaria argues that there are strong strands within the Egyptian polity and around other parts of the Middle East to indicate that the Arab Spring is truly a democratic revolution. Although he cautions that democracy results are dependent on a host of complex factors, he sees several reasons for optimism, including a strong and secular military and an independent judiciary system.

NO: Adam Shatz argues that it is far too early to determine whether the Arab Spring, as some are calling it, will lead to democracy of the type and form the west would favor. He contends that the revolt against autocratic rule may indeed lead to the exchange of one form of authoritarianism with another and that worries in parts of the United States and Israel about authoritarian, anti-Western regimes replacing governments in Egypt, Tunisia, and other places are quite justified.

For nearly 100 years, since the end of World War I and the fall of the Ottoman Empire, the Middle East has been ruled in one fashion or another by France and Britain, conservative monarchies of one form or another, military dictatorships, or de facto one-party states. Democracy in the form of multiparty elections and competition for votes has been short lived in places like Lebanon, Jordan, and of course in Iraq. Further, these regimes have enjoyed the support of various ethnic and religious factions within all of these states and from outside benefactors, most notably, the United States, the former Soviet Union, France, and Britain among others. It is also important to note that we are excluding the lone democracy in the region, Israel, from this analysis.

For most of that period, scholars and analysts across the region and around the world talked about the Middle East "not being ready for democracy" and not able to embrace such traditions. Although there were a few internal and external voices who argued against this view, the notion that democracy could not find root in the Middle East became a self-fulfilling prophecy and a prime justification in the West for supporting monarchies and nondemocratic regimes. Chief among these were Egypt under Sadat and Mubarak, Tunisia under Bella, Saudi Arabia under the House of Saud, and others states such as Jordan, the UAE, Kuwait, and Oman. In every case, whether the benefactor was the United States, the former Soviet Union, or other states, the common dynamic was authoritarian government was the norm and not the exception.

Now with the advent of uprisings in Tunisia, what many are calling the *Arab Spring* has emerged. Almost every state has seen varying levels of popular protest, from peaceful demonstrations in Morocco to outright civil war in Libya. In almost every instance, regimes have tried to at the least co-opt and at the worst violently silence the protests and shut off the contagion, but through the power of social media (see Issue 14) the "virus" has spread. In every case, the protests have been largely led by those under age 40 and the issues that drive them have centered primarily on regime corruption, economic and political justice, and democratic empowerment. The fractions involved are numerous and the role of women in several uprisings, most notably Tunisia, Egypt, and Libya, is striking.

For those who are young, it is akin to quite possibly witnessing the events of the French and American Revolutions unfold before your flat screens. Or perhaps watching the year 1848 in Europe where political and social movements converged to change regimes and the times. The difference is most certainly the immediacy of the images and information and the sheer speed of its dissemination. Where governments could at a moment throw up literal and figurative walls to keep out democratic ideas and perspectives, now the walls are porous and permeable. Youthful desires for change can be felt, organized, and activated via Twitter or Facebook and governments can do little to stop it.

The analyses are now running concurrent with events as reporters and others try to ascertain the character of the movements, the goals and aspirations of them, and also what types of governments, if successful, will come after the old regimes. Questions still abound about how "democratic" these movements are and who and what is behind them. One school of thought is that these movements are true democratic uprisings of the street fueled by the power of social media and rife with decades of unfulfilled aspirations for jobs, advancement, justice, and a voice. Others are contending that it is merely another form of factional challenge to elite control and that one elite will simply replace another with cosmetic changes but little substantive revolution taking place. Still others believe that somehow Islamic Fundamentalist movements are behind the uprisings and that countries like Iran are engineering such movements and then will highjack them for their own anti-Western, anti-U.S. ends.

Layered on top of this movement is of course the vitality of this region to the global economy, that is, oil. All one needs do is watch the price of oil on the global markets from the time of the first uprising in Tunisia through to the conflict in Libya and crackdowns in Syria to know that this Arab Spring has a central impact on oil and therefore the global economy. And, the core of that issue is of course Saudi Arabia. Policymakers, corporations, and literally billions are watching whether this movement spreads into Saudi Arabia. Quietly, they are hoping that it does not, if for no other reason than stability.

What is clear is that we are witnessing something monumental and unprecedented in the Middle East. Masses of people are risking death to protest their government's legitimacy in the name of democracy (however defined) and economic and social empowerment. In some cases, women are a clear and demonstrative voice in this movement. And it is safe to say that with the collapse of regimes in Tunisia and Egypt, and the imminent collapse in Yemen and Libya, the genie is out of the bottle.

Analysts will be discussing this Arab Spring for many years and evaluating its impact across the region and in every state, but fundamentally the Middle East has already been changed. Political and social unrest has proven a successful weapon against dictatorial regimes and thus subsequent groups will use this tool when the state fails to meet their expectations in profound ways.

In this section, the authors examine how democratic this movement is and whether it means true awakening of a democratic, diverse political culture in these societies, or just more of the same.

YES ⤶

Fareed Zakaria

How Democracy Can Work in the Middle East

When Frank Wisner, the seasoned U.S. diplomat and envoy of President Obama, met with Hosni Mubarak on Tuesday, Feb. 1, the scene must have been familiar to both men. For 30 years, American diplomats would enter one of the lavish palaces in Heliopolis, the neighborhood in Cairo from which Mubarak ruled Egypt. The Egyptian President would receive the American warmly, and the two would begin to talk about American-Egyptian relations and the fate of Middle East peace. Then the American might gently raise the issue of political reform. The President would tense up and snap back, "If I do what you want, the Islamic fundamentalists will seize power." The conversation would return to the latest twist in the peace process.

It is quite likely that a version of this exchange took place on that Tuesday. Mubarak would surely have warned Wisner that without him, Egypt would fall prey to the radicalism of the Muslim Brotherhood, Egypt's Islamist political movement. He has often reminded visitors of the U.S.'s folly in Iran in 1979, when it withdrew support for a staunch ally, the Shah, only to see the regime replaced by a nasty anti-American theocracy. But this time, the U.S. diplomat had a different response to the Egyptian President's arguments. It was time for the transition to begin.

And that was the message Obama delivered to Mubarak when the two spoke on the phone on Feb. 1. "It was a tough conversation," said an Administration official. Senior national-security aides gathered around a speakerphone in the Oval Office to listen to the call. Mubarak made it clear how difficult the uprising had been for him personally; Obama pressed the Egyptian leader to refrain from any violent response to the hundreds of thousands in the streets. But a day later, those streets—which had been remarkably peaceful since the demonstrations began—turned violent. In Cairo, Mubarak supporters, some of them wading into crowds on horseback, began battering protesters.

It was a reminder that the precise course that Egypt's revolution will take over the next few days and weeks cannot be known. The clashes between the groups supporting and opposing the government mark a new phase in the conflict. The regime has many who live off its patronage, and they could fight to keep their power. But the opposition is now energized and empowered. And the world—and the U.S.—has put Mubarak on notice.

Whatever happens in the next few days will not change the central narrative of Egypt's revolution. Historians will note that Jan. 25 marked the start of the end of Mubarak's 30-year reign. And now we'll test the theory that politicians and scholars have long debated. Will a more democratic Egypt become a radical Islamic state? Can democracy work in the Arab world?

Backward, Corrupt, Peaceable

Few thought it ever would come to this. Egypt has long been seen as a society deferential to authority, with a powerful state and a bureaucracy that might have been backward and corrupt but nonetheless kept the peace. "This a country with a remarkable record of political stability," wrote Fouad Ajami in an essay in 1995, pointing out that in the past two centuries, Egypt has been governed by just two regimes, a monarchy set up in 1805 and the Free Officers Movement that came to power in 1952 with Gamal Abdel Nasser. (France, by comparison, has been through a revolution, two empires, five republics and a quasi-fascist dictatorship in much the same period.) In the popular imagination, Egyptians are passive, meekly submitting to religion and hierarchy. But by the end of January the streets of Cairo and Alexandria and other cities were filled with a different people: crowds of energetic, strong-willed men from all walks of life and even some women, all determined to shape their destiny and become masters of their own fate.

What changed? Well, Egyptians were never as docile as their reputation suggested. Egyptian society has spawned much political activism, from Islamic radicals to Marxists to Arab nationalists to liberals. But ever since the late 1950s, the Egyptian regime has cracked down on its civil society, shutting down political parties, closing newspapers, jailing politicians, bribing judges and silencing intellectuals. Over the past three decades Egypt became a place where few serious books were written, universities were monitored, newspapers carefully followed a bland party line and people watched what they said in public. In the past 20 years, the war against Islamic terrorist groups—often genuinely brutal thugs—allowed Mubarak's regime to clamp down even harder on Egyptian society in the name of security.

Reform and Revolution

Egypt has had some successes, and ironically, one of them has helped foment change. Over the past decade, Egypt has been reforming its economy. From the mid-1990s on, Egypt found that in order to get loans from the IMF and the World Bank, it had to dismantle the most inefficient parts of its somewhat socialist economic system. In recent years, Mubarak—persuaded by his son Gamal, a Western-trained banker—appointed a set of energetic reformers to his Cabinet, who embarked on an ambitious effort to restructure the Egyptian economy, lowering taxes and tariffs, eliminating regulations and reducing subsidies. Egypt, long moribund, began growing vigorously. From 2006 to 2008, the economy expanded about 7% a year, and even last year, after the economic crisis, growth came in at almost 6%. Long isolated behind protectionist walls, with media in the regime's grip, Egypt also became more connected with the world through the new communication technologies.

Why would economic progress spur protests? Growth stirs things up, upsets the settled, stagnant order and produces inequalities and uncertainties. It also creates new expectations and demands. Tunisia was not growing as vigorously as Egypt, but there too a corrupt old order had opened up, and the resulting ferment proved too much for the regime to handle. Alexis de Tocqueville once observed that "the most dangerous moment for a bad government is when it begins to reform itself." It is a phenomenon that political scientists have dubbed "a revolution of rising expectations." Dictatorships find it difficult to handle change because the structure of power they have set up cannot respond to the new, dynamic demands coming from their people. So it was in Tunisia; so it was in Egypt. Youth unemployment and food prices might have been the immediate causes, but the underlying trend was a growing, restive population, stirred up by new economic winds, connected to a wider world. (Notice that more-stagnant countries like Syria and North Korea have remained more stable.)

Mubarak coupled the forward moves in the economy with a series of harsh, backward steps politically. Having allowed somewhat more open parliamentary elections in 2005, the regime reversed course and rigged the elections massively in 2010, reducing the Muslim Brotherhood's representation in parliament from 88 to zero. Ayman Nour, who ran against Mubarak in the presidential election in 2005, was arrested on trumped-up charges, jailed, tortured and finally released in 2009. Mubarak had allowed some freedom of speech and assembly surrounding the 2005 elections, then reversed what little opening there had been. Judges and lawyers who stood up to the regime were persecuted.

On the crucial question of political succession, Mubarak bitterly disappointed many Egyptians, including several in his Cabinet, who believed that 2011 would be the year for a transition to an Egypt without him. (Many of his aides, to be clear, hoped that their patron, Gamal Mubarak, might rise in a controlled political atmosphere. But even they thought the system would have to become far more open.) Last year, Mubarak signaled that he intended to run for a sixth term, despite being 82 and in poor health. It was a sign that whatever progress might take place with the economy, serious political reform was unthinkable.

The Case for Hope

Had Mubarak made the speech promising not to run again last year rather than on Feb. 1, he would have been hailed as a reformer ushering his country into a new era. Today, it seems too little, too late. But his reputation will depend in large part on what sort of regime succeeds him. If Egypt does descend into chaos or become an Iranian-style theocracy, people might look back at Mubarak's regime fondly. Ironically, if Egypt does better and turns into a functioning democracy, his legacy as the dictator who ruled his country before it moved to greater freedom will be more mixed.

Which will it be? Anyone making predictions with confidence is being foolhardy. Egypt is a vast, complex country and is in the midst of unprecedented change. There are certainly troubling signs. When the Pew Research Center surveyed the Arab world last April, it found that Egyptians have views that would strike the modern Western eye as extreme. Pew found that 82% of Egyptians support stoning as a punishment for adultery, 84% favor the death penalty for Muslims who leave the religion, and in the struggle between "modernizers" and "fundamentalists," 59% identify with fundamentalists.

That's enough to make one worry about the rise of an Iranian-style regime. Except that this is not all the Pew surveys show. A 2007 poll found that 90% of Egyptians support freedom of religion, 88% an impartial judiciary and 80% free speech; 75% are opposed to censorship, and, according to the 2010 report, a large majority believes that democracy is preferable to any other kind of government.

I remain convinced that fears of an Egyptian theocracy are vastly overblown. Shi'ite Iran is a model for no country—certainly not a Sunni Arab society like Egypt. The nation has seen both Mubarak and Iran's mullahs and wants neither. More likely is the prospect of an "illiberal democracy," in which Egypt becomes a country with reasonably free and fair elections, but the elected majority restricts individual rights and freedoms, curtails civil society and uses the state as its instrument of power. The danger, in other words, is less Iran than Russia.

My hope is that Egypt avoids this path. I cannot tell you in all honesty that it will. But much evidence suggests that democracy in Egypt could work. First, the army, which remains resolutely secular, will thwart any efforts to create a religious political order. The Egyptian army may well fight the efforts of democrats to dismantle some elements of the military dictatorship—since the elites of the armed forces have benefited mightily from that system—but it is powerful and popular enough to be able to draw certain lines. In Egypt, as in Turkey, the army has the opportunity to play a vital role in modernizing the society and checking the excesses of religious politics.

Egyptian civil society is rich and complex and has within it a persistent liberal strain. Since Napoleon's invasion of Egypt in 1798, Egyptians have wanted to catch up with the West. Liberal currents of thought and politics have repeatedly flourished in the country—prominently in the 1880s, the 1920s and the 1950s. Egypt's Fundamental Law of 1882 was an advance over almost all Asian and Middle Eastern constitutions at the time.

Egypt also retains some core elements of a liberal constitutional order, chief among them a judiciary that has fought excessive state power for decades. In a fascinating and timely book published in 2008, *Egypt After Mubarak*, Bruce Rutherford of Colgate University details the long and persistent struggle of the judiciary to carve out an independent role for itself, even under a military dictatorship. The recent moves toward a more open and market-based economy have also created a new business elite that has some stake in a liberal, constitutional order.

It is possible, of course, that the economic reforms will not continue. As in many countries, policies that revoke subsidies and dismantle protected industries provoke public anxiety and spirited opposition from business oligarchs (who often turn out to be those who have been protected). But given that Egypt will need economic growth, it will not be possible to turn back the basic movement toward freer markets. Such policies require better courts and laws, plus efforts to tackle corruption and improve education. And over time, they will create a middle class more independent of the state.

The Appeal, and Limits, of Islam

The real challenge remains the role of Islam, Islamic fundamentalists and the Muslim Brotherhood. Islam has a special appeal in Egypt and the broader Arab world, but it's important to understand why. Secular dictators have ruled these lands for decades and ruthlessly suppressed all political activity. The one place they could not shut down was the mosque, so it became the center of political activism and discourse, and Islam became the language of opposition.

This is not to deny that for many Egyptians, "Islam is the solution," as the Muslim Brotherhood's slogan claims. But the group has an allure in Egyptian society largely because it has been persecuted and banned for decades. Once it has to compete in the marketplace of ideas, it might find that, as in many Muslim countries, people are more worried about issues of governmental competence, corruption and growth than grand ideological statements.

Those issues, close to home, were at the heart of the protests not only in Egypt but also in Tunisia. It has been fascinating to watch as the legendary "Arab street" finally erupted spontaneously and freely. It turned out not to be consumed with the Middle East peace process and the Palestinians. Israelis have reacted to the unrest in Egypt with horror, convinced that any change will mean less security for their country. To an extent this is true. The peace between Egypt and Israel was never between two peoples but between their regimes. Israel might have to ask itself what policies it will have to pursue to create stability with a democratic Egypt. It would hardly be a cure-all, but were Israel to offer a deal that Palestinians accepted, it would surely help persuade Egyptians that Israel does not seek to oppress the Palestinian people.

The challenge for Israel is the challenge for the U.S. The Egyptian public's attitude toward America is poisoned by years of Washington's backing dictators and offering unflinching support for Israel. The U.S. too will have to ask what it will take to have better relations not merely with Egypt's military elite but with its people. And it will have to avoid the overreaction—common in Israel—that brands every move toward social conservatism as one toward jihad. Asking women to wear veils is different from making men wear suicide belts. If the U.S. is opposed to every expression of religiosity, it will find itself unable to understand or work with a new, more democratic Middle East.

The most interesting aspect of the protests in both Tunisia and Egypt has been how small America loomed in the public's imagination. Those on the street were not centrally concerned with the U.S., though Obama became a focus when it was clear that he could help in pushing Mubarak out. In Tunisia, the U.S. played an even smaller role. In a strange sense, this might be the consequence of both George W. Bush's and Obama's approaches in the region. After

9/11, Bush put a harsh spotlight on the problem of Arab dictatorships in a way that made them impossible to ignore. But he discredited his cause with a foreign policy that was deeply unpopular in the Arab world (the Iraq war, support for Israel, etc.). In 2005, Mubarak was able to tar democracy activists by pointing out that they were arguing for an American agenda for Egypt.

Obama, by contrast, pulled back from an overbearing, aggressive American role, which made it possible for Egyptian liberals and democrats to find their voices without being branded as U.S. puppets. (Even recently, the pro-Mubarak crowd warned that "outside forces" were trying to destabilize Egypt, but it didn't work.) In fact, the protests in Egypt, Tunisia, Jordan and elsewhere have resonated with the broader population of the Arab world because they came from within, having grown organically, and were concerned with the conditions of ordinary Arabs.

For five decades the Middle East has been force-fed a political discourse based on grand ideologies. For the Iranian protesters, America was not just a country or even a superpower but the "Great Satan." What is happening in Egypt and Tunisia might be a return to a more normal politics, fueled by the realities of the modern world, rooted in each country's conditions. In this sense, these might be the Middle East's first post-American revolutions.

Adam Shatz   ➔ **NO**

After Mubarak

Popular uprisings are clarifying events, and so it is with the revolt in Egypt. The Mubarak regime—or some post-Mubarak continuation of it—may survive this challenge, but the illusions that have held it in place have crumbled. The protests in Tahrir Square are a message not only to Mubarak and the military regime that has ruled Egypt since the Free Officers coup of 1952; they are a message to all the region's autocrats, particularly those supported by the West, and to Washington and Tel Aviv, which, after spending years lamenting the lack of democracy in the Muslim world, have responded with a mixture of trepidation, fear and hostility to the emergence of a pro-democracy movement in the Arab world's largest country. If these are the 'birth pangs of a new Middle East', they are very different from those Condoleezza Rice claimed to discern during Israel's war on Lebanon in the summer of 2006.

The first illusion to crumble was the myth of Egyptian passivity, a myth that had exerted a powerful hold over Egyptians. 'We're all just waiting for someone to do the job for us,' an Egyptian journalist said to me when I reported from Cairo last year (*LRB*, 27 May 2010); despite the proliferation of social movements since the 1970s, the notion of a mass revolt against the regime was inconceivable to her. When Galal Amin, a popular Egyptian sociologist, remarked that 'Egyptians are not a revolutionary nation' in a recent al-Jazeera documentary, few would have disagreed. And until the Day of Rage on 25 January many Egyptians—including a number of liberal reformers—would have resigned themselves to a caretaker regime led by the intelligence chief, Omar Suleiman, if only to save themselves from the president's son Gamal Mubarak. The first to be surprised by the uprising were the Egyptians themselves, who—in the lyrical early days of the revolt, culminating in the 'million-man march' on Tahrir Square on 1 February—discovered that they were capable of taking matters into their own hands, of overcoming their fear of the police and collectively organising against the regime. And as they acquired a thrilling sense of their own power, they would settle only for the regime's removal.

The Mubarak regime was not the only Arab government to be shaken by the protests: the reverberations were soon felt in Yemen and Jordan, and in the West Bank, where Mahmoud Abbas's police cracked down on a march called in solidarity with Egypt's pro-democracy forces. What we're seeing in Cairo is both new and old: not an Islamist revolt but a broad-based social movement bridging the secular-religious divide, a 21st-century version of the Arab nationalism that had for many years seemed a spent force. And though the Egyptian protests have found a provisional figurehead in Mohammed ElBaradei, the movement is largely leaderless, in striking contrast to the heroic age of Arab nationalism, dominated by charismatic, authoritarian figures like Nasser and Boumedienne.

The revolt that began in Tunisia and spread to Egypt is a struggle against what Algerians call *hogra*, 'contempt', a struggle fed by anger over authoritarian rule, torture, corruption, unemployment and inequality, and—a lightning rod everywhere in the Arab world—deference to the US strategic agenda. Not surprisingly, US officials are nervous that revolts could break out in other friendly states. Asked whether he expected similar unrest in Jordan, John Kerry, who was admirably forthright in calling for Mubarak to stand down, dismissed the idea: 'King Abdullah of Jordan is extraordinarily intelligent, thoughtful, sensitive, in touch with his people. The monarchy there is very well respected, even revered.'

For years, Arab rulers told their Western patrons not to worry about their subjects, as though they were obedient, if sometimes unruly children, and these patrons were only too happy to follow this advice. There was nothing to fear from the Egyptians, accustomed as they were to despotism since the Pharaonic age. Mubarak might be hated by them, but he was our man in Cairo: 'family', as Hillary Clinton put it. (The Clinton and Mubarak families have been close for years.) So long as he opened the economy to multinationals, achieved high growth rates and honoured his foreign policy commitments—allowing swift passage for US warships through the Suez Canal, interrogating radical Islamists kidnapped by the CIA as part of the extraordinary rendition programme, maintaining the peace with Israel, tightening the siege of Gaza, opposing the 'resistance' front led by Iran—American military aid would continue to flow, at a rate of $1.3 billion a year.

A façade of euphemism had to be erected to disguise the nature of Mubarak's regime, and press accounts seemed to bolster it. Reading Western—particularly American—newspapers before the recent crackdown, one would hardly have known the degree of discontent in Egypt. Mubarak was typically described as an 'authoritarian' but 'moderate' and 'responsible' leader, almost never as a dictator. Popular anger over torture—and over the regime's cosy relations with Israel—was rarely discussed. But when the police attacked peaceful protesters throughout Egypt, and especially after Mubarak's thugs—armed with grenades, knives and petrol bombs, some wearing pro-Mubarak T-shirts that seemed to have been designed for the occasion—charged through Tahrir Square on 2 February on horses and camels, the regime's face was revealed: coarse, brutal, an unwitting parody of Orientalist clichés. Newspapers not known for their candour about Egypt began to describe it with a new, hard clarity.

The crisis in Egypt has also been a crisis for the Obama administration. Unlike the 'colour' revolutions in Eastern Europe, the Lebanese protests against Syrian troops or the Green Movement in Iran, the uprising in Egypt targeted an old and trusted ally, not an enemy. Coming out in support of the Tunisian protesters made the Obama administration feel good, but it required no sacrifice.

Egypt, a pillar of US strategy in the greater Middle East, particularly in the 'peace process', was a harder case. Until late January, the US did not hesitate to call Mubarak a friend, or to extend all courtesies to visiting members of the Egyptian military. But when Egyptians went into open revolt, the US was suddenly very tight-lipped about its old friend in Cairo. A new discourse was rapidly invented. Some Western officials failed to catch on to the shift: Joe Biden was widely ridiculed for saying that Mubarak couldn't be a dictator because he was friendly with Israel; Tony Blair praised him as 'immensely courageous and a force for good'—yesterday's message. But when Blair said that Egypt's transition had to be 'managed'—presumably by the West—so as not to jeopardise the 'peace process', he was only saying openly what Washington believed.

Obama couldn't very well come out against the protesters; they embodied the values which, in his Cairo speech, he claimed the United States would always support. But the administration clearly didn't want Mubarak to be chased out of office, as Zine Abedine Ben-Ali of Tunisia had been. Instead, he had to be eased out so that a popular revolution could be averted, and a regime friendly to the US and Israel preserved: otherwise Egypt would be 'lost'. And so, even as Obama increased the pressure on Mubarak to stand down, he refused to side with the demonstrators, reserved his highest praise for the military, and insisted that Washington would not interfere in the question of who rules Egypt. But in the eyes of the demonstrators, the US could hardly pretend to be neutral: the tear gas canisters fired at them were labelled 'Made in America', as were the F-16s monitoring them from the sky. In calling for something more than a 'managed' transition under military rule, the demonstrators in Egypt were defying not just Mubarak but the US. The Mubarak regime was infuriated by Obama's statement on 1 February that the transition 'must begin now', but the emphasis on an 'orderly transition' was a hint that the US preferred continuity, or perhaps a soft coup by defectors in the army: there were, after all, shared interests at stake which no expression of 'people power' could be permitted to sabotage. The man who was sent to Cairo to deliver Washington's message to Mubarak was an old friend: Frank G. Wisner, the former ambassador to Egypt and a lobbyist in DC for the Egyptian military.

Mubarak, when he stands down, is not likely to be missed by many people in Egypt, where he has pledged to spend his last days, but he will be missed in Washington and, above all, in Tel Aviv. Mubarak and Omar Suleiman, now the interim vice president, worked closely with Israel on everything from the Gaza blockade to intelligence-gathering; they allowed Israeli warships into the Suez Canal to prevent weapons smuggling into Gaza from Sudan, and did their best to stir up tensions between Fatah and Hamas. The Egyptian public is well aware of this intimate collaboration, and ashamed of it: democratisation could spell its end. A democratic government isn't likely to abolish the peace treaty with Israel—even some of the leaders of the Muslim Brotherhood have said they would respect it. But Egyptian foreign policy would be set in Cairo rather than in Washington and Tel Aviv, and the cold peace would grow colder. A democratic government in Cairo would have to take public opinion into account, much as Erdogan's government does in Turkey: another former US client state but one that, in marked contrast to Egypt, has escaped

American tutelage, made the transition to democracy under an Islamist government, and pursued an independent foreign policy that is widely admired in the Muslim world. If Egypt became a democracy, it might work to achieve Palestinian unity, open up the crossing from Gaza and improve relations with Iran and Hizbullah: shifts which would be anathema to Israel.

Almost from the moment the demonstrations began, while much of the world rejoiced at the scenes in Tahrir Square, Binyamin Netanyahu and other high-ranking Israeli officials were urging Western politicians to stop criticising Mubarak, and raising fears of an Iranian-style revolution. For years, Israel had said it could hardly be expected to make concessions in such a dangerously undemocratic region. But as calls for Mubarak's exit grew, Israeli officials and commentators began to talk about Arab democracy as if it constituted another existential threat to the Jewish state. 'If, the day after elections [in Egypt], we have an extremist religious dictatorship, what good are democratic elections?' Shimon Peres asked, while Moshe Arens, the former defence minister, wondered in *Haaretz* whether Israel could make peace only with dictators like Mubarak. As one Israeli commentator wrote in *Yediot Ahronot*, Israel has been 'overtaken by fear: the fear of democracy. Not here, in neighbouring countries.'

Israel's fears of Egyptian democracy were instantly echoed by its supporters in the US. David Makovsky of the Washington Institute for Near East Policy worried that 'what starts as a Berlin revolution of 1989 morphs into a Tehran revolution of 1979.' Israel would then find itself with a Hizbullah-led government to the north, Hamas to the west and the Muslim Brothers to the south. To stave off such a scenario, he said, Egypt would be better off under a military regime led by Omar Suleiman during a transition that 'brings in constructive forces of Egyptian civil society'. These 'constructive forces', according to Malcolm Hoenlein, the executive vice president of the Conference of Presidents of Major American Jewish Organisations, would not include ElBaradei, whom he attacked as a 'stooge of Iran'. (ElBaradei earned the enmity of the Israel lobby for denouncing the Gaza blockade as a 'brand of shame on the forehead of every Arab, every Egyptian and every human being', and for opposing military confrontation with Iraq and Iran.) 'Things are about to go from bad to worse in the Middle East,' Richard Cohen, a columnist for the *Washington Post*, warned:

> The dream of a democratic Egypt is sure to produce a nightmare . . . The next Egyptian government—or the one after—might well be composed of Islamists. In that case, the peace with Israel will be abrogated and the mob currently in the streets will roar its approval . . . I care about democratic values, but they are worse than useless in societies that have no tradition or respect for minority rights. What we want for Egypt is what we have ourselves. This, though, is an identity crisis. We are not them.

As I write, Cohen has little to fear. A different kind of nightmare appears to be unfolding in Egypt: the brutal repression of a mass movement for democracy by a regime bent on staying in power, and confident that its backers will give it time to do the job. Seldom has the hidden complicity between Western governments and Arab authoritarianism been so starkly revealed. Protesters are being savagely beaten by the *baltagiya*—paid thugs—and opposition figures and foreign journalists have been arrested. I have just learned that Ahmed Seif, a human rights lawyer I interviewed last year in Cairo, has been jailed along with several other colleagues, accused of spying for Iran.

By 3 February, Thursday evening, Omar Suleiman seemed to be in charge. A hard, smooth-talking man, he cast himself as a national saviour in an interview on state television, defending Egypt from the 'chaos' the regime has done its best to encourage, and from a sinister conspiracy to destabilise the country on the part of 'Iranian and Hamas agents', with help from al-Jazeera. Wednesday's mob violence in Tahrir Square would be investigated, he said (he denied any government responsibility), and the 'reform' process would go forward, but first demonstrators must go home—or face the consequences. With this grimly calibrated mix of promises and threats, Suleiman became the man of the hour: later that evening it was reported that the Obama administration was drafting plans for Mubarak's immediate removal and a transitional government under his long-serving intelligence chief.

Mubarak, however, gracelessly refused to co-operate with the patrons who now find him such an embarrassment. He wanted to retire, he told Christiane Amanpour, he was 'fed up', but feared that his rapid departure would lead to 'chaos'. The longer he remains in office, the more violence we're likely to see. But even if Suleiman replaces him, it won't be an 'orderly transition'—or a peaceful one—because Egypt's pro-democracy forces want something better than Mubarakism without Mubarak; they have not sacrificed hundreds of lives in order to be ruled by the head of intelligence.

From the Obama administration we can expect criticisms of the crackdown, prayers for peace, and more calls for 'restraint' on 'both sides'—as if there were symmetry between unarmed protesters and the military regime—but Suleiman will be given the benefit of the doubt. Unlike ElBaradei, he's a man Washington knows it can deal with. The men and women congregating in Tahrir Square have the misfortune to live in a country that shares a border with Israel, and to be fighting a regime that for the last three decades has provided indispensable services to the US. They are well aware of this. They know that if the West allows the Egyptian movement to be crushed, it will be, in part, because of the conviction that 'we are not them,' and that we can't allow them to have what we have. Despite the enormous odds, they continue to fight.

EXPLORING THE ISSUE

Is the Middle East Undergoing a Democratic Revolution?

Critical Thinking and Reflection

1. How representative are these uprisings of the mass of people in the Middle East?
2. How much of these uprisings is economic and how much is political?
3. Does democratization in the Middle East mean better relations for outside states or worse?
4. How does oil impact the calculus for external states in evaluating the spread of democracy?
5. What is the logical long-term development of this phenomenon?

Is There Common Ground?

In terms of the Arab Spring, there are two clear areas of consensus. The first is that the Middle East is undergoing a revolution where masses of people are demanding more of a say in their government and society. This movement is largely based among the youth and most certainly is fueled in part by social media. The second area of agreement is that no one knows where this will ultimately lead. Some states will see this movement lead to democracy of one form or another, others will see it co-opted by nondemocratic forces like fundamentalism or the military, while others will see years of instability and factionalism which has been within these societies but dormant for years.

Additional Resources

Note: Because of the immediacy of the democratic revolutions in the Middle East, few if any in depth analyses have been written. Therefore, the key sources for review are still articles.

Abouzeid, Rania, "Has Arab Spring Made Bin Laden an Afterthought?" *TIME* (May 2, 2011)

Anderson, Liza, "Demystifying the Arab Spring," *Foreign Affairs* (May/June 2011)

Khalidi, Rashid, "The Arab Spring," *The Nation* (March 21, 2011)

Lizza, Ryan, "The Consequentialist: How Arab Spring Remade Obama's Foreign Policy," *The New Yorker* (May 2, 2011)

UNIT 5

Bonus Issues

*T*he two debates presented in this unit represent issues that are new to the expanded edition.

- Is the International Community Making Effective Progress in Securing Global Human Rights?
- Should Israel Preempt Against Iran's Nuclear Program?

ISSUE 21

Is the International Community Making Effective Progress in Securing Global Human Rights?

YES: Council on Foreign Relations, from "The Global Human Rights Regime," *Issue Brief* (May 11, 2012)

NO: Amnesty International, from *Amnesty International Report 2012: The State of the World's Human Rights* (Amnesty International, London, 2012)

Learning Outcomes

After reading this issue, you should be able to:

- Develop a basic understating of the evolution of the international community's concern for human rights.
- Distinguish between how the international community approached the human rights issue prior to and after World War II.
- Briefly describe the basic role played by the United Nations in the advancement of human rights between 1945 and 2006.
- Briefly discuss the tension between universal human rights and national sovereignty.
- Briefly discuss the different approaches to human rights taken by the Western and communist blocs during the Cold War.
- Describe recent progress made by the international community in advancing universal human rights.
- Describe current challenges faced by the international community in advancing human rights.
- Describe Amnesty International's analysis of recent failures in the international advancement of human rights.

ISSUE SUMMARY

YES: The Council on Foreign Relations, an independent nonpartisan and essentially American think tank, in *Issue Brief* summarizes the development of an elaborate global system of governmental and nongovernmental organizations developed primarily over the past few decades to promote human rights throughout the world, while recognizing that the task is still far from complete.

NO: Amnesty International's annual report on the state of human rights around the world suggests major failures in all regions ("Failed leadership has gone global in the last year . . ."), with specific restrictions on free speech in at least 91 countries and cases of torture and other ill-treatment in over 101 countries.

Human rights has become such a common phrase in our everyday vocabulary that one might think that the seeking and practice of human rights have been part of human behavior for well over a millennium. This view is probably reinforced by the fact that one of the enduring events of a high school world history class is the signing of the Magna Carta in 1215, acknowledged by most as the first successful effort by humans to limit the power of a sovereign and thus protect some of its subjects. But indeed, we can go back to the ancient Greeks for the first references to the idea that humans have fundamental rights and freedoms simply by virtue of the fact that they are members of the human race. The Greek notion of universal rights, championed by Greek philosophers or Stoics, influenced Roman thinking, which in turn ultimately spread throughout Europe. Those who read political philosophy are familiar with men like John Locke, Immanuel Kant, Hugo Grotius, Rousseau, and Voltaire.

These men's writings influenced the early attempts of citizens to rise up against their national rulers demanding protection of rights that they believed originated not with these human rulers but with a higher order. English history is replete with references to citizen demands for sovereign recognition of their rights, culminating with a revolution against the king in 1688. But it is the American revolution of 1776 and the French revolution of 1789 that have captured the headlines in the early struggle for human rights. The former was a rather modest revolution, conducted on the basic principle that individuals have a right to determine their own form of government and also their ruler. The French episode was much broader, representing a struggle for equality throughout society.

These revolutions and others that followed were characterized by one major fact. They were staged within the confines of a single country. That is, they were domestic battles launched against a national ruler and fought within the context of the nation-state system. The latter international arrangement, emerging in the early sixteenth century, laid out the norms of national governments and the behavior among them. Chief among these rules was the idea that national leaders were sovereign. That is, they had complete authority over how they ruled, including how they treated their citizens. And the rest of the world was not to interfere in the internal affairs of the country, no matter how egregious the ruler's behavior.

By the nineteenth century, however, cracks began to appear in the extreme idea of total national sovereignty, first on the issue of slavery and later on the issue of soldiers, prisoners, and other victims of war. But it was not until World War II and the initial evidence of Nazi atrocities that national leaders began to think and talk seriously about the need for global human rights. President Franklin Roosevelt in early 1941 announced to Congress America's commitment to four freedoms—of speech and expression, of religion, from economic hardship, and from fear. These freedoms were formalized later that year in the Atlantic Charter by Roosevelt and his British counterpart, Winston Churchill.

As World War II was winding down in spring 1945, world leaders met in San Francisco and created a new international organization, the United Nations, giving it responsibility for not only maintaining and restoring peace throughout the world but also entrusting it with other important responsibilities, among them identifying and securing human rights for citizens throughout the globe. Indeed, the UN Charter mentions human rights many times through the document.

The first step in identifying human rights was the UN's adoption of the Universal Declaration of Human Rights in 1948, which lays out 29 separate categories of human rights and claims them to be universal, that is, relevant for all citizens of the globe no matter where they live and no matter the form of government under which they live. How a government treats its own citizens was now assumed to be a legitimate international concern that ought be addressed by appropriate international bodies such as the United Nations. It soon became evident that the two major players in the international arena, the Western bloc and the communist or Soviet bloc of nations, had different ideas over precisely which kinds of human rights were important, however. In short, the West focused on political and civil rights, while the Eastern bloc favored economic and social rights, thus creating tensions between the two blocs.

The other stumbling block in global efforts to ensure human rights for everyone was the clash between the concept of the universality of human rights and the basic principle of the nation-state system, national sovereignty. This was not a fight between East and West. Rather it was a struggle between democratic governments and nongovernments everywhere. The former suggested that government was limited and its powers flowed from its own citizens, while the latter argued that national rulers had few if any limitations on their capacity to rule their subjects, including freedom from outside interference. More recently, the concept of universality itself has been once again called into question, as some believe that earlier documents were biased in favor of Western thinking and also ignored other religious and national cultures.

Despite the challenges caused by both the Cold War and the national sovereignty versus universal human rights argument, the international community became increasingly interested in how governments treated their own citizens as well as how others in positions of authority treated those individuals under them. In fact, the United Nations was immediately busy with the task of codifying national behavior in many different areas of human rights. Its initial action was a Convention on Genocide, passed in 1948 as the Universal Declaration was in its last day of debate. This was the first of over 60 binding human rights treaties in effect today. It also immediately created a permanent body, the United Nations Commission on Human Rights (UNCHR), which focused on the promotion and protection of human rights. In 2006, the UN replaced UNCHR with a new body, the UN Human Rights Council. The work of UNCHR can be divided into two distinct phases. From 1947 until 1967, the promotion rather than the protection of human rights was emphasized, but after 1967 it focused on an interventionist strategy of protection. UNCHR was not without its critics during its 60-year existence, as the organization was often attacked for including member states whose record of human rights compliance within their own national boundaries was horrible, and for its selective "finger-pointing," with first South Africa and later Israel being all too frequent targets of attention. The move to disband UNCHR and replace it with another UN agency gained steam and was finally accomplished in 2006, but critics have not been silenced.

The United Nations has not been the only global body to concern itself with human rights. Increasingly, other international regional governmental agencies as well as international nongovernmental organizations, many with a secular focus on one area such as child abuse or abuse of women, have joined the fight against human rights violators. It is not surprising that nongovernmental organizations are playing increasingly important roles, as its citizen members strive to fill the void caused by inaction of reluctant leaders of national governments.

One alternative approach to analyzing progress on human rights is to focus on very specific areas within the broad range of political, economic, and social rights, for progress has been significant in selected categories of rights. Two such successful examples relate to the international community's handling of perpetrators of war crimes, as the example of Slobodan Milošević of Serbia shows, or a revolutionary government's handling of deposed dictators such as revealed in the case of Hosni Mubarak of Egypt or Saddam Hussein of Iraq, not to mention half a dozen other ousted or soon-to-be-ousted dictators. It was not too long ago when those national leaders who engaged in unjust wars or abused their own citizens were never made to account for their behavior.

Another alternative approach to the question of international progress on human rights is to focus on the extent to which the global community has made significant progress on meeting the eight Millennium Development Goals spelled out over a decade ago by the United Nations. The latter organization, in fact, used a human rights framework to report in 2010 on the extent to which nations of the globe have met these goals.

In the YES selection, the Council on Foreign Relations suggests an on-balance "glass is half-full" viewpoint, namely that an "elaborate global system is being developed" for the protection of human rights. While alluding to the fact that more national governments are promoting human rights, it suggests that an increasing "dynamic and decentralized network of civil society actors" is beginning to make a significant difference. In the NO selection, Amnesty International's annual report (2012) sums up the current state of progress in human rights advocacy by asserting that "failed leadership has gone global . . . with politicians responding to protests with brutality or indifference."

YES ↩ Council on Foreign Relations

The Global Human Rights Regime

Scope of the Challenge

Although the concept of human rights is abstract, how it is applied has a direct and enormous impact on daily life worldwide. Millions have suffered crimes against humanity. Millions more toil in bonded labor. In the last decade alone, authoritarian rule has denied civil and political liberties to billions. The idea of human rights has a long history, but only in the past century has the international community sought to galvanize a regime to promote and guard them. Particularly, since the United Nations (UN) was established in 1945, world leaders have cooperated to codify human rights in a universally recognized regime of treaties, institutions, and norms.

An elaborate global system is being developed. Governments are striving to promote human rights domestically and abroad, and are partnering with multilateral institutions to do so. A particularly dynamic and decentralized network of civil society actors is also involved in the effort.

Together, these players have achieved marked success, though the institutionalization and implementation of different rights is progressing at varying rates. Response to mass atrocities has seen the greatest progress, even if enforcement remains inconsistent. The imperative to provide people with adequate public health care is strongly embedded across the globe, and substantial resources have been devoted to the challenge. The right to freedom from slavery and forced labor has also been integrated into international and national institutions, and has benefited from high-profile pressure to combat forced labor. Finally, the steady accumulation of human rights-related conventions has encouraged most states to do more to implement binding legislation in their constitutions and statutes.

Significant challenges to promoting human rights norms remain, however. To begin with, the umbrella of human rights is massive. Freedom from slavery and torture, the imperative to prevent gender and racial persecution, and the right to education and health care are only some of the issues asserted as human rights. Furthermore, nations continue to dispute the importance of civil and political versus economic, social, and cultural rights. National governments sometimes resist adhering to international norms they perceive as contradicting local cultural or social values. Western countries—especially the United States—resist international rights cooperation from a concern that it might harm business, infringe on autonomy, or limit freedom of speech. The world struggles to balance democracy's promise of human rights protection against its historically Western identification.

Moreover, implementing respect for established human rights is problematic. Some of the worst violators have not joined central rights treaties or institutions, undermining the initiatives' perceived effectiveness. Negligence of international obligations is difficult to penalize. The UN Charter promotes "fundamental freedoms," for example, but also affirms that nations cannot interfere with domestic matters. The utility of accountability measures, such as sanctions or force, and under what conditions, is also debatable. At times, to secure an end to violent conflict, negotiators choose not to hold human rights violators accountable. Furthermore, developing nations are often incapable of protecting rights within their borders, and the international community needs to bolster their capacity to do so—especially in the wake of the Arab Spring. Finally, questions remain over whether the UN, regional bodies, or other global actors should be the primary forums to advance human rights.

In the long term, strengthening the human rights regime will require a broadened and elevated UN human rights architecture. A steady coalition between the global North and South to harmonize political and economic rights within democratic institutions will also be necessary. In the meantime, regional organizations and nongovernmental organizations must play a larger role from the bottom up, and rising powers must do more to lead. Together, these changes are the world's best hope for durable and universal enjoyment of human rights.

Human Rights: Strengths and Weaknesses

Overall Assessment: *Heightened Attention, Uneven Regional Efforts, Weak Global Compliance*

The international human rights regime has made several welcome advances—including increased responsiveness in the Muslim world, attention to prevention and accountability for atrocities, and great powers less frequently standing in the way of action, notably at the UN Security Council (UNSC). Yet, despite responses to emerging cases demanding action, such as Sudan and Libya, global governance in ensuring human rights has faltered.

Many experts credit intergovernmental organizations (IGOs) for advances—particularly in civil and political rights. These scholars cite the creation of an assortment of secretariats, administrative support, and expert personnel to institutionalize and implement human rights norms. Overall, the United Nations (UN) remains the central global institution for developing international norms and legitimizing efforts to implement them, but the number of actors involved has grown exponentially.

The primary mechanisms include UNSC action, the UN Human Rights Council (UNHRC), committees of elected experts, various rapporteurs, special representatives, and working groups. War crimes tribunals—the International Criminal Court (ICC), tribunals for the former Yugoslavia and Rwanda, and hybrid courts in Sierra Leone and Cambodia—also contribute to the development and enforcement of standards. All seek to raise political will and public consciousness, assess human rights–related conduct of states and warring parties, and offer technical advice to states on improving human rights. . . .

Of all UN bodies with a similar focus, the UNHRC receives the most attention. In its former incarnation as the Commission on Human Rights, it developed a reputation for allowing the participation—and even leadership—of notorious human rights abusers, which undermined its legitimacy. Reconstituted as the UNHRC in 2006, the new forty-seven member body has a higher threshold for membership as well as a universal periodic review process, which evaluates the human rights records of states, including those on the council. Nevertheless, the UNHRC's effectiveness has been uneven. On the one hand, it took the unprecedented decision to vote to suspend Libya in 2011 and passed a pioneering resolution on sexual orientation. On the other, it maintains a disproportionate focus on Israel, ignores major abuses in other nations, avoids condemning specific rights issues, and still includes serial rights abusers in its ranks. . . .

Increasingly, the locus of activity on human rights is moving to the regional level, but at markedly different paces from place to place. Regional organizations and powers contribute to advancing human rights protections in their neighborhoods by bolstering norms, providing mechanisms for peer review, and helping countries codify human rights stipulations within domestic institutions. Regional organizations are often considered the first lines of defense, and better able to address rights issues unique to a given area. This principle is explicitly mentioned in the UN Charter, which calls on member states to "make every effort to achieve pacific settlement of local disputes through such regional arrangements or by such regional agencies" before approaching the UNSC.

Major regional organizations in the Western Hemisphere, Europe, and Africa—such as the Organization of American States (OAS), the European Union (EU), and the African Union (AU)—have integrated human rights into their mandate and established courts to which citizens can appeal if a nation violates their rights. This has led to important rulings on slavery in Niger and spousal abuse in Brazil, for example, but corruption continues to hamper implementation throughout Latin America and Africa, and a dearth of leadership in African nations has slowed institutionalization.

Meanwhile, organizations in the Middle East and Asia, such as the Association of Southeast Asian Nations (ASEAN) and the South Asian Association for Regional Cooperation, focus primarily on economic cooperation and have historically made scant progress on human rights. The Arab League, however, departed from its indifference to human rights in 2011, backing UN action against Libya and sanctioning Syria, and may prove more committed to protecting human rights in the wake of the Arab Spring.

Civil society efforts have achieved the most striking success in human rights, though they often interact with international institutions and many national governments. Nongovernmental organizations provide valuable data and supervision, which can assist both states and international organizations. NGOs also largely rely on international organizations for funding, administrative support, and expert assistance. Indeed, more than 3,000 NGOs have been named as official consultants to the UN Economic and Social Council alone, and many more contribute in more abstract ways. Domestic NGOs understand needs on the ground far better than their international counterparts. That international NGOs are beginning to recognize this is clear in two recent developments: the first is financier-philanthropist George Soros's $100 million donation to Human Rights Watch to develop field offices staffed by locals, which enabled the organization to increase its annual operating budget to $80 million. Second, the number of capacity-building partnerships between Western-based NGOs and NGOs indigenous to a country is increasing. That said, NGOs have to date been more successful in advocacy—from achieving passage of the Anti-Personnel Mine Ban Convention to calling attention to governments' atrocities against their own citizens. Yet NGOs devoted to implementing human rights compliance have been catching up—on issues from democratic transitions to gender empowerment to protecting migrants.

Norm and Treaty Creation: *Prodigious but Overemphasized*

The greatest strength of the global governance architecture has been creating norms. Myriad treaties, agreements, and statements have enshrined human rights on the international community's agenda, and some regional organizations have followed suit. These agreements lack binding clauses to ensure that action matches rhetoric, however, and many important violators have not signed on. In addition, states often attach qualifiers to their signatures that dilute their commitments.

The array of treaties establishing standards for human rights commitments is broad—from political and civil liberties to economic, social, and cultural rights to racial discrimination to the rights of women, children, migrant workers, and more recently the disabled. Other global efforts have focused on areas such as labor rights and human trafficking. Regional organizations, most notably the Council of Europe and the Organization of American States, have also promulgated related instruments, although less uniformly. In addition, member states have articulated declarations and resolutions establishing human rights standards, and increasingly so in economic affairs. The United Nations Human Rights Council, in a departure from the premise that states are to be held accountable for human rights conduct, in 2011 even passed formal guidelines for related business responsibilities. . . .

Rights Monitoring: *Proliferating Experts, Increasing Peer-Based Scrutiny*

Monitoring is imperative to matching rhetoric with action. Over the years, human rights monitoring has matured and developed considerably, though serious challenges remain, such as ensuring freedom from torture for suspected terrorists, and uniformly protecting and promoting human rights despite the biases of rights organizations or officials entrusted with doing so.

The original United Nations Commission on Human Rights and its successor Human Rights Council (UNHRC) both authorized a wide array of special procedures to monitor human rights protection in functional areas and particular countries. Since the UNHRC was established in 2006, country-specific mandates have decreased, and functional monitors addressing economic and social rather than political and civil liberties have increased.

In addition, each UN human rights treaty has an elected body of experts to which state parties must report at regular intervals on implementation. For instance, the Human Rights Committee (not to be confused with the Council) is charged with receiving reports about the implementation of the International Covenant on Civil and Political Rights (ICCPR) and making nonbinding "concluding observations" about states' overall compliance. The Human Rights Committee can also receive complaints from individuals regarding state compliance with the accord. The UN Convention against Torture's monitoring mechanism, the Committee against Torture, is similar but can also send representatives to inspect areas where torture is suspected. However, the applicability of this unique monitoring tool is limited because investigations can be undertaken only in states that have ratified the First Optional Protocol to the UN Convention against Torture, which only sixty-one of 193 UN member states have done. . . .

Capacity Building: *Vital but Underemphasized*

Capacity building—especially for human rights—is often expensive and daunting, viewed with suspicion, and the success of assistance is notoriously hard to measure. In many cases, national governments have signed international commitments to promote and protect human rights, and earnestly wish to implement them, but are incapable of doing so. For example, many experts have noted that Libya may require an entirely new judicial system, following the collapse of Muammar al-Qaddafi's regime. On the other hand, some states refuse assistance from nongovernmental organizations (NGOs) and international organizations (IGOs), suspecting that it might interfere with domestic affairs. On balance, it also remains far easier, and less costly, for the international community to condemn, expose, or shame human rights abusers rather than provide material aid for human rights capacity building.

The international community has developed various ways to offer technical assistance. Most notable is the Office of the High Commissioner for Human Rights (OHCHR), established in 1993. In addition to providing an institutionalized moral voice, OHCHR offers technical assistance to states through an array of field offices—for example, by providing training to civilian law enforcement and judicial officials through its country office in Uganda, strengthening the Cambodian legal and institutional framework for human rights, and assisting Mexico with development of a National Program on Human Rights. Such work is undercut, however, by member states' propensity to prefer unilateral support for capacity building, to favor naming and shaming over capacity building, or to oppose human rights capacity building as either a threat to sovereignty or tantamount to neocolonialism.

Regional organizations such as the Organization for Security Cooperation in Europe (OSCE), Council of Europe, Organization of American States
(OAS), European Union, and to some extent the African Union, may be more
effective than the United Nations in sharing best practices and providing
capacity-building advice to states. Often capacity building entails training
human rights protectors and defenders, but it may also include legal framework building or addressing countries' specific capacity deficits. The OSCE,
for instance, collaborates with member states on election monitoring and
offers training and education to human rights defenders through its Office
for Democratic Institutions and Human Rights. In another example, the OAS
collaborates with European partners in its judicial facilitators program, which
trains judicial officials in rural areas with limited access to justice, and assisted
Haiti in establishing a civil registry. Still, sharing resources and coordinating
between IGOs and NGOs in capacity building are limited. As mentioned, norm
creation has outstripped both monitoring and implementing norms.

Human rights capacity building also occurs on a bilateral basis. Indeed,
some developed states prefer providing bilateral assistance to working with
IGOs and multilateral institutions because resources can be better monitored
and projects more carefully tailored to support donor state interests. For
instance, the U.S. Foreign Assistance Act of 1961, which laid the basis for the
creation of the U.S. Agency for International Development (USAID), calls for
the use of development assistance to promote economic and civil rights. Since
its inception, USAID has provided billions of dollars to support good governance, transparency building, and civil society projects worldwide. It recently
gave hundreds of millions of dollars to Liberia to train judges, promote the
rule of the law, and increase government transparency.

Meanwhile, other multilateral institutions like the World Bank, International Monetary Fund, and World Trade Organization also support human
rights promotion, but tend to do so more indirectly, through poverty allevia-
tion and community enhancement schemes. Together, though, these institutions face new constraints as the international community continues to grapple
with the global financial crisis and unprecedented budget deficits. . . .

As a whole, successful capacity building forms the core of long-term
efforts to improve human rights in countries. Regardless, human rights capacity building is often underemphasized both in states with the poorest of
human rights as well as among countries or intergovernmental organizations
that are most in a position to help. While NGOs are crucial contributors to
capacity-building efforts, they cannot—and should not—shoulder the entire
burden. Broad, crosscutting partnerships are essential for such efforts to enjoy
success and produce sustainable human rights reform.

Response to Atrocities: *Significant Institutionalization, Selective Action*

Atrocities of all sorts—whether war crimes, genocide, crimes against humanity,
or ethnic cleansing—have been a major focus in the international community
over the last two decades. A number of regional and country-specific courts, as

well as the International Criminal Court (ICC), provide potential models for ending impunity. However, these courts have unevenly prosecuted violators of human rights, and have been criticized for focusing on some abuses or regions while ignoring others.

In the aftermath of the Balkans and Rwanda in the 1990s, where UN peacekeepers on the ground failed to prevent mass killing and sexual violence, efforts to establish preventive and responsive norms to atrocities accelerated. To hold perpetrators accountable, the Rome Statute established the ICC as the standing tribunal for atrocities. The ICC was largely considered an alternative to ad hoc tribunals like those for the former Yugoslavia and Rwanda, which were criticized for proceeding too slowly and for requiring redundant and complex institution building. The ICC is the result of UN efforts to evaluate the prospects for an international court to address crimes like genocide as early as 1948. . . .

As for preventive action, former UN secretary-general Kofi Annan championed stronger norms for intervention against ongoing atrocities. In the wake of the Kosovo crisis, Annan cited the need for clarifying when international intervention should legally be used to prevent atrocities in states. In response, the Canadian-sponsored International Commission on Intervention and State Sovereignty promoted the concept of the "responsibility to protect" (R2P) in 2000 and 2001. This principle sought to reframe the debate over humanitarian intervention in terms of state sovereignty. Specifically, it placed the primary responsibility on states to protect their own citizens. When states failed, responsibility would fall to the international community. Annan's *In Larger Freedom* report picked up on this concept, and R2P informed two paragraphs in the Outcome Document of 2005 UN World Summit. The latter also included an emphasis on the importance of capacity-building assistance to help states meet their R2P obligations. In the UN Security Council (UNSC), the R2P doctrine has been invoked repeatedly—first generically affirmed, then raised in semi-germane cases in 2008 (in Myanmar after a cyclone and in Kenya during post-election violence), and then more conclusively in 2011 (UNSC Resolution 1973 on Libya). . . .

In short, the international community has taken its greatest step by redefining sovereignty as answerable to legal international intervention should a state fail to shield its citizens from atrocities, or worse yet, sponsor them. However, state practice has not matched these norms, and it remains to be seen whether consensus about Libya was sui generis.

Political and Civil Rights: *Disproportionately Institutionalized, Backlash on Free Expression and Association*

Treaties that define political and civil liberties are widely ratified, but many countries have not signed on to enforcement protocols, and many continue to violate the rights of their citizens regardless of treaties. In addition, the right of people to choose their leaders and freedom of the press, religion, and association has backslid in recent years. At the same time, however, people are increasingly demanding rights and attempting to bypass repression of illiberal regimes. New technology (such as cell phones, social media, and satellite television) is also providing unprecedented opportunities to publicize abuse and organize protests, though repressive regimes are closely following with practices to censor new technology.

States resisting the spread of political and civil liberties have been challenged more by civil society than by other states or by intergovernmental organizations (IGOs). Using information and communications technology, and with the support of global nongovernmental organizations (NGOs) and occasionally the private sector, civil society have taken their demands to a new level. China's effort to control dissent, for example, has been greatly challenged by Uighur dissenters in Xinjiang, Falun Gong groups, and the decision by Google to refuse to implement comprehensive censorship in China. However, international pressure remains relevant. For example, the Obama administration's recent statement that censorship practices in China may violate World Trade Organization rules has increased pressure on China to reform.

In the United Nations, the number of member states, organs, and generic mandates related to freedom of expression and association have increased. For instance, the UN General Assembly adopted a resolution in 2007 calling for the end of capital punishment. In September 2010, the UN Human Rights Council (UNHRC) adopted another resolution, creating a special rapporteur on rights to freedom of peaceful assembly and of association. This occurred in the wake of a multiyear backlash against domestic NGOs and their international philanthropic and civil society backers in a series of autocracies. . . .

Economic Rights and Business Responsibilities: *Increased Corporate Focus and Engagement*

A long-standing debate between the global North and global South has been over whether to prioritize negative obligations of states to avoid restricting political and civil liberties or positive obligations to deliver economic and social benefits. Indicators, however, show a subtle yet important shift in the last ten of the forty-year debate.

Until the end of the twentieth century, international law frameworks placed human rights obligations on the shoulders of states. Not least through former UN secretary-general Kofi Annan's role as an ideas entrepreneur, notions of the obligation of businesses on human rights have blossomed. First, in 2000, Annan and his Harvard-based scholar-adviser John Ruggie crafted the UN Global Compact, which enumerates voluntary principles for business related to human rights and environmental stewardship. The UN then created a mandate for a special representative of the secretary-general to assess state, business, and civil society stakeholders on business conduct and human rights. In July 2011, the UN Human Rights Council (UNHRC) adopted guidelines that delineate state obligations to protect human rights, business obligations to respect them, and a joint role to provide remedies to people robbed of them. These successes do not come without challenges, however. Ruggie, who has been at the forefront of business and human rights, completed his term as special representative in mid-2011, raising the prospect that UN efforts may stall in his absence. Further, although the UN Security Council's adoption of the Global Compact guidelines is significant, implementation will be a difficult next step. Additionally, the International Labor Organization (ILO) and its counterpart, the International Organization of Employers, have jointly engaged businesses on best practices on human rights.

Nevertheless, businesses' decisions to uphold human rights standards remain largely voluntary and thus subject to market—rather than moral— forces. Even when businesses make commitments to corporate responsibility programs, no actor exists to enforce such commitments. Civil society can play a critical role in mitigating these challenges, however, by publicizing corporate human rights abuses and working directly with businesses on corporate responsibility. NGOs such as Human Rights Watch, the Institute for Human Rights and Business, the International Federation for Human Rights, Global Witness, and the International League for Human Rights exemplify these efforts. Additionally, even where businesses act in violation of domestic laws or international conventions protecting human rights, limited domestic law enforcement capabilities undermine the force of accountability standards.

The international community's efforts to address economic and social rights have advanced. Some measures evidence a redefinition of human rights, such as the mandate from the UNHRC on toxic waste. Some entail ambitious norm setting, such as the UN Convention on the Rights of Persons with Disabilities, negotiated during the George W. Bush administration and signed by the Obama administration. Most important have been efforts to address economic and social rights with tangible programming. The Global Fund to Fight AIDS, Tuberculosis, and Malaria is a landmark achievement for bridging health, economic, and discriminatory ills; for mobilizing significant resources beyond regular assessed budgets of the UN; and for involving an array of UN, private sector, philanthropic, and civil society actors in a concerted partnership. It is worth noting that the global North (and its greatest skeptic on economic and social rights, the United States) have championed this effort, supplementing it heavily through the U.S. President's Emergency Plan for AIDS Relief (PEPFAR).

Child labor, forced labor, human trafficking, and contemporary slavery have also become a focus of global governance efforts since the beginning of the twenty-first century. Such abridgments of freedom and autonomy signal a tragic combination of economic desperation, weak rule of law, and discrimination. The ILO's work to address forced labor and the most acute forms of child labor through conventions and preventive programs has now been supplemented by other efforts. New energy has been directed to mitigating the most coercive of labor practices as a result of the near simultaneous enactment of the Palermo Protocol to the UN Crime Convention on Trafficking in Persons (TIP) and the U.S. Victims of Trafficking and Violence Protection Act in 2000.

The UNHRC has also authorized special rapporteurs on both human trafficking and contemporary slavery. States, intergovernmental organizations, and NGOs have developed partnerships to address child labor, forced labor, and human trafficking. Businesses are also joining global governance efforts, moving from sector-specific partnerships (such as the travel and hospitality sector on child sex trafficking and chocolate companies on child labor in West Africa) to cross-sectoral ones (such as the Athens Ethical Principles and emerging thought-leader coalitions).

Women's and Children's Rights: *Institutional Progress but Holdouts on Implementation*

The rights of women have advanced incrementally. The United Nations (UN) system has moved beyond creating norms, such as the Convention on the Elimination of All Forms of Discrimination against Women and the Convention on the Rights of the Child to more assertive leadership and calls for implementation efforts among national governments. However, despite marked success on various fronts, the UN estimates that women continue to make up less than 10 percent of world leaders and less than one-fifth of parliamentarians. Moreover, it remains to be seen whether the Arab Spring will help or hinder the cause of gender equality. Efforts to enhance the economic and social wellbeing of women and children have also improved, but remain at risk as a result of tightened national and international aid budgets.

Arguably, the decision of the UN Development Program to commission reports by Arab experts to link gender inequality and reduced development in the Arab world, published in 2005, was an important step forward. The formation of the UN Entity for Gender Equality and the Empowerment of Women (UN Women), amalgamating four existing agencies, received an additional boost when Chile's Michelle Bachelet was appointed its first leader. The remaining question is whether the consolidation of women's rights functions will mainstream or silo them. Around the world, more women have become involved in political participation—from the first woman elected head of state in Africa to the franchise in Gulf States.

The essential role of women in peace and consensus building has moved from statements like UN Security Council Resolution (UNSCR) 1325, which recognized that women are not adequately consulted and integrated into peace processes, to reality. In December 2011, for example, the United States joined thirty-two other countries in publishing a National Action Plan (NAP) on Women, Peace and Security designed to integrate governmental efforts to implement UNSCR 1325. Ellen Johnson Sirleaf's leadership in postconflict Liberia and the July 2010 establishment of UN Women provide further evidence of the international community's improving recognition of the indispensable role of women in postconflict situations.

Moreover, attention to the acute problem of violence against women has advanced, even if it has been significantly curtailed in practice. In 1998, The International Criminal Tribunal for the former Yugoslavia (ICTY), along with the Rome Statute, established the precedent that targeted rape is a crime against humanity, though the practice has continued largely unabated in Darfur, the Democratic Republic of the Congo, Burma, and Zimbabwe. The degree to which prostitution of girls and sex trafficking of women is an act of violence is beginning to be better understood around the world. . . .

Other Group Rights: *Heightened Focus, Selective Bias*

Dedicated efforts to address the rights of particular groups have advanced for some, but stalled for others. Racism and other forms of xenophobia have been a major focus. Organization of American States (OAS) members have been negotiating over an antiracism convention proposed by Brazil since 2005, to follow in the footsteps of the United Nations Convention on the Elimination of All Forms of Racism and monitoring regime. The UN process, despite the 1991 repeal of UN General Assembly Resolution 3379 (classifying Zionism as a form of racism), has been sidetracked by the issue of Israel and its occupation of Palestinian territories. The 2001 UN World Conference against Racism in Durban came close to declaring Israel to be racist, and follow-on efforts, such as at the 2009 Review Conference, had a similarly skewed focus. In practice, however, certain great exemplars of antiracism have transcended, from South Africa's reconciliation under Nelson Mandela to Barack Obama's election in a nation in which segregation was widely institutionalized a half century earlier. Sadly, many varied instances of racism and xenophobia remain, from anti-Semitic violence in Europe to anti-white land seizure policies in Zimbabwe. . . .

In short, an increasing number of groups have been recognized by multilateral bodies, states, and publics as deserving equal access to justice. Implementation efforts are spottier. Second, cultural legacies of prejudice may persist as more and more groups lobby for rights.

→ **NO**

Amnesty International Report 2012: The State of the World's Human Rights

The Amnesty International Report 2012 documents the state of human rights during 2011. In five regional overviews . . . , the report shows how the demand for human rights continued to resound in every corner of the globe.

Millions took to the streets of their towns and cities in a mass outpouring of hope for freedom and justice. Even the most brutal repression seemed unable to silence the increasingly urgent demands for an end to tyranny as people showed they were no longer willing to endure systems of governance that were not built on accountability, transparency, justice and the promotion of equality.

Resistance to injustice and repression took many forms, often inspiring acts of enormous courage and determination from the communities and individuals facing seemingly insuperable obstacles. In the face of indifference, threats and attacks, human rights defenders pursued legal challenges at the national and international level to long-standing impunity and endemic discrimination. . . .

Africa

The popular movements across North Africa resonated with people in sub-Saharan Africa, particularly in countries with repressive governments. Trade unionists, students and opposition politicians were inspired to organize demonstrations. People took to the streets because of their political aspirations, the quest for more freedom, and a deep frustration with a life in poverty. They protested against their desperate social and economic situation and the rise in living costs.

Many of the underlying factors which led to the uprisings in North Africa and the Middle East also exist in other parts of Africa. They include authoritarian rulers who have been in power for decades and rely on a security apparatus to clamp down on dissent. Poverty and corruption are widespread, there is a lack of basic freedoms, and large groups are often marginalized from mainstream society. The brutal suppression of demonstrations during 2011 illustrated how the region's political leaders learned little from what happened to their peers in the north.

Poverty

Africa's poverty rates have been falling and progress has been made in realizing the UN Millennium Development Goals over the past decade. But millions of people are still living in poverty, without access to essential services such as clean water, sanitation, health care and education. . . .

Political Repression

Inspired by events in North Africa, anti-government protesters took to the streets in Khartoum and other towns across Sudan, from the end of January onward. They were beaten by security forces, and dozens of activists and students were arbitrarily arrested and detained. Many were reportedly tortured in detention. In Uganda, opposition politicians called on people to imitate the Egyptian protests and take to the streets, but violence marred the demonstrations. In February, the Ugandan government banned all public protests. The police and army used excessive force against protesters, and opposition leader Kizza Besigye was harassed and arrested. In Zimbabwe, a group of about 45 activists [was] arrested in February, merely for discussing events in North Africa. Six of them were initially charged with treason. In April, the Swaziland authorities repressed similar protests with excessive force.

Security forces used live ammunition against anti-government protesters in Angola, Burkina Faso, Guinea, Liberia, Malawi, Mauritania, Nigeria, Senegal, Sierra Leone and South Sudan, resulting in many casualties. The authorities usually failed to investigate the excessive use of force and nobody was held to account for the deaths caused.

Human rights defenders, journalists and political opponents in most African countries continued to be arbitrarily arrested and detained, beaten, threatened and intimidated. . . .

Governments tried to control publicly available information in Burundi, the DRC, Equatorial Guinea, Ethiopia, Gambia, Guinea, Guinea-Bissau, Liberia, Madagascar, Somalia, Sudan and Uganda. They placed restrictions on reporting certain events, closed down or temporarily suspended radio stations, blocked specific websites or banned the publication of certain newspapers. . . .

Conflict

The South Sudanese people voted overwhelmingly in favour of independence during the January referendum on self-determination. With South Sudan's independence date set for 9 July, tensions rose in the so-called transitional areas of Abyei, Southern Kordofan and Blue Nile. The envisaged separate referendum for Abyei did not take place as scheduled in January, and conflict erupted in May. The Sudanese Armed Forces (SAF), supported by militia, took control of Abyei, causing tens of thousands of people from the Dinka Ngok community to flee to South Sudan. Houses in Abyei town were looted and destroyed. Here too the UN peacekeeping mission, deployed in Abyei, failed to take any meaningful action to prevent the attacks and protect the civilian population. By the end of the year, no resolution had been found for the status of Abyei. . . .

The conflict in Darfur, Sudan, also continued unabated, forcing more people to leave their homes. Those already living in camps for internally displaced people were targeted by the Sudanese authorities because they were perceived to be supporting armed opposition groups. Rape and other forms of sexual violence continued to be reported. Sudan still refused to co-operate with the ICC. The ICC Prosecutor requested an arrest warrant for the Minister of Defence, Abdelrahim Mohamed Hussein, for war crimes and crimes against humanity committed in Darfur. . . .

No end was in sight either to the conflict in the eastern DRC. Rape and other forms of sexual violence remained endemic, and were committed both by government security forces and armed opposition groups. Other human rights abuses, such as unlawful killings, looting and abductions continued as well, primarily by armed groups. The DRC's justice system remained unable to deal with the many human rights violations committed during the conflict. Child soldiers continued to be recruited and used in various conflicts, such as in the Central African Republic, the DRC and Somalia.

Some African governments remained reluctant to ensure accountability for crimes under international law. . . .

Justice and Impunity

Many human rights violations committed by security and law enforcement forces remained unaddressed. The authorities hardly ever initiated independent and impartial investigations in reported cases of arbitrary arrests and detention; torture or other ill-treatment; unlawful killings, including extrajudicial executions; and enforced disappearances. Only very rarely were individuals held to account for committing human rights violations. As a result, people have lost confidence in law enforcement agencies and the judiciary in many countries in the region. High costs are another obstacle to accessing the formal justice system, including for people subjected to human rights violations.

Impunity for human rights violations by law enforcement officers was pervasive in Burundi, Cameroon, Republic of Congo, DRC, Eritrea, Ethiopia, Gambia, Guinea, Guinea-Bissau, Kenya, Madagascar, Malawi, Mozambique, Nigeria, Senegal, Sudan, Swaziland, Tanzania and Zimbabwe. . . .

The number of people in pre-trial detention remained very high, as most countries' justice systems could not guarantee a fair trial without undue delay. Many people arrested had no access to legal representation. Detention conditions remained appalling in many countries, with overcrowding, a lack of access to basic sanitation facilities, health care, water or food, and a lack of prison staff. Detention conditions often fell below minimum international standards and constituted inhuman, cruel and degrading treatment or punishment. In one particularly gruesome incident, nine men died of asphyxiation caused by overcrowding during their detention in a National Gendarmerie facility in Léré, Chad, in September. . . .

Marginalization

Refugees and migrants were particularly affected by human rights violations and abuses in many countries. Congolese nationals were again exposed to gender-based violence while being expelled from Angola. Mauritania arbitrarily arrested several thousand migrants before deporting them to neighbouring countries. Refugees and migrants were also subjected to human rights violations in Mozambique, including reported unlawful killings by law enforcement officials. In South Africa, refugees and migrants continued to experience violence and had their property destroyed. . . .

Girls and women continued to be subjected to rape and other forms of sexual violence in various countries in conflict or with a large number of refugees or displaced people. These included eastern Chad, the Central African Republic, Côte d'lvoire, eastern DRC and Sudan (Darfur). Members of government security forces were often responsible, and in most cases no investigations were carried out.

Discrimination

Discrimination against people based on their perceived or real sexual orientation or gender identity worsened. Politicians not only failed to protect people's right not to be discriminated against, but often used statements or actions to incite discrimination and persecution based on perceived sexual orientation. . . .

Security and Human Rights

Africa has become increasingly vulnerable to acts of terrorism from various Islamist armed groups. They include al-Qa'ida in the Islamic Maghreb (AQMI), which operated in various countries in the Sahel; the religious sect Boko Haram, which stepped up its bombing activities in Nigeria throughout the year; and al-Shabab, which is active in Kenya and Somalia. These armed groups were responsible for numerous human rights abuses, including indiscriminate attacks, unlawful killings, abductions and torture.

Time to Embrace Change

Improved respect for and protection of human rights will probably not develop as quickly and dramatically in sub-Saharan Africa as in North Africa. In some places the situation might even get worse. However, factors such as sustained economic growth, demands for better governance, an emerging middle class, stronger civil society and improved access to information and communication technology will gradually contribute to a better human rights situation. The question is whether Africa's political leadership will embrace these changes or see them as a threat to their hold on power. In 2011, most political leaders—in their reactions to protests and dissent—were part of the problem, not the solution.

Americas

. . . The demand for human rights resounded throughout the region during 2011 in the national courts, the Inter-American system and on the streets. The calls for justice from individuals, human rights defenders, civil society organizations and Indigenous Peoples continued to gain strength, frequently bringing people into direct confrontation with powerful economic and political interests. At the heart of many of these conflicts were economic development policies that left many, particularly those living in poverty and marginalized communities, at increased risk of abuse and exploitation.

The Demand for Justice and an End to Impunity

Many human rights cases made slow progress, obstructed by the absence of meaningful access to justice, a lack of independence in the judiciary, and a willingness among some sectors to resort to extreme measures to avoid accountability and to protect vested political, criminal and economic interests. Difficulty in pursuing respect for rights was often exacerbated by threats against and killings of human rights defenders, witnesses, lawyers, prosecutors and judges in countries such as Brazil, Colombia, Cuba, Guatemala, Haiti, Honduras and Venezuela. Journalists trying to expose abuses of power, human rights violations and corruption were also frequently targeted in Latin America and the Caribbean.

In some countries, however, despite obstacles and frequent setbacks, there were significant advances in the investigation and prosecution of past human rights violations and a number of former de facto military rulers and senior commanders were convicted and sentenced to prison terms. . . .

In the sphere of international justice, progress was uneven. For example, in October, the Canadian government failed to arrest former US President George W. Bush when he travelled to British Columbia, despite clear evidence that he was responsible for crimes under international law, including torture. However, in December, France extradited former de facto head of state Manuel Noriega to Panama where he had been convicted in his absence of the murder of political opponents, among other crimes.

The Inter-American Human Rights System

The Inter-American system, and in particular the Inter-American Commission on Human Rights, came under sustained attack from several states during 2011. . . .

During the second half of 2011, OAS member states continued the debate over possible reforms of the Inter-American human rights system. This debate concluded with the issuing of a report that the OAS Permanent Council was due to consider in early 2012. Although the recommendations contained in the report were described as an effort to strengthen the system, in reality some of the measures proposed could have the effect of undermining its independence and effectiveness, and have a particularly serious impact on the work of the Commission and its rapporteurs.

Public Security and Human Rights

Governments continued to exploit legitimate concerns regarding public security and high crime rates to justify or to ignore human rights violations committed by their security forces when responding to criminal activities or armed groups.

The Mexican government closed its eyes to widespread reports of torture, enforced disappearances, unlawful killings and excessive use of force by the army and, increasingly, by navy personnel, as it pursued its campaign against the drug cartels. . . .

On a lesser scale, a number of other countries in the region also used military personnel to carry out law enforcement duties. These included the Dominican Republic, El Salvador, Guatemala, Honduras and Venezuela. . . .

In the face of high levels of violent crime, law enforcement practices in Brazil continued to be characterized by discrimination, human rights abuses, corruption and military-style policing operations. . . .

In the Dominican Republic, serious human rights violations, including arbitrary detentions, torture and other cruel and inhuman or degrading treatment, unlawful killings and disappearances, were committed by the police implementing a so-called "hard line policy" in fighting crime. There was evidence that in a number of cases the police had adopted a shoot-to-kill policy, rather than trying to arrest suspects, many of whom were unarmed.

Armed Conflict

The long-running internal armed conflict in Colombia continued to inflict untold misery on civilian communities across the country. The human rights consequences of the fighting were particularly acute for rural Indigenous Peoples and Afro-descendent and peasant farmer communities, thousands of whom were forced to flee their homes. Guerrilla groups, as well as paramilitaries and the security forces sometimes acting in collusion, were all responsible for serious human rights abuses and violations of international humanitarian law. . . .

Indigenous Peoples

Human rights violations against Indigenous Peoples remained a serious concern despite some positive advances in the region.

In many cases, Indigenous Peoples were denied their right to meaningful consultation and free, prior and informed consent over large-scale development projects, including extractive industry projects, affecting them. . . .

The failure to respect the rights of Indigenous Peoples had a negative impact not only on livelihoods, but also resulted in communities being threatened, harassed, forcibly evicted or displaced, attacked or killed as the drive to exploit resources intensified in the areas where they live. . . .

The Rights of Women and Girls

States in the region failed to put the protection of women and girls from rape, threats and killings at the forefront of their political agendas. Implementation of legislation to combat gender-based violence remained a serious concern and the lack of resources available to investigate and prosecute these crimes raised questions about official willingness to address the issue. The failure to bring to justice those responsible for these crimes further entrenched impunity for gender-based violence in many countries and helped foster a climate where violence against women and girls was tolerated.

Violations of women's and girls' sexual and reproductive rights remained rife, with appalling consequences for their lives and health. Chile, El Salvador and Nicaragua continued to ban abortion in all circumstances, including for girls and women pregnant as a result of rape or who experience life-threatening complications in their pregnancies. Those seeking or providing an abortion risked lengthy imprisonment.

In other countries, access to safe abortion services was granted in law, but denied in practice by protracted judicial procedures that made access to safe abortion almost impossible, especially for those who could not afford to pay for private abortion services. Access to contraception and information on sexual and reproductive issues remained a concern, particularly for the most marginalized women and girls in the region.

Migrants: Visible Victims, Invisible Rights

Hundreds of thousands of regular and irregular migrants in a number of countries were denied the protection of the law.

In Mexico, hundreds of bodies, some identified as kidnapped migrants, were discovered in clandestine graves. . . .

Migrants' rights defenders came under unprecedented attack in Mexico, especially those working at the network of shelters providing humanitarian assistance to migrants.

In the USA, along its south-western border with Mexico, regular and irregular migrants suffered discrimination and profiling by federal, state, and local law enforcement officials. They faced discrimination when attempting to access justice and protection and encountered barriers to education and health care. . . .

Death Penalty

Forty-three prisoners were executed in the USA during the year, all by lethal injection. This brought to 1,277 the total number of executions carried out since the US Supreme Court lifted a moratorium on the death penalty in 1976. On a more positive note, however, in March, Illinois became the 16th abolitionist state in the USA and in November, the Governor of Oregon imposed a moratorium on executions in the state and called for a rethink on the death penalty. . . .

Asia-Pacific

As winds of political change blew in from the Middle East and North Africa, several governments in the Asia-Pacific region responded by increasing their efforts to retain power by repressing demands for human rights and dignity. At the same time, the success of uprisings in Tunisia and Egypt inspired human rights defenders, activists, and journalists in Asia to raise their own voices, using a combination of new technologies and old-fashioned activism to challenge violations of their rights. . . .

The dynamism of Chinese citizens invoking their rights contrasted with the situation in neighbouring Democratic People's Republic of Korea (North Korea), where there were no indications of an improvement in the country's horrific human rights situation after Kim Jong-un, in his late twenties, succeeded his father as absolute ruler of the country on 17 December. If anything, there were signs that the authorities had detained officials suspected of potentially challenging or questioning a smooth transition, and there were concerns that those detained would be sent to join the hundreds of thousands already suffering arbitrary detention, forced labour, public execution and torture and other ill-treatment in the country's numerous political prison camps.

Repression of Dissent

Few governments in the region were as brutal as the North Korean regime in repressing the voices of their own people, but violations of the right to freely express and receive opinions continued throughout the region. Several governments deliberately crushed dissenting views. In North Korea, those deviating from official ideology could end up spending the rest their lives in a bleak and remote political prison camp. Both Viet Nam and Myanmar have criminalized free expression of dissenting views, and have intelligence agencies that are dedicated to intimidating and silencing critics.

Other countries also muzzled critics, although they relied on less overtly violent means. Continuing to hold itself as an exception to international standards on the protection of freedom of speech, Singapore briefly jailed 76-year-old British author Alan Shadrake on 1 June, having charged him with contempt of court after he criticized the judiciary for imposing the death penalty.

In India, which boasts a proud history of free speech and a vibrant media, the government sought to impose new restrictions on social media including instant messaging services. Internet media also remained under pressure in Malaysia, although it was slightly less fettered than the country's heavily censored print and broadcast media.

In Thailand, the newly elected government of Yingluck Shinawatra (sister of former Prime Minister Thaksin Shinawatra) did not put a stop to the aggressive enforcement of the highly problematic lése majesté law, which prohibits any criticism of the royal family. Many of those who were targeted had posted material on the internet which prosecutors had found objectionable, or, in the case of a 61-year-old grandfather, AmponTangnoppakul, had allegedly sent text messages deemed offensive, earning a 20-year prison sentence.

Authorities in the Republic of Korea (South Korea) increasingly invoked the National Security Law to harass those perceived as opposing the government's policy on North Korea. At times, this resulted in absurd applications of the Law, as in the case of Park Jeonggeun, who faced detention and criminal prosecution for posting satirical snippets of North Korean propaganda.

Other critics demanding human rights and dignity in the region provoked more severe responses and, at times, paid the ultimate price for raising their voices. Pakistani journalists managed to maintain a boisterous and at times fractious media environment in the country despite a violent backlash from the government as well as from political parties and insurgent groups such as the Pakistani Taleban. At least nine journalists were killed during the year, including Saleem Shahzad, an online journalist who had openly criticized the country's powerful military and intelligence agencies. Other journalists told Amnesty International that they had been seriously threatened by the country's powerful and shadowy intelligence agencies, security forces, political parties or militant groups.

Journalists were not alone in being attacked for their opinions in Pakistan. Two high-profile politicians were assassinated for challenging the use of the highly problematic blasphemy laws: Salman Taseer, the outspoken Governor of Punjab, and Shahbaz Bhatti, Minister for Minorities (and sole Christian cabinet member).

Minority Groups

Pakistan, like many other countries in the Asia-Pacific region, witnessed ongoing and serious discrimination against religious and ethnic minorities. Members of minority groups were often marginalized and in many instances were the victims of direct government harassment. In numerous cases, governments failed to uphold their responsibility to protect the rights of members of minority groups. This entrenched discrimination, aggravated poverty, slowed down overall development, and in many countries, stoked violence. . . .

Sunni Muslims were victims of discrimination in China: the Uighur population, predominantly Muslim and ethnically distinct, continued to face repression and discrimination in the Xinjiang Uighur Autonomous Region. The Chinese government invoked the nebulous threat of terrorism and insurgency to repress civil and political rights and interfere with the religious practices of the Uighurs, while the influx of Han Chinese migrants and discrimination in their favour has rendered Uighurs second-class citizens in terms of cultural, economic and social achievement.

Other ethnic minorities in China also fared poorly. At least a dozen Tibetan nuns and monks or former monks set themselves on fire (six of them are believed to have died) in protest against the restrictions imposed on religious and cultural practices—restrictions that have heightened Tibetans' sense of alienation and deepened their grievances. In Inner Mongolia, too, ethnic tensions were high. Widespread protests erupted across the region after a Han Chinese coal truck driver allegedly murdered an ethnic Mongolian herder.

Armed Conflicts and Insurgencies

Ethnic and religious discrimination and the resulting political and economic grievances were behind many of the multiple armed conflicts and long-running insurgencies that afflicted hundreds of thousands of people in the region. . . .

The Taleban and other insurgent groups in Afghanistan engaged in widespread and systematic attacks on civilians, causing 77 per cent of civilian casualties in the conflict, according to the UN. . . .

Lower intensity conflicts continued on Mindanao island in the Philippines, as well as in southern Thailand—both areas where Muslim minority populations were historically disenfranchised and had to contend with poor economic development. . . .

Relatively low economic development, particularly for tribal Adivasi communities, and poor governance, fuelled insurgencies in several of India's central and eastern states. . . .

Indian forces in Jammu and Kashmir again came under criticism for violating human rights. . . .

Accountability and Justice

Impunity for past violations haunted many countries in the region, particularly those grappling with the legacy of conflicts. The failure to provide justice complicated reconciliation efforts and often established a pattern of injustice and lack of accountability for security forces. . . .

While those accused of human rights violations evaded accountability, many governments used flogging to punish alleged wrongdoers—a violation of the international prohibition of cruel, inhuman and degrading punishment. Singapore and Malaysia continued to impose caning for a variety of offences, including immigration violations. The Indonesian province of Aceh increasingly used caning as a punishment for various offences, including drinking alcohol, gambling, and being alone with someone of the opposite sex who is not a marriage partner or relative. And in the Maldives, the government retained the punishment of caning under pressure from its political opposition.

Migrants and Refugees

Insecurity, natural disasters, poverty, and lack of suitable opportunities drove hundreds of thousands of people to seek better lives elsewhere, within the region as well as outside. While many governments in the region rely on migrant labour as a matter of basic economic necessity, many governments still fell short of protecting the rights of people who were seeking work or shelter. . . .

Europe and Central Asia

. . .

Freedom of Expression

In a marked contrast to the hope and change unleashed across the Arab world, autocratic regimes in a number of the successor states to the Soviet Union strengthened their grip on power. They crushed protest, arrested opposition leaders and silenced dissenting voices. For many, the hope that accompanied the collapse of the Soviet Union 20 years ago must have seemed a distant memory.

In Belarus, protests following the alleged vote-rigging in 2010 were banned or dispersed, hundreds of protesters were arrested and fined and even more draconian restrictions on the freedom of assembly were introduced. Critical human rights NGOs were also targeted. In Azerbaijan, anti-government demonstrations were effectively outlawed, and attempts by a small number of government critics prompted a fresh wave of repression and intimidation. The demonstrations planned for March and April, to protest against corruption and call for greater civil and political freedoms, were unreasonably banned then violently dispersed despite their peaceful nature. As in Belarus, critical NGOs and reporters also felt the backlash, with five human rights organizations closed down and several journalists reporting instances of intimidation and harassment in the immediate aftermath of the protests.

In Central Asia, Turkmenistan and Uzbekistan continued to severely restrict the rights to freedom of expression and association. Genuine opposition political parties continued to be denied registration, and social activists were rarely able to operate openly. Critical journalists and human rights defenders were routinely monitored and risked beatings, detention and unfair trials. In Tajikistan, Kazakhstan and Kyrgyzstan there were unfair trials and cases of harassment for government critics and those who exposed abuses by public officials.

The picture in Russia was mixed. As elsewhere in the region, human rights defenders and journalists were harassed, intimidated and beaten for exposing abuses. Anti-government demonstrations were frequently banned and their organizers and participants subjected to short periods of detention or fined. Typically for the region, most mainstream media and TV outlets remained under the strong influence of national and local authorities. Despite this, civic activism continued to grow, with a variety of causes garnering widespread popular support— including the environment and combating abuses by public officials. The internet remained relatively uncontrolled by the authorities and grew in importance as a rival source of information and forum for the exchange of opinion.

Against this backdrop, the largest demonstrations seen in Russia since the collapse of the Soviet Union took place in December, sparked by widespread allegations, and numerous recorded instances, of electoral fraud in the parliamentary elections that returned Prime Minister Vladimir Putin's United Russia party to power with a significantly reduced share of the vote. . . .

In Turkey, critical journalists, Kurdish political activists, and others risked unfair prosecution when speaking out on the situation of Kurds in Turkey, or criticizing the armed forces. Threats of violence against prominent outspoken individuals continued and in November new regulations came into force raising further concerns regarding the arbitrary restriction of websites.

People on the Move

. . . Many European countries, including France and the UK, refused to resettle any refugees displaced by the armed conflict in Libya, despite having been parties to that conflict under the aegis of NATO.

Across the region, states continued to violate human rights through the interception, detention and expulsion of foreign nationals, including those eligible for international protection. Detention as a tool of deterrence and control was a widespread, rather than a last, legitimate, resort.

Asylum systems frequently failed those seeking protection, including because of the resort to expedited asylum determination procedures in countries such as Finland, France, Germany, the Netherlands, Sweden, Switzerland and the UK that offered inadequate safeguards against the risk of individuals being sent back to places where they faced human rights abuses. . . .

Across the region, hundreds of thousands of people remained displaced by the conflicts that accompanied the collapse of the former Yugoslavia and the Soviet Union, often unable to return owing to their legal status—or lack of it—and discrimination in access to rights including property tenure.

While negotiating new EU asylum legislation, EU member states failed to address deficiencies in their asylum systems and in arrangements for transferring asylum-seekers back to the first EU country which they had entered.

Discrimination

Although discrimination continued to affect the lives of millions of people across the region, governments failed to prioritize policies to combat it, citing other urgent needs. They quoted economic factors, in spite of many pointers that those already marginalized faced an increased risk of having the inequalities they already experienced further entrenched. Or they simply sought to walk away from their obligations, like the Dutch government, which publicly stated in July that it was the primary responsibility of citizens to free themselves from discrimination. . . .

While failing to strengthen domestic or European mechanisms to tackle discrimination, some governments were also keen to uphold existing or promote new discriminatory tools. Legislation, policies and practices discriminating against Roma in the enjoyment of their right to housing remained on many statute books, and Roma communities continued to be forcibly evicted in several countries across the region including France, Italy and Serbia. Legislative proposals discriminating against individuals on the basis of gender identity or sexual orientation were introduced in the Russian Federation and Lithuania.

The absence of comprehensive legal protection and a robust championing of rights by those in authority again led to adverse consequences in individual lives. Hostility and discrimination, often driven by radical-right populist parties, against ethnic and religious minorities, as well as people on the basis of their gender identity or sexual orientation, continued to be a matter of concern throughout the region. Lesbians, gay men, bisexual and transgender people, and Roma, migrants and Muslims, among others, were targeted in hate-motivated attacks. Hate crimes continued to be inadequately tackled because of gaps in legislation, poor reporting systems, inadequate investigations, or flaws in criminal justice systems and lack of trust towards the police. Entrenched prejudices and stereotypes also resulted in racially motivated misconduct by law enforcement officials. . . .

Torture and Other Ill-Treatment

Victims of torture and other ill-treatment were likewise too often failed by justice systems that did not hold those responsible to account. Obstacles to accountability included lack of prompt access to a lawyer, failure by prosecutors to vigorously pursue investigations, fear of reprisals, low penalties imposed on convicted police officers, and the absence of properly independent systems for monitoring complaints and investigating serious police misconduct. . . .

Conclusion

. . . However, too many people across the region still fell through the gap between the rhetoric of human rights and the reality of their implementation. Robust support for human rights was too often seen as incompatible with supporting state security or energy supply. There were challenges to the independence and authority of the European Court of Human Rights; the EU too often showed itself a toothless tiger in the face of violations committed by its member states. And individual states still failed in their primary obligation to uphold all human rights for all.

Middle East and North Africa

. . . All across the Middle East and North Africa, 2011 was marked by mass demands for change—for greater liberty to speak and to act, free from the suffocating fear of state repression; for government transparency and accountability and an end to pervasive high-level corruption; for more jobs and fairer employment opportunities and the means to seek a better standard of living; for justice and human rights, including the right to live one's life and bring up one's family in dignity and security. It was in support of such demands that hundreds of thousands of people, with women conspicuous in the vanguard, thronged onto the streets of Tunis, Cairo, Benghazi, Sana'a and many other cities and towns across the region to demand change. They continued to do so despite the carnage wrought among them by government security forces. They did so with determination, resolution and naked courage, and in doing so freed themselves from the fear that their governments had for so long sought to imbue in order to keep them quiescent and in their place. For a time at least, the notion of people's power gripped the region and shook it to its core.

Initially, the protests mostly voiced popular frustration against the failure of national leaders to address people's needs and aspirations. Those leaders responded all too characteristically by sending out their riot police and security agents to crush the protests by force; they succeeded only in pouring fuel on the flames and further igniting public outrage and defiance. As protesters were shot down in cold blood, rounded up in mass arrests, tortured and abused, so the popular mood hardened. Unintimidated by the bloodshed, more and more people rallied to the streets to demand the replacement or overthrow of national leaders who had become both discredited and despised as they sought to consolidate family dynasties to maintain their grip on power. . . .

Conflict and Intolerance of Dissent

The uprisings that dominated the headlines throughout 2011 overshadowed other deep-seated problems that retained disastrous potential for human rights in the Middle East and North Africa, and beyond.

Israel maintained its blockade of Gaza, prolonging the humanitarian crisis there, and continued aggressively to expand settlements in the Palestinian West Bank territory it has occupied since 1967. The two leading Palestinian political organizations, Fatah and Hamas, despite a reconciliation agreement signed in May remained divided and targeted each other's supporters, while Israeli forces and

Palestinian armed groups mounted tit-for-tat attacks in Gaza. It was a sorry and all too familiar tale that continued to wreak a heavy cost on so many people's lives.

Iran's government became increasingly isolated internationally and tolerated no dissent at home; human rights defenders, women's and minority rights activists were among those persecuted, and the death penalty was used on an extensive scale, ostensibly to punish criminals but also to intimidate the populace. Globally, only China carried out more executions.

Elsewhere in the region, it was unclear how the withdrawal of all US military forces from Iraq would impact security there after eight years of conflict. The issue of self-determination for the people of Western Sahara still remained as a running sore, poisoning government relations in the Maghreb.

Other patterns of human rights violations remained and were both central in driving the popular uprisings and protests and also deepened by governments' responses. Arbitrary arrests and detentions, enforced disappearances, torture and other ill-treatment, unfair trials, and unlawful killings by state forces remained common and widespread across the region. Almost without exception, those in power allowed their forces to kill and torture with impunity. In Egypt, the SCAF bowed to popular demands and disbanded the State Security Investigations service, which was notorious for torture under Hosni Mubarak. Torture, however, did not cease; the army simply took it over, even subjecting some women protesters to forced "virginity testing," while also arresting and sending thousands of civilians for trial before unfair military courts. Yet thousands of Egyptians remained stubborn in the face of the new authorities' repression and continued to demand political, social and human rights changes.

Discrimination

Discrimination on grounds of gender, ethnicity, religion, national origin and other factors, such as sexual orientation, remained. To a large extent, the sense of injustice this engendered was reflected in the wave of protests, as when stateless Bidun gathered together in Kuwait to demand that they be recognized as citizens. At the same time, the turmoil also deepened divisions. In Libya, both Libyans and foreign nationals were targeted by militias because of their skin colour. There was growing fear within the Syria's complex of different faiths and communities that the country might descend into a civil war of such bitterness and hatred as the one that tore Lebanon apart from 1975 to 1990—a war whose legacy of enforced disappearances and distrust still remains conspicuously unaddressed. In Egypt, discrimination against Copts remained rife. In Iran, religious and ethnic minorities continued to face discrimination in law and, in the case of the Baha'i minority, persecution. . . .

All across the region, migrant workers from poor and developing countries were abused and exploited even though, as in several Gulf states, they were the lifeblood of the economy. They were inadequately protected, if offered any protection at all, under local labour laws. Women domestic workers suffered worst of all—they were victims all too often of multiple discrimination, as women, as migrants, and as foreign nationals whose own governments frequently took little or no interest in their plight. . . .

EXPLORING THE ISSUE

Is the International Community Making Effective Progress in Securing Global Human Rights?

Critical Thinking and Reflection

1. Why was the international community reluctant to involve itself in human rights abuses in other countries for most of the last 500 ears?
2. Should pre-1945 global leaders be held accountable for failure of the international community to make much progress in the promotion and protection of human rights?
3. Is it fair to place blame on the United Nations for failure to protect human rights when the agency has no real enforcement mechanism?
4. Why would certain individuals today assert that their religious and national culture result in their looking at human rights differently?
5. Is Amnesty International able to be objective in its assessment of human rights problems worldwide, given that its very existence depends on such problems?
6. Do those who are seeking human rights rely too heavily on international organizations when national sovereignty is still operative?

Is There Common Ground?

Given that the list of specific human rights spelled out in the array of international documents is quite extensive, it is not surprising that the current track record of progress is viewed as mixed. And as a consequence, for the mainstream international human rights actors—be they governmental actors charged with promoting and protecting human rights, or nongovernmental advocacy groups who act as watchdogs of such actors—the typical message appears to present a cautionary tale. That is, on the one hand, each acknowledges success of certain steps taken and/or on specific human rights, while on the other hand, each posits a range of challenges that hinder progress. The difference between those formally charged with promotion and protection of human rights and those watchdogs who monitor the situation or those informal practitioners who take it upon themselves to try to solve the problem is one of degree rather than of kind. That is, the former bodies emphasize successes while lamenting impediments, while the latter group highlights abuses while acknowledging some successes. The YES and NO selections are examples of this common ground.

Additional Resources

Alson, Philip and Goodman, Ryan (authors), and Steiner, Henry J. (editor), *International Human Rights in Context: Law, Politics, Morals*, Third Edition, Oxford University press (2007).

> This interdisciplinary course book provides a wide range of primary and secondary materials and text on a large number of human rights-related topics.

Beltz, Charles R., *The Idea of Human Rights*, Oxford University Press (2011).

> This book examines the idea of human rights from a practical and advocacy approach, looking at the history and practice of human rights.

Beltz, Charles R., and Goodin, Robert E., editors, *Global Basic Rights*, Oxford University Press (2011).

> This edited book of important contributors focuses on some of the most difficult theoretical and practical questions relating to human rights.

DeLaet, Debra, *The Global Struggle for Human Rights: Universal Principles in World Politics*, Wadsworth Publishing (2005).

> This book focuses on the challenge of national sovereignty to human rights advances in the context of the universality argument, with special emphasis on gender equality, feminist perspectives, and sexual orientation.

Donnelly, Jack, *International Human Rights*, Third Edition, Westview Press (2006).

> This book is a good introduction to the many issues associated with global human rights.

Human Rights Watch, *World Report 2012: Events of 2011*, Seven Stories Press (2012).

> This 22nd annual *World Report* describes the human rights situation in over 90 countries and territories worldwide.

Ishay, Micheline, *The History of Human Rights: From Ancient Times to the Globalization Era, with a New Preface*, Second Revised Edition, University of California Press (2008).

> This is a well-written synthesis of the historical struggle since ancient times for human rights.

Lauren, Paul Gordon, *The Evolution of International Human Rights: Visions Seen*, Third Edition, University of Pennsylvania Press (2011).

> This book describes how the international community moved from centuries of indifference and active abuse into a current state of concern about human rights abuse.

Mertus, Julie, *The United Nations and Human Rights: A Guide for a New Era*, Second Edition, Routledge (2009).

> This a comprehensive guide to the role of the United Nations in the advancement of global human rights.

Neier, Aryeh, *The International Human Rights Movement: A History*, Princeton University Press (2012).

> The book chronicles the history of international efforts against human rights abuses from the seventeenth century to current struggles.

Office of the High Commissioner for Human Rights, *Human Rights and the Millennium Development Goals in Practice: A Review of Country Strategies and Reporting*, United Nations (2010).

> Using a human rights framework, this UN report analyzes the extent to which countries have made progress and meeting the eight Millennium Development Goals.

Sikkink, Kathryn, *The Justice Cascade: How Human Rights Prosecutions Are Changing World Politics*, W. W. Norton & Company (2011)

> The author argues that human rights prosecutions are a powerful tool in advancing human rights globally.

ISSUE 22

Should Israel Preempt Against Iran's Nuclear Program?

YES: Elliott Abrams, from "Israel and Iran: The Grounds for an Israeli Attack," *World Affairs Journal* (May/June 2012)

NO: Colin H. Kahl, from "Before Attacking Iran, Israel Should Learn from Its 1981 Strike on Iraq," *The Washington Post* (March 2, 2012)

Learning Outcomes

After reading this issue, you should be able to:

- Understand the positive and negative consequences of a possible Israeli attack on Iran.
- Understand the issue from a U.S. perspective.
- Appreciate the diplomatic and security implications of such an action.

ISSUE SUMMARY

YES: Elliott Abrams argues that a nuclear-armed Iran represents a unique and existential threat to the survival of the state of Israel and therefore is unacceptable. He contends that some states when faced with such a threat should act to prevent destruction since the approach and policy of the Iranian regime is clear and unequivocal in its hostility to Israel's very existence.

NO: Colin H. Kahl argues that Israel's attack on the Osirak reactor in Iraq had the reverse impact it wished. Saddam Hussein became even more determined to acquire nuclear weapons. Given the greater strength and resiliency of the Iranian regime, its geographic position, and its resources, an Israeli preemption on Iran would merely galvanize hard liners to regroup and continue the work toward nuclear weapons. And this is something that Israel or the United States cannot ultimately stop.

In a recent Congressional Research Service report (see source at the end of this section), it was reported that U.S. Secretary of Defense Leon Panetta in February 2012 "believes there is a strong likelihood that Israel will strike Iran in April, May or June" to prevent Iran from acquiring nuclear capability. The Secretary's statement was not made in a vacuum. Twice in its history Israel has used air strikes to destroy a country's acquiring nuclear capability—in Iraq in 1981 and in Syria in 2007. And Israel has let it be known awhile now that it may repeat such action to prevent a nuclear-armed Iran even as Israel for some time deferred to the United States as the latter has used diplomacy and sanctions to convince Iran to abandon its nuclear weapons program. Panetta's statement was only one of many coming from both high American and Israeli officials during the winter 2011–2012. While the strike did not come, the assertive statement from a leading American foreign policy figure underscores the volatile nature in the region, exacerbated by bellicose statements emanating from the Iranian leadership about its intentions with respect to Israel. The situation is further muddied by the fact that there is not a clear consensus on when Iran will attain the capacity to use nuclear weapons in anger.

To understand the full story, one must go back several decades to find the initial seeds of the simmering conflict. Israel's conflict with the Arab/Muslim world is long standing and deep. While we cannot rehash that entire history here, there are certain important facts that bear noting as we examine the question of should Israel preempt against Iran. For Israel, these include two noteworthy events. The first are the lessons of the 1967 Six-Day War when in response to apparent Egyptian-Syrian and Arab threats of pending conflict, Israel launched a highly successful preemptive war in which the Arab armies were destroyed and Israel's military position in the region was greatly strengthened. In fact, since that time Israel has occupied strategic preeminence in the Middle East. This event ingrained in the Israeli military and political leadership the great benefits of action rather than inaction.

The second is the vocal antipathy of the Iranian regime to the state of Israel and its leadership within the radical fundamentalist community, certainly among Shi'ites but also among some Sunni fundamentalists as well. When this position is combined with Iran's history of supporting terrorism in general and in particular Hezbollah in Lebanon and Hamas in Gaza, the origins of Israel's fear of a nuclear Iran have resonance. Combining these two facts gives the Israeli leadership cause for consternation and indeed worry should Iran acquire nuclear weapons and the capability to deliver them.

Obviously, for Iran the key lessons are quite different. When the United States invaded Iraq and removed Saddam Hussein from power, a vacuum was created in the Persian Gulf. Iran has moved decisively to fill that vacuum. Today, Iran's influence in Iraq and throughout the region has been enhanced. Furthermore, key elements in the Iranian leadership derived the lesson that only an Iranian nuclear bomb could deter a possible attack from the United States or other states in the region, that is, Israel. They view nuclear weapons as the only ultimate hedge against regime change from the U.S. and other external interests. The uprisings in Tehran after the elections and the monumental events during the recent Arab Spring have only underscored their belief that security rests with the nuclear option despite their public pronouncements that their nuclear program is only for peaceful purposes.

This context is important as we explore the question of a nuclear Iran in the coming years and Israel's options with respect to thwarting that ambition. Israel, the United States, and others have gone on record as opposing a nuclear-armed Iran. A sanctions regime has been implemented to deter Iran and high-level talks have produced numerous statements from both sides that are confrontational and escalatory with respect to the ultimate choices that each side possesses. While an Israeli attack might inhibit and indeed thwart short-term Iranian nuclear ambitions, the political and military consequences would be deep, profound, and potentially destabilizing to the region. The effects on Iran's nuclear program and regime were summed up in the above-mentioned Congressional Research Service report:

- Ultimately, is an attack more likely to prevent an Iran with nuclear weapons or help bring it about? If an attack only delayed a potential nuclear weapons program in Iran, would Israel feel compelled to take additional military action later?
- What effect might an attack have on a potential Iranian decision to weaponize its nuclear program?
- Would an attack help or hinder the ongoing international effort to use diplomacy, monitoring, sanctions, and possible threats of further military action to persuade Iran not to pursue nuclear weapons? To what extent might the large coalition that is now working with the United States to enforce sanctions against Iran fracture in the event of a strike?
- Would an attack strengthen or weaken the Iranian regime, particularly given that current trends indicate that the regime faces significant economic challenges and political divisions?

The United States and Israel along with others have been weighing those consequences along with the benefits for some months.

Finally, we must remember that in 2003, the then President George W. Bush launched a preemptive strike against Iraq because his administration believed that the Iraqi dictator Saddam Hussein had weapons of mass destruction and that these weapons posed an immediate danger to the United States. Bush had justified his decision on his previously articulated Bush Doctrine, which allowed preemptive strikes in the face of the belief in an imminent strike against a country's homeland. World public opinion turned against the United States as a consequence, and the ramifications of the ill-advised American attack on Iraq are still being felt today. While Israel has always been more immune to negative public opinion, one cannot help but wonder if such a major military initiative as a preemptive strike will lead to Israel's paying too high a price in the world court of public opinion and thus deter Israel in this case.

The U.S. position on an Israeli strike is becoming a wedge issue between the two allies when juxtaposed with the U.S. presidential election. Those strains being seen in Obama administration statements and Israeli governmental responses add a further sense of urgency to the issue. For if Israel were to strike, whether with or without American support, the U.S. government knows that they too would bear the brunt of Muslim rage at such an act and it may tip the delicate balance in those Arab states exhibiting various forms of democratic change, that is, Egypt, Tunisia, Libya, and Bahrain. Also, if Iran retaliated after an Israeli strike, would it limit the counterattack to Israeli targets or would it also include American interests and those of America's allies as targets? And one has to consider the effect on global oil prices should attacks and counter-attacks occur in the region.

Our two authors examine this question from the viewpoint of what is best for the state of Israeli U.S., and Western interests. Elliott Abrams believes that the dangers of a nuclear Iran outweigh the fallout of action. He contends that to assume a nuclear Iran would be deterred in the traditional sense by a nuclear Israel and by extension the United States and a mini-Cold War would ensure misses the fundamental character of the Iranian regime and particularly its fundamentalist leadership. Colin H. Kahl, on the other hand, argues that the consequences of such action may very well bring about the nuclear Iran that Israel fears and with it regional and international sympathy in the wake of a preemptive attack. Both authors do agree that a nuclear Iran is a potentially destabilizing influence on the entire region and may trigger a regional nuclear arms race.

YES ↵

Elliott Abrams

Israel and Iran: The Grounds for an Israeli Attack

A broad international coalition agrees that Iran must freeze its nuclear weapons program and may not develop either of the ingredients—sufficient highly enriched uranium and a usable warhead and delivery system—that could result in a bomb for the Islamic Republic. The International Atomic Energy Agency Board of Governors, the UN Security Council, and the governments of almost every influential country—including the United States, Russia, China, Germany, Britain, and France, acting as the P5+1 negotiating group—have not only reached consensus on this demand but acted upon it. Increasingly tough sanctions have been imposed on Iran to force it to stop what is obviously a military program aimed at building a usable nuclear weapon. These diplomatic steps and these tightened sanctions reflect a wide consensus about the dangers that an Iranian nuclear weapon would bring.

But those dangers, ranging from the risk of further proliferation to the likelihood that a nuclear Iran would be an even bolder supporter of terrorism, do not affect all nations equally. In fact, they are a matter of principle but not much of a danger to many countries, while of much greater interest to Iran's immediate neighbors and to the United States. And then there is Israel. The dangers it faces from an Iranian nuclear weapon are unique and, I will argue, are dangers no nation should be asked to accept.

The only case today in which a UN member country is calling for the destruction of another member is Tehran's repeated threats to obliterate Israel, and there is no reason to believe the Iranians don't mean it. Official Iranian comments about Israel are continually genocidal in nature. A good example is an article in the Iranian press in February—circulated by the Revolutionary Guard's Fars News Agency but originating at the website Alef, which has ties to the supreme leader—that calls for the destruction of the Jews. The author, Alireza Forghani, a chief strategy specialist, is a significant figure in Iran; more important is that key regime websites are promoting his views. A report at the WND news website summarizes the central paragraph of Forghani's analysis of the necessity for destroying Israel and its people this way:

> Under this pre-emptive defensive doctrine, several Ground Zero points of Israel must be destroyed and its people annihilated. Forghani cites the last census by the Israel Central Bureau of Statistics that shows Israel has

From *World Affairs*, May/June 2012. Copyright © 2012 by ©2010 American Peace Society. Reprinted by permission of World Affairs Institute. www.WorldAffairsJournal.org

a population of 7.5 million citizens of which a majority of 5.7 million are Jewish. Then it breaks down the districts with the highest concentration of Jewish people, indicating that three cities, Tel Aviv, Jerusalem and Haifa, contain over 60 percent of the Jewish population that Iran could target with its Shahab 3 ballistic missiles, killing all its inhabitants.

This call for genocide is acceptable discourse in the Islamic Republic. It follows various statements by Iran's president calling for Israel to be wiped off the map, and as recently as February 3rd, Iran's "supreme leader," Ayatollah Khamenei, again called Israel a "cancerous tumor that should be cut and will be cut."

It is not necessary to believe that Iran would launch a nuclear attack at Israel the day after acquiring that capability to understand that Israel cannot tolerate a nuclear weapon in the hands of this regime. In addition to the threat of state action, Iran could also provide such a capability to Hamas, Hezbollah, or some other terrorist group with which it has connections as a way of masking its own role in the attack. Iran could also use a newly acquired nuclear capacity to defend stepped-up terrorist activities, both against Israel proper and against Israeli and Jewish individuals and sites around the world. The recent attacks on Israeli Embassy officers in India and Georgia and the bombing of the Israeli Embassy and Jewish community headquarters in Buenos Aires in the 1990s were all conducted when Iran did not have the added protection of a nuclear weapon. Similarly, Hezbollah and Hamas rocket attacks and terrorist bombings and kidnappings have all occurred when their benefactors in Tehran did not yet have the bomb. How much more aggressive would the mullahs be if the threat of retaliation against such attacks were neutralized by nuclear warheads? Israel has paid a great price in blood and treasure to survive in the decades when it had a nuclear monopoly in the region. To confront the same hostility, terror, and aggression when that monopoly is gone could undermine its ability to survive.

No nation, of course, can defend preemptively against an unexpected sneak attack. But if Iran acquires nuclear weapons (which it has already indicated a willingness to use), it will not come as a surprise to Israel or to its main ally, the United States. Instead, Tehran's acquisition of such weaponry would give the lie to the stated determination of both nations to prevent that outcome. All the speeches about what we would and would not accept would be shown to have been mere talk; all the determination would be shown to have been mere show; and every observer would conclude that we allowed ourselves to be cowed by Iran into an inaction that would continue to have ramifications for years to come even if, by some miracle, Tehran did not soon act on its genocidal threats. We would have watched their program grow year after year, and done nothing—or nothing that worked. So the image of Israel as indestructible, resolute, tough, and ready to act— as it acted against the nuclear programs of Iraq in 1981 and Syria in 2007—would be gone, as would the United States' own image as the dominant power in the Middle East and one committed to preserving Israel's existence.

And what will the Middle East be like when Iran possesses that nuclear weapon and its top officials continue to say that Israel must be eliminated? It would be easy for Iran to bring Israeli life to a standstill by launching a missile or a plane whose mission might, just might, be a nuclear attack. The chances that miscalculation or misperception would bring war and catastrophe would be enormous.

All of this helps explain why the so-called "international community," an entity not known to be friendly to Israel, has nonetheless almost unanimously said Iran must not be permitted to acquire nuclear weapons.

The question is therefore whether we mean what we say. There is a great gap between saying an Iranian nuclear weapon is so terrible to contemplate that we will speak against it and sanction Iran's economy, and saying we will act to prevent it. While some American leaders, mostly Republican candidates for office, have said we should use military force to stop Iran, that is not the official position of the United States. In 1980, the Carter Doctrine announced that "an attempt by any outside force to gain control of the Persian Gulf region will be regarded as an assault on the vital interests of the United States of America, and such an assault will be repelled by any means necessary, including military force." No president has said anything like that regarding Iran's nukes. The more anodyne "all options are on the table" formula has not scared the ayatollahs and never will.

Given this lack of urgency, Israel would, then, be taking a very great gamble to think that the United States will save it from Iran's nukes. We might, under this president or the next, or we might not. Iranian nuclear weapons are, after all, an existential threat to Israel, not to the US. It is not America that is regularly threatened with genocide by Tehran, however much its rulers may believe it the Great Satan.

Should Israel then take it upon itself to act? There are three main arguments against such a course. The first is that it is impossible: Israel can't do the job, and would only set Iran back a few months by an attack that would nonetheless bring significant reprisals. If it is true that the "window" has already closed and Israel cannot much damage the Iranian effort, the argument is over. If it can do substantial damage, there is not much point in arguing over whether setting Iran back three or five or seven years is sufficient to justify the attack. There is no magic number here, any more than there is a magic number revealing how many years this hated regime will rule in Iran before the people rise up against it. A corollary to this argument suggests that an Israeli attack would give the regime a new lease on life by rallying all Iranians, including the presumably growing numbers of dissidents, to the flag. But who knows if this is true, especially given the fact that the attack would be over before Iranians were even aware it had happened; that civilian targets would have been spared; and that the mullahs' regime is very widely despised? It could equally be argued that an attack would have the same consequences as in the late Soviet period, when military setbacks (Afghanistan, Central America) hastened the demise of the regime by showing its weaknesses and by intensifying internal tensions. The same might be true in Iran if it were shown that its much-vaunted, immensely expensive nuclear program had now gone up in smoke, and that the years of privation and isolation under sanctions had been for naught. In any event, the goal of an attack would not be to decapitate or overthrow the regime, but only to destroy or slow down its nuclear program.

The second argument against Israeli action is that it would set off a giant Mideast war, a spreading conflagration of immeasurable size and consequence. This is not persuasive either. Who would fight for Iran, especially given that its only client and ally in the region, Syria, is currently embroiled in an internal war of its own against its own people? There will be no wider war because Arab governments do not want Iran to acquire nuclear weapons either, and would not react much to an Israeli strike. Demonstrations against Israel, which are predictable, would pass after a few days. Iran's threats to close the Strait of Hormuz or to attack American bases and allies in the Gulf are not really credible either, and are almost surely a sort of psy-op against Washington. Such actions would draw the United States into a conflict with Iran when the US acted to re-open the Strait, which it could and would do—with world support—and these actions would bring far more damage to Iran's military (especially naval) capacity than an Israeli attack would accomplish. Why would Iran down US power on the head of its Islamic revolutionary state? Why would it attack American bases and thereby kill hundreds of Americans, knowing that this would bring devastating retribution from the United States? Similarly, would Iran really attack Arab states across the Gulf, some of which have decent air forces of their own (the UAE and Saudi Arabia) and can expect to rely on American help? If the Iranian leadership would engage in such suicidal actions, it confirms the Israeli position that such an irrational group cannot be permitted to have nuclear weapons in the first place.

Israel must expect Iranian terrorist attacks, and missiles targeting its own nuclear facilities at Dimona. The real danger, and the only one that might trigger a war, is an attack by Hezbollah. If it threw all of its arsenal at Israel, another conflict perhaps larger than the 2006 war would ensue. But is it certain that Hezbollah would sacrifice its future for Iran at this juncture? Recall that its leader, Sheik Hassan Nasrallah, said after the 2006 war, "If I had known on July 11 . . . that the operation would lead to such a war, would I do it? I say no, absolutely not." And that was said when Iran and the Assad regime in Syria were riding high, and able and willing to rearm the group after the conflict—as they indeed did. With Assad desperately focused on his own survival and Iran's own prestige and power damaged by an Israeli strike, would Nasrallah push Lebanon into a war its people cannot possibly want and that would do immense and possibly irrecoverable political and military damage to Hezbollah? Israel must anticipate the worst and prepare for it, but that is not to say it will happen.

The third argument against an Israeli strike is that a nuclear-armed Iran could still be "contained." It is never explained how this would be achieved. Containment is not a diplomatic strategy but at bottom a doctrine enforced by military power: red lines are set and may not be crossed without clear consequences. If Iran gets nuclear weapons, this would mean that all such red lines had been crossed and that US warnings had been proved to be mere words. After Iran has gained status as a nuclear weapons state, how could Washington threaten war to contain it when it was unwilling to act when it did not have nuclear weapons? This cannot be seriously advanced as a realistic proposition to make Iran think twice about the course it has set.

President Obama, like many world leaders, has called an Iranian nuclear weapon "unacceptable." He is right, and that should remain the US position—not just that it would be a bad outcome, not just that we would be angered by it, but that we refuse to accept it and, as the president also once said, will prevent it. If we are unwilling to act, or to act soon enough, it should be our position that Israeli action is justifiable.

Colin H. Kahl   **NO**

Before Attacking Iran, Israel Should Learn from Its 1981 Strike on Iraq

On June 7, 1981, eight Israeli F-16 fighter jets, protected by six F-15 escorts, dropped 16 2,000-pound bombs on the nearly completed Osirak nuclear reactor at the Tuwaitha complex in Iraq. Israeli Prime Minister Menachem Begin and other prominent members of the government such as Ariel Sharon saw the reactor as central to Iraqi President Saddam Hussein's quest to build nuclear weapons, and they believed that it posed an existential threat to Israel.

The timing of the strike was justified by intelligence reports suggesting that Osirak would soon become operational. Two days later, Begin explained the raid to the public: "We chose this moment: now, not later, because later may be too late, perhaps forever. And if we stood by idly, two, three years, at the most four years, and Saddam Hussein would have produced his three, four, five bombs . . . another Holocaust would have happened in the history of the Jewish people."

Three decades later, eerily similar arguments can be heard regarding the threat of a nuclear-armed Iran. Last May, Israeli Prime Minister Benjamin Netanyahu told a joint session of the U.S. Congress that "the hinge of history may soon turn, for the greatest danger of all could soon be upon us: a militant Islamic regime armed with nuclear weapons." In a Feb. 2 speech in Israel, Deputy Prime Minister Ehud Barak channeled Begin in making the case for possible military action against Iran, arguing that "those who say 'later' may find that later is too late." And late last month, Barak sought to discredit Israeli President Shimon Peres's reported opposition to a possible strike on Iran by pointing to his dissent during the 1981 attack.

When Netanyahu meets with President Obama on Monday and addresses the annual meeting of AIPAC, the American Israel Public Affairs Committee, later that day, we should expect additional dire assessments and warnings of military action.

For Israelis considering a strike on Iran, Osirak seems like a model for effective preventive war. After all, Hussein never got the bomb, and if Israel was able to brush back one enemy hell-bent on its destruction, it can do so again. But a closer look at the Osirak episode, drawing on recent academic research and memoirs of individuals involved with Iraq's program, argues powerfully against an Israeli strike on Iran today.

To begin with, Hussein was not on the brink of a bomb in 1981. By the late 1970s, he thought Iraq should develop nuclear weapons at some point, and he hoped to use the Osirak reactor to further that goal. But new evidence suggests that Hussein had not decided to launch a full-fledged weapons program prior to the Israeli strike. According to Norwegian scholar Målfrid Braut-Hegghammer, a leading authority on the Iraqi program, "on the eve of the attack on Osirak . . . Iraq's pursuit of a nuclear weapons capability was both directionless and disorganized."

Moreover, as Emory University political scientist Dan Reiter details in a 2005 study, the Osirak reactor was not well designed to efficiently produce weapons-grade plutonium. If Hussein had decided to use Osirak to develop nuclear weapons and Iraqi scientists somehow evaded detection, it would still have taken several years—perhaps well into the 1990s—to produce enough plutonium for a single bomb. And even with sufficient fissile material, Iraq would have had to design and construct the weapon itself, a process that hadn't started before Israel attacked.

The risks of a near-term Iraqi breakthrough were further undercut by the presence of French technicians at Osirak, as well as regular inspections by the International Atomic Energy Agency. As a result, any significant diversion of highly enriched uranium fuel or attempts to produce fissionable plutonium would probably have been detected.

By demonstrating Iraq's vulnerability, the attack on Osirak actually increased Hussein's determination to develop a nuclear deterrent and provided Iraq's scientists an opportunity to better organize the program. The Iraqi leader devoted significantly more resources toward pursuing nuclear weapons after the Israeli assault. As Reiter notes, "the Iraqi nuclear program increased from a program of 400 scientists and $400 million to one of 7,000 scientists and $10 billion."

Iraq's nuclear efforts also went underground. Hussein allowed the IAEA to verify Osirak's destruction, but then he shifted from a plutonium strategy to a more dispersed and ambitious uranium-enrichment strategy. This approach relied on undeclared sites, away from the prying eyes of inspectors, and aimed to develop local technology and expertise to reduce the reliance on foreign suppliers of sensitive technologies. When inspectors finally gained access after the 1991 Persian Gulf War, they were shocked by the extent of Iraq's nuclear infrastructure and how close Hussein had gotten to a bomb.

Ultimately, Israel's 1981 raid didn't end Iraq's drive to develop nuclear weapons. It took the destruction of the Gulf War, followed by more than a decade of sanctions, containment, inspections, no-fly zones and periodic bombing—not to mention the 2003 U.S. invasion—to eliminate the program. The international community got lucky: Had Hussein not been dumb enough to invade Kuwait in 1990, he probably would have gotten the bomb sometime by the mid-1990s.

Iran's nuclear program is more advanced than Hussein's was in 1981. But the Islamic republic is still not on the cusp of entering the nuclear club. As the IAEA has documented, Iran is putting all the pieces in place to have the option to develop nuclear weapons at some point. Were Supreme Leader Ayatollah

Ali Khamenei to decide tomorrow to go for a bomb, Iran probably has the technical capability to produce a testable nuclear device in about a year and a missile-capable device in several years. But as Director of National Intelligence James Clapper told the Senate Arms Services Committee on Feb. 16, it does not appear that Khamenei has made this decision.

Moreover, Khamenei is unlikely to dash for a bomb in the near future because IAEA inspectors would probably detect Iranian efforts to divert low-enriched uranium and enrich it to weapons-grade level at declared facilities. Such brazen acts would trigger a draconian international response. Until Iran can pursue such efforts more quickly or in secret—which could be years from now—Khamenei is unlikely to act.

Also, an Israeli strike on Iran's nuclear infrastructure would be more risky and less effective than the Osirak raid. In 1981, a relatively small number of Israeli aircraft flew 600 miles across Jordanian, Saudi and Iraqi airspace to hit a single, vulnerable, above-ground target. This was no easy feat, but it is nothing compared with the complexity of a strike on Iran's nuclear infrastructure.

Such an attack would probably require dozens of aircraft to travel at least 1,000 miles over Arab airspace to reach their targets, stretching the limits of Israeli refueling capabilities. Israeli jets would then have to circumvent Iranian air defenses and drop hundreds of precision-guided munitions on the hardened Natanz enrichment facility, the Fordow enrichment site deep in a mountain near Qom, the Isfahan uranium-conversion facility, the heavy-water production plant and plutonium reactor under construction at Arak, and multiple centrifuge production facilities in and around populated areas of Tehran and Natanz.

These same aircraft would not be able to reengage any missed targets— they would need to race back to defend Israel against retaliation by Iran and its proxies, including Lebanese Hezbollah and possibly Hamas.

Unlike an attack by the U.S. military, which has much more powerful munitions and the ability to sustain a large-scale bombing campaign, an Israeli assault would probably be a one-off strike with more limited effects.

No wonder that Gen. Martin Dempsey, the chairman of the U.S. Joint Chiefs of Staff, recently told CNN that an Israeli attack would set the program back only "a couple of years" and "wouldn't achieve their long-term objectives." (Because a U.S. strike would potentially be more effective, the administration has kept that option on the table even as it has cautioned against an Israeli attack.)

Should Israel rush to war, Iran might follow Hussein's example and rebuild its nuclear program in a way that is harder to detect and more costly to stop. And while there seems to be consensus among Iranians that the country has a right to a robust civilian nuclear program, there is no domestic agreement yet on the pursuit of nuclear weapons. Even the supreme leader has hedged his bets, insisting that Iran has the right to pursue technological advances with possible military applications, while repeatedly declaring that possession or use of nuclear weapons would be a "grave sin" against Islam.

After an Israeli strike, that internal debate would be settled—hard-line arguments would win the day.

Short of invasion and regime change—outcomes beyond Israel's capabilities—it would be nearly impossible to prevent Iran from rebuilding its program. Iran's nuclear infrastructure is much more advanced, dispersed and protected, and is less reliant on foreign supplies of key technology, than was the case with Iraq's program in 1981.

Although Barak often warns that Israel must strike before Iran's facilities are so protected that they enter a "zone of immunity" from Israeli military action, Iran would be likely to reconstitute its program in the very sites—and probably new clandestine ones—that are invulnerable to Israeli attack. An Israeli strike would also end any prospect of Iran cooperating with the IAEA, seriously undermining the international community's ability to detect rebuilding efforts.

Barely a week after the Osirak raid, Begin told CBS News that the attack "will be a precedent for every future government in Israel." Yet, if history repeats itself, an Israeli attack would result in a wounded adversary more determined than ever to get a nuclear bomb. And then the world would face the same terrible choices it ultimately faced with Iraq: decades of containment to stall nuclear rebuilding efforts, invasion and occupation—or acquiescence to an implacable nuclear-armed foe.

EXPLORING THE ISSUE

Should Israel Preempt Against Iran's Nuclear Program?

Critical Thinking and Reflection

1. Would an Israeli attack solve the nuclear Iran issue or merely prolong it?
2. Would a U.S. supported strike be fuel for Islamic militancy and terrorism?
3. Will a nuclear Iran spur a regional arms race among Israel and some Arab states?
4. Can the United States prevent such a development and escalation?

Is There Common Ground?

There appears to be a consensus in the international community that a nuclear Iran would be a destabilizing force in the Persian Gulf and throughout the Middle East. Saudi Arabia and many other Arab states share that view with Israel and the United States although they do not publicly voice it. Europe, Russia, and China also share that view although their approaches to changing Iran's policy differ. It seems that ultimately many can agree on the result that they wish, a non-nuclear Iran, while they cannot agree on the methods to achieve it.

Additional Resources

Allin, Dana, and Simon, Steven, *The Sixth Crisis: Iran, Israel, America, and the Rumors of War*, Oxford University Press (2010).

This book links Iran's growing nuclear challenge, the increasing likelihood of an Israeli preventive strike, the Israel-Palestine problem, and Obama.

Bergman, Ronen, "Israel vs. Iran When Will It Erupt?" *The New York Times Magazine* (January 29, 2012).

Corsi, Jerome R., *Why Israel Can't Wait: The Coming War between Israel and Iran*, Threshold Editions (2009).

This book argues that Israel's next war is with Iran unless the United States takes a much stronger stand against Iran.

Holmes, Marschall E., and Matthews, Suzanne F., editors, *Israel's Stability, the Iranian Nuclear Threat and U.S. Relations*, Nova Science Pub Inc. (2012).

The book analyzes key factors that could influence Israel's decision to strike Iran.

Ignatius, David, "Is Israel Preparing to Attack Iran?" *The Washington Post* (February 2, 2012).

This article suggests that Israel is prepared to accept and even welcome the prospect of war with Iran alone.

Katz, Yaakov, and Hendel, Yoaz, *Israel vs. Iran: The Shadow War*, Potomac Books (2012).

This book describes Israel strategic military deliberations since 2006.

Kaye, Dalia Dassa, *Israel and Iran: A Dangerous Rivalry*, Rand Corporation (2012).

This book argues that Israel and Iran view each other as natural regional rivals, which has intensified in recent years.

Parsi, Trira, *Treacherous Alliance: The Secret Dealings of Israel, Iran, and the United States*, Yale University Press (2007).

This older book traces the history among these three countries since 1948.

Raviv, Dan, and Melman, Yossi, *Spies Against Armageddon*, Levant Books (2012).

This book describes the history of Israeli intelligence.

Roshandel, Jalil, and Lean, Nathan Chapman, *Iran, Israel, and the United States: Regime Security vs. Political Legitimacy*, Praeger (2011).

This book examines Iran's nuclear behavior and the implications for Israel.

Waltz, Kenneth N., "Why Iran Should Get the Bomb," *Foreign Affairs* (July/August 2012).

This article argues that a nuclear-armed Iran would create a more stable military balance in the Middle East.

Zanotti, Jim, et al., *Israel: Possible Military Strike against Iran's Nuclear Facilities* Congressional Research Service (March 28, 2012).

This report analyzes key factors that will likely influence Israel's decision regarding a possible strike against Iran's nuclear facilities.

Contributors to This Volume

EDITORS

JAMES E. HARF currently serves as a professor of political science as well as associate vice-president and director of the Center for Global Education at Maryville University in St. Louis. He spent most of his career at The Ohio State University where he holds the title of professor emeritus. He is coeditor of *The Unfolding Legacy of 9/11* (University Press of America, 2004) and coauthor of *World Politics and You: A Student Companion to International Politics on the World Stage*, 5th ed. (Brown & Benchmark, 1995) and *The Politics of Global Resources* (Duke University Press, 1986). His first novel, *Memories of Ivy* (Ivy House Publishing Group), about life as a university professor, was published in 2005. He also coedited a four-book series on the global issues of population, food, energy, and environment, as well as three other book series on national security education, international studies, and international business. He and a colleague have recently completed a manuscript, *The Wise Traveler Abroad: Knowledge to Enhance the Global Journey of Undergraduates and Cruise Shippers Alike*, a book about strategies for maximizing one's serious travel and study abroad adventures. As a staff member on the President Jimmy Carter's Commission on Foreign Language and International Studies in the late 1970s, he was responsible for undergraduate education recommendations. He also served 15 years as executive director of the Consortium for International Studies Education. He has been a frequent TV and radio commentator on international issues.

MARK OWEN LOMBARDI is president and chief executive officer of Maryville University in St. Louis, Missouri. He is coeditor and author of *The Unfolding Legacy of 9/11* (University Press of America 2004) and coeditor of *Perspectives on Third World Sovereignty: The Post-Modern Paradox* (Macmillan, 1996). Dr. Lombardi has authored numerous articles and book chapters on such topics as U.S. foreign policy, African political economy, the politics of the cold war, and higher education reform. He is a member of numerous civic organizations and boards locally and nationally, and he has given more than 200 speeches to local and national groups on topics ranging from higher education reform to U.S. politics, international affairs, and U.S. foreign policy. He has also appeared as a political commentator for local and national news outlets.

AUTHORS

DIVYA ABHAT is a science and environment reporter, specializing in wildlife issues in North America and the rest of the world. Originally from Mumbai, India, Abhat came to the United States for a graduate degree in journalism from the University of Missouri–Columbia and focused on international reporting and science, health, and environmental journalism.

ELLIOTT ABRAMS, a conservative policy analyst who served in both the Ronald Reagan and George W. Bush presidencies, most recently as deputy national security advisor in 2005–2009, is currently senior fellow for Middle Eastern Studies at the Council for Foreign Relations.

GRAHAM ALLISON is Douglas Dillon Professor of Government at the John F. Kennedy School of Government at Harvard University and director of the Belfer Center for Science and International Affairs.

AMNESTY INTERNATIONAL is a global nongovernmental organization of over three million supporters, members, and activists in more than 150 countries, committed to the rights, dignity, and well-being of all persons throughout the globe.

RONALD BAILEY is science correspondent for *Reason* magazine and author of *ECOSCAM: The False Prophets of Ecological Apocalypse* (1994).

LESTER R. BROWN is founder and president of Earth Policy Institute. He is described by *The Washington Post* as "one of the most influential thinkers" and is the author of numerous books on environmental issues.

LUIS CDEBACA is ambassador-at-large, U.S. Department of State, Office to Monitor and Combat Trafficking in Persons.

MARK CLAYTON is a staff writer for *The Christian Science Monitor.*

COUNCIL ON FOREIGN RELATIONS is an independent nonpartisan essentially American membership organization, think tank, and publisher, founded in 1921 for the purpose of serving as a resource for its members, government officials, business executives, journalists, educators and students, civic and religious leaders, and other interested citizens to better help them understand the world and the foreign policy choices facing the United States and other countries.

SHAUNA DINEEN is Foster Care Coordinator and Animal Care and Adoption Counselor at MSPCA. Formerly, she served as Administrative and Programs Assistant at The New England Antivivisection Society and was Editorial and Public Relations Intern at *E—The Environmental Magazine.*

PAUL B. FARRELL is author of four books and an investing and personal finance columnist for *CBS MarketWatch.* He has contributed more than 1,000 columns and appears frequently on television and radio.

DORE GOLD is a former Israeli ambassador to the United Nations and special advisor to Prime Minister Benjamin Netanyahu.

MARK L. HAAS is an associate professor of political science at Duquesne University and author of *The Ideological Origins of the Great Powers 1789–1989* (2005).

SCOTT HORTON is host of Antiwar radio on the Liberty radio network and assistant editor at Antiwar.com.

NEIL HOWE is a senior associate at the Center for Strategic and International Studies, and coauthor of *The Graying of the Great Powers: Demography and Geopolitics in the 21st Century* (2008).

KATSUHITO IWAI is a professor of economics at the University of Tokyo.

RICHARD JACKSON is a senior fellow at the Center for Strategic and International Studies, and coauthor of *The Graying of the Great Powers: Demography and Geopolitics in the 21st Century* (2008).

BRIAN MICHAEL JENKINS is a senior advisor to the president of the Rand Corporation and director of the Mineta Transportation Institute's Transportation Center.

TAMSYN JONES is a multitalented writer and reporter and with experience and interest in agriculture, environment, science, and explanatory writing. Her writing ranges from magazine and hard news stories to fact sheets and PR pieces.

COLIN H. KAHL, currently an associate professor at Georgetown University's Edmund A. Walsh School of Foreign Service and a senior fellow at the Center for a New American Security, served as deputy assistant secretary of defense for the Middle East.

HEATH A. KELLY is employed at the Victorian Infectious Diseases Laboratory in Melbourne, Australia.

STEPHEN LENDMAN is a research associate of the Centre for Research on Globalization, based in Montreal, Canada.

RICHARD S. LINDZEN is the Alfred P. Sloan professor of meteorology in the Department of Earth, Atmosphere, and Planetary Sciences at MIT.

BILL McKIBBEN is scholar in residence at Middlebury College and author of nine books, including *Deep Economy: The Wealth of Communities and the Durable Future* (2007).

MICHAEL J. MILLER is a writer for the *Catholic World Report*, an international monthly magazine. He translated the biography of Jérôme Lejeune, *Life Is a Blessing*, for Ignatius Press.

EVGENY MOROZOV is a visiting scholar at Stanford University and a Schwartz fellow at the New America Foundation. He is author of *The Net Delusion: The Dark Side of Internet Freedom* (2011).

JIM MOTAVILLI is a freelance journalist, book author, and radio personality on environmental issues. He previously spent 14 years as editor of *E—The Environmental Magazine*.

MINIX PEI is the Tom and Margot Pritzker Professor of Government at Claremont McKenna College.

TERRY M. REDDING is a communications consultant.

DANI RODRIK is a professor of international political economy at the John F. Kennedy School of Government, Harvard University.

PETER ROGERS is a professor of environmental engineering, School of Engineering and Applied Sciences, Harvard University.

DAVID ROTHKOPF is president and CEO of Garten Rothkopf, an international advisory firm specializing in emerging markets investing and risk management-related services. Previously, he served as deputy under secretary of commerce for international trade in the Clinton Administration.

NANSEN G. SALERI is president and CEO of Quantum Reservoir Input, and the oil industry's preeminent authority on reservoir management and upstream technologies.

ADAM SHATZ is the senior editor of the *London Review of Books*.

CLAY SHIRKY is an author, teacher, and consultant on the social and economic effects of Internet technologies.

HUSSEIN SOLOMON is a lecturer at the University of Pretoria and the director of the Centre of International Political Studies.

ALLAN BRIAN SSENYONGA is a Ugandan freelance writer based in Rwanda.

SCOTT STEWART is affiliated with STRATFOR, an organization that delivers intelligence and perspective to the public through situation reports, analysis, and multimedia. Stewart provides reports that assess world events and their significance.

SHIBLEY TELHAMI is the Anwar Sadat Professor for peace and development, University of Maryland, and nonresident senior fellow at Saban Center, Brookings Institute.

MIKE TRACE is chairman, International Drug Policy Consortium and former United Kingdom drug czar.

SHUJIE YAO is a professor of economics and Chinese sustainable development at the China Policy Institute, University of Nottingham.

FAREED ZAKARIA is editor of *Newsweek International*, a *Newsweek* and *Washington Post* columnist, weekly host for CNN, and a *New York Times* bestselling author. He was described in 1999 by Esquire Magazine as "the most influential foreign policy adviser of his generation" and in 2007, *Foreign Policy* and *Prospect* magazines named him one of the 100 leading public intellectuals in the world.